MSA 602
Financial Analysis, Planning, and Control

Custom Edition for Central Michigan University

Taken from:

Introduction to Management Accounting, Sixteenth Edition
Charles T. Horgren, Gary L. Sundem, David Burgstahler,
and Jeff Schatzberg

Principles of Managerial Finance, Thirteenth Edition
by Lawrence J. Gitman and Chad J. Zutter

Cover Art: Courtesy of Stockbyte and Photodisc/Getty Images.

Taken from:

Introduction to Management Accounting, Sixteenth Edition
Charles T. Horgren, Gary L. Sundem, David Burgstahler, and Jeff Schatzberg
Copyright © 2014, 2011, 2008 by Pearson Education, Inc.
Published by Prentice Hall
Upper Saddle River, NJ 07458

Principles of Managerial Finance, Thirteenth Edition
Lawrence J. Gitman and Chad J. Zutter
Copyright © 2012, 2009, 2006, 2003 by Lawrence J. Gitman
Published by Prentice Hall

This special edition published in cooperation with Pearson Learning Solutions.

All trademarks, service marks, registered trademarks, and registered service marks are the property of their respective owners and are used herein for identification purposes only.

Pearson Learning Solutions, 501 Boylston Street, Suite 900, Boston, MA 02116
A Pearson Education Company
www.pearsoned.com

Printed in the United States of America

1 2 3 4 5 6 7 8 9 10 V011 17 16 15 14 13

000200010271764990

EEB

 ISBN 10: 1-269-33928-1
ISBN 13: 978-1-269-33928-5

Contents

Unless otherwise noted, chapters are taken from: *Introduction to Management Accounting*, Sixteenth Edition, by Charles T. Horgren, Gary L. Sundem, David Burgstahler, and Jeff Schatzberg.

Chapters 2, 10 and 11 are taken from: *Principles of Managerial Finance*, Thirteenth Edition, by Lawrence J. Gitman and Chad J. Zutter.

FREQUENTLY USED SYMBOLS AND ABBREVIATIONS

AAI	Average Age of Inventory	EOQ	Economic Order Quantity
ACH	Automated Clearinghouse	EPS	Earnings Per Share
ACP	Average Collection Period	ERP	Enterprise Resource Planning
AF_j	Amount of Funds Available from Financing Source j at a Given Cost	EU	European Union
		EVA	Economic Value Added
ANPV	Annualized Net Present Value	FC	Fixed Operating Cost
A/P	Accounts Payable	FCF	Free Cash Flow
APP	Average Payment Period	FDI	Foreign Direct Investment
APR	Annual Percentage Rate	FLM	Financial Leverage Multiplier
APY	Annual Percentage Yield	FV	Future Value
A/R	Accounts Receivable	GAAP	Generally accepted accounting principles
b_j	Beta Coefficient or Index of Nondiversifiable Risk for Asset j	GATT	General Agreement on Tariffs and Trade
b_p	Portfolio Beta	g	Growth Rate
B_0	Value of a Bond	I	Interest Payment
C	Carrying Cost per Unit per Period	IP	Inflation Premium
CAPM	Capital Asset Pricing Model	IPO	Initial Public Offering
CCC	Cash Conversion Cycle	IRR	Internal Rate of Return
CD	Stated Cash Discount in Percentage Terms	JIT	Just-In-Time System
CF_0	Initial Investment	LBO	Leveraged Buyout
CF_t	Cash Inflow in Period t	m	Number of times per year interest is compounded
CV	Coefficient of Variation	M	Bond's Par Value
D_p	Preferred Stock Dividend	M/B	Market/Book Ratio
D_t	• Per-Share Dividend Expected at the End of Year t	MACRS	Modified Accelerated Cost Recovery System
	• Depreciation Expense in Year t	MNC	Multinational Company
DFL	Degree of Financial Leverage	MP	Market Price per Share
DIP	Debtor in Possession	MPR	Market Price Ratio of Exchange
DOL	Degree of Operating Leverage	MRP	Materials Requirement Planning
DPS	Dividends per Share	n	• Number of Outcomes Considered
DTC	Depository Transfer Check		• Number of Periods—Typically, Years
DTL	Degree of Total Leverage		• Years to Maturity
e	Exponential Function = 2.7183	N	• Number of Days Payment Can Be Delayed by Giving up the Cash Discount
E	Exercise Price of the Warrant		
EAR	Effective Annual Rate		• Number of Shares of Common Stock Obtainable with One Warrant
EBIT	Earnings Before Interest and Taxes		
EOM	End of the Month	N_d	Net Proceeds from the Sale of Debt (Bond)

N_n	Net Proceeds from the Sale of New Common Stock
N_p	Net Proceeds from the Sale of the Preferred Stock
NAFTA	North American Free Trade Agreement
NCAI	Net Current Asset Investment
NFAI	Net Fixed Asset Investment
NOPAT	Net operating profits after taxes
NPV	Net Present Value
O	Order Cost Per Order
OC	Operating Cycle
OCF	Operating Cash Flow
P	Price (value) of asset
P_0	Value of Common Stock
$PBDT_t$	Profits Before Depreciation and Taxes in year t
PD	Preferred Stock Dividend
P/E	Price/Earnings Ratio
PI	Profitability Index
PMT	Amount of Payment
Pr	Probability
PV	Present Value
Q	• Order Quantity in Units
	• Sales Quantity in Units
r	• Actual, Expected ($\bar{r}$), or Required Rate of Return
	• Annual Rate of Interest
	• Cost of Capital
r^*	Real Rate of Interest
r_a	Weighted Average Cost of Capital
r_d	• Required Return on Bond
	• Before-Tax Cost of Debt
r_i	After-Tax Cost of Debt
r_j	Required Return on Asset j
r_m	• Market Return
	• Return on the Market Portfolio of Assets
r_p	• Cost of Preferred Stock
	• Portfolio Return

r_r	Cost of Retained Earnings
r_s	• Required Return on Common Stock
	• Cost of Common Stock Equity
R_F	Risk-Free Rate of Interest
RADR	Risk-Adjusted Discount Rate
RE	Ratio of Exchange
ROA	Return on Total Assets
ROE	Return on Common Equity
S	• Usage in Units per Period
	• Sales in Dollars
SML	Security Market Line
t	Time
T	Firm's Marginal Tax Rate
TVW	Theoretical Value of a Warrant
V	• Value of an Asset or Firm
	• Venture Capital
V_C	Value of Entire Company
V_D	Value of All Debt
V_P	Value of Preferred Stock
V_S	Value of Common Stock
VC	Variable Operating Cost per Unit
w_j	• Proportion of the Portfolio's Total Dollar Value Represented by Asset j
	• Proportion of a Specific Source of Financing j in the Firm's Capital Structure
WACC	Weighted Average Cost of Capital
WTO	World Trade Organization
YTM	Yield to Maturity
ZBA	Zero Balance Account
σ	Standard Deviation
Σ	Summation Sign

MSA 602
FINANCIAL ANALYSIS, PLANNING, AND CONTROL

Basic Accounting: Concepts, Techniques, and Conventions

LEARNING OBJECTIVES

When you have finished studying this chapter, you should be able to:

1. Read and interpret basic financial statements.

2. Analyze typical business transactions using the balance sheet equation.

3. Distinguish between the accrual basis of accounting and the cash basis of accounting.

4. Make adjustments to the accounts under accrual accounting.

5. Explain the nature of dividends and retained earnings.

6. Select relevant items from a set of data and assemble them into a balance sheet and an income statement.

7. Distinguish between the reporting of corporate owners' equity and the reporting of owners' equity for partnerships and sole proprietorships.

8. Explain the role of auditors in financial reporting and how accounting standards are set.

9. Identify how the measurement principles of recognition, matching and cost recovery, and stable monetary unit affect financial reporting.

10. Define continuity, relevance, faithful representation, materiality, conservatism, and cost-benefit (Appendix 1 A).

11. Use T-accounts, debits, and credits to record transactions (Appendix 1 B).

▶ GENERAL MILLS

Chances are you have eaten Big-G cereals from **General Mills**, such as Wheaties or Cheerios. Or perhaps you have baked with Betty Crocker flour or Bisquick, or snacked on Bugles, Yoplait yogurt, or Häagen-Dazs ice cream. General Mills sells nearly $17 billion of these and other food products throughout the world each year. General Mills' customers want foods that are convenient, tasty, and affordable. Managers at General Mills take pride in developing and marketing food products that meet these customer demands. Just as important to the managers is whether the company is making a profit. How can the company's managers see how much profit General Mills is making? The same way you can—by reading the company's financial statements.

Financial statements are generated by a company's financial accounting system. General Mills, like all well-managed companies, has a financial accounting system that not only generates company-wide financial statements but also provides detailed information about the financial results of each product. General Mills holds managers responsible for meeting their segment's profit targets. In his 2011 letter to shareholders, Ken Powell, chairman and CEO, indicated that the company expects each segment's operating profit to grow in the "mid-single digits" annually.

Suppose you want to buy General Mills stock instead of its food products. Then you too would be interested in the company's financial performance. You would want to know the company's financial position and its prospects to judge whether it is wise to invest in General Mills stock. The company's financial statements can be a great help in making this judgment, but only if you know a bit about accounting. Accounting is the language of business. Its special vocabulary conveys the financial story of an organization. To understand corporate annual reports, you must learn this language—the words and ideas used by accountants and other managers when discussing financial matters.

This chapter explores the essence of profit-making activities and how accountants portray them in financial statements. We leave the more technical topics for the chapter appendices. As you examine what accountants do, you will also learn many of the relevant concepts and principles of accounting. Although the focus will be on profit-seeking organizations, the main ideas also apply to nonprofit organizations. ■

© ZUMA Press/Alamy

The Need for Accounting

Accountants record the financial history of a company. You can use accounting information to assess the past financial performance of a company and to help predict its future performance. In addition to businesses, all kinds of organizations—government agencies, nonprofit organizations, and others—rely on accounting to gauge their progress.

The accounting process begins by recording an organization's transactions. A **transaction** is any event that affects the financial position of an organization and requires recording. Many concepts, conventions, and rules determine what events a company records as accounting transactions and how accountants measure the financial impact of each transaction. As you learn about these concepts, conventions, and rules, you will also learn about **financial statements**, which are summaries of recorded accounting transactions.

Managers, investors, and other interest groups often want the answers to two important questions about an organization: How well did the organization perform for a given period? Where does the organization stand financially at a given point? Accountants answer these questions with three major financial statements: The income statement and statement of cash flows summarize two different aspects of performance over a period of time, and the balance sheet shows the financial position at a point in time. This chapter discusses the income statement and balance sheet.

Financial Statements—Balance Sheet and Income Statement

An efficient way to learn about accounting is to study a specific illustration. Suppose King Hardware Company began business as a **corporation**—a business organized as a separate legal entity and owned by its stockholders. The company's first transaction occurred on February 28, 20X1, when its stockholders invested a total of $100,000 cash. The following additional transactions occurred during March:

1. Acquisition of inventory for $75,000 cash.
2. Acquisition of inventory for $35,000 on open account. A purchase on open account allows the buyer to pay cash after the date of purchase, often in 30 days. Amounts owed to vendors for purchases on open accounts are **accounts payable**.
3. Merchandise carried in inventory at a cost of $100,000 was sold for $130,000. King Hardware received $10,000 in cash and recorded accounts receivable of $120,000. **Accounts receivable** are amounts due from customers for sales charged to an account instead of being paid for in cash.
4. Cash collections of a portion of accounts receivable from item 4, $15,000.
5. Cash payments of a portion of accounts payable from item 3, $20,000.
6. On March 1, King Hardware paid $3,000 cash for store rent for March, April, and May. Rent is $1,000 per month, payable quarterly in advance, beginning March 1.

General Mills cereals — from heart-healthy Cheerios to kids' favorites Cocoa Puffs and Trix — are popular throughout the world.

transaction
Any event that affects the financial position of an organization and requires recording.

financial statements
Summarized reports of accounting transactions.

Objective 1

Read and interpret basic financial statements.

corporation
A business organized as a separate legal entity and owned by its stockholders.

accounts payable
Amounts owed to vendors for purchases on open accounts.

accounts receivable
Amounts due from customers for sales charged to an account instead of being paid for in cash.

The Balance Sheet

balance sheet (statement of financial position)

A snapshot of the financial status of an organization at a point in time.

King Hardware's **balance sheet** (also called a **statement of financial position**)—a snapshot of the financial status of an organization at a specific point in time—after the first transaction, investment by stockholders, follows:

King Hardware
Balance Sheet (Statement of Financial Position) as of February 28, 20X1

Assets		Liabilities and Stockholders' Equity	
Cash	$100,000	Paid-in capital	$100,000

assets

Economic resources that a company owns and expects to provide future benefits.

liabilities

The entity's economic obligations to nonowners.

owners' equity

The excess of the assets over the liabilities.

account

Each item in a financial statement.

stockholders' equity

The owners' equity of a corporation.

The balance sheet has two sections—(1) assets and (2) liabilities plus owners' (stockholders') equity. **Assets** are economic resources that a company owns and expects to provide future benefits. **Liabilities** are the entity's economic obligations to nonowners. **Owners' equity** is the excess of the assets over the liabilities. You can think of the two sections of the balance sheet as the two sides of an equation:

$$\text{Assets} = \text{Liabilities} + \text{Owners' Equity}$$

Liabilities and owners' equity are essentially claims on the assets by creditors and owners, respectively. A company typically has multiple assets, liabilities, and owners' equity items—a large company may have thousands, or even millions, of individual assets and liabilities. The accounting process aggregates and summarizes results reported on the balance sheet. Each separate asset, liability, or owners' equity item shown on a balance sheet is an **account**—the term used for any item in a financial statement.

Because the stockholders own a corporation, we call the owners' equity of a corporation **stockholders' equity**. In turn, the stockholders' equity has two major components, (1) **paid-in capital**, the ownership claim arising from funds paid in by the owners, and (2) **retained earnings** (or **retained income**), the ownership claim arising from reinvestment of previous profits:

$$\text{assets} = \text{liabilities} + \text{stockholders' equity}$$
$$= \text{liabilities} + (\text{paid-in capital} + \text{retained earnings})$$

Objective 2

Analyze typical business transactions using the balance sheet equation.

paid-in capital

The ownership claim arising from funds paid in by the owners.

retained earnings (retained income)

The ownership claim arising from the reinvestment of previous profits.

Now let's examine how King Hardware's March transactions affect the balance sheet. The balance sheet equation, shown in Exhibit 1-1, summarizes the cumulative effect of all these transactions (including the initial investment). Note that most of the transactions are summaries of a larger set of underlying transactions. For example, the sales did not all occur in a single sales transaction. Similarly, there were multiple purchases of inventory, collections from customers, or disbursements to suppliers. Consider sales of Cheerios by General Mills. It sells millions of boxes of Cheerios and other products during a year in thousands of transactions. Accountants record each transaction in the accounting system and then add together all the sales amounts to find the total sales to report in the financial statements.

You can see in Exhibit 1-1 that King Hardware's transaction 1, the initial investment by owners, increases assets and increases stockholders' equity. That is, cash increases and so does paid-in capital—the claim arising from the owners' total initial investment in the corporation. The balance sheet after this first transaction, shown at the top of this page, contains only two accounts.

Transaction 2, the purchase of inventory for cash, is an exchange of one asset for another. This transaction changes the balances in individual assets, increasing one asset (inventory) and decreasing another asset (cash), but does not change total assets or claims on those assets. Transaction 3, the purchase of inventory on account, adds an asset (inventory) and a liability (accounts payable), increasing total assets and total liabilities and stockholders' equity to $135,000. After the first three transactions, the balance sheet now includes four accounts, cash, inventory, accounts payable, and paid-in capital:

King Hardware
Balance Sheet after Transactions 1, 2, and 3

Assets		Liabilities and Stockholders' Equity	
Cash	$ 25,000	Account payable	$ 35,000
Inventory	110,000	Paid-in capital	100,000
Total assets	$135,000	Total liabilities and stockholders' equity	$135,000

	Assets				=	Liabilities	+	Stockholders' Equity	
Transactions	Cash	+ Accounts Receivable	+ Inventory	+ Prepaid Rent	=	Accounts Payable	+	Paid-in Capital	+ Retained Earnings
1. Initial investment	+ 100,000				=			+ 100,000	
2. Acquire inventory for cash	− 75,000		+ 75,000		=				
3. Acquire inventory for credit			+ 35,000		=	+ 35,000			
4a. Sales on credit and for cash	+ 10,000	+ 120,000			=				+ 130,000 (revenue)
4b. Cost of inventory sold			− 100,000		=				− 100,000 (expense)
5. Collect from customers	+ 15,000	− 15,000			=				
6. Pay accounts of suppliers	− 20,000				=	− 20,000			
7a. Pay rent in advance	− 3,000			+ 3,000	=				
7b. Recognize expiration of rental services				− 1,000	=				− 1,000 (expense)
Balance, 3/31/X1	+ 27,000	+ 105,000	+ 10,000	+ 2,000	=	+ 15,000		+ 100,000	+ 29,000
	144,000							144,000	

Exhibit 1-1

King Hardware Co.

Analysis of Transactions (in dollars) for March 20X1

Transaction 4 is the sale of $100,000 of inventory for $130,000. This is our first example of a transaction that reflects the fundamental purpose of providing a good or service that has a value to the purchaser ($130,000) greater than the cost of providing the good or service ($100,000). In this transaction, two things happen simultaneously—the company acquires new assets, Cash and Accounts Receivable (4a), in exchange for Inventory (4b). The assets Cash and Accounts Receivable and the Retained Earnings portion of Stockholders' Equity increase by the selling price, $130,000. (Notice that the $10,000 increase in Cash plus the $120,000 increase in Accounts Receivable equals the $130,000 increase in stockholders' equity.) The asset Inventory and the Retained Earnings portion of Stockholders' Equity decrease by the cost of the items sold, $100,000. The $30,000 net increase in retained earnings represents stockholders' claims arising from the profitable sale. Transaction 4a is also our first example of a **compound entry**, a transaction that affects more than two accounts.

compound entry
A transaction that affects more than two accounts.

Transaction 5, cash collection of accounts receivable, is another example of an event that affects individual asset accounts but has no impact on liabilities or stockholders' equity. Collections are merely the transformation of one asset (Accounts Receivable) into another (Cash). Transaction 6, cash payment of accounts payable, affects assets and liabilities only. In general, collections from customers and payments to suppliers have no direct impact on stockholders' equity.

In transaction 7, the company pays cash for rent to acquire the right to use store facilities for the next 3 months. On March 1, we create the asset Prepaid Rent (7a), a measure of the future benefit from the right to use these facilities. Assets include legal rights to receive goods and services such as the future use of facilities as well as items you can see or touch such as cash or inventory. Transaction 7b recognizes that King Hardware received one-third of the 3 months of rental services during March. Because the company has "used up" $1,000 of the asset Prepaid Rent during March, we reduce both the asset and stockholders' equity by $1,000.

The balance sheet for King Hardware at the end of March follows:

revenue
Increases in ownership claims arising from the delivery of goods or services.

King Hardware Co.
Balance Sheet as of March 31, 20X1

Assets		Liabilities and Stockholders' Equity		
Cash	$ 27,000	Liabilities: Accounts payable		$ 15,000
Accounts receivable	105,000	Stockholders' equity		
Inventory	10,000	Paid-in capital	$100,000	
Prepaid rent	2,000	Retained earnings	29,000	129,000
Total	$144,000	Total		$144,000

recognize
To formally record in the accounting records during the current period.

Revenues, Expenses, and the Income Statement

expenses
Decreases in ownership claims arising from delivering goods or services or using up assets.

Let's review transaction 4 in more detail. Recall that this transaction has two phases, (a) and (b). Transaction 4a illustrates the recognition of revenue. **Revenues** are increases in ownership claims arising from the delivery of goods or services. We **recognize** revenue by formally recording it in the accounting records during the current period. We do this only after it meets two tests. First, the company must earn the revenues. That is, it must deliver the goods or render the services to customers. Second, the revenue must be realized or realizable. If the company collects payment, it has realized the revenue. If it has not collected payment but is reasonably sure that it will collect the receivable, the revenue is realizable.

income (net income, profits, earnings)
The excess of revenues over expenses.

Transaction 4b illustrates the incurrence of an expense. **Expenses** are decreases in ownership claims arising from delivering goods or services or using up assets. The expense in this case is cost of goods sold, the amount paid for the items sold to the customer.

Transactions 4a and 4b also illustrate the fundamental meaning of **income** (also called **net income**, **profits**, or **earnings**), which is the excess of revenues over expenses. As the Retained Earnings column in Exhibit 1-1 shows, increases in revenues increase stockholders' equity. In contrast, increases in expenses decrease stockholders' equity.

income statement
A statement that summarizes a company's revenues and expenses. It measures the performance of an organization by matching its accomplishments (revenue from customers) and its efforts (cost of goods sold and other expenses).

A company's **income statement** summarizes its revenues and expenses. It measures the performance of an organization by matching its accomplishments (revenue from customers, often called **sales revenue** or simply **sales**) and its efforts (cost of goods sold and other expenses) for a span of time, often a month, a quarter, or a year.

sales revenue (sales)
Revenue from customers.

The income statement is the major link between balance sheets:

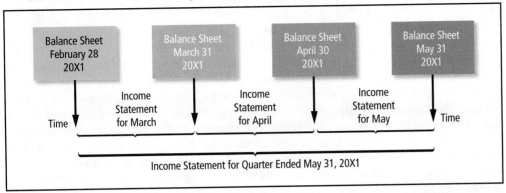

Notice that each balance sheet is a snapshot at a point in time. In contrast, each income statement summarizes events during a period that cause changes in the stockholders' equity (specifically retained earnings) section of the balance sheet. Examine the changes in retained earnings in Exhibit 1-1. The revenues and expenses during March explain why retained earnings changed from $0 at the beginning of the month to $29,000 at the end of the month. The revenues increase stockholders' equity, and expenses decrease stockholders' equity.

The following King Hardware income statement summarizes the company's revenues and expenses for the month of March:

King Hardware Co.
Income Statement for the Month Ended March 31, 20X1

Revenues (sales)		$130,000
Expenses		
Cost of goods sold	$100,000	
Rent	1,000	
Total expenses		101,000
Net income		$ 29,000

Real income statements and balance sheets use the same formats as those for King Hardware, though they usually contain more details. Consider General Mills. Simplified versions of its balance sheet and income statement follow (in millions):

General Mills, Inc.
Balance Sheet May 29, 2011

Assets		Liabilities and Stockholders' Equity	
Cash	$ 620	Liabilities	$12,063
Accounts receivable	1,162	Stockholders' equity	6,612
Other assets	16,893		
Total assets	$18,675	Total liabilities and stockholders' equity	$18,675

General Mills, Inc.
Income Statement for the Year Ended May 29, 2011

Sales	$14,880
Expenses	13,076
Net income	$ 1,804

The income statement shows that General Mills' stockholders' equity (retained earnings) increased by $1,804 million because of profitable operations in the year ended May 29, 2011. This $1,804 million is included in the $6,612 million of stockholders' equity on the May 29, 2011, balance sheet.

The Analytical Power of the Balance Sheet Equation

The balance sheet equation highlights the link between the income statement and balance sheet. Indeed, the entire accounting system is based on the simple balance sheet equation,

$$\text{Assets (A)} = \text{liabilities (L)} + \text{stockholders' equity (SE)} \qquad (1)$$

SE equals the original ownership claims plus the increase in ownership claims from profitable operations. That is, SE equals the claim arising from paid-in capital plus the claim arising from retained earnings. Therefore,

$$A = L + \text{paid-in capital} + \text{retained earnings} \tag{2}$$

For most companies, the major changes in retained earnings come from revenues and expenses—revenues increase retained earnings and expenses decrease them. Revenue and expense accounts are nothing more than current period changes in retained earnings. They are temporary retained earnings accounts that are reset to zero at the start of each new period. They summarize the revenues and expenses that occurred during the current period, summarizing the reasons for the changes in retained earnings. After a company adds the revenues less expenses for the current period to the balance in retained earnings, it resets revenue and expense accounts to zero so that it can use them to accumulate the revenues and expenses for the next period.

Notice in Exhibit 1-1 that, for each transaction, the equation is always in balance. How do we keep it in balance? If a transaction affects items on only one side of the equation, the total amount added equals the total amount subtracted on that side. If the transaction affects items on both sides, then we add or subtract equal amounts on each side.

The striking feature of the balance sheet equation is its universal applicability. Every transaction, no matter how simple or complex, can be analyzed via the equation. The top technical partners in the world's largest professional accounting firms, when confronted with the most intricate transactions of multinational companies, inevitably discuss and analyze transactions in terms of the balance sheet equation.

Accrual Basis and Cash Basis

There are two approaches to accounting: the cash basis and the accrual basis. You may not realize it, but you are probably already familiar with the cash basis. We keep our checkbooks on the cash basis. We simply record the receipts and payments of cash. Many small nonprofit organizations use the cash basis of accounting.

In contrast, corporations and many other large organizations measure income and financial position using the accrual basis of accounting. The **accrual basis** recognizes the impact of transactions on the financial statements in the periods when revenues and expenses occur instead of when the company receives or pays cash. That is, a company records revenue when it meets the criteria for recognition, and it records expenses when it uses resources to generate revenue—not necessarily when cash changes hands.

accrual basis
A process of accounting that recognizes the impact of transactions on the financial statements in the time periods when revenues and expenses occur instead of when the company pays or receives cash.

Transaction 4a in Exhibit 1-1, on page 5, shows an example of the accrual basis. King Hardware recognizes revenue when it makes sales on credit, not when it receives cash. Similarly, transactions 4b and 7b (for cost of goods sold and rent) show that King Hardware records expenses as it expends efforts or uses services to obtain the revenue, regardless of when it pays out the cash. Most users of financial statements believe that the accrual basis provides the best framework for relating accomplishments (revenues) with efforts (expenses). That is, they believe that revenue less expenses is a better measure of a company's performance during a period than is cash receipts less cash payments. Why do they believe this? Companies conduct more than 95% of all business on a credit basis, so cash receipts and payments are not the critical transactions for recognizing accomplishments and efforts. The accrual basis evolved to provide a more complete and timely, and therefore more accurate, report of the financial impact of various events.

cash basis
A process of accounting where revenue and expense recognition occur when the company receives and pays out cash.

If King Hardware used the **cash basis** of accounting instead of the accrual basis, revenue and expense recognition would occur when the company receives and pays out cash. In March, King Hardware would show $25,000 of revenue, the amount of cash collected from customers. Similarly, cost of goods sold would be the $20,000 cash payment for the purchase of inventory, and rent expense would be the $3,000 cash payment for rent rather than the $1,000 rent applicable to March. Consider the rent example for King Hardware. Under the cash basis, March must bear expenses for the entire quarter's rent of $3,000, merely because the cash outflow occurs then. Most accountants maintain that it is nonsense to say that March's rent expense was $3,000 while rent expense for April and May was zero. In contrast, the accrual basis better measures performance by assigning one-third of the total 3-month rental expenses to each of the 3 months that benefits from the use of the facilities. This method makes the economic performance of each month comparable to that of other months.

The major deficiency of the cash basis of accounting is that it fails to properly match efforts and accomplishments (expenses and revenues) to measure performance. Moreover, it omits key assets (such as accounts receivable and prepaid rent) and key liabilities (such as accounts payable) from balance sheets that measure financial position.

Nonprofit Organizations

The examples in this chapter focus on profit-seeking organizations, but nonprofit organizations, such as government agencies and charitable organizations, also use balance sheets and income statements. For many years, most nonprofit organizations used cash-basis rather than accrual accounting. However, that is changing quickly. As these organizations face more pressure to develop accurate measures of performance, they are increasingly using accrual accounting.

The basic concepts of assets, liabilities, revenues, and expenses apply to all organizations, whatever their goals and wherever they are located. However, organizations that do not seek profits do not measure income. Further, because they have no owners, there is no owners' equity. Nevertheless, they have parallels to income statements and balance sheets. For example, balance sheets of nonprofit organizations show a category of "net assets" instead of "owners' equity" to measure the difference between assets and liabilities. Instead of an income statement, nonprofit organizations have a "statement of activities" that reports changes in net assets.

Adjustments to the Accounts

Earlier, we defined a transaction as any economic event that an accountant should record. Under accrual accounting, accountants record both **explicit transactions**—day-to-day routine events, such as credit sales, credit purchases, cash received on account, and cash payments on account— and **implicit transactions**—events that day-to-day recording procedures temporarily ignore, such as expiration of prepaid rent or accrual of interest due to the passage of time. Explicit transactions are easy to identify because they record market transactions, exchanges of goods and services between the entity and another party. They are generally supported by **source documents**, clear evidence of transactions, such as sales slips and purchase invoices.

In contrast, accountants need a way to ensure that they record all implicit transactions. At the end of each accounting period accountants systematically make **adjustments** (or **adjusting entries**) to account for implicit transactions such as unpaid wages, prepaid rent, interest owed, and the like. We classify the principal adjustments into four types, each of which we will discuss in detail:

1. Expiration of Unexpired Costs
2. Recognition (Earning) of Unearned Revenues
3. Accrual of Unrecorded Expenses
4. Accrual of Unrecorded Revenues

These adjustments are an essential part of accrual accounting. They provide a more complete and timely measure of efforts, accomplishments, and financial position.

Adjustment Type I: Expiration of Unexpired Costs

You can view assets other than cash and receivables as bundles of economic services awaiting future use—prepaid or stored costs that the accounting system carries forward to future periods. The values of assets frequently decline (and eventually disappear) because of the passage of time. We illustrated this first type of adjustment in Exhibit 1-1 by recognizing the rent expense in transaction 7b. Rather than immediately charging these costs as expenses, we charge them as expenses in future periods when the company uses the services:

explicit transactions

Transactions that record day-to-day routine events—such as credit sales, credit purchases, cash received on account, and cash disbursed on account— that are supported by source documents.

implicit transactions

Transactions that record events that day-to-day recording procedures temporarily ignore, such as expiration of prepaid rent or accrual of interest due to the passage of time.

source documents

Clear evidence of transactions, such as sales slips and purchase invoices.

adjustments (adjusting entries)

Entries that record implicit transactions such as unpaid wages, prepaid rent, interest owed, and the like.

Objective 4

Make adjustments to the accounts under accrual accounting.

Acquisition		Expiration
Assets (Unexpired Costs)	Become →	Expenses (e.g., Cost of Goods Sold, Rent, Other Expenses or Losses)
Appear in Balance Sheet		**Appear in Income Statement**

unexpired cost

Any asset that managers expect to become an expense in future periods, for example, inventory and prepaid rent.

When a company uses the services represented by a particular cost, we say the cost expires. Therefore, an **unexpired cost** is any asset that managers expect to become an expense in future periods. Examples in our King Hardware illustration are inventory and prepaid rent. Other examples are equipment and various prepaid expenses, such as prepaid insurance and prepaid property taxes. When accountants say they are "writing off" an asset, they mean they are recording the decline in asset value as an expense.

The analysis of the inventory and rent transactions in Exhibit 1-1 maintains this distinction between acquisition and expiration. The unexpired costs of inventory and prepaid rent are assets until the company uses them up, at which time they become expenses.

Timing of Asset Expiration

Sometimes companies acquire and use resources almost simultaneously. Examples are advertising services and sales salaries and commissions. Conceptually, we can view these costs, at least momentarily, as assets on acquisition before we write them off as expenses. For example, suppose an eighth transaction in Exhibit 1-1 was newspaper advertising acquired for $1,000 cash. We can analyze the transaction in two phases:

	Assets			=	Liabilities	+	Stockholders' Equity	
Transaction	Cash +	Other Assets +	Unexpired Advertising	=			Paid-in Capital	Retained Earnings
8a. Acquire advertising services	−1,000		+1,000	=				
8b. Use advertising services			−1,000	=				−1,000 (expense)

In concept, the benefit of the newspaper ad is to increase sales, and this benefit expires over a period of days or weeks after the ad runs. However, when the benefit expires quickly, accountants often do not bother to take two steps to record an asset, Unexpired Advertising, and then write it off. Instead, they take a shortcut and record the expense immediately:

Transaction	Cash + Other Assets	=	Liabilities + Paid-in Capital + Retained Earnings
8. Acquire and use advertising services	−1,000	=	−1,000 (expense)

Making the entry in two steps instead of one is cumbersome from a practical bookkeeping viewpoint. But it is useful to think about how accounting entries relate to what managers actually do. Managers acquire goods and services, not expenses per se. These goods and services become expenses as managers use them to obtain revenue.

When does an asset expire and become an expense? Sometimes this question is hard to answer. For example, some accountants prefer to record as assets the amounts spent for research and development (R&D) and write them off (charge as an expense) in some systematic manner over a period of years. Why? Because they maintain that money spent for R&D creates future benefits and, thus, qualifies as an asset. But the regulators of financial accounting in the United States have ruled that all such costs have vague future benefits that are difficult to measure reliably. Thus, financial reporting rules in the United States require companies to write off R&D costs as expenses immediately. You will not find R&D costs listed as assets in U.S. balance sheets. Outside the United States, international financial accounting standards allow companies to differentiate between research costs—which they immediately expense—and development costs—which they are allowed to record as assets and write off to expense in future periods if the development costs meet some specific criteria.

long-lived assets

Assets that will provide services for more than a year.

Depreciation

To keep the expense-adjustment illustration simple, until now we have deliberately ignored the accounting for **long-lived assets**—assets that will provide services for more than a year. Equipment is an example of a long-lived asset that is essentially a bundle of future services that a company will use over a series of years. The cost of equipment becomes an expense on the income statement via depreciation, which is the cost of equipment that a company spreads over the future periods in which the company will be able to use the equipment.

useful life

The number of years the company expects to use an asset.

residual value

The predicted sales value of a long-lived asset at the end of its useful life.

To account for long-lived assets, accountants (1) predict the length of the asset's **useful life** (that is, the number of years the company expects to use the asset), (2) predict the ultimate **residual value** (that is, the predicted value of the asset at the end of its useful life) and (3) spread the cost of the asset less the residual value to the years of its useful life in some systematic way. This process of systematically spreading the equipment cost across the years of its useful life is called depreciation for physical assets—such as buildings, equipment, furniture, and fixtures—that the entity owns. (Land is not subject to depreciation. Why? Because we do not use up land.) The same process is called depletion when it is applied to natural resources and amortization when it is applied to intangible (non-physical) assets.

The most popular depreciation method for financial reporting is the **straight-line method**, which depreciates an asset by the same amount each year. Suppose King Hardware had acquired some store equipment for $14,000 on March 1. The predicted life of the equipment is 10 years, and the estimated residual value is $2,000:

straight-line method
A method that depreciates an asset by the same amount each year.

$$\text{straight-line depreciation per year} = \frac{\text{original cost} - \text{estimated residual value}}{\text{years of useful life}}$$

$$= \frac{\$14,000 - \$2,000}{10}$$

$$= \$1,200 \text{ per year, or } \$100 \text{ per month}$$

Depreciation illustrates the essence of the general concept of expense. The purchase and use of a resource (that is, a good or service, such as inventories, rent, or equipment) ordinarily consists of two basic steps: (1) the acquisition of the asset (transactions 2, 3, and 7a) and (2) the expiration of the asset as an expense (transactions 4b and 7b). When we use an asset, whether immediately or in some future period, we say part of the asset expires, and we decrease the value of the asset and decrease owners' equity by the same amount.

Summary Problem for Your Review

PROBLEM

We analyzed the King Hardware transactions for March in Exhibit 1-1 on page 5. The balance sheet showed the following balances as of March 31, 20X1:

	Assets	Liabilities and Stockholders' Equity
Cash	$ 27,000	
Accounts receivable	105,000	
Inventory	10,000	
Prepaid rent	2,000	
Accounts payable		$ 15,000
Paid-in capital		100,000
Retained earnings		29,000
	$144,000	$144,000

Here is a summary of the transactions that occurred during the next month, April:

1. Cash collections of accounts receivable, $88,000.
2. Cash payments of accounts payable, $24,000.
3. Acquisitions of inventory on open account, $80,000.
4. Merchandise carried in inventory at a cost of $70,000 was sold on open account for $85,000.
5. Adjustment for recognition of rent expense for April.

Using the accrual basis of accounting, prepare an analysis of transactions, employing the equation approach demonstrated in Exhibit 1-1.

SOLUTION

The answer is in the top half of Exhibit 1-2 ending with transaction 5. We will explain transactions 6–9 in the following sections.

Exhibit 1-2
King Hardware Co.
Analysis of Transactions (in dollars) for April 20X1

Transaction		Assets			=	Liabilities			+	Stockholders' Equity	
	Cash +	Accounts Receivable +	Inventory +	Prepaid Rent	=	Accounts Payable +	Accrued Wages Payable +	Unearned Revenue* +		Paid-in Capital +	Retained Earnings
Bal. 3/31/X1	+ 27,000	+ 105,000	+ 10,000	+ 2,000	=	+ 15,000				+ 100,000	+ 29,000
1.	+ 88,000	– 88,000			=						
2.	– 24,000				=	– 24,000					
3.			+ 80,000		=	+ 80,000					
4a.		+ 85,000			=						+ 85,000 (revenue)
4b.			– 70,000		=						– 70,000 (expense)
5.				– 1,000	=						– 1,000 (expense)
6.	+ 3,000				=			+ 3,000*			
7.	– 6,000				=						– 6,000 (expense)
8.					=		+ 600				– 600 (expense)
9.	– 18,000				=						– 18,000 (dividend)
4/30/X1	+ 70,000	+ 102,000	+ 20,000	+ 1,000	=	+ 71,000	+ 600	+ 3,000		+ 100,000	+ 18,400

193,000 (Assets)   193,000 (Liabilities + Stockholders' Equity)

*Some accountants would call this account "Customer Deposits," "Advances from Customers," "Deferred Sales Revenue," or "Unrealized Sales Revenue."

Adjustment Type II: Recognition (Earning) of Unearned Revenues

Now let's examine a second type of adjustment. Consider the following transaction for King Hardware in April:

6. Some customers paid $3,000 cash in advance for merchandise that they ordered but that King Hardware did not expect to deliver until mid-May.

See transaction 6 in Exhibit 1-2. We call this $3,000 **unearned revenue** or **deferred revenue**. Why? Because King Hardware collected cash from customers and recorded the amount received before the company earned it by delivering the merchandise. Unearned revenue is a liability because King Hardware is obligated to deliver the merchandise ordered or to refund the money if it does not deliver the merchandise. Some companies call this account *advances from customers* or *customer deposits*. Advance collections of rent and magazine subscriptions are other examples.

unearned revenue (deferred revenue)
Collections from customers that companies receive and record before they earn the revenue.

Sometimes it is easier to see how accountants analyze transactions by visualizing the financial positions of both parties to a contract. For instance, consider the rent transaction of March 1. You are already familiar with the King Hardware analysis. The $1,000 monthly entries for King Hardware are examples of the first type of adjustments, the expiration of unexpired costs. Compare this financial impact on King Hardware with the impact on the landlord who receives the rental payment:

	Owner of Property (Landlord, Lessor)			King Hardware (Tenant, Lessee)		
	A	= L	+ SE	A	= L +	SE
	Cash	Unearned Rent Revenue	Rent Revenue	Cash	Prepaid Rent	Rent Expense
a. Explicit transaction (advanced payment of 3 months' rent)	+3,000 =	+3,000		−3,000	+3,000 =	
b. March adjustment (for 1 month's rent)	=	−1,000	+1,000		−1,000 =	−1,000
c. April adjustment (for 1 month's rent)	=	−1,000	+1,000		−1,000 =	−1,000
d. May adjustment (for 1 month's rent)	=	−1,000	+1,000		−1,000 =	−1,000

From the viewpoint of the owner of the rental property, the first transaction recognizes unearned revenue. This is a liability because the owner is obligated to deliver the rental services (or to refund the money if it does not deliver the services).

As you can see from the preceding table, adjustments for the expiration of unexpired costs (Type I) and adjustments for the recognition of unearned revenues (Type II) are mirror images of each other. If one party to a contract has a prepaid expense, the other has unearned revenue. We can make a similar analysis for a 3-year magazine subscription. The buyer recognizes a prepaid expense (asset) and uses adjustments of Type I to spread the initial cost to expense over the 3-year life of the services. In turn, the magazine publisher must initially recognize its liability, unearned subscription revenue. It then changes the unearned revenue to earned revenue (i.e., increases rent revenue and decreases unearned revenue) when the company delivers magazines throughout the life of the subscription—adjustment Type II.

Adjustment Type III: Accrual of Unrecorded Expenses

Let's proceed now to the third type of adjustment: accrual of unrecorded expenses. To **accrue** something means to accumulate and record a receivable or payable during a given period even though no explicit transaction occurs. Examples of **accrued expenses**—expenses reported on the income statement before a company pays for them with cash—are the wages of employees

accrue
To accumulate a receivable or payable during a given period, even though no explicit transaction occurs.

accrued expenses
Expenses reported on the income statement before a company pays for them with cash.

for partial payroll periods and the interest that accumulates on borrowed money before the interest payment is made. The liability corresponding to such expenses, such as wages payable or interest payable, grows as time passes—it is accruing (or accumulating). Computerized accounting systems can make daily or even "real-time" recordings in the accounts for many accruals. However, such frequent entries are often costly and unnecessary. Instead, accountants usually make adjustments to bring each expense and corresponding liability account up to date only periodically, such as at the end of a period for which they are preparing formal financial statements.

Accounting for Payment of Wages

Consider the following two transactions relating to wages paid by King Hardware to its employees:

7. King Hardware paid employees $1,500 each Friday in April, for total wages of $6,000. (For simplicity, we ignored wages in March.) King Hardware recognizes these payments for employee services by increasing Wages Expense and decreasing Cash.
8. King Hardware incurred 2 days of wages totaling $600 near the end of April, but it did not pay the employees until after April 30. Accordingly, the accountant increased Wages Expense and increased a liability, Accrued Wages Payable.

Most companies pay their employees at predetermined times. For example, the University of Washington pays employees on the tenth and twenty-fifth of each month for the half-month period ending 10 days earlier. King Hardware pays its employees each Friday for services rendered during that week. Here is a sample calendar for April:

April						
S	M	T	W	T	F	S
	1	2	3	4	5	6
7	8	9	10	11	12	13
14	15	16	17	18	19	20
21	22	23	24	25	26	27
28	29	30				

The cumulative total wages paid on the Fridays during April were $6,000. King Hardware accounts for wages expense using the shortcut procedure described earlier for goods and services that a company routinely consumes in the period of their purchase. Transaction 7 in Exhibit 1-2 (and summarized next) shows King Hardware's entry for April's wages through April 26:

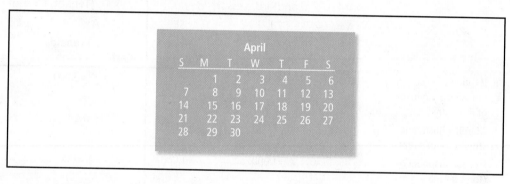

		Assets (A)	=	Liabilities (L)	+	Stockholders' Equity (SE)
		Cash	=			Wages Expense
7.	Routine entry for explicit transactions	−6,000	=			−6,000

Accounting for Accrual of Wages

King Hardware's wages of $1,500 per week are $300 per day for a 5-day work week. At the end of April, in addition to the $6,000 already paid and recorded, King Hardware owes $600 for the time employees worked during the last 2 days of April but will not pay the employees for these services until the next regular weekly payday, May 3. Thus, to bring the financial statements up to date through April 30, an accrual is necessary to record wages owed but not yet recorded. Periodic adjustments ensure that the financial statements apply accrual accounting to measure revenues, expenses, assets, and liabilities on a timely basis. King Hardware accounts for this implicit transaction with entry 8:

	A	=	L	+	SE
			Accrued Wages Payable		Wages Expense
8. Adjustment for the accrual of unrecorded wages		=	+600		−600

Accrued expenses, such as accrued wages payable, arise when payment follows the rendering of services. Other examples of accrued expenses include sales commissions, property taxes, income taxes, and interest on borrowed money. In all of these, the payment generally comes after the company recognizes the expense. Consider interest expense, which is an amount paid for the use of money. It is similar to the rent you pay for the use of buildings or automobiles. The interest accumulates (accrues) as time unfolds, regardless of when the company actually pays the interest in cash. So when General Mills showed interest expense of $346 million on its 2011 income statement, it means that it accrued $346 million of interest that year, not necessarily that it paid $346 million in cash.

Adjustment Type IV: Accrual of Unrecorded Revenues

The final type of adjustment, the recognition of **accrued revenues**—revenues that a company has earned but has not yet received in cash—does not appear in Exhibit 1-2. It is the mirror image of the accrual of unrecorded expenses. Suppose Security State Bank lends $50,000 in cash to King Hardware on a 3-month promissory note with interest at 1% per month payable at the end of the 3 months. The following tabulation shows the effect of the adjustment for interest at the end of the first month (.01 × $50,000 = $500) on both King Hardware (the accrual of unrecorded expenses, adjustment type III covered in the previous section) and Security State Bank (the accrual of unrecorded revenues, the subject of this section):

accrued revenues
Revenues that a company has earned but has not yet received in cash.

Security State Bank (Lender)					King Hardware Co. (Borrower)				
A	=	L	+	SE	A	=	L	+	SE
Accrued Interest Receivable				Interest Revenue			Accrued Interest Payable		Interest Expense
+500	=			+500		=	+500		−500

No cash changes hands at the end of the first month, but King Hardware records interest expense and Security State Bank records interest revenue.

This completes our discussion of the four types of accruals. We summarize these in Exhibit 1-3, which shows accruals of expenses or revenues in the columns and the timing of the accrual compared to the cash flows in the rows.

	Expense	Revenue
Payment precedes recognition of expense or revenue	I Expiration of unexpired costs. Illustration: The write-off of prepaid rent as rent expense (Exhibit 1-2, entry 5)	II Recognition (earning) of unearned revenues. Illustration: The mirror image of Type I, whereby the landlord recognizes rent revenue and decreases unearned rent revenue (rent collected in advance)
Recognition of expense or revenue precedes payments	III Accrual of unrecorded expenses. Illustration: Wage expense for wages earned by employees but not yet paid (Exhibit 1-2, entry 8)	IV Accrual of unrecorded revenues. Illustration: Interest revenue earned but not yet collected by a financial institution

Exhibit 1-3
Four Major Types of Accounting Adjustments Before Preparation of Financial Statements

Making Managerial Decisions

The manager of the DVD division of a large electronics firm complained, "I don't understand all this accrual stuff. Why can't you just measure my performance based on cash in and cash out?" Provide a brief answer to this question.

Answer

Accrual accounting more accurately matches accomplishment with effort. When you buy a machine that will last 5 years, do you think the entire cost of the machine should be charged against your performance at the time of purchase? Or when you sell a carton of DVD players on credit to a long-standing customer who is virtually certain to pay, should your credit for the sale await eventual collection of the cash? Accrual accounting gives you credit for accomplishments when you achieve them and charges for the expenses associated with those accomplishments. Thus, it provides a much better measure of performance than does "cash in and cash out."

Dividends and Retained Earnings

Objective 5

Explain the nature of dividends and retained earnings.

We have now covered all the entries in Exhibit 1-2 that show how revenues increase and expenses decrease the retained earnings portion of stockholders' equity. Now, let's look at transaction 9, which shows another type of transaction that decreases retained earnings—payment of dividends:

9. Cash dividends of $18,000 were declared by the board of directors and disbursed to stock-holders on April 29.

Dividends Are Not Expenses

cash dividends (dividends)

Distributions of cash to stockholders that reduce retained earnings.

Cash dividends (often called simply **dividends**) are distributions of cash to stockholders. Dividends reduce retained earnings, but they are not expenses like rent and wages. Companies do not deduct them from revenues when measuring income because dividends do not help to generate sales or conduct operations. Cash dividends simply distribute assets (cash) to the owners of those assets (stockholders). They reduce both assets (cash) and owners' claims on those assets (retained earnings).

A company's board of directors decides when to pay dividends and how much to pay. The amount of cash dividends declared by the board of directors of a company depends on many factors. A company's cash position and future needs for cash to pay debts or to purchase additional assets are usually more important than the balance in retained earnings. A company with a large retained earnings balance but little cash will find it difficult to pay dividends. Many companies try to maintain a stable dividend policy, paying dividends consistently even if they encounter a few years of little or no net income. For example, General Mills has paid shareholder dividends, uninterrupted and without reduction, for 112 consecutive years.

Nature of Retained Earnings

Let's examine the retained earnings account in more detail. On page 4 we explained that you can think of the entire right-hand side of the balance sheet equation as claims against the total assets. The liabilities are the claims of creditors. The stockholders' equity represents the claims of owners arising out of their initial investment (paid-in capital) and subsequent profitable operations (retained earnings). On August 12, 2012, General Mills had retained earnings of $10.3 billion, nearly seven times its paid-in capital of $1.3 billion. As a company grows, the Retained Earnings account can soar if the company does not pay large dividends. Retained Earnings is frequently the largest stockholders' equity account, especially for older companies. For example, General Electric had retained earnings of $142 billion on September 30, 2012, compared to paid-in capital of less than $1 billion. In contrast, Amgen, a biotech company that had huge investments before it began generating any profits, had paid-in capital of $28 billion and a retained deficit (negative retained earnings) of $9 billion.

Some users of financial statements have the mistaken impression that retained earnings represents a pot of cash awaiting distribution to stockholders. Rather, retained earnings (and also paid-in capital) is a general claim against, or undivided interest in, total assets, not a specific claim against cash or against any other particular asset. Do not confuse the assets themselves with the claims of stockholders against the assets.

We can illustrate this for King Hardware by looking at cash and retained earnings at three points in time (from the top line and bottom line of Exhibit 1-1 on page 5, and the bottom line of Exhibit 1-2 on page 12):

	Cash	Retained Earnings
February 28, 20X1	$100,000	$ 0
March 31, 20X1	27,000	29,000
April 30, 20X1	70,000	18,400

On February 28, King Hardware had $100,000 in cash (all from investments by stockholders) and no retained earnings because King Hardware had not yet begun operations and, thus, had generated no profits or losses. By March 31, cash had fallen by $73,000 to $27,000, primarily because the company had used cash to buy inventories. Meanwhile, retained earnings increased by $29,000 because of profitable operations. Finally, during April, cash increased by $43,000 (mainly because King Hardware began to collect its accounts receivable), while retained earnings fell by $10,600, mainly because King Hardware paid more dividends than it earned in net income. You can see that cash can increase while retained earnings decreases, and vice versa. It is clear that there is no direct relationship between retained earnings and available cash.

Preparing Financial Statements

We will use the data from the balance sheet equation in Exhibit 1-2 (p. 12) to prepare King Hardware's April financial statements. The balance sheet and income statement, shown in Exhibits 1-4 and 1-5, are similar to those illustrated earlier. The balance sheet uses the totals at the bottom of Exhibit 1-2, and the income statement uses the revenue and expense entries in the retained earnings column.

Objective 6

Select relevant items from a set of data and assemble them into a balance sheet and an income statement.

Assets		Liabilities and Stockholders' Equity		
Cash	$ 70,000	Liabilities		
Accounts receivable	102,000	Accounts payable	$ 71,000	
Inventory	20,000	Accrued wages payable	600	
Prepaid rent	1,000	Unearned revenue	3,000	$ 74,600
		Stockholders' equity		
		Paid-in capital	$100,000	
		Retained earnings	18,400	118,400
Total assets	$193,000	Total liabilities and stockholders' equity		$193,000

Exhibit 1-4
King Hardware Company
Balance Sheet as of April 30, 20X1

Sales		$85,000
Cost of goods sold		70,000
Gross profit		$15,000
Operating expenses		
Rent	$1,000	
Wages	6,600	7,600
Net income		$ 7,400

Exhibit 1-5
King Hardware Company
Income Statement for the Month Ended April 30, 20X1

Exhibit 1-6

King Hardware Company
*Changes in Retained Earnings for
the Month Ended April 30, 20X1*

Retained earnings, March 31, 20X1	$29,000
Net income for April	7,400
Total	$36,400
Dividends	18,000
Retained earnings, April 30, 20X1	$18,400

Exhibit 1-6 shows the linkage between the balance sheet and income statement. It lists the items affecting retained earnings during April. It starts with the beginning balance, adds net income for the period, and deducts cash dividends, to arrive at the ending balance. This explanation of changes in retained earnings is often included as part of a **statement of stockholders' equity**, which shows the changes in each individual stockholders' equity account (including retained earnings) during the period. Accountants call the income statement in Exhibit 1-5 a "multiple-step" statement because it includes a subtotal for gross profit. As described in Chapter 4 on page 148, gross profit (sometimes called gross margin) is the excess of sales over the cost of the inventory that was sold. A "single-step" statement would merely list all the expenses, including cost of goods sold, and deduct the total from sales. More complex multiple-step income statements may have additional subtotals.

Sole Proprietorships and Partnerships

statement of stockholders' equity

A statement that shows the changes in each stockholders' equity account during the period.

Objective 7

Distinguish between the reporting of corporate owners' equity and the reporting of owners' equity for partnerships and sole proprietorships.

sole proprietorship

A business entity with a single owner.

partnership

An organization that joins two or more individuals together as co-owners.

To this point, the discussion has focused on the accounting for a corporation. However, the basic accounting concepts also apply to a **sole proprietorship**—a business entity with a single owner—or a **partnership**—an organization that joins two or more individuals together as co-owners. Accounting for assets, liabilities, revenues, and expenses is identical for all forms of businesses. The basic concepts relating to owners' equity are also identical, except that financial statements for proprietorships and partnerships rarely make distinctions between paid-in capital and retained earnings. Let's compare the owners' equity section of King Hardware as of April 30 to similar presentations for a sole proprietorship owned by Alice Walsh or a partnership owned equally by Susan Zingler and John Martin:

Owners' Equity for a Corporation		
Stockholders' equity		
Capital stock (paid-in capital)	$100,000	
Retained earnings	18,400	
Total stockholders' equity		$118,400

Owners' Equity for a Sole Proprietorship	
Alice Walsh, capital	$118,400

Owners' Equity for a Partnership	
Susan Zingler, capital	$ 59,200
John Martin, capital	59,200
Total partners' equity	$118,400

This example shows that, unlike corporations, sole proprietorships and partnerships do not distinguish between paid-in capital (i.e., amounts invested by owners) and retained earnings. Instead, they typically accumulate a single amount for each owner's original investment, subsequent investments, share of net income, and withdrawals.

net worth

A synonym for owners' equity.

Some accountants call owners' equity **net worth**. This is unfortunate because naïve users of financial statements might interpret this as meaning that owners' equity is a measure of the market value of the business to an outside buyer. It is not. The market value of a business depends on future profit projections that may have little relationship to the existing assets, liabilities, or stockholders' equity of the entity as measured by its accounting records. For example, General Mills' shareholders' equity (or net worth) in June 2011, was just over $6.6 billion, while its market value was approximately $37 billion.

Making Managerial Decisions

When entrepreneurs start a company, they must decide whether the company will be a sole proprietorship, a partnership, or a corporation. As the accountant for such a start-up company, explain how the accounting system would differ for each of the three types of organizational structures.

Answer

Most important aspects of the accounting system are the same for all three types of organizational structures. The only difference will be in the owners' equity section. For a sole proprietorship, there is only one owners' equity account. A partnership has one owners' equity account for each partner. This requires the accountant to attribute all increases or decreases in owners' equity to a particular partner. For example, income will be split among the partners according to a predetermined formula. Finally, a corporation divides owners' equity into paid-in capital and retained earnings to distinguish resources contributed by the owners from those generated by profitable operations.

Generally Accepted Accounting Principles

Accounting is commonly misunderstood as being a precise discipline that produces exact measurements of a company's financial position and performance. As a result, many individuals regard accountants as little more than mechanical tabulators who grind out financial reports after processing an imposing amount of detail in accordance with stringent predetermined rules. Although accountants take methodical steps with masses of data, their rules of measurement allow much room for judgment—accounting is more an art than a science. These judgments are guided by a set of principles on which there is general agreement, not on rules that can be "proved." These principles and procedures that together make up accepted accounting practice at any given time—generally accepted accounting principles (GAAP)—were introduced in Chapter 3 on page 98.

Objective 8

Explain the role of auditors in financial reporting and how accounting standards are set.

Auditor's Independent Opinion

To ensure that companies abide by GAAP, the financial statements of publicly held corporations are subject to an independent audit. An **audit** is an examination or in-depth inspection of financial statements and companies' records made by an independent registered public accounting firm in accordance with auditing standards approved by the Public Company Accounting Oversight Board (PCAOB) in the United States. The PCAOB is a part of the **Securities and Exchange Commission (SEC)**, a government agency that regulates U.S. financial markets, including financial reporting. After auditing a company's financial statements, an accounting firm issues an **independent opinion**—the accountant's assurance that management's financial statements are in conformity with GAAP. The audit opinion typically includes the following key phrasing found in General Mills' 2012 annual report:

> *In our opinion, the consolidated financial statements referred to above present fairly, in all material respects, the financial position of General Mills, Inc. and subsidiaries as of May 27, 2012 and May 29, 2011, and the results of their operations and their cash flows for each of the fiscal years in the three-year period ended May 27, 2012, in conformity with U. S. generally accepted accounting principles.*

Audit opinions are not infallible guarantees of financial truth. Why? Financial statements may seem precise because their numbers all add up. However, they are the result of a complex measurement process that rests on a large number of assumptions and conventions. Further, it is impossible for auditors to examine every bit of data that goes into the financial statements.

audit
An "examination" or in-depth inspection of financial statements and companies' records made in accordance with auditing standards.

Securities and Exchange Commission (SEC)
A government agency that regulates the financial markets in the United States, including financial reporting.

independent opinion
The accountant's assurance that management's financial statements are in conformity with GAAP.

Although audits are not perfect, financial statement users rely on them as being honest and impartial assessments of the financial statements. However, in the last decade the shareholders of several companies, including **Enron**, **WorldCom**, **Washington Mutual**, **Fannie Mae**, and **Tyco**, accused auditors of being either negligent or deceitful (and sometimes both). These companies experienced financial troubles after receiving a "clean bill of health" from their auditors. In response to the scandals in the early 2000s, the U.S. Congress passed the Sarbanes-Oxley Act (SOX) as described in Chapter 3, p. 98. SOX required independent audits of companies' internal control systems—the policies that protect and ensure efficient use of a company's assets. One function of internal controls is to make sure that a company's financial records and reports are accurate. Management must file a statement attesting to the quality of its internal control system, and auditors examine both the system and management's statement about it. Then they issue an opinion, such as the following one about General Mills:

> *We also have audited General Mills, Inc.'s internal control over financial reporting as of May 27, 2012, based on criteria established in Internal Control—Integrated Framework issued by the Committee of Sponsoring Organizations of the Treadway Commission (COSO). . . We conducted our audits in accordance with the standards of the Public Company Accounting Oversight Board (United States). . . . [I]n our opinion, General Mills, Inc. maintained, in all material respects, effective internal control over financial reporting as of May 27, 2012.*

Accounting Standard Setters

Financial Accounting Standards Board (FASB)
The body that sets GAAP in the United States.

International Accounting Standards Board (IASB)
The group that establishes international GAAP.

Auditors and the investing public rely on GAAP determined by the **Financial Accounting Standards Board (FASB)** in the United States and the **International Accounting Standards Board (IASB)** in much of the rest of the world. The FASB, consisting of 7 full-time members plus a staff of more than 60 members, is an independent creation of the private sector. Its mission is to "establish and improve standards of financial accounting and reporting for the guidance and education of the public, including issuers, auditors, and users of financial information." The IASB is a similar independent organization whose pronouncements, called International Financial Reporting Standards (IFRS) as discussed in Chapter 3 on page 98, define GAAP in the European Union and more than 100 other countries. In 2008 the SEC started accepting financial statements based on IFRS for non-U.S. companies whose stock is traded in U.S. capital markets. It also defined a "road-map" for eventual adoption of international standards by U.S. companies as well. The FASB and IASB are currently working on converging their separate standards into one set of world-wide standards.

The SEC has the ultimate responsibility for specifying GAAP for U.S. companies with publicly traded stock. However, the SEC has informally delegated much rule-making power to the FASB. If and when the pending move to international standards occurs, such power will also be delegated to the IASB. This public sector–private sector relationship may be sketched as follows:

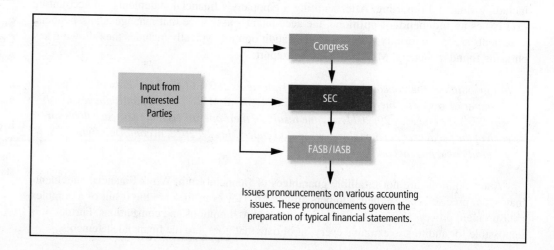

Business First

Corporate Citizenship Awards

The media have criticized many businesses recently for their greed and lack of ethics. While some companies deserve such criticism, many more go out of their way to prove their integrity and good citizenship through their dealings with customers, suppliers, employees, and the community. To recognize some of these activities, for the last 12 years *Corporate Responsibility Magazine* has annually named the 100 best corporate citizens of the year. Three companies have made the list all 12 years: Intel, Cisco Systems, and Starbucks. In 2011 the top 10 companies were Johnson Controls Inc., Campbell Soup Co., International Business Machines Corp., Bristol-Meyers Squibb Co., Mattel, Inc., 3M Co., Accenture, Kimberly-Clark Corp., Hewlett-Packard Co., and Nike Inc. What these companies have in common with those included on past lists is a commitment to social responsibility, including an assessment of concern for stakeholders in seven areas: environment, climate change, human rights, philanthropy, employee relations, finance, and governance.

CRO also maintains that good corporate social policies can lead to improved financial performance. According to an analysis of the 2009 "100 Best," companies on the list outperformed the companies not on the list by 26% in the last 3 years. Especially in the recession of 2008–2009, which was caused partly by falling trust in businesses and their leaders, companies found it important to make transparent their commitment to social responsibility. This was made clear by Richard Clark, CEO of Merck: "We've really stepped back and made sure that we are more transparent about our business. I think we have always done good things, but I don't know we have always communicated them internally or externally the best way we should. It's even more important today because we are operating in a very difficult environment, and our reputation is being challenged. We need to go the extra mile now so our stakeholders can see what we do and regain their trust." Sandra Leung, senior vice president of Bristol Myers-Squibb explained why corporate social responsibility can lead to a more productive workforce: "People like working at a place that has a vision and has respect for the environment as well as sustainability. They have respect for a company where they know their concerns will be not only heard but addressed."

Corporate social responsibility cannot rescue a failing company. But it can be an important competitive advantage, as Dan Henkle, senior vice president of social responsibility of Gap, said: "Making our company a good corporate citizen and increasingly transparent is a competitive imperative. It's that simple."

Sources: LaMotta, Lisa, "The 100 Best Corporate Citizens," Forbes.com (March 6, 2009); and *Corporate Responsibility Magazine* Web site (http://thecro.com/files/100Best2011_List_revised.pdf).

The FASB and IASB issue pronouncements on accounting issues that govern the preparation of financial statements. However, both Congress and the SEC can overrule the standard setters if they disagree with a particular accounting standard. Such disagreements are rare because setting accounting standards usually involves a long due process that includes many discussions among the affected parties: public regulators (Congress and SEC in the United States, the European Commission and others abroad), private regulators (FASB and IASB), companies, the public accounting profession, representatives of investors, and other interested groups. In the United States, Congress and the SEC generally make their opinions known long before the FASB or IASB approves standards.

Ethics

Regardless of what the accounting standards say, they do no good if accountants fail to follow them. A hallmark of the accounting profession has been its ethics and integrity. Most accountants and auditors are highly ethical and truthfully report their financial results in accordance with GAAP. The media have feasted on a few recent allegations of untruthful reporting in companies such as Washington Mutual, AIG, and Freddie Mac, but these are the exceptions. The Business First box above highlights some of the companies that have outstanding records for corporate citizenship.

Confidence in financial information is important to the smooth functioning of the world's capital markets, and confidence in financial statements depends on the competence and integrity of accountants and auditors. The leading professional organization of accountants in the United States, the American Institute of CPAs (AICPA), has a code of professional conduct that specifies the ethical obligations of accountants. The accounting problems in recent years have just highlighted the importance of accurate financial information and, therefore, the importance of recognizing and adhering to these ethical standards.

Three Measurement Principles

Objective 9

Identify how the measurement principles of recognition, matching and cost recovery, and stable monetary unit affect financial reporting.

GAAP in the United States is based on a conceptual framework that the FASB first established in the 1970s and is currently revising in a joint effort with the IASB. Among the most important concepts are three broad measurement or valuation principles that underlie accrual accounting: recognition (when to record revenue), matching and cost recovery (when to record expense), and the stable monetary unit (what unit of measure to use).

Recognition

recognition

The principle that specifies when a company should record revenue in the accounting records.

The first principle, **recognition**, introduced on page 6, specifies when a company should record revenue in the accounting records.[1] We indicated that companies recognize revenue when it is both earned and realized or realizable. Consequently, most companies recognize revenue when they deliver goods or services to customers. However, in some industries revenue recognition is not so straightforward. Suppose Oracle sells some software to a client and promises to help until the installation is complete. When has Oracle earned the revenue? At the point of sale? At the time the installation is complete? Or some time between? This might be further complicated if the customer is a small start-up company that may run out of cash before it is able to pay for the software. How certain must Oracle be that it will receive payment before it can recognize the revenue? These are judgment issues, and Oracle's accountants together with its auditor will decide when earning and realization are sufficiently complete to recognize the revenue.

Matching and Cost Recovery

matching

The linking of revenues (as measured by the selling prices of goods and services delivered) with the expenses incurred to generate them (as measured by the cost of goods and services used).

The timing of revenue recognition is important because it leads to the recording of expenses through the concept of **matching**—the linking of revenues (as measured by the selling prices of goods and services delivered) with the expenses incurred to generate them (as measured by the cost of goods and services used).

Accountants apply matching as follows:

1. Identify the revenue recognized during the period.
2. Record expenses that relate directly to the recognized revenue, such as sales commissions or costs of goods sold.
3. Record expenses that are costs of operations during a specific time period that have no measurable benefit for a future period and, thus, must be linked to the current period's revenues. Examples are administrative salaries, wages of janitors, and costs of supplies used.

cost recovery

A concept in which companies carry forward as assets such items as inventories, prepayments, and equipment because they expect to recover the costs of these assets in the form of cash inflows (or reduced cash outflows) in future periods.

The heart of recognizing expense is the **cost recovery** concept. That is, companies carry forward as assets such items as inventories, prepayments, and equipment. Why? Because companies expect to recover the costs of these assets in the form of cash inflows (or reduced cash outflows) in future periods. At the end of each period, accountants examine evidence to assure themselves that they should not write off these assets—these unexpired costs—as an expense of the current period. For instance, in our chapter example, King Hardware carried forward the asset Prepaid Rent of $2,000 on March 31 because the accountant is virtually certain that it represents a future benefit. Why? Because King is planning to use the rented facilities in April and May and without the prepayment, King would have to pay $2,000 for rent in April and May. So the presence of the prepayment is a benefit in the sense that it reduces future cash outflows by $2,000.

Stable Monetary Unit

The monetary unit (for example, the dollar in the United States, the yen in Japan, or the euro in the European Union) is the principal means for measuring assets, liabilities, and stockholders' equity. It is the common denominator for quantifying the effects of a wide variety of transactions.

Such measurement assumes that the monetary unit—the dollar, for example—is an unchanging yardstick. Yet, we all know that a 2010 dollar does not have the same purchasing power as a 2000 or 1990 dollar. Therefore, users of accounting statements that include dollars from different years must recognize the limitations of the basic measurement unit.

---

[1] At the time this book went to press the FASB and IASB were jointly working on a project to change how revenue is recognized. If the boards adopt the proposal, it will emphasize the earning of revenue and minimize the effect of realization. However, for most transactions in this textbook, the new standard will not affect when companies recognize revenue.

Some accountants have criticized the FASB and IASB for not making explicit and formal adjustments to remedy the defects of the measuring unit. Supporters of the status quo maintain that price-level adjustments would lessen objectivity and would be confusing to users. They claim that critics have exaggerated the price-level problem and that the adjustments would not significantly affect the vast bulk of corporate statements. Why? Because many accounts, such as cash, receivables, and payables, are already in current or nearly current dollars, and inflation rates have been low in recent years.

On the other hand, although inflation rates in developed countries have recently run only 1%–4%, those in some developing countries have been 10%–20%, enough to have a large effect, especially on long-lived assets. In addition, companies in countries with hyperinflation have felt the need to inflation-adjust their accounting numbers for them to make any sense at all. However, even low inflation rates can create large changes in value when the inflation persists over a long time period. The most troublesome aspect of adjusting accounting numbers for inflation, however, is how to interpret the results after we measure them. Investors and managers in the United States are accustomed to the conventional statements. The intelligent interpretation of statements adjusted for changes in the price level would require extensive changes in the habits of users, and, therefore, price-level adjustment faces widespread opposition. Rather than explicitly adjusting values for inflation, most users prefer to live with an "elastic" measuring stick.

The body of GAAP contains more than the measurement conventions just discussed. We introduce some other major concepts, including going concern, objectivity, materiality, and cost benefit, in Appendix 1A.

Summary Problem for Your Review

PROBLEM

Suppose a friend approaches you after learning that you have taken an accounting course. She makes the following remarks regarding financial statements. Do you agree or disagree? Explain fully.

1. "If I purchase 100 shares of the outstanding common stock of General Mills, I invest my money directly in that corporation. General Mills must record that transaction."
2. "Sales revenue is the cash coming in from customers and the various expenses show the cash going out for goods and services. The difference is net income."
3. Consider the following 2011 accounts of Nike (in millions):

Paid-in capital	$3,947
Retained earnings	5,801
Other	95
Total stockholders' equity	$9,843

A shareholder commented, "Why can't Nike pay higher wages and dividends? It can use its nearly $6 billion of retained earnings to do so."
4. "If Nike were sold to another company, the Nike shareholders would receive $9,843 billion, the total shareholders' equity."

SOLUTION

1. Money is invested directly in a corporation only upon original issuance of the stock by the corporation. For example, a corporation might issue 100,000 shares of stock at $80 per share, bringing in $8 million to the corporation. This is a transaction between the corporation and the stockholders. It affects the corporate financial position:

Cash	$8,000,000	Stockholders' equity	$8,000,000

In turn, an original stockholder (A) may later sell 100 shares of that stock to another individual (B) for $92 per share. This is a private transaction; no cash comes to the corporation. The corporation records the fact that B now owns the 100 shares originally owned by A, but the corporate financial position is unchanged. Accounting focuses on the business entity; the private dealings of the owners have no direct effect on the financial position of the entity and hence are unrecorded (except for detailed records of the owners' identities).

2. Cash receipts and disbursements are not the fundamental basis for the accounting recognition of revenues and expenses. If a company delivers goods or renders services to a customer, a receivable is generally sufficient justification for recognizing revenue. Similarly, if a company uses up goods or services, an obligation in the form of a payable is justification for recognizing expense. This approach to the measurement of net income is the accrual basis. Companies recognize revenue as they earn and realize it. They recognize expenses or losses when they use goods or services in obtaining revenue (or when they can no longer justify carrying forward such goods or services as an asset because they have no potential future benefit). Companies deduct the expenses and losses from the revenue, and the result of this matching process is net income, the net increase in stockholders' equity from the conduct of operations.

3. Retained earnings is not cash. It is a stockholders' equity account that represents the accumulated increase in ownership claims because of profitable operations less the decrease from payment of cash dividends. The erroneous linking of retained earnings and cash is a common misinterpretation. As a general rule, there is no direct relationship between the individual items on the two sides of the balance sheet. For example, Nike had less than $2 billion of cash when its retained earnings were nearly $6 billion. **IBM** has an even larger difference between cash and retained earnings, with a recent $11 billion cash balance when its retained earnings were more than $100 billion. Similarly, General Mills had retained earnings of $10,290 million, which was nearly 7 times larger than its cash balance of $1,508 million.

4. Stockholders' equity is not a market value. It is the difference between assets and liabilities measured at historical cost expressed in an unchanging monetary unit. Intervening changes in markets and general price levels in inflationary times may mean that financial statements list assets at amounts far below their market values.

Market values for publicly traded companies are determined by daily trading conducted in the financial marketplaces, such as the New York Stock Exchange. Numerous factors affect these values, including the expectations of (a) price appreciation and (b) cash flows in the form of dividends. The focus is on the future; investors examine the present and the past only as clues to what may be forthcoming. Therefore, the present stockholders' equity is usually of only incidental concern. For example, stockholders' equity for Nike in 2012 was slightly more than $10 per share, while the company's market price per common share was more than $100.

Highlights to Remember

1. **Read and interpret basic financial statements.** This chapter introduces two basic financial statements: the balance sheet (or statement of financial position) and income statement. Their main elements are assets, liabilities, owners' equity, revenues, and expenses. Income statement and balance sheets are linked because the revenues and expenses appearing on an income statements are components of stockholders' equity on the balance sheet. Revenues increase stockholders' equity, and expenses decrease stockholders' equity.

2. **Analyze typical business transactions using the balance sheet equation.** The balance sheet equation provides a framework for recording accounting transactions: assets = liabilities + owners' equity.

3. **Distinguish between the accrual basis of accounting and the cash basis of accounting.** The accrual basis is the heart of accounting. Under accrual accounting, companies recognize revenues as they earn and realize them, and they record expenses as they use resources, not necessarily when they receive or pay cash. Do not confuse expense with the term *cash payment*, or revenue with the term *cash receipt*.

4. **Make adjustments to the accounts under accrual accounting.** At the end of each accounting period, companies make adjustments so that they can present financial statements on an accrual basis. The major adjustments are for (a) expiration of unexpired costs, (b) recognition (earning) of unearned revenues, (c) accrual of unrecorded expenses, and (d) accrual of unrecorded revenues.

5. **Explain the nature of dividends and retained earnings.** Dividends are not expenses; they are distributions of assets that reduce ownership claims. Similarly, retained earnings is not cash; it is a claim against total assets.

6. **Select relevant items from a set of data and assemble them into a balance sheet and an income statement.** After a company records transactions and makes adjustments, it can compile the data into financial statements. The balances in the accounts comprise the balance sheet. The changes in the retained earnings account form the basis for the income statement. Therefore, the changes in retained earnings link the income statement with the balance sheet.

7. **Distinguish between the reporting of corporate owners' equity and the reporting of owners' equity for partnerships and sole proprietorships.** Entities can be organized as corporations, partnerships, or sole proprietorships. The type of organization does not affect most accounting entries. Only the owners' equity section will differ among organizational types.

8. **Explain the role of auditors in financial reporting and how accounting standards are set.** Auditors examine companies' records and financial statements to ensure they comply with GAAP. Accounting standards are set in the United States by the Financial Accounting Standards Board (FASB) and in most other countries by the International Accounting Standards Board (IASB).

9. **Identify how the measurement principles of recognition, matching and cost recovery, and stable monetary unit affect financial reporting.** Three major conventions that affect accounting are recognition, matching and cost recovery, and stable monetary unit. Recognition determines when companies record revenues in the income statement, matching and cost recovery specify when to record expenses, and stable monetary units justify use of a unit of currency (the dollar in the United States) to measure accounting transactions.

Appendix 1A: Additional Accounting Concepts

This appendix describes several concepts that are prominent parts of the body of GAAP: continuity or going concern, relevance and faithful representation, materiality, conservatism, and cost-benefit.

Objective 10

Define continuity, relevance, faithful representation, materiality, conservatism, and cost-benefit.

The Continuity or Going Concern Convention

continuity convention (going concern convention)
The assumption that an organization will continue to exist and operate.

The **continuity** or **going concern convention** is the assumption that an organization will continue to exist and operate. This notion implies that a company will use existing resources, such as plant assets, to fulfill the general purposes of a continuing entity rather than sell them in tomorrow's real estate or equipment markets. It also implies that the company will pay existing liabilities at maturity in an orderly manner.

Suppose some old specialized equipment has a net book value of $10,000, a replacement cost of $12,000, and a realizable value of $7,000 on the used-equipment market. Accountants often cite the continuity convention as the justification for adhering to net book value, $10,000 in this example, as the primary basis for valuing assets such as inventories, land, buildings, and equipment. Some critics of these accounting practices believe that such valuations are not as informative as their replacement cost ($12,000) or their realizable values on sale ($7,000). Defenders of using $10,000 as an appropriate asset valuation argue that a going concern will generally use the asset as originally intended. Therefore, the net book value (the acquisition cost less depreciation) is the preferable basis for accountability and evaluation of performance. Hence, other values are not germane because the company is using, not replacing or disposing of, the asset.

The opposite view to this going concern or continuity convention is an immediate-liquidation assumption, whereby a company values all items on a balance sheet at the amounts appropriate if it

relevance

The capability of information to make a difference to the decision maker.

predictive value

A quality of information that allows it to help users form their expectations about the future.

confirmatory value

A quality of information that allows it to confirm or change existing expectations.

faithful representation

A quality of information that ensures that it captures the economic substance of the transactions, events, or circumstances it describes. It requires information to be complete, neutral, and free from material errors.

comparability

A characteristic of information produced when all companies use similar concepts and measurements and use them consistently.

consistency

Using the same accounting policies and procedures from period to period.

verifiability

A characteristic of information that can be checked to ensure it is correct.

Timeliness

The quality that information must reach decision makers while it can still influence their decisions.

understandable

A criterion that requires accountants to present information clearly and concisely.

materiality

The accounting convention that justifies the omission of insignificant information when its omission or misstatement would not mislead a user of the financial statements.

conservatism convention

Selecting the method of measurement that yields the gloomiest immediate results.

were to sell its assets and pay off its liabilities in piecemeal fashion within a few days or months. A company would use this liquidation approach to valuation only when it is in severe financial trouble.

Relevance and Faithful Representation

Relevance and faithful representation are the two main qualities that make accounting information useful for decision making. **Relevance** refers to whether the information makes a difference to a decision maker. If information has no impact on a decision, it is not relevant to that decision. The two things that can make information relevant are predictive value and confirmatory value. Information has **predictive value** if users of financial statements can use the information to help them form their expectations about the future. Information has **confirmatory value** if it can either confirm or change existing expectations.

Users of financial statements want assurance that management has accurately and truthfully reported its financial results. Consequently, in addition to relevance, accountants want information to exhibit **faithful representation**—that is, it should truly capture the economic substance of the transactions, events, or circumstances it describes. Faithful representation requires information to be complete, neutral, and free from material errors. Information is complete if it contains all the information necessary to faithfully represent an economic phenomenon. It is neutral if it is unbiased—that is, the information is not slanted to influence behavior in a particular direction. Finally, information should be free from material errors, which means that estimates are based on appropriate inputs, which in turn are based on the best information available.

Four characteristics can enhance both relevance and faithful representation. The first such characteristic is **comparability**—requiring all companies to use similar concepts and measurements and to use them consistently. Comparability requires **consistency**, using the same accounting policies and procedures from period to period. The second enhancing characteristic is **verifiability**, which means that information can be checked to ensure it is correct. That is, knowledgeable and independent observers would agree that the information presented has been appropriately measured. **Timeliness** is obviously desirable. Information must reach decision makers while it can still influence their decisions. Finally, information should be **understandable**, which requires accountants to present information clearly and concisely.

Materiality

Because accounting is a practical art, accountants often temper their reports by applying judgments about **materiality**. A financial statement item is material if its omission or misstatement would be likely to mislead a user of the financial statements. Items with a sufficiently small value are immaterial. For example, accountants write off as expenses many small outlays that they should theoretically record as assets. Why? Because they are small enough to be immaterial. For example, many corporations have a rule that requires the immediate write-off to expense of all outlays under a specified minimum of, for example, $100, regardless of the useful life of the asset acquired. In such a case, a company might acquire coat hangers that will last many years but never add them to its balance sheet as assets. Why? The resulting $100 understatement of assets and stockholders' equity would be too trivial to affect any user decisions. The cost of recording and annually depreciating a $100 asset is greater than the benefit of more accurate financial statements.

When is an item material? There will probably never be a definitive answer. What is trivial to IBM may be material to a two-person start-up company. A working rule is that an item is material if its proper accounting would probably affect the decision of a knowledgeable user. In sum, although materiality is an important convention, it is difficult to use anything other than prudent judgment to tell whether an item is material.

Conservatism Convention

Conservatism is a hallmark of accounting. The **conservatism convention** means selecting the method of measurement that yields the gloomiest immediate results. This attitude affects such working rules as "Anticipate no gains, but provide for all possible losses," and "If in doubt, write it off."

Accountants have traditionally regarded the historical costs of acquiring an asset as the ceiling for its valuation. Asset values may be increased (written up) only when the asset is sold or exchanged, but the asset value may be reduced (written down) without an exchange. For example, companies write down inventories (and recognize a loss) when replacement costs decline, but they never write them up when replacement costs increase.

Critics maintain that conservatism is inherently inconsistent. If replacement market prices are sufficiently objective and verifiable to justify write-downs, why aren't they just as valid for write-ups? Furthermore, the critics maintain that conservatism is not a fundamental concept. Accounting reports should try to present the most accurate picture feasible—neither too high nor too low. Accountants defend their attitude by saying that erring in the direction of conservatism would usually have less severe economic consequences than erring in the direction of overstating assets and net income.

In a way, conservatism is a double-edged sword. Conservatism that leads to understating net income in one period subsequently creates an overstatement of net income in a future period. For example, suppose a company writes down inventory from $100 to $80. The company's operating income falls by $20 in the period of the write-down, but it increases by $20 in the period it sells the inventory.

Cost-Benefit

Accounting systems vary in complexity from the minimum crude records kept to satisfy government authorities to the sophisticated budgeting and feedback systems that are at the heart of management planning and control. Recent innovations include huge, multimillion dollar enterprise resource planning (ERP) systems. As companies change their accounting systems, the potential benefits should exceed the additional costs. Often, the benefits are difficult to measure, but the **cost-benefit criterion** at least implicitly underlies the decisions about the design of accounting systems. Sometimes, the reluctance to adopt suggestions for new ways of measuring financial position and performance is because of inertia. More often, it is because the apparent benefits do not exceed the costs of gathering and interpreting the information. Some companies, such as Hershey Foods, have found out too late that huge investments in accounting systems such as ERP sometimes do not deliver the benefits promised.

cost-benefit criterion
An approach that implicitly underlies the decisions about the design of accounting systems. As companies change their accounting systems, the potential benefits should exceed the costs of gathering and interpreting the information.

Appendix 1B: Using Ledger Accounts

This chapter focused on the balance sheet equation, the general framework used by accountants to record economic transactions. This appendix focuses on some of the main techniques that accountants use to record the transactions illustrated in the chapter.

Objective 11

Use T-accounts, debits, and credits to record transactions.

The Account

To begin, consider how the accountant would record the King Hardware transactions that you encountered in the chapter. Exhibit 1-1 (p. 5) showed their effects on the elements of the balance sheet equation:

	A		=	L	+	SE
	Cash	Inventory		Accounts Payable		Paid-in Capital
1. Initial investment by owners	+100,000		=			+100,000
2. Acquire inventory for cash	−75,000	+75,000	=			
3. Acquire inventory on credit		+35,000	=	+35,000		

This balance-sheet-equation approach emphasizes the concepts, but it can become unwieldy if many transactions occur. Changes in the balance sheet equation can occur many times daily. In large retail businesses, such as Target, Costco, and Macy's, thousands of repetitive transactions occur hourly. In practice, accountants use **ledger accounts** to keep track of how these transactions affect each particular asset, liability, revenue, expense, and so forth. We use simplified versions of ledger accounts called **T-accounts**. We call them T-accounts because they take the form of the capital letter *T*. Increases in the account go on one side of the vertical line of the T-account, and decreases go on the other side. Asset accounts have positive balances on the left side of the T-account. Entries on the left side increase the asset accounts and entries on the right side decrease them. Liabilities and stockholders' equity accounts have positive balances on the

ledger accounts
A method of keeping track of how transactions affect each particular asset, liability, revenue, and expense.

T-accounts
Simplified versions of ledger accounts that take the form of the capital letter *T*.

right-side. We increase them by recording entries on the right side and decrease them by recording entries on the left side. The following T-accounts illustrate the preceding transactions:

Assets		=	Liabilities + Stockholders' Equity	
Cash			**Accounts Payable**	
Increases	Decreases		Decreases	Increases
(1) 100,000	(2) 75,000			(3) 35,000
Bal. 25,000				
Inventory			**Paid-in Capital**	
Increases	Decreases		Decreases	Increases
(2) 75,000				(1) 100,000
(3) 35,000				
Bal. 110,000				

double-entry system

A method of record keeping in which each transaction affects at least two accounts.

We made the T-account entries using a **double-entry system**, whereby each transaction affects at least two accounts. Each T-account is similar to a column in the balance sheet equation. To keep assets equal to liabilities plus stockholders' equity, the amount of the left-side entries to the T-accounts must always equal the amount of the right-side entries.

Each T-account summarizes the changes in a particular asset, liability, or stockholders' equity. We key each transaction in some way, such as by the numbering in parentheses used in this illustration or by date or both. This keying facilitates the rechecking (auditing) process by helping accountants trace transactions to their original sources. You can compute the balance of any account by totaling each side of the account and deducting the smaller total amount from the larger. Accounts exist to keep an up-to-date summary of the changes in specific assets, liabilities, and stockholders' equity. Accountants can prepare a balance sheet at any time if they keep the accounts up to date. The accounts contain all the necessary information. For example, the balance sheet for King Hardware after the first three transactions is as follows:

Assets		Liabilities and Stockholders' Equity	
Cash	$ 25,000	Liabilities	
Inventory	110,000	Accounts payable	$ 35,000
		Stockholders' equity	
		Paid-in capital	100,000
Total assets	$135,000	Total liabilities and stockholders' equity	$135,000

General Ledger

general ledger

A collection of the group of accounts that supports the items shown in the major financial statements.

We show King Hardware's general ledger in Exhibit 1-7. A **general ledger** is a collection of the group of accounts that supports the items shown in the major financial statements.[2] Exhibit 1-7 is merely a recasting of the facts that we analyzed in Exhibit 1-1. Study Exhibit 1-7 by comparing its analysis of each transaction against its corresponding analysis in Exhibit 1-1 on page 5.

Debits and Credits

debit

An entry on the left side of an account.

credit

An entry on the right side of an account.

When placing transaction amounts in the appropriate accounts, accountants often use the technical terms debit and credit. **Debit** means one thing and one thing only—"left side of an account." **Credit** means one thing and one thing only—"right side of an account." Neither debit nor credit has a connotation of "good" or "bad." In our everyday conversation, we sometimes use the words *debit* and *credit* in a general sense that may completely diverge from their technical accounting uses. When you study accounting, forget these general uses of the words. Merely think right-side or left-side entries to T-accounts and whether the right side or left side increases or decreases the type of account you are analyzing.

---

[2] The general ledger is usually supported by various subsidiary ledgers that provide details for accounts in the general ledger. For instance, an accounts receivable subsidiary ledger would contain a separate account for each credit customer. For example, the accounts receivable balance of $1,162 million that appears in the General Mills 2011 balance sheet is a single account in the company's general ledger. However, that single balance is the sum of the detailed individual accounts receivable balances of thousands of credit customers.

Assets
(increases on left, decreases on right)

Cash

(1)	100,000	(2)	75,000
(4a)	10,000	(6)	20,000
(5)	15,000	(7a)	3,000
3/31 Bal.	17,000		

Accounts Receivable

(4a)	120,000	(5)	15,000
3/31 Bal.	105,000		

Inventory

(2)	75,000	(4b)	100,000
(3)	35,000		
3/31 Bal.	10,000		

Prepaid Rent

(7a)	3,000	(7b)	1,000
3/31 Bal.	2,000		

Liabilities and Stockholders' Equity
(decreases on left, increases on right)

Accounts Payable

(6)	20,000	(3)	35,000
		3/31 Bal.	15,000

Paid-in Capital

	(1)	100,000
	3/31 Bal.	100,000

Retained Earnings

	3/31 Bal.	29,000*

Sales

	(4a)	130,000

*Expense and Revenue Accounts

Cost of Goods Sold

(4b)	100,000

Rent Expense

(7b)	1,000

Exhibit 1-7
General Ledger of King Hardware Co.

For example, an accountant making an entry for transaction 4b would say "debit (or charge) Cost of Goods Sold $100,000 and credit Inventory $100,000." This is an abbreviated way of saying, "Place $100,000 on the left (debit) side of the Cost of Goods Sold T-account and place $100,000 on the right (credit) side of the Inventory T-account." Note that the total dollar amounts of the debits (entries on the left side of the account[s] affected) will always equal the total dollar amount of credits (entries on the right side of the account[s] affected) because the accounting equation must always stay in balance.

You can use *debit* and *credit* as verbs, adjectives, or nouns. The instruction "debit $1,000 to cash" uses *debit* as a verb, meaning that you should place $1,000 on the left side of the cash account. When you say "make a debit to cash," *debit* is a noun. In the statement "cash has a debit balance of $12,000," *debit* is an adjective that indicates that the balance is on the left (rather than right) side of the account.

Assets generally have left-side (debit) balances. Why do expenses also carry debit balances? Expense accounts are places to temporarily record reductions in stockholders' equity. Because stockholders' equity normally has a right-side balance, we place entries on the left side to decrease the account.

The following table summarizes the following rules: (1) debits are on the left, (2) credits are on the right, (3) debits increase and credits decrease assets, and (4) credits increase and debits decrease liabilities and stockholders' equities.

Assets		=	Liabilities		+	Stockholders' Equity	
Increase	Decrease		Decrease	Increase		Decrease	Increase
+	–		–	+		–	+
debit	credit		debit	credit		debit	credit
left	right		left	right		left	right

Because revenues increase stockholders' equity, we record them as credits. Because expenses decrease stockholders' equity, we record them as debits.

Accounting Vocabulary

This chapter and its appendices introduce more new terms than any other, so be sure that you understand them thoroughly.

account, p. 4
accounts payable, p. 3
accounts receivable, p. 3
accrual basis, p. 8
accrue, p. 13
accrued expenses, p. 13
accrued revenues, p. 15
adjusting entries, p. 9
adjustments, p. 9
assets, p. 4
audit, p. 19
balance sheet, p. 4
cash basis, p. 8
cash dividends, p. 16
comparability, p. 26
compound entry, p. 6
confirmatory value, p. 26
conservatism convention, p. 26
consistency, p. 26
continuity convention, p. 25
corporation, p. 3
cost recovery, p. 22
cost-benefit criterion, p. 27
credit, p. 28

debit, p. 28
deferred revenue, p. 13
dividends, p. 16
double-entry system, p. 28
earnings, p. 6
expenses, p. 6
explicit transactions, p. 9
faithful representation, p. 26
Financial Accounting Standards
   Board (FASB), p. 20
financial statements, p. 3
general ledger, p. 28
going concern
   convention, p. 25
implicit transactions, p. 9
income, p. 6
income statement, p. 6
independent opinion, p. 19
International Accounting
   Standards Board
   (IASB), p. 20
ledger accounts, p. 27
liabilities, p. 4
long-lived assets, p. 10

matching, p. 22
materiality, p. 26
net income, p. 6
net worth, p. 18
owners' equity, p. 4
paid-in capital, p. 4
partnership, p. 18
predictive value, p. 26
profits, p. 6
recognition, p. 22
recognize, p. 6
relevance, p. 26
residual value, p. 10
retained earnings, p. 4
retained income, p. 4
revenue, p. 6
sales, p. 6
sales revenue, p. 6
Securities and Exchange
   Commission (SEC), p. 19
sole proprietorship, p. 18
source documents, p. 9
statement of financial
   position, p. 4

Assignment Material

The assignment material for each remaining chapter is divided as follows:

- Fundamental Assignment Material
    General Exercises and Problems
    Understanding Published Financial Reports
- Additional Assignment Material
    Questions
    Critical Thinking Exercises
    General Exercises and Problems
    Understanding Published Financial Reports
    Nike 10-K Problem
- Excel Application Exercise
- Collaborative Learning Exercise
- Internet Exercise

The general exercises and problems subgroups focus on concepts and procedures that are applicable to a wide variety of specific settings. Many instructors believe that these "traditional" types of exercises and problems have proved their educational value over many years of use in introductory textbooks. The understanding published financial reports subgroups focus on real-life situations. They have the same basic aims as the general exercises and problems subgroups. Indeed, some instructors may confine their assignments to the understanding published financial reports subgroups. The distinctive characteristic of the latter subgroups is the use of actual companies and news events to enhance the student's interest in accounting. Many students and instructors get more satisfaction out of a course that frequently uses actual situations as a means of learning accounting methods and concepts.

Fundamental Assignment Material   MyAccountingLab

GENERAL EXERCISES AND PROBLEMS

1-A1 Balance Sheet Equation
For each of the following independent cases, compute the amounts (in thousands) for the items indicated by letters, and show your supporting computations:

	Case		
	1	2	3
Revenues	$140	$ K	$300
Expenses	120	170	270
Dividends declared	0	5	Q
Additional investment by stockholders	0	30	35
Net income	E	20	P
Retained earnings			
Beginning of year	40	55	90
End of year	D	J	110
Paid-in capital			
Beginning of year	25	10	N
End of year	C	H	85
Total assets			
Beginning of year	80	F	L
End of year	90	275	M
Total liabilities			
Beginning of year	A	90	105
End of year	B	G	95

1-A2 Analysis of Transactions; Preparation of Statements

The Montha Company was incorporated on April 1, 20X1. Montha had 10 holders of common stock. Chenda Montha, who was the president and CEO, held 51% of the shares. The company rented space in chain discount stores and specialized in selling running shoes. Montha's first location was a store in Centerville Mall.

The following events occurred during April:

a. The company was incorporated. Common stockholders invested $150,000 cash.
b. Purchased merchandise inventory for cash, $35,000.
c. Purchased merchandise inventory on open account, $25,000.
d. Merchandise carried in inventory at a cost of $40,000 was sold for $110,000, $35,000 for cash and $75,000 on open account. Montha carries and will collect these accounts receivable.
e. Collection of a portion of the preceding accounts receivable, $20,000.
f. Payments of a portion of accounts payable, $18,000. See transaction c.
g. Special display equipment and fixtures were acquired on April 1 for $36,000. Their expected useful life was 36 months with no terminal scrap value. Straight-line depreciation was adopted. This equipment was removable. Montha paid $12,000 as a down payment and signed a promissory note for $24,000.
h. On April 1, Montha signed a rental agreement with Centerville Mall. The agreement called for rent of $2,000 per month, payable quarterly in advance. Therefore, Montha paid $6,000 cash on April 1.
i. The rental agreement also called for a payment of 10% of all sales. This payment was in addition to the flat $2,000 per month. In this way, Centerville Mall would share in any success of the venture and be compensated for general services such as cleaning and utilities. This payment was to be made in cash on the last day of each month as soon as the sales for the month were tabulated. Therefore, Montha made the payment on April 30.
j. Wages, salaries, and sales commissions were all paid in cash for all earnings by employees. The amount was $49,000.
k. Depreciation expense for April was recognized. See transaction g.
l. The expiration of an appropriate amount of prepaid rental services was recognized. See transaction h.

1. Prepare an analysis of Montha Company's transactions, employing the equation approach demonstrated in Exhibit 1-1. Two additional columns will be needed, one for Equipment and Fixtures and one for Note Payable. Show all amounts in thousands.
2. Prepare a balance sheet as of April 30, 20X1, and an income statement for the month of April. Ignore income taxes.
3. Given these sparse facts, analyze Montha's performance for April and its financial position as of April 30, 20X1.

1-A3 Cash Basis Versus Accrual Basis

Refer to the preceding problem. If Montha Company measured income on the cash basis, what revenue would be reported for April? Which basis (accrual or cash) provides a better measure of revenue? Why?

UNDERSTANDING PUBLISHED FINANCIAL REPORTS

1-B1 Balance Sheet Equation

Nordstrom operates 207 fashion specialty retail stores in 28 states. The company's actual data (slightly simplified) follow for its fiscal year ended January 29, 2011 (in millions of dollars):

Assets, beginning of period	$6,579
Assets, end of period	E
Liabilities, beginning of period	A
Liabilities, end of period	5,441
Paid-in capital, beginning of period	1,066
Paid-in capital, end of period	D
Retained earnings, beginning of period	506
Retained earnings, end of period	C
Revenues	9,700
Costs and expenses	B
Net income	613
Dividends	266
Additional investments by stockholders	102

Find the unknowns (in millions), showing computations to support your answers.

1-B2 Analysis of Transactions; Preparation of Statements

The Volvo Group, headquartered in Gothenburg, Sweden, is one of the world's leading manufacturers of trucks, buses, and construction equipment, in addition to autos. Volvo's actual condensed balance sheet data for January 1, 2012, follows (in millions of Swedish kroner, SEK):

Assets		Liabilities and Stockholders' Equity	
Cash and cash equivalents	SEK 30,379	Accounts payable	SEK 56,546
Receivables	81,472	Other liabilities	211,017
Inventories	44,599		
Property, plant, and equipment	53,657	Stockholders' equity	85,681
Other assets	143,137		
Total	SEK 353,244	Total	SEK 353,244

Suppose the following summarizes some major transactions of the truck division of Volvo during January, 2012 (in millions):

a. Sold trucks for cash of SEK 190 and on open account of SEK 460 for a grand total of SEK 650. Volvo carried the trucks in inventory for SEK 390.
b. Acquired inventory on account, SEK 500.
c. Collected receivables, SEK 300.
d. On January 2, used SEK 250 cash to prepay some rent and insurance for 2012.
e. Payments on accounts payable (for inventories), SEK 450.
f. Paid selling and administrative expenses in cash, SEK 110.
g. A total of SEK 90 of prepaid expenses for rent and insurance expired in January 2012.
h. Recognized depreciation expense of SEK 20 for January.

1. Prepare an analysis of these truck transactions on the balance sheet of Volvo, employing the equation approach demonstrated in Exhibit 1-1 on page 5. Show all amounts in millions of SEK. (For simplicity, only a few major transactions are illustrated here.)
2. Prepare an income statement for these transactions for the month ended January 31, 2012, and a balance sheet as of January 31, 2012, that incorporates these transactions. Ignore income taxes.

1-B3 Cash Basis Versus Accrual Basis

Refer to the preceding problem. If Volvo measured income on the cash basis, what revenue would the company report for January from the transactions listed? Which basis (accrual or cash) provides a better measure of revenue? Why?

Additional Assignment Material

QUESTIONS

1-1 What types of questions are answered by the income statement and balance sheet?

1-2 Define *assets* and *liabilities*.

1-3 How are the income statement and balance sheet related?

1-4 Criticize the following statement: "Net income is the difference in the ownership capital account balances at two points in time."

1-5 Distinguish between the accrual basis and the cash basis of accounting.

1-6 How do adjusting entries differ from routine entries?

1-7 Explain why some accountants want to record research expenditures as an asset on acquisition.

1-8 Why is it better to refer to the costs, rather than values, of assets such as plant or inventories?

1-9 "Depreciation is cost allocation, not valuation." Do you agree? Explain.

1-10 What types of companies would you expect to have unearned revenues (or deferred revenues) on their balance sheets?

1-11 What is meant by an account labeled "Accrued wages?" Would it be on an income statement or a balance sheet?

1-12 Criticize the following statement: "As a stockholder, I have a right to more dividends. You have millions stashed away in retained earnings. It's about time that you let the true owners get their hands on that pot of gold."

1-13 Criticize the following statement: "Dividends are distributions of profits."

1-14 "I don't need to know accounting principles because my business is a sole proprietorship." Comment on this statement.

1-15 Explain the relationship between the FASB and the SEC in the United States.

1-16 "The FASB sets standards in the United States, so there is little need to learn International Financial Reporting Standards (IFRS)." Do you agree? Explain.

1-17 Why are ethics and integrity important to accountants?

1-18 When do accountants recognize revenue? Why is this so important in an accrual accounting system?

1-19 What is the major criticism of the dollar (or euro or yen or any other monetary unit) as the principal accounting measure?

1-20 Study Appendix 1A. What does the accountant mean by going concern?

1-21 Study Appendix 1A. What does the accountant mean by relevance? By faithful representation?

1-22 Study Appendix 1A. What is the role of cost-benefit (economic feasibility) in the development of accounting principles?

1-23 Study Appendix 1B. Describe the role of debits and credits in a double-entry bookkeeping system.

CRITICAL THINKING EXERCISES

1-24 Accounting Valuation of Fixed Assets

Consider two types of assets held by Weyerhaeuser Company: 1) timber-growing land purchased in 1912 when the company was known as Weyerhaeuser Timber Company and 2) machinery purchased and installed at its paper processing plant in Saskatchewan, Canada, in 2012. How close do you suppose the December 31, 2013, balance sheet value of each asset is to the market value of the asset at that date?

1-25 Marketing, the Income Statement, and the Balance Sheet

The marketing manager of a major electronics company said, "The balance sheet isn't of much use to me. It is so static. But the income statement is a primary tool for managing my dynamic business." Why would a marketing manager find the income statement more useful than the balance sheet?

1-26 Revenue Recognition and Evaluation of Sales Staff

Revenue on an accrual-accounting basis must be both earned and realized (or realizable) before accountants recognize it in the income statement. Companies recognize revenue in cash-basis accounting only when they have received the cash. Is an accrual-basis or cash-basis recognition of revenue more relevant for evaluating the performance of a sales staff? Why?

1-27 Relationship Between the Balance Sheet and the Income Statement

Suppose a company has no transactions with its owners during 20X0. That is, paid-in capital remains unchanged, and retained earnings increases by the entire amount of the net income. During 20X0 the company's net income is $50,000. At the beginning of the year, the company's balance sheet equation was as follows:

$$\text{assets} = \text{liabilities} + \text{stockholders' equity}$$

$$\$450,000 = \$200,000 + \$250,000$$

What do you know about the balance sheet equation at the end of 20X0?

1-28 Concepts of Relevance and Faithful Representation

The FASB and IASB both state that relevance and faithful representation are crucial concepts for financial reporting. Why are these concepts so important?

GENERAL EXERCISES AND PROBLEMS

1-29 True or False

Use T or F to indicate whether each of the following statements is true or false. Change each false statement into one that is true.

1. A large cash balance is the best evidence of previous profitable operations.
2. Accounts receivable should be classified as a liability.
3. Machinery used in the business should be recorded at replacement cost.
4. It is not possible to determine changes in the condition of a business from a single balance sheet.
5. From a single balance sheet, you can find stockholders' equity for a period of time but not for a specific day.
6. Retained earnings is just one part of stockholders' equity.

1-30 Simple Balance Sheet

Fill in the missing numbers from the following simple balance sheet for Cabo Company:

Assets		Liabilities and Stockholders' Equity	
Cash	$?	Accounts payable	$ 10,000
Accounts receivable	15,000	Long-term debt	?
Plant and equipment	75,000	Stockholders' equity	$ 45,000
Total assets	$100,000	Total Liabilities and stockholders' equity	$?

1-31 Nature of Retained Earnings

This is an exercise on the relationships among assets, liabilities, and ownership equities.

1. Prepare an opening balance sheet of

Cash	$1,000	Paid-in capital	$1,000

2. Purchase inventory for $500 cash. Prepare a balance sheet. A heading is unnecessary in this and subsequent requirements.
3. Sell the entire inventory for $850 cash. Prepare a balance sheet. Where is the retained earnings in terms of relationships within the balance sheet? That is, what is the meaning of the retained earnings? Explain in your own words.
4. Buy inventory for $400 cash and equipment for $750 cash. Prepare a balance sheet. Where is the retained earnings in terms of relationships within the balance sheet? That is, what is the meaning of the retained earnings? Explain in your own words.
5. Buy inventory for $350 on open account. Prepare a balance sheet. Where is the retained earnings and account payable in terms of the relationships within the balance sheet? That is, what is the meaning of the account payable and the retained earnings? Explain in your own words.

1-32 Income Statement

Here is a proposed income statement of a children's clothing store:

Kids 2 Klad
Statement of Profit and Loss, December 31, 20X1

Revenues:		
Sales	$1,300,000	
Increase in market value of land and building	50,000	
Cash received from loan	200,000	$1,550,000
Deduct expenses:		
Advertising	$ 100,000	
Sales commissions	60,000	
Utilities	20,000	
Wages	150,000	
Dividends	200,000	
Cost of clothes purchased	800,000	1,330,000
Net profit		$ 220,000

List and describe any shortcomings of this statement.

1-33 Income Statement, Balance Sheet, and Dividends

LaPlace Company had retained earnings of $56,780 at the beginning of 2013. During the year the company had total revenues of $530,000, total expenses (including taxes) of $495,000, bought property and equipment for $340,000, and paid cash dividends of $12,000. Compute LaPlace Company's retained earnings at the end of 2013.

1-34 Customer and Airline

Suppose **Macy's** decided to hold a managers' meeting in Honolulu in February. To take advantage of special fares, Macy's purchased airline tickets in advance from **Delta Airlines** at a total cost of $55,000. Macy's acquired the tickets on December 1 for cash. Using the balance-sheet-equation format, analyze the impact of the December payment and the February travel on the financial position of both Macy's and Delta.

1-35 Tenant and Landlord

Madison Hardware, a franchise of **Ace Hardware Corporation**, pays quarterly rent of $15,000 to Baldwin Commercial Real Estate at the beginning of each quarter for its location in Baldwin Mall. Using the balance-sheet-equation format, analyze the effects of the following on the tenant's and the landlord's financial position:

1. Madison Hardware pays $15,000 rent on July 1.
2. Adjustment for July.
3. Adjustment for August.
4. Adjustment for September.

1-36 Adjustments

1. Steinberg Company sells annual subscriptions to its investment-advice magazine for €50. Suppose it sold 5,000 subscriptions in December, 2012, for magazines to be delivered quarterly in 2013. How would Steinberg Company show this on its December 31, 2012, balance sheet? How would it affect the company's 2012 income statement? How would it affect the income statement for the first 6 months of 2013?

2. Steinberg Company pays its salaried personnel monthly on the fifth day of the following month. That is, it pays January's salaries on February 5. The company's total salaries for 2012 were €240,000, spread evenly over the 12 months. How will this affect the December 31, 2012, balance sheet? When will the December salaries (which are paid on January 5) be charged as expenses on the income statement?

1-37 Find Unknowns

The following data pertain to Andaman Tours, a travel company in Thailand where the currency is the baht (B). Total assets at January 1, 20X0, were B80,000, and at December 31, 20X0, they were B125,000. During 20X0, sales were B265,000, cash dividends were B16,000, and operating expenses (exclusive of costs of goods sold) were B50,000. Total liabilities at December 31, 20X0, were B45,000, and at January 1, 20X0, they were B30,000. There was no additional capital paid in during 20X0. Calculate the following items. (These need not be computed in any particular order.)

1. Stockholders' equity, for January 1, 20X0
2. Net income for 20X0
3. Cost of goods sold for 20X0

1-38 Balance Sheet Equation; Solving for Unknowns

Compute the unknowns (X, Y, Z, A, and B) in each of the individual cases, columns 1–7, in Exhibit 1-8. Each column is independent of the others.

1-39 Fundamental Transaction Analysis and Preparation of Statements

Three former **RIM** employees decided to go into business for themselves and open a store near an office park to sell wireless equipment to young professionals. Their first products were cell phones, PDAs, netbook and notebook computers, and computer accessories. The business was incorporated as Connectivity Plus. The following transactions occurred during April:

a. On April 1, 20X1, each of the three invested $12,000 in cash in exchange for 1,000 shares of stock each.

b. The corporation quickly acquired $40,000 in inventory, half of which had to be paid for in cash. The other half was acquired on open accounts that were payable after 30 days.

c. A store was rented for $500 monthly. A lease was signed for one year on April 1. The first 2 months' rent was paid in advance. Monthly payments were to be made on the second of each month.

d. Advertising during April was purchased on open account for $3,000 from a newspaper owned by one of the stockholders. Additional advertising services of $6,000 were acquired for cash.

e. Sales were $62,000. Merchandise was sold for twice its purchase cost. Sales of $52,000 were on open account, and the remaining $10,000 were for cash.

f. Wages and salaries incurred in April amounted to $11,000, of which $4,000 was paid in cash.

Given	1	2	3	4	5	6	7
Assets at beginning of period		$ 9,000				B	$ 8,200
Assets at end of period		11,000					9,900
Liabilities at beginning of period		6,000				$12,000	4,000
Liabilities at end of period		Y					6,000
Stockholders' equity at beginning of period	$9,000	X				A	X
Stockholders' equity at end of period	X	5,000				10,000	Y
Sales			$16,000		X	14,000	20,000
Inventory at beginning of period			6,000	$ 8,000		Z	
Inventory at end of period			7,000	6,000		7,000	
Purchase of inventory			10,000	12,000		6,000	
Gross profit			Y		$3,000	6,000	A
Cost of goods sold*			X	X	4,500	X	B
Other expenses			4,000			4,000	4,700
Net profit	4,000	Z	Z			Y	Z
Dividends	2,000	0				1,500	400
Additional investments by stockholders						5,000	0

*Note that cost of goods sold = beginning inventory + purchases − ending inventory.

Exhibit 1-8
Data for Exercise 1-38

g. Miscellaneous services paid for in cash were $2,510.

h. On April 1, fixtures and equipment were purchased for $6,000 with a down payment of $1,000 plus a $5,000 note payable in one year.

i. See transaction h and make the April 30 adjustment for interest expense accrued at 9.6%. (The interest is not due until the note matures.)

j. See transaction h and make the April 30 adjustment for depreciation expense on a straight-line basis. The estimated life of the fixtures and equipment is 10 years with no expected residual value. Straight-line depreciation here would be $6,000 ÷ 10 years = $600 per year, or $50 per month.

k. Cash dividends of $6,000 were declared and disbursed to stockholders on April 29.

1. Using the accrual basis of accounting, prepare an analysis of transactions, employing the equation approach demonstrated in Exhibit 1-1 on page 5. Use the following headings: Cash, Accounts Receivable, Inventory, Prepaid Rent, Fixtures and Equipment, Accounts Payable, Notes Payable, Accrued Wages Payable, Accrued Interest Payable, Paid-in Capital, and Retained Earnings.

2. Prepare a balance sheet and a multiple-step income statement. Also show the components of the change in retained earnings.

3. What advice would you give the owners based on the information compiled in the financial statements?

1-40 Measurement of Income for Tax and Other Purposes

The following are the summarized transactions of dentist Frieda Rivera, DDS for 20X1, her first year in practice:

a. Acquired equipment and furniture for $84,000. Its expected useful life is 6 years. Dr. Rivera will use straight-line depreciation, assuming zero terminal disposal value.

b. Fees collected, $79,000. These fees included $2,000 paid in advance by some patients on December 31, 20X1.

c. Rent is paid at the rate of $500 monthly, payable quarterly on the twenty-fifth of March, June, September, and December for the following quarter. Total disbursements during 20X1 for rent were $7,500 including an initial payment on January 1.

d. Fees billed but uncollected, December 31, 20X1, $20,000.

e. Utilities expense paid in cash, $700. Additional utility bills unpaid at December 31, 20X1, $100.

f. Salary expense for dental assistant and secretary, $16,000 paid in cash. In addition, $1,000 was earned but unpaid on December 31, 20X1.

Dr. Rivera may elect either the cash basis or the accrual basis of measuring income for income tax purposes, provided that she uses it consistently in subsequent years. Under either alternative, the original cost of the equipment and furniture must be written off over its 6-year useful life rather than being regarded as a lump-sum expense in the first year.

1. Prepare income statements for the year on both the cash and accrual bases, using one column for each basis.

2. Which basis do you prefer as a measure of Dr. Rivera's performance? Why? What do you think is the justification for the government's allowing the use of the cash basis for income tax purposes?

1-41 Debits and Credits

Study Appendix 1B. Determine for the following transactions whether the account named in parentheses is to be debited or credited:

1. Paid rent in advance (Prepaid Expenses), $1,200
2. Bought merchandise on open account (Accounts Payable), $5,000
3. Borrowed money from First National Bank (Notes Payable), $12,000
4. Sold merchandise (Merchandise Inventory), $1,000
5. Paid O'Brien Associates $3,000 owed them (Accounts Payable)
6. Paid dividends (Cash), $500
7. Delivered merchandise to customers (Merchandise Inventory), $3,000
8. Received cash from customers on accounts due (Accounts Receivable), $2,000

1-42 True or False

Study Appendix 1B. Use T or F to indicate whether each of the following statements is true or false. For each false statement, explain why it is false.

1. Purchase of inventory on account should be credited to Inventory and debited to Accounts Payable.
2. Increases in asset accounts must always be entered on the right.
3. Increases in stockholders' equity should always be entered as credits.
4. Decreases in liability accounts should be recorded on the right.
5. Debit entries must always be recorded on the left. Credit entries can be recorded either on the right or on the left.
6. Money borrowed from the bank should be credited to Cash and debited to Notes Payable.
7. Decreases in accounts must be shown on the credit side.
8. Both increases in liabilities and decreases in assets should be entered on the right.
9. Asset credits should be entered on the right and liability credits on the left.
10. Payments on mortgages should be debited to Cash and credited to Mortgages Payable. Mortgages are liabilities.

1-43 Use of T-Accounts

Study Appendix 1B. The Eastside Tennis Club had the following transactions during June:

a. Collected $600 of dues that had been billed in May.
b. Sold an old computer for $150 cash and a promise to pay $200 in one month. The balance sheet value of the computer was $350.
c. Bought a postage meter on credit for $210.
d. Received the $200 promised in transaction b.

1. Set up T-accounts for the following accounts:
   Cash
   Dues Receivable
   Accounts Receivable
   Equipment
   Accounts Payable
2. Make entries for each of the four transactions into the T-accounts. Label each entry a, b, c, or d.

1-44 Use of T-Accounts
Study Appendix 1B. Refer to problem 1-A2. Make entries for April in T-accounts. Key your entries and check to see that the ending balances agree with the financial statements.

1-45 Use of T-Accounts
Study Appendix 1B. Refer to problem 1-39. Use T-accounts to present an analysis of April transactions. Key your entries and check to see that the ending balances agree with the financial statements.

UNDERSTANDING PUBLISHED FINANCIAL REPORTS

1-46 Balance Sheet Effects
JPMorgan Chase & Co., one of the largest financial institutions in the United States with total assets of nearly $2,266 billion, showed the following items (among others) on its balance sheet at January 1, 2012 (in millions):

Cash (an asset)	$ 59,602
Total deposits (a liability)	$1,127,806

1. Suppose you deposited $5,000 in the bank. How would your deposit affect each of the bank's assets, liabilities, and stockholders' equities? How much would your deposit affect each of your personal assets, liabilities, and owners' equities? Be specific.
2. Suppose JPMorgan Chase makes a $950,000 loan to Evergreen Hospital for remodeling purposes. How would this loan affect each of the bank's assets, liabilities, and stockholders' equities? Be specific.
3. Suppose you borrowed $20,000 from JPMorgan Chase on a personal loan. How would such a transaction affect your personal assets, liabilities, and owners' equities?

1-47 Preparation of Balance Sheet for Costco
Costco Wholesale Corporation operates more than 590 membership warehouses and employs more than, 164,000 people. Its annual report included the following items at August 28, 2011 (in millions of dollars):

Accrued liabilities	$ 2,093
Cash and cash equivalents	4,009
Total stockholders' equity	b
Total liabilities	c
Long-term debt	1,253
Total revenues	88,915
Accounts receivable	965
Common stock	4,518
Inventories	a
Accounts payable	6,544
Property, net of accumulated depreciation	12,432
Retained earnings	7,111
Other assets	2,717
Other liabilities	4,298
Other stockholders' equity	944
Total assets	26,761

Prepare a condensed balance sheet including amounts for the following:

a. Inventory
b. Total stockholders' equity
c. Total liabilities

1-48 Net Income and Retained Earnings

Google Inc. is a well-known Internet company. The following data are from its financial statement for the year ended December 31, 2011 (in millions):

Google, Inc.			
Retained earnings, end of year	$37,605	Dividends paid	$?
Revenues	37,905	Retained earnings, beginning of year	27,868
Net interest income	584	Operating costs and expenses	26,163
Provision for income taxes	2,589	Cash	9,983

1. Prepare Google's income statement for the year. The final three lines of the income statement were labeled as income before taxes, provision for income taxes, and net income.
2. Compute the change in retained earnings, and use that to determine the amount of dividends paid.
3. Comment briefly on the relative size of the cash dividend.

1-49 Earnings Statement, Retained Earnings

Dell, Inc. is a global information technology company headquartered in Round Rock, Texas. The following is a reproduction of the terms and amounts in the financial statements contained in the company's annual report for the fiscal year ended February 3, 2012 (in millions):

Net revenue	$62,071	Retained earnings at	
Cash	13,852	beginning of year	$24,744
Interest and other expenses	191	Cost of products and services	48,260
Income tax provision	748	Retained earnings at end of year	28,236
Accounts payable	11,656		
Research, development and engineering expenses	856	Selling and administrative expenses	8,524

Choose the relevant data and prepare the income statement for the fiscal year. The final three lines of the income statement should be labeled earnings before income taxes, income tax provision, and net income. Also, using the retained earnings account, compute the amount of cash dividends paid during the fiscal year ending February 3, 2012.

1-50 Sole Proprietorship and Corporation

Makaw Company is a sole proprietorship with the following simplified balance sheet:

Assets		Liabilities and Owner's Equity	
Cash	$ 30,000	Accounts payable	$ 15,000
Accounts receivable	25,000	Other liabilities	35,000
Equipment	145,000	Makaw, capital	150,000
Total assets	$200,000	Total liabilities and owners' equity	$200,000

Tom Makaw decided to incorporate his company on May 31, 20X1, by selling 5,000 shares of stock for $10 each and keeping 10,000 shares for himself. Prepare a balance sheet for the new corporation.

NIKE 10-K PROBLEM

1-51 Interpreting the Income Statement and Balance Sheet

Turn to Nike's income statement and balance sheet. Answer the following questions using the two statements:

1. Compute Nike's percentage increase in revenues and in total assets in fiscal 2011. Which increased more?
2. Illustrate the balance sheet equation, using total assets, total liabilities, and shareholders' equity from Nike's May 31, 2011, balance sheet.

3. Nike's retained earnings decreased from $6,095 million to $5,801 million during fiscal 2011. A decrease of $1,858 was due to transactions not discussed in this chapter. Explain the remainder of the change in retained earnings.

4. Did Nike's net income grow by a larger percentage in fiscal 2011 or fiscal 2010?

EXCEL APPLICATION EXERCISE

1-52 Monthly Transactions Using the Balance Sheet Equation

Goal: Create an Excel spreadsheet to analyze the monthly transactions of a company using the balance sheet equation. Use the results to answer questions about your findings.

Scenario: Montha Company has asked you to prepare a transaction analysis report to help the company analyze what transpired during its first month of operation. The company would like you to record the transactions and calculate the appropriate totals using the balance sheet equation. The background data for your analysis appears in Fundamental Assignment Material 1-A2 on page 32. Prepare the transaction analysis using a format similar to Exhibit 1-1 on page 5.

When you have completed your spreadsheet, answer the following questions:

1. What are the total Assets of the firm at the end of April, 20X1?
2. Did the Stockholders' Equity increase or decrease during the month of April, 20X1? What caused the change?
3. Discuss what occurred in the Cash account and its implications.

Step-by-Step:
1. Open a new Excel spreadsheet.
2. In column A, create a bold-faced heading that contains the following:
   Row 1: Chapter 1 Decision Guideline
   Row 2: Montha Company
   Row 3: Transaction Analysis (in Dollars) for April 20X1
   Row 4: Today's Date
3. Merge and center the four heading rows across columns A–L.
4. In row 7, create the following bold-faced column headings:
   Column B: Assets
   Column H: Liabilities
   Column J: Stockholders' Equity
5. Merge and center the Assets heading across columns B–G.
6. Merge and center the Liabilities heading across columns H–I.
7. Merge and center the Stockholders' Equity heading across columns J–L.
8. Create a border around each of the headings created in row 7.
   Border tab: Presets: Outline
9. In row 8, create the following center-justified column headings:
   Column B: Cash
   Column C: A/R
   Column D: Inven.
   Column E: Ppd. Rent
   Column F: Equip.
   Column G: Acc. Dep.
   Column H: A/P
   Column I: N/P
   Column J: PIC
   Column K: Revenue
   Column L: Expense
10. Create a border around each of the column headings created in row 8.
    Border tab: Presets: Outline
11. In column A, create the following row headings:
    Row 9: Transactions:
    Row 10: a. Incorporation
    Row 11: b. Inven. for cash
    Row 12: c. Inven. for credit
    Row 13: d1. Merch. sold
    Row 14: d2. COGS

Row 15: e. Collect A/R
Row 16: f. Payment of A/P
Row 17: g. Equip. purchased
Row 18: h. Prepaid rent
Row 19: i. Add'l. rental fees
Row 20: j. Wage expense
Row 21: k. Depreciation exp.
Row 22: l. Rent expense
Skip a row.
Row 24: Balance, 4/30/X1
Skip two rows.
Row 27: Totals

Note: Adjust width of row A to accommodate row headings.

12. Use the data from Fundamental Assignment Material 1-A2 and enter the amounts for transactions a–h and j in the appropriate columns.

13. Use formulas to compute the adjusting entries needed for transactions i, k, and l.

14. Use formulas to calculate the totals in each of the columns for row 24, Balance, 4/30/X1.

15. Use formulas to generate totals for Assets, Liabilities, and Stockholders' Equity in row 27.
Print the total for Assets in column B.
Merge and center the total across columns B–G.
Print the total for Liabilities in column H.
Merge and center the total across columns H–I.
Print the total for Stockholders' Equity in column J.
Merge and center the total across columns J–L.
Change the format of the three total amounts to display as bold-faced.

16. Format all amounts in rows 10–22 as follows:
Number tab: Category: Currency
Decimal places: 0
Symbol: None
Negative numbers: Black with parentheses

17. Format amounts on row 24 as follows:
Number tab: Category: Accounting
Decimal places: 0
Symbol: $

18. Format amounts on row 27 as follows:
Number tab: Category: Currency
Decimal places: 0
Symbol: $
Negative numbers: Black with parentheses

19. Modify the Page Setup by selecting File, Page Setup.
Page tab: Orientation: Landscape
Sheet tab: Gridlines: Checked

20. Save your work, and print a copy for your files.

COLLABORATIVE LEARNING EXERCISE

1-53 Implicit Transactions

Form groups of from three to six "players." Each group should have a die and paper (or board) with four columns labeled as follows:

1. Expiration of unexpired costs
2. Realization of unearned revenues
3. Accrual of unrecorded expenses
4. Accrual of unrecorded revenues

The players should select an order in which they wish to play. Then, the first player rolls the die. If he or she rolls a 5 or 6, the die passes to the next player. If he or she rolls a 1, 2, 3, or 4, he or she must, within 20 seconds, name an example of a transaction that fits in the corresponding category; for example, if a 2 is rolled, the player must give an example of realization of unearned revenues.

Each time a correct example is given, the player receives one point. If someone doubts the correctness of a given example, he or she can challenge it. If the remaining players unanimously agree that the example is incorrect, the challenger gets a point and the player giving the example does not get a point for the example and is out of the game. If the remaining players do not unanimously agree that the answer is incorrect, the challenger loses a point and the player giving the example gets a point for a correct example. If a player fails to give an example within the time limit or gives an incorrect example, he or she is out of the game (except for voting when an example is challenged), and the remaining players continue until everyone has failed to give a correct example within the time limit. Each correct answer should be listed under the appropriate column. The player with the most points is the group winner. When all groups have finished a round of play, a second level of play can begin. All the groups should get together and list all the examples for each of the four categories by group. Discussion can establish the correctness of each entry; the faculty member or an appointed discussion leader will be the final arbitrator of the correctness of each entry. Each group gets one point for each correct example and loses one point for each incorrect entry. The group with the most points is the overall winner.

INTERNET EXERCISE

1-54 McDonald's Financial Statements

Go to www.mcdonalds.com to find the **McDonald's** home page. Click on the "Corporate Info" heading under "Our Story." Then select the "Investors" heading. Finally click on "Annual Reports" and select the most recent report.

Answer the following questions:

1. First open the balance sheet. Name two items on the McDonald's balance sheet that most likely represent unexpired (prepaid) costs. Name two items that most likely represent accruals of unrecorded expenses.
2. Has McDonald's grown in the past year? What did you look at to determine this?
3. Now look at McDonald's income statement. Did the company's sales (revenues) grow during the past year? By how much? Did its income increase or decrease? By how much? Do the sales and income changes bode well or poorly for McDonald's future?
4. Which financial statements provide evidence that McDonald's is a corporation, not a sole proprietorship or partnership?
5. Where can you find evidence in the McDonald's annual report that the financial statements were prepared using GAAP?

Financial Statements and Ratio Analysis

LEARNING GOALS

When you have finished studying this chapter, you should be able to:

1. Review the contents of the stockholders' report and the procedures for consolidating international financial statements.

2. Understand who uses financial ratios and how.

3. Use ratios to analyze a firm's liquidity and activity.

4. Discuss the relationship between debt and financial leverage and the ratios used to analyze a firm's debt.

5. Use ratios to analyze a firm's profitability and its market value.

6. Use a summary of financial ratios and the DuPont system of analysis to perform a complete ratio analysis.

► WHY THIS CHAPTER MATTERS TO YOU

In your *professional* life

ACCOUNTING You need to understand the stockholders' report and preparation of the four key financial statements; how firms consolidate international financial statements; and how to calculate and interpret financial ratios for decision making.

INFORMATION SYSTEMS You need to understand what data are included in the firm's financial statements to design systems that will supply such data to those who prepare the statements and to those in the firm who use the data for ratio calculations.

MANAGEMENT You need to understand what parties are interested in the stockholders' report and why; how the financial statements will be analyzed by those both inside and outside the firm to assess various aspects of performance; the caution that should be exercised in using financial ratio analysis; and how the financial statements affect the value of the firm.

MARKETING You need to understand the effects your decisions will have on the financial statements, particularly the income statement and the statement of cash flows, and how analysis of ratios, especially those involving sales figures, will affect the firm's decisions about levels of inventory, credit policies, and pricing decisions.

OPERATIONS You need to understand how the costs of operations are reflected in the firm's financial statements and how analysis of ratios, particularly those involving assets, cost of goods sold, or inventory, may affect requests for new equipment or facilities.

In your *personal* life
A routine step in personal financial planning is to prepare and analyze personal financial statements, so that you can monitor progress toward your financial goals. Also, you need to understand and analyze corporate financial statements to build and monitor your investment portfolio.

ABERCROMBIE & FITCH

The Value of Casual Luxury

Kimimasa Mayama/Bloomberg/
Getty Images

A May 15, 2010, post on an investment website, Motley Fool, provided a valuation analysis for clothing retailer Abercrombie & Fitch. Abercrombie's stock price had been trending down for several weeks, and given that recent months had only just seen the end of one of the worst recessions in two generations, Motley Fool analysts did not expect the firm's financial condition to be particularly impressive. However, they noted that Abercrombie's current ratio was a healthy 2.79, and its quick ratio was also strong at 1.79. Furthermore, analysts noted that Abercrombie's receivables collection period had quickened to 43 days in the prior year, and they concluded their report with a relatively positive outlook for the stock.

Just a few days later, Abercrombie & Fitch announced that it would scale back planned overseas store openings, the markets where it had been enjoying the most rapid growth. In addition, the company reported that its gross profit margin declined in the most recent quarter. Markets responded to this information by sending Abercrombie stock down 7 percent on that day.

Valuing the shares of a company is a difficult task. Analysts try to simplify that task by drawing data from financial reports produced by the company and calculating a variety of financial ratios using those data. These ratios help analysts answer questions such as, Does the firm have enough liquidity to pay the bills that will come due in the short term? and, How effectively does the firm collect cash from its customers? In this chapter, you will learn about the main financial statements that analysts rely on for this type of analysis, and you will see how information from those statements can be used to assess the overall performance of a company.

LG 1 2.1 The Stockholders' Report

Every corporation has many and varied uses for the standardized records and reports of its financial activities. Periodically, reports must be prepared for regulators, creditors (lenders), owners, and management. The guidelines used to prepare and maintain financial records and reports are known as **generally accepted accounting principles (GAAP).** *These accounting practices and procedures are authorized by the accounting profession's rule-setting body, the* **Financial Accounting Standards Board (FASB).**

In addition, the *Sarbanes-Oxley Act of 2002,* enacted in an effort to eliminate the many disclosure and conflict-of-interest problems of corporations, established the **Public Company Accounting Oversight Board (PCAOB),** a not-for-profit corporation that oversees auditors of public corporations. The PCAOB is charged with protecting the interests of investors and furthering the public interest in the preparation of informative, fair, and independent audit reports. The expectation is that it will instill confidence in investors with regard to the accuracy of the audited financial statements of public companies.

Publicly owned corporations with more than $5 million in assets and 500 or more stockholders are required by the Securities and Exchange Commission (SEC)—the federal regulatory body that governs the sale and listing of securities—to provide their stockholders with an annual **stockholders' report.** The stockholders' report summarizes and documents the firm's financial activities during the past year. It begins with a letter to the stockholders from the firm's president and/or chairman of the board.

generally accepted accounting principles (GAAP)
The practice and procedure guidelines used to prepare and maintain financial records and reports; authorized by the *Financial Accounting Standards Board (FASB).*

Financial Accounting Standards Board (FASB)

The accounting profession's rule-setting body, which authorizes generally *accepted accounting principles (GAAP).*

Public Company Accounting Oversight Board (PCAOB)
A not-for-profit corporation established by the *Sarbanes-Oxley Act of 2002* to protect the interests of investors and further the public interest in the preparation of informative, fair, and independent audit reports.

stockholders' report
Annual report that publicly owned corporations must provide to stockholders; it summarizes and documents the firm's financial activities during the past year.

GLOBAL focus

More Countries Adopt International Financial Reporting Standards

in practice In the United States, public companies are required to report financial results using GAAP. However, accounting standards vary around the world, and that makes comparing the financial results of firms located in different countries quite challenging. In recent years, many countries have adopted a system of accounting principles known as International Financial Reporting Standards (IFRS), which are established by an independent standards-setting body known as the International Accounting Standards Board (IASB). These standards are designed with the goal of making financial statements everywhere understandable, reliable, comparable, and accurate. More than 80 countries now require listed firms to comply with IFRS, and dozens more permit or require firms to follow IFRS to some degree.

Why hasn't the United States followed the global trend of IFRS adoption? Some argue that GAAP is still the "gold standard," and a movement to IFRS would lower the overall quality of financial reporting made by U.S. firms. It is true that IFRS generally requires less detail than GAAP. Even so, the Securities and Exchange Commission has expressed its view that U.S. investors will benefit as GAAP and IFRS converge though there is no expectation that firms in the United States will be required to switch to IFRS in the near future.

▶ What costs and benefits might be associated with a switch to IFRS in the United States?

The Letter to Stockholders

The **letter to stockholders** is the primary communication from management. It describes the events that are considered to have had the greatest effect on the firm during the year. It also typically discusses management philosophy, corporate governance issues, strategies, and actions, as well as plans for the coming year.

letter to stockholders

Typically, the first element of the annual stockholders' report and the primary communication from management.

The Four Key Financial Statements

The four key financial statements required by the SEC for reporting to shareholders are (1) the income statement, (2) the balance sheet, (3) the statement of stockholders' equity, and (4) the statement of cash flows. The financial statements from the 2012 stockholders' report of Bartlett Company, a manufacturer of metal fasteners, are presented and briefly discussed in this section. Most likely, you have studied these four financial statements in an accounting course, so the purpose of looking at them here is to refresh your memory of the basics, rather than provide an exhaustive review.

income statement

Provides a financial summary of the firm's operating results during a specified period.

INCOME STATEMENT The **income statement** provides a financial summary of the firm's operating results during a specified period. Most common are income statements covering a 1-year period ending at a specified date, ordinarily December 31 of the calendar year. Many large firms, however, operate on a 12-month financial cycle, or *fiscal year,* that ends at a time other than December 31. In addition, monthly income statements are typically prepared for use by management, and quarterly statements must be made available to the stockholders of publicly owned corporations.

Table 2.1 presents Bartlett Company's income statements for the years ended December 31, 2012 and 2011. The 2012 statement begins with *sales revenue*—the total dollar amount of sales during the period—from which the *cost of goods sold* is deducted. The resulting *gross profit* of $986,000 represents the amount remaining to satisfy operating, financial, and tax costs. Next, *operating expenses,* which include selling expense, general and administrative expense, lease expense, and depreciation expense, are deducted from gross profits. The resulting *operating profits* of $418,000 represent the profits earned from producing and selling products; this amount does not consider financial and tax costs. (Operating profit is often called *earnings before interest and taxes,* or *EBIT.*) Next, the financial cost—*interest expense*—is subtracted from operating profits to find *net profits* (or *earnings*) *before taxes*. After subtracting $93,000 in 2012 interest, Bartlett Company had $325,000 of net profits before taxes.

Next, taxes are calculated at the appropriate tax rates and deducted to determine *net profits* (or *earnings*) *after taxes.* Bartlett Company's net profits after taxes for 2012 were $231,000. Any preferred stock dividends must be subtracted from net profits after taxes to arrive at *earnings*

focus on ETHICS

Taking Earnings Reports at Face Value

in practice Near the end of each quarter, Wall Street's much anticipated "earnings season" arrives. During earnings season, many companies unveil their quarterly performance. Interest is high, as media outlets rush to report the latest announcements, analysts slice and dice the numbers, and investors buy and sell based on the news. The most anticipated performance metric for most companies is earnings per share (EPS), which is typically compared to the estimates of the analysts that cover a firm. Firms that beat analyst estimates often see their share prices jump, while those that miss estimates, by even a small amount, tend to suffer price declines.

Many investors are aware of the pitfalls of judging firms based on reported earnings. Specifically, the complexity of financial reports makes it easy for managers to mislead investors. Sometimes, the methods used to mislead investors are within the rules, albeit not the spirit, of acceptable accounting practices. Other times, firms break the rules to make their numbers. The practice of manipulating earnings to mislead investors is known as earnings management.

Some firms are notorious for consistently beating analysts' estimates. For example, for one 10-year period (1995–2004), General Electric Co. (GE) beat Wall Street earnings estimates every quarter, often by only a penny or two per share. However, in 2009, the U.S. Securities and Exchange Commission (SEC) fined GE $50 million for improper accounting practices, including recording sales that had not yet occurred. When GE went back to correct the problems identified by the SEC, they found that net earnings between 2001 and 2007 were a total of $280 million lower than originally reported.

In one of his famous letters to the shareholders of Berskshire Hathaway, Warren Buffett offers three bits of advice regarding financial reporting.[a] First, he warns that weak visible accounting practices are typically a sign of bigger problems. Second, he suggests that, when you can't understand management, the reason is probably that management doesn't want you to understand them. Third, he warns that investors should be suspicious of projections because earnings and growth do not typically progress in an orderly fashion. Finally, Buffett notes that "Managers that always promise to 'make the numbers' will at some point be tempted to make up the numbers."

▶ Why might financial managers be tempted to manage earnings?
▶ Is it unethical for managers to manage earnings if they disclose their activities to investors?

[a] www.berkshirehathaway.com/letters/2002pdf.pdf

---

available for common stockholders. This is the amount earned by the firm on behalf of the common stockholders during the period.

Dividing earnings available for common stockholders by the number of shares of common stock outstanding results in *earnings per share (EPS).* EPS represent the number of dollars earned during the period on behalf of each outstanding share of common stock. In 2012, Bartlett Company earned $221,000 for its common stockholders, which represents $2.90 for each outstanding share. The actual cash **dividend per share (DPS),** which is the dollar amount of cash distributed during the period on behalf of each outstanding share of common stock, paid in 2012 was $1.29.

BALANCE SHEET The **balance sheet** presents a summary statement of the firm's financial position at a given time. The statement balances the firm's *assets* (what it owns) against its financing, which can be either *debt* (what it owes) or *equity* (what was provided by owners). Bartlett Company's balance sheets as of December 31 of 2012 and 2011 are presented in Table 2.2. They show a variety of asset, liability (debt), and equity accounts.

An important distinction is made between short-term and long-term assets and liabilities. The **current assets** and **current liabilities** are *short-term* assets and liabilities. This means that they are expected to be converted into cash (current assets) or paid (current liabilities) within 1 year or less. All other assets and liabilities, along with stockholders' equity, which is assumed to have an infinite life, are considered *long-term,* or *fixed,* because they are expected to remain on the firm's books for more than 1 year.

As is customary, the assets are listed from the most liquid—*cash*—down to the least liquid. *Marketable securities* are very liquid short-term investments, such as U.S. Treasury bills or certificates of deposit, held by the firm. Because they are highly liquid, marketable securities are viewed as a form of cash ("near cash"). *Accounts receivable* represent the total monies owed the firm by its customers on credit sales. *Inventories* include raw materials, work in process (partially finished goods), and finished goods held by the firm. The entry for *gross fixed assets* is the original cost of all fixed (long-term) assets owned by the firm.[1] *Net fixed assets* represent the difference between

dividend per share (DPS)
The dollar amount of cash distributed during the period on behalf of each outstanding share of common stock.

balance sheet
Summary statement of the firm's financial position at a given point in time.

current assets
Short-term assets, expected to be converted into cash within 1 year or less.

current liabilities
Short-term liabilities, expected to be paid within 1 year or less.

[1.] For convenience the term *fixed assets* is used throughout this text to refer to what, in a strict accounting sense, is captioned "property, plant, and equipment." This simplification of terminology permits certain financial concepts to be more easily developed.

	For the years ended December 31	
	2012	**2011**
Sales revenue	$3,074	$2,567
Less: Cost of goods sold	2,088	1,711
Gross profits	$ 986	$ 856
Less: Operating expenses		
Selling expense	$ 100	$ 108
General and administrative expenses	194	187
Lease expense[a]	35	35
Depreciation expense	239	223
Total operating expense	$ 568	$ 553
Operating profits	$ 418	$ 303
Less: Interest expense	93	91
Net profits before taxes	$ 325	$ 212
Less: Taxes	94	64
Net profits after taxes	$ 231	$ 148
Less: Preferred stock dividends	10	10
Earnings available for common stockholders	$ 221	$ 138
Earnings per share (EPS)[b]	$2.90	$1.81
Dividend per share (DPS)[c]	$1.29	$0.75

[a]Lease expense is shown here as a separate item rather than being included as part of interest expense, as specified by the FASB for financial reporting purposes. The approach used here is consistent with tax reporting rather than financial reporting procedures.

[b]Calculated by dividing the earnings available for common stockholders by the number of shares of common stock outstanding—76,262 in 2012 and 76,244 in 2011. Earnings per share in 2012: $221,000 ÷ 76,262 = $2.90 ; in 2011: $138,000 ÷ 76,244 = $1.81 .

[c]Calculated by dividing the dollar amount of dividends paid to common stockholders by the number of shares of common stock outstanding. Dividends per share in 2012: $98,000 ÷ 76,262 = $1.29 ; in 2011: $57,183 ÷ 76,244 = $0.75 .

TABLE 2.1
Bartlett Company Income Statements ($000)

long-term debt
Debt for which payment is not due in the current year.

paid-in capital in excess of par
The amount of proceeds in excess of the par value received from the original sale of common stock.

retained earnings
The cumulative total of all earnings, net of dividends, that have been retained and reinvested in the firm since its inception.

gross fixed assets and *accumulated depreciation*—the total expense recorded for the depreciation of fixed assets. The net value of fixed assets is called their *book value.*

Like assets, the liabilities and equity accounts are listed from short-term to long-term. Current liabilities include *accounts payable,* amounts owed for credit purchases by the firm; *notes payable,* outstanding short-term loans, typically from commercial banks; and *accruals,* amounts owed for services for which a bill may not or will not be received. Examples of accruals include taxes due the government and wages due employees. **Long-term debt** represents debt for which payment is not due in the current year. *Stockholders' equity* represents the owners' claims on the firm. The *preferred stock* entry shows the historical proceeds from the sale of preferred stock ($200,000 for Bartlett Company).

Next, the amount paid by the original purchasers of common stock is shown by two entries, common stock and paid-in capital in excess of par on common stock. The *common stock* entry is the *par value* of common stock. **Paid-in capital in excess of par** represents the amount of proceeds in excess of the par value received from the original sale of common stock. The sum of the common stock and paid-in capital accounts divided by the number of shares outstanding represents the original price per share received by the firm on a single issue of common stock. Bartlett Company therefore received about $8.12 per share from the sale of its common stock.

Finally, **retained earnings** represent the cumulative total of all earnings, net of dividends, that have been retained and reinvested in the firm since its inception. It is important to recognize that retained earnings are not cash but rather have been utilized to finance the firm's assets.

Bartlett Company's balance sheets in Table 2.2 show that the firm's total assets increased from $3,270,000 in 2011 to $3,597,000 in 2012. The $327,000 increase was due primarily to the $219,000 increase in current assets. The asset increase, in turn, appears to have been financed

Personal Finance Example 2.1

Jan and Jon Smith, a mid-30s married couple with no children, prepared a personal income and expense statement, which is similar to a corporate income statement. A condensed version of their income and expense statement follows.

**Jan and Jon Smith's Income and Expense Statement
for the Year Ended December 31, 2012**

Income

Salaries	$72,725
Interest received	195
Dividends received	120
(1) Total income	$73,040

Expenses

Mortgage payments	$16,864
Auto loan payments	2,520
Utilities	2,470
Home repairs and maintenance	1,050
Food	5,825
Car expense	2,265
Health care and insurance	1,505
Clothes, shoes, accessories	1,700
Insurance	1,380
Taxes	16,430
Appliance and furniture payments	1,250
Recreation and entertainment	4,630
Tuition and books for Jan	1,400
Personal care and other items	2,415
(2) Total expenses	$61,704
(3) Cash surplus (or deficit) [(1) − (2)]	$11,336

During the year, the Smiths had total income of $73,040 and total expenses of $61,704, which left them with a cash surplus of $11,336. They can use the surplus to increase their savings and investments.

primarily by an increase of $193,000 in total liabilities. Better insight into these changes can be derived from the statement of cash flows, which we will discuss shortly.

STATEMENT OF RETAINED EARNINGS The *statement of retained earnings* is an abbreviated form of the statement of stockholders' equity. Unlike the **statement of stockholders' equity,** which shows all equity account transactions that occurred during a given year, the **statement of retained earnings** reconciles the net income earned during a given year, and any cash dividends paid, with the change in retained earnings between the start and the end of that year. Table 2.3 presents this statement for Bartlett Company for the year ended December 31, 2012. The statement shows that the company began the year with $1,012,000 in retained earnings and had net profits after taxes of $231,000, from which it paid a total of $108,000 in dividends, resulting in year-end retained earnings of $1,135,000. Thus the net increase for Bartlett Company was $123,000 ($231,000 net profits after taxes minus $108,000 in dividends) during 2012.

STATEMENT OF CASH FLOWS The **statement of cash flows** is a summary of the cash flows over the period of concern. The statement provides insight into the firm's operating, investment, and

statement of stockholders' equity
Shows all equity account transactions that occurred during a given year.

statement of retained earnings
Reconciles the net income earned during a given year, and any cash dividends paid, with the change in retained earnings between the start and the end of that year. An abbreviated form of the statement of stockholders' *equity.*

statement of cash flows
Provides a summary of the firm's operating, investment, and financing cash flows and reconciles them with changes in its cash and marketable securities during the period.

	December 31	
Assets	**2012**	**2011**
Cash	$363	$288
Marketable securities	68	51
Accounts receivable	503	365
Inventories	289	300
Total current assets	$1,223	$1,004
Land and buildings	$2,072	$1,903
Machinery and equipment	1,866	1,693
Furniture and fixtures	358	316
Vehicles	275	314
Other (includes financial leases)	98	96
Total gross fixed assets (at cost)[a]	$4,669	$4,322
Less: Accumulated depreciation	2,295	2,056
Net fixed assets	$2,374	$2,266
Total assets	$3,597	$3,270
Liabilities and Stockholders' Equity		
Accounts payable	$382	$270
Notes payable	79	99
Accruals	159	114
Total current liabilities	$620	$483
Long-term debt (includes financial leases)[b]	1,023	967
Total liabilities	$1,643	$1,450
Preferred stock—cumulative 5%, $100 par, 2,000 shares authorized and issued[c]	$ 200	$200
Common stock—$2.50 par, 100,000 shares authorized, shares issued and outstanding in 2012: 76,262; in 2011: 76,244	191	190
Paid-in capital in excess of par on common stock	428	418
Retained earnings	1,135	1,012
Total stockholders' equity	$1,954	$1,820
Total liabilities and stockholders' equity	$3,597	$3,270

[a]In 2012, the firm has a 6-year financial lease requiring annual beginning-of-year payments of $35,000. Four years of the lease have yet to run.

[b]Annual principal repayments on a portion of the firm's total outstanding debt amount to $71,000.

[c]The annual preferred stock dividend would be $5 per share (5% × $100 par), or a total of $10,000 annually ($5 per share × 2,000 shares).

TABLE 2.2
Bartlett Company Balance Sheets ($000)

earnings balance (January 1, 2012)	$1,012
Retained Net profits after taxes (for 2012)	231
Less: Cash dividends (paid during 2012)	
Preferred stock	10
Common stock	98
Total dividends paid	$ 108
Retained earnings balance (December 31, 2012)	$1,135

TABLE 2.3
Bartlett Company Statement of Retained Earnings ($000) for the Year Ended December 31, 2012

Personal Finance Example 2.2

The following personal balance sheet for Jan and Jon Smith—the couple introduced earlier, who are married, in their mid-30s, and have no children—is similar to a corporate balance sheet.

Jan and Jon Smith's Balance Sheet: December 31, 2012

Assets		Liabilities and Net Worth	
Cash on hand	$ 90	Credit card balances	$ 665
Checking accounts	575	Utility bills	120
Savings accounts	760	Medical bills	75
Money market funds	800	Other current liabilities	45
Total liquid assets	$2,225	Total current liabilities	$ 905
Stocks and bonds	$2,250	Real estate mortgage	$ 92,000
Mutual funds	1,500	Auto loans	4,250
Retirement funds, IRA	2,000	Education loan	3,800
Total investments	$5,750	Personal loan	4,000
Real estate	$120,000	Furniture loan	800
Cars	14,000	Total long-term liabilities	$104,850
Household furnishings	3,700	Total liabilities	$105,755
Jewelry and artwork	1,500	Net worth (N/W)	41,420
Total personal property	$139,200	Total liabilities	
Total assets	$147,175	and net worth	$147,175

The Smiths have total assets of $147,175 and total liabilities of $105,755. Personal net worth (N/W) is a "plug figure"—the difference between total assets and total liabilities—which in the case of Jan and Jon Smith is $41,420.

---

financing cash flows and reconciles them with changes in its cash and marketable securities during the period. Bartlett Company's statement of cash flows for the year ended December 31, 2012, is presented in Table 2.4 (see page 52).

Notes to the Financial Statements

Included with published financial statements are explanatory notes keyed to the relevant accounts in the statements. These **notes to the financial statements** provide detailed information on the accounting policies, procedures, calculations, and transactions underlying entries in the financial statements. Common issues addressed by these notes include revenue recognition, income taxes, breakdowns of fixed asset accounts, debt and lease terms, and contingencies. Since passage of Sarbanes-Oxley, notes to the financial statements have also included some details about compliance with that law. Professional securities analysts use the data in the statements and notes to develop estimates of the value of securities that the firm issues, and these estimates influence the actions of investors and therefore the firm's share value.

notes to the financial statements
Explanatory notes keyed to relevant accounts in the statements; they provide detailed information on the accounting policies, procedures, calculations, and transactions underlying entries in the financial statements.

Consolidating International Financial Statements

So far, we've discussed financial statements involving only one currency, the U.S. dollar. The issue of how to consolidate a company's foreign and domestic financial statements has bedeviled the accounting profession for many years. The current policy is described in **Financial Accounting Standards Board (FASB) Standard No. 52,** which mandates that U.S.–based companies translate their foreign-currency-denominated assets and liabilities into dollars, for consolidation with the parent company's financial statements. This is done by using a technique called the **current rate (translation) method,** under which all of a U.S. parent company's foreign-currency-denominated assets and liabilities are converted into dollar values using the

Cash Flow from Operating Activities	
Net profits after taxes	$231
Depreciation	239
Increase in accounts receivable	(138)[a]
Decrease in inventories	11
Increase in accounts payable	112
Increase in accruals	45
Cash provided by operating activities	$500
Cash Flow from Investment Activities	
Increase in gross fixed assets	(347)
Change in equity investments in other firms	0
Cash provided by investment activities	($347)
Cash Flow from Financing Activities	
Decrease in notes payable	(20)
Increase in long-term debts	56
Changes in stockholders' equity[b]	11
Dividends paid	(108)
Cash provided by financing activities	($ 61)
Net increase in cash and marketable securities	$ 92

[a]As is customary, parentheses are used to denote a negative number, which in this case is a cash outflow.

[b]Retained earnings are excluded here because their change is actually reflected in the combination of the "net profits after taxes" and "dividends paid" entries.

TABLE 2.4
Bartlett Company Statement of Cash Flows ($000) for the Year Ended December 31, 2012

Financial Accounting Standards Board (FASB) Standard No. 52
Mandates that U.S.–based companies translate their foreign-currency-denominated assets and liabilities into dollars, for consolidation with the parent company's financial statements. This is done by using the current rate (*translation*) method.

current rate (translation) method
Technique used by U.S.–based companies to translate their foreign-currency-denominated assets and liabilities into dollars, for consolidation with the parent company's financial statements, using the year-end (current) exchange rate.

ratio analysis
Involves methods of calculating and interpreting financial ratios to analyze and monitor the firm's performance.

exchange rate prevailing at the fiscal year ending date (the current rate). Income statement items are treated similarly. Equity accounts, on the other hand, are translated into dollars by using the exchange rate that prevailed when the parent's equity investment was made (the historical rate). Retained earnings are adjusted to reflect each year's operating profits or losses.

→ **Review Questions**

2–1 What roles do GAAP, the FASB, and the PCAOB play in the financial reporting activities of public companies?

2–2 Describe the purpose of each of the four major financial statements.

2–3 Why are the notes to the financial statements important to professional securities analysts?

2–4 How is the *current rate (translation) method* used to consolidate a firm's foreign and domestic financial statements?

LG 2 **2.2 Using Financial Ratios**

The information contained in the four basic financial statements is of major significance to a variety of interested parties who regularly need to have relative measures of the company's performance. *Relative* is the key word here, because the analysis of financial statements is based on the use of *ratios* or *relative values*. Ratio analysis involves methods of calculating and interpreting financial ratios to analyze and monitor the firm's performance. The basic inputs to ratio analysis are the firm's income statement and balance sheet.

Interested Parties

Ratio analysis of a firm's financial statements is of interest to shareholders, creditors, and the firm's own management. Both current and prospective shareholders are interested in the firm's current and future level of risk and return, which directly affect share price. The firm's creditors are interested primarily in the short-term liquidity of the company and its ability to make interest and principal payments. A secondary concern of creditors is the firm's profitability; they want assurance that the business is healthy. Management, like stockholders, is concerned with all aspects of the firm's financial situation, and it attempts to produce financial ratios that will be considered favorable by both owners and creditors. In addition, management uses ratios to monitor the firm's performance from period to period.

Types of Ratio Comparisons

Ratio analysis is not merely the calculation of a given ratio. More important is the *interpretation* of the ratio value. A meaningful basis for comparison is needed to answer such questions as "Is it too high or too low?" and "Is it good or bad?" Two types of ratio comparisons can be made, cross-sectional and time-series.

CROSS-SECTIONAL ANALYSIS   Cross-sectional analysis involves the comparison of different firms' financial ratios at the same point in time. Analysts are often interested in how well a firm has performed in relation to other firms in its industry. Frequently, a firm will compare its ratio values to those of a key competitor or group of competitors that it wishes to emulate. This type of cross-sectional analysis, called **benchmarking,** has become very popular.

Comparison to industry averages is also popular. These figures can be found in the *Almanac of Business and Industrial Financial Ratios, Dun & Bradstreet's Industry Norms and Key Business Ratios, RMA Annual Statement Studies, Value Line,* and industry sources. It is also possible to derive financial ratios for yourself using financial information reported in financial databases, such as Compustat. Table 2.5 illustrates a brief cross-sectional ratio analysis by comparing several ratios as of early 2010 for two select firms to each other and the median value for their particular industry.

Analysts have to be very careful when drawing conclusions from ratio comparisons. It's tempting to assume that if one ratio for a particular firm is above the industry norm, this is a sign that the firm is performing well, at least along the dimension measured by that ratio. However, ratios may be above or below the industry norm for both positive and negative reasons, and it is necessary to determine why a firm's performance differs from its industry peers. *Thus, ratio analysis on its own is probably most useful in highlighting areas for further investigation.*

cross-sectional analysis
Comparison of different firms' financial ratios at the same point in time; involves comparing the firm's ratios to those of other firms in its industry or to industry averages.

benchmarking
A type of *cross-sectional* analysis in which the firm's ratio values are compared to those of a key competitor or group of competitors that it wishes to emulate.

	Current ratio	Quick ratio	Inventory turnover	Average collection period (days)	Total asset turnover	Debt ratio	Net profit margin (%)	Return on total assets (%)	Return on Common Equity (%)
Dell	1.3	1.2	40.5	58.9	1.6	0.8	2.7	4.3	25.4
Hewlett-Packard	1.2	1.1	13.8	80.6	1.0	0.6	6.7	6.7	18.9
Computers	2.5	2.1	5.8	61.3	0.9	0.4	−3.1	−2.2	−2.6
Home Depot	1.3	0.4	4.3	5.3	1.6	0.5	4.0	6.5	13.7
Lowe's	1.3	0.2	3.7	0.0	1.4	0.4	3.7	5.4	9.3
Building Materials	2.8	0.8	3.7	5.3	1.6	0.3	4.0	6.5	13.7
Kroger	1.0	0.3	12.0	4.3	3.3	0.8	0.1	0.3	1.4
Whole Foods Market	1.3	1.0	25.6	7.0	3.6	0.4	2.3	8.0	14.5
Grocery Stores	1.3	0.7	11.1	7.5	2.4	0.6	2.1	3.1	9.8
Sears	1.3	0.3	3.7	5.4	1.8	0.6	0.5	0.9	2.6
Wal-Mart	0.9	0.3	9.0	3.7	2.4	0.6	3.5	8.4	20.3
Merchandise Stores	1.7	0.6	4.1	3.7	2.3	0.5	1.5	4.9	10.8

[a]The data used to calculate these ratios are drawn from the Compustat North American database.

TABLE 2.5
Financial Ratios for Select Firms and Their Industry Median Values[a]

Example 2.3

In early 2013, Mary Boyle, the chief financial analyst at Caldwell Manufacturing, a producer of heat exchangers, gathered data on the firm's financial performance during 2012, the year just ended. She calculated a variety of ratios and obtained industry averages. She was especially interested in inventory turnover, which reflects the speed with which the firm moves its inventory from raw materials through production into finished goods and to the customer as a completed sale. Generally, higher values of this ratio are preferred, because they indicate a quicker turnover of inventory and more efficient inventory management. Caldwell Manufacturing's calculated inventory turnover for 2012 and the industry average inventory turnover were as follows:

	Inventory Turnover, 2012
Caldwell Manufacturing	14.8
Industry average	9.7

Mary's initial reaction to these data was that the firm had managed its inventory significantly *better than* the average firm in the industry. The turnover was nearly 53% faster than the industry average. On reflection, however, she realized that a very high inventory turnover could be a sign that the firm is not holding enough inventories. The consequence of low inventory could be excessive stockouts (insufficient inventory to meet customer needs). Discussions with people in the manufacturing and marketing departments did, in fact, uncover such a problem: Inventories during the year were extremely low, the result of numerous production delays that hindered the firm's ability to meet demand and resulted in disgruntled customers and lost sales. A ratio that initially appeared to reflect extremely efficient inventory management was actually the symptom of a major problem.

time-series analysis
Evaluation of the firm's financial performance over time using financial ratio analysis.

TIME-SERIES ANALYSIS   Time-series analysis evaluates performance over time. Comparison of current to past performance, using ratios, enables analysts to assess the firm's progress. Developing trends can be seen by using multiyear comparisons. Any significant year-to-year changes may be symptomatic of a problem, especially if the same trend is not an industry-wide phenomenon.

COMBINED ANALYSIS   The most informative approach to ratio analysis combines cross-sectional and time-series analyses. A combined view makes it possible to assess the trend in the behavior of the ratio in relation to the trend for the industry. Figure 2.1 depicts this type of approach using the average collection period ratio of Bartlett Company, over the years 2009–2012. This ratio reflects the average amount of time (in days) it takes the firm to collect bills, and lower values of this ratio generally are preferred. The figure quickly discloses that (1) Bartlett's effectiveness in

Figure 2.1
Combined Analysis
Combined cross-sectional and time-series view of Bartlett Company's average collection period, 2009–2012

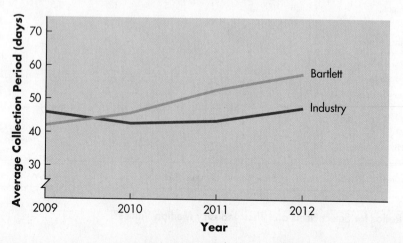

collecting its receivables is poor in comparison to the industry, and (2) Bartlett's trend is toward longer collection periods. Clearly, Bartlett needs to shorten its collection period.

Cautions About Using Ratio Analysis

Before discussing specific ratios, we should consider the following cautions about their use:

1. Ratios that reveal large deviations from the norm merely indicate *the possibility* of a problem. Additional analysis is typically needed to determine whether there is a problem and to isolate the *causes* of the problem.
2. A single ratio does not generally provide sufficient information from which to judge the *overall* performance of the firm. However, if an analysis is concerned only with certain *specific* aspects of a firm's financial position, one or two ratios may suffice.
3. The ratios being compared should be calculated using financial statements dated at the same point in time during the year. If they are not, the effects of *seasonality* may produce erroneous conclusions and decisions.
4. It is preferable to use *audited financial statements* for ratio analysis. If they have not been audited, the data in them may not reflect the firm's true financial condition.
5. The financial data being compared should have been developed in the same way. The use of differing accounting treatments—especially relative to inventory and depreciation—can distort the results of ratio comparisons, regardless of whether cross-sectional or time-series analysis is used.
6. Results can be distorted by *inflation*, which can cause the book values of inventory and depreciable assets to differ greatly from their replacement values. Additionally, inventory costs and depreciation write-offs can differ from their true values, thereby distorting profits. Without adjustment, inflation tends to cause older firms (older assets) to appear more efficient and profitable than newer firms (newer assets). Clearly, in using ratios, you must be careful when comparing older to newer firms or a firm to itself over a long period of time.

In more depth

To read about *Perils of Ratio Analysis*, go to www.myaccountinglab.com

MyAccountingLab

Categories of Financial Ratios

Financial ratios can be divided for convenience into five basic categories: liquidity, activity, debt, profitability, and market ratios. Liquidity, activity, and debt ratios primarily measure risk. Profitability ratios measure return. Market ratios capture both risk and return.

As a rule, the inputs necessary for an effective financial analysis include, at a minimum, the income statement and the balance sheet. We will use the 2012 and 2011 income statements and balance sheets for Bartlett Company, presented earlier in Tables 2.1 and 2.2, to demonstrate ratio calculations. Note, however, that the ratios presented in the remainder of this chapter can be applied to almost any company. Of course, many companies in different industries use ratios that focus on aspects peculiar to their industry.

→ Review Questions

2–5 With regard to financial ratio analysis, how do the viewpoints held by the firm's present and prospective shareholders, creditors, and management differ?

2–6 What is the difference between cross-sectional and time-series ratio analysis? What is benchmarking?

2–7 What types of deviations from the norm should the analyst pay primary attention to when performing cross-sectional ratio analysis? Why?

2–8 Why is it preferable to compare ratios calculated using financial statements that are dated at the same point in time during the year?

LG 3

2.3 Liquidity Ratios

The **liquidity** of a firm is measured by its ability to satisfy its short-term obligations *as they come due*. Liquidity refers to the solvency of the firm's *overall* financial position—the ease with which it can pay its bills. Because a common precursor to financial distress and bankruptcy is low or declining liquidity, these ratios can provide early signs of cash flow problems and impending business failure. Clearly it is desirable that a firm is able to pay its bills, so having enough liquidity for day-to-day operations is important. However, liquid assets, like cash held at

liquidity
A firm's ability to satisfy its short-term obligations as they come due.

Determinants of Liquidity Needs

Glance back at the first column of data in Table 2.5 that shows the current ratio for a variety of companies and industries. Notice that the industry with the highest current ratio (that is, most liquidity) is building materials, a business that is notoriously sensitive to business cycle swings. The current ratio for that industry is 2.8, indicating that the typical firm in that business has almost three times as much in current assets as in current liabilities. Two of the largest competitors in that industry, The Home Depot and Lowe's, operate with a current ratio of 1.3, less than half the industry average. Does this mean that these firms have a liquidity problem? Not necessarily. Large enterprises generally have well-established relationships with banks that can provide lines of credit and other short-term loan products in the event that the firm has a need for liquidity. Smaller firms may not have the same access to credit, and therefore they tend to operate with more liquidity.

banks and marketable securities, do not earn a particularly high rate of return, so shareholders will not want a firm to *overinvest* in liquidity. Firms have to balance the need for safety that liquidity provides against the low returns that liquid assets generate for investors. The two basic measures of liquidity are the current ratio and the quick (acid-test) ratio.

Current Ratio

quick (acid-test) ratio
A measure of liquidity calculated by dividing the firm's current assets minus inventory by its current liabilities.

The **current ratio,** one of the most commonly cited financial ratios, measures the firm's ability to meet its short-term obligations. It is expressed as follows:

$$\text{Current ratio} = \text{Current assets} \div \text{Current liabilities}$$

The current ratio for Bartlett Company in 2012 is

$$\$1,223,000 \div \$620,000 = 1.97$$

A higher current ratio indicates a greater degree of liquidity. How much liquidity a firm needs depends on a variety of factors, including the firm's size, its access to short-term financing sources like bank credit lines, and the volatility of its business. For example, a grocery store whose revenues are relatively predictable may not need as much liquidity as a manufacturing firm who faces sudden and unexpected shifts in demand for its products. The more predictable a firm's cash flows, the lower the acceptable current ratio. Because Bartlett Company is in a business with a relatively predictable annual cash flow, its current ratio of 1.97 should be quite acceptable.

Personal Finance Example 2.4

Individuals, like corporations, can use financial ratios to analyze and monitor their performance. Typically, personal finance ratios are calculated using the personal income and expense statement and personal balance sheet for the period of concern. Here we use these statements, presented in the preceding personal finance examples, to demonstrate calculation of Jan and Jon Smith's liquidity ratio for calendar year 2012.

The personal *liquidity ratio* is calculated by dividing total liquid assets by total current debt. It indicates the percent of annual debt obligations that an individual can meet using current liquid assets. The Smiths' total liquid assets were $2,225. Their total current debts are $21,539 (total current liabilities of $905 + mortgage payments of $16,864 + auto loan payments of $2,520 + appliance and furniture payments of $1,250). Substituting these values into the ratio formula, we get:

$$\text{Liquidity ratio} = \frac{\text{Total liquid assets}}{\text{Total current debts}} = \frac{\$2,225}{\$21,539} = 0.1033, \text{ or } 10.3\%$$

That ratio indicates that the Smiths can cover only about 10% of their existing 1-year debt obligations with their current liquid assets. Clearly, the Smiths plan to meet these debt obligations from their income, but this ratio suggests that their liquid funds do not provide a large cushion. One of their goals should probably be to build up a larger fund of liquid assets to meet unexpected expenses.

The Importance of Inventories

Glance back at the first column of data in Table 2.5 that shows the current ratio for a variety of companies and industries. Notice that the industry with the highest current ratio (that is, most liquidity) is building materials, a business that is notoriously sensitive to business cycle swings. The current ratio for that industry is 2.8, indicating that the typical firm in that business has almost three times as much in current assets as in current liabilities. Two of the largest competitors in that industry, The Home Depot and Lowe's, operate with a current ratio of 1.3, less than half the industry average. Does this mean that these firms have a liquidity problem? Not necessarily. Large enterprises generally have well-established relationships with banks that can provide lines of credit and other short-term loan products in the event that the firm has a need for liquidity. Smaller firms may not have the same access to credit, and therefore they tend to operate with more liquidity.

Quick (Acid-Test) Ratio

The **quick (acid-test) ratio** is similar to the current ratio except that it excludes inventory, which is generally the least liquid current asset. The generally low liquidity of inventory results from two primary factors: (1) Many types of inventory cannot be easily sold because they are partially completed items, special-purpose items, and the like; and (2) inventory is typically sold on credit, which means that it becomes an account receivable before being converted into cash. An additional problem with inventory as a liquid asset is that the times when companies face the most dire need for liquidity, when business is bad, are precisely the times when it is most difficult to convert inventory into cash by selling it. The quick ratio is calculated as follows:

$$\text{Quick ratio} = \frac{\text{Current assets} - \text{Inventory}}{\text{Current liabilities}}$$

The quick ratio for Bartlett Company in 2012 is

$$\frac{\$1,223,000 - \$289,000}{\$620,000} = \frac{\$934,000}{\$620,000} = 1.51$$

As with the current ratio, the quick ratio level that a firm should strive to achieve depends largely on the nature of the business in which it operates. The quick ratio provides a better measure of overall liquidity only when a firm's inventory cannot be easily converted into cash. If inventory is liquid, the current ratio is a preferred measure of overall liquidity.

→ Review Questions

2–9 Under what circumstances would the current ratio be the preferred measure of overall firm liquidity? Under what circumstances would the quick ratio be preferred?

2–10 In Table 2.5, most of the specific firms listed have current ratios that fall below the industry average. Why? The exception to this general pattern is Whole Foods Market, which competes at the very high end of the retail grocery market. Why might Whole Foods Market operate with greater-than-average liquidity?

LG 3 ## 2.4 Activity Ratios

Activity ratios measure the speed with which various accounts are converted into sales or cash—inflows or outflows. In a sense, activity ratios measure how efficiently a firm operates along a variety of dimensions such as inventory management, disbursements, and collections. A number of ratios are available for measuring the activity of the most important current accounts, which include inventory, accounts receivable, and accounts payable. The efficiency with which total assets are used can also be assessed.

activity ratios
Measure the speed with which various accounts are converted into sales or cash—inflows or outflows.

Inventory Turnover

Inventory turnover commonly measures the activity, or liquidity, of a firm's inventory. It is calculated as follows:

inventory turnover
Measures the activity, or liquidity, of a firm's inventory.

Who Gets Credit?

Notice in Table 2.5 the vast differences across industries in the average collection periods. Companies in the building materials, grocery, and merchandise store industries collect in just a few days, whereas firms in the computer industry take roughly two months to collect on their sales. The difference is primarily due to the fact that these industries serve very different customers. Grocery and retail stores serve individuals who pay cash or use credit cards (which to the store are essentially the same as cash). Computer manufacturers sell to retail chains, businesses, and other large organizations that negotiate agreements that allow them to pay for the computers they order well after the sale is made.

$$\text{Inventory turnover} = \text{Cost of goods sold} \div \text{Inventory}$$

Applying this relationship to Bartlett Company in 2012 yields

$$\$2,088,000 \div \$289,000 = 7.2$$

The resulting turnover is meaningful only when it is compared with that of other firms in the same industry or to the firm's past inventory turnover. An inventory turnover of 20 would not be unusual for a grocery store, whose goods are highly perishable and must be sold quickly, whereas an aircraft manufacturer might turn its inventory just four times per year.

Another inventory activity ratio measures how many days of inventory the firm has on hand. Inventory turnover can be easily converted into an **average age of inventory** by dividing it into 365. For Bartlett Company, the average age of inventory in 2012 is 50.7 days (365÷7.2). This value can also be viewed as the average number of days' sales in inventory.

average age of inventory
Average number of days' sales in inventory.

Average Collection Period

average collection period
The average amount of time needed to collect accounts receivable.

The **average collection period,** or average age of accounts receivable, is useful in evaluating credit and collection policies. It is arrived at by dividing the average daily sales into the accounts receivable balance:[2]

$$\text{Average collection period} = \frac{\text{Accounts receivable}}{\text{Average sales per day}}$$
$$= \frac{\text{Accounts receivable}}{\dfrac{\text{Annual sales}}{365}}$$

The average collection period for Bartlett Company in 2012 is

$$\frac{\$503,000}{\dfrac{\$3,074,000}{365}} = \frac{\$503,000}{\$8,422} = 59.7 \text{ days}$$

On the average, it takes the firm 59.7 days to collect an account receivable.

The average collection period is meaningful only in relation to the firm's credit terms. If Bartlett Company extends 30-day credit terms to customers, an average collection period of 59.7 days may indicate a poorly managed credit or collection department, or both. It is also possible that the lengthened collection period resulted from an intentional relaxation of credit-term enforcement in response to competitive pressures. If the firm had extended 60-day credit terms,

---

2. The formula as presented assumes, for simplicity, that all sales are made on a credit basis. If this is not the case, *average credit sales per day* should be substituted for average sales per day.

Sell It Fast

Observe in Table 2.5 that the grocery business turns over assets faster than any of the other industries listed. That makes sense because inventory is among the most valuable assets held by these firms, and grocery stores have to sell baked goods, dairy products, and produce quickly or throw them away when they spoil. It's true that some items in a grocery store have a shelf life longer than anyone really wants to know (think Twinkies), but on average a grocery store has to replace its entire inventory in just a few days or weeks, and that contributes to the rapid turnover of the firm's total assets.

the 59.7-day average collection period would be quite acceptable. Clearly, additional information is needed to evaluate the effectiveness of the firm's credit and collection policies.

Average Payment Period

The **average payment period,** or average age of accounts payable, is calculated in the same manner as the average collection period:

$$\text{Average payment period} = \frac{\text{Accounts payable}}{\text{Average purchases per day}}$$

$$= \frac{\text{Accounts payable}}{\dfrac{\text{Annual purchases}}{365}}$$

average payment period
The average amount of time needed to pay accounts payable.

The difficulty in calculating this ratio stems from the need to find annual purchases,[3] a value not available in published financial statements. Ordinarily, purchases are estimated as a given percentage of cost of goods sold. If we assume that Bartlett Company's purchases equaled 70 percent of its cost of goods sold in 2012, its average payment period is

$$\frac{\$382,000}{\dfrac{0.70 \times \$2,088,000}{365}} = \frac{\$382,000}{\$4,004} = 95.4 \text{ days}$$

This figure is meaningful only in relation to the average credit terms extended to the firm. If Bartlett Company's suppliers have extended, on average, 30-day credit terms, an analyst would give Bartlett a low credit rating because it was taking too long to pay its bills. Prospective lenders and suppliers of trade credit are interested in the average payment period because it provides insight into the firm's bill-paying patterns.

Total Asset Turnover

The **total asset turnover** indicates the efficiency with which the firm uses its assets to generate sales. Total asset turnover is calculated as follows:

total asset turnover
Indicates the efficiency with which the firm uses its assets to generate sales.

$$\text{Total asset turnover} = \text{Sales} \div \text{Total assets}$$

The value of Bartlett Company's total asset turnover in 2012 is

$$\$3,074,000 \div \$3,597,000 = 0.85$$

This means the company turns over its assets 0.85 times per year.

Generally, the higher a firm's total asset turnover, the more efficiently its assets have been used. This measure is probably of greatest interest to management because it indicates whether the firm's operations have been financially efficient.

---

3. Technically, annual *credit* purchases—rather than annual purchases—should be used in calculating this ratio. For simplicity, this refinement is ignored here.

→ **Review Question**

2–11 To assess the firm's average collection period and average payment period ratios, what additional information is needed, and why?

LG 4 **2.5 Debt Ratios**

The *debt position* of a firm indicates the amount of other people's money being used to generate profits. In general, the financial analyst is most concerned with long-term debts because these commit the firm to a stream of contractual payments over the long run. The more debt a firm has, the greater its risk of being unable to meet its contractual debt payments. Because creditors' claims must be satisfied before the earnings can be distributed to shareholders, current and prospective shareholders pay close attention to the firm's ability to repay debts. Lenders are also concerned about the firm's indebtedness.

financial leverage
The magnification of risk and return through the use of fixed-cost financing, such as debt and preferred stock.

In general, the more debt a firm uses in relation to its total assets, the greater its *financial leverage*. **Financial leverage** is the magnification of risk and return through the use of fixed-cost financing, such as debt and preferred stock. The more fixed-cost debt a firm uses, the greater will be its expected risk and return.

Example 2.5

Patty Akers is in the process of incorporating her new business. After much analysis she determined that an initial investment of $50,000—$20,000 in current assets and $30,000 in fixed assets—is necessary. These funds can be obtained in either of two ways. The first is the *no-debt plan*, under which she would invest the full $50,000 without borrowing. The other alternative, the *debt plan*, involves investing $25,000 and borrowing the balance of $25,000 at 12% annual interest.

Patty expects $30,000 in sales, $18,000 in operating expenses, and a 40% tax rate. Projected balance sheets and income statements associated with the two plans are summarized in Table 2.6. The no-debt plan results in after-tax profits of $7,200, which represent a 14.4% rate of return on Patty's $50,000 investment. The debt plan results in $5,400 of after-tax profits, which represent a 21.6% rate of return on Patty's investment of $25,000. The debt plan provides Patty with a higher rate of return, but the risk of this plan is also greater, because the annual $3,000 of interest must be paid whether Patty's business is profitable or not.

Balance Sheets	No-debt plan	Debt plan
Current assets	$20,000	$20,000
Fixed assets	30,000	30,000
Total assets	$50,000	$50,000
Debt (12% interest)	$0	$25,000
(1) Equity	50,000	25,000
Total liabilities and equity	$50,000	$50,000

Income Statements		No-debt plan		Debt plan
Sales		$30,000		$30,000
Less: Operating expenses		18,000		18,000
Operating profits		$12,000		$12,000
Less: Interest expense		0	0.12 × $25,000 =	3,000
Net profits before taxes		$12,000		$9,000
Less: Taxes (rate = 40%)		4,800		3,600
(2) Net profits after taxes		$7,200		$5,400
Return on equity [(2) ÷ (1)]		$\frac{\$7,200}{\$50,000} = 14.4\%$		$\frac{\$5,400}{\$25,000} = 21.6\%$

TABLE 2.6
Financial Statements Associated with Patty's Alternatives

CHAPTER 2 • FINANCIAL STATEMENTS AND RATIO ANALYSIS **61**

The example demonstrates that *with increased debt comes greater risk as well as higher potential return.* Therefore, the greater the financial leverage, the greater the potential risk and return. Here, we emphasize the use of financial debt ratios to assess externally a firm's debt position.

There are two general types of debt measures: measures of the degree of indebtedness and measures of the ability to service debts. The **degree of indebtedness** measures the amount of debt relative to other significant balance sheet amounts. A popular measure of the degree of indebtedness is the debt ratio.

The second type of debt measure, the **ability to service debts**, reflects a firm's ability to make the payments required on a scheduled basis over the life of a debt. The term to *service debts* simply means to pay debts on time. The firm's ability to pay certain fixed charges is measured using **coverage ratios.** Typically, higher coverage ratios are preferred (especially by the firm's lenders), but a very high ratio might indicate that the firm's management is too conservative and might be able to earn higher returns by borrowing more. In general, the lower the firm's coverage ratios, the less certain it is to be able to pay fixed obligations. If a firm is unable to pay these obligations, its creditors may seek immediate repayment, which in most instances would force a firm into bankruptcy. Two popular coverage ratios are the times interest earned ratio and the fixed-payment coverage ratio.

degree of indebtedness
Measures the amount of debt relative to other significant balance sheet amounts.

ability to service debts
The ability of a firm to make the payments required on a scheduled basis over the life of a debt.

Debt Ratio

The **debt ratio** measures the proportion of total assets financed by the firm's creditors. The higher this ratio, the greater the amount of other people's money being used to generate profits. The ratio is calculated as follows:

$$\text{Debt ratio} = \text{Total liabilities} \div \text{Total assets}$$

The debt ratio for Bartlett Company in 2012 is

$$\$1,643,000 \div \$3,597,000 = 0.457 = 45.7\%$$

This value indicates that the company has financed close to half of its assets with debt. The higher this ratio, the greater the firm's degree of indebtedness and the more financial leverage it has.

Times Interest Earned Ratio

The **times interest earned ratio,** sometimes called the *interest coverage ratio,* measures the firm's ability to make contractual interest payments. The higher its value, the better able the firm is to fulfill its interest obligations. The times interest earned ratio is calculated as follows:

$$\text{Times interest earned ratio} = \text{Earnings before interest and taxes} \div \text{interest}$$

The figure for *earnings before interest and taxes (EBIT)* is the same as that for *operating profits* shown in the income statement. Applying this ratio to Bartlett Company yields the following 2012 value:

$$\text{Time interest earned ratio} = \$418,000 \div \$93,000 = 4.5$$

The times interest earned ratio for Bartlett Company seems acceptable. A value of at least 3.0—and preferably closer to 5.0—is often suggested. The firm's earnings before interest and taxes could shrink by as much as 78 percent and the firm would still be able to pay the $93,000 in interest it owes. Thus it has a large margin of safety.

times interest earned ratio
Measures the firm's ability to make contractual interest payments; sometimes called the interest coverage ratio.

Fixed-Payment Coverage Ratio

The **fixed-payment coverage ratio** measures the firm's ability to meet all fixed-payment obligations, such as loan interest and principal, lease payments, and preferred stock dividends. As is true of the times interest earned ratio, the higher this value the better. The formula for the fixed-payment coverage ratio is

fixed-payment coverage ratio
Measures the firm's ability to meet all fixed-payment obligations.

$$\text{Fixed-payment coverage ratio} = \frac{\text{Earnings before interest and taxes} + \text{Lease payments}}{\text{Interest} + \text{Lease payments} + \{(\text{Principal payments} + \text{Preferred stock dividends}) \times [1/(1 - T)]\}}$$

where T is the corporate tax rate applicable to the firm's income. The term $1/(1 - T)$ is included to adjust the after-tax principal and preferred stock dividend payments back to a before-tax equivalent that is consistent with the before-tax values of all other terms. Applying the formula to Bartlett Company's 2012 data yields

$$\frac{\text{Fixed-payment}}{\text{coverage ratio}} = \frac{\$418,000 + \$35,000}{\$93,000 + \$35,000 + \{(\$71,000 + \$10,000) \times [1/(1 - 0.29)]\}}$$

$$= \frac{\$453,000}{\$242,000} = 1.9$$

Because the earnings available are nearly twice as large as its fixed-payment obligations, the firm appears safely able to meet the latter.

Like the times interest earned ratio, the fixed-payment coverage ratio measures risk. The lower the ratio, the greater the risk to both lenders and owners, and the greater the ratio, the lower the risk. This ratio allows interested parties to assess the firm's ability to meet additional fixed-payment obligations without being driven into bankruptcy.

→ Review Questions

2–12 What is *financial leverage?*

2–13 What ratio measures the firm's *degree of indebtedness?* What ratios assess the firm's *ability to service debts?*

LG 5   2.6 Profitability Ratios

There are many measures of profitability. As a group, these measures enable analysts to evaluate the firm's profits with respect to a given level of sales, a certain level of assets, or the owners' investment. Without profits, a firm could not attract outside capital. Owners, creditors, and management pay close attention to boosting profits because of the great importance the market places on earnings.

Common-Size Income Statements

common-size income statement
An income statement in which each item is expressed as a percentage of sales.

A useful tool for evaluating profitability in relation to sales is the **common-size income statement.** Each item on this statement is expressed as a percentage of sales. Common-size income statements are especially useful in comparing performance across years because it is easy to see if certain categories of expenses are trending up or down as a percentage of the total volume of business that the company transacts. Three frequently cited ratios of profitability that come directly from the common-size income statement are (1) the gross profit margin, (2) the operating profit margin, and (3) the net profit margin.

Common-size income statements for 2012 and 2011 for Bartlett Company are presented and evaluated in Table 2.7 on page 63. These statements reveal that the firm's cost of goods sold increased from 66.7 percent of sales in 2011 to 67.9 percent in 2012, resulting in a worsening gross profit margin. However, thanks to a decrease in total operating expenses, the firm's net profit margin rose from 5.4 percent of sales in 2011 to 7.2 percent in 2012. The decrease in expenses more than compensated for the increase in the cost of goods sold. A decrease in the firm's 2012 interest expense (3.0 percent of sales versus 3.5 percent in 2011) added to the increase in 2012 profits.

Gross Profit Margin

gross profit margin
Measures the percentage of each sales dollar remaining after the firm has paid for its goods.

The **gross profit margin** measures the percentage of each sales dollar remaining after the firm has paid for its goods. The higher the gross profit margin, the better (that is, the lower the relative cost of merchandise sold). The gross profit margin is calculated as follows:

$$\text{Gross profit margin} = \frac{\text{Sales} - \text{Cost of goods sold}}{\text{Sales}} = \frac{\text{Gross profits}}{\text{Sales}}$$

	For the Years Ended December 31		Evaluation[a] 2011–2012
	2012	**2011**	
Sales revenue	100.0%	100.0%	Same
Less: Cost of goods sold	67.9	66.7	Worse
(1) Gross profit margin	32.1 %	33.3 %	Worse
Less: Operating expenses			
Selling expense	3.3%	4.2%	Better
General and administrative expenses	6.8	6.7	Worse
Lease expense	1.1	1.3	Better
Depreciation expense	7.3	9.3	Better
Total operating expense	18.5 %	21.5 %	Better
(2) Operating profit margin	13.6%	11.8%	Better
Less: Interest expense	3.0	3.5	Better
Net profits before taxes	10.6%	8.3%	Better
Less: Taxes	3.1	2.5	Worse[b]
Net profits after taxes	7.5%	5.8%	Better
Less: Preferred stock dividends	0.3	0.4	Better
(3) Net profit margin	7.2 %	5.4 %	Better

[a]Subjective assessments based on data provided.

[b]Taxes as a percentage of sales increased noticeably between 2011 and 2012 because of differing costs and expenses, whereas the average tax rates (taxes ÷ net profits before taxes) for 2011 and 2012 remained about the same—30% and 29%, respectively.

TABLE 2.7
Bartlett Company Common-Size Income Statements

Bartlett Company's gross profit margin for 2012 is

$$\frac{\$3,074,000 - \$2,088,000}{\$3,074,000} = \frac{\$986,000}{\$3,074,000} = 32.1\%$$

This value is labeled (1) on the common-size income statement in Table 2.7.

Operating Profit Margin

The **operating profit margin** measures the percentage of each sales dollar remaining after all costs and expenses *other than* interest, taxes, and preferred stock dividends are deducted. It represents the "pure profits" earned on each sales dollar. Operating profits are "pure" because they measure only the profits earned on operations and ignore interest, taxes, and preferred stock dividends. A high operating profit margin is preferred. The operating profit margin is calculated as follows:

$$\text{Operating profit margin} = \text{Operating profits} \div \text{Sales}$$

Bartlett Company's operating profit margin for 2012 is

$$\$418,000 \div \$3,074,000 = 13.6\%$$

$$\frac{\$418,000}{\$3,074,000} = 13.6\%$$

This value is labeled (2) on the common-size income statement in Table 2.7.

Net Profit Margin

The **net profit margin** measures the percentage of each sales dollar remaining after all costs and expenses, *including* interest, taxes, and preferred stock dividends, have been deducted. The higher the firm's net profit margin, the better. The net profit margin is calculated as follows:

$$\text{Net profit margin} = \text{Earnings available for common stockholders} \div \text{Sales}$$

operating profit margin
Measures the percentage of each sales dollar remaining after all costs and expenses *other than* interest, taxes, and preferred stock dividends are deducted; the "pure profits" earned on each sales dollar.

net profit margin
Measures the percentage of each sales dollar remaining after all costs and expenses, *including* interest, taxes, and preferred stock dividends, have been deducted.

Bartlett Company's net profit margin for 2012 is:

$$\$221,000 \div \$3,074,000 = 0.072 = 7.2\%$$

$$\frac{\$221,000}{\$3,074,000} = 7.2\%$$

This value is labeled (3) on the common-size income statement in Table 2.7.

The net profit margin is a commonly cited measure of the firm's success with respect to earnings on sales. "Good" net profit margins differ considerably across industries. A net profit margin of 1 percent or less would not be unusual for a grocery store, whereas a net profit margin of 10 percent would be low for a retail jewelry store.

Earnings Per Share (Eps)

The firm's *earnings per share (EPS)* is generally of interest to present or prospective stockholders and management. As we noted earlier, EPS represents the number of dollars earned during the period on behalf of each outstanding share of common stock. Earnings per share is calculated as follows:

$$\text{Earnings per share} = \frac{\text{Earnings available for common stockholders}}{\text{Number of shares of common stock outstanding}}$$

Bartlett Company's earnings per share in 2012 is

$$\$221,000 \div 76,262 = \$2.90$$

This figure represents the dollar amount earned *on behalf of* each outstanding share of common stock. The dollar amount of cash *actually distributed* to each shareholder is the *dividend per share (DPS),* which, as noted in Bartlett Company's income statement (Table 2.1), rose to $1.29 in 2012 from $0.75 in 2011. EPS is closely watched by the investing public and is considered an important indicator of corporate success.

Return on Total Assets (Roa)

return on total assets (ROA)
Measures the overall effectiveness of management in generating profits with its available assets; also called the *return on investment (ROI).*

The **return on total assets (ROA),** often called the *return on investment (ROI),* measures the overall effectiveness of management in generating profits with its available assets. The higher the firm's return on total assets the better. The return on total assets is calculated as follows:

$$\text{ROA} = \text{Earnings available for common stockholders} \div \text{Total assets}$$

Bartlett Company's return on total assets in 2012 is

$$\frac{\$221,000}{\$3,597,000} = 6.1\%$$

$$\$221,000 \div \$3,597,000 = 0.061 = 6.1\%$$

This value indicates that the company earned 6.1 cents on each dollar of asset investment.

Return on Common Equity (Roe)

return on common equity (ROE)
Measures the return earned on the common stockholders' investment in the firm.

The **return on common equity (ROE)** measures the return earned on the common stockholders' investment in the firm. Generally, the owners are better off the higher is this return. Return on common equity is calculated as follows:

$$\text{ROE} = \text{Earnings available for common stockholders} \div \text{Common stock equity}$$

This ratio for Bartlett Company in 2012 is

$$\$221,000 \div \$1,754,000 = 0.126 = 12.6\%$$

$$\frac{\$221,000}{\$1,754,000} = 12.6\%$$

Note that the value for common stock equity ($1,754,000) was found by subtracting the $200,000 of preferred stock equity from the total stockholders' equity of $1,954,000 (see Bartlett

Company's 2012 balance sheet in Table 2.2). The calculated ROE of 12.6 percent indicates that during 2012 Bartlett earned 12.6 cents on each dollar of common stock equity.

→ Review Questions

2–14 What three ratios of profitability are found on a *common-size income statement?*

2–15 What would explain a firm's having a high gross profit margin and a low net profit margin?

2–16 Which measure of profitability is probably of greatest interest to the investing public? Why?

2.7 Market Ratios

Market ratios relate the firm's market value, as measured by its current share price, to certain accounting values. These ratios give insight into how investors in the marketplace feel the firm is doing in terms of risk and return. They tend to reflect, on a relative basis, the common stockholders' assessment of all aspects of the firm's past and expected future performance. Here we consider two widely quoted market ratios, one that focuses on earnings and another that considers book value.

market ratios
Relate a firm's market value, as measured by its current share price, to certain accounting values.

Price/Earnings (P/E) Ratio

The **price/earnings (P/E) ratio** is commonly used to assess the owners' appraisal of share value. The P/E ratio measures the amount that investors are willing to pay for each dollar of a firm's earnings. The level of this ratio indicates the degree of confidence that investors have in the firm's future performance. The higher the P/E ratio, the greater the investor confidence. The P/E ratio is calculated as follows:

price/earnings (P/E) ratio
Measures the amount that investors are willing to pay for each dollar of a firm's earnings; the higher the P/E ratio, the greater the investor confidence.

$$\text{P/E ratio} = \text{Market price per share of common stock} \div \text{Earnings per share}$$

If Bartlett Company's common stock at the end of 2012 was selling at $32.25, using the EPS of $2.90, the P/E ratio at year-end 2012 is

$$\$32.25 \div \$2.90 = 11.1$$

This figure indicates that investors were paying $11.10 for each $1.00 of earnings. The P/E ratio is most informative when applied in cross-sectional analysis using an industry average P/E ratio or the P/E ratio of a benchmark firm.

Market/Book (M/B) Ratio

The **market/book (M/B) ratio** provides an assessment of how investors view the firm's performance. It relates the market value of the firm's shares to their book—strict accounting—value. To calculate the firm's M/B ratio, we first need to find the *book value per share of common stock:*

market/book (M/B) ratio
Provides an assessment of how investors view the firm's performance. Firms expected to earn high returns relative to their risk typically sell at higher M/B multiples.

$$\text{Book value per share of common stock} = \frac{\text{Common stock equity}}{\text{Number of shares of common stock outstanding}}$$

Substituting the appropriate values for Bartlett Company from its 2012 balance sheet, we get

$$\text{Book value per share of common stock} = \frac{\$1,754,000}{76,262} = \$23.00$$

The formula for the market/book ratio is

$$\text{Market/book (M/B) ratio} = \frac{\text{Market price per share of common stock}}{\text{Book value per share of common stock}}$$

Substituting Bartlett Company's end of 2012 common stock price of $32.25 and its $23.00 book value per share of common stock (calculated above) into the M/B ratio formula, we get

$$\$32.25 \div \$23.00 = 1.40$$

This M/B ratio means that investors are currently paying $1.40 for each $1.00 of book value of Bartlett Company's stock.

The stocks of firms that are expected to perform well—improve profits, increase their market share, or launch successful products—typically sell at higher M/B ratios than the stocks of firms with less attractive outlooks. Simply stated, firms expected to earn high returns relative to their risk typically sell at higher M/B multiples. Clearly, Bartlett's future prospects are being viewed favorably by investors, who are willing to pay more than their book value for the firm's shares. Like P/E ratios, M/B ratios are typically assessed cross-sectionally to get a feel for the firm's return and risk compared to peer firms.

→ Review Question

2–17   How do the *price/earnings (P/E) ratio* and the *market/book (M/B) ratio* provide a feel for the firm's return and risk?

LG 6 2.8 A Complete Ratio Analysis

Analysts frequently wish to take an overall look at the firm's financial performance and status. Here we consider two popular approaches to a complete ratio analysis: (1) summarizing all ratios and (2) the DuPont system of analysis. The summary analysis approach tends to view *all aspects* of the firm's financial activities to isolate key areas of responsibility. The DuPont system acts as a search technique aimed at finding the *key areas* responsible for the firm's financial condition.

Summarizing all Ratios

We can use Bartlett Company's ratios to perform a complete ratio analysis using both cross-sectional and time-series analysis approaches. The 2012 ratio values calculated earlier and the ratio values calculated for 2010 and 2011 for Bartlett Company, along with the industry average ratios for 2012, are summarized in Table 2.8 (see pages 68 and 69), which also shows the formula used to calculate each ratio. Using these data, we can discuss the five key aspects of Bartlett's performance—liquidity, activity, debt, profitability, and market.

LIQUIDITY   The overall liquidity of the firm seems to exhibit a reasonably stable trend, having been maintained at a level that is relatively consistent with the industry average in 2012. The firm's liquidity seems to be good.

ACTIVITY   Bartlett Company's inventory appears to be in good shape. Its inventory management seems to have improved, and in 2012 it performed at a level above that of the industry. The firm may be experiencing some problems with accounts receivable. The average collection period seems to have crept up above that of the industry. Bartlett also appears to be slow in paying its bills; it pays nearly 30 days slower than the industry average. This could adversely affect the firm's credit standing. Although overall liquidity appears to be good, the management of receivables and payables should be examined. Bartlett's total asset turnover reflects a decline in the efficiency of total asset utilization between 2010 and 2011. Although in 2012 it rose to a level considerably above the industry average, it appears that the pre-2011 level of efficiency has not yet been achieved.

Debt

Bartlett Company's indebtedness increased over the 2010–2012 period and is currently above the industry average. Although this increase in the debt ratio could be cause for alarm, the firm's ability to meet interest and fixed-payment obligations improved, from 2011 to 2012, to a level that outperforms the industry. The firm's increased indebtedness in 2011 apparently caused deterioration in its ability to pay debt adequately. However, Bartlett has evidently improved its income in 2012 so that it is able to meet its interest and fixed-payment obligations at a level consistent with the average in the industry. In summary, it appears that although 2011 was an off year, the company's improved ability to pay debts in 2012 compensates for its increased degree of indebtedness.

PROFITABILITY   Bartlett's profitability relative to sales in 2012 was better than the average company in the industry, although it did not match the firm's 2010 performance. Although the *gross* profit margin was better in 2011 and 2012 than in 2010, higher levels of operating and interest expenses in 2011 and 2012 appear to have caused the 2012 *net* profit margin to fall below that of 2010. However, Bartlett Company's 2012 net profit margin is quite favorable when compared to the industry average.

The firm's earnings per share, return on total assets, and return on common equity behaved much as its net profit margin did over the 2010–2012 period. Bartlett appears to have experienced either a sizable drop in sales between 2010 and 2011 or a rapid expansion in assets during that period. The exceptionally high 2012 level of return on common equity suggests that the firm is performing quite well. The firm's above-average returns—net profit margin, EPS, ROA, and ROE—may be attributable to the fact that it is more risky than average. A look at market ratios is helpful in assessing risk.

MARKET   Investors have greater confidence in the firm in 2012 than in the prior 2 years, as reflected in the price/earnings (P/E) ratio of 11.1. However, this ratio is below the industry average. The P/E ratio suggests that the firm's risk has declined but remains above that of the average firm in its industry. The firm's market/book (M/B) ratio has increased over the 2010–2012 period, and in 2012 it exceeds the industry average. This implies that investors are optimistic about the firm's future performance. The P/E and M/B ratios reflect the firm's increased profitability over the 2010–2012 period: Investors expect to earn high future returns as compensation for the firm's above-average risk.

In summary, the firm appears to be growing and has recently undergone an expansion in assets, financed primarily through the use of debt. The 2011–2012 period seems to reflect a phase of adjustment and recovery from the rapid growth in assets. Bartlett's sales, profits, and other performance factors seem to be growing with the increase in the size of the operation. In addition, the market response to these accomplishments appears to have been positive. In short, the firm seems to have done well in 2012.

Dupont System of Analysis

The **DuPont system of analysis** is used to dissect the firm's financial statements and to assess its financial condition. It merges the income statement and balance sheet into two summary measures of profitability, return on total assets (ROA) and return on common equity (ROE). Figure 2.2 (see page 70) depicts the basic DuPont system with Bartlett Company's 2012 monetary and ratio values. The upper portion of the chart summarizes the income statement activities; the lower portion summarizes the balance sheet activities.

DuPont system of analysis
System used to dissect the firm's financial statements and to assess its financial condition.

DUPONT FORMULA   The DuPont system first brings together the *net profit margin,* which measures the firm's profitability on sales, with its *total asset turnover,* which indicates how efficiently the firm has used its assets to generate sales. In the **DuPont formula,** the product of these two ratios results in the *return on total assets (ROA):*

$$\text{ROA} = \text{Net profit margin} \times \text{Total asset turnover}$$

Substituting the appropriate formulas into the equation and simplifying results in the formula given earlier,

$$\text{ROA} = \frac{\text{Earnings available for common stockholders}}{\text{Sales}} \times \frac{\text{Sales}}{\text{Total assets}} = \frac{\text{Earnings available for common stockholders}}{\text{Total assets}}$$

DuPont formula
Multiplies the firm's *net profit margin by its total asset turnover* to calculate the firm's *return on total assets (ROA).*

When the 2012 values of the net profit margin and total asset turnover for Bartlett Company, calculated earlier, are substituted into the DuPont formula, the result is

$$\text{ROA} = 7.2\% \times 0.85 = 6.1\%$$

This value is the same as that calculated directly in an earlier section (page 64). The DuPont formula enables the firm to break down its return into profit-on-sales and efficiency-of-asset-use components. Typically, a firm with a low net profit margin has a high total asset turnover, which results in a reasonably good return on total assets. Often, the opposite situation exists.

Ratio	Formula	Year 2010[a]	Year 2011[b]	Year 2012[b]	Industry Average 2012[c]	Cross-Sectional 2012	Evaluation[d] Time-Series 2010–2012	Overall
Liquidity								
Current ratio	$\dfrac{\text{Current assets}}{\text{Current liabilities}}$	2.04	2.08	1.97	2.05	OK	OK	OK
Quick (acid-test) ratio	$\dfrac{\text{Current assets} - \text{Inventory}}{\text{Current liabilities}}$	1.32	1.46	1.51	1.43	OK	Good	Good
Activity								
Inventory turnover	$\dfrac{\text{Cost of goods sold}}{\text{Inventory}}$	5.1	5.7	7.2	6.6	Good	Good	Good
Average collection period	$\dfrac{\text{Accounts receivable}}{\text{Average sales per day}}$	43.9 days	51.2 days	59.7 days	44.3 days	Poor	Poor	Poor
Average payment period	$\dfrac{\text{Accounts payable}}{\text{Average purchases per day}}$	75.8 days	81.2 days	95.4 days	66.5 days	Poor	Poor	Poor
Total assets turnover	$\dfrac{\text{Sales}}{\text{Total assets}}$	0.94	0.79	0.85	0.75	OK	OK	OK
Debt								
Debt ratio	$\dfrac{\text{Total liabilities}}{\text{Total assets}}$	36.8%	44.3%	45.7%	40.0%	OK	OK	OK
Times interest earned ratio	$\dfrac{\text{Earnings before interest and taxes}}{\text{Interest}}$	5.6	3.3	4.5	4.3	Good	OK	OK
Fixed-payment coverage ratio	$\dfrac{\text{Earnings before interest and taxes} + \text{Lease payments}}{\text{Int.} + \text{Lease pay.} + \{(\text{Prin.} + \text{Pref. div.}) \times [1/(1 - T)]\}}$	2.4	1.4	1.9	1.5	Good	OK	Good
Profitability								
Gross profit margin	$\dfrac{\text{Gross profits}}{\text{Sales}}$	31.4%	33.3%	32.1%	30.0%	OK	OK	OK
Operating profit margin	$\dfrac{\text{Operating profits}}{\text{Sales}}$	14.6%	11.8%	13.6%	11.0%	Good	OK	Good
Net profit margin	$\dfrac{\text{Earnings available for common stockholders}}{\text{Sales}}$	8.2%	5.4%	7.2%	6.2%	Good	OK	Good

Ratio	Formula	Year 2010[a]	Year 2011[b]	Year 2012[b]	Industry Average 2012[c]	Evaluation[d] Cross-Sectional 2012	Evaluation[d] Time-Series 2010–2012	Evaluation[d] Overall
Profitability (cont.)								
Earnings per share (EPS)	$\dfrac{\text{Earnings available for common stockholders}}{\text{Number of shares of common stock outstanding}}$	$3.26	$1.81	$2.90	$2.26	Good	OK	Good
Return on total assets (ROA)	$\dfrac{\text{Earnings available for common stockholders}}{\text{Total assets}}$	7.8%	4.2%	6.1%	4.6%	Good	OK	Good
Return on common equity (ROE)	$\dfrac{\text{Earnings available for common stockholders}}{\text{Common stock equity}}$	13.7%	8.5%	12.6%	8.5%	Good	OK	Good
Market								
Price/earnings (P/E) ratio	$\dfrac{\text{Market price per share of common stock}}{\text{Earnings per share}}$	10.5	10.0[e]	11.1	12.5	OK	OK	OK
Market/book (M/B) ratio	$\dfrac{\text{Market price per share of common stock}}{\text{Book value per share of common stock}}$	1.25	0.85[e]	1.40	1.30	OK	OK	OK

[a]Calculated from data not included in this chapter.

[b]Calculated by using the financial statements presented in Tables 2.1 and 2.2.

[c]Obtained from sources not included in this chapter.

[d]Subjective assessments based on data provided.

[e]The market price per share at the end of 2011 was $18.06.

TABLE 2.8
Summary of Bartlett Company Ratios (2010–2012, Including 2012 Industry Averages)

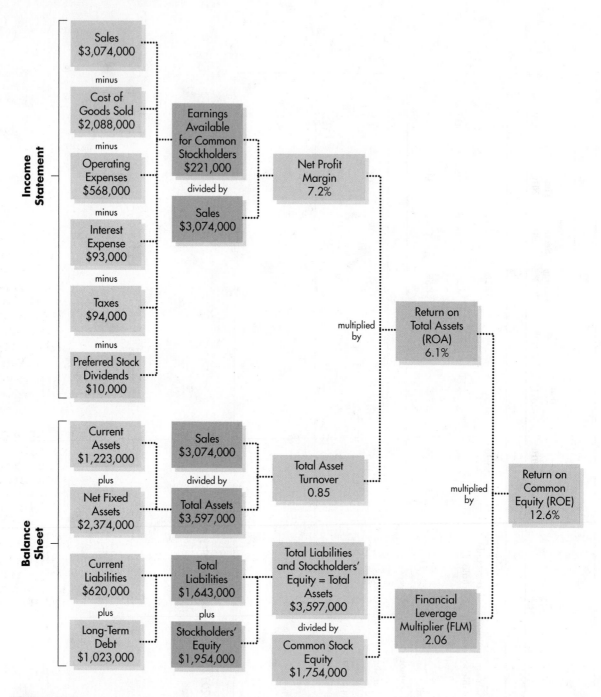

Figure 2.2
DuPont System of Analysis
The DuPont system of analysis with application to Bartlett Company (2012

MODIFIED DUPONT FORMULA The second step in the DuPont system employs the **modified DuPont formula.** This formula relates the firm's *return on total assets (ROA)* to its *return on common equity (ROE)*. The latter is calculated by multiplying the return on total assets (ROA) by the **financial leverage multiplier (FLM),** which is the ratio of total assets to common stock equity:

$$ROE = ROA \times FLM$$

Substituting the appropriate formulas into the equation and simplifying results in the formula given earlier,

$$\text{ROE} = \frac{\text{Earnings available for common stockholders}}{\text{Total assets}} \times \frac{\text{Total assets}}{\text{Common stock equity}} = \frac{\text{Earnings available for common stockholders}}{\text{Common stock equity}}$$

Use of the financial leverage multiplier (FLM) to convert the ROA into the ROE reflects the impact of financial leverage on owners' return. Substituting the values for Bartlett Company's ROA of 6.1 percent, calculated earlier, and Bartlett's FLM of 2.06 ($3,597,000 total assets ÷ $1,754,000 common stock equity) into the modified DuPont formula yields

$$\text{ROE} = 6.1\% \times 2.06 = 12.6\%$$

The 12.6 percent ROE calculated by using the modified DuPont formula is the same as that calculated directly (page 64).

APPLYING THE DUPONT SYSTEM   The advantage of the DuPont system is that it allows the firm to break its return on equity into a profit-on-sales component (net profit margin), an efficiency-of-asset-use component (total asset turnover), and a use-of-financial-leverage component (financial leverage multiplier). The total return to owners therefore can be analyzed in these important dimensions.

The use of the DuPont system of analysis as a diagnostic tool is best explained using Figure 2.2. Beginning with the rightmost value—the ROE—the financial analyst moves to the left, dissecting and analyzing the inputs to the formula to isolate the probable cause of the resulting above-average (or below-average) value.

Example 2.6

For the sake of demonstration, let's ignore all industry average data in Table 2.8 and assume that Bartlett's ROE of 12.6% is actually below the industry average. Moving to the left in Figure 2.2, we would examine the inputs to the ROE—the ROA and the FLM—relative to the industry averages. Let's assume that the FLM is in line with the industry average, but the ROA is below the industry average. Moving farther to the left, we examine the two inputs to the ROA—the net profit margin and total asset turnover. Assume that the net profit margin is in line with the industry average, but the total asset turnover is below the industry average. Moving still farther to the left, we find that whereas the firm's sales are consistent with the industry value, Bartlett's total assets have grown significantly during the past year. Looking farther to the left, we would review the firm's activity ratios for current assets. Let's say that whereas the firm's inventory turnover is in line with the industry average, its average collection period is well above the industry average.

We can readily trace the possible problem back to its cause: Bartlett's low ROE is primarily the consequence of slow collections of accounts receivable, which resulted in high levels of receivables and therefore high levels of total assets. The high total assets slowed Bartlett's total asset turnover, driving down its ROA, which then drove down its ROE. By using the DuPont system of analysis to dissect Bartlett's overall returns as measured by its ROE, we found that slow collections of receivables caused the below-industry-average ROE. Clearly, the firm needs to better manage its credit operations.

→ **Review Questions**

2–18   Financial ratio analysis is often divided into five areas: *liquidity, activity, debt, profitability,* and *market* ratios. Differentiate each of these areas of analysis from the others. Which is of the greatest concern to creditors?

2–19   Describe how you would use a large number of ratios to perform a complete ratio analysis of the firm.

2–20   What three areas of analysis are combined in the *modified DuPont formula?* Explain how the *DuPont system of analysis* is used to dissect the firm's results and isolate their causes.

Matter of fact

Dissecting ROA

Return to Table 2.5, and examine the total asset turnover figures for Dell and The Home Depot. Both firms turn their assets 1.6 times per year. Now look at the return on assets column. Dell's ROA is 4.3 percent, but The Home Depot's is significantly higher at 6.5 percent. If the two firms are equal in terms of the efficiency with which they manage their assets (that is, equal asset turns), why is The Home Depot more profitable relative to assets? The answer lies in the DuPont formula. Notice that Home Depot's net profit margin is 4.0 percent compared to Dell's 2.7 percent. That drives the superior ROA figures for The Home Depot.

modified DuPont formula
Relates the firm's return on total assets (ROA) to its return on common equity (ROE) using the financial leverage multiplier (FLM).

financial leverage multiplier (FLM)
The ratio of the firm's total assets to its common stock equity.

Summary

FOCUS ON VALUE

Financial managers review and analyze the firm's financial statements periodically, both to uncover developing problems and to assess the firm's progress toward achieving its goals. These actions are aimed at **preserving and creating value for the firm's owners**. Financial ratios enable financial managers to monitor the pulse of the firm and its progress toward its strategic goals. Although financial statements and financial ratios rely on accrual concepts, they can provide useful insights into important aspects of risk and return (cash flow) that affect share price.

REVIEW OF LEARNING GOALS

LG 1   **Review the contents of the stockholders' report and the procedures for consolidating international financial statements.** The annual stockholders' report, which publicly owned corporations must provide to stockholders, documents the firm's financial activities of the past year. It includes the letter to stockholders and various subjective and factual information. It also contains four key financial statements: the income statement, the balance sheet, the statement of stockholders' equity (or its abbreviated form, the statement of retained earnings), and the statement of cash flows. Notes describing the technical aspects of the financial statements follow. Financial statements of companies that have operations whose cash flows are denominated in one or more foreign currencies must be translated into dollars in accordance with *FASB Standard No. 52*.

LG 2   **Understand who uses financial ratios and how.** Ratio analysis enables stockholders, lenders, and the firm's managers to evaluate the firm's financial performance. It can be performed on a cross-sectional or a time-series basis. Benchmarking is a popular type of cross-sectional analysis. Users of ratios should understand the cautions that apply to their use.

LG 3   **Use ratios to analyze a firm's liquidity and activity.** Liquidity, or the ability of the firm to pay its bills as they come due, can be measured by the current ratio and the quick (acid-test) ratio. Activity ratios measure the speed with which accounts are converted into sales or cash—inflows or outflows. The activity of inventory can be measured by its turnover: that of accounts receivable by the average collection period and that of accounts payable by the average payment period. Total asset turnover measures the efficiency with which the firm uses its assets to generate sales.

LG 4   **Discuss the relationship between debt and financial leverage and the ratios used to analyze a firm's debt.** The more debt a firm uses, the greater its financial leverage, which magnifies both risk and return. Financial debt ratios measure both the degree of indebtedness and the ability to service debts. A common measure of indebtedness is the debt ratio. The ability to pay fixed charges can be measured by times interest earned and fixed-payment coverage ratios.

LG 5   **Use ratios to analyze a firm's profitability and its market value.** The common-size income statement, which shows each item as a percentage of sales, can be used to determine gross profit margin, operating profit margin, and net profit margin. Other measures of profitability include earnings per share, return on total assets, and return on common equity. Market ratios include the price/earnings ratio and the market/book ratio.

LG 6   **Use a summary of financial ratios and the DuPont system of analysis to perform a complete ratio analysis.** A summary of all ratios can be used to perform a complete ratio analysis using cross-sectional and time-series analysis. The DuPont system of analysis is a diagnostic tool used to find the key areas responsible for the firm's financial performance. It enables the firm to break the return on common equity into three components: profit on sales, efficiency of asset use, and use of financial leverage.

Opener-in-Review

In the chapter opener you read about how financial analysts gave Abercrombie's stock a relatively positive outlook based on a current ratio of 2.79, a quick ratio of 1.79, and a receivables collection period of 43 days. Based on what you learned in this chapter, do you agree with the analysts' assessment? Explain why or why not.

Self-Test Problems   (Solutions in Appendix)

LG 2   LG 4   LG 5   ST2–1   Ratio formulas and interpretations   Without referring to the text, indicate for each of the following ratios the formula for calculating it and the kinds of problems, if any, the firm may have if that ratio is too high relative to the industry average. What if the ratio is too low relative to the industry average? Create a table similar to the one that follows and fill in the empty blocks.

Ratio	Too High	Too Low
Current ratio =		
Inventory turnover =		
Times interest earned =		
Gross profit margin =		
Return on total assets =		
Price/earnings (P/E) ratio =		

LG 3   LG 4   LG 5   ST2–2   Balance sheet completion using ratios   Complete the 2012 balance sheet for O'Keefe Industries using the information that follows it.

O'Keefe Industries Balance Sheet December 31, 2012

Assets		Liabilities and Stockholders' Equity	
Cash	$ 32,720	Accounts payable	$ 120,000
Marketable securities	25,000	Notes payable	_____
Accounts receivable	_____	Accruals	20,000
Inventories	_____	Total current liabilities	_____
Total current assets	_____	Long-term debt	_____
Net fixed assets	_____	Stockholders' equity	$ 600,000
Total assets $	_____	Total liabilities and stockholders' equity	$ _____

The following financial data for 2012 are also available:

1. Sales totaled $1,800,000.
2. The gross profit margin was 25%.
3. Inventory turnover was 6.0.
4. There are 365 days in the year.
5. The average collection period was 40 days.
6. The current ratio was 1.60.
7. The total asset turnover ratio was 1.20.
8. The debt ratio was 60%.

Warm-Up Exercises

All problems are available in *MyAccountingLab*

LG 1 **E2–1** You are a summer intern at the office of a local tax preparer. To test your basic knowledge of financial statements, your manager, who graduated from your alma mater 2 years ago, gives you the following list of accounts and asks you to prepare a simple income statement using those accounts.

Accounts	($000,000)
Depreciation	25
General and administrative expenses	22
Sales	345
Sales expenses	18
Cost of goods sold	255
Lease expense	4
Interest expense	3

   a. Arrange the accounts into a well-labeled income statement. Make sure you label and solve for gross profit, operating profit, and net profit before taxes.
   b. Using a 35% tax rate, calculate taxes paid and net profit after taxes.
   c. Assuming a dividend of $1.10 per share with 4.25 million shares outstanding, calculate EPS and additions to retained earnings.

LG 1 **E2–2** Explain why the income statement can also be called a "profit-and-loss statement." What exactly does the word *balance* mean in the title of the balance sheet? Why do we balance the two halves?

LG 1 **E2–3** Cooper Industries, Inc., began 2012 with retained earnings of $25.32 million. During the year it paid four quarterly dividends of $0.35 per share to 2.75 million common stockholders. Preferred stockholders, holding 500,000 shares, were paid two semiannual dividends of $0.75 per share. The firm had a net profit after taxes of $5.15 million. Prepare the statement of retained earnings for the year ended December 31, 2012.

LG 3 **E2–4** Bluestone Metals, Inc., is a metal fabrication firm that manufactures prefabricated metal parts for customers in a variety of industries. The firm's motto is "If you need it, we can make it." The CEO of Bluestone recently held a board meeting during which he extolled the virtues of the corporation. The company, he stated confidently, had the capability to build any product and could do so using a lean manufacturing model. The firm would soon be profitable, claimed the CEO, because the company used state-of-the-art technology to build a variety of products while keeping inventory levels low. As a business press reporter, you have calculated some ratios to analyze the financial health of the firm. Bluestone's current ratios and quick ratios for the past 6 years are shown in the table below:

	2007	2008	2009	2010	2011	2012
Current ratio	1.2	1.4	1.3	1.6	1.8	2.2
Quick ratio	1.1	1.3	1.2	0.8	0.6	0.4

   What do you think of the CEO's claim that the firm is lean and soon to be profitable? (*Hint*: Is there a possible warning sign in the relationship between the two ratios?)

LG 5 **E2–5** If we know that a firm has a net profit margin of 4.5%, total asset turnover of 0.72, and a financial leverage multiplier of 1.43, what is its ROE? What is the advantage to using the DuPont system to calculate ROE over the direct calculation of earnings available for common stockholders divided by common stock equity?

Problems   All problems are available in *MyAccountingLab*

LG 1   **P2-1**   **Reviewing basic financial statements**   The income statement for the year ended December 31, 2012, the balance sheets for December 31, 2012 and 2011, and the statement of retained earnings for the year ended December 31, 2012, for Technica, Inc., are given below and on the following page. Briefly discuss the form and informational content of each of these statements.

Technica, Inc. Income Statement for the Year Ended December 31, 2012

Sales revenue	$600,000
Less: Cost of goods sold	460,000
Gross profits	$140,000
Less: Operating expenses	
General and administrative expenses	$ 30,000
Depreciation expense	30,000
Total operating expense	$ 60,000
Operating profits	$ 80,000
Less: Interest expense	10,000
Net profits before taxes	$ 70,000
Less: Taxes	27,100
Earnings available for common stockholders	$ 42,900
Earnings per share (EPS)	$2.15

Technica, Inc. Balance Sheets

	December 31	
Assets	**2012**	**2011**
Cash	$15,000	$16,000
Marketable securities	7,200	8,000
Accounts receivable	34,100	42,200
Inventories	82,000	50,000
Total current assets	$138,300	$116,200
Land and buildings	$150,000	$150,000
Machinery and equipment	200,000	190,000
Furniture and fixtures	54,000	50,000
Other	11,000	10,000
Total gross fixed assets	$415,000	$400,000
Less: Accumulated depreciation	145,000	115,000
Net fixed assets	$270,000	$285,000
Total assets	$408,000	$401,200
Liabilities and Stockholders' Equity		
Accounts payable	$ 57,000	$ 49,000
Notes payable	13,000	16,000
Accruals	5,000	6,000
Total current liabilities	$ 75,000	$71,000
Long-term debt	$150,000	$160,000
Common stock equity (shares outstanding: 19,500 in 2012 and 20,000 in 2011)	$110,200	$120,000
Retained earnings	73,100	50,200
Total stockholders' equity	$183,300	$170,200
Total liabilities and stockholders' equity	$408,300	$401,200

**Technica, Inc. Statement of Retained Earnings
for the Year Ended December 31, 2012**

Retained earnings balance (January 1, 2012)	$50,200
Plus: Net profits after taxes (for 2012)	42,900
Less: Cash dividends (paid during 2012)	20,000
Retained earnings balance (December 31, 2012)	$73,100

LG 1 **P2-2** **Financial statement account identification** Mark each of the accounts listed in the following table as follows:

a. In column (1), indicate in which statement—income statement (IS) or balance sheet (BS)—the account belongs.

b. In column (2), indicate whether the account is a current asset (CA), current liability (CL), expense (E), fixed asset (FA), long-term debt (LTD), revenue (R), or stockholders' equity (SE).

	(1)	(2)
Account name	**Statement**	**Type of account**
Accounts payable	_____	_____
Accounts receivable	_____	_____
Accruals	_____	_____
Accumulated depreciation	_____	_____
Administrative expense	_____	_____
Buildings	_____	_____
Cash	_____	_____
Common stock (at par)	_____	_____
Cost of goods sold	_____	_____
Depreciation	_____	_____
Equipment	_____	_____
General expense	_____	_____
Interest expense	_____	_____
Inventories	_____	_____
Land	_____	_____
Long-term debts	_____	_____
Machinery	_____	_____
Marketable securities	_____	_____
Notes payable	_____	_____
Operating expense	_____	_____
Paid-in capital in excess of par	_____	_____
Preferred stock	_____	_____
Preferred stock dividends	_____	_____
Retained earnings	_____	_____
Sales revenue	_____	_____
Selling expense	_____	_____
Taxes	_____	_____
Vehicles	_____	_____

LG 1 **P2-3** **Income statement preparation** On December 31, 2012, Cathy Chen, a self-employed certified public accountant (CPA), completed her first full year in business. During the year, she billed $360,000 for her accounting services. She had two employees, a bookkeeper and a clerical assistant. In addition to her *monthly* salary of $8,000, Ms. Chen paid *annual* salaries of $48,000 and $36,000 to the bookkeeper and the clerical assistant, respectively. Employment taxes and benefit costs for Ms. Chen and her employees totaled $34,600 for the year. Expenses for office supplies, including postage, totaled $10,400 for the year. In addition, Ms.

Chen spent $17,000 during the year on tax-deductible travel and entertainment associated with client visits and new business development. Lease payments for the office space rented (a tax-deductible expense) were $2,700 *per month*. Depreciation expense on the office furniture and fixtures was $15,600 for the year. During the year, Ms. Chen paid interest of $15,000 on the $120,000 borrowed to start the business. She paid an average tax rate of 30% during 2012.

a. Prepare an income statement for Cathy Chen, CPA, for the year ended December 31, 2012.

b. Evaluate her 2012 financial performance.

Personal Finance Problem

LG 1   P2–4   Income statement preparation   Adam and Arin Adams have collected their personal income and expense information and have asked you to put together an income and expense statement for the year ended December 31, 2012. The following information is received from the Adams family.

Adam's salary	$45,000	Utilities	$ 3,200
Arin's salary	30,000	Groceries	2,200
Interest received	500	Medical	1,500
Dividends received	150	Property taxes	1,659
Auto insurance	600	Income tax, Social Security	13,000
Home insurance	750	Clothes and accessories	2,000
Auto loan payment	3,300	Gas and auto repair	2,100
Mortgage payment	14,000	Entertainment	2,000

a. Create a personal *income and expense statement* for the period ended December 31, 2012. It should be similar to a corporate income statement.

b. Did the Adams family have a cash surplus or cash deficit?

c. If the result is a surplus, how can the Adams family use that surplus?

LG 1   P2–5   Calculation of EPS and retained earnings   Philagem, Inc., ended 2012 with a net profit *before* taxes of $218,000. The company is subject to a 40% tax rate and must pay $32,000 in preferred stock dividends before distributing any earnings on the 85,000 shares of common stock currently outstanding.

a. Calculate Philagem's 2012 earnings per share (EPS).

b. If the firm paid common stock dividends of $0.80 per share, how many dollars would go to retained earnings?

LG 1   P2–6   Balance sheet preparation   Use the *appropriate items* from the following list to prepare in good form Owen Davis Company's balance sheet at December 31, 2012

Item	Value ($000) at December 31, 2012	Item	Value ($000) at December 31, 2012
Accounts payable	$ 220	Inventories	$ 375
Accounts receivable	450	Land	100
Accruals	55	Long-term debts	420
Accumulated depreciation	265	Machinery	420
Buildings	225	Marketable securities	75
Cash	215	Notes payable	475
Common stock (at par)	90	Paid-in capital in excess	
Cost of goods sold	2,500	of par	360
Depreciation expense	45	Preferred stock	100
Equipment	140	Retained earnings	210
Furniture and fixtures	170	Sales revenue	3,600
General expense	320	Vehicles	25

Personal Finance Problem

LG 1 **P2-7** **Balance sheet preparation** Adam and Arin Adams have collected their personal asset and liability information and have asked you to put together a balance sheet as of December 31, 2012. The following information is received from the Adams family.

Cash	$ 300	Retirement funds, IRA	$ 2,000
Checking	3,000	2011 Sebring	15,000
Savings	1,200	2010 Jeep	8,000
IBM stock	2,000	Money market funds	1,200
Auto loan	8,000	Jewelry and artwork	3,000
Mortgage	100,000	Net worth	76,500
Medical bills payable	250	Household furnishings	4,200
Utility bills payable	150	Credit card balance	2,000
Real estate	150,000	Personal loan	3,000

a. Create a personal balance sheet as of December 31, 2012. It should be similar to a corporate balance sheet.
b. What must the total assets of the Adams family be equal to by December 31, 2012?
c. What was their net working capital (NWC) for the year? (Hint: NWC is the difference between total liquid assets and total current liabilities.)

LG 1 **P2-8** Impact of net income on a firm's balance sheet Conrad Air, Inc., reported net income of $1,365,000 for the year ended December 31, 2013. Show how Conrad's balance sheet would change from 2012 to 2013 depending on how Conrad "spent" those earnings as described in the scenarios that appear below.

Conrad Air, Inc. Balance Sheet as of December 31, 2012

Assets		Liabilities and Stockholders' Equity	
Cash	$120,000	Accounts payable	$ 70,000
Marketable securities	35,000	Short-term notes	55,000
Accounts receivable	45,000	Current liabilities	$ 125,000
Inventories	130,000	Long-term debt	2,700,000
Current assets	$ 330,000	Total liabilities	$2,825,000
Equipment	$2,970,000	Common stock	$ 500,000
Buildings	1,600,000	Retained earnings	1,575,000
Fixed assets	$4,570,000	Stockholders' equity	$2,075,000
Total assets	$4,900,000	Total liabilities and equity	$4,900,000

a. Conrad paid no dividends during the year and invested the funds in marketable securities.
b. Conrad paid dividends totaling $500,000 and used the balance of the net income to retire (pay off) long-term debt.
c. Conrad paid dividends totaling $500,000 and invested the balance of the net income in building a new hangar.
d. Conrad paid out all $1,365,000 as dividends to its stockholders.

LG 1 **P2-9** **Initial sale price of common stock** Beck Corporation has one issue of preferred stock and one issue of common stock outstanding. Given Beck's stockholders' equity account that follows, determine the original price per share at which the firm sold its single issue of common stock.

	Stockholders' Equity ($000)
Preferred stock	$ 125
Common stock ($0.75 par, 300,000 shares outstanding)	225
Paid-in capital in excess of par on common stock	2,625
Retained earnings	900
Total stockholders' equity	$3,875

LG 1 **P2–10 Statement of retained earnings**   Hayes Enterprises began 2012 with a retained earnings balance of $928,000. During 2012, the firm earned $377,000 after taxes. From this amount, preferred stockholders were paid $47,000 in dividends. At year-end 2012, the firm's retained earnings totaled $1,048,000. The firm had 140,000 shares of common stock outstanding during 2012.

   a. Prepare a statement of retained earnings for the year ended December 31, 2012, for Hayes Enterprises. (Note: Be sure to calculate and include the amount of cash dividends paid in 2012.)

   b. Calculate the firm's 2012 earnings per share (EPS).

   c. How large a per-share cash dividend did the firm pay on common stock during 2012?

LG 1 **P2–11 Changes in stockholders' equity**   Listed are the equity sections of balance sheets for years 2011 and 2012 as reported by Mountain Air Ski Resorts, Inc. The overall value of stockholders' equity has risen from $2,000,000 to $7,500,000. Use the statements to discover how and why this happened.

Mountain Air Ski Resorts, Inc.
Balance Sheets (partial)

Stockholders' equity	2011	2012
Common stock ($1.00 par)		
Authorized—5,000,000 shares		
Outstanding—1,500,000 shares 2012		$1,500,000
— 500,000 shares 2011	$ 500,000	
Paid-in capital in excess of par	500,000	4,500,000
Retained earnings	1,000,000	1,500,000
Total stockholders' equity	$2,000,000	$7,500,000

The company paid total dividends of $200,000 during fiscal 2012.

   a. What was Mountain Air's net income for fiscal 2012?

   b. How many new shares did the corporation issue and sell during the year?

   c. At what average price per share did the new stock sold during 2012 sell?

   d. At what price per share did Mountain Air's original 500,000 shares sell?

LG 2 **LG 3**
LG 4 **LG 5**

P2–12 Ratio comparisons   Robert Arias recently inherited a stock portfolio from his uncle. Wishing to learn more about the companies in which he is now invested, Robert performs a ratio analysis on each

Ratio	Island Electric Utility	Burger Heaven	Fink Software	Roland Motors
Current ratio	1.10	1.3	6.8	4.5
Quick ratio	0.90	0.82	5.2	3.7
Debt ratio	0.68	0.46	0.0	0.35
Net profit margin	6.2%	14.3%	28.5%	8.4%

Assuming that his uncle was a wise investor who assembled the portfolio with care, Robert finds the wide differences in these ratios confusing. Help him out.

a. What problems might Robert encounter in comparing these companies to one another on the basis of their ratios?

b. Why might the current and quick ratios for the electric utility and the fast-food stock be so much lower than the same ratios for the other companies?

c. Why might it be all right for the electric utility to carry a large amount of debt, but not the software company?

d. Why wouldn't investors invest all of their money in software companies instead of in less profitable companies? (Focus on risk and return.)

LG 3 **P2–13** **Liquidity management** Bauman Company's total current assets, total current liabilities, and inventory for each of the past 4 years follow:

Item	2009	2010	2011	2012
Total current assets	$16,950	$21,900	$22,500	$27,000
Total current liabilities	9,000	12,600	12,600	17,400
Inventory	6,000	6,900	6,900	7,200

a. Calculate the firm's current and quick ratios for each year. Compare the resulting time series for these measures of liquidity.

b. Comment on the firm's liquidity over the 2009–2010 period.

c. If you were told that Bauman Company's inventory turnover for each year in the 2009–2012 period and the industry averages were as follows, would this information support or conflict with your evaluation in part b? Why?

Inventory turnover	2009	2010	2011	2012
Bauman Company	6.3	6.8	7.0	6.4
Industry average	10.6	11.2	10.8	11.0

Personal Finance Problem

LG 3 **P2–14** **Liquidity ratio** Josh Smith has compiled some of his personal financial data in order to determine his liquidity position. The data are as follows.

Account	Amount
Cash	$3,200
Marketable securities	1,000
Checking account	800
Credit card payables	1,200
Short-term notes payable	900

a. Calculate Josh's *liquidity ratio.*

b. Several of Josh's friends have told him that they have liquidity ratios of about 1.8. How would you analyze Josh's liquidity relative to his friends?

LG 3 **P2–15** **Inventory management** Wilkins Manufacturing has annual sales of $4 million and a gross profit margin of 40%. Its *end-of-quarter inventories* are

Quarter	Inventory
1	$ 400,000
2	800,000
3	1,200,000
4	200,000

a. Find the average quarterly inventory and use it to calculate the firm's inventory turnover and the average age of inventory.

b. Assuming that the company is in an industry with an average inventory turnover of 2.0, how would you evaluate the activity of Wilkins' inventory?

LG 3 **P2–16 Accounts receivable management** An evaluation of the books of Blair Supply, which follows, gives the end-of-year accounts receivable balance, which is believed to consist of amounts originating in the months indicated. The company had annual sales of $2.4 million. The firm extends 30-day credit terms.

Month of origin	Amounts receivable
July	$ 3,875
August	2,000
September	34,025
October	15,100
November	52,000
December	193,000
Year-end accounts receivable	$300,000

a. Use the year-end total to evaluate the firm's collection system.

b. If 70% of the firm's sales occur between July and December, would this affect the validity of your conclusion in part a? Explain.

LG 3 **P2–17 Interpreting liquidity and activity ratios** The new owners of Bluegrass Natural Foods, Inc., have hired you to help them diagnose and cure problems that the company has had in maintaining adequate liquidity. As a first step, you perform a liquidity analysis. You then do an analysis of the company's short-term activity ratios. Your calculations and appropriate industry norms are listed.

Ratio	Bluegrass	Industry norm
Current ratio	4.5	4.0
Quick ratio	2.0	3.1
Inventory turnover	6.0	10.4
Average collection period	73 days	52 days
Average payment period	31 days	40 days

a. What recommendations relative to the amount and the handling of inventory could you make to the new owners?

b. What recommendations relative to the amount and the handling of accounts receivable could you make to the new owners?

c. What recommendations relative to the amount and the handling of accounts payable could you make to the new owners?

d. What results, overall, would you hope your recommendations would achieve? Why might your recommendations not be effective?

LG 4 **P2–18 Debt analysis** Springfield Bank is evaluating Creek Enterprises, which has requested a $4,000,000 loan, to assess the firm's financial leverage and financial risk. On the basis of the debt ratios for Creek, along with the industry averages (see top of page 82) and Creek's recent financial statements (following), evaluate and recommend appropriate action on the loan request.

Creek Enterprises Income Statement for the Year Ended December 31, 2012

Sales revenue	$30,000,000
Less: Cost of goods sold	21,000,000
Gross profits	$ 9,000,000
Less: Operating expenses	
Selling expense	$ 3,000,000
General and administrative expenses	1,800,000
Lease expense	200,000
Depreciation expense	1,000,000
Total operating expense	$ 6,000,000
Operating profits	$ 3,000,000
Less: Interest expense	1,000,000
Net profits before taxes	$ 2,000,000
Less: Taxes (rate = 40%)	800,000
Net profits after taxes	$ 1,200,000
Less: Preferred stock dividends	100,000
Earnings available for common stockholders	$ 1,100,000

Industry averages	
Debt ratio	0.51
Times interest earned ratio	7.30
Fixed-payment coverage ratio	1.85

Creek Enterprises Balance Sheet December 31, 2012

Assets		Liabilities and Stockholders' Equity	
Cash	$ 1,000,000	Accounts payable	$ 8,000,000
Marketable securities	3,000,000	Notes payable	8,000,000
Accounts receivable	12,000,000	Accruals	500,000
Inventories	7,500,000	Total current liabilities	$16,500,000
Total current assets	$23,500,000	Long-term debt (includes	
Land and buildings	$11,000,000	financial leases)[b]	$20,000,000
Machinery and equipment	20,500,000	Preferred stock (25,000	
Furniture and fixtures	8,000,000	shares, $4 dividend)	$ 2,500,000
Gross fixed assets (at cost)[a]	$39,500,000	Common stock (1 million	
Less: Accumulated depreciation	13,000,000	shares at $5 par)	5,000,000
Net fixed assets	$26,500,000	Paid-in capital in excess of	
Total assets	$50,000,000	par value	4,000,000
		Retained earnings	2,000,000
		Total stockholders' equity	$13,500,000
		Total liabilities and	
		stockholders' equity	$50,000,000

[a]The firm has a 4-year financial lease requiring annual beginning-of-year payments of $200,000. Three years of the lease have yet to run.

[b]Required annual principal payments are $800,000.

LG 5 **P2–19 Common-size statement analysis** A common-size income statement for Creek Enterprises' 2011 operations follows. Using the firm's 2012 income statement presented in Problem 2–18, develop the 2012 common-size income statement and compare it to the 2011 statement. Which areas require further analysis and investigation?

**Creek Enterprises Common-Size Income Statement
for the Year Ended December 31, 2011**

Sales revenue ($35,000,000)	100.0%
Less: Cost of goods sold	65.9
Gross profits	34.1 %
Less: Operating expenses	
Selling expense	12.7%
General and administrative expenses	6.3
Lease expense	0.6
Depreciation expense	3.6
Total operating expense	23.2
Operating profits	10.9%
Less: Interest expense	1.5
Net profits before taxes	9.4%
Less: Taxes (rate = 40%)	3.8
Net profits after taxes	5.6%
Less: Preferred stock dividends	0.1
Earnings available for common stockholders	5.5 %

LG 4 **LG 5** **P2–20** **The relationship between financial leverage and profitability**
Pelican Paper, Inc., and Timberland Forest, Inc., are rivals in the manufacture of craft papers. Some financial statement values for each company follow. Use them in a ratio analysis that compares the firms' financial leverage and profitability.

Item	Pelican Paper, Inc.	Timberland Forest, Inc.
Total assets	$10,000,000	$10,000,000
Total equity (all common)	9,000,000	5,000,000
Total debt	1,000,000	5,000,000
Annual interest	100,000	500,000
Total sales	25,000,000	25,000,000
EBIT	6,250,000	6,250,000
Earnings available for common stockholders	3,690,000	3,450,00

a. Calculate the following debt and coverage ratios for the two companies. Discuss their financial risk and ability to cover the costs in relation to each other.
   (1) Debt ratio
   (2) Times interest earned ratio
b. Calculate the following profitability ratios for the two companies. Discuss their profitability relative to each other.
   (1) Operating profit margin
   (2) Net profit margin
   (3) Return on total assets
   (4) Return on common equity
c. In what way has the larger debt of Timberland Forest made it more profitable than Pelican Paper? What are the risks that Timberland's investors undertake when they choose to purchase its stock instead of Pelican's?

LG 6 **P2–21** **Ratio proficiency**   McDougal Printing, Inc., had sales totaling $40,000,000 in fiscal year 2012. Some ratios for the company are listed below. Use this information to determine the dollar values of various income statement and balance sheet accounts as requested.

McDougal Printing, Inc.
Year Ended December 31, 2012

Sales	$40,000,000
Gross profit margin	80%
Operating profit margin	35%
Net profit margin	8%
Return on total assets	16%
Return on common equity	20%
Total asset turnover	2
Average collection period	62.2 days

Calculate values for the following:
a. Gross profits
b. Cost of goods sold
c. Operating profits
d. Operating expenses
e. Earnings available for common stockholders
f. Total assets
g. Total common stock equity
h. Accounts receivable

LG 6 **P2–22 Cross-sectional ratio analysis** Use the financial statements below and on page 85 for Fox Manufacturing Company for the year ended December 31, 2012, along with the industry average ratios below to:

a. Prepare and interpret a complete ratio analysis of the firm's 2012 operations.

Fox Manufacturing Company Income Statement
for the Year Ended December 31, 2012

Sales revenue	$600,000
Less: Cost of goods sold	460,000
Gross profits	$140,000
Less: Operating expenses	
General and administrative expenses	$30,000
Depreciation expense	30,000
Total operating expense	60,000
Operating profits	$ 80,000
Less: Interest expense	10,000
Net profits before taxes	$ 70,000
Less: Taxes	27,100
Net profits after taxes (earnings available for common stockholders)	$ 42,900
Earnings per share (EPS)	$2.15

Ratio	Industry average, 2012
Current ratio	2.35
Quick ratio	0.87
Inventory turnover[a]	4.55
Average collection period[a]	35.8 days
Total asset turnover	1.09
Debt ratio	0.300
Times interest earned ratio	12.3
Gross profit margin	0.202
Operating profit margin	0.135
Net profit margin	0.091
Return on total assets (ROA)	0.099
Return on common equity (ROE)	0.167
Earnings per share (EPS)	$3.10

[a]Based on a 365-day year and on end-of-year figures.

Fox Manufacturing Company Balance Sheet
December 31, 2012

Assets

Cash	$ 15,000
Marketable securities	7,200
Accounts receivable	34,100
Inventories	82,000
Total current assets	$138,300
Net fixed assets	270,000
Total assets	$408,300

Liabilities and Stockholders' Equity

Accounts payable	$ 57,000
Notes payable	13,000
Accruals	5,000
Total current liabilities	$ 75,000
Long-term debt	$150,000
Common stock equity (20,000 shares outstanding)	$110,200
Retained earnings	73,100
Total stockholders' equity	$183,300
Total liabilities and stockholders' equity	$408,300

LG 6 **P2–23 Financial statement analysis** The financial statements of Zach Industries for the year ended December 31, 2012, follow.

Zach Industries Income Statement
for the Year Ended December 31, 2012

Sales revenue	$160,000
Less: Cost of goods sold	106,000
Gross profits	$ 54,000
Less: Operating expenses	
Selling expense	$ 16,000
General and administrative expenses	10,000
Lease expense	1,000
Depreciation expense	10,000
Total operating expense	$ 37,000
Operating profits	$ 17,000
Less: Interest expense	6,100
Net profits before taxes	$ 10,900
Less: Taxes	4,360
Net profits after taxes	$ 6,540

Zach Industries Balance Sheet December 31, 2012

Assets

Cash	$ 500
Marketable securities	1,000
Accounts receivable	25,000
Inventories	45,500
Total current assets	$ 72,000
Land	$ 26,000
Buildings and equipment	90,000
Less: Accumulated depreciation	38,000
Net fixed assets	$ 78,000
Total assets	$150,000

Liabilities and Stockholders' Equity

Accounts payable	$ 22,000
Notes payable	47,000
Total current liabilities	$ 69,000
Long-term debt	22,950
Common stock[a]	31,500
Retained earnings	26,550
Total liabilities and stockholders' equity	$150,000

[a]The firm's 3,000 outstanding shares of common stock closed 2012 at a price of $25 per share.

a. Use the preceding financial statements to complete the following table. Assume the industry averages given in the table are applicable for both 2011 and 2012.

Ratio	Industry average	Actual 2011	Actual 2012
Current ratio	1.80	1.84	_____
Quick ratio	0.70	0.78	_____
Inventory turnover[a]	2.50	2.59	_____
Average collection period[a]	37.5 days	36.5 days	_____
Debt ratio	65%	67%	_____
Times interest earned ratio	3.8	4.0	_____
Gross profit margin	38%	40%	_____
Net profit margin	3.5%	3.6%	_____
Return on total assets	4.0%	4.0%	_____
Return on common equity	9.5%	8.0%	_____
Market/book ratio	1.1	1.2	_____

[a]Based on a 365-day year and on end-of-year figures.

b. Analyze Zach Industries' financial condition as it is related to (1) liquidity, (2) activity, (3) debt, (4) profitability, and (5) market. Summarize the company's overall financial condition.

LG 6 **P2–24 Integrative—Complete ratio analysis** Given the following financial statements (following and on page 87), historical ratios, and industry averages, calculate Sterling Company's financial ratios for the most recent year. (Assume a 365-day year.)

Sterling Company Income Statement for the Year Ended December 31, 2012

Sales revenue	$10,000,000
Less: Cost of goods sold	7,500,000
Gross profits	$ 2,500,000
Less: Operating expenses	
Selling expense	$300,000
General and administrative expenses	650,000
Lease expense	50,000
Depreciation expense	200,000
Total operating expense	$ 1,200,000
Operating profits	$ 1,300,000
Less: Interest expense	200,000
Net profits before taxes	$ 1,100,000
Less: Taxes (rate = 40%)	440,000
Net profits after taxes	$ 660,000
Less: Preferred stock dividends	50,000
Earnings available for common stockholders	$ 610,000
Earnings per share (EPS)	$3.05

Sterling Company Balance Sheet December 31, 2012

Assets		Liabilities and Stockholders' Equity	
Cash	$ 200,000	Accounts payable[b]	$ 900,000
Marketable securities	50,000	Notes payable	200,000
Accounts receivable	800,000	Accruals	100,000
Inventories	950,000	Total current liabilities	$ 1,200,000
Total current assets	$ 2,000,000	Long-term debt (includes	
Gross fixed assets (at cost)[a]	$12,000,000	financial leases)[c]	$ 3,000,000
Less: Accumulated depreciation	3,000,000	Preferred stock (25,000 shares,	
Net fixed assets	$ 9,000,000	$2 dividend)	$ 1,000,000
Other assets	1,000,000	Common stock (200,000	
Total assets	$12,000,000	shares at $3 par)[d]	600,000
		Paid-in capital in excess of	
		par value	5,200,000
		Retained earnings	1,000,000
		Total stockholders' equity	$ 7,800,000
		Total liabilities and	
		stockholders' equity	$12,000,000

[a]The firm has an 8-year financial lease requiring annual beginning-of-year payments of $50,000. Five years of the lease have yet to run.

[b]Annual credit purchases of $6,200,000 were made during the year.

[c]The annual principal payment on the long-term debt is $100,000.

[d]On December 31, 2012, the firm's common stock closed at $39.50 per share.

Analyze its overall financial situation from both a cross-sectional and a time-series viewpoint. Break your analysis into evaluations of the firm's liquidity, activity, debt, profitability, and market.

Historical and Industry Average Ratios for Sterling Company

Ratio	Actual 2010	Actual 2011	Industry average, 2012
Current ratio	1.40	1.55	1.85
Quick ratio	1.00	0.92	1.05
Inventory turnover	9.52	9.21	8.60
Average collection period	45.6 days	36.9 days	35.5 days
Average payment period	59.3 days	61.6 days	46.4 days
Total asset turnover	0.74	0.80	0.74
Debt ratio	0.20	0.20	0.30
Times interest earned ratio	8.2	7.3	8.0
Fixed-payment coverage ratio	4.5	4.2	4.2
Gross profit margin	0.30	0.27	0.25
Operating profit margin	0.12	0.12	0.10
Net profit margin	0.062	0.062	0.053
Return on total assets (ROA)	0.045	0.050	0.040
Return on common equity (ROE)	0.061	0.067	0.066
Earnings per share (EPS)	$1.75	$2.20	$1.50
Price/earnings (P/E) ratio	12.0	10.5	11.2
Market/book (M/B) ratio	1.20	1.05	1.10

LG 6 **P2–25 DuPont system of analysis** Use the following ratio information for Johnson International and the industry averages for Johnson's line of business to:
a. Construct the DuPont system of analysis for both Johnson and the industry.
b. Evaluate Johnson (and the industry) over the 3-year period.
c. Indicate in which areas Johnson requires further analysis. Why?

Johnson	2010	2011	2012
Financial leverage multiplier	1.75	1.75	1.85
Net profit margin	0.059	0.058	0.049
Total asset turnover	2.11	2.18	2.34

Industry Averages			
Financial leverage multiplier	1.67	1.69	1.64
Net profit margin	0.054	0.047	0.041
Total asset turnover	2.05	2.13	2.15

LG 6 **P2–26 Complete ratio analysis, recognizing significant differences** Home Health, Inc., has come to Jane Ross for a yearly financial checkup. As a first step, Jane has prepared a complete set of ratios for fiscal years 2011 and 2012. She will use them to look for significant changes in the company's situation from one year to the next.

Home Health, Inc. Financial Ratios

Ratio	2011	2012
Current ratio	3.25	3.00
Quick ratio	2.50	2.20
Inventory turnover	12.80	10.30
Average collection period	42.6 days	31.4 days
Total asset turnover	1.40	2.00
Debt ratio	0.45	0.62
Times interest earned ratio	4.00	3.85
Gross profit margin	68%	65%
Operating profit margin	14%	16%
Net profit margin	8.3%	8.1%
Return on total assets	11.6%	16.2%
Return on common equity	21.1%	42.6%
Price/earnings ratio	10.7	9.8
Market/book ratio	1.40	1.25

a. To focus on the degree of change, calculate the year-to-year proportional change by subtracting the year 2011 ratio from the year 2012 ratio, then dividing the difference by the year 2011 ratio. Multiply the result by 100. Preserve the positive or negative sign. The result is the percentage change in the ratio from 2011 to 2012. Calculate the proportional change for the ratios shown here.

b. For any ratio that shows a year-to-year difference of 10% or more, state whether the difference is in the company's favor or not.

c. For the most significant changes (25% or more), look at the other ratios and cite at least one other change that may have contributed to the change in the ratio that you are discussing.

 LG 1   **P2-27 ETHICS PROBLEM** Do some reading in periodicals and/or on the Internet to find out more about the Sarbanes-Oxley Act's provisions for companies. Select one of those provisions, and indicate why you think financial statements will be more trustworthy if company financial executives implement this provision of SOX.

Spreadsheet Exercise

The income statement and balance sheet are the basic reports that a firm constructs for use by management and for distribution to stockholders, regulatory bodies, and the general public. They are the primary sources of historical financial information about the firm. Dayton Products, Inc., is a moderate-sized manufacturer. The company's management has asked you to perform a detailed financial statement analysis of the firm.

The income statements for the years ending December 31, 2012 and 2011, respectively, are presented in the table below. (Note: Purchases of inventory during 2012 amounted to $109,865.)

Annual Income Statements (Values in millions)

	For the year ended	
	December 31, 2012	December 31, 2011
Sales	$178,909	$187,510
Cost of goods sold	?	111,631
Selling, general, and administrative expenses	12,356	12,900
Other tax expense	33,572	33,377
Depreciation and amortization	12,103	7,944
Other income (add to EBIT to arrive at EBT)	3,147	3,323
Interest expense	398	293
Income tax rate (average)	35.324%	37.945%
Dividends paid per share	$1.47	$0.91
Basic EPS from total operations	$1.71	$2.25

You also have the following balance sheet information as of December 31, 2012 and 2011, respectively.

Annual Balance Sheets (Values in millions)

	December 31, 2012	December, 31, 2011
Cash and equivalents	$ 7,229	$ 6,547
Receivables	21,163	19,549
Inventories	8,068	7,904
Other current assets	1,831	1,681
Property, plant, and equipment, gross	204,960	187,519
Accumulated depreciation and depletion	110,020	97,917
Other noncurrent assets	19,413	17,891
Accounts payable	13,792	22,862
Short-term debt payable	4,093	3,703
Other current liabilities	15,290	3,549
Long-term debt payable	6,655	7,099
Deferred income taxes	16,484	16,359
Other noncurrent liabilities	21,733	16,441
Retained earnings	74,597	73,161
Total common shares outstanding	6.7 billion	6.8 billion

TO DO

a. Create a spreadsheet similar to Table 2.1 to model the following:
   (1) A multiple-step comparative income statement for Dayton, Inc., for the periods ending December 31, 2012 and 2011. You must calculate the cost of goods sold for the year 2012.
   (2) A common-size income statement for Dayton, Inc., covering the years 2012 and 2011.

b. Create a spreadsheet similar to Table 2.2 to model the following:
   (1) A detailed, comparative balance sheet for Dayton, Inc., for the years ended December 31, 2012 and 2011.
   (2) A common-size balance sheet for Dayton, Inc., covering the years 2012 and 2011.

c. Create a spreadsheet similar to Table 2.8 to perform the following analysis:
   (1) Create a table that reflects both 2012 and 2011 operating ratios for Dayton, Inc., segmented into (a) liquidity, (b) activity, (c) debt, (d) profitability, and (e) market. Assume that the current market price for the stock is $90.
   (2) Compare the 2012 ratios to the 2011 ratios. Indicate whether the results "outperformed the prior year" or "underperformed relative to the prior year."

MyAccountingLab Visit www.myaccountinglab.com for **Chapter Case: Assessing Martin Manufacturing's Current Financial Position,** Group Exercises, and numerous online resources.

3

Managerial Accounting, the Business Organization, and Professional Ethics

LEARNING OBJECTIVES

When you have finished studying this chapter, you should be able to:

1. Explain why accounting is essential for decision makers and managers.

2. Describe the major users and uses of accounting information.

3. Explain the role of budgets and performance reports in planning and control.

4. Describe the cost-benefit and behavioral issues involved in designing an accounting system.

5. Discuss the role accountants play in the company's value-chain functions.

6. Identify current trends in management accounting.

7. Explain why ethics and standards of ethical conduct are important to accountants.

▶ STARBUCKS

If you had asked most people a decade or two ago whether consumers around the world would pay a premium price for a "better" cup of coffee, few would have answered yes. Nevertheless, the expansion of Starbucks since its founding in 1971 in Seattle's Pike Place Market has been nothing short of phenomenal. In 2011, Starbucks' total revenues—the amount the company received for all items sold— were $11.7 billion, compared with only $700 million in 1996. Net income—the profit that Starbucks made—was $1.7 billion, up from only $42 million in 1996. Total assets—the recorded value of the items owned by Starbucks—grew from less than $900 million in 1996 to more than $7.3 billion in 2011. These numbers are accounting measures of the cumulative success of numerous managers of Starbucks stores in many countries. Managers use these figures, along with more detailed accounting numbers, to make day-to-day decisions and to measure performance.

Starbucks has established a worldwide reputation to match its financial success. Interbrand ranked Starbucks among the 100 best global brands for 2011. Starbucks ranked seventy-third on *Fortune* magazine's "100 Best Companies to Work For." *Corporate Responsibility* magazine placed it thirty-ninth in its list of "100 Best Corporate Citizens." Finally, in 2011 *Fortune* named Starbucks the sixteenth most admired company in the world and named founder and CEO Howard Schultz the businessperson of the year.

How did Starbucks accomplish all this? As we embark on our journey into the world of management accounting, we will explore what it takes for a company such as Starbucks to ensure that when Mei-Hwa Zhang walks into a Starbucks in Beijing, she has much the same quality experience as Mohammad Kumar does in a Starbucks in Kuwait or Franz Mueller does in Zurich. All Starbucks' managers, from baristas to store managers to the chief executive officer, use accounting reports to assess how well their units meet corporate goals and objectives. Accounting provides a common language to help managers around the world communicate and coordinate their actions. By the time you finish reading this book, you will be comfortable with the language of accounting. You will know why it is necessary to understand accounting information in order to use it wisely in your decisions. You will also understand the role of performance evaluation systems in communicating strategy and coordinating actions throughout an organization.

Managerial accounting information is used in all sorts of decisions. For example, consider decisions you might face as a manager in the following situations:

- Suppose you are a Boeing engineer preparing manufacturing specifications for a component of its new 787 Dreamliner airplane. There are three possible ways to organize the assembly of the component. Which is the most cost-effective approach?
- Suppose you are a product manager at General Mills and you are designing a new marketing plan for Cheerios. Market research predicts that distributing free samples in the mail will increase annual sales by 4%. Will profits from the added sales be more than the cost of producing and distributing the free samples?
- Bank of America offers free checking to customers with no minimum balance requirement in their MyAccess™ checking account. How much does it cost the bank to provide this free service?
- Kitsap County Special Olympics holds a series of athletic events for disabled youth. As executive director, you must set a goal for the group's annual fund drive based on the estimated cost to support its planned activities.
- Madison Park Cafe currently is open only for dinner, but the owner is considering opening for lunch. The average lunch is priced at about $15, and the café expects to serve about 40 lunches per day. Can the chef produce a luncheon menu that meets the café's quality standards at an average cost that yields a reasonable profit?
- Amazon.com offers free 2-day shipping on all orders for subscribers that pay a single $79 annual fee. Does the fee plus the profits from increased sales to subscribers exceed the cost of providing free shipping?

For all these decisions, managers rely on managerial accounting information.

In this chapter, we provide an overview of management accounting in all types of organizations. Larry White, former chair of the **Institute of Management Accountants (IMA),** the largest U.S. professional organization focused on internal accounting, sums up the role of management accounting as follows: "Management accountants are committed to helping their organization achieve its strategic goals by providing decision support, planning, and control for business operations with a high level of ethics and professional competence." ■

© Richard Ellis/ZUMA Wire Service/Newscom

Starbucks' coffee shops have strategic locations throughout the world, including this one in Beijing.

Institute of Management Accountants (IMA)
The largest U.S. professional organization of accountants focused on internal accounting.

management accounting
The branch of accounting that produces information for managers within an organization. It is the process of identifying, measuring, accumulating, analyzing, preparing, interpreting, and communicating information that helps managers fulfill organizational objectives.

Management Accounting and Your Career

In this book we focus on **management accounting**, which is the process of identifying, measuring, accumulating, analyzing, preparing, interpreting, and communicating information that helps managers fulfill organizational objectives. In contrast, **financial accounting** produces information for external parties, such as stockholders, suppliers, banks, and government regulatory agencies. Exhibit 3-1 summarizes the major differences between management accounting and financial accounting.

This book is written primarily for managers who are not accounting specialists. All managers use information from accounting systems. By learning about accounting systems, you will better understand the relationships among different components of an organization. You also learn why it is essential to understand the system that generates accounting information in order to use that information in any of a wide variety of functional decisions (including purchasing, manufacturing, inventory management, hiring, marketing, and pricing, among others). You will learn to evaluate whether your accounting system is providing the information you need for your decisions. You will learn to evaluate performance measures generated by your accounting system and assess whether the performance measures create appropriate incentives. In sum, a thorough understanding of accounting is essential for managers in any organization.

When accounting is mentioned, most people think first of financial accounting. Independent auditors—**certified public accountants (CPAs)** in the United States and **chartered accountants (CAs)** in many other nations—provide assurance to external users about the reliability of companies'

Objective 1

Explain why accounting is essential for decision makers and managers.

financial accounting
The branch of accounting that develops information for external decision makers, such as stockholders, suppliers, banks, and government regulatory agencies.

certified public accountant (CPA)
In the United States, independent accountants who assure the reliability of companies' published financial statements.

	Management Accounting	Financial Accounting
Primary users	Organization managers at various levels	Outside parties such as investors and government agencies but also organization managers
Freedom of choice of accounting measures	No constraints other than requiring the benefits of improved management decisions to exceed information costs	Constrained by generally accepted accounting principles (GAAP)
Behavioral implications in selecting accounting measures	Choice should consider how measurements and reports will influence managers' daily behavior	Choice based on how to measure and communicate economic phenomena; behavioral considerations are secondary, although executive compensation based on reported results may have behavioral impacts
Time focus of reports	Future orientation: formal use of budgets as well as historical records. Example: 20X2 budget versus 20X2 actual performance	Past orientation: historical evaluation; example: 20X2 actual performance versus 20X1 actual performance
Time span of reports	Flexible, varying from hourly to 10–15 years	Less flexible; usually one year or one quarter
Types of reports	Detailed reports include details about products, departments, territories, etc.	Summary reports: primarily report on the entity as a whole
Influence of other functional areas	Field is less sharply defined; heavier use of economics, decision sciences, and behavioral sciences	Field is more sharply defined; lighter use of related disciplines

Exhibit 3-1

Distinctions Between Management Accounting and Financial Accounting

chartered accountant (CA)

In many countries, the equivalent to the CPA in the United States—independent accountants who assure the reliability of companies' financial statements.

certified management accountant (CMA)

The management accountant's counterpart to the CPA.

published financial statements. Another, even larger, group of people work in private industry and government as management accounting specialists. Though management accountants often help to produce financial statements for external users, they primarily produce accounting information for internal users. The **certified management accountant (CMA)** designation is the management accountant's counterpart to the CPA. The Institute of Management Accountants (IMA) oversees the CMA program. CMAs must pass an examination covering (1) financial planning, performance, and control, and (2) financial decision making.[1] Like the CPA designation, the CMA confers status and often opens the door to higher-level positions. A survey by *Financial Executive* magazine showed that 33% of CEOs in companies with revenues greater than $500 million had risen through the finance/accounting ranks, compared with 26% from operations and 21% from sales and marketing.

Roles of Accounting Information

One basic purpose of accounting information is to help you make decisions. Every day, you and your organization face a new and continually changing set of decisions, and many of these decisions rely on accounting information. When you understand how your decisions affect costs and revenues, you will be a better decision maker.

A second basic purpose of accounting is to help you plan and control your organization's operations. Plans describe how the organization will achieve its objectives. Control is the process of implementing plans and evaluating whether your organization is achieving its objectives. When you understand how people respond to the incentives created by performance evaluation and control systems, you will be better able to assess which system creates the most appropriate incentives.

Objective 2

Describe the major users and uses of accounting information.

---

[1]For information about the IMA and the CMA exam, see www.imanet.org.

Organizations address these two purposes by designing and implementing **accounting systems**, which are formal mechanisms for gathering, organizing, and communication information about an organization's activities. The organization of this book reflects how accounting systems address these two basic purposes. Chapters 4 through 5, focuses on the decision-making purpose of accounting information. These chapters help you determine what costs are relevant for different decisions and how accounting systems generate relevant costs for managers, demonstrating a key concept in management accounting: "Different costs for different purposes." Chapters 6 through 9, deals with planning and control systems. These chapters show how measuring performance affects managers' incentives, leading to a second key concept: "You get what you measure."Chapter 12, focuses on relevant costs for long-term capital investment decisions describes systems to generate detailed product costing information.

As you progress in your study of management accounting and in your career, you move from understanding how to use information from existing accounting systems to creating systems that produce information useful to your particular decisions. Early in your studies, you initially react to the systems that are described to you, making sure that you understand how each system works and how to use the information it produces in your decisions. Early in your career, you may have little opportunity to influence the management accounting system, and your initial goal is simply to understand and use the information from the accounting system. As you advance in your studies, you learn about increasingly complex systems designed to provide information for a variety of purposes. As you learn about specific alternatives, you also develop the ability to design new alternatives that provide better information for your decision-making and performance evaluation purposes. Finally, you develop the proficiency and understanding required to evaluate the relative advantages of alternative accounting systems. You will likely see a parallel progression in the use of management accounting in your career. As you advance, you are able to suggest changes to improve the existing systems, and eventually you may be in a position to influence the systems implemented by your organization. The more you can influence management accounting systems, the more important it is to understand their role.

Information for Decision Making and Planning and Control

What types of accounting information do managers need for decision making and performance evaluation and control? For **decision making**—choosing among alternative courses of action to achieve some objective—accounting information helps answer problem-solving questions. For performance evaluation and control, accounting helps answer scorecard and attention-directing questions:

1. Scorecard questions: Is the company doing well or poorly? **Scorekeeping** is the accumulation, classification, and reporting of data that help users understand and evaluate organizational performance. Scorekeeping information must be accurate and reliable to be useful. For example, Starbucks produces numerous reports to evaluate results for stores and divisions.
2. Attention-directing questions: Which areas require additional investigation? **Attention directing** involves reporting and interpreting information that helps managers to focus on operating problems, imperfections, inefficiencies, and opportunities. For example, a manager who sees that a Starbucks store has reported profits of $120,000 when budgeted profit was $150,000 will look for explanations as to why the store did not achieve its budget.
3. Problem-solving questions: Of the alternatives being considered, which is the best? The **problem-solving** aspect of accounting involves analysis of alternative courses of action and identification of the best course to follow. For example, Starbucks experiments with adding various items to its menu. After an analysis of how a new product will affect revenues and costs, management decides which items to add and which to delete.

The scorecard and attention-directing uses of information are closely related. The same information that helps a manager understand and evaluate performance may also serve an attention-directing function for the manager's superior. For example, by pinpointing where actual results differ from plans, performance reports show managers how they are doing and where to

accounting system
A formal mechanism for gathering, organizing, and communicating information about an organization's activities.

decision making
Choosing among alternative courses of action designed to achieve some objective.

scorekeeping
The accumulation, classification, and reporting of data that help users understand and evaluate performance.

attention directing
Reporting and interpreting information that helps managers to focus on operating problems, imperfections, inefficiencies, and opportunities.

problem solving
Analysis of possible courses of action and identification of the best course to follow.

take action. Companies produce most scorecard and attention-directing information on a routine basis every day, month, quarter, or year.

In contrast, specific decisions often require problem-solving information beyond the information routinely generated for scorekeeping and attention directing. When organizations make decisions (such as how to price products and special orders, whether to make or to buy components, whether to add or drop a product, how to adjust product mix, or whether to keep or replace equipment), specially-prepared information is often required. For example, Starbucks uses problem-solving information when deciding whether to run ads during the Super Bowl™ broadcast.

Decision making is the core of the management process. Decisions range from the routine (setting daily production schedules) to the non-routine (launching a new product line), and accountants are information specialists who aid the decision makers. Managers use accounting information for all types of decisions. Accountants must make sure that they produce information that is useful for these decisions and managers must work with accountants to get the information that is needed.

Making Managerial Decisions

What type of information—scorekeeping, attention-directing, or problem-solving—would managers use for each of the following decisions? Why?

1. Deciding whether to replace a traditional assembly line with a fully automated robotic process
2. Evaluating the performance of a division for the preceding year
3. Identifying which products exceeded their budgeted profitability and which ones fell short of their budgets

Answers

1. Problem-solving. This is a one-time decision for which managers need information about the potential impacts of each of the alternatives under consideration.
2. Scorekeeping. This is a routine evaluation of an organizational unit for which managers want systematic data on a regular basis.
3. Attention-directing. To identify products that need attention, managers want information that highlights deviations of actual results from pre-specified expectations in the budget.

planning

Setting objectives for an organization and determining how to attain them.

control

Implementing plans and using feedback to evaluate the attainment of objectives.

Another essential element of the management process is planning and controlling the organization's operations. **Planning** provides the answers to two questions: What objectives does the organization want to achieve? When and how will the organization achieve these objectives? **Control** refers to implementing plans and using feedback to evaluate the attainment of objectives. Thus, feedback is crucial to the cycle of planning and control. Planning determines action, action generates feedback, and the control phase uses this feedback to influence further planning and actions. Timely, systematic reports provided by the accounting system are a primary source of useful feedback.

The left side of Exhibit 3-2 demonstrates the planning and control cycle of current operations that could be used by a particular Starbucks store. The planning section in Exhibit 3-2 shows an objective for the store (increase profitability) and how it will be attained (product growth and improved marketing). The control section shows the actions that are intended to increase profitability and how Starbucks will evaluate the actions. The Starbucks store will implement its plan to expand the number of drinks on its menu and increase advertising. Management will evaluate these actions based on three performance measures, the increase in drinks sold, increase in advertising expenditures, and the increase in revenue. Managers will then use the performance evaluation results for further planning and implementation.

Management by Exception

The right side of Exhibit 3-2 shows that the accounting system formalizes plans by expressing them as budgets. A **budget** is a quantitative expression of a plan of action and an aid to coordinating and implementing plans. Budgets are the chief devices for disciplining management planning. Without budgets, planning may not get the front-and-center focus that it deserves. The Starbucks store expresses its plan for product growth and improved marketing through revenue and advertising budgets.

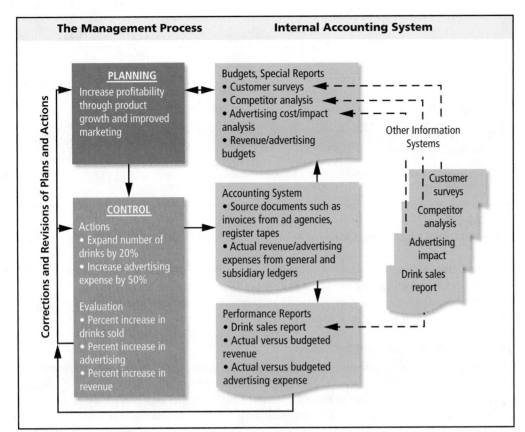

Exhibit 3-2
Starbucks Store—Accounting Framework for Planning and Control

The accounting system records, measures, and classifies actions to produce performance reports (the last box in Exhibit 3-2). **Performance reports** provide feedback by comparing results with plans and by highlighting **variances**, which are deviations from plans. Organizations use performance reports to judge managers' decisions and the productivity of organizational units. Performance reports compare actual results to budgets, thereby motivating managers to achieve the objectives. For example, managers of the Starbucks store evaluate the effectiveness of its advertising plan by comparing the increase in revenue and profits to the increase in advertising costs. Based on their evaluation, managers at Starbucks make corrections and revisions to their plans.

Exhibit 3-3 shows a simple performance report for a hypothetical Starbucks store, the Mayfair Starbucks. The first column of Exhibit 3-3 is the budget for March 20X1. It is based on a predicted level of sales and the estimated costs needed to support that level of sales. After managers and their superiors agree on a budget, it becomes the managers' target for the month. As the store sells its products and incurs costs, Starbucks' accounting system collects the revenue and cost information. At the end of each month (or more often if managers need more frequent feedback), the accounting department prepares a store-level performance report, such as the one in Exhibit 3-3. Managers use the performance report to help evaluate the store's operations.

The Mayfair store report shows that the store met its targeted sales, but the $2,500 unfavorable variance for ingredients shows that these costs were $2,500 over budget. Other variances show that store labor costs were $400 under budget and other labor was $50 over budget. At the Mayfair store, management would undoubtedly focus attention on ingredients, which had by far the largest unfavorable variance. However, it may also be worthwhile to investigate the $400 favorable labor variance. By investigating favorable variances, managers may find better ways of doing things.

Performance reports spur investigation of exceptions—items for which actual amounts differ significantly from budgeted amounts. Managers then revise operations to conform with the plans or revise the plans. This process is **management by exception**, which means concentrating more on areas that deviate from the plan and less on areas that conform with plans. Thus, the management-by-exception approach frees managers from needless concern with those phases of operations that adhere to plans and are running smoothly. However, well-conceived plans incorporate enough discretion or flexibility so that the manager feels free to pursue any unforeseen opportunities.

budget
A quantitative expression of a plan of action and an aid to coordinating and implementing the plan.

performance reports
Feedback provided by comparing results with plans and by highlighting variances.

variances
Deviations from plans.

management by exception
Concentrating more on areas that deviate from the plan and less on areas that conform with plans and are presumed to be running smoothly.

	Budget	Actual	Variance
Sales	$50,000	$50,000	$ 0
Less:			
Ingredients	$22,000	$24,500	$2,500 U
Store labor (baristas, etc.)	12,000	11,600	400 F
Other labor (managers, supervisors)	6,000	6,050	50 U
Utilities, maintenance, etc.	4,500	4,500	0
Total expenses	$44,500	$46,650	$2,150 U
Total operating income	$ 5,500	$ 3,350	$2,150 U

U = unfavorable—actual cost greater than budgeted; actual revenue or profit less than budgeted
F = favorable—actual cost less than budgeted; actual revenue or profit greater than budgeted

Exhibit 3-3
Mayfair Starbucks Store—Performance Report for the Month Ended March 31, 20X1

Notice that although budgets aid planning and performance reports aid control, it is not accountants but operating managers and their subordinates who use accounting reports to plan and control operations. Accounting assists the managerial planning and control functions by providing prompt measurements of actions and by systematically pinpointing trouble spots.

Influences on Accounting Systems

Accounting systems vary across organizations—systems must meet the needs of each particular organization. In order to reduce costs and complexity, many organizations use a general-purpose accounting system that attempts to meet the needs of both external and internal users. However, as outlined in Exhibit 3-1, there are important differences between management accounting information and financial accounting information. Systems developed primarily for external reporting may not produce the most useful information for managers.

There are three categories of requirements imposed on accounting systems designed to meet the requirements of external users. First, public companies' financial reports for external users must adhere to a set of standards known as **generally accepted accounting principles (GAAP)** as determined by the Financial Accounting Standards Board (FASB) in the United States and the International Accounting Standards Board (IASB) in most of the rest of the world. Second, every company is also subject to various taxes, and therefore subject to various reporting requirements specified by tax rules and regulations. Third, many companies are subject to other government regulations.

There are many other governmental regulations that influence accounting systems. For example, in 2002 the **Sarbanes-Oxley Act** added several levels of regulation in the United States. Driven by corporate bankruptcies blamed in part on accounting lapses (as well as deficiencies in corporate governance, lax securities regulation, and executive greed), the act requires more top-management oversight of a company's accounting policies and procedures. By requiring chief executive officers to sign a statement certifying the accuracy of the company's financial statements, the act makes accounting numbers the concern of all managers, not just the accountants. Sarbanes-Oxley requires external auditors to examine and prepare a separate report on a company's system of **internal controls**—policies to protect and make the most efficient use of an organization's assets.

Another example of broad regulation is the **Foreign Corrupt Practices Act**, a U.S. law forbidding bribery and other corrupt practices but also requiring companies to maintain reasonably detailed accounting records and to have an appropriate system of internal controls. The word *Foreign* in the title is somewhat misleading because the act's provisions apply to all publicly held companies, even if they do not conduct business outside the United States. This law requires that companies maintain their accounting records in reasonable detail and accuracy. Most companies have **internal auditors** who review and evaluate accounting systems, including companies' internal controls, and conduct **management audits**—reviews to determine whether managers are implementing the policies and procedures specified by top management. A final specific area of regulation is government contracting. Universities, defense contractors, and others contracting with the U.S. government must comply with numerous reporting requirements.

The requirements of external reporting should not take precedence over the scorekeeping, attention-directing, and problem-solving information that is generated to meet the needs of

generally accepted accounting principles (GAAP)
A set of standards to which public companies' published financial statements must adhere.

Sarbanes-Oxley Act
A 2002 law that requires top-management oversight of a company's accounting policies and procedures.

internal controls
Policies to protect and make the most efficient use of an organization's assets.

Foreign Corrupt Practices Act
A U.S. law forbidding bribery and other corrupt practices. The law also requires all publicly held companies to maintain their accounting records in reasonable detail and accuracy and have an appropriate system of internal controls.

internal auditors
Accountants who review and evaluate accounting systems, including their internal controls.

management audit
A review to determine whether managers are implementing the policies and procedures specified by top management.

internal users. In later chapters, we will see many examples where a general-purpose accounting system designed to meet external reporting requirements does not generate the information needed for management decisions. As a decision-maker, you must recognize when information from the existing accounting system is not sufficient for your decision and be prepared to ask for additional information to be generated. Your requests for more information should be balanced against the cost of obtaining the information. As explained in the following section, you should only incur the cost to acquire additional information when the expected benefit of an improved decision exceeds the cost of the information.

Cost-Benefit and Behavioral Considerations

Managers should keep two important ideas in mind when designing accounting systems: (1) the cost-benefit balance and (2) behavioral implications.

The **cost-benefit balance**—weighing estimated costs against probable benefits—is the primary consideration in choosing among accounting systems and methods. We will refer again and again to cost-benefit considerations throughout this book. Accounting systems are economic goods—like office supplies or labor—available at various costs. Which system does a manager want to buy: a simple file drawer for amassing receipts and canceled checks, an elaborate budgeting system based on computerized models of the organization and its subunits, or something in between?

The answer depends on a straightforward concept that often becomes complex when applied to real decisions. The concept is that the manager should purchase the system that provides the largest excess of benefits over cost. Real-world applications of this concept are often complex because the expected benefits are difficult to assess. For example, consider a manager at University Clinic who is considering installing a HorizonMIS®-computerized system from American Medical Systems of Ohio for managing a medical practice. With this system, users enter a piece of information only once and the system automatically integrates it with billing, insurance claims, and patient history records. Such a system is efficient and is subject to few errors, but should it be purchased? The expected benefits from the new system come from improved decisions or better controls, and it can be very difficult to develop a comprehensive assessment of these benefits, a point that will be illustrated repeatedly in later chapters.

Management accounting reports influence the decisions of managers. The system must provide accurate, timely reports in a form useful to managers. If a report is too complex, too difficult to use, or arrives too late, the manager may not use the report in making decisions. A report that goes unused creates no benefits.

Managers should also consider **behavioral implications**, that is, the system's effect on employees' decisions and behavior. For example, consider a performance report that a manager's superiors use to evaluate the operations for which the manager is responsible. If the report unfairly attributes excessive costs to the manager's operations, the manager may lose confidence in the system and not let it influence future decisions.

In a nutshell, think of management accounting as a balance between costs and benefits of accounting information coupled with an awareness of the importance of behavioral effects. Therefore, management accountants must understand related disciplines, such as economics, the decision sciences, and the behavioral sciences, to make intelligent decisions about the best information to supply to managers.

Planning and Control for Product Life Cycles and the Value Chain

To effectively plan and control production of goods or services, accountants and other managers must consider the product's life cycle. **Product life cycle** refers to the various stages through which a product passes: conception and product development; introduction into the market; maturation of the market; and, finally, withdrawal from the market. At each stage, managers face differing costs and potential returns. Exhibit 3-4 shows a typical product life cycle.

In the planning process, managers predict revenues and costs over the entire life cycle—however long or short. Then accounting systems track actual costs and revenues throughout the life cycle. Periodic comparisons between planned costs and revenues and actual costs and revenues allow managers to assess the current profitability of a product, determine its current product life-cycle stage, and make any needed changes in strategy.

Objective 4

Describe the cost-benefit and behavioral issues involved in designing an accounting system.

cost-benefit balance
Weighing estimated costs against probable benefits, the primary consideration in choosing among accounting systems and methods.

behavioral implications
The accounting system's effect on the behavior, specifically the decisions, of managers.

product life cycle
The various stages through which a product passes, from conception and development to introduction into the market to maturation and, finally, withdrawal from the market.

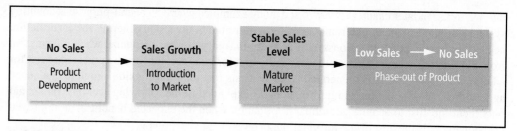

Exhibit 3-4
Typical Product Life Cycle

For example, suppose **Pfizer** is developing a new drug to reduce high blood pressure. There will be substantial development costs and no revenue during the product development stage. Most of the revenues from the product will be received during the introduction and mature market stages when there will also be production costs. During the phase-out of the product, there will be little revenue, but Pfizer will need to keep the drug on the market for those who have come to rely on it. Thus, the product pricing strategy must recognize the need for revenues during the introduction and mature market stages to cover both development and phase-out costs as well as the direct costs of producing the drug.

Product life cycles range from a few months (for fashion clothing or faddish toys) to many years (for automobiles or refrigerators). Some products, such as many computer software packages, have long development stages and relatively short market lives. Others, such as **Boeing** 737 airplanes, have a market life many times longer than their development stage. Many companies are working to shorten the product development phase, both to reduce the time during which a product generates no revenue and to bring products to market on a more timely basis.

The Value Chain

In addition to considering a product's life cycle, managers must recognize those activities necessary for a company to create the goods or services that it sells. These activities comprise the **value chain**, the set of business functions or activities that add value to the products or services of an organization. As shown in Exhibit 3-5 these functions include the following:

- Research and development: generation of ideas related to new products, services, or processes
- Design: detailed design and engineering of products, services, or processes
- Production: coordination and assembly of resources to produce a product or deliver a service
- Marketing: methods by which customers learn about the value and features of products or services (for example, advertising or selling activities)
- Distribution: mechanisms by which a company delivers products or services to the customer
- Customer service: support activities provided to the customer

Not all functions are of equal importance to the success of a company. Senior management must decide which functions enable the company to gain and maintain a competitive edge. For example, managers at **Dell Computers** consider the design function a critical success factor. The features designed into Dell's computers create greater value and higher quality. In addition, the design of efficient processes used to make and deliver computers lowers costs and speeds up delivery to its customers. Dell also performs the other value-chain functions, but it concentrates on being the best process designer in the computer market.

Accountants play a role in supporting all the value-chain functions. Most obvious is the production stage, where accountants facilitate cost planning and control through the use of budgets and performance reporting and help track the effects of continuous improvement programs. However, accounting can also have a great influence on the two pre-production value-chain functions. For example, accountants provide estimated revenue and cost data during the research and development stage and during the design stage of the value chain. Managers use these data to decide which ideas will move to the production stage and which will be dropped. These data also

---

Objective 5

Discuss the role accountants play in the company's value-chain functions.

value chain
The set of business functions or activities that add value to the products or services of an organization.

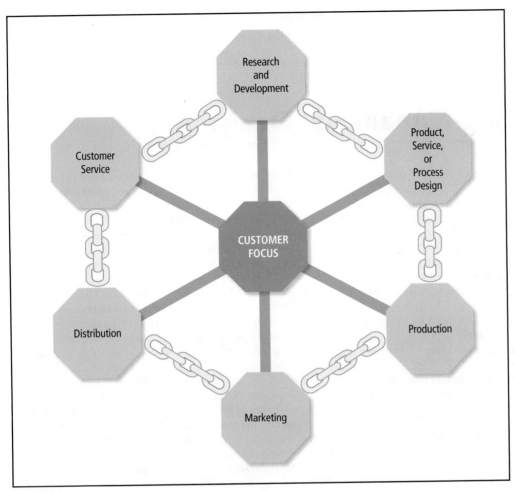

Exhibit 3-5
The Value Chain of Business Functions

enable managers and engineers to reduce the life-cycle costs of products or services by changing product and process designs. Accountants can give managers feedback on ideas for cost reductions long before the company must make a commitment to purchase expensive equipment.

Accountants also play a role in post-production value-chain functions. For example, accountants analyze the trade-off between the increased revenue expected from a marketing program and its cost. In addition, accounting information can influence decisions about distributing products or services to customers. Should a company sell its products directly to a chain of retail stores, or should it sell to a wholesaler? What transportation system should be used—trucks or trains? Accountants provide important information about the costs of each alternative. Finally, accountants provide cost data for customer service activities, such as warranty and repair costs and the costs of goods returned. Managers compare these costs to the benefits generated by better customer service. As you can see, cost management is important throughout the value chain.

Note that customer focus is at the center of Exhibit 3-5. Each value-chain function should focus on activities that create value for the customer. Successful businesses never lose sight of the importance of maintaining a focus on the needs of their customers. For example, one of the main principles in **Starbucks**' mission statement is to "develop enthusiastically satisfied customers all of the time." Customers are also the focus at **Wal-Mart**, as explained by Sam Walton, founder and former chairman:

There is only one boss—the customer. Customers can fire everybody in the company from the chairman on down, simply by spending their money somewhere else.

The value chain and the concepts of adding value and focusing on the customer are essential for success. Therefore, we will return to the value chain and use it as a focus for discussion throughout this book.

Making Managerial Decisions

Measuring costs at various stages of the value chain is important to **Starbucks**. Suppose that you are a Starbucks manager or accountant. For each of the following activities, indicate the value-chain function that is being performed and what accounting information might be helpful to managers in the function:

1. Process engineers investigate methods to reduce the time to roast coffee beans and to better preserve their flavor.
2. A direct-to-your-home mail-order system is established to sell custom-blended coffees.
3. Arabica coffee beans are purchased and transported to company processing plants.
4. Focus groups investigate the feasibility of a new line of Frappuccino drinks.
5. A telephone hotline is established for mail-order customers to call with questions and comments on the quality and speed of delivery.
6. Each company-owned retail store undertakes a campaign to provide information to customers about the processes used to make its coffee products.

Answers

1. Research and development or design. Both the generation of ideas for new processes and the design of new production processes are important parts of the value chain. Managers need the costs of various possible production processes to decide among the alternatives.

2. Distribution. This provides an additional way to deliver products to customers. Managers need information on the costs of a mail-order system to compare to the added profit from mail-order sales.
3. Production. Starbucks purchases only premium beans, but the company is still concerned about the purchase price of beans and transportation. These are part of product costs incurred during production.
4. Research and development or marketing. These costs (mostly wages) are incurred prior to management's final decision to design and produce a new product. Predicted revenues and costs from the Frappuccino market can help managers design a drink that is both marketable and profitable.
5. Customer service. These costs include all expenditures made after Starbucks has delivered the product to the customer; in this case, Starbucks obtains feedback on the quality and speed of delivery. Managers will trade off the cost of the hotline and the value of the information generated from the calls.
6. Marketing. These costs are for activities that enhance the existing or potential customers' awareness and opinion of the product. Like many advertising expenses, it is easy to estimate the costs of such a program but hard to quantify the benefits.

Accounting's Position in the Organization

How do management accountants fit into an organizational structure? Consider the following four work activities of management accountants:

- Collecting and compiling information
- Preparing standardized reports
- Interpreting and analyzing information
- Being involved in decision making

The role of management accountants in organizations is evolving. Management accountants are spending less time on the first two, data collection and reporting activities, and more time on the last two, analysis and decision-making activities. In essence, the management accountant is becoming an internal consultant on information-related issues—that is, an advisor for managers about what information is available, what additional information would be useful, and how to analyze the information and use it in decision making.

Line and Staff Authority

As an organization grows, it must divide responsibilities among a number of managers and executives, each with specific responsibilities. **Line managers** are directly involved with making and selling the organization's products or services. Their decisions lead directly to meeting (or not meeting) the organization's objectives. In contrast, **staff managers** are advisory—they have no authority over line managers, but they support the line managers by providing information and advice. The organization chart in Exhibit 3-6 shows how a traditional manufacturing company divides responsibilities between line and staff managers. The line managers in manufacturing are supported by corporate-level staff (in sales, engineering, human resources, and finance) and by factory-level staff (in receiving, inspection, tool room, purchasing, production control, and maintenance).

Many modern organizations have abandoned the type of hierarchical structure shown in Exhibit 3-6 in favor of a "flatter" organization. For example, **W. L. Gore & Associates**, maker of GORE-TEX® and other products using fluoropolymer technologies, has gone so far as to eliminate all job titles so everyone shares the same title, "associate." Gore also limits the size of organizational units to 150 associates. In these flatter organizations, specialization by individuals is giving way to decision making by cross-functional teams. In such an organization, management accountants are still the information specialists. However, they are not isolated in one branch of the organization chart and do not sit in their offices and issue reports. Instead, the management accountants are physically located with the line managers, and they work together to determine the optimal information support for the managers. We highlight some other recent changes in the role of accountants in the Business First box on p. 104.

line managers

Managers who are directly involved with making and selling the organization's products or services.

staff managers

Managers who are advisory to the line managers. They have no authority over line managers, but they support the line managers by providing information and advice.

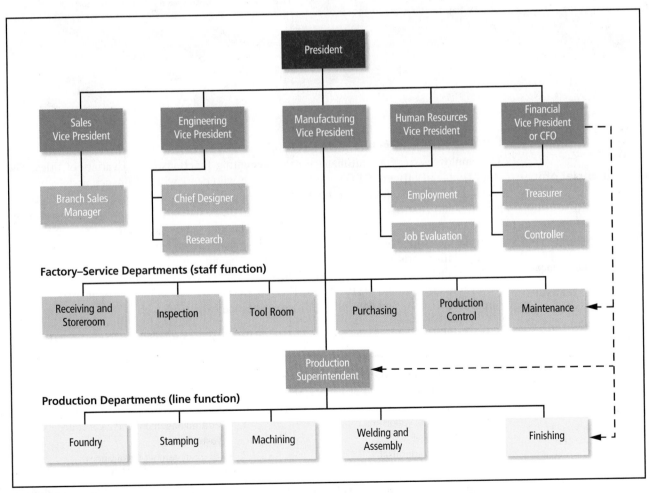

Exhibit 3-6

Partial Organization Chart of a Manufacturing Company

The Accountant's Role at the Marmon Group

The Marmon Group illustrates nearly all the reasons why management accounting is a vital and growing function in today's leading companies. Marmon, a Berkshire Hathaway company, is an international association of about 140 manufacturing, distribution, and service companies that employ more than 16,000 people and operate primarily in North America, Europe, and China. Because operations are spread over many different countries with thousands of diverse products and services (such as workers' gloves, water coolers, railroad tank cars, medical products, and credit services for banks), managers at Marmon make extensive use of management accounting information when undertaking important decisions.

What exactly is the role of management accountants at Marmon? According to Jim Smith, Marmon's former director of cost management, "The role of the management accountant is changing dramatically in most of our companies." In the past, Marmon's management accountants were basically clerical workers who spent most of their time analyzing monthly cost variances. Now, however, Marmon's management accountants work closely with operating and sales managers, providing cost information in a format that makes sense to those managers. Says Smith, "In the past few years the management accountant has become much more of a financial and business strategy adviser to senior management. Operating and sales managers are demanding meaningful cost information, and management accountants are helping them see how their actions affect costs and the bottom line."

Management accountants have become more important to Marmon because recessions and foreign competition have awakened the understanding in most managers that managing costs is an important function. Measurement of product costs or the cost of servicing a particular customer has become essential to Marmon's profitability.

"To help manage costs," says Smith, "accountants and managers are shying away from using one cost, often the cost used for financial reporting purposes, as the only important cost." Instead, they are now using costs relevant for each specific decision. As Smith said, "Depending on the decision, any of the cost methods described in *Introduction to Management Accounting* are relevant." He believes this is a very positive change, "since it allows and, in fact, requires the management accountant to understand all of the functions in a business and how each one adds value to the product or service."

Source: The Marmon Group Web site (www.marmon.com); discussions with James Smith, former director of cost management, the Marmon Group.

Controller and Treasurer Functions

chief financial officer (CFO)

The top executive who deals with all finance and accounting issues in an organization. The CFO generally oversees the accounting function.

treasurer

The executive who is concerned mainly with the company's financial matters, such as raising and managing cash.

controller (comptroller)

The accounting officer of an organization who deals mainly with operating matters, such as aiding management decision making.

The employees carrying out management accounting functions have a variety of titles. The **chief financial officer (CFO)**, the top executive who deals with all finance and accounting issues in an organization, oversees the accounting function in most organizations. Both the treasurer and controller generally report to the CFO, as shown in Exhibit 3-6. The **treasurer** is concerned mainly with the company's financial matters such as raising and managing cash, while the **controller** (also called **comptroller** in many government organizations) is concerned mainly with operating matters such as aiding management decision making. In a small company, one person may perform both treasury and controllership functions. Nevertheless, it is useful to differentiate the two roles. The Financial Executives Institute, an association of corporate treasurers and controllers, distinguishes the two as follows:

Controllership

1. Planning for control
2. Reporting and interpreting
3. Evaluating and consulting
4. Tax administration
5. Government reporting
6. Protection of assets
7. Economic appraisal

Treasurership

1. Provision of capital
2. Investor relations
3. Short-term financing
4. Banking and custody
5. Credit management and cash collections
6. Investments
7. Risk management (insurance)

Management accounting is the primary means of implementing the first three functions of controllership, including advice and help in budgeting, analyzing variances, pricing, and making special decisions.

Adaptation to Change

Businesses in the twenty-first century differ from those in the twentieth century. Markets have become more competitive, and access to information has become more important. Many companies today derive their competitive advantage from their information, not their physical facilities. Companies such as **Amazon.com** and **Netflix** pride themselves on managing the information obtained from their customers and suppliers. Such companies work to continually improve their accounting information. The information that supported traditional companies in the 1980s and 1990s does not adequately support the modern business environment.

Objective 6

Identify current trends in management accounting.

We next discuss four major business trends that are influencing management accounting today:

1. Shift from a manufacturing-based to a service-based economy in the United States
2. Increased global competition
3. Advances in technology
4. Changes in business process management

Service Sector

Accountants in manufacturing organizations developed many of the basic ideas of management accounting. These ideas, however, have evolved so that they apply to all types of organizations, including service and nonprofit organizations. **Service organizations**, for our purposes, are organizations that do not make or sell tangible goods but instead provide other forms of value. Public accounting firms, law firms, management consultants, real estate firms, transportation companies, banks, insurance companies, and hotels are examples of profit-seeking service organizations. Most nonprofit organizations, such as hospitals, schools, libraries, museums, and government agencies, are also service organizations.

service organizations
Organizations that do not make or sell tangible goods but instead provide other forms of value.

Common characteristics of service organizations include the following:

1. *Labor is a major component of costs:* The highest proportions of expenses in service organizations, such as schools and law firms, are typically wages, salaries, and payroll-related costs, not the costs relating to the use of equipment and physical facilities.
2. *Output is usually difficult to measure:* Because service outputs are intangible, they are often hard to measure. For example, the output of a university might be defined as the number of degrees granted, but many contend that the real output is the knowledge and beliefs the students develop during their time at the university.
3. *Service organizations cannot store their major inputs and outputs:* Services cannot usually be stockpiled. For example, an airline cannot save an empty airline seat for a later flight, and a hotel's available labor force and rooms are either used or unused as each day passes.

The service sector now accounts for more than 80% of the employment in the United States. Service industries are extremely competitive, and their managers increasingly rely on accounting information. Many examples in this book are from service companies.

Managers and accountants in service companies, whether profit-seeking or nonprofit organizations, have much in common. They raise and spend money. They prepare budgets and design and implement control systems. They have an obligation to use resources wisely. Used intelligently, accounting information contributes to efficient operations and helps organizations achieve their objectives.

Simplicity is the watchword for accounting systems in service industries and nonprofit organizations. Why? Because many of the decision makers using these systems, such as physicians, professors, or government officials, are too busy to try to grapple with a complex system. For them to use the information, it must be in a form that is easy to understand. In fact, simplicity is an important consideration in the design of any accounting system. Complexity generates costs of gathering and interpreting data, and the costs of complexity often exceed the prospective benefits.

Global Competition

Global competition has increased in recent years as many countries have lowered international barriers to trade, such as tariffs and duties. In addition, there has been a worldwide trend toward deregulation. The result has been a shift in the balance of economic power in the world.

electronic commerce (e-commerce)

Conducting business online.

business-to-consumer (B2C)

Electronic commerce from business to consumer.

business-to-business (B2B)

Electronic commerce from one business to another business.

enterprise resource planning (ERP) systems

Integrated information systems that support all functional areas of a company.

eXtensible Business Reporting Language (XBRL)

An XML-based accounting language that helps communicate financial information electronically.

business process reengineering

The fundamental rethinking and radical redesign of business processes to improve performance in areas such as cost, quality, service, and speed.

computer-aided design (CAD)

The use of computer technology for the design of real or virtual objects.

computer-aided manufacturing (CAM)

The use of computer-based software tools in manufacturing or prototyping.

computer-integrated manufacturing (CIM) systems

Systems that use computer-aided design, computer-aided manufacturing, robots, and computer-controlled machines.

just-in-time (JIT) philosophy

A philosophy to eliminate waste by reducing the time products spend in the production process and eliminating the time products spend on activities that do not add value.

Nowhere has this been more evident than in the United States. To regain their competitive edge, many U.S. companies redesigned their accounting systems to provide more accurate and timely information about the cost of activities, products, or services. Improved cost information helps managers better understand and predict the effects of their decisions.

Advances in Technology

The dominant influence on management accounting over the past two decades has been technological change, affecting both the production and the use of accounting information. The increasing capabilities and decreasing cost of computer processing and storage has changed how accountants gather, store, manipulate, and report data. In many cases, databases allow managers to access data directly and to generate their own reports and analyses. Today managers and accountants work together to assure the availability of the data needed for decisions and to be sure managers know how to assemble and use the data.

Electronic commerce, or **e-commerce**—conducting business online—including both **business-to-consumer (B2C)** and **business-to-business (B2B)** transactions—continues to grow at nearly 50% a year. The growth in B2B activities is especially significant as many companies have discovered that B2B creates real savings. For example, some companies have reduced procurement processing costs by as much as 70% by automating the process.

A major effect of technology on accounting systems has been the growing use of **enterprise resource planning (ERP)** systems—integrated information systems that support all functional areas of a company. Accounting is just one part of such a system. For example, Oracle describes its JD Edwards EnterpriseOne ERP system as one that "helps you integrate all aspects of your business—including customer relationship management, enterprise asset management, enterprise resource planning, supply chain management, and supplier relationship management." Other well-known ERP system providers are SAP, Microsoft Dynamics, and The Sage Group. Accountants must work with managers throughout the organization to ensure that the ERP system provides the financial information that managers need.

Finally, the development and widespread adoption of **eXtensible Business Reporting Language (XBRL)**, an XML-based accounting language, helps communicate financial information electronically. This language is greatly influencing both internal and external reporting by making comparisons across companies much simpler.

Changes in Business Process Management

Because management accounting supports business decisions, accounting systems must adapt to changes in management practices. Some companies implement sweeping changes in operations through **business process reengineering**, the fundamental rethinking and radical redesign of business processes to improve performance in areas such as cost, quality, service, and speed. Companies reduce process time by redesigning, simplifying, and automating the production process. They use **computer-aided design (CAD)** to design products that can be manufactured efficiently and **computer-aided manufacturing (CAM)** to direct and control production equipment. **Computer-integrated manufacturing (CIM) systems** use CAD, CAM, robots, and computer-controlled machines. The costs of such a system are quite different from those of a less-automated system. Companies that install a full CIM system use very little labor. Instead, they acquire the robots and computer-controlled machines needed to perform the routine jobs that were previously accomplished by assembly-line workers.

One management change leading to increased efficiency in business processes has been the adoption of a **just-in-time (JIT) philosophy**. Originally, JIT referred to an inventory system that minimized inventories by arranging for materials and subcomponents to arrive just as they were needed for production and for goods to be made just in time to ship them to customers—no sooner and no later. But JIT has become the cornerstone of a broad management philosophy. It originated in Japanese companies such as Toyota and Kawasaki. Now many large U.S. companies use JIT, including Hewlett-Packard, Goodyear, General Motors, Intel, and Xerox, as well as many smaller firms. The essence of the JIT philosophy is to eliminate waste by (1) reducing the time that products spend in the production process and (2) eliminating the time that products spend in activities that do not add value (such as inspection and waiting time).

Another management approach focused on efficiency is **lean manufacturing**, which applies continuous process improvements to eliminate waste from the entire enterprise.

For example, Matsushita Electric's Saga plant on Japan's Kyushu island decreased the time it takes to produce a finished product from $2\frac{1}{2}$ days to 40 minutes by replacing conveyor belts with clusters of robots. As with JIT, lean ideas are now being extended beyond manufacturing to other business processes.

A focus on quality is also important in today's competitive environment. Many companies have implemented **total quality management (TQM)** initiatives. TQM minimizes costs by maximizing quality. It focuses on prevention of defects and customer satisfaction. Recently the focus on quality has shifted to **Six Sigma**, a disciplined, *data-driven approach* to eliminating defects in any process. Used by about 35% of major U.S. companies, Six Sigma is essentially a continuous process-improvement effort designed to reduce costs by improving quality. Pioneered in the 1980s by Motorola, Six Sigma has also been implemented by companies such as General Electric in the United States and Samsung in Korea to transform their business. Six Sigma seeks to ensure that internal processes are running as efficiently as possible. Staff functions, such as legal departments, also use Six Sigma today. For example, law departments in both DuPont and Tyco use Six Sigma to "improve compliance, reduce risk, contain costs, and align the law department more closely with the objectives of the business." Management accountants play a major role in Six Sigma applications as both the experts on the measurements being used and as full members of the cross-functional teams that lead the efforts.

Why do these business process changes affect management accounting? They all directly affect costs, and accountants often measure the actual cost savings, predict anticipated cost savings, and develop costs for products or services for different production environments. For example, one midwestern factory saved production time by redesigning its plant layout to reduce the distance products traveled from one operation to the next during production from 1,384 feet to just 350 feet. Accountants measured the cost the company saved by the reduced production time. As another example, a British company reduced the time to manufacture a vacuum pump from 3 weeks to 6 minutes by switching from long assembly lines to manufacturing cells that accomplish all production steps in quick succession. Again, accountants measured the benefits created by the reduced production time. In general, when companies change their production processes to accomplish economic objectives, accountants predict and measure the economic impact.

lean manufacturing

Applying continuous process improvements to eliminate waste from the entire enterprise.

total quality management (TQM)

An approach to quality that focuses on prevention of defects and on customer satisfaction.

Six Sigma

A data-driven continuous process improvement effort designed to eliminate defects and improve quality.

Making Managerial Decisions

Suppose you are a manager of a DuPont chemical plant. The plant has just undertaken a business process reengineering project and, as a result, has substantially changed its production process. It is much more automated, with newly acquired equipment replacing labor-intensive operations. The plant is also making more use of electronic commerce and moving toward a JIT inventory policy. You have a meeting with your accountant to discuss possible changes in your accounting system. What types of accounting-system changes might be warranted?

Answer

Major changes in production processes generally lead to different information needs. The old accounting system may have focused on accounting for labor, while the new system should focus on the use of the automated equipment. This will direct attention to the most important costs in the process and make sure that they are monitored and controlled. Problem-solving needs will also be different. Initially, the plant's managers will probably want comparative data on the cost of the new process versus the cost of the old. In the future, they will need information about how best to use capacity that the plant owns (the equipment) rather than how much labor to use for the planned level of production.

Implications for the Study of Management Accounting

As you read the remainder of this book, remember that accounting systems change as the world changes. Companies currently apply the techniques described in this book. However, to adapt to changes, you must understand why companies are using the techniques, not just how they are using them. Resist the temptation to simply memorize rules and techniques, and instead develop your understanding of the underlying concepts and principles. This understanding will continue to be useful no matter what new conditions you encounter.

Ethical Conduct for Professional Accountants

Objective 7

Explain why ethics and standards of ethical conduct are important to accountants.

ethics

The field that deals with human conduct in relation to what is morally good and bad, right and wrong. It is the application of values to decision making. These values include honesty, fairness, responsibility, respect, and compassion.

Business processes and accounting systems change. However, the need for accountants to maintain high ethical standards of professional conduct will never change. The Institute of Management Accountants says that **ethics** "deals with human conduct in relation to what is morally good and bad, right and wrong. It is the application of values to decision making. These values include honesty, fairness, responsibility, respect, and compassion."

We like to think of ethics as simply doing what is right. One way to decide whether an action is unethical is to ask yourself whether you would be embarrassed to read about your action in the newspaper the next day. Another warning sign that an action may be unethical is when the justification for the action is "Everybody else is doing it," the phrase Warren Buffett has described as "the five most dangerous words in business." He goes on to say that this excuse should always raise a red flag: "Why would somebody offer such a rationale for an act if there were a good reason available? Clearly the advocate harbors at least a small doubt about the act if he utilizes this verbal crutch."

Why is it so important for accountants to have integrity? Think of it this way: If you buy a car, you can see many of the quality details. Further, if something goes wrong with the car, you will certainly know it. But accounting information is different. Users can't see its quality. Users might not know for years that something was wrong with the information—probably not until it's too late to do anything about it. Thus, users rely on the integrity of accountants to assure the integrity of information. If you cannot trust the information, then it is nearly worthless.

In the remainder of this section, we discuss ethical standards and formal codes of conduct that often help resolve ethical issues. We also provide examples of clearly unethical behavior. Finally, we turn to the difficult issue of ethical dilemmas, situations where conflicting values make it unclear which is the ethical action.

Standards of Ethical Conduct

IMA Statement of Ethical Professional Practice

A code of conduct developed by the Institute of Management Accountants; this code includes competence, confidentiality, integrity, and credibility.

code of conduct

A document specifying the ethical standards of an organization.

Ethical standards require CPAs and CMAs to adhere to codes of conduct regarding competence, confidentiality, integrity, and credibility. Exhibit 3-7 contains the **IMA Statement of Ethical Professional Practice**, a code of conduct developed by the Institute of Management Accountants. Professional accounting organizations have procedures for reviewing alleged behavior that is not consistent with the standards.

The ethical organization also has policies in place to motivate ethical actions. Integrity and outspoken support for ethical standards by senior managers, in both word and deed, are the greatest motivators of ethical behavior throughout an organization. A **code of conduct**—a document specifying the ethical standards of an organization—is the centerpiece of most ethics programs. (See the Business First box, "Ethics and Corporate Codes of Conduct," on p. 111.) But having a code is not sufficient. Actual policies and practices influence behavior. This means that managers' evaluations must include an assessment of ethical conduct. Organizations cannot tolerate unethical behavior, even if it appears to lead to great financial performance. For example, Enron, WorldCom, Tyco, Global Crossing, Adelphia, Xerox, and others were accused of creating accounting entries to make their financial reports look better than their actual performances. In some cases, accountants participated in these fraudulent activities. In other cases, they simply did not step up and challenge what they surely knew (or at least should have known) was misleading information.

Fortunately, there are also many examples of accountants who stood up and reported wrongdoing to their supervisors despite the personal costs. In the spring of 2001, Sherron Watkins began working directly for Enron CFO Andrew Fastow. When she discovered the off-the-books liabilities that have now become famous, she wrote a memo to CEO Kenneth Lay and met with him personally, explaining to him "an elaborate accounting hoax." Later she discovered that, rather than the hoax being investigated, her report had generated a memo from

Members of IMA shall behave ethically. A commitment to ethical professional practice includes: overarching principles that express our values and standards that guide our conduct.

Principles

IMA's overarching ethical principles include: Honesty, Fairness, Objectivity, and Responsibility. Members shall act in accordance with these principles and shall encourage others within their organizations to adhere to them.

Standards

A member's failure to comply with the following standards may result in disciplinary action.

I Competence

Each member has a responsibility to:
1. Maintain an appropriate level of professional expertise by continually developing knowledge and skills.
2. Perform professional duties in accordance with relevant laws, regulations, and technical standards.
3. Provide decision support information and recommendations that are accurate, clear, concise, and timely.
4. Recognize and communicate professional limitations or other constraints that would preclude responsible judgment or successful performance of an activity.

II Confidentiality

Each member has a responsibility to:
1. Keep information confidential except when disclosure is authorized or legally required.
2. Inform all relevant parties regarding appropriate use of confidential information. Monitor subordinates' activities to ensure compliance.
3. Refrain from using confidential information for unethical or illegal advantage.

III Integrity

Each member has a responsibility to:
1. Mitigate actual conflicts of interest. Regularly communicate with business associates to avoid apparent conflicts of interest. Advise all parties of any potential conflicts.
2. Refrain from engaging in any conduct that would prejudice carrying out duties ethically.
3. Abstain from engaging in or supporting any activity that might discredit the profession.

IV Credibility

Each member has a responsibility to:
1. Communicate information fairly and objectively.
2. Disclose all relevant information that could reasonably be expected to influence an intended user's understanding of the reports, analyses, or recommendations.
3. Disclose delays or deficiencies in information, timeliness, processing, or internal controls in conformance with organizational policy and/or applicable law.

Resolution of Ethical Conflict

In applying the Standards of Ethical Professional Practice, you may encounter problems identifying unethical behavior or resolving an ethical conflict. When faced with ethical issues, you should follow your organization's established policies on the resolution of such conflict. If these policies do not resolve the ethical conflict, you should consider the following courses of action:

1. Discuss the issue with your immediate supervisor except when it appears that the supervisor is involved. In that case, present the issue to the next level. If you cannot achieve a satisfactory resolution, submit the issue to the next management level. If your immediate superior is the chief executive officer or equivalent, the acceptable reviewing authority may be a group such as the audit committee, executive committee, board of directors, board of trustees, or owners. Contact with levels above the immediate superior should be initiated only with your superior's knowledge, assuming he or she is not involved. Communication of such problems to authorities or individuals not employed or engaged by the organization is not considered appropriate, unless you believe there is a clear violation of the law.
2. Clarify relevant ethical issues by initiating a confidential discussion with an IMA Ethics Counselor or other impartial advisor to obtain a better understanding of possible courses of action.
3. Consult your own attorney as to legal obligations and rights concerning the ethical conflict.

Source: IMA (Institute of Management Accountants, www.imanet.org). Adapted with permission.

Exhibit 3-7
IMA Statement of Ethical Professional Practice

Enron's legal counsel titled "Confidential Employee Matter" that included the following: "... how to manage the case with the employee who made the sensitive report.... Texas law does not currently protect corporate whistle-blowers...." In addition, her boss confiscated her hard drive, and she was demoted. In the end, Watkins proved to be right. Watkins made the ethical decision to reveal the wrongdoings and did not look back. In June 2002, Cynthia Cooper, vice president of internal audit for WorldCom, told the company's board of directors that fraudulent accounting entries had turned a $662 million loss into a $2.4 billion profit in 2001. This disclosure led to additional discoveries totaling $9 billion in erroneous accounting entries—the largest accounting fraud in history. Cooper was proud of WorldCom and highly committed to its success. Nevertheless, when she and her internal audit team discovered the unethical actions of superiors she admired, she did not hesitate to do the right thing.

Most companies make ethics a top priority. For example, Starbucks includes ethical principles in the first line of its mission statement: "To establish Starbucks as the premier purveyor of the finest coffee in the world while maintaining our uncompromising principles as we grow." Ben & Jerry's, the ice cream company, has a reputation for high ethical standards that focus on its external social obligations, as recognized in its mission statement: "To operate the Company in a way that actively recognizes the central role that business plays in the structure of society by initiating innovative ways to improve the quality of life of a broad community—local, national, and international." There are many more companies with high ethical standards than there are with ethical violations, though the latter receive most of the publicity.

Ethical Dilemmas

The ethical standards of the profession leave much room for individual interpretation and judgment. A first step is to ask two questions: Is this action unethical? Would it be unethical not to take this action? If the answers to these questions are clear, then the ethical action is clear. For example, if WorldCom's accountants had asked whether their recording of expenses as assets was unethical, they would have answered "yes." However, a manager's ethical choice becomes more complex when there are no legal guidelines or clear-cut ethical standards. Ethical dilemmas exist when managers must choose an alternative and there are (1) significant value conflicts among differing interests, (2) several alternatives are justifiable, and (3) there are significant consequences for stakeholders in the situation.

Suppose you are an accountant and your boss has asked you to supply the company's banker with a profit forecast for the coming year. A badly needed bank loan rides on the prediction. Your boss is absolutely convinced that profits will be at least $500,000—anything less than that and the loan is not likely to be approved.

Your analysis reveals three possible outcomes: First, if the planned introduction of a new product goes extraordinarily well, profits will exceed $500,000. Second, if there is a modestly successful introduction, there will be a $100,000 profit. You believe this is the most likely outcome. Third, if the product fails, the company stands to lose $600,000. Without the loan, the new product cannot be taken to the market, and there is no way the company can avoid a loss for the year. Bankruptcy is a real possibility.

What forecast would you make? The ethical dilemma arises here because of uncertainty and disagreement about the prospects for the new product. If your boss is correct that profits will exceed $500,000, it would be unethical to make a forecast of less than $500,000. Such a forecast seems to guarantee that the loan will not be obtained, leading to financial problems, perhaps even bankruptcy. This would hurt stockholders, management, employees, suppliers, and customers. On the other hand, if you are correct that the most likely outcome is a profit of $100,000, a forecast of $500,000 may not be fair and objective. It may mislead the bank.

There is no easy answer to this dilemma. It is one of those gray areas where either action includes risks. But remember that a series of gray areas can create a black area. That is, a series of actions that push the boundary of ethical behavior can add up to a clearly unethical situation. Accountants must draw the line someplace, and it is usually better to err on the side of full disclosure than to withhold important information. Enron repeatedly pushed boundaries by reporting only optimistic information. If its managers had done this once or twice, it might not have created a problem. But the pattern of exclusively optimistic projections eventually deteriorated into completely unrealistic, and unethical, projections.

Business First

Ethics and Corporate Codes of Conduct

The Sarbanes-Oxley Act of 2002 requires companies "to disclose whether or not, and if not, the reason therefore, such issuer has adopted a code of ethics for senior financial officers, applicable to its principal financial officer and comptroller or principal accounting officer, or persons performing similar functions." This has created increased interest in corporate codes of conduct. However, a code of conduct means different things to different companies. Some of the items included in companies' codes of conduct include maintaining a dress code, avoiding illegal drugs, following instructions of superiors, being reliable and prompt, maintaining confidentiality, not accepting personal gifts from stakeholders as a result of company role, avoiding racial or sexual discrimination, avoiding conflict of interest, complying with laws and regulations, not using an organization's property for personal use, and reporting illegal or questionable activity. Even before Enron and other corporate scandals, more than 80% of U.S. companies had a code of conduct, according to a survey by the Financial Executives Institute (FEI). But the codes differed in type and in level of enforcement.

One company had only one rule: "Don't do anything you would be embarrassed to read about in tomorrow's newspaper." Others have detailed lists of dos and don'ts. Some companies use consulting firms to advise them on their codes. Although the codes and their development differ, the goal is generally the same—to motivate employees to act with integrity.

To encourage development of codes of conduct, the FEI includes examples of codes on its Web site. Two extremes among those presented are those of Wiremold and CSX Corporation. Wiremold has a simple, seven-point code: (1) respect others, (2) tell the truth, (3) be fair, (4) try new ideas, (5) ask why, (6) keep your promises, and (7) do your share. In contrast, CSX has 26 paragraphs detailing expectations

of employees under the following headings: Employee Relationships and Conflicts of Interest, Political Contributions and Public Service Involvement, Misrepresentations and False Statements, Employee Discrimination and Harassment, Competition, and Safety and the Environment.

FEI also lists inquiries about corporate codes of conduct among the questions to expect at shareholder annual meetings. As stated on FEI's Web site, "If there's any single issue that overlays the recent corporate and accounting scandals, it is a deficiency in ethical behavior among some company executives. Corporate governance consultants and academics agree that a company needs to have a code of conduct and ethics in place, by which the entire staff and management should conduct themselves in relation to their business activities.... In all probability, shareholders will ask questions relating to board committees or subcommittees focused on ethical matters."

While having a code of conduct is important, it is not sufficient. After all, Enron's code of conduct specified that "business is to be conducted in compliance... with the highest professional and ethical standards." Top management must set the tone and get out the message. Management must recognize and reward honesty and integrity. As Clarence Otis, CFO of Darden Restaurants, says, "Our senior managers care about honesty and integrity and doing things right, and that influences how they do their job." The corporate culture, more than codes of conduct, is the real influence on the ethical climate of an organization. Codes of conduct can be a part, but only a part, of developing a culture of integrity.

Sources: Sarbanes-Oxley Act of 2002, HR 3763; RedHawk Productions Web site (http://redhawkproductions.com); Financial Executives Institute Web site (www.fei.org); D. Blank, "A Matter of Ethics," *Internal Auditor*, February 2003, pp. 27–31; Enron Corporation, *2000 Corporate Responsibility Report*, p. 3.

To maintain high ethical standards, accountants and others need to recognize situations that create pressures for unethical behavior. Four such temptations, summarized in *Financial Executive*, are as follows:

1. ***Emphasis on short-term results.*** This may have been the largest issue in the recent spate of ethical breakdowns. If "making the numbers" is goal number one, accountants may do whatever is necessary to produce the expected profit numbers.

2. ***Ignoring the small stuff.*** Most ethical compromises start out small. The first step may seem insignificant, but large misdeeds are often the result of many small steps. Toleration of even small lapses can lead to large problems.

3. ***Economic cycles.*** A down market can reveal what an up market conceals. When Enron was flying high at the turn of the century, no one seemed to question its financial reports. When the economy took a downward turn, managers made ethical compromises to keep pace with expectations of an up market. The result was a huge crisis when scrutiny revealed many questionable practices. Similarly, later in the decade companies such as AIG, Fannie Mae, and Freddie Mac were accused of accounting compromises after the

economy started to sour in 2008. Companies need to be especially vigilant to prevent ethical lapses in good times when such lapses are more easily concealed, and thereby avoid revelation of lapses in bad times when their effects are especially damaging.

4. *Accounting rules.* Accounting rules have become more complex and less intuitive, making abuse of the rules harder to identify. Ethical accountants do not just meet the "letter of the law," they seek full and fair disclosure—conveying to users the real economic performance and financial position of the company.

Few organizations are intentionally unethical. Even **Arthur Andersen**, the accounting firm destroyed by failed audits at Enron, **Sunbeam**, **Global Crossing**, and others, had a formal ethical structure, including a partner in charge of ethics. Nevertheless, other pressures, especially the pressure for growing revenues, overrode some of the ethical controls and caused bad decisions.

Resolution of Ethical Conflicts

Ethical dilemmas also arise when you only observe, rather than commit, unethical behavior. If you discover unethical behavior in an organization, you are obligated to try to halt that behavior. However, you still have confidentiality issues to confront. The section on Resolution of Ethical Conflict in Exhibit 3-7 provides guidance. Most often you can bring the issue to the attention of your supervisor or a special ethics officer (often called an ombudsperson) in the organization. However, if there is not an ethics officer and you suspect your supervisor is involved in unethical activity, your decision becomes more complex. As was the case for Cynthia Cooper at WorldCom described on p. 110, you may need to go all the way to the board of directors. If the case involves legal issues and the board is not responsive, approaching the Securities and Exchange Commission (the body that regulates corporate reporting) or other legal authorities may be necessary.

Summary Problem for Your Review

PROBLEM

Yang Electronics Company (YEC) developed a high-speed, low-cost copying machine marketed primarily for home use. However, as YEC customers learned how easy and inexpensive it was to make copies with it, sales to small businesses soared. Unfortunately, the heavier use by these companies caused breakdowns in a component of the equipment that had been designed only for light use. The copiers were warranted for 2 years, regardless of the amount of usage. Consequently, YEC began to experience high costs for replacing the damaged component.

As the quarterly meeting of YEC's board of directors approached, the CFO asked Mark Chua, assistant controller, to prepare a report on the situation. It was hard to predict the exact effects, but it seemed that many business customers were starting to switch away from the YEC copier to more expensive copiers sold by competitors. It was also clear that the increased warranty costs would significantly affect YEC's profitability. Mark summarized the situation in writing as best he could for the board.

Alice Martinez, YEC's CFO, was concerned about the impact of the report on the board. She did not disagree with the analysis, but she thought it would make management look bad and might even lead the board to discontinue the product. She was convinced from conversations with the head of engineering that the copier could be slightly redesigned to meet the needs of high-volume users, so discontinuing it may pass up a potentially profitable opportunity.

Martinez called Chua into her office and asked him to delete the part of his report dealing with the component failures. She said it was all right to mention this orally to the board, noting that engineering is nearing a solution to the problem. However, Chua felt strongly that such a revision in his report would mislead the board about a potentially significant negative impact on the company's earnings.

Use the IMA Statement of Ethical Professional Practice in Exhibit 3-7 to explain why Martinez's request to Chua is unethical. How should Chua resolve this situation?

SOLUTION

Martinez's request violates requirements for competence, integrity, and credibility. It violates competence because she is asking Chua to prepare a report that is not complete and clear, and omits potentially relevant information. Therefore, the board will not have all the information it should to make a decision about the component failure problem.

The request violates integrity because the revised report may subvert the attainment of the organization's objectives to achieve Martinez's objectives. Management accountants are specifically responsible for communicating unfavorable as well as favorable information.

Finally, the revised report would not be credible. It would not disclose all relevant information that could be expected to influence the board's understanding of operations and, therefore, its decisions.

Chua's responsibility is to discuss this issue with increasingly higher levels of authority within YEC. First, he should let Martinez know about his misgivings. Possibly the issue can be resolved by her withdrawing the request. If not, he should inform her that he intends to take up the matter with the company president, and even the board, if necessary, until the issue is resolved. So that Chua does not violate the standard of confidentiality, he should not discuss the matter with persons outside of YEC.

Highlights to Remember

1. **Explain why accounting is essential for decision makers and managers.** Decision makers in all functional areas of an organization must understand the accounting information that they are using in their decisions and the incentives created by accounting systems.

2. **Describe the major users and uses of accounting information.** Internal managers use accounting information for making short-term planning and control decisions, for making nonroutine decisions, and for formulating overall policies and long-range plans. External users, such as investors and regulators, use published financial statements to make investment decisions, regulatory rulings, and many other decisions. Managers use accounting information to answer scorekeeping, attention-directing, and problem-solving questions.

3. **Explain the role of budgets and performance reports in planning and control.** Budgets and performance reports are essential tools for planning and control. Budgets result from the planning process. Managers use them to translate the organization's goals into action. A performance report compares actual results to the budget. Managers use these reports to monitor, evaluate, and reward performance and, thus, exercise control.

4. **Describe the cost-benefit and behavioral issues involved in designing an accounting system.** Management accounting information systems should be judged by a cost-benefit criterion—the benefits of better decisions and better incentives should exceed the cost of the system. Behavioral factors—how the system affects managers and their decisions—greatly influence the benefits from a management accounting system.

5. **Discuss the role accountants play in the company's value-chain functions.** Accountants play a key role in planning and control. Throughout the company's value chain, accountants gather and report cost and revenue information for decision makers.

6. **Identify current trends in management accounting.** Many factors have caused changes in accounting systems in recent years. Most significant are a shift to a service-based economy, increased global competition, advances in technology, and changed business processes. Without continuous adaptation and improvement, accounting systems would soon become obsolete.

7. **Explain why ethics and standards of ethical conduct are important to accountants.** Users of accounting information expect accountants to adhere to high standards of ethical conduct. Most users cannot directly assess the quality of that information, and if they cannot rely on accountants to produce unbiased information, the information will have little value to them. That is why professional accounting organizations, as well as most companies, have codes of ethical conduct. Many ethical dilemmas, however, require more than codes and rules. They call for value judgments, not the simple application of standards.

Accounting Vocabulary

accounting system, p. 95
attention directing, p. 95
behavioral implications, p. 99
budget, p. 97
business process reengineering,
   p. 106
business-to-business (B2B),
   p. 106
business-to-consumer (B2C),
   p. 106
certified management
   accountant (CMA), p. 94
certified public accountant
   (CPA), p. 93
chartered accountant (CA),
   p. 93
chief financial officer (CFO),
   p. 104
code of conduct, p. 108
computer-aided design (CAD),
   p. 106
computer-aided manufacturing
   (CAM), p. 106

computer-integrated
   manufacturing (CIM)
   systems, p. 106
control, p. 96
controller (comptroller), p. 104
cost-benefit balance, p. 99
decision making, p. 95
electronic commerce
   (e-commerce), p. 106
enterprise resource planning
   (ERP) system, p. 106
ethics, p. 108
eXtensible Business Reporting
   Language (XBRL), p. 106
financial accounting, p. 93
Foreign Corrupt Practices Act,
   p. 98
generally accepted accounting
   principles (GAAP), p. 98
IMA Statement of Ethical
   Professional Practice,
   p. 108
Institute of Management
   Accountants (IMA), p. 93
internal auditors, p. 98

internal controls, p. 98
just-in-time (JIT) philosophy,
   p. 106
lean manufacturing, p. 107
line managers, p. 103
management accounting,
   p. 93
management audit, p. 98
management by exception,
   p. 97
performance reports, p. 97
planning, p. 96
problem solving, p. 95
product life cycle, p. 99
Sarbanes-Oxley Act, p. 98
scorekeeping, p. 95
service organizations, p. 105
Six Sigma, p. 107
staff managers, p. 103
total quality management
   (TQM), p. 107
treasurer, p. 104
value chain, p. 100
variances, p. 97

MyAccountingLab Fundamental Assignment Material

The assignment material for each chapter is divided into two groups: fundamental and additional. The fundamental assignment material consists of two sets of parallel problems that convey the essential concepts and techniques of the chapter. The additional assignment material covers the chapter in more detail and includes questions, critical thinking exercises, exercises, problems, cases, a problem based on Nike's 10-K, an Excel application exercise, a collaborative learning exercise, and an Internet exercise.

3-A1 Scorekeeping, Attention Directing, and Problem Solving

For each of the following activities, identify the primary function that the accountant is performing—scorekeeping, attention directing, or problem solving—and explain why it best fits that category.

1. Preparing a schedule of depreciation for forklift trucks in the receiving department of a General Electric factory in Scotland
2. Analyzing, for a Sony production superintendent, the impact on costs of purchasing some new assembly equipment
3. Preparing a scrap report for the finishing department of a Toyota parts factory
4. Interpreting why the Colville Timber Resource Company did not adhere to its production schedule
5. Explaining the stamping department's performance report
6. Preparing a monthly statement of European sales for the Ford Motor Company's vice president of marketing
7. Preparing, for the manager of production control of a Mittal Steel plant, a cost comparison of two computerized manufacturing control systems
8. Interpreting variances on the performance report for the University of Michigan's purchasing department.

9. Analyzing, for an **Airbus** manufacturing manager, the desirability of having some parts for the A380 airplane made in Korea

10. Preparing the budget for the dermatology department of **Providence Hospital**

3-A2 Management by Exception

Beta Alpha Psi, the accounting honorary fraternity, held a homecoming party. The fraternity expected attendance of 80 persons and prepared the following budget:

Room rental	$ 170
Food	660
Entertainment	570
Decorations	210
Total	$1,610

After Beta Alpha Psi paid all the bills for the party, the total cost came to $1,885, or $275 over budget. Details are $170 for room rental; $875 for food; $570 for entertainment; and $270 for decorations. Ninety-six persons attended the party.

1. Prepare a performance report for the party that shows how actual costs differed from the budget. That is, include in your report the budgeted amounts, actual amounts, and variances.

2. Suppose the fraternity uses a management-by-exception rule. Which costs deserve further examination? Why?

3-A3 Professional Ethics

Exhibit 3-7 on page 109 lists four main categories of ethical standards for management accountants: competence, confidentiality, integrity, and credibility. For each of the following situations, indicate which of these four should influence the manager and what the appropriate action should be:

1. At a dinner party, a guest asked a **General Mills** manager how a major new cereal was doing. The manager had just read a report that said sales lagged much below expectation. What should he say?

2. Felix just graduated from business school with an accounting major and joined the controller's department of Pioneer Enterprises. His boss asked him to evaluate a market analysis for a potential new product prepared by the marketing department. Felix knows very little about the industry, and he never had a class to teach him how to make a market analysis. Should he just do the best he can on the analysis without asking for help?

3. Mary Sue prepared a budget for a division of Southeastern Electronics. Her supervisor, the division manager, was not happy that she included results for an exciting new product that was to be introduced in a month. He asked her to leave the results for the product out of the budget. That way, the financial results for the product would boost actual profits well above the amount budgeted, resulting in favorable reviews for the division and its managers. What should Mary Sue do?

3-B1 Scorekeeping, Attention Directing, and Problem Solving

For each of the following activities, identify the function the accountant is performing—scorekeeping, attention directing, or problem solving. Explain each of your answers.

1. Estimating the operating costs and outputs that could be expected for each of two large metal-stamping machines offered for sale by different manufacturers; only one of these machines is to be acquired by your company

2. Recording daily material purchase vouchers

3. Analyzing the expected costs of acquiring and using each of two alternate types of welding equipment

4. Preparing a report of overtime labor costs by production department

5. Estimating the costs of moving corporate headquarters to another city

6. Interpreting increases in nursing costs per patient-day in a hospital

7. Analyzing deviations from the budget of the factory maintenance department

8. Assisting in a study by the manufacturing vice president to determine whether to buy certain parts needed in large quantities for manufacturing products or to acquire facilities for manufacturing these parts

9. Preparing estimated costs for a new marketing campaign
10. Recording overtime hours of the product finishing department
11. Compiling data for a report showing the ratio of advertising expenses to sales for each branch store
12. Investigating reasons for increased returns and allowances for drugs purchased by a hospital
13. Preparing a schedule of fuel costs by months and government departments
14. Computing and recording end-of-year adjustments for expired fire insurance on the factory warehouse

3-B2 Management by Exception

Cost of fireworks	$40,000
Labor cost	10,000
Other costs	7,000
Total costs	$57,000

The Skokomish Indian tribe sells fireworks for the 5 weeks preceding July 4. The tribe's stand on Highway 101 near Hoodsport had budgeted sales of $80,000. Expected expenses were as follows: Actual sales were $79,440, almost equal to the budget. The tribe spent $39,400 for fireworks, $13,100 for labor, and $6,900 for other costs.

1. Compute budgeted profit and actual profit.
2. Prepare a performance report to help identify those costs that were significantly different from the budget.
3. Suppose the tribe uses a management-by-exception rule. What costs deserve further explanation? Why?

3-B3 Ethical Code of Conduct

According to the **Financial Executives Institute**, "corporate governance consultants and academics agree that a company needs to have a code of conduct" for its employees. Most companies, even many of those who experienced ethical breakdowns, have such a code. Answer the following questions about corporate codes of conduct.

1. What is a corporate code of conduct?
2. What types of issues are covered in a corporate code of conduct? At what level of detail?

MyAccountingLab

3. In some cases, codes of conduct were not effective. What, besides simply having a code, is necessary for a code of conduct to be effective?

Additional Assignment Material

QUESTIONS

3-1 Who uses information from an accounting system?

3-2 "The emphases of financial accounting and management accounting differ." Explain.

3-3 "The field is less sharply defined. There is heavier use of economics, decision sciences, and behavioral sciences." Identify the branch of accounting described in the quotation.

3-4 Distinguish among scorekeeping, attention directing, and problem solving.

3-5 "Generally accepted accounting principles (GAAP) assist the development of management accounting systems." Do you agree? Explain.

3-6 "The Foreign Corrupt Practices Act applies to bribes paid outside the United States." Do you agree? Explain.

3-7 Why is the Sarbanes-Oxley Act controversial?

3-8 Why is integrity so important to accountants?

3-9 "Integrity is more important for business professionals than it is for business students." Do you agree? Explain.

3-10 Give three examples of service organizations. What distinguishes service organizations from other types of organizations?

3-11 What two major considerations affect the design of all accounting systems? Explain each.

3-12 "The accounting system is intertwined with operating management. Business operations would be in a hopeless tangle without the recordkeeping that is so often regarded with disdain." Do you agree? Explain, giving examples.

3-13 Distinguish among a budget, a performance report, and a variance.

3-14 "Management by exception means abdicating management responsibility for planning and control." Do you agree? Explain.

3-15 Why are accountants concerned about product life cycles?

3-16 Name the six primary business functions (excluding support functions) that make up the value chain, and briefly describe each.

3-17 "Accountants in every company should measure and report on every function in the company's value chain." Do you agree? Explain.

3-18 Distinguish between the duties of line managers and staff managers.

3-19 The role of management accountants is changing, especially in companies with a "flatter" organizational structure. What are some of the changes?

3-20 Does every company have both a controller and a treasurer? Explain.

3-21 Describe the two parts of the qualifying examination for becoming a CMA.

3-22 "The problem with accounting is that accountants never get to become top managers such as CEOs." Do you agree? Explain.

3-23 How are changes in technology affecting management accounting?

3-24 What is the essence of the JIT philosophy?

3-25 Briefly describe how a change in a plant's layout can make its operation more efficient.

3-26 Standards of ethical conduct for management accountants have been divided into four major responsibilities. Describe each of the four in 20 words or fewer.

3-27 "Why are there ethical dilemmas? I thought accountants had standards that specified what ethical behavior is." Discuss this quote.

CRITICAL THINKING EXERCISES

3-28 Finance and Management Accounting

Often there is confusion between the roles played by the controller and treasurer in an organization. In many small companies, a single person performs activities related to both functions.

Distinguish between the controller and the treasurer functions by listing typical activities that are associated with each.

3-29 Accounting's Position in the Organization: Controller and Treasurer

For each of the following activities, indicate whether it is more likely to be performed by the controller or by the treasurer. Explain each answer.

1. Prepare divisional financial statements.
2. Help managers prepare budgets.
3. Advise which alternative action is least costly.
4. Meet with financial analysts from Wall Street.
5. Arrange short-term financing.
6. Prepare tax returns.
7. Arrange insurance coverage.
8. Prepare credit checks on customers.

3-30 Marketing and Management Accounting

A cross-functional team of managers, including the management accountant, performs each of the following activities. However, depending on the nature of the decision to be made, one functional area will take the leadership role. Which of these activities is primarily a marketing decision? What would the management accountant contribute to each of the marketing decisions?

1. **Porsche Motor Company** must decide whether to buy a part for one of its cars or to make the part at one of its plants.
2. **Airbus** must decide the price to charge for spare parts it sells over the Internet using its Spare Parts Web site.
3. **St. Luke's Hospital** must decide how to finance the purchase of expensive new medical analysis equipment.
4. **Amazon.com** must forecast the impact on video sales of a new advertising program.
5. **Mission Foods**, a leading producer and distributor of tortillas to retail and food service industries, must decide whether to accept a special order for tortilla chips by a large, national retail chain.
6. **Target Stores** must decide whether to close one of its retail stores that is currently operating at a loss.

3-31 Production and Management Accounting

A cross-functional team of managers, including the management accountant, performed each of the following activities. However, depending on the nature of the decision to be made, one functional area will take the leadership role. Which of these activities is primarily a production decision? What would the management accountant contribute to each of the production decisions?

1. **Saab Automobile AB** must decide whether to buy a part for one of its cars or to make the part at one of its plants.
2. **Boeing Company** must decide the price for spare parts it sells over the Internet using its Spare Parts Web site.
3. **St. Mary's Hospital** must decide how to finance the purchase of expensive new medical analysis equipment.
4. **Amazon.com** must forecast how a new advertising program will affect DVD sales.
5. **Mission Foods**, a leading producer and distributor of tortillas to retail and food service industries, must decide whether to accept a special order for tortilla chips by a large, national retail chain.
6. **Kmart** must evaluate its overall vision and strategic goals in the light of competitive pressures from **Target**, **Sears**, and **Wal-Mart**.
7. **Dell Computers** must decide whether to spend money on training workers to perform setups and changeovers faster. This will free up capacity to be used to make more computers without purchasing more equipment.
8. **Ford Motor Company** must decide whether to keep or replace 4-year-old equipment used in one of its Escape plants.

EXERCISES

3-32 Management Accounting and Financial Accounting

Consider the following short descriptions. Indicate whether each of the following descriptions more closely relates to a major feature of financial accounting or management accounting:

1. Field is less sharply defined
2. Provides internal consulting advice to managers
3. Has less flexibility
4. Is characterized by detailed reports
5. Has a future orientation
6. Is constrained by GAAP
7. Behavioral impact is secondary

3-33 Planning and Control, Management by Exception

Study the framework for planning and control of a **Starbucks** store in Exhibit 3-2 on page 97. Suppose that for next year a particular store budgeted revenue of $356,400, an 8% increase over the current revenue of $330,000. The actions listed in Exhibit 3-2 resulted in six new budgeted products and a total advertising budget of $33,000. Actual results were as follows:

New products added	7
Advertising	$ 35,640
Revenues	$351,400

1. Prepare a performance report for revenues and advertising costs using the format of Exhibit 3-3 on page 98.
2. Suppose the remaining cost elements of net income were not available until several months after the store implemented the plan. The net income results were disappointing to management—profits declined even though revenues increased because costs increased by more than revenues. List some factors that might have caused costs to increase so much and that management may not have considered when it formulated the store's plan.

3-34 Line Versus Staff and Value-Chain Responsibility

For each of the following, indicate whether the employee has line or staff responsibility. Also indicate whether the employee primarily provides support for other value-chain functions or performs a specific value-chain business function.

1. President
2. District sales manager
3. Market research analyst
4. Cost accountant
5. Head of the legal department
6. Production superintendent

3-35 Microsoft's Value Chain

Microsoft is the world's largest software company. For each of the following value-chain functions, discuss briefly what Microsoft managers would do to achieve that function and how important it is to the overall success of Microsoft.

R&D	Product (service) and process design
Production	Marketing
Distribution	Customer service
Support functions	

3-36 Objectives of Management Accounting

The Institute of Management Accountants (IMA) is composed of nearly 70,000 members. The IMA "Objectives of Management Accounting" states, "The management accountant participates, as part of management, in assuring that the organization operates as a unified whole in its long-run, intermediate, and short-run best interests."

Based on your reading in this chapter, prepare a 100-word description of the principal ways that accountants participate in managing an entity.

3-37 Cost-Benefit of the Ethical Environment

A poor ethical environment results in costs to the company. On the other hand, a good ethical environment creates benefits. List several costs of a poor ethical environment and benefits of a good ethical environment.

3-38 Early Warning Signs of Ethical Conflict

The following statements are early warning signs of ethical conflict:

- "I don't care how you do it, just get it done!"
- "No one will ever know."

List several other statements that are early warning signs of ethical conflict.

PROBLEMS

3-39 Management and Financial Accounting

Lillian Choi, an able mechanical engineer, was informed that she would be promoted to assistant factory manager. Lillian was pleased but uncomfortable. In particular, she knew little about accounting. She had taken one course in financial accounting.

Lillian planned to enroll in a management accounting course as soon as possible. Meanwhile, she asked Walt Greenspan, a cost accountant, to state three or four of the principal distinctions between financial and management accounting.

Prepare Walt's written response to Lillian.

3-40 Use of Accounting Information in Hospitals

Most U.S. hospitals do not derive their revenues directly from patients. Instead, revenues come through third parties, such as insurance companies and government agencies. Until the 1980s, these payments generally reimbursed the hospital's costs of serving patients. Such payments, however, are now generally flat fees for specified services. For example, the hospital might receive $7,000 for an appendectomy or $28,000 for heart surgery—no more, no less.

How might the method of payment change the demand for accounting information in hospitals? Relate your answer to the decisions of top management.

3-41 Costs and Benefits

Marks & Spencer, a huge retailer in the United Kingdom with sales of more than £9 billion, was troubled by its paper bureaucracy. Looked at in isolation, each document seemed reasonable, but overall a researcher reported that there was substantial effort in each department to verify the information. Basically, the effort seemed out of proportion to any value received, and, eventually, the company simplified or eliminated many of the documents.

Describe the rationale that should govern systems design. How should a company such as Marks & Spencer decide what documents it needs and which can be eliminated?

3-42 Importance of Accounting

Some companies are run by engineers and other technical specialists. For example, a manager in a division that is now part of **ArvinMeritor**, an automotive parts supplier, once said that "there'd be sixty or seventy guys talking technical problems, with never a word on profits." Other companies, especially consumer products companies such as **General Mills**, fill top management positions primarily with marketing executives. And still others, like **Berkshire Hathaway** with Warren Buffett as CEO, have top managers with strong finance skills.

How might the role of management accountants differ in these types of companies?

3-43 Changes in Accounting Systems

In the last decade, **Boeing** has made several significant changes to its accounting system. None of these changes were for reporting to external parties. Management believed, however, that the new system gave more accurate costs of the airplanes and other products produced.

1. Boeing had been a very successful company using its old accounting system. What might have motivated it to change the system?
2. When Boeing changed its system, what criteria might its managers have used to decide whether to invest in the new system?
3. Is changing to a system that provides more accurate product costs always a good strategy? Why or why not?

3-44 Value Chain

Nike is an Oregon-based company that focuses on the design, development, and worldwide marketing of high-quality sports footwear, apparel, equipment, and accessory products. Nike is the largest seller of athletic footwear and athletic apparel in the world. The company sells its products to more than 20,000 retail accounts in the United States and through a mix of independent distributors, licensees, and subsidiaries in approximately 170 countries around the world. Nike contracts with hundreds of factories around the world to manufacture virtually all the company's products. Nike produces most footwear and branded apparel products outside the United States.

1. Identify one decision that Nike managers make in each of the six value-chain functions.
2. For each decision in requirement 1, identify one piece of accounting information that would aid the manager's decision.

3-45 Role of Controller

Juanita Veracruz, newly hired controller of Braxton Industries, had been lured away from a competitor to revitalize the controller's department. Her first day on the job proved to be an eye-opener. One of her first interviews was with Adrian Belton, production supervisor in the Cleveland factory. Belton commented, "I really don't want to talk to anyone from the controller's office. The only time we see those accountants is when our costs go over their budget. They wave what they call a 'performance report,' but it's actually just a bunch of numbers they make up. It has nothing to do with what happens on the shop floor. Besides, my men can't afford the time to fill out all the paperwork those accountants want, so I just plug in some numbers and send it back. Now, if you'll let me get back to important matters...." Veracruz left quickly, but she was already planning for her next visit with Belton.

1. Identify some of the problems in the relationship between the controller's department and the production departments (assuming that the Cleveland factory is representative of the production departments).
2. What should Juanita Veracruz do next?

3-46 The Accountant's Role in an Organization

The Business First box on page 104 described the role of accountants in the **Marmon Group**, a collection of operating companies that manufacture such diverse products as copper tubing, water purification products, railroad tank cars, and store fixtures, and provide services such as credit information for banks. Others have described accountants as "internal consultants." Using the information in the Business First box, discuss how accountants at Marmon can act as internal consultants. What kind of background and knowledge would an accountant require to be an effective internal consultant?

3-47 Ethics and Accounting Personnel

McMillan Shipping Company has an equal opportunity employment policy. This policy has the full support of the company's president, Rosemary Creighton, and is included in all advertisements for employee positions.

Hiring in the accounting department is done by the controller, D. W. "Butch" Brigham. The assistant controller, Jack Merton, also interviews candidates, but Brigham makes all decisions. In the last year, the department hired 5 new people from a pool of 175 applicants. Thirteen had been interviewed, including four minority candidates. The five hired included three sons of Brigham's close friends and no minorities. Merton had felt that at least two of the minority candidates were very well qualified and that the three sons of Brigham's friends were definitely not among the most qualified.

When Merton questioned Brigham concerning his reservations about the hiring practices, he was told that these decisions were Brigham's and not his, so he should not question them.

1. Explain why Brigham's hiring practices were probably unethical.
2. What should Merton do about this situation?

3-48 Ethical Issues

Suppose you are controller of a medium-sized oil exploration company in western Texas. You adhere to the standards of ethical conduct for management accountants. How would those standards affect your behavior in each of the following situations?

1. Late one Friday afternoon you receive a geologist's report on a newly purchased property. It indicates a much higher probability of oil than had previously been expected. You are the only one to read the report that day. At a party on Saturday night, a friend asks about the prospects for the property.
2. An oil industry stock analyst invites you and your spouse to spend a week in Tahiti free of charge. All she wants in return is to be the first to know about any financial information your company is about to announce to the public.
3. It is time to make a forecast of the company's annual earnings. You know that some additional losses will be recognized before the company prepares final statements. The company's president has asked you to ignore these losses in making your prediction because a lower-than-expected earnings forecast could adversely affect the chances of obtaining a loan that is being negotiated and that will be completed before actual earnings are announced.
4. You do not know whether a particular expense is deductible for income tax purposes. You are debating whether to research the tax laws or simply to assume that the item is deductible. After all, if you are not audited, no one will ever know the difference. If you are audited, you can plead ignorance of the law.

3-49 Hundred Best Corporate Citizens

Each year *Corporate Responsibility* magazine publishes its list of the 100 best corporate citizens. The magazine rates companies on performance in seven stakeholder categories: (1) environment, (2) climate change, (3) human rights, (4) employee relations, (5) corporate governance, (6) philanthropy, and (7) financial. In 2011, the top 10 corporate citizens were Johnson Controls, Campbell Soup, International Business Machines, Bristol-Myers Squibb, Mattel, 3M, Accenture, Kimberly-Clark, Hewlett-Packard, and Nike.

For each of the seven dimensions on which the magazine reported ratings, give a one-sentence description of what you think would make for good corporate citizenship. Based on your knowledge of these 10 companies, however limited that is, predict the top 2 companies in each of the seven rated categories.

CASES

3-50 Line and Staff Authority

Fidelity Leasing Company (FLC) leases office equipment to a variety of customers. The company's organization chart is shown on the following page. The responsibilities of the four positions in blue in the chart are:

- J. P. Chen, assistant controller—special projects. Chen works on projects assigned to him by the controller. The most recent project was to design a new accounts payable system.
- Betty Hodge, leasing contracts manager. Hodge coordinates and implements leasing transactions. Her department handles all transactions after the sales department gets a signed contract. This includes requisitioning equipment from the purchasing department, maintaining appropriate insurance, delivering equipment, issuing billing statements, and seeking renewal of leases.

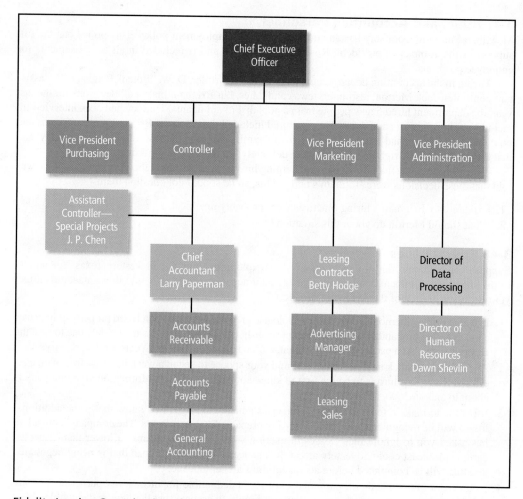

Fidelity Leasing Organization Chart

- Larry Paperman, chief accountant. Paperman supervises all the accounting functions. He produces reports for the four supervisors in the functional areas.
- Dawn Shevlin, director of human resources. Shevlin works with all departments of FLC in hiring personnel. Her department advertises all positions and screens candidates, but the individual departments conduct interviews and make hiring decisions. Shevlin also coordinates employee evaluations and administers the company's salary schedule and fringe benefit program.

1. Distinguish between line and staff positions in an organization and discuss why conflicts might arise between line and staff managers.
2. For each of the four managers described, identify whether their position is a line or staff position and explain why you classified it that way. Also, indicate any potential conflicts that might arise with other managers in the organization.

3-51 Professional Ethics and Toxic Waste

Alberta Mining Company extracts and processes a variety of ores and minerals. One of its operations is a coal-cleaning plant that produces toxic wastes. For many years, the wastes have been properly disposed of through Canadian Disposal, an experienced company. However, disposal of the toxic wastes is becoming an economic hardship because increasing government regulations caused the cost of such disposal to quadruple in the last 6 years.

Rachel O'Casey, director of financial reporting for Alberta Mining, was preparing the company's financial statements for the current year. In researching the material needed for preparing a footnote on environmental contingencies, Rachel found the following note scribbled in pencil at the bottom of a memo to the general manager of the coal-cleaning plant. The body of the memo gave details on the increases in the cost of toxic waste disposals:

Ralph—We've got to keep these costs down or we won't meet budget. Can we mix more of these wastes with the shipments of refuse to the Oak Hill landfill? Nobody seems to notice the coal-cleaning fluids when we mix it in well.

Rachel was bothered by the note. She considered ignoring it, pretending that she had not seen it. But after a couple of hours, her conscience would not let her do it. Therefore, she pondered the following three alternative courses of action:

- Seek the advice of her boss, the vice president of finance for Alberta.
- Anonymously release the information to the local newspaper.
- Give the information to an outside member of Alberta's board of directors, whom she knew because he lived in her neighborhood.

1. Discuss why Rachel has an ethical responsibility to take some action about her suspicion of the illegal dumping of toxic wastes.
2. For each of the three alternative courses of action, explain whether the action is appropriate.
3. Assume that Rachel sought the advice of the vice president of finance and discovered that he both knew about and approved of the dumping of toxic wastes. What steps should she take to resolve the conflict in this situation?

NIKE 10K PROBLEM

3-52 Information in Nike's 10K Report

U.S. companies file 10K reports annually with the SEC. These reports contain the company's annual financial reports and much additional information about the company. Examine **Nike's** 10K report that is presented. Answer the following questions about Nike:

1. What is Nike's principal business activity?
2. What proportion of Nike revenue comes from sales in the United States? What proportion from other countries? How many retail outlets does Nike have in the United States?
3. Who is Nike's CFO? What is his accounting background?
4. Where does Nike manufacture most of its footwear? What ethical issues might result from this manufacturing philosophy?

EXCEL APPLICATION EXERCISE

3-53 Budgets and Performance Evaluation

Goal: Create an Excel spreadsheet to prepare a performance report, and use the results to answer questions about your findings.

Scenario: Beta Alpha Psi, the accounting honorary fraternity, has asked you to prepare a performance report about a homecoming party that it recently held. The background data for Beta Alpha Psi's performance report appears in the Fundamental Assignment Material 1-A2.

When you have completed your spreadsheet, answer the following questions:

1. Based on the formatting option used in the exercise, do the negative (red) variances represent amounts that are over or under budget?
2. Which cost/costs changed because the number of attendees increased?
3. Did the fraternity stay within the budgeted amount for food on a per person basis?

Step-by-Step:
1. Open a new Excel spreadsheet.
2. In column A, create a bold-faced heading that contains the following:
   Row 1: Chapter 3 Decision Guideline
   Row 2: Beta Alpha Psi Homecoming Party
   Row 3: Performance Report
   Row 4: Today's Date
3. Merge and center the date across columns A–D.
4. In row 7, create the following bold-faced, right-justified column headings:
   Column B: Budget
   Column C: Actual
   Column D: Variance

5. In column A, create the following row headings:
   Row 8: Room rental
   Row 9: Food
   Row 10: Entertainment
   Row 11: Decorations
   Row 12: Total costs
   Skip a row.
   Row 14: Attendees
   Skip a row.
   Row 16: Food per person

6. Use the data from Fundamental Assignment Material 3-A2 and enter the budget and actual amounts for room, food, entertainment, decorations, and attendees.

7. Use budget minus actual formulas to generate variances for each of the cost categories.

8. Use the SUM function to generate total costs for the budget, actual, and variance columns.

9. Use a formula to generate the "per person" food amount for the budget and actual columns.

10. Format all amounts as follows:

Number tab:	Category:	Currency
	Decimal places:	0
	Symbol:	None
	Negative numbers:	Red with parentheses

11. Change the format of the food per person amounts to display two decimal places and a dollar symbol.

12. Change the format of the room rental and total cost amounts to display a dollar symbol.

13. Change the format of the total costs data (row 12) to display as bold faced.

14. Change the format of the total costs heading to display as indented:

Alignment tab:	Horizontal:	Left (Indent)
	Indent:	1

15. Save your work, and print a copy for your files.

COLLABORATIVE LEARNING EXERCISE

3-54 The Future Management Accountant

Students should gather in groups of three to six. One-third of each group should read each of the following articles. (Alternatively, you can do this exercise as a whole class, with one-third of the class reading each article.)

- Roth, R. T., "The CFO's Great Balancing Act," *Financial Executive*, July/August 2004, pp. 60–61.
- Johnsson, M, "The Changing Role of the CFO," *Strategic Finance*, June 2002, pp. 54–57, 67.
- Russell, K., G. Siegel, and C. Kulesza, "Counting More, Counting Less: Transformations in the Management Accounting Profession," *Strategic Finance*, September 1999, pp. 39–44.

1. Individually, write down the three most important lessons you learned from the article you read.

2. As a group, list all the lessons identified in requirement 1. Combine those that are essentially the same.

3. Prioritize the list you developed in requirement 2 in terms of their importance to someone considering a career in management accounting.

4. Discuss whether this exercise has changed your impression of management accounting and, if so, how your impression has changed.

INTERNET EXERCISE

3-55 Institute of Management Accountants

The Institute of Management Accountants (IMA) is a major professional organization geared toward managerial accounting and finance. The IMA has chapters throughout the United States as well as international chapters. The IMA is very concerned about ethics. Log on to www.imanet.org, the Web site for the IMA.

1. Click on About IMA and follow the link that shows the mission statement for the IMA. What is the mission of the IMA?

2. Click on IMA Membership, then Resources and Benefits, and then on the Professional Development link. How many courses does IMA offer to enhance effectiveness on the job, satisfy CPE requirements, and advance careers of members?

3. Click on the Ethics Center & Helpline link under Resources and Publications. Follow the Learn More link under the Ethical Practices heading to the Statement of Ethical Professional Practice. Read the code and comment on its importance to management accountants.

Introduction to Cost Behavior and Cost-Volume-Profit Relationships

LEARNING OBJECTIVES

When you have finished studying this chapter, you should be able to:

1. Explain how cost drivers affect cost behavior.

2. Show how changes in cost-driver levels affect variable and fixed costs.

3. Explain step- and mixed-cost behavior.

4. Create a cost-volume-profit (CVP) graph and understand the assumptions behind it.

5. Calculate break-even sales volume in total dollars and total units.

6. Calculate sales volume in total dollars and total units to reach a target profit.

7. Differentiate between contribution margin and gross margin.

8. Explain the effects of sales mix on profits (Appendix 4A).

9. Compute cost-volume-profit (CVP) relationships on an after-tax basis (Appendix 4B).

▶ BOEING COMPANY

In 1915, William Boeing, a Seattle timberman, assembled his first airplane in a boathouse. In 1954 Boeing introduced its first four-engine 707. The Boeing family of jets has grown to include the 727, 737, 747, 757, 767, 777, and the company delivered its first 787-Dreamliner in 2011. Today, the Boeing Company is the world's largest aerospace company, the second largest producer of commercial jets, and the second largest military contractor. Boeing builds 40 to 50 commercial jetliners each month and had annual revenue of $68.7 billion in 2011. The company produces aircraft that carry from about 100 to well over 500 passengers and has about half of the world's market share in airplane sales.

How will Boeing maintain its competitive edge and profitability? With intense competition from Airbus, Boeing knows that it can improve profits more by controlling (reducing) costs than by increasing prices to customers—especially when many of its customers are only beginning to recover from the steep decline in airline profits in 2008 and 2009. So, should Boeing develop new and bigger airplanes or produce more of its current line of planes with improvements in features and efficiencies that will lower customers' operating costs? Which alternative has lower costs for Boeing and its customers? To answer these questions, Boeing has to understand its own costs as well as the costs of its customers.

Consider a recent Boeing decision regarding development and production of a new airplane. Back in 1999, the company started an R&D program for the Sonic Cruiser. The Sonic Cruiser emphasized speed—it was designed to reduce travel time by about 20%. An important part of the development decision was the assessment of customers' costs—both of operating their existing fleet of planes and of the costs of the new Sonic Cruisers. In early 2001, discussions with airlines in North America, Asia, and Europe confirmed the design offered exactly what airlines and passengers were looking for: the ability to fly quickly and directly to their destinations while avoiding time-consuming and costly stops at major hubs. In late 2002, after more than 3 years of research, the company had completed the design of the new airplane and was faced with the final decision to launch. A decision to launch would involve a huge immediate investment in costly plant and equipment resources. To pay for these assets and make a profit, Boeing had to be confident that its customers would be willing to pay more for the airplane than it cost Boeing to design, produce, and sell it.

But production ultimately hinged on whether customers were willing to pay enough to cover the cost of producing a faster airplane that used the most up-to-date technology. Despite the years of development activities, Boeing decided not to proceed with the Sonic Cruiser. Why? Boeing made its decision after a careful analysis of its own production costs and the airlines' operating costs. According to Alan Mulally, CEO of Boeing Commercial Airplanes at the time, the airlines made it clear that they wanted a cheaper plane rather than a faster plane. Therefore, Boeing management decided to dedicate its resources to developing the 787-Dreamliner—a "super-efficient" jetliner constructed primarily from composite materials rather than aluminum and other metals.

© European Pressphoto Agency (EPA)/Alamy

This chapter begins your study of costs. One of the main goals of management accounting is to help managers understand **cost behavior**—how the activities of an organization affect its costs—as they make crucial decisions about their production and service activities. For example, how much would it cost Boeing to produce each 787? How much cost does Delta Airlines incur when it adds one more passenger at the last moment to an existing flight, or when it adds one more flight to the schedule? What does it cost Toyota to develop a new line of luxury autos, as it did with Lexus? How much does it cost to produce one more Prius? How will an increase in Arizona's population affect the costs to run the state's department of motor vehicles? What does it cost Nestlé Purina to meet Wal-Mart's specifications for shipments of pet-care products? What activities contribute most to Nestlé Purina's cost to serve Wal-Mart stores? These are all specific forms of the general question: What will be the incremental effects if an organization changes its activities? ∎

The design and production of an airplane is a complex process. This is the first assembled Boeing 787 Dreamliner airplane at its production facility at Everett, Washington.

cost behavior
How the activities of an organization affect its costs.

Identifying Activities, Resources, Costs, and Cost Drivers

Different types of costs behave in different ways. Consider the costs of making the 737-MAX— Boeing's newest version of the most popular single-aisle airplane ever produced. As Boeing produces more airplanes, it buys and uses more resources, such as electrical wire, seats, aluminum, and labor. Therefore, each additional airplane requires Boeing to incur more of these resource costs. In contrast, the cost of other resources such as the factory and salaries of key managers stay the same, regardless of the number of airplanes made. To predict costs for decision making and to control costs on a day-to-day basis, Boeing managers identify

- key activities performed,
- resources used in performing these activities,
- costs of the resources used, and
- **cost drivers**, measures of activities that require the use of resources and thereby cause costs.

Exhibit 4-1 shows how activities link resources and their costs with the output of products or services. For example, an activity that requires resources and therefore causes costs for Boeing is installing seats. This activity uses many resources, but let's consider just two: 1) the seats themselves, which Boeing purchases from a subcontractor, and 2) labor for installing the seats. One measure of activity, number of seats installed, is an appropriate cost driver for the cost of the seats. A different measure of activity, labor hours used in installing the seats, is a cost driver for the cost of labor resources.

An organization may have many activities as part of its value chain and many cost drivers for those activities. For example, one manufacturer of pet foods has a plant in Denver with more

cost driver
A measure of activities that requires the use of resources and thereby cause costs.

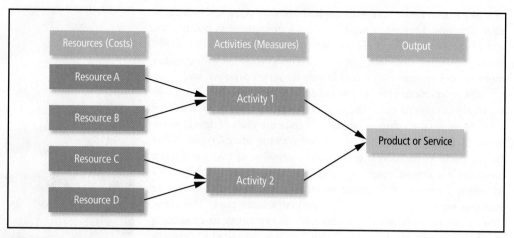

Exhibit 4-1
Linking Resource Costs to Outputs via Activities

than 50 production activities and a total of 21 cost drivers. Exhibit 4-2 lists examples of resource costs and potential cost drivers for activities in each of the value-chain functions. How well we identify the most appropriate cost drivers determines how well managers understand cost behavior and how well managers can control costs.

In this chapter we focus on a simple situation of one activity and one cost driver for the production of a particular product or service. The activity includes all aspects of the production and sale of the product or service. The cost driver is the number of units produced and sold, which we assume drives all the resource costs. Therefore, the analysis will examine how decisions about the volume of production and sales affect costs. This simplified analysis is useful to managers who want an estimate of the general relationship between production volume and costs. In later chapters, we will consider more specific and detailed analysis of costs.

Value-Chain Functions and Resource Costs	Example Cost Drivers
Research and development	
• Salaries of sales personnel, costs of market surveys	Number of new product proposals
• Salaries of product and process engineers	Complexity of proposed products
Design of products, services, and processes	
• Salaries of product and process engineers	Number of engineering hours
• Cost of computer-aided design equipment used to develop prototype of product for testing	Number of distinct parts per product
Production	Labor hours
• Labor wages	Number of people supervised
• Supervisory salaries	Number of mechanic hours
• Maintenance wages	Number of machine hours
• Depreciation of plant and machinery, supplies	Kilowatt hours
• Energy cost	
Marketing	Number of advertisements
• Cost of advertisements	Sales dollars
• Salaries of marketing personnel, travel costs, entertainment costs	
Distribution	Labor hours
• Wages of shipping personnel	Weight of items delivered
• Transportation costs including depreciation of vehicles and fuel	
Customer service	Hours spent servicing products
• Salaries of service personnel	Number of service calls
• Costs of supplies, travel	

Exhibit 4-2
Examples of Value-Chain Functions, Resource Costs, and Cost Drivers

Variable-Cost and Fixed-Cost Behavior

Accountants classify costs as variable or fixed depending on whether the cost changes with respect to a particular cost driver. A **variable cost** changes in direct proportion to changes in the cost driver. In contrast, changes in the cost driver do not affect a **fixed cost**. Suppose the cost driver is units of goods or services produced. A 10% increase in units produced would result in a 10% increase in variable costs. However, the fixed costs would remain unchanged.

Consider an example of variable costs for Watkins Products, the 140-year-old health food company. If Watkins pays its sales personnel a 20% straight commission on sales, the total cost of sales commissions to Watkins is 20% of sales dollars—a variable cost with respect to sales revenues. Or suppose Long Lake Bait Shop buys bags of fish bait from a supplier for $2 each. The total cost of fish bait is $2 times the number of bags purchased—a variable cost with respect to units (number of bags) purchased. Notice that variable costs do not change *per unit of the cost driver*, but the *total variable costs* change in direct proportion to the cost-driver activity.

Now consider an example of a fixed cost. Suppose Sony rents a factory for $500,000 per year to produce DVD players. The number of DVD players produced does not affect the *total fixed cost* of $500,000. The *unit cost* of rent applicable to each DVD player, however, does depend on the total number of DVD players produced. If Sony produces 50,000 DVD players, the unit cost will be $500,000 ÷ 50,000 = $10. If Sony produces 100,000 DVD players, the unit cost will be $500,000 ÷ 100,000 = $5. Therefore, while the fixed cost *per-unit of the cost-driver* becomes progressively smaller as the volume increases, the *total fixed cost* does not change with volume.

The term "fixed cost" describes the behavior of cost with respect to the cost driver, but a fixed cost can change due to factors other than changes in the cost driver. For example, heating costs are commonly fixed and do not change with respect to the production volume cost driver. Nonetheless, heating costs change with respect to factors not related to the cost driver, such as changes in the price of oil or electricity, or unusually warm or unusually cold weather.

Pay special attention to the fact that the terms "variable" or "fixed" describe the behavior of the total dollar cost, not the per-unit cost, which has the opposite behavior. Total variable costs increase as the cost driver increases but variable costs per unit remain constant. Total fixed costs remain constant as cost driver activity increases but fixed costs per unit decrease. Exhibit 4-3 summarizes these relationships.

Objective 2

Show how changes in cost-driver levels affect variable and fixed costs.

variable cost

A cost that changes in direct proportion to changes in the cost-driver level.

fixed cost

A cost that is not affected by changes in the cost-driver level.

Making Managerial Decisions

Test your understanding of the distinction between variable and fixed costs by answering the following questions.

1. A producer of premium ice cream uses "gallons of ice cream produced" as a cost driver for the production activity. One of the main resources this activity uses is dairy ingredients. Is the cost of dairy ingredients a variable or a fixed cost with respect to production volume?

2. Another resource used by this activity is supervisory salaries. If supervisory salaries do not change with the level of production of ice cream, is the supervisory salaries cost variable or fixed with respect to production volume?

Answer

The way to determine whether the cost of a resource is fixed or variable with respect to a cost driver is to ask the question, "If the level of the cost driver changes, what will happen to the cost?"

If the company increases or decreases its production of ice cream, the cost of dairy ingredients will increase or decrease in proportion to production volume. Thus, the cost of dairy ingredients is a variable cost. If the production of ice cream increases or decreases, supervisory salaries will not change. Thus, the cost of supervisory salaries is a fixed cost.

Exhibit 4-3
Cost Behavior of Fixed and Variable Costs

| | **If Cost-Driver Level Increases (or Decreases)** | |
Type of Cost	Total Cost	Cost per Unit*
Fixed costs	No change	Decrease (or increase)
Variable costs	Increase (or decrease)	No change

*Per unit of activity volume, for example, product units, passenger-miles, orders processed, or sales dollars

To plan and control costs, managers focus on the activities required to make, sell, and deliver products or services and the resources needed to support these activities. Consider one of the many activities performed as part of the production function at Boeing's plant—receiving parts that production workers install on an airplane. Managers need to know how the receiving activity affects production costs. For example, how does the increase or decrease in receiving activity affect the lease payment for renting the equipment used to move parts from the receiving area to the production floor? How does it affect the cost of fuel for the moving equipment? Similarly, how does it affect costs of receiving labor, supplies, and other resources?

Consider the behavior of just two of these resource costs, equipment and fuel costs, ignoring other resource costs such as labor and supplies. Suppose equipment costs of $45,000 are fixed and do not vary with increases or decreases in the number of parts received, while fuel cost is a variable cost that increases or decreases by $.80 with each part received. Exhibit 4-4 shows how these resource costs relate to the receiving activity.

Exhibit 4-5 illustrates the relationship between the receiving activity and resource costs. The equipment costs represent the total fixed lease cost of $45,000. The fuel costs are variable at $0.80 per part received. We can use the descriptions of cost behavior in Exhibits 4-4 and 4-5 to find total fuel and equipment cost at any other level of receiving activity. For example, the total equipment and fuel costs of receiving 30,000 parts is $45,000 + (30,000 × $.80) = $69,000. Similarly, the total cost of receiving 27,500 parts is $45,000 + (27,500 × $.80) = $67,000. Notice how we used the respective costs in these calculations. We used the total cost of $45,000 for the fixed equipment lease cost and the unit cost of $.80 for variable fuel cost.

Exhibit 4-4
Receiving Activity and
Resources Used

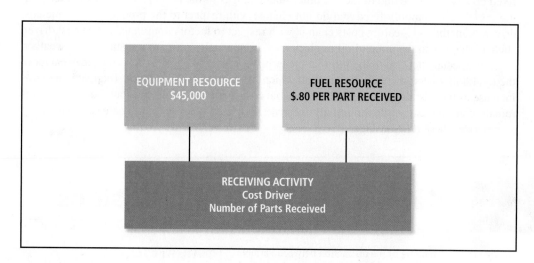

Exhibit 4-5
Total Fuel and Equipment
Lease Costs

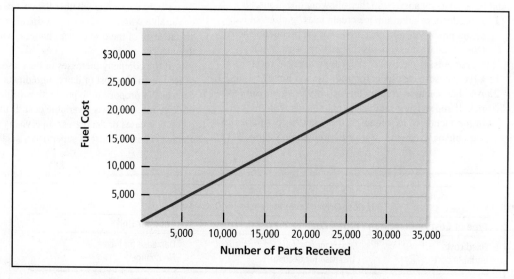

Exhibit 4-5
(continued)

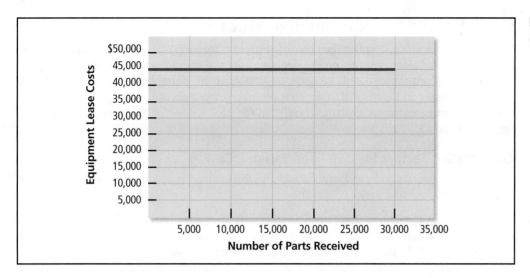

Summary Problem for Your Review

PROBLEM

The manager at the **Boeing** plant is looking at a monthly report of plant costs. He notices that the receiving activity costs vary substantially from month to month and is interested in knowing more about why the total cost and unit cost of the receiving activity change. The number of parts received has ranged from 10,000 to 30,000 parts per month over the last several months.

1. Prepare a table that shows the cost of equipment, the cost of fuel, the total of equipment and fuel costs, and the cost per-part-received for 10,000 to 30,000 parts per month, using increments of 5,000 parts per month.

2. Prepare brief explanations of why the total and unit cost patterns change.

SOLUTION

1. The table can be developed using the relationships shown in Exhibit 4-5.

(1) Parts Received	(2) Equipment Cost	(3) $.80 × (1) Fuel Cost	(4) (2) + (3) Total Cost	(5) (4) ÷ (1) Cost per Part Received
10,000	$45,000	$ 8,000	$53,000	$5.30
15,000	45,000	12,000	57,000	3.80
20,000	45,000	16,000	61,000	3.05
25,000	45,000	20,000	65,000	2.60
30,000	45,000	24,000	69,000	2.30

2. Column (4) shows the total cost of the receiving activity, which shows a pattern of increasing total cost. The increase in total cost is less than proportional to the activity cost driver because total cost includes both the fixed cost component from Column (2) as well as the variable cost component from Column (3). For example, a 50% increase in the number of parts received from 10,000 parts to 15,000 parts results in a 50% increase in the variable cost component in column (3) but the total cost in column (4) increases by far less than 50% because the fixed cost in column (2) does not change.

Column (5) shows the cost per part received, which shows a pattern of decreasing cost per part. The decreasing cost per part is entirely due to the fixed equipment cost being spread over increasing numbers of parts received, the cost driver. For example, consider the change in cost per part as the number of parts received increases from 10,000 to 15,000 parts. The fixed cost per part moves from $4.50 at 10,000 parts received ($45,000 ÷ 10,000) to $3.00 at 15,000 parts received ($45,000 ÷ 15,000). The variable cost per part remains constant at $0.80. Thus, the sum of the fixed and variable costs per part in column (5) decreases from $5.30 ($4.50 + $.80) to $3.80 ($3.00 + $.80) due entirely to the decline in the fixed cost per part.

Cost Behavior: Further Considerations

decision context

The circumstances surrounding
the decision for which the cost
will be used.

For a variety of reasons, cost behavior cannot always be accurately described as simply variable or fixed. Cost behavior depends on the **decision context**, the circumstances surrounding the decision for which the cost will be used, as illustrated by examples in the discussion that follows. Further, cost behavior also depends on management decisions—management choices determine cost behavior, as explained briefly in the final section of this chapter and in more detail in Chapter 5.

Complicating Factors for Fixed and Variable Costs

In this section, we illustrate and explain some of the factors that complicate cost behavior for fixed and variable costs.

relevant range

The limits of the cost-driver
level within which a specific
relationship between costs and
the cost driver is valid.

FIXED COSTS   Although we described fixed costs as unchanging regardless of changes in the cost driver, this description holds true only within limits. For example, rent costs for a production building are generally fixed within a limited range of activity but may rise if activity increases enough to require additional rental space or may decline if activity decreases so much that it allows the company to rent less space. The **relevant range** is the limits of the cost-driver level within which a specific relationship between costs and the cost driver is valid.

Suppose that total monthly fixed costs are $100,000 for a General Electric lightbulb plant as long as production is between 40,000 and 85,000 cases of lightbulbs per month. However, if production falls below 40,000 cases, changes in production processes will slash fixed costs to $60,000 per month. On the other hand, if operations rise above 85,000 cases, rentals of additional facilities will boost fixed costs to $115,000 per month. Exhibit 4-6 graphs these assumptions about cost behavior. The top figure shows a refined analysis that reflects all the complexities described previously. The bottom figure shows a simplified analysis that focuses only on the cost in the relevant range, ignoring the issue of cost behavior outside the relevant range. Within the relevant range highlighted in yellow, the refined and simplified analyses coincide. However, the refined description at the top of Exhibit 4-6 explicitly shows the rental costs at the levels of activity outside the relevant range. The simplified description at the bottom of the exhibit shows only the rental costs for the relevant range and uses a dashed line outside the relevant range to remind the user that the graphed cost is outside the limits of the relevant range.

Exhibit 4-6
Fixed Costs and Relevant
Range

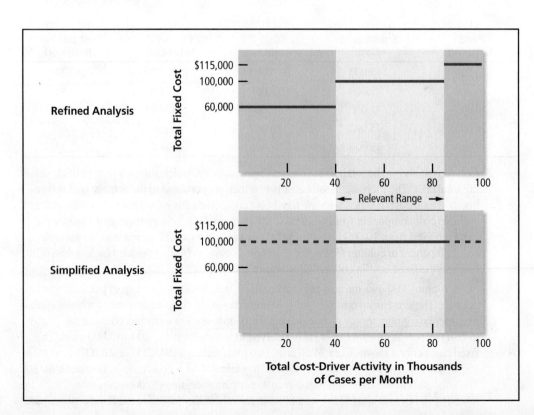

As a decision maker, it is essential to recognize when your decision will move outside the relevant range. In that case, it is essential that you obtain the information included in the refined analysis, showing how costs behave outside the relevant range.

VARIABLE COSTS   The idea of a relevant range is obviously important for fixed costs, but a corresponding issue may also arise for variable costs. For example, if **GE** obtains volume discounts for purchasing larger quantities of input materials such as glass and tungsten, the materials cost per case for the GE lightbulb plant would be lower, and the slope of the variable cost function would be lower, at higher levels of production. As another example, labor cost per case will decrease at higher levels of production if expansion to achieve higher levels of production results in a new production process with higher labor efficiency. When costs vary with changes in the cost driver but not in direct proportion to the change in the cost driver, the variable cost function does not produce a straight-line graph.

Step- and Mixed-Cost Behavior Patterns

Some costs are neither purely fixed nor purely variable. For example, two types of costs that combine characteristics of both fixed- and variable-cost behavior are step costs and mixed costs.

STEP COSTS   Costs that change abruptly at different levels of activity because the resources are available only in indivisible chunks are **step costs**. For decisions where the range of activity is limited to a single step of the cost function, we consider the cost a fixed cost. For decisions where the range of activity encompasses many steps, the cost behaves more like a variable cost.

Panel A of Exhibit 4-7 illustrates a decision where a step cost could be treated as a fixed cost. In this example, when oil and gas exploration activity reaches a certain level, the company must lease an additional rig. Each additional rig leased defines a new step in the cost function, which supports a new, higher volume of exploration activity. This step cost behaves as a fixed cost as long as all the decision alternatives remain within the relevant range of a single step, such as within the highlighted relevant range of the second step in the cost function shown in Panel A of Exhibit 4-7.

Panel B of Exhibit 4-7 illustrates a decision where a step cost could be treated as a variable cost. The cost function shows the wage cost of cashiers at a supermarket where the individual cost steps are uniform. Each cashier can serve an average of 20 shoppers per hour. In a decision about staffing, where the number of shoppers is expected to range from 40 per hour to 440 per hour, the required number of cashiers to match the number of shoppers would range between 2 and 22. Because the range of the number of shoppers in this decision spans a large number of equal-sized steps, this step cost behaves much like a variable cost, and for this decision there is only a small loss of accuracy when we assume the step cost is variable.

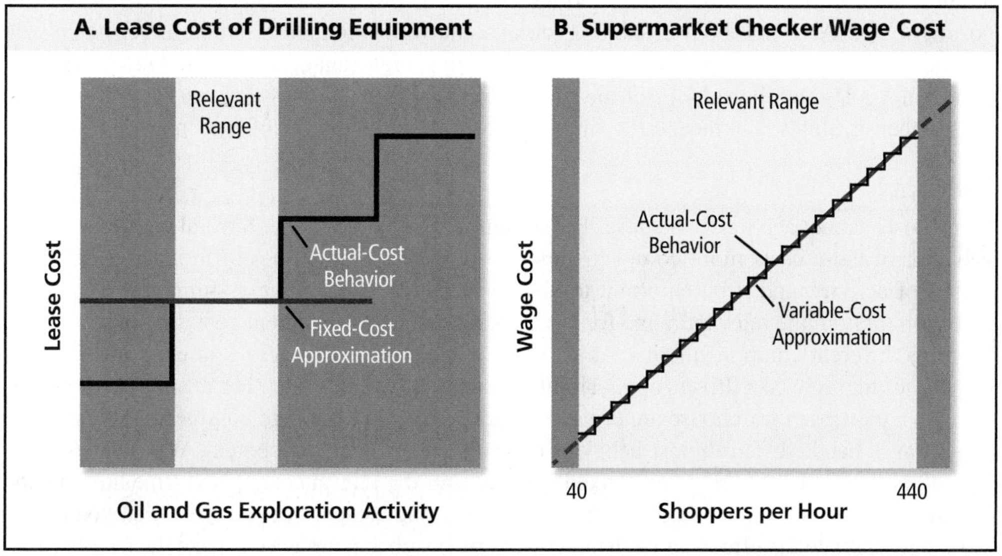

Objective 3

Explain step- and mixed-cost behavior.

step cost
A cost that changes abruptly at different intervals of activity because the resources and their costs come in indivisible chunks.

Exhibit 4-7
Step-Cost Behavior

Note that the decision context dictates whether a step cost can be treated as fixed or variable. For example, in the cashier staffing example, suppose we are deciding whether to implement a promotional offer expected to attract 5 more shoppers per hour during mid-afternoon when there are currently about 70 shoppers per hour. Because this decision will not span more than one step in the cashier cost function, for this decision we can assume cashier wages are a fixed cost.

mixed cost

A cost that contains elements of both fixed- and variable-cost behavior.

MIXED COSTS   Many costs are **mixed costs**, which contain elements of both fixed- and variable-cost behavior. The fixed-cost element is unchanged over the relevant range of activity levels while the variable-cost element of the mixed cost varies proportionately with cost-driver activity. You might think of the fixed cost element as the cost of creating the capacity to operate and the variable cost element as the additional cost of actually using that capacity.

For example, the cost of providing diagnostic imaging services at the Mayo Clinic is a mixed cost. There is a substantial fixed cost of having expensive imaging equipment available and ready for use. There is also a variable cost associated with actual use of the equipment, such as the costs of power, technicians to operate the equipment, and physicians to interpret the results. As another example, the cost of running an evening dinner cruise on the Seine River in Paris is a mixed cost. There is a fixed cost of having the boat and crew available to travel along the river. There is also a variable cost of having service staff, food, and beverages to match the number of passengers on the cruise.

Effect of Time Horizon and Magnitude on Cost Behavior

Whether costs behave as fixed or variable often depends on the time frame affected by a decision and on the magnitude of the change in cost-driver activity. For long time spans or large changes in activity level, more costs behave as variable. For short time spans or small changes in activity level, more costs behave as fixed. The preceding discussion of step costs shows how cashier wage costs can be variable in large magnitude decisions about staffing but fixed in small magnitude decisions.

To illustrate the effects of time horizon, suppose a United Airlines plane with several empty seats is scheduled to depart from its gate. A potential passenger is running down a corridor bearing a transferable ticket from a competing airline. Unless the gate attendant holds the airplane for an extra 2 minutes, the passenger will miss the departure and will not switch to United for the planned trip. What are the variable costs in the gate agent's decision whether to delay the departure and place one more passenger in an otherwise empty seat? Virtually all the costs in this situation are fixed. The number of passenger meals carried on the flight will not change at the last moment, and the flight crew salaries and maintenance costs will not change. Only the cost of jet fuel will change, but this change will be relatively small, and the additional fuel used when one more passenger is added is far less than proportional to the increase in the number of passengers. This is a decision that has a short time horizon, a small change in the cost driver (number of passengers), and therefore mainly fixed costs.

Now consider decisions that United makes that involve longer time horizons and larger magnitudes, such as the decision whether to temporarily add a few extra flights to serve the city hosting the NCAA Final Four basketball tournament. In this longer term and larger magnitude decision, many more costs are variable with respect to the relevant cost driver and fewer costs are fixed. Fuel costs and the salaries of the flight and maintenance crews now vary with respect to the number of flights, and meal costs vary with respect to the number of passengers.

Summary

Many costs cannot accurately be described as simply fixed or variable. Several factors make the behavior of these costs more complex. First, cost behavior sometimes differs across different ranges of activity, and it is important to always consider whether the assumptions about cost behavior apply in the relevant range for your decision. Second, different cost drivers sometimes apply to different components of cost, as in the United Airlines flight cost example. Further, sometimes multiple cost drivers apply simultaneously to the same cost. For example, labor costs at an Amazon.com warehouse are driven by package weight, package volume, and the number of packages handled. Third, cost behavior depends on the decision context. Whether costs are "fixed" or "variable" or "step" or "mixed" depends on the relevant range, the time horizon and magnitude of the decision, and other characteristics of the context. It is essential that you understand and evaluate the effects of decision context on cost behavior as you make decisions.

Cost-Volume-Profit Analysis

For the remainder of this chapter, we consider only decisions where costs are fixed, variable, or mixed. The models developed assume the fixed cost components of cost do not change with the cost driver and the variable cost components change in direct proportion to a single cost driver. These models serve as useful starting points in decisions where the assumptions do not hold exactly but are reasonable approximations. For example, the models apply to step costs where the decision spans a large enough number of steps and the steps in the cost function are proportional to the cost driver so that the steps can be reasonably approximated as a variable cost.

Consider situations where managers are trying to evaluate the effects of changes in the volume of goods or services produced. For example, managers might be interested in upward changes such as increased sales expected from increases in promotion or advertising. On the other hand, managers might be interested in downward changes such as decreased sales expected due to a new competitor entering the market or due to a decline in economic conditions. While such changes in volume have many effects, managers are always interested in the relationship between volume and revenue (sales), expenses (costs), and net income (net profit). We call this **cost-volume-profit (CVP) analysis**.

cost-volume-profit (CVP) analysis
The study of the effects of output volume on revenue (sales), expenses (costs), and net income (net profit).

CVP Scenario

Amy Winston, the manager of food services for one of Boeing's plants, is trying to decide whether to rent a line of snack vending machines. Although individual snack items have various acquisition costs and selling prices, Winston has decided that an average selling price of $1.50 per unit and an average acquisition cost of $1.20 per unit will suffice for purposes of this analysis. She predicts the following revenue and expense relationships:

	Per Unit	Percentage of Sales
Selling price	$1.50	100%
Variable cost of each item	1.20	80
Selling price less variable cost	$ .30	20%
Monthly fixed expenses		
Rent	$ 3,000	
Wages for replenishing and servicing	13,500	
Other fixed expenses	1,500	
Total fixed expenses per month	$18,000	

Graphing the CVP Relationship

Exhibit 4-8 is a graph of the cost-volume-profit relationship in our vending machine example. Most students find it easiest to begin the study of CVP relationships with graphs. After introducing the relationships with a graph, we will turn to equations that describe the same CVP concepts. The equations are usually the better way to find the quantitative answer to a specific question. On the other hand, when you need to explain a CVP model to an audience, graphs more quickly convey the break-even point and more easily show profits expected over a range of volume.

As you read the following procedure for constructing the graph, visualize the revenues and costs that correspond to the points and lines you are plotting.

1. Draw the axes. The horizontal axis is sales volume and the vertical axis is dollars of cost and revenue.
2. Plot revenue. Select a convenient value at the upper end of the relevant range for sales volume, say, 100,000 units, and plot point A for total sales dollars at that volume: 100,000 × $1.50 = $150,000. Draw the revenue line from the origin (the point corresponding to $0 and 0 units) to point A.
3. Plot fixed costs. Draw the horizontal line showing the $18,000 fixed portion of cost. The point where the horizontal fixed cost line intersects the vertical axis is point B.

Objective 4

Create a cost-volume-profit (CVP) graph and understand the assumptions behind it.

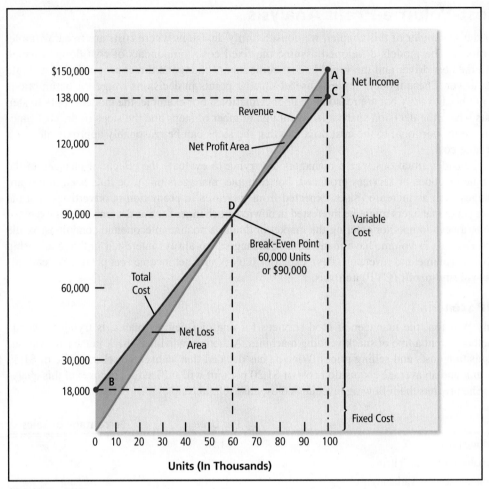

Exhibit 4-8
Cost-Volume-Profit (CVP) Graph

4. Plot fixed costs plus variable costs. Determine the variable portion of cost at the volume you used to plot point A: 100,000 units × $1.20 = $120,000. Plot point C, the fixed plus variable costs for 100,000 units, $18,000 + $120,000 = $138,000. Then draw a line between this point and point B, the fixed plus variable costs for 0 units, $18,000 + $0 = $18,000. This line shows the total cost (fixed cost plus variable cost) at volumes between 0 and 100,000 units.

break-even point

The level of sales at which revenue equals total cost and net income is zero.

5. Locate the **break-even point**—the volume of sales at which revenue equals total cost and therefore income is zero. Graphically, this is the point at 60,000 units where the sales revenue line and the total cost line cross. At 60,000 units, total revenue (60,000 × $1.50 = $90,000) is equal to total cost ([60,000 × $1.20] + $18,000 = $90,000). On the graph, the break-even point is labeled point D.

CVP analysis is sometimes also referred to as break-even analysis. However, this term is misleading. Why? Because CVP analysis reveals more than just the break-even point. At any volume of activity, the vertical distance between the revenue line and the total cost line represents the profit or loss at that volume.

Throughout the remainder of the book, we will see that CVP analysis plays an important role in management decision making and in planning for the effects of changes in competitive and economic conditions on sales, costs, and net income. The business press frequently discusses break-even points, especially during economic downturns. The Business First box on p. 137 describes efforts to lower break-even points by some high-tech and auto-industry firms.

Tech Firms and Auto Makers Lower Break-Even Points During Economic Recession

One might think that because the goal of business is to make a profit, not just break even, the term breakeven would not often be used in business. However when economic conditions result in declining sales, companies are keenly aware of the break-even point.

In the recession that began in 2008, many companies reported on their attempts to achieve profitability in spite of declining sales. They often focused on how their efforts to control costs reduced their break-even points. If a company faces rapidly falling sales, it must restructure its costs to be able to break even at a lower volume. Restructuring costs can involve reducing both fixed and variable costs.

Consider Sony's PlayStation 3. It costs Sony about $500 to make a PS3 but the sales price is about $300 and with competitive pressure from Nintendo Wii and Microsoft Xbox 360, raising the price was not an option. So how could Sony lower its costs to break even? The two actions Sony considered were reducing variable cost and fixed cost. To lower its variable cost, Sony reduced the number of parts and the cost for the console's central processing unit. Reducing the number of parts also lowered Sony's fixed costs, such as assembly equipment and salaries of purchasing agents responsible for vendor negotiations.

At the same time, automakers worldwide faced dramatic declines in sales, forcing equally dramatic restructuring of their operations to lower their costs in hopes of breaking even. For example, to deal with the ongoing downturn in auto sales, "Toyota embarked on efforts to make its domestic factory lines more flexible and introduce other changes to be able to break even at capacity utilization of 70 percent, equivalent to daily production of 12,000 units." Until the recession, the break-even level of car sales for the "Big Three" U.S. automakers was about 16 million per year. By early 2009, the annual sales rate was at a pace of 9 million, far below the break-even point. Among the actions taken to reduce the break-even sales level by GM, Chrysler, and Ford were massive plant closings, layoffs, and reduction of the number of models produced. Many of the associated costs were fixed and thus not dependent on unit sales. The main idea for automakers was to reduce both fixed costs and variable costs, thus lowering breakeven and eventually returning to profitability.

Sources: "Sony PS3 Costs Less To Make, But Still A Money Loser," *Techweb*, December 30, 2008; "Car Sales Not as Horrid In March," *USA Today*, April 2, 2009; "Toyota aims to lower break-even point for Japan operations," *Reuters*, December 24, 2010.

It is important to remember that CVP analysis is based on a set of important assumptions. Some of these assumptions follow:

1. We can classify costs into variable and fixed categories. The variable costs vary in direct proportion to activity level. Fixed costs do not change with activity level.
2. We expect no change in costs due to changes in efficiency or productivity.
3. The behavior of revenues and costs is linear over the relevant range. This means that selling prices per unit and variable costs per unit do not change with the level of sales. Note that almost all break-even graphs show revenue and cost lines extending back to the vertical axis as shown in Exhibit 4-8. As illustrated by the earlier discussion of Exhibits 4-6 and 4-7, this approach is misleading in cases where the relevant range does not extend all the way back to zero volume.
4. In multiproduct companies, the sales mix remains constant. The **sales mix** is the relative proportions or combinations of quantities of different products that constitute total sales. (See Appendix 4A for more on sales mixes.)
5. The inventory level does not change significantly during the period. That is, the number of units sold equals the number of units produced.

sales mix
The relative proportions or combinations of quantities of products that constitute total sales.

Computing the Break-Even Point

We next illustrate how to compute the break-even point using an equation that describes the CVP relationship. The discussion begins with the general approach, and then moves to a method that focuses on the contribution margin, which often leads more quickly to solutions.

Objective 5

Calculate break-even sales volume in total dollars and total units.

GENERAL EQUATION APPROACH We begin with a general approach that you can adapt to any conceivable cost-volume-profit situation. You are familiar with a typical income statement. We can express an income statement in equation form as follows:

$$\text{sales} - \text{variable expenses} - \text{fixed expenses} = \text{net income} \qquad (1)$$

That is,

$$\left(\frac{\text{Unit sales}}{\text{price}} \times \frac{\text{number}}{\text{of units}}\right) - \left(\frac{\text{unit}}{\text{variable cost}} \times \frac{\text{number}}{\text{of units}}\right) - \frac{\text{fixed}}{\text{expenses}} = \frac{\text{net}}{\text{income}}$$

To find the break-even point, set net income on the right-hand-side of the equation to zero:

$$\text{sales} - \text{variable expenses} - \text{fixed expenses} = 0$$

Let $N =$ number of units to be sold to break even. Then, for the vending machine example,

$$\$1.50\,N - \$1.20\,N - \$18,000 = 0$$
$$\$.30\,N = 18,000$$
$$N = \$18,000 \div \$.30$$
$$N = 60,000 \text{ units}$$

To express the break-even point in terms of dollar sales rather than number of units, multiply the number of units (60,000) by the selling price per unit ($1.50) to find the break-even point in terms of dollar sales, $90,000.

unit contribution margin (marginal income per unit)
The sales price per unit minus the variable cost per unit.

CONTRIBUTION-MARGIN METHOD The general equation can also be reformulated in terms of the **unit contribution margin** or **marginal income per unit** that every unit sold generates, which is the unit sales price minus the variable cost per unit. For the vending machine snack items, the unit contribution margin is $.30:

Unit sales price	$1.50
− Unit variable cost	1.20
= Unit contribution margin	$ .30

total contribution margin
Total number of units sold times the unit contribution margin.

When do we reach the break-even point? When we sell enough units to generate a **total contribution margin** (total number of units sold × unit contribution margin) that is sufficient to cover the total fixed costs. Think about the contribution margin of the snack items. Each unit sold generates extra revenue of $1.50 and extra cost of $1.20. Fixed costs are unaffected. If we sell zero units, we incur a loss equal to the fixed cost of $18,000. Each additional unit sold reduces the loss by $.30 until sales reach the break-even point. After that point, each unit sold adds (or contributes) $.30 to profit.

To find the break-even number of units, divide the fixed costs of $18,000 by the unit contribution margin of $.30. The number of units that we must sell to break even is $18,000 ÷ $.30 = 60,000 units. The sales revenue at the break-even point is 60,000 units × $1.50 per unit, or $90,000.

Instead of using per unit variable costs and contribution margins, it is sometimes more convenient to use percentages. The variable cost percentage and the contribution margin percentage can be computed using either total or per unit costs:

variable-cost percentage
Total variable costs divided by total sales.

Variable-cost percentage = total variable costs ÷ total sales

= variable cost per unit ÷ sales price per unit

contribution-margin percentage
Total contribution margin divided by sales or 100% minus the variable cost percentage.

Contribution-margin percentage = total contribution margin ÷ total sales

= contribution margin per unit ÷ sales price per unit

variable-cost ratio
Variable cost percentage expressed as a ratio.

Note that the contribution-margin percentage = 100% − variable cost percentage. We can also express these percentages as ratios, the **variable-cost ratio** and **contribution-margin ratio**, which are simply the percentages multiplied by 100.

contribution-margin ratio
Contribution margin percentage expressed as a ratio.

Now let's solve for break-even sales dollars in our vending machine example without computing the unit break-even point by using the contribution-margin ratio or percentage:

$$\frac{\text{contribution margin}}{\text{ratio or percentage}} = \frac{\text{contribution margin per unit}}{\text{sales price per unit}} = \frac{\$.30}{\$1.50} = .20 \text{ or } 20\%$$

Let S = sales in dollars needed to break even. Then variable expenses = .80S. Setting the right-hand-side of equation (1) to the break-even level of zero net income,

$$\text{sales} - \text{variable expenses} - \text{fixed expenses} = 0$$
$$S - .80S - \$18,000 = 0$$
$$.20S = \$18,000$$
$$S = \$18,000 \div .20$$
$$S = \$90,000$$

The 20% contribution-margin ratio or percentage implies that $.20 of each sales dollar is available for the recovery of fixed expenses. Thus, we need $18,000 ÷ .20 = $90,000 of sales to break even.

The condensed income statement at the break-even point is

	Total	Per Unit	Percentage
Units	60,000		
Sales	$90,000	$1.50	100%
Variable costs	72,000	1.20	80
Contribution margin*	$18,000	$ .30	20%
Fixed costs	18,000		
Net income	$ 0		

*Sales less variable costs

The preceding income statement shows three different ways the term **contribution margin** can be used. The term can refer to total contribution margin ($18,000), unit contribution margin ($.30 per unit), or contribution-margin ratio or percentage (.20 or 20%). The context generally makes it clear which meaning is intended.

The contribution margin method is often used to evaluate the overall effect of changes in volume for companies that sell multiple products with different unit prices and different unit variable costs. You can use the preceding formula to assess the effect of a change in dollar volume of sales. For example, you can use the formula to assess the effect of an increase in dollar sales for a grocery store selling hundreds of products at many different prices assuming that the variable-cost percentage stays the same. Note that the variable-cost percentage might change if the sales mix changes, an issue that we discuss further in Appendix 4A.

contribution margin
A term used for either total contribution margin, unit contribution margin, or contribution margin percentage.

RELATIONSHIP BETWEEN THE TWO METHODS   The contribution-margin method is a specific version of the general equation method. Look at the last three lines in the two solutions given for equation 1. They read

Break-Even Volume	
Units	Dollars
$.30N = \$18,000	.20S = \$18,000
$N = \dfrac{\$18,000}{\$.30}$	$S = \dfrac{\$18,000}{.20}$
N = 60,000 units	S = $90,000

From these equations, we can derive the following shortcut formulas:

$$\text{break-even volume in units} = \frac{\text{fixed expenses}}{\text{unit contribution margin}} \qquad (2)$$

$$\text{break-even volume in dollars} = \frac{\text{fixed expenses}}{\text{contribution-margin ratio}} \qquad (3)$$

Should you use the general equation method or the contribution-margin method? Use whichever is easier for you to understand or apply to a particular case. Both yield the same results, so the choice is a matter of personal preference.

Making Managerial Decisions

Managers use CVP analysis to predict the effect of changes in sales or costs on the break-even point. Using shortcut formulas (2) and (3), answer the following questions. Remember that the contribution margin per unit equals the sales price per unit minus the variable costs per unit.

1. What would be the effect on the unit and dollar break-even level if fixed costs increase (and there are no other changes)?
2. What would be the effect on the unit and dollar break-even level if variable cost per unit decreases (and there are no other changes)?
3. What would be the effect on the unit and dollar break-even level if sales volume increases? (Think carefully before answering this question.)

Answers

1. The break-even level in both units and sales dollars would increase if fixed costs increase.
2. The break-even level in both units and sales dollars would decrease if variable cost per unit decreases.
3. The actual (or even planned) volume of sales in units has nothing to do with determining the break-even point. This is why unit sales volume does not appear in either equation (2) or (3).

Effects of Changes in Fixed Expenses or Contribution Margin

In addition to determining profit at various volume levels, we can use CVP to examine the effects of changes in fixed costs, variables costs, or selling prices.

CHANGES IN FIXED EXPENSES Changes in fixed expenses cause changes in the break-even point. For example, if we double the $3,000 monthly rent of the vending machines, what is the monthly break-even point in number of units and dollar sales?

The fixed expenses increase from $18,000 to $21,000, so

$$\text{break-even volume in units} = \frac{\text{fixed expenses}}{\text{unit contribution margin}}$$
$$= \frac{\$21,000}{\$.30}$$
$$= 70,000 \text{ units}$$

$$\text{break-even volume in dollars} = \frac{\text{fixed expenses}}{\text{contribution-margin ratio}}$$
$$= \frac{\$21,000}{.20}$$
$$= \$105,000$$

Note that a one-sixth increase in fixed expenses increases the break-even point by one-sixth, from 60,000 to 70,000 units and from $90,000 to $105,000. This type of relationship always exists between fixed expenses and the break-even point, assuming everything else remains constant.

Companies frequently lower their break-even points by reducing their total fixed costs. For example, when demand for cars fell because of the slumping economy in 2008 and 2009, the "Big Three" auto companies closed factories to decrease fixed costs such as property taxes, insurance, depreciation, and managers' salaries. If they had merely produced fewer cars and trucks with the same fixed costs, their volume would have fallen below the break-even point. By reducing fixed costs, the companies lowered their break-even points and reduced their losses.

CHANGES IN UNIT CONTRIBUTION MARGIN Companies can also reduce their break-even points by increasing their unit contribution margins, by either increasing unit sales prices or decreasing unit variable costs, or both.

For example, assume the fixed costs for the vending machine example remain at $18,000. (1) If Winston increases the selling price from $1.50 to $1.60 per unit and the original variable costs per unit are unchanged at $1.20 per unit, find the monthly break-even point in number of units and in dollar sales. (2) If Winston reduces variable costs per unit by $.10 per unit and the selling price remains unchanged at $1.50 per unit, find the monthly break-even point in number of units and in dollar sales.

Here's what happens to the break-even point:

1. If Winston increases the selling price from $1.50 to $1.60 per unit and the original variable expenses are unchanged, the unit contribution margin would increase from $1.50 − $1.20 = $.30 to $1.60 − $1.20 = $.40, and the break-even point would fall to $18,000 ÷ $.40 = 45,000 units. The break-even point in dollars would also change because of the selling price per unit and contribution-margin ratio change. The contribution-margin ratio would be $.40 ÷ $1.60 = .25. The break-even point in dollars would be 45,000 units × $1.60 = $72,000 or, using the formula,

$$\text{break-even volume in dollars} = \frac{\$18,000}{.25} = \$72,000$$

2. The variable expenses decrease from $1.20 to $1.10 per unit, the unit contribution margin increases from $.30 to $.40, and the contribution-margin ratio become $.40 ÷ $1.50 = .26667. The original fixed expenses of $18,000 would stay the same, but the denominators would change from those previously used. Thus,

$$\text{break-even point in units} = \frac{\$18,000}{\$.40} = 45,000 \text{ units}$$

$$\text{break-even point in dollars} = \frac{\$18,000}{.26667} = \$67,500$$

Note that the break-even point in units in (2) is the same as the break-even point in units in (1), because both examples have the same fixed costs and the same contribution margin. However, the break-even points in dollars differ, because the selling prices per unit differ.

You can see that small percentage changes in price or variable costs can lead to large percentage changes in the unit contribution margin and, hence, to large changes in the break-even point.

Target Net Profit and an Incremental Approach

Managers also use CVP analysis to determine the sales volume needed to reach a target profit. For example, in our vending example, suppose Winston considers $1,440 per month the minimum acceptable net income. How many units will she have to sell to justify the adoption of the vending machine plan? How does the number of units "translate" into dollar sales?

To compute the target sales volume in units needed to meet the desired or target net income, we adapt the general approach (equation 1 on p. 137) by setting profit on the right-hand side to the target net income:

$$\text{target sales} - \text{variable expenses} - \text{fixed expenses} = \text{target net income} \qquad (4)$$

or

$$\text{target sales volume in units} = \frac{\text{fixed expenses} + \text{target net income}}{\text{unit contribution margin}}$$

$$= \frac{\$18,000 + \$1,440}{\$.30} = 64,800 \text{ units} \qquad (5)$$

The only real difference from the normal break-even analysis is that we are solving for a target net income of $1,440 instead of a target of $0, which is the definition of break-even net income.

Another way of finding the volume required to achieve a target level of net income is to start with the break-even point and adopt an incremental approach. The phrase **incremental effect** refers to the change in total results (such as revenue, expenses, or income) under a new condition in comparison with some given or known condition. In this case, the known condition is the 60,000-unit break-even point. The change or increment in net income for every unit of sales beyond 60,000 is the unit contribution margin of $1.50 − $1.20 = $.30. The incremental volume required to generate incremental profit of $1,440 is $1,440 ÷ $.30 = 4,800 units. Thus, the volume required to achieve target profit of $1,440 must exceed the break-even volume by 4,800 units; it would therefore be

60,000 + 4,800 = 64,800 units. Multiply 64,800 units by sales price of $1.50 per unit to get the volume in dollar sales, $97,200.

To solve directly for sales dollars with the incremental approach, start at the break-even point in dollar sales of $90,000. Every sales dollar beyond that point contributes $.20 to net profit. Divide $1,440 by $.20 to find the incremental dollar sales ($7,200) required to produce incremental net profit of $1,440. Thus, the total dollar sales is $90,000 + $7,200 = $97,200.

Finally, you can solve directly for the volume in dollar sales using the formula

$$\text{target sales volume in dollars} = \frac{\text{fixed expenses} + \text{target net income}}{\text{contribution-margin ratio}}$$

$$= \frac{\$18,000 + \$1,440}{.20} = \$97,200 \qquad (6)$$

The following table summarizes these alternative computations:

	Break-Even Point	Increment	New Condition
Volume in units	60,000	4,800	64,800
Sales	$90,000	$7,200	$97,200
Variable expenses	72,000	5,760	77,760
Contribution margin	$18,000	$1,440	$19,440
Fixed expenses	18,000	—	18,000
Net income	$ 0	$1,440	$ 1,440

Multiple Changes in Key Factors

So far, we have seen changes in only one CVP factor at a time. In the real world, managers often make decisions about the probable effects of multiple factor changes. For example, Boeing may cut the price of its airplanes to increase sales volume, affecting total revenue and total variable costs. Mars might decrease the size of its Snickers candy bar, saving variable costs and increasing the unit contribution margin, but also decreasing sales volume. Or Medtronic might automate the production of its insulin infusion pump, replacing variable costs of labor with fixed costs of equipment.

Consider our vending example. Suppose Winston is considering locking the vending machines from 6:00 PM to 6:00 AM, which she estimates will save $2,460 in wages monthly. However, she also estimates the cutback from 24-hour service would reduce volume by 10,000 units because many nighttime employees use the machines. Should the machines remain available 24 hours per day? We will perform the analysis for two months representing the lowest and highest predicted sales volume: (1) 62,000 units and (2) 90,000 units.

We will consider two approaches. The first is to construct and solve equations for conditions that prevail under each alternative and select the volume level that yields the highest net income.

Regardless of the current volume level, be it 62,000 or 90,000 units, if we accept the prediction that sales will decline by 10,000 units, closing from 6:00 PM to 6:00 AM will decrease net income by $540:

	Decline from 62,000 to 52,000 Units		Decline from 90,000 to 80,000 Units	
Units	62,000	52,000	90,000	80,000
Sales	$93,000	$78,000	$135,000	$120,000
Variable expenses	74,400	62,400	108,000	96,000
Total contribution margin	$18,600	$15,600	$ 27,000	$ 24,000
Fixed expenses	18,000	15,540	18,000	15,540
Net income	$ 600	$ 60	$ 9,000	$ 8,460
Change in net income		($540)		($540)

A second approach—an incremental approach—is quicker and simpler. Simplicity is important to managers because it keeps the analysis from being cluttered by irrelevant and potentially confusing data.

What does the insightful manager see in this situation? The effect of a 10,000 unit decline in volume does not depend on whether the initial volume is 62,000 or 90,000 units. The essence of this decision is whether the savings in fixed costs exceed the loss in total contribution-margin dollars.

Savings in fixed expenses	$2,460
Less: Lost contribution margin, 10,000 units at $.30	−3,000
Prospective decline in net income	$ −540

As in the first analysis, the incremental analysis also shows that locking the vending machines from 6:00 PM to 6:00 AM would cause a $540 decrease in monthly net income. Whichever way you analyze it, locking the machines is not a sound financial decision.

Nonprofit Application

The managers of nonprofit organizations also benefit from the study of CVP relationships. For example, administrators of nonprofit hospitals are concerned about the behavior of costs as the volume of patients fluctuates. Many nonprofit organizations do not derive revenue from selling goods or services, so their revenue function is not simply number of units sold multiplied by selling price per unit. For example, some nonprofit organizations receive a fixed allocation of funds to cover their costs, and must plan operations based on that fixed budget. Other nonprofit organizations use CVP analysis to plan how to adjust operations in response to changes in the level of donations received. Still other nonprofits receive a fixed allocation of funds and a revenue subsidy that covers a portion of the cost of the services provided. CVP analysis can be adapted to reflect the source or form of the organization's revenue.

To illustrate CVP analysis for a nonprofit organization with a fixed budget allocation, suppose a city has a $100,000 lump-sum budget appropriation to conduct a counseling program for drug addicts. The variable costs for counseling are $400 per patient per year. Fixed costs are $60,000 in the relevant range of 50 to 150 patients. If the city spends the entire budget appropriation, how many patients can it serve in a year?

We can use the break-even equation to solve the problem. Let N be the number of patients, substitute the $100,000 lump-sum budget for sales, and note that the lump-sum budget equals variable expenses plus fixed expenses if the city completely spends its budget.

$$\text{sales} = \text{variable expenses} + \text{fixed expenses}$$
$$\$100{,}000 \text{ lump sum} = \$400N + \$60{,}000$$
$$\$400N = \$100{,}000 - \$60{,}000$$
$$N = \$40{,}000 \div \$400$$
$$N = 100 \text{ patients}$$

The city can serve 100 patients. Now, suppose the city cuts the total budget appropriation for the following year by 10%. Fixed costs will be unaffected, but service will decline.

$$\text{sales} = \text{variable expenses} + \text{fixed expenses}$$
$$\$90{,}000 = \$400N + \$60{,}000$$
$$\$400N = \$90{,}000 - \$60{,}000$$
$$N = \$30{,}000 \div \$400$$
$$N = 75 \text{ patients}$$

The percentage reduction in service is $(100 - 75) \div 100 = 25\%$, which is more than the 10% reduction in the budget. Unless the city restructures its operations, the service volume must fall by 25% to stay within budget.

A graphical presentation of this analysis is in Exhibit 4-9. Note that lump-sum revenue is a horizontal line on the graph.

CVP Analysis and Spreadsheets

Spreadsheets simplify analysis of multiple changes in key factors in a CVP model. Managers use a spreadsheet-based CVP modeling program to study combinations of changes in selling prices,

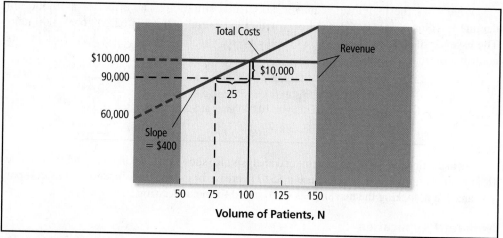

Exhibit 4-9
Graphical Presentation of Nonprofit Application

unit variable costs, fixed costs, and desired profits. Spreadsheets quickly calculate results for alternative assumptions and can display results both numerically and graphically.

Consider Exhibit 4-10, which is a sample spreadsheet that computes the required sales level for all possible combinations of three fixed cost levels ($4,000, $6,000, or $8,000), three variable cost percentages (40%, 44%, or 48% of sales), and three target income levels ($2,000, $4,000, or $6,000). For the 27 different combinations of fixed costs, variable costs, and target income, the spreadsheet calculates the required sales levels rapidly and without error. Further, managers can quickly substitute different numbers for fixed costs (column A), variable cost percentage (column B), and target net income (row 3 of columns C, D, and E) and the spreadsheet will immediately re-compute the required sales level.

In addition to speed and accuracy, spreadsheets allow a more sophisticated approach to CVP analysis than the one illustrated in this chapter. The assumptions we listed on page 137 are necessary to simplify the analysis enough to construct a CVP model by hand. Computer models can be more complex and include multiple cost drivers, nonlinear relationships between costs and cost drivers, varying sales mixes, and analyses for multiple relevant ranges.

	A	B	C	D	E
1				Sales Required to Earn	
2	Fixed	Variable Cost		Annual Net Income of	
3	Cost	as % of Sales	$ 2,000	$ 4,000	$ 6,000
4					
5	$4,000	0.40	$10,000*	$13,333	$16,667
6	$4,000	0.44	$10,714*	$14,286	$17,857
7	$4,000	0.48	$11,538*	$15,385	$19,231
8	$6,000	0.40	$13,333	$16,667	$20,000
9	$6,000	0.44	$14,286	$17,857	$21,429
10	$6,000	0.48	$15,385	$19,231	$23,077
11	$8,000	0.40	$16,667	$20,000	$23,333
12	$8,000	0.44	$17,857	$21,429	$25,000
13	$8,000	0.48	$19,231	$23,077	$26,923

*(A5 + C3)/(1 − B5) = ($4,000 + $2,000)/(1 − $.40) = $10,000
(A6 + C3)/(1 − B6) = ($4,000 + $2,000)/(1 − $.44) = $10,714
(A7 + C3)/(1 − B7) = ($4,000 + $2,000)/(1 − $.48) = $11,538

Exhibit 4-10
Spreadsheet Analysis of CVP Relationships

The use of computer models is a cost-benefit issue. The validity of these models depends on the accuracy of the underlying assumptions about revenue and cost behavior. More complex models often require fewer assumptions and, thus, are valid in more general circumstances. However, sometimes the costs of modeling exceed the value of the improved quality of management decisions. In small organizations, simplified CVP models often are accurate enough; the cost of more sophisticated modeling may exceed the benefit.

Additional Uses of CVP Analysis

Margin of Safety

CVP analysis can help managers assess risk. One measure of risk is the **margin of safety**. The margin of safety measures how far sales can fall before losses occur and is the difference between the level of planned sales and the break-even point. The margin of safety can be defined in either units or dollars:

> **margin of safety**
> Planned unit sales less the break-even unit sales; a measure of how far sales can fall below the planned level before losses occur.

$$\text{margin of safety in units} = \text{planned unit sales} - \text{break-even unit sales}$$

$$\text{margin of safety in dollars} = \text{planned dollar sales} - \text{break-even dollar sales}$$

For example, if Amy Winston in our vending machine example predicts sales volume of 80,000 units or $120,000, the margin of safety in units is 20,000 units and the margin of safety in dollars is $30,000:

$$\text{margin of safety in units} = 80,000 \text{ units} - 60,000 \text{ units} = 20,000 \text{ units}$$

$$\text{margin of safety in dollars} = \$120,000 - \$90,000 = \$30,000$$

The larger the margin of safety, the less likely it is that volume will fall to the point where the company has an operating loss, that is, below the break-even point. Conversely, a smaller margin of safety indicates greater risk of incurring a loss.

Operating Leverage

In addition to weighing the varied effects of changes in fixed and variable costs, managers need to consider the firm's **cost structure**—the combination of variable- and fixed-cost resources used to carry out the organization's activities. There is typically a tradeoff between variable and fixed costs in choosing a cost structure. Lower variable costs are often achieved by incurring higher fixed costs. For example, highly-automated factories with high fixed overhead costs typically have lower variable labor costs compared to less automated factories. Firms with higher fixed costs and lower variable costs are said to have greater **operating leverage**—the sensitivity of a firm's profit to changes in volume of sales. In highly leveraged companies with lower variable costs, small changes in sales volume result in large changes in net income. In companies with less leverage and higher variable costs, changes in sales volume have a smaller effect on income.

> **cost structure**
> The combination of variable- and fixed-cost resources used to carry out the organization's activities.

> **operating leverage**
> The sensitivity of a firm's profit to changes in volume of sales.

Exhibit 4-11 shows cost behavior relationships at two firms, one with higher operating leverage and one with lower leverage. The firm with higher leverage has fixed costs of $14,000 and variable cost per unit of $.10. The firm with lower leverage has fixed costs of only $2,000 but variable costs of $.25 per unit. For both firms, the sales price is $.30 per unit.

The amount by which profit changes with sales volume is determined by the respective contribution margins. The contribution margin per unit for the firm with higher operating leverage is $.30 − $.10 = $.20 per unit. The contribution margin per unit for the firms with lower operating leverage is $.30 − $.25 = $.05 per unit. Thus, each unit change in sales results in a $.20 change in profit for the firm with higher operating leverage and a $.05 change in profit for the firm with lower operating leverage.

To illustrate the effect of operating leverage in the preceding example, suppose expected sales at both companies are 80,000 units. At this sales level, both firms have net incomes of $2,000. If sales fall short of 80,000 units, profits drop more sharply for the more highly leveraged cost structure. If sales exceed 80,000 units, however, profits also increase more sharply. For example, at sales of 70,000 units, the higher-leveraged firm has zero profits, compared to $1,500 for the lower-leveraged firm. At sales of 90,000 units, however, net income is $4,000 for the higher-leveraged firm but only $2,500 for the lower-leveraged firm.

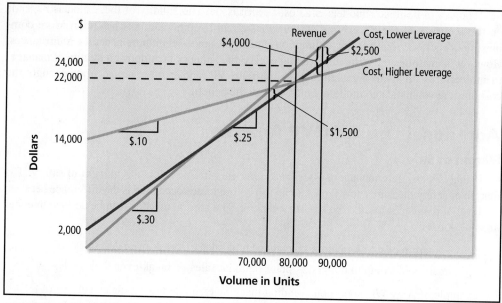

Exhibit 4-11
High Versus Low Operating Leverage

degree of operating leverage
The ratio of contribution margin to profit, defined at a specific volume of sales.

The effect of operating leverage on the variability of profit is captured by **degree of operating leverage**—the ratio of contribution margin to profit, defined at a specific volume of sales. The degree of operating leverage at a specific volume describes how a percentage change in sales will translate into a percentage change in profit.

For example, for the firm with lower operating leverage in Exhibit 4-11, the degree of operating leverage at 80,000 units is contribution margin at 80,000 units (80,000 × $.05) divided by profit at 80,000 units ($2,000), or $4,000/$2,000 = 2. In our example, a degree of operating leverage of 2 means that the percentage change in profit will be 2 times the percentage change in sales. If sales volume increases by 12.5%, increasing by 10,000 units from 80,000 units to 90,000 units, profit will increase by 2 × 12.5% = 25%, moving from $2,000 at 80,000 units to $2,500 at 90,000 units. Similarly, if sales volume decreases by 12.5%, decreasing from 80,000 units to 70,000 units, profit will decrease by 2 × −12.5% = −25%, moving from $2,000 to $1,500.

For the firm with higher operating leverage in Exhibit 4-11, the degree of operating leverage at 80,000 units is $16,000/$2,000 = 8, which means that the percentage change in profit will be 8 times the percentage change in sales. If sales volume increases by 12.5%, increasing by 10,000 units from 80,000 units to 90,000 units, profit will increase by 8 × 12.5% = 100%, moving from $2,000 at 80,000 units to $4,000 at 90,000 units. Similarly, if sales volume decreases by 12.5%, profit will decrease by 8 × −12.5% = −100%, moving from $2,000 to $0.

The higher-leverage cost structure is more risky. Why? Because it results in more variability of income—it might lead to a higher net income but it also might lead to a larger net loss. The lower-leverage alternative is less risky because variations in sales volume lead to smaller variability in net income. Is lower risk always better? Not necessarily. Suppose in the preceding example that managers are sure that volume will be greater than 80,000 units. Then the higher operating leverage (and higher risk) cost structure is better because it will yield higher profits. On the other hand, suppose there is a possibility that volume will be lower than 80,000 units. For volume lower than 80,000 units, the lower operating leverage (and lower risk) cost structure yields higher profits. Thus, if managers are unsure whether volume will be greater or lower than 80,000 units, they should evaluate the expected profit and should also take into account the effects of risk.

Best Cost Structure

Analyzing and managing the organization's cost structure is an important management responsibility. For example, purchasing automated machinery may raise fixed costs but reduce the variable cost, labor cost per unit. Conversely, it may be wise to reduce fixed costs to obtain a more favorable combination. For example, a company may decide to compensate its sales force via sales commissions rather than pay them salaries, thus reducing salaries (a fixed cost) but increasing sales commissions (a variable cost). Another example of exchanging a fixed cost for a variable cost is a contract **Blockbuster** signed with **Disney** and other major studios. Instead of buying video tapes for $65 each, a fixed cost for each tape, Blockbuster paid only a $7 fixed cost and an additional variable cost equal to a percentage of the rental revenues. You can see one result of this contract in the Business First box on p. 149.

A thorough understanding of cost-volume-profit relationships is essential in choosing a cost structure. The best combination of variable- and fixed-cost resources depends on many factors—the current level of sales, expected level of future sales, and the set of alternatives available now and in the future.

Generally, companies that spend heavily on the fixed costs of advertising are willing to do so because they have high contribution-margin percentages (e.g., airlines, cigarette, and cosmetic companies). Conversely, companies with low contribution-margin percentages usually spend less for advertising and promotion (e.g., manufacturers of industrial equipment). As a result, two companies with the same unit sales volumes at the same unit prices could have different attitudes toward risking an advertising outlay. Assume the following:

	Perfume Company	Janitorial Service Company
Unit sales volume	200,000 bottles	200,000 square feet
Dollar sales at $10 per unit	$2,000,000	$2,000,000
Variable costs	200,000	1,700,000
Total contribution margin	$1,800,000	$ 300,000
Contribution-margin percentage	90%	15%

Suppose each company can increase sales volume by 10% by spending $100,000 for advertising:

	Perfume Company	Janitorial Service Company
Increase in sales volume, 20,000 × $10	$200,000	$200,000
Increase in total contribution margin, 90%, 15%	180,000	30,000

By spending $100,000 on advertising, the perfume company would increase the total contribution margin by $180,000, thus increasing total profit by $180,000 − $100,000 = $80,000. In contrast, the janitorial service company would increase the total contribution margin by only $30,000, resulting in a change in total profit of $30,000 − $100,000 = −$70,000.

Note that when the contribution margin as a percentage of sales is low, large increases in volume are necessary to generate increases in net profits. At the same time, decreases in volume also generate smaller decreases in profit when contribution-margin percentages are low. High contribution-margin ratios have the opposite effect—large increases in profits if sales grow but large decreases in profits if sales fall.

The best cost structure depends on multiple factors. The best cost structure is not necessarily the cost structure with the greatest margin of safety, or the lowest break-even point, or the highest operating leverage, or the lowest operating leverage. The best cost structure depends on the impact of risk and on the expected volume of sales, both in the current time period and in future time periods. Further, as explained in later chapters, the expected volume of sales may be different for different cost structures. Managers must have a thorough understanding of all these factors in order to choose the best cost structure.

Contribution Margin and Gross Margin

Objective 7

Differentiate between contribution margin and gross margin.

gross margin (gross profit)
The excess of sales over the total cost of goods sold.

cost of goods sold
The cost of the merchandise that a company acquires or produces and sells.

This chapter has focused on the contribution margin. However, accountants also use a similar term, *gross margin*, to mean something quite different. Too often people confuse the terms *contribution margin* and *gross margin*. **Gross margin**, also called **gross profit**, is the excess of sales over the cost of goods sold. **Cost of goods sold** is the cost of the merchandise that a company acquires or produces and then sells. Compare the gross margin with the contribution margin:

$$\text{gross margin} = \text{sales price} - \text{cost of goods sold}$$
$$\text{contribution margin} = \text{sales price} - \text{all variable expenses}$$

Exhibit 4-12 shows costs divided on two different dimensions. As shown at the bottom of the exhibit, the gross margin uses the division on the production or acquisition cost versus selling and administrative cost dimension, and the contribution margin uses the division based on the variable-cost versus fixed-cost dimension.

In our vending-machine illustration, the contribution margin and the gross margin are identical because the cost of goods sold is the only variable cost:

Sales	$1.50
Variable costs: acquisition cost of unit sold	1.20
Contribution margin and gross margin are equal	$ .30

Now, suppose the firm had to pay a commission of $.12 per unit sold:

		Contribution Margin	Gross Margin
Sales		$1.50	$1.50
Acquisition cost of unit sold	$1.20		1.20
Variable commission	.12		
Total variable expense		1.32	
Contribution margin		$ .18	
Gross margin			$ .30

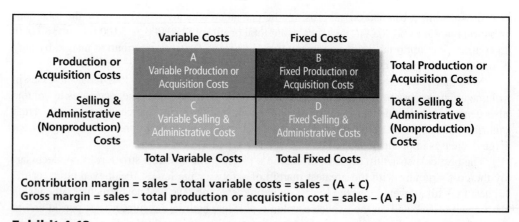

Contribution margin = sales – total variable costs = sales – (A + C)
Gross margin = sales – total production or acquisition cost = sales – (A + B)

Exhibit 4-12
Costs for Gross Margin and Contribution Margin

Business First

Did Blockbuster Violate Disney Contract? Accounting Disagreement or Ethical Issue?

In early 2003, the Walt Disney Company sued Blockbuster, claiming that Blockbuster had violated a 1997 agreement between the two companies. Prior to the agreement, Blockbuster purchased videos from Disney for about $65 each and kept all the rental revenue. Under the pact, Blockbuster agreed to purchase movies from Disney for $7 a copy and then pay the studio a portion of the revenue from each rental.

The contract allowed Blockbuster to buy more copies of each video, which led to the guarantee that customers could rely on Blockbuster to have a copy of any movie the customer wanted or else the rental was free. With this policy, Blockbuster increased its market share of the video rental market from 28% to 40%. Essentially, Blockbuster turned a fixed cost, $65 per tape, into primarily a variable cost, with a small $7 fixed-cost portion and a larger variable-cost portion that depended on how much revenue Blockbuster generated from its rentals.

The arrangement was similar to that between the owners of shopping malls and many of their retail store tenants. Each store pays a monthly rental fee plus a percentage of its sales. Just as shopping mall owners rely on their tenants to truthfully report their sales, Disney relied on Blockbuster to correctly account for its video rentals.

In addition, Blockbuster and Disney also agreed on when Blockbuster could sell old rental tapes. Since these were so inexpensive for Blockbuster, selling them could be a lucrative business. But Disney did not want these low-cost tapes competing with its own videotape sales. Thus, it placed restrictions on when Blockbuster could sell them.

In the suit, Disney claimed that Blockbuster improperly deducted "promotional" credits from its gross rental fees, failed to account for "hundreds of thousands" of missing videos, and sold videos prematurely. Disney had to rely on Blockbuster to correctly account for its rental revenues and inventory of tapes. Blockbuster claimed that its accounting was in accordance with the original agreement.

This is an example where good ethics and good accounting are both important. The original agreement promised benefits to both companies—more rental income for Disney on hit movies and a lower operating leverage cost-structure for Blockbuster. But such a contract will not work if each party cannot trust the other. It's not clear who is right in this case, but both companies were hurt by the allegations. At a minimum, both will need to include better monitoring provisions in future contracts because other companies will suspect Disney of trying to get more than it deserves and Blockbuster of playing accounting tricks to minimize its payment to Disney.

Source: "Disney Sues Blockbuster Over Contract," *New York Times*, January 4, 2003; "Disney Sues Top Video Chain," *Los Angeles Times*, January 3, 2003.

Summary Problem for Your Review

PROBLEM

The budgeted income statement of Port Williams Gift Shop follows:

Net revenue	$800,000
Less expenses, including $400,000 of fixed expenses	880,000
Net loss	$ (80,000)

The manager believes that an additional outlay of $200,000 for advertising will increase sales but is wondering how much sales will have to increase in order to achieve 1) breakeven, or 2) a $40,000 profit.

1. At what sales volume in dollars will the shop break even after spending $200,000 on advertising?
2. What sales volume in dollars will result in a net profit of $40,000 after spending the $200,000 on advertising?

SOLUTION

1. Note that all data are in dollars, not units. The variable costs are $880,000 − $400,000 = $480,000 and the variable-cost ratio is $480,000 ÷ $800,000 = .60.

149

(Remember to divide variable costs by sales, not by total costs.) Therefore, the contribution-margin ratio is .40. Let S = break-even sales in dollars. Then

$$\text{Sales} - \text{variable costs} - \text{fixed costs} = \text{net profit}$$

$$S - .60S - (\$400{,}000 + \$200{,}000) = 0$$

$$.40S = \$600{,}000$$

$$S = \frac{\$600{,}000}{.40} = \frac{\text{fixed costs}}{\text{contribution-margin ratio}}$$

$$S = \$1{,}500{,}000$$

2. $$\text{required sales} = \frac{(\text{fixed costs} + \text{target net profit})}{\text{contribution-margin ratio}}$$

$$\text{required sales} = \frac{(\$600{,}000 + \$40{,}000)}{.40} = \frac{\$640{,}000}{.40}$$

$$\text{required sales} = \$1{,}600{,}000$$

Alternatively, we can use an incremental approach and reason that all dollar sales beyond the $1.5 million break-even point will result in a 40% contribution to net profit. Divide $40,000 by .40. Therefore, sales must be $100,000 beyond the $1.5 million break-even point to produce a net profit of $40,000.

Highlights to Remember

1. **Explain how cost drivers affect cost behavior.** A cost driver is an output measure that causes the use of costly resources. When the level of an activity changes, the level of the cost driver or output measure will also change, causing changes in costs.

2. **Show how changes in cost-driver levels affect variable and fixed costs.** Cost behavior refers to how costs change as levels of an organization's activities change. If the cost of the resource used changes in proportion to changes in the cost-driver level, the resource is a variable-cost resource (its costs are variable). If the cost of the resource used does not change because of cost-driver level changes, the resource is a fixed-cost resource (its costs are fixed).

3. **Explain step- and mixed-cost behavior.** Step and mixed costs combine aspects of variable- and fixed-cost behavior. Graphs of step costs look like steps. Costs remain fixed within a given range of activity or cost-driver level, but then rise or fall abruptly when the cost-driver level moves outside this range. Mixed costs involve a fixed element and a variable element of cost behavior. Unlike step costs, mixed costs have a single fixed cost at all levels of activity and in addition have a variable cost element that increases proportional to the level of activity.

4. **Create a cost-volume-profit (CVP) graph and understand the assumptions behind it.** We can approach CVP analysis (sometimes called break-even analysis) graphically or with equations. We create a CVP graph by drawing revenue and total cost lines as functions of the volume of activity. Be sure to recognize the limitations of CVP analysis and that it assumes efficiency, sales mix, and inventory levels are all held constant.

5. **Calculate break-even sales volume in total dollars and total units.** To calculate the break-even point in total units, divide the fixed costs by the unit contribution margin. To calculate the break-even point in total dollars (sales dollars), divide the fixed costs by the contribution-margin ratio.

6. **Calculate sales volume in total dollars and total units to reach a target profit.** Managers use CVP analysis to compute the sales needed to achieve a target profit or to examine the effects on profit of changes in factors such as fixed costs, variable costs, or cost-driver volume.

7. **Differentiate between contribution margin and gross margin.** The contribution margin—the difference between sales price and variable costs—is an important concept. Do not confuse it with gross margin, the difference between sales price and cost of goods sold.

Appendix 4A: Sales-Mix Analysis

Objective 8

Explain the effects of sales mix on profits.

The cost-volume-profit analysis in this chapter focused on the case of a single product. However, nearly all companies produce more than one product or service. For these companies, volume is determined not just by total sales but also by sales mix, which you will recall from p. 137 is the relative proportions or combinations of quantities of products that comprise total sales. If the proportions of the mix change, the cost-volume-profit relationships also change.

Suppose Ramos Company has two products, wallets (W) and key cases (K) and the following budget:

	Wallets (W)	Key Cases (K)	Total
Sales in units	300,000	75,000	375,000
Sales @ $8 and $5	$2,400,000	$375,000	$2,775,000
Variable expenses @ $7 and $3	2,100,000	225,000	2,325,000
Contribution margins @ $1 and $2	$ 300,000	$150,000	$ 450,000
Fixed expenses			180,000
Net income			$ 270,000

What is the break-even point for Ramos? The answer depends on the mix of products. For example, you can use the approach outlined in the chapter to find the break-even point if the mix is 100% W or 100% K. For instance, suppose Ramos Company sells only key cases, and fixed expenses stay at $180,000.

$$\text{break-even point in units of K} = \frac{\text{fixed expenses}}{\text{contribution margin per unit}}$$

$$= \frac{\$180,000}{\$2}$$

$$= 90,000 \text{ key cases}$$

If Ramos sells only wallets,

$$\text{break-even point in units of W} = \frac{\$180,000}{\$1} = 180,000 \text{ wallets}$$

We can also generalize the approach used in the chapter to find breakeven for any other fixed proportion of key cases and wallets. For example, consider a sales mix of four wallets for every key case. Letting K and W denote the number of units of key cases and wallets, respectively, the assumed sales mix implies $W = 4K$. The calculation of total volume to break even is as follows:

$$\text{sales} - \text{variable expenses} - \text{fixed expenses} = \text{zero net income}$$

$$[\$8(4K) + \$5(K)] - [\$7(4K) + \$3(K)] - \$180,000 = 0$$

$$\$32K + \$5K - \$28K - \$3K - \$180,000 = 0$$

$$\$6K = \$180,000$$

$$K = 30,000$$

$$W = 4K = 120,000$$

The break-even point for a sales mix of four wallets for every key case is 30,000 key cases and 120,000 wallets, or 150,000 total units.

These examples show that each sales mix has a break-even point. The break-even point if Ramos produces only wallets is 180,000 wallets, the break-even point if Ramos produces only key cases is 90,000 key cases, and the break-even point if Ramos produces four wallets for every key case is a total of 150,000 units (30,000 key cases and 120,000 wallets).

Changes in sales mix affect the break-even point and the expected net income at various sales levels. For example, consider a revised Ramos budget where the budgeted number of units remains at 375,000 units but the mix is revised to 325,000 wallets and 50,000 key cases:

	Wallets (W)	Key Cases (K)	Total
Sales in units	325,000	50,000	375,000
Sales @ $8 and $5	$2,600,000	$250,000	$2,850,000
Variable expenses @ $7 and $3	2,275,000	150,000	2,425,000
Contribution margins @ $1 and $2	$ 325,000	$100,000	$ 425,000
Fixed expenses			180,000
Net income			$ 245,000

The revised budget shows that the change in sales mix results in net income of $245,000, rather than $270,000 for the original mix of 300,000 wallets and 75,000 key cases. Although both budgets have identical total numbers of units, the revised budget has a smaller proportion of sales of the product bearing the higher unit contribution margin, key cases. Relative to the original budget, the revised budget has 25,000 fewer key cases with a contribution margin of $2 per unit ($5 − $3) and 25,000 more wallets with a contribution margin of $1 per unit ($8 − $7). As a result, budgeted net income is $25,000 lower in the revised budget.

The effect of sales mix on profit is often an important element of strategy. For example, a recent annual report for **Neenah Paper Inc.** described the role of product mix in its strategy to grow margins and improve profitability: "Margin improvement will come through optimizing our product mix, faster growth of higher margin products, new product sales generated through innovation/R&D efforts and overall benefits of volume and scale efficiencies."

Contribution margins help guide executives who must decide to emphasize or deemphasize particular products. For example, given limited production facilities or limited time of sales personnel, should we emphasize wallets or key cases? Contribution margins, along with other factors, affect these decisions. Including the importance of the contribution margin per unit of time (or per unit of other constrained resource) rather than per unit of product.

Appendix 4B: Impact of Income Taxes

Objective 9

Compute cost-volume-profit (CVP) relationships on an after-tax basis.

Thus far we have ignored income taxes, but most companies must pay income taxes. Income taxes do not affect the break-even point. Why? Because there is no income tax at a level of zero income. However, income taxes do affect calculation of the volume required to achieve a specified after-tax target profit.

Reconsider the vending machine example from earlier in this chapter. If the vending machine company pays income tax at a rate of 40%, the before-tax income of $1,440 corresponds to after-tax net income of $864, as shown by the following calculations:

Income before income tax	$1,440	100%
Income tax	576	40%
After-tax net income	$ 864	60%

This example illustrates the general relationship between income before tax and net income after tax:

$$\text{after-tax net income} = \text{income before income taxes} \times (1 - \text{tax rate})$$

or

$$\text{income before income taxes} = \frac{\text{after-tax net income}}{1 - \text{tax rate}}$$

The only change required to introduce taxes into the general equation illustrated in the chapter for calculation of volume required to achieve a given target income is to substitute $\frac{\text{target after-tax net income}}{1 - \text{tax rate}}$ on the right-hand side of the equation:

$$\text{target sales} - \text{variable expenses} - \text{fixed expenses} = \frac{\text{target after-tax net income}}{1 - \text{tax rate}}$$

Return to the target income example from the chapter where selling price is \$1.50 per unit, variable cost is \$1.20 per unit, and total fixed cost is \$18,000. Assume that target after-tax net income is \$864. The equation to find N, the number of units to be sold to achieve the after-tax income target of \$864 is as follows:

$$\$1.50N - \$1.20N - \$18,000 = \frac{\$864}{1 - .4}$$

$$\$0.30N - \$18,000 = \$1,440$$

$$\$0.30N = \$1,440 + \$18,000$$

$$\$0.30N = \$19,440$$

$$N = 64,800 \text{ units}$$

Sales of 64,800 units produce an after-tax profit of \$864 as shown here, which of course corresponds to the volume required to produce before-tax profit of \$1,440, as shown in the chapter.

Now suppose the target after-tax net income is \$1,800. The volume required for this higher level of after-tax income would rise to 70,000 units:

$$\$1.50N - \$1.20N - \$18,000 = \frac{\$1,800}{1 - .4}$$

$$\$0.30N - \$18,000 = \$3,000$$

$$\$0.30N = \$3,000 + \$18,000$$

$$\$0.30N = \$21,000$$

$$N = 70,000 \text{ units}$$

The formula from the chapter for the effect of a change in volume on income can also be adapted to show the effect on after-tax net income:

$$\text{change in net income} = \left(\begin{array}{c}\text{change in volume}\\\text{in units}\end{array}\right) \times \left(\begin{array}{c}\text{contribution margin}\\\text{per unit}\end{array}\right) \times (1 - \text{tax rate})$$

Apply this formula to verify how net income should change when we increase volume from a level of 64,800 units (which produced \$864 after-tax net income) to a level of 70,000 units in our example:

$$\text{change in net income} = (70,000 - 64,800) \times \$.30 \times (1 - .4)$$

$$= 5,200 \times .30 \times .60 = 5,200 \times \$.18$$

$$= \$936$$

The formula verifies our earlier calculations. When volume increases from 64,800 units to 70,000 units, after-tax net income increases by \$936, moving from \$864 to \$1,800.

Accounting Vocabulary

break-even point, p. 136
contribution margin, p. 139
contribution-margin
    percentage, p. 138
contribution-margin
    ratio, p. 138
cost behavior, p. 127
cost driver, p. 127
cost of goods sold, p. 148
cost structure, p. 145
cost-volume-profit (CVP)
    analysis, p. 135

decision context, p. 132
degree of operating
    leverage, p. 146
fixed cost, p. 129
gross margin, p. 148
gross profit, p. 148
incremental effect, p. 141
margin of safety, p. 145
marginal income
    per unit, p. 138
mixed cost, p. 134
operating leverage, p. 145

relevant range, p. 132
sales mix, p. 137
step cost, p. 133
total contribution
    margin, p. 138
unit contribution
    margin, p. 138
variable cost, p. 129
variable-cost
    percentage, p. 138
variable-cost ratio, p. 138

MyAccountingLab **Fundamental Assignment Material**

4-A1 Fixed- and Variable-Cost Behavior

Maintaining a clean working environment is important to Napco, an industrial parts manufacturer. Cleaning the plant is the responsibility of the maintenance department. The 50,000 square foot plant is thoroughly cleaned from four to eight times a month depending on the level and stage of production. For the most recent month, March, the plant was cleaned four times. The production schedule for the next quarter (April through June) indicates that the plant will need to be cleaned five, six, and eight times respectively.

Two of the resources needed to clean the plant are labor and cleaning supplies. The cost driver for both resources is number of times the plant is cleaned. Plant cleaning laborers are full-time employees who are paid the same wages regardless of the number of times the plant is cleaned. Cleaning supplies is a variable cost. The March cost of labor was $21,000 and cleaning supplies used cost $8,000.

1. Prepare a table that shows how labor cost, cleaning supplies cost, total cost, and total cost per cleaning changes in response to the number of times the plant is cleaned. What is the predicted total cost of plant cleaning for the next quarter?
2. Suppose Napco can hire an outside cleaning company to clean the plant as needed. The charge rate for cleaning is $5,700 per plant cleaning. If the outside cleaning company is hired, Napco can lay off the workers who are now cleaning the plant and will spend nothing for cleaning supplies. Will Napco save money with the outside cleaning company over the next quarter? Prepare a schedule that supports your answer.

4-A2 Cost-Volume-Profit and Vending Machines

Vendmart Food Services Company operates and services snack vending machines located in restaurants, gas stations, and factories in four southwestern states. The machines are rented from the manufacturer. In addition, Vendmart must rent the space occupied by its machines. The following expense and revenue relationships pertain to a contemplated expansion program of 80 machines.

Fixed monthly expenses follow:

Machine rental: 80 machines @ $22.10	$1,768
Space rental: 80 locations @ $20.00	1,600
Part-time wages to service the additional 80 machines	500
Other fixed costs	132
Total monthly fixed costs	$4,000

Other data follow:

	Per Unit (Snack)	Per $100 of Sales
Selling price	$1.00	100%
Cost of snack	.68	68
Contribution margin	$.32	32%

These questions relate to the given data unless otherwise noted. Consider each question independently.

1. What is the monthly break-even point in number of units (snacks)? In dollar sales?
2. If 45,000 units were sold, what would be the company's net income?
3. If the space rental cost was doubled, what would be the monthly break-even point in number of units? In dollar sales?
4. Refer to the original data. If, in addition to the fixed space rent, Vendmart Food Services Company paid the vending machine manufacturer $.07 per unit sold, what would be the monthly break-even point in number of units? In dollar sales?
5. Refer to the original data. If, in addition to the fixed rent, Vendmart paid the machine manufacturer $.11 for each unit sold in excess of the break-even point, what would the new net income be if 45,000 units were sold?

4-A3 Exercises in Cost-Volume-Profit Relationships

Upcraft Moving Company specializes in hauling heavy goods over long distances. The company's revenues and expenses depend on revenue-miles, a measure that combines both weights and mileage.

Summarized budget data for next year are based on predicted total revenue miles of 500,000. At that level of volume, and at any level of volume between 300,000 and 700,000 revenue miles, the company's fixed costs are $50,000. The selling price and variable costs are as follows:

Per Revenue-Mile	
Average selling price (revenue)	$2.00
Average variable expenses	1.60

1. Compute the budgeted net income. Ignore income taxes.
2. Management is trying to decide how various possible conditions or decisions might affect net income. Compute the new net income for each of the following changes. Consider each case independently.
    a. A 30% increase in sales price.
    b. A 30% increase in revenue miles.
    c. A 30% increase in variable expenses.
    d. A 30% increase in fixed expenses.
    e. An average decrease in selling price of $.05 per revenue mile and a 15% increase in revenue miles. Refer to the original data.
    f. An average increase in selling price of $.01 and a 30% decrease in revenue miles.
    g. A 30% increase in fixed expenses in the form of more advertising and a 15% increase in revenue miles.

4-A4 Types of Cost Behavior
Identify the following planned costs as (a) variable costs, (b) fixed costs, (c) mixed costs, or (d) step costs. For variable costs and mixed costs, indicate the most likely cost driver.

1. Public relations employee compensation to be paid by Intel
2. Crew supervisor in a Lands' End mail-order house; a new supervisor is added for every 12 workers employed
3. Sales commissions based on revenue dollars; payments to be made to advertising salespersons employed by radio station WCCO, Minneapolis
4. Jet fuel costs of Southwest Airlines
5. Total costs of renting trucks by the city of Nashville; charge is a lump sum of $300 per month plus $.20 per mile
6. Straight-line depreciation on desks in the office of an attorney
7. Advertising costs, a lump sum, planned by ABC, Inc.
8. Rental payment by the Internal Revenue Service on a five-year lease for office space in a private office building
9. Advertising allowance granted to wholesalers by 7-Up Bottling on a per-case basis
10. Compensation of lawyers employed internally by Microsoft
11. Total repairs and maintenance of a university classroom building

4-B1 Fixed- and Variable-Cost Behavior
Applejack Fine Dining has 970 restaurants across the United States. Maintaining a clean environment for customers is a key success factor at Applejack. Each restaurant is cleaned regularly after closing. In addition to regular cleaning, from 5 to 20 times a month, depending on various factors including the amount of business, a special treatment is given to the floors consisting of breaking down the old wax and rewaxing. So the total number of times a restaurant is cleaned varies from 35 to 50 times a month.

The two most costly resources needed to clean an Applejack restaurant are labor and supplies. The cost driver for both resources is number of times a restaurant is cleaned. Cleaning laborers are paid the same wages regardless of the number of times a restaurant is cleaned. Cleaning supplies is a variable cost. The cost of supplies used per regular cleaning and per special cleaning is about the same.

Suppose one of the local Applejack restaurants in Orlando has 6,000 square feet. In October, the restaurant was cleaned 35 times. The cost of cleaning labor was $21,000 for October, and cleaning supplies cost $16,800. The months of November and December are typically much busier, so the restaurant manager expects to clean 45 times and 50 times in November and December, respectively.

1. Prepare a table that shows how labor cost, cleaning supplies cost, total cost, and total cost per cleaning changes in response to number of times the restaurant is cleaned. Use volumes of 35, 40, 45, and 50 times cleaned. What is the predicted total cost of cleaning for November and December?

2. Suppose Applejack can hire an outside cleaning company to clean the restaurant as needed. The charge rate for cleaning is $.25 per square foot. If the outside cleaning company is hired, Applejack can lay off the workers who are now cleaning and will spend nothing on cleaning supplies. Will Applejack save money with the outside cleaning company over the next two months? Prepare a schedule that supports your answer. What information would you need to make a recommendation about hiring the outside cleaning company on a permanent basis?

4-B2 Cost-Volume-Profit at a Day Care Facility

Luke Morrison opened Luke's Corner, a small day care facility, just over 2 years ago. After a rocky start, Luke's Corner has been thriving. Morrison is now preparing a budget for November 20X7.

Monthly fixed costs for Luke's Corner are as follows:

Rent	$ 800
Salaries	1,400
Other fixed costs	140
Total fixed costs	$ 2,340

The salary is for Anna Dukes, the only employee, who works with Morrison by caring for the children. Morrison does not pay himself a salary, but he receives the excess of revenues over costs each month.

The cost driver for variable costs is "child-days." One child-day is one day in day care for one child, and the variable cost is $12 per child-day. The facility is open from 6:00 AM to 6:00 PM weekdays (that is, Monday–Friday), and there are 22 weekdays in November 20X7. An average day has 8 children attending Luke's Corner. State law prohibits Luke's Corner from having more than 14 children, a limit it has never reached. Morrison charges $30 per day per child, regardless of how long the child is at the facility.

1. What is the break-even point for November in child-days? In revenue dollars?
2. Suppose attendance for November 20X7 is equal to the average, resulting in $22 \times 8 = 176$ child-days. What amount will Morrison have left after paying all expenses?
3. Suppose both costs and attendance are difficult to predict. Compute the amount Morrison will have left after paying all expenses for each of the following situations. Consider each case independently.
   a. Average attendance is 9 children per day instead of 8, generating 198 child-days.
   b. Variable costs increase to $14 per child-day.
   c. Rent increases by $220 per month.
   d. Morrison spends $300 on advertising (a fixed cost) in November, which increases average daily attendance to 9.5 children.
   e. Morrison begins charging $33 per day on November 1, and average daily attendance slips to 7 children.

4-B3 Exercises in Cost-Volume-Profit Relationships

Each problem is unrelated to the others.

1. Given: Selling price per unit, $25; total fixed expenses, $9,100; variable expenses per unit, $18. Find break-even sales in units.
2. Given: Sales, $43,000; variable expenses, $30,100; fixed expenses, $8,400; net income, $4,500. Find break-even sales in dollars.
3. Given: Selling price per unit, $29; total fixed expenses, $30,400; variable expenses per unit, $13. Find total sales in units to achieve a profit of $8,000, assuming no change in selling price.
4. Given: Sales, $51,000; variable expenses, $18,000; fixed expenses, $18,000; net income, $15,000. Assume no change in selling price; find net income if activity volume increases by 20%.
5. Given: Selling price per unit, $48; total fixed expenses, $106,000; variable expenses per unit, $36. Assume that variable expenses are reduced by 25% per unit, and the total fixed expenses are increased by 15%. Find the sales in units to achieve a profit of $23,000, assuming no change in selling price.

4-B4 Identifying Cost Behavior Patterns

At a seminar, a cost accountant spoke on identification of different kinds of cost behavior. Tammy Li, a hospital administrator who heard the lecture, identified several hospital costs of concern to her. After her classification, Li presented you with the following list of costs and asked you to (1) classify its behavior as one of the following: variable, step, mixed, or fixed; and (2) identify a likely cost driver for each variable or mixed cost.

1. Operating costs of X-ray equipment ($95,000 a year plus $3 per film)
2. Health insurance for all full-time employees
3. Costs incurred by Dr. Rath in cancer research
4. Repairs made on hospital furniture
5. Training costs of an administrative resident
6. Straight-line depreciation of operating room equipment
7. Costs of services of King Hospital Consulting
8. Nursing supervisors' salaries (a supervisor is needed for each 45 nursing personnel)

Additional Assignment Material

MyAccountingLab

QUESTIONS

4-1 "Cost behavior is simply identification of cost drivers and their relationships to costs." Comment.

4-2 Give two rules of thumb to use when analyzing cost behavior.

4-3 Give three examples of variable costs and of fixed costs.

4-4 Why is the word *immediately* used in the definition of *fixed cost* and not in the definition of *variable cost*?

4-5 "It is confusing to think of fixed costs on a per-unit basis." Do you agree? Why or why not?

4-6 "All costs are either fixed or variable. The only difficulty in cost analysis is determining which of the two categories each cost belongs to." Do you agree? Explain.

4-7 "The relevant range pertains to fixed costs, not variable costs." Do you agree? Explain.

4-8 Identify the major simplifying assumption that underlies CVP analysis.

4-9 "Classification of costs into variable and fixed categories depends on the decision situation." Explain.

4-10 "Contribution margin is the excess of sales over fixed costs." Do you agree? Explain.

4-11 Why is *break-even analysis* a misnomer?

4-12 "Companies in the same industry generally have about the same break-even point." Do you agree? Explain.

4-13 "It is essential to choose the right CVP method—equation, contribution margin, or graphical. If you pick the wrong one, your analysis will be faulty." Do you agree? Explain.

4-14 Describe three ways of lowering a break-even point.

4-15 "Incremental analysis is quicker, but it has no other advantage over an analysis of all costs and revenues associated with each alternative." Do you agree? Why or why not?

4-16 Define operating leverage and explain why a highly leveraged company may be risky.

4-17 Suppose a company with high operating leverage is also operating at near capacity for all its fixed-cost resources. How could an increase in sales volume result in decreasing economies of scale for this company?

4-18 What is the relationship between the margin of safety and the break-even point?

4-19 "The contribution margin and gross margin are always equal." Do you agree? Explain.

4-20 "CVP relationships are unimportant in nonprofit organizations." Do you agree? Explain.

4-21 Study Appendix 4A. A company sold two products. Total budgeted sales and total actual sales in number of units were identical. Actual unit variable costs and sales prices were the same as budgeted. Actual total contribution margin was lower than budgeted. What could be the reason for the lower contribution margin?

4-22 Study Appendix 4B. Given a target after-tax net income, present the CVP formula for computing the income before income taxes.

4-23 Study Appendix 4B. Present the CVP formula for computing the effects of a change in volume on after-tax income.

CRITICAL THINKING EXERCISES

4-24 Mixed Costs and the Sales Force

Wysocki Company pays its sales force a fixed salary plus a 5% commission on all sales. Explain why sales force costs would be considered a mixed cost.

4-25 Marketing Function of Value-Chain and Cost Behavior

Refer to Exhibit 4-2. For the two examples of marketing costs given in Exhibit 4-2, describe their cost behavior in relation to the cost driver listed.

4-26 Production Function of Value-Chain and Cost Behavior

Refer to Exhibit 4-2. For the labor wages and depreciation of plant and machinery examples of production costs given in Exhibit 4-2, describe their cost behavior in relation to the cost driver listed.

4-27 Tenneco Automotive's Value Chain

Tenneco is a leading auto parts company that makes Walker exhaust systems and Monroe ride-control equipment (shocks, struts) for vehicle manufacturers and the replacement market, with annual revenues in excess of $5.9 billion. After reporting weak earnings, the company undertook a strategy to reduce its break-even point by 25% by selling excess capacity, reducing head count, and introducing new high-contribution-margin products. The company's senior vice president listed the key elements of the company's strategy, stating, "We are gaining momentum and transforming our North American aftermarket business with new products, new technology, new positioning strategies, and new pricing." For each of these "new" elements of Tenneco's aftermarket business strategy, list the value-chain function that is most applicable.

EXERCISES

4-28 Identifying Cost Drivers

The following list identifies several potential cost drivers for a manufacturing company that makes eight products. The company uses a JIT production system so it stores finished products for a very limited time. The eight products vary substantially in size from small (plastic casings for pens) to large (plastic casings for truck instrument panels). The company uses order-processing labor to process all orders from customers.

- Number of setups
- Setup time
- Square feet
- Cubic feet
- Cubic feet weeks
- Number of orders
- Number or order line items

For each of the following situations (activity and related resource), identify the best cost driver from the list and briefly justify your choice.

1. To produce a product, production mechanics must set up machinery. It takes about the same time to set up for a production run regardless of the product being produced. What is the best cost driver for the resources used during the setup activity?
2. Instead of the situation described in number 1, what driver should the company use for the setup activity if it takes longer to set up for complex products, such as the instrument panel casings, than for simple products, such as pen casings?
3. What driver should the company use for warehouse occupancy costs (depreciation and insurance)? The company uses the warehouse to store finished products.
4. What driver should the company use for the warehouse occupancy costs if it did not use a JIT system (that is, the company maintains inventories), and upon inspection one of the products had a thick layer of dust on it?
5. What driver should the company use for order processing cost? All orders are similar in terms of types of products ordered and it takes about the same time to process each type of product.
6. What driver should the company use for order processing cost if orders vary substantially in terms of types of products ordered and it takes about the same time to process each type of product?

4-29 Basic Review Exercises

Fill in the blanks for each of the following independent cases (ignore income taxes):

	Sales	Variable Expenses	Contribution Margin	Fixed Expenses	Net Income
1.	$960,000	$533,000	$ —	$310,000	$ —
2.	550,000	—	300,000	—	46,000
3.	—	500,000	520,000	200,000	—

4-30 Variable- and Fixed-Cost Behavior

Refer to Exhibits 4-2 and 4-3 on pages 128 and 129. Part of a company's marketing function is as described in Exhibit 4-2. Two of the many marketing-function activities are advertising and selling. The annual cost behavior of the resources used to perform the advertising activity is depicted in the following diagram. With respect to the cost driver number of advertisements, which of the two costs is fixed? Which cost is variable? What is the total cost of advertising if the number of advertisements is 46? 92? Does the total cost of advertising double in response to a doubling of the cost driver level? Why or why not?

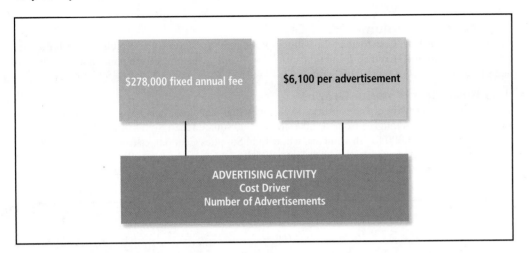

4-31 Variable- and Fixed-Cost Behavior

Refer to Exhibits 4-2 and 4-3 on pages 128 and 129. Part of a company's marketing function is as described in Exhibit 4-2. Two of the many marketing-function activities are advertising and selling. The annual cost behavior of the resources used to perform the selling activity is depicted in the following diagram. With respect to the cost driver sales dollars, which of the two costs is fixed? Which cost is variable? What is the total cost of the selling activity if sales dollars are $24,000,000? What is the total cost of selling if sales dollars are $12,000,000? Does the total cost of selling decrease by half in response to a 50% decrease in the cost driver level? Why or why not?

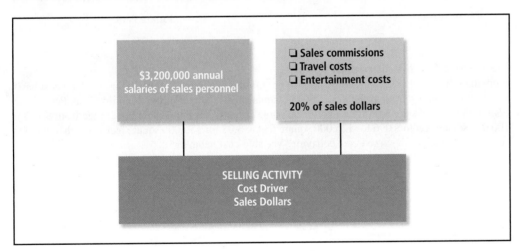

4-32 Basic Review Exercises

Fill in the blanks for each of the following independent cases:

Case	(a) Selling Price per Unit	(b) Variable Cost per Unit	(c) Total Units Sold	(d) Total Contribution Margin	(e) Total Fixed Costs	(f) Net Income
1	$26	$—	125,000	$750,000	$675,000	$ —
2	10	6	100,000	—	320,000	—
3	21	18	—	63,000	—	14,000
4	30	20	60,000	—	—	12,000
5	—	12	86,000	172,000	125,000	—

4-33 Basic Cost-Volume-Profit Graph

Refer to Exercise 4-32. Construct a cost-volume-profit graph for Case 2 that depicts the total revenue, total variable cost, total fixed cost, and total cost lines. Estimate the break-even point in total units sold and the net income for 100,000 units sold.

4-34 Basic Cost-Volume-Profit Graph

Refer to Exercise 4-32. Construct a cost-volume-profit graph for Case 4 that depicts the total revenue, total variable cost, total fixed cost, and total cost lines. Estimate the break-even point in total units sold and the net income (loss) for 50,000 units sold.

4-35 Basic Cost-Volume Graphs

From the following two graphs, construct two graphs that depict the cost behavior on a per-square-foot basis for volumes ranging from 100,000 to 200,000 square feet. (Note that the Total Labor Cost in these graphs is $24,000 for all volumes, while Total Supplies Cost ranges from $5,000 for 100,000 square feet to $10,000 for 200,000 square feet.) Which of the two constructed graphs show fixed-cost behavior? Variable-cost behavior?

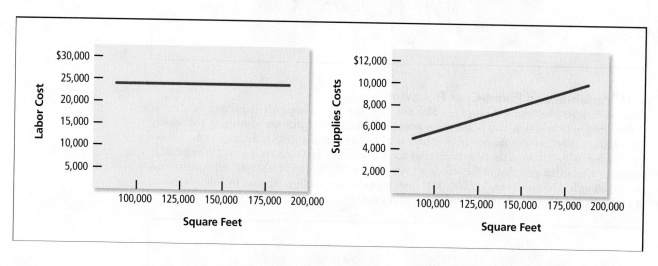

4-36 Basic Cost-Volume Graphs

From the following two graphs, construct two graphs that depict the cost behavior on a total cost basis for volumes ranging from 100,000 to 150,000 square feet. (Note that the Supplies Costs Per Square Foot in these graphs are $.06 for all volumes, while Labor Costs Per Square Foot range from $.12 for 100,000 square feet to $.096 for 125,000 square feet to $.08 for 150,000 square feet.) Which of the two constructed graphs show fixed-cost behavior? Variable-cost behavior?

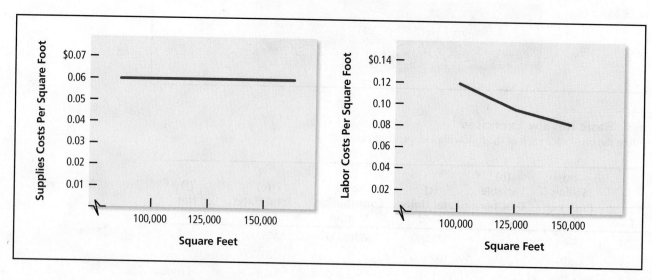

4-37 Step Costs

Which of the following are step costs? Why?

a. Rent on a warehouse that is large enough for all anticipated orders
b. Teachers for a private elementary school; one teacher is needed for every 15 students

c. Sheet steel for a producer of machine parts; steel is purchased in carload shipments, where each carload contains enough steel for 1,000 parts

4-38 Mixed Costs

The following cost function is a mixed cost. Explain why it is a mixed cost and not a fixed, variable, or step cost.

$$\text{Total cost} = \$8,000 + \$52 \times \text{units produced}$$

4-39 Various Cost-Behavior Patterns

In practice, there is often a tendency to simplify approximations of cost-behavior patterns, even though the "true" underlying behavior is not simple. Choose from the following graphs A–H the one that matches the numbered items. Indicate by letter which graph best fits each of the situations described. Next to each number-letter pair, identify a likely cost driver for that cost.

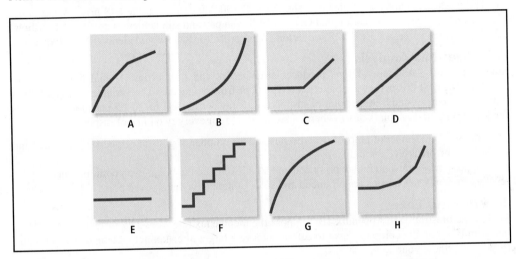

The vertical axes of the graphs represent total dollars of costs incurred, and the horizontal axes represent levels of cost driver activity during a particular time period. The graphs may be used more than once.

1. Cost of machining labor that tends to decrease as workers gain experience
2. Price of an increasingly scarce raw material as the quantity used increases
3. Guaranteed annual wage plan, whereby workers get paid for 40 hours of work per week even at zero or low levels of production that require working only a few hours weekly
4. Water bill, which entails a flat fee for the first 10,000 gallons used and then an increasing unit cost for every additional 10,000 gallons used
5. Availability of quantity discounts, where the cost per unit falls as each price break is reached
6. Depreciation of office equipment
7. Cost of sheet steel for a manufacturer of farm implements
8. Salaries of supervisors, where one supervisor is added for every 12 phone solicitors
9. Natural gas bill consisting of a fixed component, plus a constant variable cost per thousand cubic feet after a specified number of cubic feet are used

4-40 Hospital Costs and Pricing

Olympia Hospital has overall variable costs of 25% of total revenue and fixed costs of $45 million per year.

1. Compute the break-even point expressed in total revenue.
2. A patient-day is often used to measure the volume of a hospital. Suppose there are to be 37,500 patient-days next year. Compute the average daily revenue per patient-day necessary to achieve the break-even total revenue computed in item 1.

4-41 Cost-Volume-Profit at a Hospital

Children's Hospital predicts variable costs of 70% of total revenue and fixed costs of $42 million per year for the coming year.

1. Compute the break-even point expressed in total revenue.
2. Children's Hospital expects total revenue of $150 million from 200,000 patient-days. Compute expected profit (a) if costs behave as expected, and (b) if variable costs are 10% greater than predicted.

4-42 Motel Rentals

Super 8, the world's largest budget hotel chain, was founded in 1972. It now has more than 120,000 rooms in more than 2,000 locations (average is 61 rooms) in the United States and Canada. Suppose a particular

Super 8 has annual fixed costs of $900,000 for its 100-room motel, average daily room rents of $54, and average variable costs of $9 for each room rented. It operates 365 days per year.

1. How much net income on rooms will Super 8 generate (a) if the motel is completely full throughout the entire year and (b) if the motel is half full?
2. Compute the break-even point in number of rooms rented. What percentage occupancy for the year is needed to break even?

4-43 Variable Cost to Break Even

General Mills makes Nature Valley granola bars, Cheerios cereal, Yoplait yogurt, Häagen-Dazs ice cream, and many other food products. Suppose the product manager of a new General Mills cereal has determined that the appropriate wholesale price for a carton of the cereal is $48. Fixed costs of the production and marketing of the cereal are $19 million.

1. The product manager estimates that she can sell 800,000 cartons at the $48 price. What is the largest variable cost per carton that General Mills can pay and still achieve a profit of $1 million?
2. Suppose the variable cost is $25 per carton. What profit (or loss) would General Mills expect?

4-44 Sales-Mix Analysis

Study Appendix 4A. Eames Farms produces strawberries and raspberries. Annual fixed costs are $15,300. The cost driver for variable costs is "pints of fruit produced." The variable cost is $.85 per pint of strawberries and $.90 per pint of raspberries. Strawberries sell for $1.05 per pint, raspberries for $1.30 per pint. Five pints of strawberries are produced for every two pints of raspberries.

1. Compute the number of pints of strawberries and the number of pints of raspberries produced and sold at the break-even point.
2. Suppose only strawberries are produced and sold. Compute the break-even point in pints.
3. Suppose only raspberries are produced and sold. Compute the break-even point in pints.

4-45 Income Taxes

Review the illustration in Appendix 4B. Suppose the income tax rate were 25% instead of 40%. How many units would the company have to sell to achieve a target after-tax net income of (a) $864 and (b) $1,440? Show your computations.

4-46 Income Taxes and Cost-Volume-Profit Analysis

Study Appendix 4B. Suppose Wooliscroft Construction Company has a 32% income tax rate, a contribution-margin ratio of 45%, and fixed costs of $664,000. What sales volume is necessary to achieve an after-tax income of $136,000?

PROBLEMS

4-47 Terry's Pub, Cost-Volume-Profit Analysis in a Small Business

Terry Shevlin recently opened Terry's Pub in the University District. Because of licensing restrictions, the only liquor he can sell is beer. The average price of beer at Terry's Pub is $5.00 per glass, and each glass costs Terry an average of $4.10. Terry has hired a bartender and waiter at $3,000 and $4,000 per month, respectively. His rent, utilities, and other fixed operating costs are $3,000 per month.

Terry is considering selling hamburgers during the lunch hour. He feels that this will increase his daytime business, which is currently quite small. It will also allow him to be more competitive with other local bars that offer a wider variety of food and beverages.

Terry would like to sell the hamburgers for $1.24 each in order to be attractive to customers. Terry will buy buns for $1.44 a dozen and ground beef for $1.20 per pound. Each pound of ground beef will make three hamburgers. Other ingredients will cost an average of $.12 per hamburger. Terry will also need to hire a part-time cook at $1,200 per month. Other additional fixed costs will run about $360 a month.

1. If Terry sells only beer, how many glasses of beer does he have to sell each month to make a monthly profit of $500?
2. If Terry sells only beer, how many glasses of beer does he have to sell each month to make a monthly profit of 5% of sales?
3. Suppose Terry decides to add hamburgers to his menu. How many hamburgers does he need to sell to break even on the hamburgers? Assume that there is no effect on beer sales.
4. The main reason Terry wanted to add hamburgers was to attract more customers. Suppose that 3,000 extra customers per month came for lunch because of the availability of hamburgers and that each bought an average of 1 hamburger and 1.6 beers. Compute the added profit (or loss) generated by these extra customers.
5. Terry was not sure how many new customers would be attracted by the hamburgers. Give Terry some advice about how many new customers would be needed to just break even on the new business if each new customer bought one hamburger and one beer. Include an assessment of the consequences of volume falling below or above this break-even point.

6. Terry could offer a higher quality hamburger if he spends 50% more on the ingredients. He could then charge $2.24 for them. Explain how Terry could determine whether the higher quality hamburgers would be more profitable than the regular hamburgers.

4-48 Super Valu Grocery Chain, Variable and Fixed Costs

Maintaining a clean shopping environment is a key success factor for Super Valu, a large grocery chain based in Minnesota. Three of the most costly resources needed to clean a supermarket are labor, equipment, and cleaning supplies. The cost driver for all these resources is "number of times cleaned." Wages for cleaning laborers (called porters) and rent for cleaning equipment are the same regardless of the number of times the supermarket is cleaned. Supplies used for each regular daily cleaning and for each special cleaning are about the same.

A typical store has 48,000 square feet. Regular cleaning is performed each day from midnight until 7:00 AM. Special cleaning of floors and fixtures is performed in the various departments as needed. Special cleaning varies from 10 to 30 times a month depending on the amount of traffic through the store. Thus, the number of times a store is cleaned varies from 40 to 60 times a month.

Suppose that in one of Super Valu's stores in Minneapolis, cleaning was performed 60 times during March. For the month, the cost of labor and rent on equipment was $21,000 and cleaning supplies used cost $12,000. The sales budget for the next quarter (April through June) and better weather conditions indicate that the store will need to be cleaned 50, 46, and 35 times in April, May, and June respectively.

1. Prepare a table that shows how labor cost, rent, cleaning supplies cost, total cost, and total cost per cleaning changes in response to the number of times the store is cleaned. Show costs for 35, 40, 45, 50, 55, and 60 cleanings. What is the predicted total cost of cleaning the Minneapolis store for the next quarter?
2. Prepare a single graph that can be used to predict the fixed, variable, and total cleaning cost of the Super Valu store.
3. Suppose the manager of the Super Valu store can hire an outside cleaning company to clean the store as needed. The charge rate is $720 per cleaning. If the outside cleaning company is hired, Super Valu can lay off the workers who are now cleaning the store, eliminate the need for equipment rent, and stop purchasing cleaning supplies. Will Super Valu save money with the outside cleaning company over the next quarter? Prepare a schedule that supports your answer.

4-49 Fixed Costs and Relevant Range

Bridger Canyon Systems Group (BCSG) has substantial year-to-year fluctuations in billings to clients. Top management has the following policy regarding the employment of key professional personnel:

If Gross Annual Billings Are	Number of Persons to Be Employed	Key Professional Annual Salaries and Benefits
$2,000,000 or less	10	$1,000,000
$2,000,001–2,400,000	11	$1,100,000
$2,400,001–2,800,000	12	$1,200,000

Top management believes that the group should maintain a minimum of 10 individuals for a year or more even if billings drop drastically below $2 million.

For the past 5 years, gross annual billings for BCSG have fluctuated between $2,020,000 and $2,380,000. Expectations for next year are that gross billings will be between $2,100,000 and $2,300,000. What amount should the group budget for key professional personnel salaries? Graph the relationships on an annual basis, using the two approaches (refined and simplified) illustrated in Exhibit 4-6 on page 132. Indicate the relevant range on each graph. You need not use graph paper; simply approximate the graphical relationships.

4-50 Comparing Contribution Margin Percentages

Following are actual statements of operating income for Microsoft and Procter & Gamble (in millions):

Microsoft		Procter & Gamble	
Revenues	$60,420	Net sales	$83,503
Cost of revenue	11,598	Cost of products sold	40,695
Research and development	8,164	Selling, general, and administrative expenses	25,725
Sales and Marketing	13,039		
General and administrative	5,127	Operating income	$17,083
Operating income	$22,492		

Assume that the only variable cost for Microsoft is "cost of revenue" and for Procter & Gamble the only variable cost is "cost of products sold."

1. Compute the contribution-margin percentage of Microsoft and that of Procter & Gamble. Why do you suppose the percentages are so different?
2. Suppose each company increases its revenue by $10 million. Compute the increase in operating income for each company.
3. Explain how the contribution margin percentage helps you predict the effects on operating income of changes in sales volume. What assumptions do you make in forming such a prediction?

4-51 Cost Structure and Risk Sharing

Marge Porter is the manager of Stanford's traditional Sunday Flicks, sponsored by the Stanford Student Association. The admission price is deliberately set at a very low $3. Each Sunday, a film has two showings and a maximum of 500 tickets can be sold for each showing. The rental of the auditorium is $330 and labor is $435, including $90 for Porter. Porter must pay the film distributor a guarantee, ranging from $300 to $900, or 50% of gross admission receipts, whichever is higher.

Before and during the show, she sells refreshments; these sales average 12% of gross admission receipts and yield a contribution margin of 40%.

1. On June 3, Porter screened *The Descendants*. The film grossed $2,250. The guarantee to the distributor was $750, or 50% of gross admission receipts, whichever is higher. What operating income was produced for the Student Association?
2. Recompute the results if the film grossed $1,400.
3. The "four-wall" concept is increasingly being adopted by movie producers. In this plan, the movie's producer pays a guaranteed fixed rental to the theater owner for, say, a week's showing of a movie and the producer receives the ticket receipts less the fixed rental. As a theater owner, how would you evaluate a "four-wall" offer?

4-52 CVP for Promotion of a Rock Concert

TJB Productions, Ltd., is promoting a rock concert in London. The bands will receive a flat fee of £7.3 million. The concert will be shown worldwide on closed-circuit television. TJB will collect 100% of the receipts and will return 20% to the individual local closed-circuit theater managers. TJB expects to sell 1.3 million seats at a net average price of £15 each. TJB will also receive £270,000 from the London arena (which has sold out its 19,700 seats, ranging from £175 for box seats to £20 for general admission, for a gross revenue of £1.2 million); TJB will not share the £270,000 with the local promoters.

1. The general manager of TJB Productions is trying to decide what amount to spend for advertising. What is the most TJB could spend and still break even on overall operations, assuming sales of 1.3 million tickets?
2. If TJB desires an operating income of £490,000, how many seats would it have to sell? Assume that the average price is £15 and fixed costs consist of the £7.3 million fee for the bands and £3.7 million for advertising, for total fixed costs of £11 million.

4-53 Cost Drivers at Boeing

Consider the Boeing plant discussed on pages 126–127. Suppose Boeing has a cost-reduction program for this plant to reduce the costs of activities, such as receiving parts for its airplanes, by 10%.

At a meeting of the receiving department operating managers and the accounting staff, complaints were made that cost-reduction was not completely the responsibility of the receiving department because some factors were beyond the department's control. Managers pointed out that the total cost of fuel is a function of fuel price per gallon and the gallons used. Furthermore, neither the price paid for fuel nor the lease cost is controllable by receiving department employees. Managers argue that the factors such as fuel and equipment usage were not explicitly tracked and costed. These operating measures were the ones managers believed to be the ones that should be used as cost drivers.

You have been asked to refine the way variable and fixed costs are calculated by using the more relevant cost drivers for fuel and equipment—"gallons" and "hours operated." You have collected the following data for the most recent period.

Equipment cost	$45,000
Fuel cost	$24,000
Hours equipment operated	1,500
Gallons of fuel used	6,000
Parts received	30,000
Target cost goal after 10% cost reduction (90% × $69,000)	$62,100

1. Draw a diagram similar to Exhibit 4-4 on page 130 that shows the relationships between the receiving activity and the resources used and that incorporates the new cost drivers recommended by operating

managers. On the diagram, show the total level of each cost driver, the fuel consumption rate in gallons used per part received, and the equipment consumption rate in hours per part received.

2. Refer to your answer to requirement 1. If the number of parts received increased from 30,000 to 40,000, which number(s) would most likely change: total gallons used, total hours operated, or gallons per part received? Derive an equation that calculates total fuel cost as a function of fuel cost per gallon and fuel consumption rate. Predict the total cost of the receiving activity if the number of parts received is 40,000.

3. The managers in the receiving department have a plan that will improve fuel efficiency. What is the predicted total cost of receiving 30,000 parts if the fuel consumption rate is reduced by 20% (assume fuel costs per gallon will not change)? Will the receiving department achieve Boeing's 10% cost-reduction goal? Why or why not?

4. Comment on the benefits of the new cost-driver model compared to the one based solely on one cost driver—"number of parts received."

5. Can you think of other refinements in the cost-driver model based on the data that are given?

4-54 Basic CVP Relationships, Restaurant

Joann Swanson owns and operates a restaurant. Her fixed costs are $17,000 per month. She serves luncheons and dinners. The average total bill (excluding tax and tip) is $18 per customer. Swanson's present variable costs average $9.50 per meal.

1. How many meals must she serve to attain a profit before taxes of $8,500 per month?
2. What is the break-even point in number of meals served per month?
3. Suppose Swanson's rent and other fixed costs rise to a total of $25,420 per month and variable costs also rise to $11.40 per meal. If Swanson increases her average price to $22, how many meals must she serve to make $8,500 profit per month?
4. Assume the same situation described in requirement 3. Swanson's accountant tells her she may lose 15% of her customers if she increases her prices. If this should happen, what would be Swanson's profit per month? Assume that the restaurant had been serving 3,000 customers per month.
5. Assume the same situation described in requirement 4. To help offset the anticipated 15% loss of customers, Swanson hires a pianist to perform for 4 hours each night for $2,300 per month. Assume that this would increase the total monthly meals from 2,550 to 2,800. Would Swanson's total profit change? By how much?

4-55 Changing Fixed Costs to Variable Costs at Blockbuster Video

When John F. Antioco took charge of Blockbuster Video, he changed the company's strategy. Traditionally, Blockbuster had bought videos from the movie studios for an average cost of about $65 each, planning to rent them out often enough to make a profit. Mr. Antioco replaced this strategy with one that allows Blockbuster to purchase videos for an average of $7 each and pay the studio 40% of any rental fee received. With this arrangement, Blockbuster can afford to stock more copies of each video and guarantee customers that the movie they want will be in stock—or the rental is free. Suppose that Blockbuster rents videos for $2 a day. In each of the following questions, consider only the direct costs of the videos, not the costs of operating the rental store.

1. Under the traditional strategy, how many days must each video be rented before Blockbuster will break even on the video?
2. Under the new strategy, how many days must each video be rented before Blockbuster will break even on the video?
3. Suppose customers rented a particular copy of *Moneyball* for 50 days. What profit would Blockbuster make on rentals under the traditional strategy? Under the new strategy?
4. Suppose customers rented a particular copy of *The Descendants* for only 6 days. What profit would Blockbuster make on rentals under the traditional strategy? Under the new strategy?
5. Comment on how the new arrangement affects the risks Blockbuster accepts when purchasing an additional copy of a particular video.

4-56 CVP and Financial Statements for a Mega-Brand Company

Procter & Gamble Company is a Cincinnati-based company that produces household products under brand names such as Gillette, Bounty, Crest, Folgers, and Tide. The company's 2011 income statement showed the following (in millions):

Net sales	$82,559
Costs of products sold	40,768
Selling, general, and administrative expense	25,973
Operating income	$15,818

Suppose that the cost of products sold is the only variable cost; selling, general, and administrative expenses are fixed with respect to sales.

Suppose Procter & Gamble has a 10% decrease in sales next year and there is no change in costs except for decreases associated with the lower volume of sales. Compute the predicted operating income for Procter & Gamble and its percentage decrease. Explain why the percentage decrease in income differs from the percentage decrease in sales.

4-57 Bingo and Operating Leverage

Many churches sponsor bingo games, a tradition stemming from the time when only specific nonprofit institutions were allowed to sponsor games of chance. Reverend Donovan Dukes, the pastor of a new parish in Orange County, is investigating the desirability of conducting weekly bingo nights. The parish has no hall, but a local hotel would be willing to commit its hall for a lump-sum rental of $950 per night. The rent would include cleaning, setting up and taking down the tables and chairs, and so on.

1. A local printer would provide bingo cards in return for free advertising. Local merchants would donate door prizes. The services of clerks, callers, security force, and others would be donated by volunteers. Admission would be $8.00 per person, entitling the player to one card; extra cards would be $.50 each. Many persons buy extra cards so there would be an average of five cards played per person. What is the maximum in total cash prizes that the church may award and still break even if 200 persons attend each weekly session?
2. Suppose the total cash prizes are $1,050. What will be the church's operating income if 50 persons attend? If 200 persons attend? If 350 persons attend? Briefly explain the effects of the cost behavior on income.
3. After operating for 10 months, Reverend Dukes is thinking of negotiating a different rental arrangement but keeping the prize money unchanged at $1,050. Suppose the rental arrangement is $700 per night plus $1 per person. Compute the operating income for attendance of 50, 200, and 350 persons, respectively. Explain why the results differ from those in requirement 2.

4-58 Operating Leverage at eBay

In 2011, eBay had $11.6 billion in revenue and net income over $3.2 billion. eBay's mission is to "provide a global trading platform where practically anyone can trade practically anything." However, eBay has not always had profits in the billions.

Consider eBay's situation during the early years. In the first quarter of 2001, eBay reported revenue of $154 million and operating expenses of $123 million, for an operating profit of $31 million. In the first quarter of 2002, eBay reported that revenue had increased 59%, to $245 million. Assume that during both years, eBay's fixed costs were $37 million and all other costs were variable costs.

1. Compute eBay's operating income for the first quarter of 2002 assuming that variable costs were the same percentage of revenue in 2002 as in 2001. Compute the percentage increase in operating income between 2001 and 2002.
2. Explain how eBay managed to increase its income so much with only a 59% increase in revenue.

4-59 Adding a Product

Arnold's Brew Pub, located near Southwestern State University, serves as a gathering place for the university's more social scholars. Arnold sells draft beer and all brands of bottled beer at a contribution margin of $.72 a beer.

Arnold is considering also selling hamburgers during selected hours. His reasons are twofold. First, sandwiches would attract daytime customers. A hamburger and a beer are a quick lunch. Second, he has to meet competition from other local bars, some of which provide more extensive menus.

Arnold analyzed the costs of adding hamburgers as follows:

Per Month		**Per Hamburger**	
Monthly Fixed Expenses		**Variable Expenses**	
Wages of part-time cook	$1,452	Rolls	$.11
Other	330	Meat @ $2.66 per pound (seven hamburgers per pound)	.38
Total	$1,782		
		Other	.22
		Total	$.71

Arnold planned a selling price of $1.25 per hamburger to lure many customers. For all questions, assume a 30-day month.

1. What are the monthly and daily break-even points, in number of hamburgers?
2. What are the monthly and daily break-even points, in dollar sales?
3. At the end of 2 months, Arnold finds he has sold 3,800 hamburgers. What is the operating profit per month on hamburgers?
4. Arnold thinks that at least 75 extra beers are sold per day because he has these hamburgers available. This means that 75 extra people come to the bar or that 75 buy an extra beer because they are attracted by the hamburgers. How does the sale of hamburgers combined with the accompanying effect on beer sales affect Arnold's monthly operating income?
5. Refer to requirement 3. How many extra beers would have to be sold per day so that the overall effect of the hamburger sales on monthly operating income would be zero?

4-60 Government Organization

A social welfare agency has a government budget appropriation for 20X7 of $900,000. The agency's major mission is to help disabled persons who are unable to hold jobs. On the average, the agency supplements each person's income by $5,000 annually. The agency's fixed costs are $280,000. There are no other costs.

1. How many disabled persons were helped during 20X7?
2. For 20X8, the agency's budget appropriation has been reduced by 15%. If the agency continues the same level of monetary support per person, how many disabled persons will be helped in 20X8? Compute the percentage decline in the number of persons helped.
3. Assume a budget reduction of 15%, as in requirement 2. The manager of the agency has discretion as to how much to supplement each disabled person's income. She does not want to reduce the number of persons served. On average, what is the amount of the supplement that can be given to each person? Compute the percentage decline in the annual supplement.

4-61 Gross Margin and Contribution Margin

Eastman Kodak Company is a provider of imaging technology products and services to the photographic, graphic communications, and health-care markets. A condensed 2011 income statement follows (in millions):

Sales	$6,022
Cost of goods sold	5,135
Gross margin	887
Other operating expenses	1,487
Loss from continuing operations	$ (600)

Assume that $1,400 million of the cost of goods sold is a fixed cost representing depreciation and other production costs that do not change with the volume of production. In addition, $1,000 million of the other operating expenses is fixed.

1. Compute the total contribution margin for 2011 and the contribution margin percentage. Explain why the contribution margin differs from the gross margin.
2. Suppose that sales for Eastman Kodak are predicted to increase by 10% and that the cost behavior is expected to continue. Compute the predicted operating income (loss).
3. What assumptions were necessary to compute the predicted operating income in requirement 2?

4-62 Choosing Equipment for Different Volumes

MetroCinemas owns and operates a nationwide chain of movie theaters. The 500 properties in the chain vary from low-volume, small-town, single-screen theaters to high-volume, big-city, multiscreen theaters.

The management is considering installing machines that will make popcorn on the premises. These machines would allow the theaters to sell freshly popped popcorn rather than the prepopped, prebagged corn that it currently sells. This proposed feature would be properly advertised and is intended to increase patronage at the company's theaters.

The machines can be purchased in several different sizes. The annual rental costs and operating costs vary with the size of the machines. The machine capacities and costs are as follows:

	Popper Model		
	Standard	**Deluxe**	**Jumbo**
Annual capacity	50,000 boxes	120,000 boxes	300,000 boxes
Costs			
Annual machine rental	$7,840	$11,200	$20,200
Popcorn cost per box	.14	.14	.14
Cost of each box	.09	.09	.09
Other variable costs per box	.22	.14	.05

1. Calculate the volume level in boxes at which the standard and deluxe poppers would earn the same operating profit (loss).
2. The management can estimate the number of boxes to be sold at each of its theaters. Present a decision rule that would enable MetroCinemas management to select the most profitable machine without having to make a separate cost calculation for each theater. That is, at what anticipated range of unit sales should the theater use the standard model? The deluxe model? The jumbo model?
3. Could the management use the average number of boxes sold per seat for the entire chain and the capacity of each theater to develop this decision rule? Explain your answer.

4-63 Sales Compensation, Variable/Fixed Costs, and Ethics

Most companies compensate their sales forces with a combination of a fixed salary and a commission that is a percentage of sales. Consider two companies competing for the same customers—for example, Kellogg's and Post cereals. Suppose that Kellogg's pays its sales force a large fixed salary and a small commission, while Post pays its sales force a small fixed salary and a large commission. The total pay on average was the same for both companies.

1. Compare the sales cost structure of Kellogg's with that of Post. Which has the larger fixed cost? Which has the larger variable cost? How will this affect each company's risk? (Focus on how the company's profits change with changes in volume.)
2. What incentives does each pay system provide for the sales force?
3. Might either incentive system create potential ethical dilemmas for the sales personnel? Explain.

4-64 Sales-Mix Analysis

Study Appendix 4A. The Colorado Catering Company specializes in preparing Mexican dinners that it freezes and ships to restaurants in the Denver area. When a diner orders an item, the restaurant heats and serves it. The budget data for 20X5 are as follows:

	Product	
	Chicken Tacos	**Beef Enchiladas**
Selling price to restaurants	$4	$5
Variable expenses	3	3
Contribution margin	$1	$2
Number of units	200,000	100,000

The company prepares the items in the same kitchens, delivers them in the same trucks, and so forth. Therefore, decisions about the individual products do not affect the fixed costs of $680,000.

1. Compute the planned net income for 20X5.
2. Compute the break-even point in units, assuming that the company maintains its planned sales mix.
3. Compute the break-even point in units if the company a) sells only tacos, or b) sells only enchiladas.
4. Suppose the company sells 225,000 units of tacos and 75,000 units of enchiladas, for a total of 300,000 units. Compute the net income. Compute the new break-even point with this new sales mix. What is the major lesson of this problem?

4-65 Hospital Patient Mix

Study Appendix 4A. Hospitals measure their volume in terms of patient-days. We calculate patient-days by multiplying the number of patients by the number of days that the patients are hospitalized.

Suppose a large hospital has fixed costs of $52.8 million per year and variable costs of $750 per patient-day. Daily revenues vary among classes of patients. For simplicity, assume that there are two classes: (1) self-pay patients (S) who pay an average of $1,250 per day and (2) non–self-pay patients (G) who are the responsibility of insurance companies and government agencies and who pay an average of $950 per day. Twenty-five percent of the patients are self-pay.

1. Compute the break-even point in patient-days, assuming that the hospital maintains its planned mix of patients.
2. Suppose that the hospital achieves 172,000 patient-days but that 40% of the patient-days were self-pay (instead of 25%). Compute the net income. Compute the break-even point.

4-66 Income Taxes on Hotels

Study Appendix 4B. The Regal Hotel in downtown Phoenix has annual fixed costs applicable to rooms of $8.7 million for its 570-room hotel, average daily room rates of $90, and average variable costs of $42 daily for each room rented. It operates 365 days per year. The hotel is subject to an income tax rate of 25%.

1. How many rooms must the hotel rent to earn a net income after taxes of $801,000? Of $400,500?
2. Compute the break-even point in number of rooms rented. What percentage occupancy for the year is needed to break even?
3. Assume that the volume level of rooms rented is 200,000. The manager is wondering how much income could be generated if 6,000 additional rooms are rented. Compute the additional net income after taxes.

4-67 Tax Effects

Study Appendix 4B. Decca Company is a wholesaler of compact discs. The projected after-tax net income for the current year is $90,000, based on a sales volume of 170,000 CDs. Decca has been selling the CDs at $15 each. The variable costs consist of the $8 unit purchase price and a handling cost of $4 per unit. Decca's annual fixed costs are $714,000, and the company is subject to a 40% income tax rate.

Management is planning for the coming year when it expects that the unit purchase price will increase 25%.

1. Compute Decca Company's break-even point for the current year.
2. An increase of 15% in projected unit sales volume for the current year would result in an increased after-tax income for the current year of how much?
3. Compute the volume of sales in dollars that Decca Company must achieve in the coming year to maintain the same after-tax net income as projected for the current year if unit selling price remains at $15.
4. To cover a 25% increase in the unit purchase price for the coming year and still maintain the current contribution-margin ratio, Decca Company must establish a selling price per unit for the coming year of how much?

CASES

4-68 Hospital Costs

Gother City Hospital is unionized. In 20X6, nurses received an average annual salary of $45,000. The hospital administrator is considering changes in the contract with nurses for 20X7. In turn, the hospital may also change the way it charges nursing costs to each department.

The hospital holds each department accountable for its financial performance, and it records revenues and expenses by departments. Consider the expenses of the obstetrics department in 20X6.

Variable expenses (based on 20X6 patient-days) are as follows:

Meals	$ 610,000
Laundry	260,000
Laboratory	900,000
Pharmacy	850,000
Maintenance	150,000
Other	530,000
Total	$3,300,000

Fixed expenses (based on number of beds) are as follows:

Rent	$3,000,000
General administrative services	2,200,000
Janitorial	200,000
Maintenance	150,000
Other	350,000
Total	$5,900,000

Management assigns nurses to departments on the basis of annual patient-days as follows:

Volume Level in Patient-Days	Number of Nurses
10,000–12,000	30
12,001–16,000	35

Total patient-days are the number of patients multiplied by the number of days they are hospitalized. The hospital charges each department for the salaries of the nurses assigned to it.

During 20X6, the obstetrics department had a capacity of 60 beds, billed each patient an average of $810 per day, and had revenues of $12.15 million.

1. Compute the 20X6 volume of activity in patient-days.
2. Compute the 20X6 patient-days that would have been necessary for the obstetrics department to recoup all fixed expenses except nursing expenses.
3. Compute the 20X6 patient-days that would have been necessary for the obstetrics department to break even including nurses' salaries as a fixed cost.
4. Suppose obstetrics must pay $200 per patient-day for nursing services. This plan would replace the two-level, fixed-cost system employed in 20X6. Compute what the break-even point in patient-days would have been in 20X6 under this plan.

4-69 CVP in a Modern Manufacturing Environment

A division of Hewlett-Packard Company changed its production operations from one where a large labor force assembled electronic components to an automated production facility dominated by computer-controlled robots. The change was necessary because of fierce competitive pressures. Improvements in quality, reliability, and flexibility of production schedules were necessary just to match the competition. As a result of the change, variable costs fell and fixed costs increased, as shown in the following assumed budgets:

	Old Production Operation	New Production Operation
Unit variable cost		
Material	$ .88	$ .88
Labor	1.22	.22
Total per unit	$2.10	$1.10
Monthly fixed costs		
Rent and depreciation	$450,000	$ 875,000
Supervisory labor	80,000	175,000
Other	50,000	90,000
Total per month	$580,000	$1,140,000

Expected volume is 600,000 units per month, with each unit selling for $3.10. Capacity is 800,000 units.

1. Compute the budgeted profit at the expected volume of 600,000 units under both the old and the new production environments.
2. Compute the budgeted break-even point under both the old and the new production environments.

3. Discuss the effect on profits if volume falls to 500,000 units under both the old and the new production environments.
4. Discuss the effect on profits if volume increases to 700,000 units under both the old and the new production environments.
5. Comment on the riskiness of the new operation versus the old operation.

4-70 Multiproduct Break Even in a Restaurant

Study Appendix 4A. An article in *Washington Business* included an income statement for **La Brasserie**, a French restaurant in Washington, D.C. A simplified version of the statement follows:

Revenues	$2,098,400
Cost of sales, all variable	1,246,500
Gross profit	851,900
Operating expenses	
Variable	222,380
Fixed	170,940
Administrative expenses, all fixed	451,500
Net income	$ 7,080

The average dinner tab at La Brasserie is $40, and the average lunch tab is $20. Assume that the variable cost of preparing and serving dinner is also twice that of a lunch. The restaurant serves twice as many lunches as dinners. Assume that the restaurant is open 305 days a year.

1. Compute the daily break-even volume in lunches and dinners for La Brasserie. Compare this to the actual volume reflected in the income statement.
2. Suppose that an extra annual advertising expenditure of $15,000 would increase the average daily volume by three dinners and six lunches, and that there is plenty of capacity to accommodate the extra business. Prepare an analysis for the management of La Brasserie, explaining whether this would be desirable.
3. La Brasserie uses only premium food, and the cost of food makes up 25% of the restaurant's total variable costs. Use of average rather than premium ingredients could cut the food cost by 20%. Assume that La Brasserie uses average-quality ingredients and does not change its prices. How much of a drop-off in volume could it endure and still maintain the same net income? What factors in addition to revenue and costs would influence the decision about the quality of food to use?

4-71 Effects of Changes in Costs, Including Tax Effects

Study Appendix 4B. Pacific Fish Company is a wholesale distributor of salmon. The company services grocery stores in the Chicago area.

Average selling price per pound	$	5.00
Average variable costs per pound		
Cost of salmon	$	2.50
Shipping expenses		.50
Total		$3.00
Annual fixed costs		
Selling		$ 210,000
Administrative		356,250
Total		$ 566,250
Expected annual sales volume (390,000 pounds)		$1,950,000
Tax rate		40%

Small but steady growth in sales has been achieved by Pacific Fish over the past few years, while salmon prices have been increasing. The company is formulating its plans for the coming fiscal year. Presented next are the data used to project the current year's after-tax net income of $128,250.

Fishing companies have announced that they will increase prices of their products by an average of 15% in the coming year, owing mainly to increases in labor costs. Pacific Fish Company expects that all other costs will remain at the same rates or levels as in the current year.

1. What is Pacific Fish Company's break-even point in pounds of salmon for the current year?
2. What selling price per pound must Pacific Fish Company charge to cover the 15% increase in the cost of salmon and still maintain the current contribution-margin ratio?
3. What volume of sales in dollars must the Pacific Fish Company achieve in the coming year to maintain the same net income after taxes as projected for the current year if the selling price of salmon remains at $5 per pound and the cost of salmon increases 15%?
4. What strategies might Pacific Fish Company use to maintain the same net income after taxes as projected for the current year?

NIKE 10-K PROBLEM

4-72 Operating Leverage
Examine **Nike**'s 10K report.

1. In Item 7 of the 10K, review the section titled Operating Segments. Prepare a table that compares the percent change in "Total revenue" to the change in "Pre-tax income" from 2010 to 2011 for the six major regions (ignore the Global Brand Divisions segment). Note that generally earnings before interest and taxes changes by a larger percentage than revenue. For example, in Western Europe, revenue declined by 2% but earnings declined by 16%. (The exception to this general observation is the "Central and Eastern Europe" region where revenue and earnings moved in opposite directions—revenue increased but earnings before interest and taxes decreased). How can operating leverage help explain the greater percent change in earnings than the percent change in total revenues?
2. What might explain the decrease in income despite the increase in revenue for the Central and Eastern region?
3. Would you expect Nike's operating leverage to be high or low? Explain. Which assets do you think contribute to Nike's ability to leverage operating overhead?

EXCEL APPLICATION EXERCISE

4-73 CVP and Break Even
Goal: Create an Excel spreadsheet to perform CVP analysis and show the relationship between price, costs, and break-even points in terms of units and dollars. Use the results to answer questions about your findings.

Scenario: Phonetronix is a small manufacturer of telephone and communications devices. Recently, company management decided to investigate the profitability of cellular phone production. They have three different proposals to evaluate. Under all the proposals, the fixed costs for the new phone would be $110,000. Under proposal A, the selling price of the new phone would be $99 and the variable cost per unit would be $55. Under proposal B, the selling price of the phone would be $129 and the variable cost would remain the same. Under proposal C, the selling price would be $99 and the variable cost would be $49.

When you have completed your spreadsheet, answer the following questions:

1. What are the break-even points in units and dollars under proposal A?
2. How did the increased selling price under proposal B impact the break-even points in units and dollars compared to the break-even points calculated under proposal A?
3. Why did the change in variable cost under proposal C not impact the break-even points in units and dollars as significantly as proposal B did?

Step-by-Step:
1. Open a new Excel spreadsheet.
2. In column A, create a bold-faced heading that contains the following:
   Row 1: Chapter 4 Decision Guideline
   Row 2: Phonetronix
   Row 3: Cost-Volume-Profit (CVP) Analysis
   Row 4: Today's Date
3. Merge and center the four heading rows across columns A–D.

4. In row 7, create the following bold-faced, right-justified column headings:
   Column B: Proposal A
   Column C: Proposal B
   Column D: Proposal C

   Note: Adjust cell widths when necessary as you work.

5. In column A, create the following row headings:
   Row 8: Selling price
   Row 9: Variable cost
   Row 10: Contribution margin
   Row 11: Contribution-margin ratio
   Skip a row.
   Row 13: Fixed cost
   Skip a row.
   Row 15: Breakeven in units
   Skip a row.
   Row 17: Breakeven in dollars

6. Use the scenario data to fill in the selling price, variable cost, and fixed cost amounts for the three proposals.

7. Use the appropriate formulas from this chapter to calculate contribution margin, contribution-margin ratio, breakeven in units, and breakeven in dollars.

8. Format all amounts as follows:

Number tab:	Category:	Currency
	Decimal places:	0
	Symbol:	None
	Negative numbers:	Red with parenthesis

9. Change the format of the selling price, contribution margin, fixed cost, and breakeven in dollars amounts to display a dollar symbol.

10. Change the format of both contribution margin headings to display as indented:

Alignment tab:	Horizontal:	Left (Indent)
	Indent:	1

11. Change the format of the contribution-margin amount cells to display a top border, using the default line style.

Border tab:	Icon:	Top Border

12. Change the format of the contribution-margin ratio amounts to display as a percentage with two decimal places.

Number tab:	Category:	Percentage
	Decimal places:	2

13. Change the format of all break-even headings and amounts to display as bold-faced.

14. Activate the ability to use heading names in formulas under Tools → Options:

Calculation tab:	Check the box:	Accept labels in formulas

15. Replace the cell-based formulas with "word-based" equivalents for each formula used in Proposal A.

Example: Contribution margin for proposal B would be:
= ('Selling price' 'Proposal B') − ('Variable cost' 'Proposal B')

Note: The tic marks used in the example help avoid naming errors caused by data having similar titles (i.e., "contribution margin" and "contribution-margin ratio"). The parentheses help clarify groupings.

Help: Ask the Answer Wizard about "Name cells in a workbook."

Select "Learn about labels and names in formulas" from the right-hand panel.

16. Save your work, and print a copy for your files.

COLLABORATIVE LEARNING EXERCISE

4-74 CVP for a Small Business

Form into groups of two to six students. Each group should select a very simple business, one with a single product or one with approximately the same contribution-margin percentage for all products. Some possibilities are

A child's lemonade stand
A retail DVD rental store
An espresso cart
A retail store selling compact discs
An athletic shoe store
A cookie stand in a mall

However, you are encouraged to use your imagination rather than just select one of these examples. The following tasks might be split up among the group members:

1. Make a list of all fixed costs associated with running the business you selected. Estimate the amount of each fixed cost per month (or per day or per year, if one of them is more appropriate for your business).
2. Make a list of all variable costs associated with making or obtaining the product or service your company is selling. Estimate the cost per unit for each variable cost.
3. Given the fixed and variable costs you have identified, compute the break-even point for your business in either units or dollar sales.
4. Assess the prospects of your business making a profit.

INTERNET EXERCISE

4-75 Cost Behavior at Southwest Airlines

It is critical that managers understand how costs and revenues behave. One company that is affected by changes in costs and may not have the capability to rapidly change revenues because of competition is **Southwest Airlines**. Let's take a closer look at SWA and its costs and revenues. Log on to SWA's Web site at www.southwest.com. This Web site serves many purposes for the airline, such as providing flight schedules, making reservations and selling tickets, and displaying vacation and airfare specials.

1. Click on the Air icon and then on "See Where We Fly," which provides a map showing the cities served by Southwest. What is the closest city to your current location served by SWA? Click on that city as the departure city and then select any city you like for the arrival city. Now select a date about a month from now for leaving and one for returning. Click to continue to the next screen. What types of fares are available? Why do you think that there are different types of fares offered? Click on one of the fare-type captions to see if Southwest places any restrictions on this fare. If there are any restrictions, what purpose do they serve?
2. Return to the reservations screen and select a departure date that is less than a week away. What types of fare choices are available now? Are the rates the same as those that you found for a trip more than a month away? Why do you think that the choices remaining are for the most part the higher-priced ones? Is there any advantage to the fare(s) still available? Who is the most likely user of a ticket purchased at the last minute?

3. Now that you have looked at the revenue side, let's focus on the expense side. Individuals on the same flight may pay different prices for the ticket. Do you think that the cost of flying a passenger differs because of the price that he or she pays for the ticket? Why or why not?

4. Return to SWA's home page. Take a look at the costs that SWA actually incurs. Find the list of information available "About Southwest" near the bottom of the page and click on "Investor Relations." Click on the most recent "Annual Report" icon, which takes you to Southwest's most recent 10-K report. Open the 10K report and notice the summary information that the company has provided in the "Selected Financial Data" section. Give the most recent year's operating revenues and operating expenses. How much has each changed over the prior year? What does this imply for Southwest's profitability?

5. Now look further down the page and find "Operating Expenses per ASM." (ASM stands for *available seat miles*, a measure of capacity.) What kinds of costs do you suppose are included in operating expenses per ASM? Which of these costs is primarily fixed with respect to ASM? Which is primarily variable? What other cost drivers might be important causes of costs for Southwest?

5

Measurement of Cost Behavior

LEARNING OBJECTIVES

When you have finished studying this chapter, you should be able to:

1. Explain management influences on cost behavior.

2. Measure and mathematically express cost functions and use them to predict costs.

3. Describe the importance of activity analysis for measuring cost functions.

4. Measure cost behavior using the engineering analysis, account analysis, high-low, visual-fit, and least-squares regression methods.

▶ AMERICA WEST

US Airways and **America West** came together in 2006 to create the fifth largest domestic airline. US Airways, US Airways Shuttle, and US Airways Express now operate approximately 3,000 flights per day and serve more than 200 communities in the United States, Canada, Mexico, the Caribbean, Latin America, Europe, and the Middle East. Before its merger with US Airways, America West rode the wave of a booming economy to increased revenues in the late 1990s. As a result, management decided to expand by introducing service to new destinations including Acapulco, Miami, and Detroit, and by adding more daily flights to existing markets including Las Vegas, Mexico City, and Boston. To accomplish this, the company had to expand its labor force, add new aircraft, and spend more than $40 million on new technology.

Management took very seriously the decision to invest large amounts of money in aircraft and equipment. It knew that the decision would have a significant influence on costs, and thus profits, for many years. Management also knew that most of the costs would be fixed but the revenues would fluctuate with the economy. If the economy were bad, revenues would decline and may not cover these costs.

How does an airline protect itself against losses when the economy experiences a downturn? According to Richard Goodmanson, former president and chief executive officer of America West, "management has a goal to have from 5% to 10% of the fleet of aircraft leased and thus subject to annual renewal. This enhances the company's ability to decrease capacity (and related costs) in the event of an industry downturn." This example illustrates that understanding how costs behave, as well as how managers' decisions can influence costs, helped the airline improve its cost control.

Chapter 4 demonstrated the importance of understanding the cost structure of an organization and the relationships between an organization's activities and its costs, revenues, and profits. This chapter focuses on the **measurement of cost behavior**, which means understanding and quantifying how an organization's activities affect its costs. Recall that activities use resources, and these resources have costs. We measure this relationship between activity and cost using cost drivers. Understanding relationships between costs and their cost drivers allows managers in all types of organizations—profit seeking, nonprofit, and government—to do the following:

measurement of cost behavior
Understanding and quantifying how activities of an organization affect its levels of costs.

- Evaluate strategic plans and operational improvement programs.
- Make proper short-run pricing decisions.
- Make short-run operating decisions.
- Plan or budget the effects of future activities. (Chapters 6 and 7)

- Design effective management control systems. (Chapters 8 and 9)
- Make proper long-run decisions. (Chapter 12)
- Design useful and accurate product costing systems.

As you can see, understanding cost behavior is fundamental to management accounting. There are numerous real-world cases in which managers have made very poor decisions to drop product lines, close manufacturing plants, or bid too high or too low on jobs because they had erroneous cost-behavior information. This chapter, therefore, deserves careful study. ■

Cost Drivers and Cost Behavior

Accountants and managers often assume that cost behavior is linear over some relevant range of activity or cost-driver levels. We can graph **linear-cost behavior** with a straight line because we assume each cost to be either fixed or variable. Recall that the relevant range specifies the interval of cost-driver activity within which a specific relationship between a cost and its driver will be valid. Managers usually define the relevant range based on their previous experience operating the organization at different levels of activity.

In this chapter, we focus on costs for which the primary cost driver is the volume of a product produced or service provided, as such costs are easy to trace to products or services. Examples of volume-driven costs include the costs of printing labor, paper, ink, and binding to produce all the copies of this textbook. The number of copies printed affects the total printing labor, paper, ink, and binding costs. We can trace the use of these resources to the number of copies of the text printed by using schedules, payroll records, and other documents that show how much of each resource was used to produce the copies of this text.

Activities not directly related to volume also affect costs. Such costs often have multiple cost drivers. For the publisher of this textbook, the wages and salaries of the editorial staff are not easy to trace to outputs. These editorial personnel produce many different textbooks, and it would be very difficult to determine exactly what portion of their wages and salaries went into a specific book, such as *Introduction to Management Accounting*.

Understanding and measuring costs that are difficult to trace to outputs is a challenging exercise. In practice, many organizations use a linear relationship with a single cost driver to describe each cost, even though many costs have multiple causes. This approach is easier and less expensive than using nonlinear relationships or multiple cost drivers. If we use it carefully, this method often provides cost estimates that are sufficiently accurate for most decisions. This scheme may seem at odds with reality and economic theory, but the added benefit of understanding "true" cost behavior may be less than the cost of determining it, which is consistent with the cost-benefit approach to decision making.

Accountants often describe cost behavior in visual or graphical terms. Exhibit 5-1 shows linear-cost behavior, the relevant range, and an activity or resource cost driver. Note the similarity to the cost-volume-profit (CVP) graphs of Chapter 4.

Additionally, many cost graphs display mixed-cost behavior. For example, consider the monthly facilities maintenance department cost of the Parkview Medical Center (PMC), shown in Exhibit 5-2. Salaries of the maintenance personnel and costs of equipment are fixed at $10,000 per month. In addition, cleaning supplies and repair materials vary at a rate of $5 per patient-day[1] delivered by the hospital.

The chief administrator at PMC used knowledge of the facilities maintenance department cost behavior to do the following:

1. Plan costs: In May, the hospital expected to service 3,000 patient-days. May's predicted facilities maintenance department costs are $10,000 fixed costs plus the variable cost of $15,000 (3,000 patient-days times $5 per patient-day) for a total of $25,000.
2. Provide feedback to managers: In May, the actual facilities maintenance costs were $34,000 in a month when PMC serviced 3,000 patient-days as planned. The administrator wanted to know why the hospital overspent by $9,000 ($34,000 less the planned $25,000) so that managers could take corrective action.

© Marianna Day Massey/Newscom

America West airplanes on the ground at the company's Phoenix hub.

linear-cost behavior
Activity that can be graphed with a straight line because costs are assumed to be either fixed or variable.

---

[1]A patient-day is one patient spending 1 day in the hospital. One patient spending 5 days in the hospital is 5 patient-days of service.

Exhibit 5-1
Linear-Cost Behavior

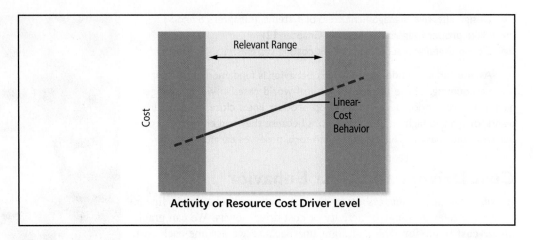

3. Make decisions about the most efficient use of resources: For example, managers might weigh the long-run trade-offs of increased fixed costs of highly efficient floor cleaning equipment against the variable costs of extra cleaning supplies needed to clean the floors manually.

We can see that managers not only passively measure how costs behave, they also actively influence the cost structure of an organization. Let's explore in more detail how managers influence cost behavior.

Management Influence on Cost Behavior

In addition to measuring and evaluating current cost behavior, managers can influence cost behavior through decisions about such factors as product or service attributes, capacity, technology, and policies to create incentives to control costs.

Product and Service Decisions and the Value Chain

Throughout the value chain, managers influence cost behavior. This influence occurs through their choices of process and product design, quality levels, product features, distribution channels, and so on. Each of these decisions contributes to the organization's performance, and managers should consider the costs and benefits of each decision. For example, **Hertz**, the car rental company, would add a feature to its services only if the cost of the feature—for example, GPS navigation systems in its vehicles—could be more than recovered in profit from increased business and/or extra fees it could charge for the feature.

Capacity Decisions

capacity costs
The fixed costs of being able to achieve a desired level of production or to provide a desired level of service while maintaining product or service attributes, such as quality.

Strategic decisions about the scale and scope of an organization's activities generally result in fixed levels of capacity costs. **Capacity costs** are the fixed costs of being able to achieve a desired level of production or service while maintaining product or service attributes, such as quality. Most companies make a capacity decision infrequently. They consider capacity decisions

Exhibit 5-2
Mixed-Cost Behavior

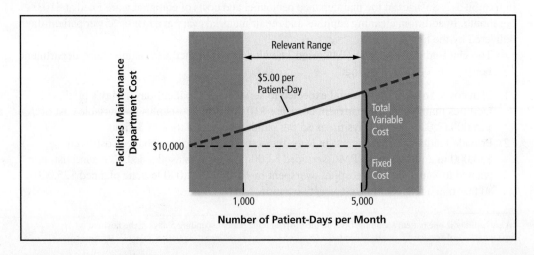

as strategic because large amounts of resources are involved. An incorrect capacity decision can have serious consequences for the competitiveness of a company. However, some companies make capacity decisions so frequently that they almost become routine operating decisions, such as opening a new **Starbucks** or **McDonald's**. In this case, the decision to open a new Starbucks is still strategic, but it becomes highly structured.

Companies in industries with long-term variations in demand must be careful when making capacity decisions. Companies may not be able to fully recover fixed capacity costs when demand falls during an economic downturn. Additionally, capacity decisions can entail an ethical commitment to a company's employees. Most companies try to keep a stable employment policy so that they do not need to fire or lay off employees unless there are huge shifts in demand. In the economic downturn of 2008, news stories about companies "downsizing" and initiating extensive layoffs abounded. But other companies managed the decrease in demand without imposing large financial and emotional costs on their employees. Companies that plan their capacity to allow flexibility in meeting demand generally are better able to survive economic hard times, without the upheaval caused by widespread firings and layoffs.

Committed Fixed Costs

Even if a company has chosen to minimize fixed capacity costs, every organization has some costs to which it is committed, perhaps for quite a few years. A company's **committed fixed costs** usually arise from the possession of facilities, equipment, and a basic organizational structure. They include mortgage or lease payments, interest payments on long-term debt, property taxes, insurance, and salaries of key personnel. Only major changes in the philosophy, scale, or scope of operations could change these committed fixed costs in future periods. Recall the example of the facilities maintenance department for the Parkview Medical Center. The capacity of the facilities maintenance department was a management decision, and in this case the decision determined the magnitude of the equipment cost. Suppose PMC were to increase permanently its patient-days per month beyond the relevant range of 5,000 patient-days. Because PMC would need more capacity, the committed equipment cost would rise to a new level per month.

committed fixed costs
Costs arising from the possession of facilities, equipment, and a basic organization.

Discretionary Fixed Costs

Some costs are fixed at certain levels only because management decided to incur these levels of cost to meet the organization's goals. These **discretionary fixed costs** have no obvious relationship to levels of capacity or output activity. Companies determine them as part of the periodic planning process. Each planning period, management will determine how much to spend on discretionary items such as advertising and promotion costs, public relations, research and development costs, charitable donations, employee training programs, and management consulting services. These costs then become fixed until the next planning period.

discretionary fixed costs
Costs determined by management as part of the periodic planning process in order to meet the organization's goals. They have no obvious relationship with levels of capacity or output activity.

Managers can alter discretionary fixed costs—up or down—even within a budget period, if they decide that different levels of spending are desirable. Conceivably, managers could eliminate such discretionary costs almost entirely for a given year in dire times, whereas they could not reduce committed costs. Discretionary fixed costs may be essential to the long-run achievement of the organization's goals, but managers can vary spending levels broadly in the short run.

Consider Marietta Corporation, which is experiencing financial difficulties. Sales for its major products are down, and Marietta's management is considering cutting back on costs temporarily. Marietta's management must determine which of the following fixed costs it can reduce or eliminate and how much money each would save:

Fixed Costs	Planned Amounts
Advertising and promotion	$ 50,000
Depreciation	400,000
Employee training	100,000
Management salaries	800,000
Mortgage payment	250,000
Property taxes	600,000
Research and development	1,500,000
Total	$3,700,000

Can Marietta reduce or eliminate any of these fixed costs? The answer depends on Marietta's long-run outlook. Marietta could reduce costs but also greatly reduce its ability to compete in the future if it cuts fixed costs carelessly. Suppose rearranging these costs by categories of committed and discretionary costs yields the following analysis:

Fixed Costs	Planned Amounts
Committed	
Depreciation	$ 400,000
Mortgage payment	250,000
Property taxes	600,000
Total committed	$1,250,000
Discretionary (potential savings)	
Advertising and promotion	$ 50,000
Employee training	100,000
Management salaries	800,000
Research and development	1,500,000
Total discretionary	$2,450,000
Total committed and discretionary	$3,700,000

Eliminating all discretionary fixed costs would save Marietta $2,450,000 per year. However, Marietta might be unwise to cut all discretionary costs completely. This could severely impair the company's long-run prospects and its future competitive position. Nevertheless, distinguishing committed and discretionary fixed costs would be the company's first step in identifying where costs could be reduced.

Technology Decisions

One of the most critical decisions that managers make is choosing the type of technology the organization will use to produce its products or deliver its services. Choice of technology (for example, labor-intensive versus robotic manufacturing, personal banking services versus automated tellers, or online versus in-store sales) positions the organization to meet its current goals and to respond to changes in the environment (for example, changes in customer needs or actions by competitors). The use of high-technology methods rather than labor usually means a much greater fixed-cost component and higher operating leverage, as discussed in Chapter 4. Higher operating leverage creates greater risks for companies with wide variations in demand.

Cost-Control Incentives

Finally, the incentives that management creates for employees can affect future costs. Managers use their knowledge of cost behavior to set cost expectations, and employees may receive compensation or other rewards that are tied to meeting these expectations. For example, the administrator of Parkview Medical Center could give the supervisor of the facilities maintenance department a favorable evaluation if the supervisor maintained quality of service and kept department costs below the expected amount for the actual level of patient-days. This feedback motivates the supervisor to watch department costs carefully and to find ways to reduce costs without reducing service quality.

Cost Functions

As a manager, you will use cost functions often as a planning and control tool. A few of the reasons why cost functions are important are listed here:

1. Planning and controlling the activities of an organization require useful and accurate estimates of future fixed and variable costs.
2. Understanding relationships between costs and their cost drivers allows managers in all types of organizations—profit seeking, nonprofit, and government—to make better operating, marketing, and production decisions; to plan and evaluate actions; and to determine appropriate costs for short-run and long-run decisions.

The first step in estimating or predicting costs is **cost measurement**—measuring cost behavior as a function of appropriate cost drivers. The second step is to use these cost measures to estimate future costs at expected levels of cost-driver activity. We begin by looking at the form of cost functions and the criteria for choosing the most appropriate cost drivers.

cost measurement
Estimating or predicting costs as a function of appropriate cost drivers.

Form of Cost Functions

To describe the relationship between a cost and its cost driver(s), managers often use an algebraic equation called a **cost function**. When there is only one cost driver, the cost function is similar to the algebraic CVP relationships discussed in Chapter 4. Consider the mixed cost graphed in Exhibit 5-2 on page 178, the facilities maintenance department cost:

Objective 2

Measure and mathematically express cost functions and use them to predict costs.

cost function
An algebraic equation used by managers to describe the relationship between a cost and its cost driver(s).

$$\begin{array}{l}\text{monthly facilities} \\ \text{maintenance} \\ \text{department costs} \end{array} = \begin{array}{l}\text{monthly fixed} \\ \text{maintenance cost} \end{array} + \begin{array}{l}\text{monthly variable} \\ \text{maintenance cost} \end{array}$$

$$= \begin{array}{l}\text{monthly fixed} \\ \text{maintenance cost} \end{array} + \left(\begin{array}{l}\text{variable cost per} \\ \text{patient-day} \end{array} \times \begin{array}{l}\text{number of patient-days} \\ \text{in the month} \end{array} \right)$$

Let

Y = monthly facilities maintenance department cost

F = monthly fixed maintenance cost

V = variable cost per patient-day

X = cost-driver activity in number of patient-days per month

We can rewrite the mixed-cost function as

$$Y = F + VX \tag{1}$$

or

$$Y = \$10{,}000 + \$5.00X$$

This mixed-cost function has the familiar form of a straight line—it is called a linear cost function. When we graph a cost function, F is the intercept—the point on the vertical axis where the cost function begins. In Exhibit 5-2, the intercept is the \$10,000 fixed cost per month. V, the variable cost per unit of activity, is the slope of the cost function. In Exhibit 5-2, the cost function slopes upward at the rate of \$5 for each additional patient-day.

In our example, we use patient-days as the relevant cost driver. How did we choose this cost driver? Why not use number of patients, or number of operations, or facility square footage? In general, how do we develop cost functions?

Developing Cost Functions

Managers should apply two criteria to obtain useful and accurate cost functions: plausibility and reliability.

1. The cost function must be plausible, that is, believable. Personal observation of costs and activities, when it is possible, provides the best evidence of a plausible relationship between a resource cost and its cost driver. Some cost relationships, by nature, are not directly observable, so the cost analyst must be confident that the proposed relationship is valid. Many costs may move together with a number of cost drivers, but no cause-and-effect relationships may exist. A cause-and-effect relationship (that is, the cost driver causes the organization to incur the resource cost) is desirable for cost functions to be useful and accurate. For example, consider three possible cost drivers for the total cost of a **US Airways** round-trip flight from Phoenix to San Diego: miles flown, number of passengers, and passenger-miles (number of passengers times miles flown). Which of these possible cost drivers makes most sense, if only one cost driver were used for total cost? The answer is passenger-miles—the cost driver used by almost all airlines because both distance AND number of passengers flown impact cost incurrence.

2. In addition to being plausible, a cost function's estimates of costs at actual levels of activity must reliably conform to observed costs. We assess reliability in terms of "goodness of fit"—how well the cost function explains past cost behavior. If the fit is good and conditions do not change in the future, the cost function should be a reliable predictor of future costs.

Managers use these criteria together in choosing a cost function. Each is a check on the other. A manager needs to fully understand operations and the way accountants record costs to determine a plausible and reliable cost function that links cause and effect. For example, companies often perform maintenance when output is low because that is the best time to take machines out of service. Therefore, daily or weekly records of maintenance costs and outputs may show that higher maintenance costs occur when output is low. However, lower output does not cause increased maintenance costs, nor does increased output cause lower maintenance costs. A more plausible explanation is that over a longer period increased output causes higher maintenance costs. Understanding the nature of maintenance costs should lead managers to a plausible and reliable estimate of the long-run cost function.

Making Managerial Decisions

A cost function is a mathematical expression of how cost drivers affect a particular cost. However, an intuitive understanding of cost functions is just as important as being able to write the mathematical formula. Suppose you have been using a cost function to predict total order-processing activity costs. The cost function is total costs = $25,000 + $89 × (number of orders processed). This formula is based on data that are in the range of 0–700 orders processed. Now, you want to predict the total cost for 680 orders. You have a few fundamental questions to answer before you are comfortable using the cost function in this situation. What does it mean when a cost function is linear? Why do managers want to know whether a cost is linear? What is the importance of the relevant range?

Answer

A linear cost function means that there are two parts to the cost. One part is fixed—that is, it's independent of the cost driver. The other part varies in proportion to the cost driver—that is, if the cost driver increases by X%, this part of the cost also increases by X%. Knowing that a cost is linear allows a manager to separate the cost into fixed and variable components—a simplification that helps you understand how decisions will affect costs. Incidentally, the predicted total cost for 680 orders is $25,000 + ($89 × 680) = $85,520. As long as the operating conditions that existed when the data were collected have not changed significantly, then knowing that the number of orders processed is within the relevant range— 0–700, in this case—gives you confidence in the predicted total cost.

Choice of Cost Drivers: Activity Analysis

Objective 3

Describe the importance of activity analysis for measuring cost functions.

activity analysis
The process of identifying appropriate cost drivers and their effects on the costs of making a product or providing a service.

How do managers construct plausible and reliable cost functions? Well, you cannot have a good cost function without knowing the right cost drivers, so constructing a cost function starts with choosing cost drivers—the X in equation (1) on page 181. Managers use **activity analysis** to identify appropriate cost drivers and their effects on the costs of making a product or providing a service. The final product or service may have several cost drivers because production may involve many separate activities. The greatest benefit of activity analysis is that it helps management accountants identify the appropriate cost drivers for each cost.

Consider Northwestern Computers, which makes two products for personal computers: a plug-in music board (Mozart-Plus) and a hard-disk drive (Powerdrive). These two products consist of material costs, labor costs, and support costs. In the past, most of the work on Northwestern's products was done by hand. In such a situation, labor costs were the primary driver of support costs. Support costs were twice as much as labor costs, on average.

Northwestern has just finished upgrading the production process. Now the company uses computer-controlled assembly equipment, which has increased the costs of support activities, such as engineering and maintenance, and has reduced labor cost. Its cost function has now changed; specifically, labor cost is now only 5% of the total costs at Northwestern. An activity analysis has shown that the number of components added to products (a measure of product complexity), not labor cost, is the primary cost driver for support costs. Northwestern estimated support costs to be $20 per component. Mozart-Plus has five component parts, and Powerdrive has nine.

Suppose Northwestern wants to predict how much support cost it will incur in producing one Mozart-Plus and how much for one Powerdrive. Using the old cost driver, labor cost, the prediction of support costs would be as follows:

	Mozart-Plus	Powerdrive
Prior labor cost per unit	$ 8.50	$130.00
Predicted support cost		
2 × direct labor cost	$17.00	$260.00

Using the more appropriate cost driver based on the new production process, the number of components added to products, the predicted support costs are as follows:

	Mozart-Plus	Powerdrive
Predicted support cost at $20 per component		
$20 × 5 components	$100.00	
$20 × 9 components		$180.00
Difference in predicted support cost between the old and new cost function	$ 83.00 higher	$ 80.00 lower

By using an appropriate cost driver, Northwestern can predict its support costs much more accurately. Managers will make better decisions with this more accurate information. For example, they can relate prices charged for products more closely to the costs of production. To see how an actual organization uses activity analysis, see the Business First box on page 184.

One major question remains in our discussion of the measurement of cost behavior: How are the estimates of fixed costs and variable cost per cost-driver unit determined? Equation (1) on page 181 denotes these amounts by F = monthly fixed maintenance cost and V = variable cost per patient-day. In practice, organizations use several methods of measuring cost functions and determining values for F and V. Let's look at each of these methods.

Methods of Measuring Cost Functions

After determining the most plausible drivers behind different costs, managers can choose from a broad selection of methods for approximating cost functions. These methods include (1) engineering analysis, (2) account analysis, (3) high-low analysis, (4) visual-fit analysis, and (5) least-squares regression analysis. These methods are not mutually exclusive; managers frequently use two or more together to confirm conclusions about cost behavior. The first two methods rely primarily on logical analysis of the cost environment, whereas the last three involve explicit analysis of prior cost data.

Objective 4

Measure cost behavior using the engineering analysis, account analysis, high-low, visual-fit, and least-squares regression methods.

Engineering Analysis

The first method, **engineering analysis**, measures cost behavior according to what costs should be in an on-going process. It entails a systematic review of materials, supplies, labor, support services, and facilities needed for products and services. Analysts can even use engineering analysis successfully for new products and services, as long as the organization has had experience with similar costs. Why? Because they can base measures on information from personnel who are directly involved with the product or service. In addition to actual experience, analysts learn about new costs from experiments with prototypes, accounting and industrial engineering literature, the experience of competitors, and the advice of management consultants. From this information, cost analysts estimate what future costs should be. If the cost analysts are experienced and understand the activities of the organization, then their engineering cost predictions may be quite useful and reliable for decision making. The disadvantages of engineering cost analysis are that the efforts are costly and may not be timely.

engineering analysis
The systematic review of materials, supplies, labor, support services, and facilities needed for products and services; measuring cost behavior according to what costs should be, not by what costs have been.

Business First

Activity Analysis in Health-Care Organizations

Manufacturing companies were the first organizations to use activity analysis. However, its use has spread to many service industries and nonprofit organizations. For example, Hosparus (formerly called the Alliance of Community Hospices and Palliative Care Services), a health-care organization formed by the merger of two hospices in Kentucky and one in Indiana, has used activity analysis to better understand its costs.

Hosparus is a Medicare/Medicaid-certified program providing medical care to the terminally ill. In addition to seeing to the medical needs of its patients, Hosparus has social workers, home health aides, volunteers, and chaplains. It also provides an 18-month bereavement program for families of patients.

Many of Hosparus's costs were related directly to patients, and understanding these costs posed no problems. However, support costs were large, and Hosparus had little information about what caused these costs.

The organization undertook an activity analysis to determine the appropriate cost drivers for support costs. This consisted of two basic tasks: (1) identify the activities being performed and (2) select a cost driver for each activity.

To identify the activities and the costs related to each activity, Hosparus formed a cross-functional team. The team identified 14 activities. The next step was to select a cost driver for each activity. Some of the activities and their related cost drivers were as follows:

Activity	Cost Driver
Referral	Number of referrals
Admission	Number of admissions
Bereavement	Number of deaths
Accounting/finance	Number of patient-days
Billing	Number of billings
Volunteer services	Number of volunteers

Using the cost information from the activity analysis, management was able to learn how much each different activity cost and could recognize that patients requiring use of expensive activities were more expensive to treat.

Another organization, a retirement and assisted-living community with 70 living units, took such an activity analysis one step further. Using an activity analysis similar to that of Hosparus, this organization took the resultant detailed cost information and conducted sensitivity analysis on profitability. Using optimization software called "Solver" from Microsoft Excel the organization was able to construct modified income statements that explicitly displayed how changes in its underlying cost activities would affect its profits. It was subsequently able to maximize its profits by optimizing the levels of these various activities, thus developing an organizational strategy that was best for its cost environment.

Sources: Adapted from Sidney J. Baxendale and Victoria Dornbusch, "Activity-Based Costing for a Hospice," *Strategic Finance*, March 2000, pp. 65–70; Sidney J. Baxendale, Mahesh Gupta, and P. S. Raju, "Profit Enhancement: Using an ABC Model," *Management Accounting Quarterly*, Winter 2005, pp. 11–21; and Hosparus's Web site (http://www.hosparus.org).

Nearly any organization can use this approach to measuring cost behavior. For example, Weyerhaeuser Company, producer of wood products, used engineering analysis to determine the cost functions for its 14 corporate service departments. These cost functions measure the cost of corporate services used by three main business groups. For example, Weyerhaeuser found that its accounts payable costs for each division are a function of three cost drivers: the number of hours spent on each division, number of documents, and number of invoices.

Now consider Parkview Medical Center, introduced earlier in the chapter. An assistant to the hospital administrator interviewed facilities maintenance personnel and observed their activities on several random days for a month. From these data, she confirmed that the most plausible cost driver for facilities maintenance cost is the number of patient-days. She also estimated from current department salaries and equipment charges that monthly fixed costs approximated $10,000 per month. Using interviews and observing supplies usage during the month, she estimated that variable costs are $5 per patient-day. She gave this information to the hospital administrator but cautioned that the cost measures may be incorrect for the following reasons:

1. The month observed may be abnormal.
2. The facilities maintenance personnel may have altered their normal work habits because the assistant was observing them.

3. The facilities maintenance personnel may not have told the complete truth about their activities because of their concerns about the use of the information they revealed.

However, if we assume the observed and estimated information is correct, we could predict facilities maintenance costs in any month by first forecasting that month's expected patient-days and then entering that figure into the following algebraic, mixed-cost function:

$$Y = \$10,000 \text{ per month} + (\$5 \times \text{patient-days})$$

For example, if the administrator expects 3,000 patient-days next month, the prediction of facilities maintenance costs would be as follows:

$$Y = \$10,000 + (\$5 \times 3,000 \text{ patient-days}) = \$25,000$$

Account Analysis

In contrast to engineering analysis, users of **account analysis** look to the accounting system for information about cost behavior. The simplest method of account analysis classifies each account as a variable or fixed cost with respect to a selected cost driver. The cost analyst then looks at each cost account balance and estimates either the variable cost per unit of cost-driver activity or the periodic fixed cost.

To illustrate this approach to account analysis, let's return to the facilities maintenance department at Parkview Medical Center and analyze costs for a recent month. The following table shows costs recorded in a month with 3,700 patient-days:

account analysis
Classifying each account as a variable cost or as a fixed cost with respect to a selected cost driver.

Monthly Cost	January Amount
Supervisor's salary and benefits	$ 3,800
Hourly workers' wages and benefits	14,674
Equipment depreciation and rentals	5,873
Equipment repairs	5,604
Cleaning supplies	7,472
Total facilities maintenance cost	$37,423

Recall that the most plausible and reliable driver for these costs is the number of patient-days serviced per month. Next, the analyst determines which costs may be fixed and which may be variable. Assume that the analyst has made the following judgments:

Monthly Cost	Amount	Fixed	Variable
Supervisor's salary and benefits	$ 3,800	$3,800	
Hourly workers' wages and benefits	14,674		$14,674
Equipment depreciation and rentals	5,873	5,873	
Equipment repairs	5,604		5,604
Cleaning supplies	7,472		7,472
Total facilities maintenance costs	$37,423	$9,673	$27,750

Measuring total facilities maintenance cost behavior, then, requires only simple arithmetic. First add up all the fixed costs to get the total fixed cost per month. Then divide the total variable costs by the units of cost-driver activity to get the variable cost per unit of cost driver.

$$\text{Fixed cost per month} = \$9,673$$

$$\text{Variable cost per patient-day} = \$27,750 \div 3,700 \text{ patient-days}$$

$$= \$7.50 \text{ per patient-day}$$

The algebraic, mixed-cost function, measured by account analysis, is

$$Y = \$9,673 \text{ per month} + (\$7.50 \times \text{patient-days})$$

Account analysis methods are less expensive to conduct than engineering analyses, but they require recording of relevant cost accounts and cost drivers. In addition, like engineering analysis, account analysis is subjective because the analysts decide whether each cost is variable or fixed based on their own judgment.

Summary Problem for Your Review

PROBLEM

The Dependable Insurance Company processes a variety of insurance claims for losses, accidents, thefts, and so on. Account analysis using one cost driver has estimated the variable cost of processing the claims for each automobile accident at 0.5% (.005) of the dollar value of all claims related to a particular accident. This estimate seemed reasonable because high-cost claims often involve more analysis before settlement. To control processing costs better, however, Dependable conducted an activity analysis of claims processing. The analysis suggested that there are three main cost drivers for the costs of processing claims for automobile accidents. The drivers and cost behavior are as follows:

> 0.2% of Dependable Insurance policyholders' property claims
> + 0.6% of other parties' property claims
> + 0.8% of total personal injury claims

Data from two recent automobile accident claims follow:

	Automobile Claim No. 607788	Automobile Claim No. 607991
Policyholder claim	$ 4,500	$23,600
Other party claim	0	3,400
Personal injury claim	12,400	0
Total claim amount	$16,900	$27,000

1. Estimate the cost of processing each claim using data from (a) the single-cost-driver analysis and (b) the three-cost-driver analysis.
2. How would you recommend that Dependable Insurance estimate the cost of processing claims?

SOLUTION

1. Costs are summarized in the table here.

	Automobile Claim No. 607788		Automobile Claim No. 607991	
	Claim Amount	Processing Cost	Claim Amount	Processing Cost
Using single-cost-driver analysis				
Total claim amount	$16,900		$27,000	
Estimated processing cost at 0.5%		$ 84.50		$135.00
Using three-cost-driver analysis				
Policyholder claim	$ 4,500		$23,600	
Estimated processing cost at 0.2%		$ 9.00		$ 47.20
Other party claim	0		3,400	
Estimated processing cost at 0.6%		0		20.40
Personal injury claim	12,400		0	
Estimated processing cost at 0.8%		99.20		0
Total estimated processing cost		$108.20		$ 67.60

2. The three-cost-driver analysis estimates of processing costs are considerably different from those using a single cost driver. If the activity analyses are reliable, then automobile claims that include personal injury losses are more costly to process than property damage claims. If these estimates are relatively inexpensive to keep current and to use, then it seems reasonable to adopt the three-cost-driver approach. Dependable will have more accurate cost estimates and will be better able to plan its claims processing activities. However, Dependable processes many different types of claims. Extending activity analysis to identify multiple cost drivers for all types of claims would result in a complicated system for predicting costs—much more complex (and costly) than simply using the total dollar value of claims. Whether to undertake an activity analysis for all types of policies depends on cost-benefit considerations. Managers can address such considerations by first adopting activity analysis for one type of claim and assessing the usefulness and cost of the more accurate information.

High-Low, Visual-Fit, and Least-Squares Methods

When enough relevant cost data are available, we can use historical data to estimate the cost function mathematically. Three popular methods are the high-low, visual-fit, and least-squares methods. All three methods are more objective than the engineering-analysis and account-analysis methods. Each is based on hard evidence and uses cost and activity information from multiple periods. In particular, least-squares regression is a powerful statistical tool that yields both accurate estimates of the cost function and precise measures of probable error inherent in the estimation.

While there are situations where one of the three data-based methods is the best way to develop estimates of the cost function, account analysis and engineering analysis will probably remain popular methods of estimating cost behavior because the three mathematical methods require relevant past cost data. Products, services, technologies, and organizations are changing rapidly in response to increased global competition and technological advances. In some cases, by the time enough historical data are collected to support these analyses, the data are obsolete—the organization has changed, the production process has changed, or the product has changed. These methods should only be used when the historical data are from a past environment that still closely resembles the future environment for which a manager wants to predict costs. Another concern is that historical data may hide past inefficiencies that the company could reduce if it could identify them. That being said, the three mathematical methods have their advantages when relevant data exist, in particular the least-squares analysis.

DATA FOR ILLUSTRATION In discussing the high-low, visual-fit, and least-squares regression methods, we will continue to use the Parkview Medical Center's facilities maintenance department costs. The following table shows monthly data collected on facilities maintenance department costs and on the number of patient-days serviced over the past year:

Facilities Maintenance Department Data

Month	Facilities Maintenance Department Cost (Y)	Number of Patient-Days (X)
January	$37,000	3,700
February	23,000	1,600
March	37,000	4,100
April	47,000	4,900
May	33,000	3,300
June	39,000	4,400
July	32,000	3,500
August	33,000	4,000
September	17,000	1,200
October	18,000	1,300
November	22,000	1,800
December	20,000	1,600

high-low method

A simple method for measuring a linear-cost function from past cost data, focusing on the highest-activity and lowest-activity points, and fitting a line through these two points.

HIGH-LOW METHOD When sufficient cost data are available, the cost analyst may use historical data to measure the cost function mathematically. The simplest of the three methods to measure a linear-cost function from past cost data is the **high-low method** shown in Exhibit 5-3.

The first step in the high-low method is to plot the historical data points on a graph. This visual display helps the analyst see whether there are obvious errors in the data. Even though many points are plotted, the focus of the high-low method is normally on the highest and lowest activity points. However, if one of these points is an outlier that seems in error or non-representative of normal operations, we should use the next-highest or next-lowest activity point. For example, we should not use a point from a period with abnormally low activity caused by a labor strike or fire. Why? Because that point is not representative of a normal relationship between cost and cost driver.

After selecting the representative high and low points, we can draw a line between them, extending the line to the vertical (Y) axis of the graph. Note that this extension in Exhibit 5-3 is a dashed line, as a reminder that costs may not be linear outside the range of activity for which we have data (the relevant range). Also, managers usually are concerned with how costs behave within the relevant range, not with how they behave either at zero activity or at impossibly high activity levels. Cost measurements within the relevant range may not be reliable measures or predictors of costs outside the relevant range.

The point at which the line intersects the Y-axis is the intercept, F, or estimate of fixed cost. The slope of the line measures the variable cost, V, per patient-day. The clearest way to measure the intercept and slope with the high-low method is to use algebra:

Month	Facilities Maintenance Department Cost (Y)	Number of Patient-Days (X)
High: April	$47,000	4,900
Low: September	17,000	1,200
Difference	$30,000	3,700

Variable cost per patient-day,

$$V = \frac{\text{change in costs}}{\text{change in activity}} = \frac{\$47,000 - \$17,000}{4,900 - 1,200 \text{ patient-days}}$$

$$V = \frac{\$30,000}{3,700} = \$8.1081 \text{ per patient-day}$$

Exhibit 5-3
High-Low Method

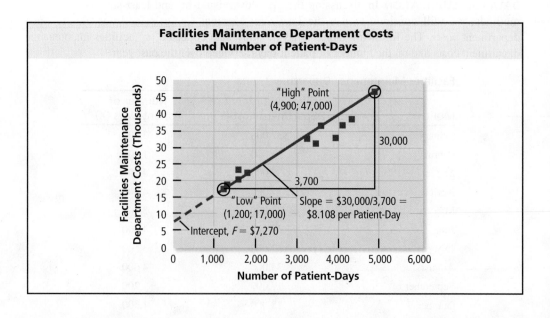

Fixed cost per month, F = total mixed cost less total variable cost

At X (high): $F = \$47,000 - (\$8.1081 \times 4,900 \text{ patient-days})$

$= \$47,000 - \$39,730$

$= \$7,270 \text{ per month}$

At X (low): $F = \$17,000 - (\$8.1081 \times 1,200 \text{ patient-days})$

$= \$17,000 - \$9,730$

$= \$7,270 \text{ per month}$

Therefore, the facilities maintenance department cost function, measured by the high-low method, is

$$Y = \$7,270 \text{ per month} + (\$8.1081 \times \text{patient-days})$$

The high-low method is easy to apply and illustrates mathematically how a change in a cost driver can change total cost. The cost function that resulted in this case is plausible. Before the widespread availability of computers, managers often used the high-low method to measure a cost function quickly. Today, however, the high-low method is not used as often because it makes inefficient use of information, basing the cost function on only two periods' cost experience, regardless of how many relevant data points have been collected.

Summary Problem for Your Review

PROBLEM

The Reetz Company has its own photocopying department. Reetz's photocopying costs include costs of copy machines, operators, paper, toner, utilities, and so on. We have the following cost and activity data:

Month	Total Photocopying Cost	Number of Copies
1	$25,000	320,000
2	29,000	390,000
3	24,000	300,000
4	23,000	310,000
5	28,000	400,000

1. Use the high-low method to measure the cost behavior of the photocopy department in formula form.
2. What are the benefits and disadvantages of using the high-low method for measuring cost behavior?

SOLUTION

1. The lowest and highest activity levels are in months 3 (300,000 copies) and 5 (400,000 copies).

$$\text{Variable cost per copy} = \frac{\text{change in cost}}{\text{change in activity}} = \frac{\$28,000 - \$24,000}{400,000 - 300,000}$$

$$= \frac{\$4,000}{100,000} = \$0.04 \text{ per copy}$$

Fixed cost per month = total cost less variable cost

at 400,000 copies: $\$28,000 - (\$0.04 \times 400,000) = \$12,000$ per month

at 300,000 copies: $\$24,000 - (\$0.04 \times 300,000) = \$12,000$ per month

Therefore, the photocopy cost function is

$Y(\text{total cost}) = \$12,000 \text{ per month} + (\$0.04 \times \text{number of copies})$

2. The benefits of using the high-low method are as follows:
- The method is easy to use.
- Not many data points are needed.

The disadvantages of using the high-low method are as follows:
- The choice of the high and low points is subjective.
- The method does not use all available data.
- The method may not be reliable.

visual-fit method

A method in which the cost analyst visually fits a straight line through a plot of all the available data.

VISUAL-FIT METHOD In the **visual-fit method**, we draw a straight line through a plot of all the available data, using judgment to fit the line as close as possible to all the plotted points. If the cost function for the data is linear, it is possible to draw a straight line through the scattered points that comes reasonably close to most of them and thus captures the general tendency of the data. We can extend that line back until it intersects the vertical axis of the graph.

Exhibit 5-4 shows this method applied to the facilities maintenance department cost data for the past 12 months. By measuring where the line intersects the cost axis, we can visually estimate the monthly fixed cost—in this case, about $10,000 per month. To find the variable cost per patient-day, select any activity level (for example 1,000 patient-days) and visually find the total cost at that activity level ($17,000). Then, divide the variable cost (which is total cost less fixed cost) by the units of activity.

$$\text{Variable cost per patient-day} = (\$17,000 - \$10,000) / 1,000 \text{ patient-days}$$
$$= \$7 \text{ per patient-day}$$

The linear-cost function measured by the visual-fit method is

$$Y = \$10,000 \text{ per month} + (\$7 \times \text{patient-days})$$

Although the visual-fit method uses all the data, the placement of the line and the measurement of the fixed and variable costs are subjective. This subjectivity is the main reason that many companies with sufficient data prefer to use least-squares regression analysis rather than the visual-fit method.

least-squares regression (regression analysis)

Measuring a cost function objectively by using statistics to fit a cost function to all the data.

LEAST-SQUARES REGRESSION METHOD Least-squares regression (or simply **regression analysis**) measures a cost function more objectively and explicitly than does the visual-fit method. Least-squares regression analysis uses statistics rather than human eyesight to fit a cost function to all the historical data. A simple regression uses one cost driver to measure a cost function, while a multiple regression uses two or more cost drivers. We will discuss only simple regression analysis in this chapter.

Exhibit 5-4
Visual-Fit Method

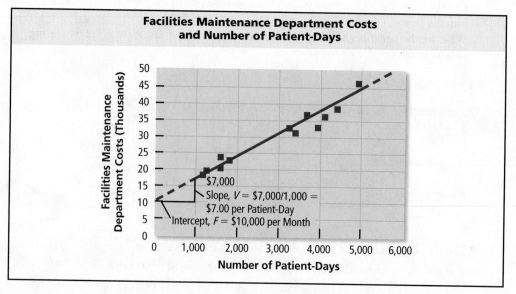

Appendix 5 presents some statistical properties of regression and shows how to use spreadsheet software to conduct a regression analysis.

Regression analysis measures cost behavior more reliably than other data-based cost measurement methods. It also yields important statistical information about the reliability of its cost estimates. These statistics allow analysts to assess their confidence in the cost measures and thereby select the best cost driver. One such measure of reliability, or goodness of fit, is the **coefficient of determination, R^2** (or R-squared), which measures how much of the fluctuation of a cost is explained by changes in the cost driver. Appendix 5 explains R^2 and discusses how to use it to select the best cost driver.

coefficient of determination (R^2)
A measurement of how much of the fluctuation of a cost is explained by changes in the cost driver.

Exhibit 5-5 shows the linear, mixed-cost function for facilities maintenance costs as measured mathematically by regression analysis. The fixed-cost measure is $9,329 per month. The variable-cost measure is $6.951 per patient-day. The linear-cost function is as follows:

Facilities maintenance department cost = $9,329 per month + ($6.951 × number of patient-days)

or

$$Y = \$9{,}329 + (\$6.951 \times \text{patient-days})$$

Compare the cost measures produced by each of the five approaches:

Method	Fixed Cost per Month	Variable Cost per Patient-Day
Engineering analysis	$10,000	$5.000
Account analysis	9,673	7.500
High-low	7,270	8.108
Visual-fit	10,000	7.000
Regression	9,329	6.951

Because the regression-cost measures are grounded in statistical theory, they are more reliable than those obtained from the other data-based methods. Thus, managers have more confidence in cost predictions from the regression-cost function.

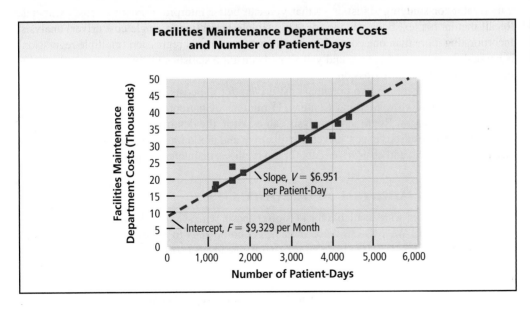

Facilities Maintenance Department Costs and Number of Patient-Days

Exhibit 5-5
Least-Squares Regression Method

Highlights to Remember

1. **Explain management influences on cost behavior.**   Managers can affect the costs and cost behavior patterns of their companies through the decisions they make. Decisions on product and service features, capacity, technology, and cost-control incentives, for example, can all affect cost behavior.

2. **Measure and mathematically express cost functions and use them to predict costs.** The first step in estimating or predicting costs is measuring cost behavior. This is done by finding a cost function. This is an algebraic equation that describes the relationship between a cost and its cost driver(s). To be useful for decision-making purposes, cost functions should be plausible and reliable.

3. **Describe the importance of activity analysis for measuring cost functions.**   Activity analysis is the process of identifying the best cost drivers to use for cost estimation and prediction and determining how they affect the costs of making a product or service. This is an essential step in understanding and predicting costs.

4. **Measure cost behavior using the engineering analysis, account analysis, high-low, visual-fit, and least-squares regression methods.**   Once analysts have identified cost drivers, they can use one of several methods to determine the cost function. Engineering analysis focuses on what costs should be by systematically reviewing the materials, supplies, labor, support services, and facilities needed for a given level of production. Account analysis involves examining all accounts in terms of an appropriate cost driver and classifying each account as either fixed or variable with respect to the driver. The cost function consists of the variable cost per cost-driver unit multiplied by the amount of the cost driver plus the total fixed cost. The high-low, visual-fit, and regression methods all use historical data to determine cost functions. Of these three methods, regression is the most reliable.

Appendix 5: Applying and Interpreting Least-Squares Regression

While we can perform regression analysis of historical cost data by hand, it would be unusual to find cost analysts doing so. Rather, spreadsheets or statistical analysis software are almost always used because they are faster, less prone to error, and produce explicit statistical analyses of the results. Therefore, we focus on interpreting regression results from a spreadsheet analysis.

This appendix is not a substitute for a good statistics class. More properly, think of it as a motivator for studying statistics so that you can better interpret regression cost estimates. Recall that in this text book we consider only simple regression (a single cost driver) analysis. Incorporating more than one cost driver into a cost function via regression (multiple regression) is beyond the scope of this text, and you should consult a statistics textbook to learn about this more advanced form of regression.

Assume that there are two potential cost drivers for the costs of the facilities maintenance department in Parkview Medical Center: (1) number of patient-days and (2) total value of hospital room charges. Regression analysis can assist in the determination of which activity is the better (more descriptive) cost driver in explaining and predicting costs. Exhibit 5-6 shows the past 12 months' cost and cost-driver data for the facilities maintenance department.

Regression Analysis Procedures

Most spreadsheet software available for PCs offers basic regression analysis in the data analysis or tools commands. We will use these spreadsheet commands to illustrate regression analysis because many readers will already be familiar with spreadsheet software.

Entering Data

First, create a spreadsheet with the historical cost data in rows and columns. Each row should be data from one period. Each column should be a cost category or a cost driver. For ease of analysis, all the potential cost drivers should be in adjacent columns. Each row and column should be complete (no missing data) and without errors.

Exhibit 5-6
Facilities Maintenance
Department Data

Month	Facilities Maintenance Cost (Y)	Number of Patient-Days (X_1)	Value of Room Charges (X_2)
January	$37,000	3,700	$2,183,000
February	23,000	1,600	2,735,000
March	37,000	4,100	2,966,000
April	47,000	4,900	2,846,000
May	33,000	3,300	2,967,000
June	39,000	4,400	2,980,000
July	32,000	3,500	3,023,000
August	33,000	4,000	2,352,000
September	17,000	1,200	1,825,000
October	18,000	1,300	1,515,000
November	22,000	1,800	1,547,000
December	20,000	1,600	2,117,000

Plotting Data

There are two main reasons why the first step in regression analysis should be to plot the cost against each of the potential cost drivers. First, plots may show obvious nonlinear trends in the data; if so, linear regression analysis may not be appropriate for the entire range of the data. Second, plots help identify outliers that should be excluded from the analysis—costs that are in error or are otherwise obviously inappropriate. For example, costs may have been abnormally high (or abnormally low) in one month because of an unusual event such as a strike or mechanical breakdown, in which case the abnormal cost for that month should not be used in estimating the normal cost relation.

Plotting with spreadsheets uses graph commands on the columns of cost and cost-driver data. These graph commands typically offer many optional graph types (such as bar charts and pie charts), but the most useful plot for regression analysis usually is called the XY graph. This graph is the type shown earlier in this chapter—the X-axis is the cost driver, and the Y-axis is the cost. The XY graph should be displayed without lines drawn between the data points (called data symbols)—an optional command. (Consult your spreadsheet manual for details because each spreadsheet program is different.)

Regression Output

The format of the regression output is different for each software package. However, every package will identify the cost to be explained ("dependent variable") and the cost driver ("independent variable") in the cost function.

Producing regression output with spreadsheets is simple: Just select the regression command, specify (or highlight) the X-dimension(s) (the cost driver[s]), and specify the Y-dimension or "series" (the cost). Next, specify where the output will be displayed on the spreadsheet, and select Ok. The following is a regression analysis of facilities maintenance department costs using one of the two possible cost drivers, number of patient-days, X_1.

Facilities Maintenance Department Cost Explained by Number of Patient-Days

Regression Output	
Constant	9,329
R^2	0.955
X coefficient(s)	6.951

Interpretation of Regression Output

The fixed-cost measure, labeled "constant" or "intercept" by most programs, is $9,329 per month. The variable cost measure, labeled "X coefficient" (or something similar in other spreadsheets), is $6.951 per patient-day. The linear cost function is

$$Y = \$9,329 \text{ per month} + (\$6.951 \times \text{patient-days})$$

As mentioned in the chapter, it is important to consider plausibility and reliability in evaluating a cost function and its estimates. Plausibility simply refers to whether the estimated cost function makes economic sense. We can assess this by examining the sign of the variable cost estimate. In the preceding cost function, this estimate is +$6.951. The positive sign in this cost function implies that as patient-days increase, facilities maintenance costs also increase (specifically, by $6.951 per patient-day). We assess the economic plausibility of this positive relationship by asking ourselves whether it makes economic sense that an increase in patient-days should increase facilities maintenance costs. Based on our economic intuition, a positive relationship appears to make sense (that is, we would expect that increasing patient-days would increase the cost of cleaning supplies and repair materials such that total facilities maintenance costs increase). While plausibility appears to be a simple and straightforward item to assess, it is the most important element to assess in a cost function. We would not want to use a cost function to estimate and predict costs if it did not exhibit plausibility (even if it displayed good reliability) because, without plausibility, we do not fundamentally understand the cost function, which makes cost estimation and prediction suspect.

Regarding reliability, the computer output usually gives a number of statistical measures that indicate how well each cost driver explains the cost and how reliable the cost predictions are likely to be when using the cost function. A full explanation of the output is beyond the scope of this text. However, one of the most important statistics, the coefficient of determination, or R^2, is an important measure of reliability—how well the cost function fits the actual cost data. In general, the better a cost driver is at explaining a cost, the closer the data points will lie to the line, and the higher will be the R^2, which varies between 0 and 1. An R^2 of 0 means that the cost driver does not explain variability in the cost data, whereas an R^2 of 1 means that the cost driver explains the variability perfectly. The R^2 of the relationship measured with number of patient-days as the cost driver is 0.955, which is quite high. This value indicates that the number of patient-days explains facilities maintenance department cost extremely well. In fact, the number of patient-days explains 95.5% of the past fluctuations in facilities maintenance department cost. Such a regression is highly reliable.

In contrast, performing a regression analysis on the relationship between facilities maintenance department cost and value of hospital room charges produces the following results:

Facilities Maintenance Department Cost Explained by Value of Hospital Room Charges	
Regression Output	
Constant	$ 924
R^2	0.511
X coefficient(s)	0.012

While the positive sign of the variable cost estimate (+.012) appears to satisfy plausibility (that is, as hospital room charges increase we would expect facilities maintenance costs to also increase), the R^2 value, 0.511, indicates that the cost function using value of hospital room charges fits the facilities maintenance department cost worse than does the cost function using number of patient-days.

To use the information generated by regression analysis fully, an analyst must understand the meaning of the statistics and must be able to determine whether the statistical assumptions of regression are satisfied by the cost data. Indeed, one of the major reasons why cost analysts study statistics is to understand the assumptions of regression analysis better. With this understanding, analysts can provide their organizations with the best estimates of cost behavior.

Summary Problem for Your Review

PROBLEM

Comtell makes computer peripherals (disk drives, tape drives, and printers). Until recently, managers predicted production scheduling and control (PSC) costs to vary in proportion to labor costs according to the following cost function:

$$\text{PSC costs} = 200\% \text{ of labor cost}$$

or

$$Y = 2 \times \text{labor cost}$$

Because PSC costs have been growing at the same time that labor cost has been shrinking, Comtell is concerned that its cost estimates are neither plausible nor reliable. Comtell's controller has just completed regression analysis to determine the most appropriate drivers of PSC costs. She obtained two cost functions using different cost drivers:

$$Y = 2 \times \text{labor cost}$$
$$R^2 = 0.233$$

and

$$Y = \$10,000 \text{ per month} + (11 \times \text{number of components used})$$
$$R^2 = 0.782$$

1. How should the controller determine which cost function better predicts PSC costs?
2. During a subsequent month, Comtell's labor costs were $12,000, and it used 2,000 product components. Actual PSC costs were $31,460. Using each of the preceding cost functions, prepare reports that show predicted and actual PSC costs and the difference or variance between the two.
3. What is the meaning and importance of each cost variance?

SOLUTION

1. The controller should examine both the plausibility and the reliability of each cost function. Both costs seem plausible with positive signs on their respective variable cost estimates as we would expect. Regarding reliability, a statistical test of which function better explains past PSC costs compares the R^2 of each function. The second function, based on the number of components used, has a considerably higher R^2, so it better explains the past PSC costs. If the environment is essentially unchanged in the future, the second function probably will predict future PSC costs better than the first.

   A useful predictive test would be to compare the cost predictions of each cost function with actual costs for several months that were not used to measure the cost functions. The function that more closely predicted actual costs is probably the more reliable function.

2. Note that more actual cost data would be desirable for a better test, but the procedure would be the same. PSC cost predicted on a labor-cost basis follows:

Predicted Cost	Actual Cost	Variance
2 × $12,000 = $24,000	$31,460	$7,460 underestimate

PSC cost predicted on a component basis follows:

Predicted Cost	Actual Cost	Variance
$10,000 + ($11 × 2,000) = $32,000	$31,460	$540 overestimate

3. The cost function that relies on labor cost underestimated PSC cost by $7,460. The cost function that uses the number of components closely predicted actual PSC costs (off by $540). Planning and control decisions would have been based on more accurate information using this prediction than using the labor-cost-based prediction. An issue is whether the benefits of collecting data on the number of components used exceeded the added cost of the data collection.

Accounting Vocabulary

account analysis, p. 185
activity analysis, p. 182
capacity costs, p. 178
coefficient of determination
(R²), p. 191
committed fixed costs, p. 179

cost function, p. 181
cost measurement, p. 181
discretionary fixed
costs, p. 179
engineering analysis, p. 183
high-low method, p. 188

least-squares regression, p. 190
linear-cost behavior, p. 177
measurement of cost
behavior, p. 176
visual-fit method, p. 190

MyAccountingLab ## Fundamental Assignment Material

5-A1 Activity Analysis

Dogwood Signs makes customized wooden signs for businesses and residences. These signs are made of wood, which the owner glues and carves by hand or with power tools. After carving the signs, she paints them or applies a natural finish. She has a good sense of her labor and materials cost behavior, but she is concerned that she does not have good measures of other support costs. Currently, she predicts support costs to be 75% of the cost of materials. Close investigation of the business reveals that $70 times the number of power tool operations is a more plausible and reliable support cost relationship.

Consider estimated support costs of the following two signs that Dogwood Signs is making:

	Sign A	Sign B
Materials cost	$300	$800
Number of power tool operations	10	2
Support cost	?	?

1. Prepare a report showing the support costs of both signs using each cost driver and showing the differences between the two.
2. What advice would you give Dogwood Signs about predicting support costs?

5-A2 Division of Mixed Costs into Variable and Fixed Components

Molly Flutie, president of First Tool, Co., has asked for information about the cost behavior of manufacturing support costs. Specifically, she wants to know how much support cost is fixed and how much is variable. The following data are the only records available:

Month	Machine Hours	Support Costs
May	1,700	$ 22,000
June	1,600	21,000
July	1,500	19,500
August	1,400	18,500
September	1,300	18,000

1. Find monthly fixed support cost and the variable support cost per machine hour by the high-low method.
2. Explain how your analysis for requirement 1 would change if new October data were received and machine hours were 1,650 and support costs were $24,000.
3. A least-squares regression analysis gave the following output:

$$\text{Regression equation: } Y = \$4,050 + \$10.50X$$

What recommendations would you give the president based on these analyses?

5-B1 Activity Analysis

DeHart Technology, an Idaho manufacturer of printed circuit boards, has always estimated the support cost of its circuit boards with a 100% "markup" over its material costs. An activity analysis suggests that support costs are driven primarily by the number of manual operations performed on each board, estimated at $6 per manual operation. Compute the estimated support costs of the following two typical circuit boards using the traditional markup and the activity analysis results:

	Board Z15	Board Q52
Material cost	$46.00	$65.00
Manual operations	19	8

Why are the cost estimates different?

5-B2 Division of Mixed Costs into Variable and Fixed Components

The president and the controller of Toluca Transformer Company (Mexico) have agreed that refinement of the company's cost measurements will aid planning and control decisions. They have asked you to measure the function for mixed-cost behavior of repairs and maintenance from the following sparse data. Currency is the Mexican peso (P).

Monthly Activity in Machine Hours	Monthly Repair and Maintenance Cost
7,900	P202,000,000
11,900	P272,000,000

Additional Assignment Material

MyAccountingLab

QUESTIONS

5-1 What is a cost driver? Give three examples of costs and their possible cost drivers.

5-2 Explain linear-cost behavior.

5-3 "Step costs can be fixed or variable, depending on your perspective." Explain.

5-4 Explain how mixed costs are related to both fixed and variable costs.

5-5 How do management's product and service choices affect cost behavior?

5-6 Why are fixed costs also called capacity costs?

5-7 How do committed fixed costs differ from discretionary fixed costs?

5-8 Why are committed fixed costs the most difficult of the fixed costs to change?

5-9 What are the primary determinants of the level of committed costs? Discretionary costs?

5-10 "Planning is far more important than day-to-day control of discretionary costs." Do you agree? Explain.

5-11 How can a company's choice of technology affect its costs?

5-12 Explain the use of incentives to control cost.

5-13 Why is it important for managers and accountants to measure cost functions?

5-14 Explain plausibility and reliability of cost functions. Which is preferred? Explain.

5-15 What is activity analysis?

5-16 What is engineering analysis? Account analysis?

5-17 Describe the methods for measuring cost functions using past cost data.

5-18 How could account analysis be combined with engineering analysis?

5-19 Explain the strengths and weaknesses of the high-low and visual-fit methods.

5-20 In the high-low method, does the high and low refer to cost-driver levels or to total cost levels? Explain.

5-21 Why is regression analysis usually preferred to the high-low method?

5-22 "You never know how good your fixed- and variable-cost measures are if you use account analysis or if you visually fit a line on a data plot. That's why I like least-squares regression analysis." Explain.

5-23 (Study Appendix 5) Why should an analyst always plot cost data in addition to applying least-squares regression analysis?

5-24 (Study Appendix 5) What can we learn from R^2, the coefficient of determination?

5-25 At a conference, a consultant stated, "Before you can control, you must measure." An executive complained, "Why bother to measure when work rules and guaranteed employment provisions in labor contracts prevent discharging workers, using part-time employees, and using overtime?" Evaluate these comments.

CRITICAL THINKING EXERCISES

5-26 Committed and Discretionary Fixed Costs in Manufacturing

Among the fixed costs of Howarth Company are depreciation and research and development (R&D). Using these two costs as examples, explain the difference between committed and discretionary fixed costs.

5-27 Cost Functions and Decision Making

Why is it important that decision makers in a corporation know the cost function for producing the company's products?

5-28 Statistical Analysis and Cost Functions

What advantages does using regression analysis have over the visual-fit method for determining cost functions?

EXERCISES

5-29 Plotting Data

The following graph was constructed and data plotted to apply the visual-fit method. Then, the predicted total order-department costs for processing 90 orders was computed. Comment on the accuracy of the analysis. Do your own analysis and explain any differences. Assume the data in parentheses are accurate in thousands of dollars and number of orders.

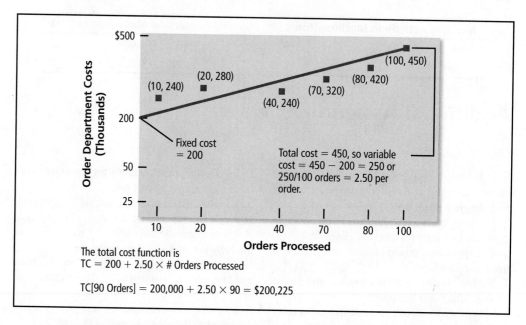

The total cost function is
TC = 200 + 2.50 × # Orders Processed

TC[90 Orders] = 200,000 + 2.50 × 90 = $200,225

5-30 Cost Function for Travel Services

One Travel provides travel services on the Internet. 2011 was an important year for One Travel as it reported positive operating income after 3 years of operating losses. In the first quarter of 2010, One Travel reported an operating loss of $11 million on sales revenue of $74 million. In the first quarter of 2011, sales revenue had more than doubled to $154 million, and One Travel had operating income of $61 million. Assume that fixed costs were the same in 2011 as in 2010.

1. Compute the operating expenses for One Travel in the first quarter of 2010 and in the first quarter of 2011.
2. Determine the cost function for One Travel, that is, the total fixed cost and the variable cost as a percentage of sales revenue. Use the same form as equation (1) on page 181.
3. Explain how One Travel's operating income could increase by $72 million with an increase in sales of $80 million, while it had an operating loss of $11 million on its $74 million of sales in the first quarter of 2010.

5-31 Predicting Costs

Given the following four cost behaviors and expected levels of cost-driver activity, predict total costs:

1. Fuel costs of driving vehicles, $0.40 per mile, driven 16,000 miles per month
2. Equipment rental cost, $5,000 per piece of equipment per month for seven pieces for 3 months
3. Ambulance and EMT personnel cost for a soccer tournament, $1,200 for each 200 tournament participants; the tournament is expecting 2,400 participants
4. Purchasing department cost, $7,500 per month plus $5 per material order processed at 4,000 orders in one month

5-32 Identifying Discretionary and Committed Fixed Costs

Identify and compute total discretionary fixed costs and total committed fixed costs from the following list prepared by the accounting supervisor for Kasay Building Supply:

Advertising	$21,000
Depreciation	48,000
Health insurance for the company's employees	24,000
Management salaries	87,500
Payment on long-term debt	48,500
Property tax	30,000
Grounds maintenance	7,000
Office remodeling	24,000
Research and development	45,500

5-33 Cost Effects of Technology

American Sports, an outdoor sports retailer, is planning to add a Web site for online sales. The estimated costs of two alternative approaches are as follows:

	Alternative 1	Alternative 2
Annual fixed cost	$155,000	$315,000
Variable cost per order	$ 9	$ 7
Expected number of orders	45,000	45,000

At the expected level of orders, which online approach has the lower cost? What is the indifference level of orders, or the "break-even" level of orders? What is the meaning of this level of orders?

5-34 Mixed Cost, Choosing Cost Drivers, and High-Low and Visual-Fit Methods

Cedar Rapids Implements Company produces farm implements. Cedar Rapids is in the process of measuring its manufacturing costs and is particularly interested in the costs of the manufacturing maintenance activity, since maintenance is a significant mixed cost. Activity analysis indicates that maintenance activity consists primarily of maintenance labor setting up machines using certain supplies. A setup consists of preparing the necessary machines for a particular production run of a product. During setup, machines must still be running, which consumes energy. Thus, the costs associated with maintenance include labor, supplies, and energy. Unfortunately, Cedar Rapids' cost accounting system does not trace these costs to maintenance activity separately. Cedar Rapids employs two full-time maintenance mechanics to perform maintenance. The annual salary of a maintenance mechanic is $42,000 and is considered a fixed cost. Two plausible cost drivers have been suggested: "units produced" and "number of setups."

Data had been collected for the past 12 months and a plot was made for the cost driver—units of production. The maintenance cost figures collected include estimates for labor, supplies, and energy. Cory Fielder, controller at Cedar Rapids, noted that some types of activities are performed each time a batch of goods is processed rather than each time a unit is produced. Based on this concept, he has gathered data on the number of setups performed over the past 12 months. The plots of monthly maintenance costs versus the two potential cost drivers follow:

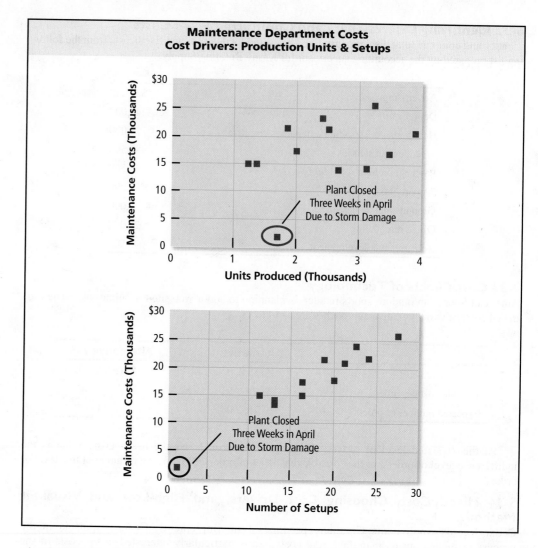

1. Find monthly fixed maintenance cost and the variable maintenance cost per driver unit using the visual-fit method based on each potential cost driver. Explain how you treated the April data.

2. Find monthly fixed maintenance cost and the variable maintenance cost per driver unit using the high-low method based on each potential cost driver.

3. Which cost driver best meets the criteria for choosing cost functions? Explain.

5-35 Account Analysis

Heavenly Computers is a company started by two engineering students to assemble and market personal computers to faculty and students. The company operates out of the garage of one of the students' homes. From the following costs of a recent month, compute the total cost function and total cost for the month:

Telephone	$ 60, fixed
Utilities	250, fixed: 30% attributable to the garage, 70% to the house
Advertising	85, fixed
Insurance	110, fixed
Materials	5,500, variable, for five computers
Labor	2,150: $1,400 fixed plus $750 for hourly help for assembling five computers

5-36 Linear Cost Functions

Let Y = total costs, X_1 = production volume, and X_2 = number of setups. Which of the following are linear cost functions? Which are mixed cost functions?

a. $Y = \$8X_1$

b. $Y = \$1,500$

c. $Y = \$8,500 + \$1.50X_1$

d. $Y = \$3,000 + \$6X_1 + \$30X_2$

e. $Y = \$9,000 + \$3(X_1 \times X_2)$

f. $Y = \$5,000 + \$4.00X_1$

5-37 High-Low Method

North Manchester Foundry produced 55,000 tons of steel in March at a cost of £1,150,000. In April, the foundry produced 35,000 tons at a cost of £950,000. Using only these two data points, determine the cost function for North Manchester.

5-38 Economic Plausibility of Regression Analysis Results

The head of the warehousing division of Lachton, Co., was concerned about some cost behavior information given to him by the new assistant controller, who was hired because of his recent training in cost analysis. His first assignment was to apply regression analysis to various costs in the department. One of the results was presented as follows:

A regression on monthly data was run to explain building maintenance cost as a function of direct labor hours as the cost driver. The results are

$$Y = \$7,810 - \$.47X$$

I suggest that we use the building as intensively as possible to keep the maintenance costs down.

The department head was puzzled. How could increased use cause decreased maintenance cost? Explain this counterintuitive result to the department head. What step(s) did the assistant controller probably omit in applying and interpreting the regression analysis?

PROBLEMS

5-39 Controlling Risk, Capacity Decisions, Technology Decisions

Consider the following hypothetical situation in the computer industry. HP had been outsourcing production to Acer and using overtime for as much as 20% of production—HP's plants and assembly lines were running at 100% of capacity and demand was sufficient for an additional 20%. HP had considered increasing its capacity by building new, highly automated assembly lines and plants. However, the investment in high technology and capacity expansion was rejected.

Assume that all material and labor costs are variable with respect to the level of production and that all other costs are fixed. Consider one of HP's plants that makes the Pavillion model. The increase in annual fixed costs to convert the plant to use fully automated assembly lines is $20 million. The resulting labor costs would be significantly reduced and there would be no need for overtime or outsourced production. The annual costs, in millions of dollars, of the build option and the existing costs that include outsourcing and overtime are given in the following tables:

	Build Option		
Percent of current capacity	60	100	120
Material costs	$18	$30	$36
Labor costs	6	10	12
Other costs	40	40	40
Total costs	$64	$80	$88

	HP's Existing Costs Using Outsourcing/Overtime		
Percent of current capacity	60	100	120
Material costs	$18	$30	$ 36
Labor costs	18	30	44
Other costs	20	20	20
Total costs	$56	$80	$100

1. Prepare a line graph showing total costs for the two options: (a) build new assembly lines, and (b) continue to use overtime and outsource production of Pavillions. Give an explanation of the cost behavior of the two options.

2. Which option enables HP's management to control risk better? Explain. Assess the cost-benefit trade-offs associated with each option.

3. A solid understanding of cost behavior is an important prerequisite to effective managerial control of costs. Suppose you are an executive at HP. Currently the production (and sales) level is approaching the 100% level of capacity, and the economy is expected to remain strong for at least 1 year. While sales and profits are good now, you are aware of the variability inherent in the computer business. Would you recommend committing HP to building automated assembly lines in order to service potential near-term increases in demand? Or would you recommend against building, looking to the possible future downturn in business? Discuss your reasoning.

5-40 Step Costs

Algona Beach Jail requires a staff of at least 1 guard for every 4 prisoners. The jail will hold 48 prisoners. Algona Beach attracts numerous tourists and transients in the spring and summer. However, the town is rather sedate in the fall and winter. The jail's fall–winter population is generally between 12 and 16 prisoners. The numbers in the spring and summer can fluctuate from 12 to 48, depending on the weather, among other factors (including phases of the moon, according to some longtime residents).

Algona Beach has four permanent guards, hired on a year-round basis at an annual salary of $36,000 each. When additional guards are needed, they are hired on a weekly basis at a rate of $600 per week. (For simplicity, assume that each month has exactly 4 weeks.)

1. Prepare a graph with the weekly planned cost of jail guards on the vertical axis and the number of prisoners on the horizontal axis.

2. What would be the budgeted amount for jail guards for the month of January? Would this be a fixed or a variable cost?

3. Suppose the jail population of each of the 4 weeks in July was 25, 38, 26, and 43, respectively. The actual amount paid for jail guards in July was $19,800. Prepare a report comparing the actual amount paid for jail guards with the amount that would be expected with efficient scheduling and hiring.

4. Suppose Algona Beach treated jail-guard salaries for nonpermanent guards as a variable expense of $150 per week per prisoner. This variable cost was applied to the number of prisoners in excess of 16. Therefore, the weekly cost function was as follows:

$$\text{Weekly jail-guard cost} = \$3{,}000 + \$150 \times (\text{total prisoners} - 16)$$

Explain how this cost function was determined.

5. Prepare a report similar to that in requirement 3 except that the cost function in requirement 4 should be used to calculate the expected amount of jail-guard salaries. Which report, this one or the one in requirement 3, is more accurate? Is accuracy the only concern?

5-41 Government Service Cost Analysis

Auditors for the Internal Revenue Service (IRS) scrutinize income tax returns after they have been prescreened with the help of computer tests for normal ranges of deductions claimed by taxpayers. The IRS uses an expected cost of $5 per tax return, based on measurement studies that allow 15 minutes per return. Each agent has a workweek of 5 days of 8 hours per day. Eighteen auditors are employed at a salary of $790 each per week.

The audit supervisor has the following data regarding performance for the most recent 4-week period, when 8,300 returns were processed:

Actual Cost of Auditors	Expected Cost for Processing Returns	Difference or Variance
$56,880	?	?

1. Compute the expected cost and the variance.

2. The supervisor believes that audit work should be conducted more productively and that superfluous personnel should be transferred to field audits. If the foregoing data are representative, how many auditors should be transferred?

3. List some possible reasons for the variance.

4. Describe some alternative cost drivers for processing income tax returns.

5-42 Cost Analysis at US Airways

US Airways is one of the nation's leading commercial air carriers, with hubs in Phoenix and Las Vegas. The following are some of the costs incurred by US Airways. For each cost, select an appropriate cost driver and indicate whether the cost is likely to be fixed, variable, or mixed in relation to your cost driver.

    a. Airplane fuel
    b. Flight attendants' salaries
    c. Baggage handlers' salaries
    d. In-flight meals
    e. Pilots' salaries
    f. Airplane depreciation
    g. Advertising

5-43 Separation of Mixed Costs into Variable and Fixed Components

A staff meeting has been called at SportsLab, a drug-testing facility retained by several professional and college sports leagues and associations. The chief of testing, Dr. Hyde, has demanded an across-the-board increase in prices for a particular test because of the increased testing and precision that are now required.

    The administrator of the laboratory has asked you to measure the mixed-cost behavior of this particular testing department and to prepare a short report she can present to Dr. Hyde. Consider the following limited data:

	Average Test Procedures per Month	Average Monthly Cost of Test Procedures
Monthly averages, 20X7	400	$ 60,000
Monthly averages, 20X8	500	80,000
Monthly averages, 20X9	600	140,000

5-44 School Cost Behavior

Oceanview School, a private high school, is preparing a planned income statement for the coming academic year ending August 31, 2013. Tuition revenues for the past two years ending August 31 were as follows: 2012, $840,000; and 2011, $880,000. Total expenses for 2012 were $830,000 and in 2011 were $844,000. No tuition rate changes occurred in 2011 or 2012, nor are any expected to occur in 2013. Tuition revenue is expected to be $830,000 for 2013. What net income should be planned for 2013, assuming that the implied cost behavior remains unchanged?

5-45 Activity Analysis

Washta Software develops and markets computer software for the agriculture industry. Because support costs are a large portion of the cost of software development, the director of cost operations of Washta, Vera Soren, is especially concerned with understanding the effects of support cost behavior. Soren has completed a preliminary activity analysis of one of Washta's primary software products: FertiMix (software to manage fertilizer mixing). This product is a software template that is customized for specific customers, who are charged for the basic product plus customizing costs. The activity analysis is based on the number of customized lines of FertiMix code. Currently, support cost estimates are based on a fixed rate of 65% of the basic cost. Data are shown for two recent customers:

	Customer	
	Mystical Plants	Todal Blooms
Basic cost of FertiMix	$8,000	$8,000
Lines of customized code	520	160
Estimated cost per line of customized code	$ 20	$ 20

1. Compute the support cost of customizing FertiMix for each customer using each cost-estimating approach.
2. If the activity analysis is reliable, what are the pros and cons of adopting it for all Washta's software products?

5-46 High-Low, Regression Analysis

On November 15, 2009, Sandra Cook, a newly hired cost analyst at Peterson Company, was asked to predict overhead costs for the company's operations in 2010, when 530 units are expected to be produced. She collected the following quarterly data:

Quarter	Production in Units	Overhead Costs
1/06	73	$ 715
2/06	76	709
3/06	68	640
4/06	133	1,124
1/07	122	995
2/07	125	1,105
3/07	122	1,113
4/07	130	1,036
1/08	121	982
2/08	126	1,060
3/08	112	990
4/08	81	951
1/09	81	829
2/09	119	1,044
3/09	87	985

1. Using the high-low method to estimate costs, prepare a prediction of overhead costs for 2010.
2. Sandy ran a regression analysis using the data she collected. The result was

$$Y = \$347 + \$5.76X$$

Using this cost function, predict overhead costs for 2010.
3. Which prediction do you prefer? Why?

5-47 Interpretation of Regression Analysis

Study Appendix 3. The tent division of New York Outdoor Equipment Company has had difficulty controlling its use of supplies. The company has traditionally regarded supplies as a purely variable cost. Nearly every time production was above average, however, the division spent less than predicted for supplies; when production was below average, the division spent more than predicted. This pattern suggested to Winnie Tsang, the new controller, that part of the supplies cost was probably not related to production volume, or was fixed.

She decided to use regression analysis to explore this issue. After consulting with production personnel, she considered two cost drivers for supplies cost: (1) number of tents produced, and (2) square feet of material used. She obtained the following results based on monthly data.

	Cost Driver	
	Number of Tents	**Square Feet of Material Used**
Constant	2,500	2,000
Variable coefficient	0.071	0.073
R^2	0.803	0.485

1. Which is the preferred cost function? Explain.
2. What percentage of the fluctuation of supplies cost depends on square feet of materials? Do fluctuations in supplies cost depend on anything other than square feet of materials? What proportion of the fluctuations is not explained by square feet of materials?

5-48 Regression Analysis

Study Appendix 3. Mr. Liao, CEO of a manufacturer of fine china and stoneware, is troubled by fluctuations in productivity and wants to compute how manufacturing support costs are related to the various sizes of batches of output. The following data show the results of a random sample of 10 batches of one pattern of stoneware:

Sample	Batch Size, X	Support Costs, Y
1	15	$180
2	12	140
3	20	230
4	17	190
5	12	160
6	25	300
7	22	270
8	9	110
9	18	240
10	30	320

1. Plot support costs, Y, versus batch size, X.
2. Using regression analysis, measure the cost function of support costs and batch size.
3. Predict the support costs for a batch size of 25.
4. Using the high-low method, repeat requirements 2 and 3. Should the manager use the high-low or regression method? Explain.

5-49 Choice of Cost Driver

Study Appendix 5. Richard Ellis, the director of cost operations of American Micro Devices, wishes to develop an accurate cost function to explain and predict support costs in the company's printed circuit board assembly operation. Mr. Ellis is concerned that the cost function that he currently uses—based on direct labor costs—is not accurate enough for proper planning and control of support costs. Mr. Ellis directed one of his financial analysts to obtain a random sample of 25 weeks of support costs and three possible cost drivers in the circuit-board assembly department: direct labor hours, number of boards assembled, and average cycle time of boards assembled. (Average cycle time is the average time between start and certified completion—after quality testing—of boards assembled during a week.) Much of the effort in this assembly operation is devoted to testing for quality and reworking defective boards, all of which increase the average cycle time in any period. Therefore, Mr. Ellis believes that average cycle time will be the best support-cost driver. Mr. Ellis wants his analyst to use regression analysis to demonstrate which cost driver best explains support costs.

Week	Circuit Board Assembly Support Costs, Y	Direct Labor Hours, X_1	Number of Boards Completed, X_2	Average Cycle Time (Hours), X_3
1	$66,402	7,619	2,983	186.44
2	56,943	7,678	2,830	139.14
3	60,337	7,816	2,413	151.13
4	50,096	7,659	2,221	138.30
5	64,241	7,646	2,701	158.63
6	60,846	7,765	2,656	148.71
7	43,119	7,685	2,495	105.85
8	63,412	7,962	2,128	174.02
9	59,283	7,793	2,127	155.30
10	60,070	7,732	2,127	162.20
11	53,345	7,771	2,338	142.97
12	65,027	7,842	2,685	176.08
13	58,220	7,940	2,602	150.19
14	65,406	7,750	2,029	194.06
15	35,268	7,954	2,136	100.51
16	46,394	7,768	2,046	137.47
17	71,877	7,764	2,786	197.44
18	61,903	7,635	2,822	164.69
19	50,009	7,849	2,178	141.95
20	49,327	7,869	2,244	123.37
21	44,703	7,576	2,195	128.25
22	45,582	7,557	2,370	106.16
23	43,818	7,569	2,016	131.41
24	62,122	7,672	2,515	154.88
25	52,403	7,653	2,942	140.07

1. Plot support costs, Y, versus each of the possible cost drivers, X_1, X_2, and X_3.
2. Use regression analysis to measure cost functions using each of the cost drivers.
3. According to the criteria of plausibility and reliability, which is the best cost driver for support costs in the circuit board assembly department?
4. Interpret the economic meaning of the best cost function.

5-50 Use of Cost Functions for Pricing

Study Appendix 3. Read the previous problem. If you worked that problem, use your measured cost functions. If you did not work the previous problem, assume the following measured cost functions:

$$Y = \$9,000/\text{week} + (\$6 \times \text{direct labor hours}); R^2 = .10$$

$$Y = \$20,000/\text{week} + (\$14 \times \text{number of boards completed}); R^2 = .40$$

$$Y = \$5,000/\text{week} + (\$350 \times \text{average cycle time}); R^2 = .80$$

1. Which of the support cost functions would you expect to be the most reliable for explaining and predicting support costs? Why?
2. Assume that American Micro Devices prices its products by adding a percentage markup to its product costs. Product costs include assembly labor, components, and support costs. Using each of the cost functions, compute the circuit board portion of the support cost of an order that used the following resources:

   a. Effectively used the capacity of the assembly department for 3 weeks
   b. Assembly labor hours: 20,000
   c. Number of boards: 6,000
   d. Average cycle time: 180 hours

3. Which cost driver would you recommend that American Micro Devices use? Why?
4. Assume that the market for this product is extremely cost competitive. What do you think of American Micro Devices' pricing method?

5-51 Review of Chapters 4 and 5

Curtis Institute of Music (CIM) provides instrumental music education to children of all ages. Payment for services comes from two sources: (1) a contract with Imagine That School to provide private music lessons for up to 140 band students a year (where a year is 9 months of education) for a fixed fee of $150,000, and (2) payment from individuals at a rate of $120 per month for 9 months of education each year. In the 2012–2013 school year, CIM made a profit of $1,000 on revenues of $270,000:

Revenues:		
Imagine That School contract	$150,000	
Private students	120,000	
Total revenues		$270,000
Expenses:		
Administrative staff	$ 64,000	
Teaching staff	100,000	
Facilities	51,000	
Supplies	54,000	
Total expenses		269,000
Profit		$ 1,000

CIM conducted an activity analysis and found that teaching staff wages and supplies costs are variable with respect to student-months. (A student-month is one student educated for 1 month.) Administrative staff and facilities costs are fixed within the range of 1,800–2,300 student-months. At volumes between 2,300 and 2,800 student-months, an additional facilities charge of $2,800 would be incurred. During the last year, a total of 2,200 student-months of education were provided, 1,000 of which were for private students and 1,200 of which were offered under the contract with Imagine That School.

1. Compute the following using cost information from year 2012–2013 operations:
   Fixed cost per year
   Variable cost per student-month

2. Suppose that in 2013–2014 Imagine That School decreased its use of CIM to 90 students (that is, 810 student-months). The fixed contract price of $150,000 was still paid. If everything else stayed as it was in 2012–2013, what profit or loss would be made in 2013–2014?

3. Suppose that at the beginning of 2013–2014 Imagine That School decided not to renew its contract with CIM, and the management of CIM decided to try to maintain business as usual with only private students. How many students (each signing up for 9 months) would CIM require to continue to make a profit of $1,000 per year?

CASES

5-52 Government Health Cost Behavior

Dr. Stephanie White, the chief administrator of Uptown Clinic, a community mental health agency, is concerned about the dilemma of coping with reduced budgets in the next year and into the foreseeable future, despite increasing demand for services. In order to plan for reduced budgets, she first must identify where costs can be cut or reduced and still keep the agency functioning. The following are some data about fixed costs from the past year:

Program Area	Costs
Administrative salaries	
Administrator	$60,000
Assistant	35,000
Two secretaries	42,000
Supplies	35,000
Advertising and promotion	9,000
Professional meetings, dues, and literature	14,000
Purchased services	
Accounting and billing	15,000
Custodial and maintenance	13,000
Security	12,000
Consulting	10,000
Community mental health services	
Salaries (two social workers)	46,000
Transportation	10,000
Outpatient mental health treatment	
Salaries	
Psychiatrist	86,000
Two social workers	70,000

1. Identify which costs you think are likely to be discretionary costs and which are committed costs.
2. One possibility is to eliminate all discretionary costs. How much would be saved? What do you think of this recommendation?
3. How would you advise Dr. White to prepare for reduced budgets?

5-53 Activity Analysis

The costs of the systems support (SS) department (and other service departments) of Southeast Pulp and Paper have always been charged to the three business divisions (forest management, lumber products, and paper products) based on the number of employees in each division. This measure is easy to obtain and update, and until recently none of the divisions had complained about the charges. The paper products division has recently automated many of its operations and has reduced the number of its employees. At the same time, however, to monitor its new process, paper products has increased its requests for various reports provided by the SS department. The other divisions have begun to complain that they are being charged more than their fair share of SS department costs. Based on activity analysis of possible cost drivers, cost analysts have suggested using the number of reports prepared as a means of charging for SS costs and have gathered the following information:

	Forest Management	Lumber Products	Paper Products
2011 number of employees	762	457	502
2011 number of reports	410	445	377
2011 SS costs: $300,000			
2012 number of employees	751	413	131
2012 number of reports	412	432	712
2012 SS costs: $385,000			

1. Discuss the plausibility and probable reliability of each of the cost drivers—number of employees or number of reports.
2. What are the 2011 and 2012 SS costs per unit of cost driver for each division using each cost driver? Do the forest management and lumber products divisions have legitimate complaints? Explain.
3. What are the incentives that are implied by each cost driver?
4. Which cost driver should Southeast Pulp and Paper use to charge its divisions for SS services? For other services? Why?

5-54 Identifying Relevant Data

eComp.com manufactures personal digital assistants (PDAs). Because these very small computers compete with laptops that have more functions and flexibility, understanding and using cost behavior is very critical to eComp.com's profitability. eComp.com's controller, Kelly Hudson, has kept meticulous files on various cost categories and possible cost drivers for most of the important functions and activities of eComp.com. Because most of the manufacturing at eComp.com is automated, labor cost is relatively fixed. Other support costs comprise most of eComp.com's costs. Partial data that Hudson has collected over the past 25 weeks on one of these support costs, logistics operations (materials purchasing, receiving, warehousing, and shipping), follow:

Week	Logistics Costs, Y	Number of Orders, X
1	$23,907	1,357
2	18,265	1,077
3	24,208	1,383
4	23,578	1,486
5	22,211	1,292
6	22,862	1,425
7	23,303	1,306
8	24,507	1,373
9	17,878	1,031
10	18,306	1,020
11	20,807	1,097
12	19,707	1,069
13	23,020	1,444
14	20,407	733
15	20,370	413
16	20,678	633
17	21,145	711
18	20,775	228
19	20,532	488
20	20,659	655
21	20,430	722
22	20,713	373
23	20,256	391
24	21,196	734
25	20,406	256

1. Plot logistics costs, *Y*, versus number of orders, *X*. What cost behavior is evident? What do you think happened in week 14?
2. What is your recommendation to Kelly Hudson regarding the relevance of the past 25 weeks of logistics costs and number of orders for measuring logistics cost behavior?
3. Hudson remarks that one of the improvements that eComp.com has made in the past several months was to negotiate JIT deliveries from its suppliers. This was made possible by substituting an automated ordering system for the previous manual (labor-intensive) system. Although fixed costs increased, the variable cost of placing an order was expected to drop greatly. Do the data support this expectation? Do you believe that the change to the automated ordering system was justified? Why or why not?

NIKE 10-K PROBLEM

5-55 Step and Mixed Costs and Cost Drivers

Refer to **Nike**'s 10-K report "Item 1. Business." Nike's contract manufacturers make the vast majority of Nike's footwear. Assume these costs are variable to Nike. Nike's largest fixed costs are associated with its distribution system. Consider one of Nike's three distribution and customer service facilities in the United States. List several examples of step-fixed costs and mixed costs at these centers. For each of the following activities at a distribution center, list one plausible cost driver:

1. Receiving activity
2. Unpacking incoming cases of footwear
3. Picking and packing cases of footwear for shipment to retail accounts
4. Processing orders from retail accounts
5. Providing customer service to retail accounts
6. Processing order changes from retail accounts

EXCEL APPLICATION EXERCISE

5-56 Fixed and Variable Cost Data

Goal: Create an Excel spreadsheet to calculate fixed and variable cost data for evaluating alternative approaches. Use the results to answer questions about your findings.

Scenario: American Sports has asked you to evaluate two alternative cost approaches for its new Web site. It would like you to calculate fixed and variable costs at different numbers of orders. The background data for your analysis appear in Exercise 5-33, on page 199.

When you have completed your spreadsheet, answer the following questions:

1. At what number of orders are the total costs for the two approaches the same? What does this mean?
2. Which alternative should be selected if the expected number of orders is less than the break-even level of orders? If the expected number of orders is greater than the break-even level of orders?
3. What conclusion regarding cost predictions can be drawn from your analysis?

Step-by-Step:
1. Open a new Excel spreadsheet.
2. In column A, create a bold-faced heading that contains the following:
   Row 1: Chapter 5 Decision Guideline
   Row 2: American Sports
   Row 3: Analysis of Alternative Cost Approaches
   Row 4: Today's Date
3. Merge and center the four heading rows across columns A–K.
4. In row 7, create the following bold-faced, right-justified column headings:
   Column A: Number of Orders
   Column B: Alternative 1
   Column C: Alternative 2

   Note: Adjust column widths as necessary.

5. In column A, rows 8–12, enter order levels from 40,000 to 80,000 in 10,000-unit increments.

6. Use the scenario data to create formulas in columns B and C for calculating the total costs (fixed plus variable costs) for each alternative at the order level in column A.

7. Format all amounts as follows:

Number tab:	Category:	Number
	Decimal places:	0
	Use 1000 Separator (,):	Checked

8. Modify the Page Setup by selecting File, Page Setup.

Page tab:	Orientation:	Landscape
Margins tab:	Top:	.5
	Bottom:	.5

9. Select the data in columns A–C, rows 7–12, and start the Chart Wizard either by inserting a chart (Insert, Chart) or by clicking the Chart Wizard icon on the toolbar.

Step 1 of 4—Chart Type

a. **Custom Types tab:**
b. Chart Type: Smooth Lines
c. Click "Next >" button

Note: List is alphabetical.

Step 2 of 4—Chart Source Data

d. **Data Range tab:**
e. Modify Data range to: = *SheetName*!$B$7:$C$12
f. Series in: Columns
g. **Series tab:**
h. Category (X) axis labels: = *SheetName*!$A$8:$A$12
i. Click "Next >" button

Step 3 of 4—Chart Options

j. **Titles tab:**
k. Chart Title: Analysis of Alternative Cost Approaches
l. Category (X) axis: Number of Orders
m. Value (Y) axis: Total Costs
n. **Gridlines tab:**
o. Category (X) axis: Major Gridlines (checked)
p. Value (Y) axis: Major Gridlines (checked)
q. Click "Next >" button

Step 4 of 4—Chart Location

r. As object in SheetName Checked
s. Click "Finish" button

10. Move the chart so the upper-left corner is on the left margin, row 14.
Left-click the upper-left handle and drag it to the designated location.

11. Resize the chart so the lower-right corner fills cell K37.
Left-click the lower-right handle and drag it to the designated location.

12. Format the Y-axis amounts (Total Costs) to display a dollar symbol by doing the following:
Double-click any cost amount on the Y-axis to open the "Format Axis" dialog box.

Scale tab:	Minimum:	300,000
Number tab:	Category:	Currency
	Decimal Places:	0
	Symbol:	$

13. Save your work, and print a copy for your files.

Note: Select cell A8 before printing if you want both the data and the chart to print. If you want only the chart to print, ignore the "Select cell A8" instruction.

Print your spreadsheet using landscape in order to ensure that all columns appear on one page.

COLLABORATIVE LEARNING EXERCISE

5-57 Cost-Behavior Examples

Select about 10 students to participate in a "cost-behavior bee." The game proceeds like a spelling bee—when a participant is unable to come up with a correct answer, he or she is eliminated from the game. The last one in the game is the winner.

The object of the game is to identify a type of cost that fits a particular cost-behavior pattern. The first player rolls a die.[2] If a 1 or a 6 comes up, the die passes to the next player (and the roller makes it to the next round). If a 2, 3, 4, or 5 comes up, the player has to identify one of the following types of costs:

If a 2 is rolled, identify a variable cost.
If a 3 is rolled, identify a fixed cost.
If a 4 is rolled, identify a mixed cost.
If a 5 is rolled, identify a step cost.

A scribe should label four columns on the board, one for each type of cost, and list the costs that are mentioned for each category. Once a particular cost has been used, it cannot be used again.

Each player has a time limit of 10 seconds to produce an example. (For a tougher game, make the time limit 5 seconds.) The instructor is the referee, judging if a particular example is acceptable. It is legitimate for the referee to ask a player to explain why he or she thinks the cost mentioned fits the category before making a judgment.

After each player has had a turn, a second round begins with the remaining players taking a turn in the same order as in the first round. The game continues through additional rounds until all but one player has failed to give an acceptable answer within the time limit. The remaining player is the winner.

INTERNET EXERCISE

5-58 Cost Behavior at Southwest Airlines

In this exercise, we will look at some costs and see if we can determine the type of behavior associated with those costs. While firms are concerned about trying to label costs as either variable or fixed to help in planning, very few costs are completely variable or fixed. The information provided by firms to external users also often precludes a user from determining specifics about the cost behaviors—they don't want to give the competitors too much information!

Log on to the **Southwest Airlines** Web site at www.southwest.com. Click on the information icon "About Southwest," and then click on "Investor Relations." This will take you to the site where you can then access the financial information.

1. Click on the most recent "Southwest Airlines One Report" tab. Then click on the "performance" tab, then "past performance," and find the page where the 10-year summary starts. Go to this section of the report. What type of information do you find there?
2. When you look at the operating revenue information, what do you see? Look at the information provided concerning operating expenses. Is it categorized in the same manner as the revenues? If the information is not in the same categories, why do you think Southwest did not match it up in the same manner?
3. Now look at the section on consolidated operating statistics. Southwest measures activity in revenue passenger miles (RPMs) and capacity in available seat miles (ASMs). Which of these is larger? How are the RPM and ASM determined? Is it possible for the two numbers to be the same? What information is provided for each of these items in the consolidated operating statistics section?
4. Using data from 2008 through 2011 and employing the high-low method, compute the fixed operating expense per year and the variable operating expense per RPM. Assume that half of the increase in operating expenses between 2008 and 2011 represents increases in fuel prices, which should be omitted from the analysis. Compare the total operating expense after omitting the increase caused by higher fuel prices and the variable expense for 2011. Is this relationship what you expected? Why or why not?
5. Airlines are often considered to be high-fixed-cost companies. Is this consistent with your findings in requirement 4? Explain why the high-low method this time might overestimate the amount of variable costs.

---

[2]Instead of rolling a die, players could draw one of the four cost categories out of a hat (or similar container) or from a deck of four 3 × 5 cards. This eliminates the chance element that can let some players proceed to a later round without having to give an example of a particular cost behavior. However, the chance element can add to the enjoyment of the game.

Introduction to Budgets and Preparing the Master Budget

LEARNING OBJECTIVES

When you have finished studying this chapter, you should be able to:

1. Explain how budgets facilitate planning and coordination.

2. Anticipate possible human relations problems caused by budgets.

3. Explain potentially dysfunctional incentives in the budget process.

4. Explain the difficulties of sales forecasting.

5. Explain the major features and advantages of a master budget.

6. Follow the principal steps in preparing a master budget.

7. Prepare the operating budget and the supporting schedules.

8. Prepare the financial budget.

9. Use a spreadsheet to develop a budget (Appendix 6).

▶ RITZ-CARLTON

If you have ever traveled, you know that there is a big difference between staying in a cheap motel and staying in a five-star, world-class hotel. The cheap motel takes care of your basic needs, but the five-star hotel surrounds you in comfort and luxury, catering to your every whim. No one understands the difference better than the managers of the **Ritz-Carlton** chain of hotels. After all, the word *ritzy*, which means elegant and luxurious, is derived from the name of the Ritz Hotel. Thanks to fierce competition in the industry, though, Ritz-Carlton managers have their share of challenges in maintaining standards that keep their hotels successful.

What does it take to run a world-class hotel successfully? Good location, exquisite food, luxury, personalized service, and quality are all essential ingredients. But you might be surprised to learn that the budgeting process is also a key to success. According to Ralph Vick, former general manager of the Phoenix Ritz-Carlton, "Budgets are crucial to the ultimate financial success of our hotels." Why are budgets so important? Mainly because they serve as a road map to help managers understand, plan, and control operations. Ritz-Carlton wants to give its managers the best tools possible. As a result, the company takes the budgeting process very seriously.

At the Ritz-Carlton hotels, all employees, from the hotel manager, to the controller, to the newest housekeeper, are involved in the budgeting process. Working in teams, managers set budget targets for the expenses they can control. These target figures help not only in planning, but also in controlling and evaluating employee performance. Managers compare actual results with budgeted target figures, and they evaluate performance based on the differences. In addition to financial reports, Ritz-Carlton managers also use nonfinancial measures, such as quality and customer satisfaction, to evaluate and reward employees.

Planning is the key to good management. This statement is certainly true for Ritz-Carlton, and it is also true for other types of organizations—small, family-owned companies; large corporations; government agencies; and nonprofit organizations. All organizations need budgets to make the best and most profitable use of their resources. Budgeting can cover such diverse issues as how much time to spend inspecting a product and how much money the company will allot to research and development in the coming year. In this chapter, we look at the benefits (and costs) of budgets and illustrate the construction of a comprehensive, detailed budget. ■

© Holger Burmeister/Alamy

Budgets and the Organization

Many people associate the word *budget* primarily with limitations on spending. For example, management often gives each unit in an organization a spending budget and then expects them to stay within the limits prescribed by the budget. However, budgeting can play a much more important role than simply limiting spending. Budgeting moves planning to the forefront of the manager's mind. Well-managed organizations make budgeting an integral part of the formulation and execution of their strategy.

A Ritz-Carlton hotel projects an image of quality. High quality is expensive so during the master budgeting process Ritz-Carlton managers must assess the planned expenditures for quality-enhancing features versus the added revenues these features will bring.

Objective 1

Explain how budgets facilitate planning and coordination.

In Chapter 3, we defined a budget as a quantitative expression of a plan of action. Sometimes plans are informal, perhaps even unwritten, and informal plans sometimes work in a small organization. However, as an organization grows, seat-of-the-pants planning is not enough. Budgets impose the formal structure—a budgetary system—that is needed for all but the smallest organizations. There are numerous examples of seemingly healthy businesses that failed because managers did not bother to construct budgets that would have identified problems in advance or they failed to monitor and adjust budgets to changing conditions. While there will always be debate about the costs and benefits of budgeting, as indicated in the Business First box on page 214, the vast majority of managers continue to use budgeting as an effective cost-management tool.

Advantages of Budgeting

Budgeting is the process of formulating an organization's plans. We will discuss four major advantages of effective budgeting:

1. Budgeting compels managers to think ahead by formalizing their responsibilities for planning.
2. Budgeting provides an opportunity for managers to reevaluate existing activities and evaluate possible new activities.
3. Budgeting aids managers in communicating objectives and coordinating actions across the organization.
4. Budgeting provides benchmarks to evaluate subsequent performance.

Let's look more closely at each of these benefits.

FORMALIZATION OF PLANNING Budgeting forces managers to devote time to planning. On a day-to-day basis, managers often move from extinguishing one business brush fire to another, leaving no time for thinking beyond the next day's problems. As a result, planning takes a backseat to, or is obliterated by, daily pressures. The budgeting process formalizes the need to anticipate and prepare for changing conditions.

To prepare a budget, a manager should set objectives and establish policies to aid their achievement. The objectives are the destination points, and budgets are the road maps guiding us to those destinations. In the absence of goals and objectives, results are difficult to interpret, managers do not foresee problems, and company operations lack direction.

EVALUATION OF ACTIVITIES Budgeting typically uses the current activities of the organization as a starting point for planning, but how managers use this starting point varies widely. At one extreme, in some organizations the budget process automatically assumes that activities for the new budget period will be the same as the activities for the previous period. At the other extreme,

Business First

Budgeting: Value Driver or Value Buster?

There is an ongoing debate about the costs and benefits of budgeting, focusing on four issues: (1) The budgeting process is time-consuming and expensive; (2) even the best-prepared budgets become inaccurate because marketplace change is frequent and unpredictable; (3) evaluating performance against a budget causes managers to bias their budgets, resulting in inaccurate planning; and (4) budget targets create incentives for individuals to take actions to meet targets even when the actions make the firm as a whole worse off.

Some studies suggest that the annual budgeting process can take up to 30% of management's time. For example, estimates place Ford Motor Company's cost of budgeting at $1.2 billion a year. Companies can justify such large budgeting costs only when there are corresponding large benefits. Companies that either fail to incorporate budgeting in their planning activities or react to changing economic conditions by ignoring the budget rather than adapting the budget to the changes will not reap some of the major benefits of budgeting. Consequently, these companies may find that large costs of budgeting are not justified.

Skeptical managers sometimes claim, "I face too many uncertainties and complications to make budgeting worthwhile for me." While it is true that budgeting is more difficult in uncertain or complicated environments, it is also true that these are the environments where the potential benefits are largest. When conditions are changing rapidly, a budget provides a framework for systematic response rather than chaotic reaction.

When managers anticipate that budget information will be used to set targets used in their subsequent performance evaluations, they have an incentive to provide budget information that is biased to make it easier to meet the targets. Biases severely limit the usefulness of budget information for planning and coordination. Moreover, widespread understanding and acceptance of built-in biases can create a pernicious "culture of lying" within the organization.

When managers realize that meeting budget targets affects their rewards, either explicitly through bonus plans or implicitly through promotion and recognition, they have incentives to take actions to meet the targets. This can be a positive motivation, but it can also lead to unethical behavior, such as "cooking the books" or putting pressure on employees to meet targets using whatever means possible. For example, the director of the Office of Federal Housing Enterprise Oversight (OFHEO)

denounced "an arrogant and unethical culture" at Fannie Mae, the giant mortgage finance company. An OFHEO report cited a corporate culture that allowed managers to disregard accounting standards when they got in the way of achieving earnings targets that were tied to bonuses. In other cases, managers have taken actions to ship faulty or incomplete products to meet budgeted sales targets, despite clear adverse effects on customer relations and the reputation of the firm.

Most companies that have experienced problems with their budgeting process are not abandoning traditional budgeting but instead are modifying their approach to budgeting. For example, some companies now separate planning budgets from control budgets, comparing actual performance to benchmarks based on performance of peers and best-in-class operations. Further, most managers still agree that budgeting, when correctly used, has significant value to management. More than 92% of the companies in a recent survey use budgets, and they rank budgeting among their top three cost-management tools.

Companies such as Allstate, Owens Corning, Sprint, Battelle, and Texaco are modifying their approach to budgeting by implementing new technologies. For example, Battelle's Pacific Northwest National Laboratory uses an intranet to reduce the time and expense of developing the annual budget. The new system enables support staff and managers to input their budget plans directly on this corporate intranet. In addition to decreasing the cost of budgeting, managers at Battelle report that the new system "results in higher quality and more accurate budgeting, reporting, and analysis." Many companies are tying their budgeting process more closely to their overall strategy and have expanded their performance measures beyond traditional financial measures to also consider nonfinancial measures, such as time to market for new products or services.

Sources: Adapted from R. Banham, "Better Budgets," *Journal of Accountancy*, February 2000, pp. 37–40; J. Hope and R. Fraser, "Who Needs Budgets?" *Harvard Business Review*, February 2003, pp. 108–115; P. Smith, C. Goranson, and M. Astley, "Intranet Budgeting," *Strategic Finance*, May 2003, pp. 30–33; T. Hatch and W. Stratton, "Scorecarding in North America: Who is Doing What?" Paper presented at the CAM-I/CMS 3rd quarter meeting, Portland, Oregon, September 10, 2002; M. Jensen, "Corporate Budgeting Is Broken, Let's Fix It," *Harvard Business Review*, November 2001, pp. 94–101; M. Jensen, "Paying People to Lie: the Truth About the Budgeting Process," *European Financial Management*, Vol. 9 No. 3, (2003), pp. 379–406; and "Fannie Mae Ex-Officials May Face Legal Action over Accounting," *Wall Street Journal*, May 24, 2006, p. A1.

zero-base budget
A budget that requires justification of expenditures for every activity, including continuing activities.

some organizations use a form of **zero-base budget**, which starts with the assumption that current activities will not automatically be continued. The term zero-base comes from the fundamental assumption that the budget for every activity starts at zero. The advantage of a zero-base system is that managers reevaluate all activities (including whether existing activities should be continued) in each new budget.

In practice, budgeting for most organizations falls somewhere between these two extremes. An effective budget process encourages managers to think carefully about whether to continue current activities and methods, whether there are opportunities to modify activities, and whether to add new activities to help the organization better achieve its goals in response to changing conditions. Used in this way, budgeting encourages managers to review whether a particular plan allocates resources optimally among the firm's various activities.

COMMUNICATION AND COORDINATION The most effective budget processes facilitate communication both from the top down and from the bottom up. Top management communicates the strategic goals and objectives of the organization in its budgetary directives. Lower-level managers and employees contribute their own ideas and provide feedback on the goals and objectives. The result is two-way communication about opportunities and challenges that lie ahead.

Budgets also help managers coordinate activities across the organization. For example, a budget allows purchasing personnel to integrate their plans with production requirements, while production managers use the sales budget and delivery schedule to help them anticipate and plan for the employees and physical facilities they will need. Similarly, financial officers use the sales budget, purchasing requirements, and other planned expenditures to anticipate the company's need for cash. Thus, budgeting forces managers to communicate and coordinate their department's activities with those of other departments and the company as a whole.

PERFORMANCE EVALUATION Budgeted performance goals generally provide a better basis for evaluating actual results than would a simple comparison with past performance. Relying only on historical results for judging current performance may allow inefficiencies in past performance to continue undetected. Changes in economic conditions, technology, personnel, competition, and other factors also limit the usefulness of comparisons with the past. For example, sales of $100 million this year, for a company that had sales of $80 million the previous year, may or may not indicate that company objectives have been met—perhaps conditions imply that the sales goal for this year should have been $110 million.

Making Managerial Decisions

Level 3 Communications is "a facilities-based provider of a broad range of communications services." The company has had losses for a number of years, which it attributes to a difficult competitive environment. For example, the 2011 annual report states, "Although the pricing for data services is currently relatively stable, the IP market is generally characterized by price compression and high unit growth rates depending upon the type of service. The Company experienced price compression in the high-speed IP market in 2011 and expects that aggressive pricing for its highspeed IP services will continue." The company has had a steady stream of large losses, $1,114 million in 2007, $318 million in 2008, $618 million in 2009, and $622 million in 2010.

Level 3's loss for 2011 was $756 million. Suppose the company budgeted to break even for 2011. Evaluate operating performance for 2011.

Answer

Level 3's performance in 2011 is consistent with what might be expected based on the losses that have occurred over the previous 4 years. However, if the company budgeted for break even in 2011, then performance is much worse than budgeted. This situation illustrates that a comparison to past results can provide a very different conclusion than a comparison to budget.

Potential Problems in Implementing Budgets

In this section, we discuss three problems that can limit, in some cases severely, the advantages of budgeting:

Objective 2

Anticipate possible human relations problems caused by budgets.

1. Low levels of participation in the budget process and lack of acceptance of responsibility for the final budget
2. Incentives to lie and cheat in the budget process
3. Difficulties in obtaining accurate sales forecasts

BUDGET PARTICIPATION AND ACCEPTANCE OF THE BUDGET The advantages of budgeting are fully realized only when employees throughout the organization accept and take responsibility for the final budget. The main factors affecting budget acceptance are as follows:

1. The perceived attitude of top management.
2. The level of participation in the budget process.
3. The degree of alignment between the budget and other performance goals.

The attitude of top management will heavily influence lower-level managers' and employees' attitudes toward budgets. If top management does not use budgets effectively in controlling operations and adapting to change, others in the organization may come to view budgeting as irrelevant. Even with the support of top management, however, budgets—and the managers who implement them—can run into opposition.

Lower-level managers sometimes have negative attitudes toward budgets because they believe the primary purpose of the budget is to limit spending. These negative attitudes are reinforced when companies evaluate managerial performance by comparing actual expenditures against amounts budgeted without substantive input from the managers. Ensuring that managers at all levels participate in setting budgets is one way to reduce negative attitudes and improve the quality of planning decisions. Budgets created with the active participation of all affected employees—called **participative budgeting**—are generally more effective than budgets imposed on subordinates. For example, Ritz-Carlton's budgeting system involves all hotel employees and is thus a participative system. Employee "buy-in" to the budget is so important at Ritz-Carlton that self-directed employee teams at all levels of the company have the authority to change operations based on budgets as they see fit.

participative budgeting
Budgets formulated with the active participation of all affected employees.

Misalignment between the performance goals stressed in budgets versus the performance measures the company uses to reward employees and managers can also limit the advantages of budgeting. For example, suppose a company rewards managers based on actual profit compared to budgeted profit and also on quality (defect rate) and timely delivery to customers (percent on time). Increased quality and more timely deliveries typically require higher costs, so the message conveyed by the budget system (minimize cost) may be misaligned with the incentives provided by the compensation system (maximize quality and timely delivery). Companies can manage the apparent misalignment by clearly specifying and communicating the tradeoff between costs and quality measures. This is particularly important for performance goals where the short-term impact on current performance relative to budget is negative but the long-term impact due to improved customer satisfaction is positive. We explore these issues in more detail in Chapter 8.

There is often too much concern with the mechanics of budgets and too little attention paid to the fact that the effectiveness of any budgeting system depends directly on whether the affected managers and employees understand and accept the budget. Management should seek to create an environment where there is a true two-way flow of information in the budget process so that lower level managers and employees perceive that their input has a real effect on budget outcomes. Top management must emphasize the importance of budgets in planning and communication and demonstrate how budgets can help each manager and employee achieve better results. Only then will the budgets become a positive aid in motivating employees at all levels to work toward goals, set objectives, measure results accurately, and direct attention to the areas that need investigation.

Objective 3

Explain potentially dysfunctional incentives in the budget process.

INCENTIVES TO LIE AND CHEAT   Effective budgets provide targets for managers and motivate them to achieve the organization's objectives. However, misuse of budgets can lead to undesirable incentives—what Professor Michael Jensen calls incentives to lie and cheat. Not only do such incentives lead managers to make poor decisions, they undercut attempts to maintain high ethical standards in the organization.

Let's first consider lying. What incentives might cause managers to create biased budgets—essentially to lie about their plans? Managers may want to increase the resources allocated to their department—resources such as space, equipment, and personnel—and larger budgets may justify such allocations. Why do managers want more resources? Day-to-day managing is easier when the department has more resources to achieve its output targets. Further, it is common for managers of larger units with more resources to have higher pay, higher status, and greater prospects for promotion. Recognizing these incentives allows organizations to implement budgets in a way that minimizes bias. For example, when employees understand, accept, and participate in the budget process, they are less likely to introduce biased information. Also, decision makers can be aware of expected bias when they make decisions based on budget information.

budgetary slack (budget padding)
Overstatement of budgeted cost or understatement of budgeted revenue to create a budget goal that is easier to achieve.

When organizations use budgets as a target for performance evaluations, managers have additional incentives to lie. Managers have incentives to create **budgetary slack** or **budget padding**—that is, overstate their budgeted costs or understate their budgeted revenues to create a budget target that is easier to achieve. Budgetary slack also helps buffer managers from budget cuts imposed by higher-level management and provides protection against cost increases or revenue shortfalls due to unforeseen events.

These incentives can lead to the following cycle that destroys the value of budget information: Lower-level managers bias their budgets to create budgetary slack. Knowing that lower-level managers face these incentives, upper-level managers correct for this bias in their inputs to the budget process. Lower-level managers, recognizing that upper-level managers are making this correction, then incorporate additional bias to compensate. Upper-level managers then introduce larger corrections to compensate for the increased bias. This cycle of increasing bias and increasing bias corrections causes increasing distortion in budget information. Inputs from both upper-level and lower-level managers become increasingly meaningless, and the budget process spirals out of control.

Now let's add one more complication—managerial bonuses based on making budget. Suppose a manager with a $100,000 annual salary will receive a bonus ranging from 80% to 120% of a target bonus of $50,000 if her division achieves between 80% and 120% of its budgeted profit target, as shown in Exhibit 6-1. In this example, representative of bonus plans commonly encountered in practice, there is a minimum level of division profit below which no bonus is paid (the bonus drops from a $40,000 bonus at 80% of budgeted profit to zero bonus at any profit level below 80% of budgeted profit) and a maximum level of division profit above which the maximum bonus is capped (above 120% of budgeted profit, the bonus is capped at $60,000).

We should first recognize that within the relevant range of 80%–120% of profits this system creates appropriate incentives to work harder, more efficiently, and more effectively to achieve desired results. But suppose, despite a manager's best efforts, it appears that reported profit will fall below 80% of the target profit in Exhibit 6-1. What inappropriate incentives does this bonus system provide for the manager? There are incentives to "cheat," to make results appear better than they actually are. The incentive to cheat is particularly strong when the division is in danger of falling just short of 80% of the profit target, so that a small increase in reported profit would lead to a large jump in the amount of the bonus.

An extreme form of cheating is to "cook the books," that is, report false profit numbers. The division manager may accomplish this by recording fictitious sales or omitting costs. For example, a few years ago **Enron** and other energy companies recorded questionable sales of energy contracts, and **WorldCom** increased reported income by treating expenses as capital investments. Such actions have serious ethical and legal consequences, but sometimes the pressure to meet profit targets has been great enough to motivate managers to go to such extremes.

Managers may instead choose less extreme actions to increase reported profits. They may increase current sales by offering customers discounts that cause them to accelerate purchases from future periods to the current period, or offer better credit terms that are costly to the company through increased financing costs or increased credit risk. Managers may cut discretionary expenditures, such as research and development (R&D) and advertising, trading future sales for current profits. These short-term actions allow managers to achieve their current bonus, but cheat the company and its shareholders whenever the actions are not in the company's best long-run interests.

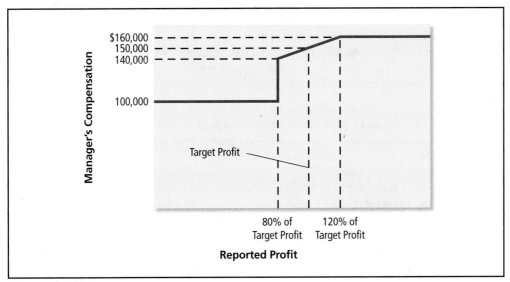

Exhibit 6-1
Bonus Payments Tied to Profit Levels

This compensation system can also create incentives to *decrease* profits when the manager sees actual profits exceeding 120% of the profit target in Exhibit 6-1 or when profits fall so far short of the 80% profit target that there is no hope of achieving a bonus. In these cases, managers may move current sales into the next year by encouraging customers to defer purchases until the next year, thus effectively transferring current income to the future. They might also speed up actual expenditures (for example, moving maintenance planned for future years into the current year) or accelerate recognition of expenses (for example, writing off costs of equipment that remains in use), taking as current period expenses some costs that rightly belong to future periods.

Why would managers take actions to decrease current reported profit? First, moving this year's sales into next year or moving next year's expenses into this year increases next year's income, ensuring a higher level of reported profit (and probably a higher bonus) next year. Second, by decreasing this year's income, the manager may avoid increasing performance expectations for the next year—and thus may avoid a higher budgeted profit target for next year.

To minimize the incentives to cheat, performance-linked payment plans should avoid "discontinuities" in payments. Note that in Exhibit 6-1 the manager's payment jumps up (that is, it is discontinuous) at 80% of the target profit level and the payment levels off (is discontinuous again) at the maximum bonus level. To minimize incentives to transfer income between periods, we can make bonuses and total payments increase continuously over the entire range of possible performance so that there is no point at which a small change in profit has a large effect on pay.

Perhaps the most serious concern raised by these inappropriate incentives for lying and cheating is that they foster cynicism about the budget process and create a culture of unethical behavior in the organization. When managers know that the budget and evaluation processes encourage employees to provide biased information and make questionable decisions, not only does information quality suffer, but a lack of trust begins to pervade the organization.

How can organizations avoid unwanted incentives in budgetary systems? The main way to avoid lying in preparing the budget is to reward good budget forecasts as well as good performance against the budget. It is also important to motivate managers to take personal responsibility for their budgets and motivate their superiors to take the budgeting process seriously.

Objective 4

Explain the difficulties of sales forecasting.

DIFFICULTIES OF OBTAINING ACCURATE SALES FORECASTS   The third problem that limits the advantages of budgets is the difficulty of obtaining accurate sales forecasts. The sales budget is the foundation of budgeting. Why? Because the accuracy of all components of the budget depends on the accuracy of budgeted sales, as illustrated later in the chapter. At the **Ritz-Carlton** hotels, the process of developing the sales budget involves forecasting levels of room occupancy, group events, banquets, and other activities. Upper management initially sets the sales targets. Then, employee teams in each department provide their inputs. Once everyone agrees on a sales forecast, managers prepare monthly departmental budgets based on the sales forecast.

sales forecast
A prediction of sales under a given set of conditions.
sales budget
The sales forecast that is the result of decisions to create conditions that will generate a desired level of sales.

The sales budget is conceptually distinct from sales forecasts. A **sales forecast** is a prediction of sales under a given set of conditions. The **sales budget** is the specific sales forecast that is the result of decisions to create the conditions that will generate a desired level of sales. For example, you may have various forecasts of sales corresponding to various levels of advertising. The sales forecast for the one level of advertising you decide to implement becomes the sales budget.

The top sales executive usually directs the preparation of sales forecasts. Important factors considered by sales forecasters include the following:

1. Past patterns of sales: Past experience combined with detailed past sales by product line, geographic region, and type of customer can help predict future sales.
2. Estimates made by the sales force: A company's sales force is often the best source of information about the desires and plans of customers.
3. General economic conditions: The financial press regularly publishes predictions for many economic indicators, such as gross domestic product and industrial production indexes (local and foreign). Knowledge of how sales relate to these indicators can aid sales forecasting.
4. Competitors' actions: Sales depend on the strength and actions of competitors. To forecast sales, a company should consider the likely strategies and reactions of competitors, such as changes in their prices, product quality, or services.
5. Changes in the firm's prices: A company should consider the effects of planned price changes on customer demand. Normally, lower prices increase unit sales while higher prices decrease unit sales.

6. Changes in product mix: Changing the mix of products often can affect not only sales levels but also overall contribution margin. Identifying the most profitable products and devising methods to increase their sales is a key part of successful management.
7. Market research studies: Some companies hire marketing experts to gather information about market conditions and customer preferences. Such information is useful to managers making sales forecasts and product-mix decisions.
8. Advertising and sales promotion plans: Advertising and other promotional costs affect sales levels. A sales forecast should be based on anticipated effects of promotional activities.

Sales forecasting usually combines various techniques. In addition to the opinions of the sales staff, statistical analysis of correlations between sales and economic indicators (prepared by economists and members of the market research staff) provide valuable help. The opinions of line management also heavily influence the final sales forecasts. No matter how many technical experts a company uses in forecasting, the sales budget should ultimately be the responsibility of line management. Line managers who participate fully in setting the sales budget will be more committed to achieving the budget goals.

Governments and other nonprofit organizations face a similar problem in forecasting revenues from taxes, contributions, or other sources. For example, city revenues may depend on a variety of factors, such as property taxes, traffic fines, parking fees, license fees, and city income taxes. In turn, property taxes depend on the extent of new construction and general increases in real estate values. Thus, forecasting revenues for a government or nonprofit organization may require just as much sophistication as sales forecasts of a for-profit firm.

Types of Budgets

Businesses use several different types of budgets. The most forward-looking and least detailed budget is the **strategic plan**, which sets the overall goals and objectives of the organization. While the strategic plan does not deal with a specific time frame and does not produce forecasted financial statements, it provides the overall framework for the **long-range plan**. Long-range plans typically produce forecasted financial statements for 5- to 10-year periods. Decisions made during long-range planning include addition or deletion of product lines, design and location of new plants, acquisitions of buildings and equipment, and other long-term commitments. Companies coordinate their long-range plan with their **capital budget**, which details the planned expenditures for facilities, equipment, new products, and other long-term investments. Short-term plans and budgets guide day-to-day operations.

The **master budget** is a detailed and comprehensive analysis of the first year of the long-range plan. It quantifies targets for sales, purchases, production, distribution, and financing in the form of forecasted financial statements and supporting operating schedules. These schedules provide detailed information beyond what appears in the forecasted financial statements. Thus, the master budget includes forecasts of sales, expenses, balance sheets, and cash receipts and disbursements.

Many companies break their annual budgets into 4 quarterly or even 12 monthly budgets. A **continuous budget** or **rolling budget** is a master budget that simply adds a month (or quarter) in the future as the month (or quarter) just ended is dropped. Continuous budgets force managers to always think about the next full year, not just the remainder of the current fiscal year, so budgeting becomes an ongoing process instead of a once-a-year exercise.

Components of the Master Budget

The two major parts of a master budget are the operating budget and the financial budget. The **operating budget**—sometimes called the **profit plan**—focuses on the income statement and its supporting schedules or, in an organization with no sales revenues, on budgeted expenses and supporting schedules. In contrast, the **financial budget** focuses on the effects that the operating budget and other plans (such as capital expenditures and repayments of debt) will have on cash balances. The distinction between the operating budget and the financial budget is important because of the distinction between profitability and financial position. There are many examples of firms with strong profits where a weak cash position placed them in bankruptcy. There are also many examples of firms whose strong financial position allowed them to survive periods of temporary unprofitability.

strategic plan
A plan that sets the overall goals and objectives of the organization.

long-range plan
Forecasted financial statements for 5- to 10-year periods.

capital budget
A budget that details the planned expenditures for facilities, equipment, new products, and other long-term investments.

Objective 5

Explain the major features and advantages of a master budget.

master budget
An extensive analysis of the first year of the long-range plan. It summarizes the planned activities of all subunits of an organization.

continuous budget (rolling budget)
A common form of master budget that adds a month in the future as the month just ended is dropped.

operating budget (profit plan)
A major part of a master budget that focuses on the income statement and its supporting schedules.

financial budget
The part of a master budget that focuses on the effects that the operating budget and other plans (such as capital budgets and repayments of debt) have on cash balances.

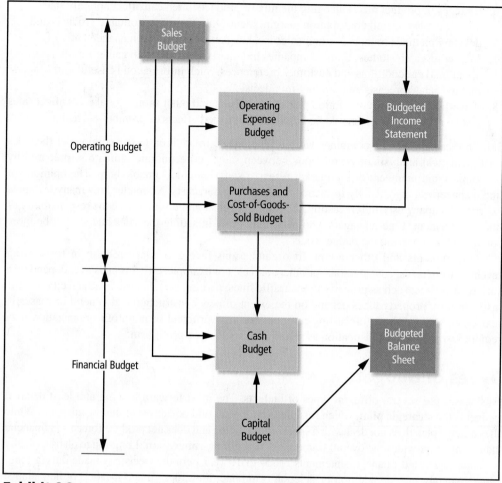

Exhibit 6-2
Preparation of the Master Budget for a Merchandising Company

The terms used to describe specific budget schedules vary from organization to organization. However, most master budgets share common elements. The usual master budget for a merchandising company has the following components as shown in Exhibit 6-2:

A. Operating budget
   1. Sales budget
   2. Operating expense budget
   3. Purchases and cost-of-goods-sold budget
   4. Budgeted income statement
B. Financial budget
   1. Cash budget
   2. Capital budget
   3. Budgeted balance sheet

Other companies add to or adapt these categories depending on the nature of their operations. For example, manufacturing companies add budgets for raw material, work-in-process, and finished good inventories, and budgets for each type of resource activity, such as labor, materials, and factory overhead. Similarly, a consulting company might adapt the operating expense budget to focus on its major cost—consultant salaries. In addition to the master budget, there are countless forms of special budgets and related reports. For example, a report might detail goals and objectives for improvements in quality or customer satisfaction during the budget period.

Preparing the Master Budget

Let's return to Exhibit 6-2 and trace the preparation of the master budget components. Although the process involves a large number of detailed calculations, always keep the big picture in mind. Remember that the master budgeting process provides an opportunity to review key decisions regarding all aspects of the company's value chain. Early drafts of the budget often lead to decisions that, in turn, lead to revisions in subsequent budget drafts. This cycle may be repeated several times before the budget is finalized.

The Cooking Hut

We illustrate the budgeting process using the Cooking Hut Company (CHC), a retailer of a wide variety of kitchen and dining room items, such as coffeemakers, silverware, and table linens. Although master budgets normally cover a full year, for the sake of brevity this illustration shows only the first 3 months of CHC's fiscal year, April–June. Exhibit 6-3 is the closing balance sheet for the previous fiscal year ending March 31, 20X1.

SALES BUDGET Preparation of the master budget for the first 3 months of the new fiscal year requires a sales budget for 1 month beyond the 3 months because CHC bases its budgeted inventory purchases on the following month's sales. The sales budget for the next 4 months is as follows:

April	$50,000
May	$80,000
June	$60,000
July	$50,000

The master budget also requires information about actual sales in the previous month because CHC collects cash for the credit sales in the month following the sale. On average, 60% of sales are cash sales and the remaining 40% are credit sales. Sales in March were $40,000 and the $16,000 of accounts receivable on March 31 represents credit sales made in March (40% of $40,000). Uncollectible accounts are negligible and thus ignored. For simplicity's sake, we also ignore all local, state, and federal taxes for this illustration.

PLANNED INVENTORY LEVELS Because deliveries from suppliers and customer demands are uncertain, at the end of each month CHC wants to have on hand a base inventory of $20,000 plus additional inventory equal to 80% of the expected cost of goods sold for the following month. The cost of goods sold averages 70% of sales. Therefore, the inventory on March 31 is $20,000 + (.8 × .7 × April sales of $50,000) = $20,000 + $28,000 = $48,000. On average, CHC

Exhibit 6-3
The Cooking Hut Company
Balance Sheet March 31, 20X1

Assets		
Current assets		
Cash	$10,000	
Accounts receivable, net (.4 × March sales of $40,000)	16,000	
Merchandise inventory, $20,000 +.8 × (.7 × April sales of $50,000)	48,000	
Unexpired insurance (for April–December 20X1)	1,800	$ 75,800
Plant assets		
Equipment, fixtures, and other	$37,000	
Accumulated depreciation	12,800	24,200
Total assets		$100,000
Liabilities and Owners' Equity		
Current liabilities		
Accounts payable (.5 × March purchases of $33,600)	$16,800	
Accrued wages and commissions payable ($1,250 + $3,000)	4,250	$ 21,050
Owners' equity		78,950
Total liabilities and owners' equity		$100,000

pays for 50% of each month's purchases during the month of purchase and 50% during the next month. Therefore, the accounts payable balance on March 31 is 50% of March purchases, or $.5 \times \$33,600 = \$16,800$.

WAGES AND COMMISSIONS CHC pays wages and commissions twice each month, with payments lagged half a month after they are earned. Each payment consists of two components: (i) one-half of monthly fixed wages of $2,500, and (ii) commissions equal to 15% of sales, which we assume are uniform throughout each month. To illustrate the wage and commission payments, the March 31 balance of accrued wages and commissions payable is $(.5 \times \$2,500) + .5 \times (.15 \times \$40,000) = \$1,250 + \$3,000 = \$4,250$. Because of the half-month lag, CHC will pay this $4,250 balance on April 15.

CAPITAL EXPENDITURES AND OPERATING EXPENDITURES CHC's only planned capital expenditure is the purchase of new fixtures for $3,000 cash in April. CHC has monthly operating expenses as follows:

Miscellaneous expenses	5% of sales, paid as incurred
Rent	$2,000, paid as incurred
Insurance	$200 expiration per month
Depreciation, including new fixtures	$500 per month

CASH BALANCES Because collections lag credit sales, CHC often struggles to come up with the cash to pay for purchases, employee wages, and other outlays. To meet cash needs, CHC uses short-term loans from local banks, paying them back when excess cash is available. CHC maintains a minimum $10,000 cash balance at the end of each month for operating purposes and can borrow or repay loans only in multiples of $1,000. Assume that borrowing occurs at the beginning and repayments occur at the end of the month. Also assume that interest of 1% per month is paid in cash at the end of each month.

Steps in Preparing the Master Budget

Objective 6

Follow the principal steps in preparing a master budget.

The principal steps in preparing the master budget are as follows:

Supporting Budgets and Schedules

1. Using the data given, prepare the following budgets and schedules for each of the months of the planning horizon:
   Schedule a. Sales budget
   Schedule b. Cash collections from customers
   Schedule c. Purchases and cost-of-goods-sold budget
   Schedule d. Cash disbursements for purchases
   Schedule e. Operating expense budget
   Schedule f. Cash disbursements for operating expenses

Operating Budget

2. Using the supporting budgets and schedules, prepare a budgeted income statement for the 3 months ending June 30, 20X1.

Financial Budget

3. Prepare the following budgets and forecasted financial statements:
   a. Capital budget
   b. Cash budget, including details of borrowings, repayments, and interest for each month of the planning horizon
   c. Budgeted balance sheet as of June 30, 20X1

Organizations with effective budget systems have specific guidelines for the steps and timing of budget preparation. Although the details differ, the guidelines invariably include the preceding steps. As we follow these steps to prepare CHC's master budget, be sure that you understand the source of each figure in each schedule and budget.

Step 1: Preparing Basic Data

STEP 1A: SALES BUDGET The sales budget is the starting point for budgeting because planned inventory levels, purchases, and operating expenses all depend on the expected level of sales. Schedule a includes information about actual March sales because March credit sales affect cash collections in April.

Objective 7

Prepare the operating budget and the supporting schedules.

Schedule a: Sales Budget

	March	April	May	June	April–June Total
Total Sales	$40,000	$50,000	$80,000	$60,000	$190,000

STEP 1B: CASH COLLECTIONS FROM CUSTOMERS Schedule b uses the sales budget to plan when CHC will collect cash. In turn, we will use Schedule b to prepare the cash budget in step 3. Cash collections from customers include the current month's cash sales plus collection of the previous month's credit sales.

Schedule b: Cash Collections from Customers

	April	May	June
Cash sales (60% of current month sales)	$30,000	$48,000	$36,000
Collection of last month's credit sales (40% of previous month sales)	16,000	20,000	32,000
Total collections	$46,000	$68,000	$68,000

STEP 1C: PURCHASES BUDGET The elements of the purchases budget are tied together by a simple intuitive identity that ignores minor complications such as returns and defects but relates the fundamental uses of inventory to the sources: Inventory is either sold or else carried over to the next period as ending inventory. Inventory comes from either beginning inventory or purchases. Therefore, cost of goods sold plus ending inventory equals beginning inventory plus purchases.

We budget cost of goods sold by multiplying the cost of merchandise sold percentage (70%) by budgeted sales. The total merchandise needed is the sum of budgeted cost of goods sold plus the desired ending inventory. Finally, we compute required purchases by subtracting beginning inventory from the total merchandise needed:

Schedule c: Purchases Budget

	March	April	May	June	April–June Total
Budgeted cost of goods sold[†]		$35,000	$ 56,000	$42,000	$133,000
Plus: Desired ending inventory[**]		64,800	53,600	48,000	
Total merchandise needed		$99,800	$109,600	$90,000	
Less: Beginning inventory		48,000[‡]	64,800	53,600	
Purchases	$33,600*	$51,800	$ 44,800	$36,400	

[†].7 × April sales of $50,000 = $35,000; .7 × May sales of $80,000 = $56,000; .7 × June sales of $60,000 = $42,000
** $20,000 + (.80 × next month cost of goods sold)
[‡]Ending inventory from March was $48,000 as shown in Exhibit 6-3.
* Purchases for March were ending inventory ($48,000 as shown in Exhibit 6-3) plus cost of goods sold (.7 × March sales of $40,000) less beginning inventory ($42,400 = $20,000 + [.8 × March cost of goods sold of $28,000]).

STEP 1D: DISBURSEMENTS FOR PURCHASES We use the purchases budget to develop Schedule d. In our example, disbursements are 50% of the current month's purchases and 50% of the previous month's purchases.

Schedule d: Cash Disbursements for Purchases

	April	May	June
50% of last month's purchases	$16,800	$25,900	$22,400
Plus 50% of this month's purchases	25,900	22,400	18,200
Disbursements for purchases	$42,700	$48,300	$40,600

STEP 1E: OPERATING EXPENSE BUDGET Month-to-month changes in sales volume and other cost-driver activities directly influence many operating expenses. Examples of expenses driven by sales volume include sales commissions and delivery expenses—these are included in miscellaneous expenses for CHC. Other expenses, such as rent, insurance, depreciation, and wages, are not influenced by sales (within appropriate relevant ranges), and we regard them as fixed. Schedule e summarizes operating expenses for CHC.

Schedule e: Operating Expense Budget

	March	April	May	June	April–June Total
Wages (fixed)	$2,500	$ 2,500	$ 2,500	$ 2,500	
Commissions (15% of current month's sales)	6,000	7,500	12,000	9,000	
Total wages and commissions	$8,500	$10,000	$14,500	$11,500	$36,000
Miscellaneous expenses (5% of current sales)		2,500	4,000	3,000	9,500
Rent (fixed)		2,000	2,000	2,000	6,000
Insurance (fixed)		200	200	200	600
Depreciation (fixed)		500	500	500	1,500
Total operating expenses		$15,200	$21,200	$17,200	$53,600

STEP 1F: DISBURSEMENTS FOR OPERATING EXPENSES   Disbursements for operating expenses are based on the operating expense budget. Disbursements include 50% of last month's wages and commissions, 50% of this month's wages and commissions, and miscellaneous and rent expenses. There is no monthly cash disbursement for Insurance (which is paid annually at the beginning of the year) nor for depreciation (which does not involve any periodic cash disbursement). We will use the total of these disbursements for each month in preparing the cash budget.

Schedule f: Disbursements for Operating Expenses

	April	May	June
Wages and commissions			
50% of last month's expenses	$ 4,250	$ 5,000	$ 7,250
50% of this month's expenses	5,000	7,250	5,750
Total wages and commissions	$ 9,250	$12,250	$13,000
Miscellaneous expenses	2,500	4,000	3,000
Rent	2,000	2,000	2,000
Total disbursements	$13,750	$18,250	$18,000

Step 2: Preparing the Operating Budget

Steps 1a, 1c, and 1e, along with interest expense from the cash budget (which we will construct in step 2), provide information to construct the budgeted income statement in Exhibit 6-4. Budgeted income from operations is often a benchmark for judging management performance.

Exhibit 6-4

The Cooking Hut Company
*Budgeted Income Statement
for Three Months Ending
June 30, 20X1*

		Data	Source of Data
Sales		$190,000	Schedule a
Cost of goods sold		133,000	Schedule c
Gross margin		$ 57,000	
Operating expenses:			
Wages and commissions	$36,000		Schedule e
Rent	6,000		Schedule e
Miscellaneous	9,500		Schedule e
Insurance	600		Schedule e
Depreciation	1,500	53,600	Schedule e
Income from operations		$ 3,400	
Interest expense		410	Cash budget
Net income		$ 2,990	

Step 3: Preparation of Financial Budget

The second major part of the master budget is the financial budget, which consists of the capital budget, cash budget, and ending balance sheet.

STEP 3A: CAPITAL BUDGET   In our illustration, the $3,000 planned purchase of new fixtures in April is the only item in the capital budget. More complex capital budgets are illustrated in Chapter 12.

STEP 3B: CASH BUDGET   The **cash budget** is a statement of planned cash receipts and disbursements. Cash budgets help management avoid either unnecessary idle cash or unnecessary cash deficiencies. The cash budget is heavily affected by the level of operations summarized in the budgeted income statement.

The cash budget in Exhibit 6-5 has the following major sections, where the letters x, y, and z refer to the lines that summarize the effects of that section:

- The available cash balance (x) is the amount by which the beginning cash balance exceeds CHC's $10,000 minimum cash balance. Companies maintain a minimum cash balance to allow for fluctuations in the level of cash during the month—daily balances during the month typically fluctuate relative to the beginning and ending cash balances—and also to provide for unexpected cash needs.
- Net cash receipts and disbursements (y):
  1. Cash receipts depend on collections from customers' accounts receivable, cash sales, and on other operating cash income sources, such as interest received on notes receivable. Trace total collections from Schedule b to Exhibit 6-5.
  2. Disbursements for purchases depend on the credit terms extended by suppliers and the bill-paying habits of the buyer. Trace disbursements for merchandise from Schedule d to Exhibit 6-5.

Objective 8

Prepare the financial budget.

cash budget
A statement of planned cash receipts and disbursements.

	April	May	June
Beginning cash balance	$ 10,000	$ 10,410	$ 10,720
Minimum cash balance desired	10,000	10,000	10,000
Available cash balance (x)	$ 0	$ 410	$ 720
Cash receipts and disbursements			
Collections from customers (Schedule b*)	$ 46,000	$ 68,000	$ 68,000
Payments for merchandise (Schedule d)	(42,700)	(48,300)	(40,600)
Payments for operating expenses (Schedule f)	(13,750)	(18,250)	(18,000)
Purchase of new fixtures (Step 3a)	(3,000)		
Net cash receipts and disbursements (y)	$ (13,450)	$ 1,450	$ 9,400
Excess (deficiency) of cash before financing ($x + y$)	(13,450)	$ 1,860	$ 10,120
Borrowing (at beginning of month)	$ 14,000[†]		
Repayments (at end of month)		$ (1,000)	$ (9,000)
Interest payments (1% per month, end of month[‡])	(140)	(140)	(130)
Total cash increase (decrease) from financing (z)	$ 13,860	$ (1,140)	$ (9,130)
Ending cash balance (beginning + y + z)	$ 10,410	$ 10,720	$ 10,990

Exhibit 6-5
The Cooking Hut Company
Cash Budget for Three Months Ending June 30, 20X1

[*]Letters x, y, and z are keyed to the explanation in the text.
[†]Borrowing and repayment of principal are made in multiples of $1,000, at an interest rate of 1% per month.
[‡]Interest computations: $14,000 × .01 = $140; $14,000 × .01 = $140; $13,000 × .01 = $130.

3. Payroll depends on wages and commission terms and on payroll dates. Some costs and expenses depend on contractual terms for installment payments, mortgage payments, rents, leases, and miscellaneous items. Trace disbursements for operating expenses from Schedule f to Exhibit 6-5.

4. Other disbursements include outlays for fixed assets, long-term investments, dividends, and the like. An example is the $3,000 expenditure for new fixtures.

- The total cash increase (decrease) from financing (z) depends on the total available cash balance (x) and the net cash receipts and disbursements (y). If cash available plus net cash receipts less disbursements is negative, borrowing is necessary—Exhibit 6-5 shows that CHC will borrow $14,000 in April to cover the planned deficiency. If cash available plus net cash receipts less disbursements is sufficiently positive, CHC can repay loans—it repays $1,000 and $9,000 in May and June, respectively. This section of the cash budget also generally contains the outlays for interest expense. Trace the calculated interest expense, which in our example is the same as the cash interest payments for the 3 months, to Exhibit 6-4, which then will be complete.

- The ending cash balance is the beginning cash balance $+ y + z$. Financing, z, has either a positive (borrowing) or a negative (repayment) effect on the cash balance. The illustrative cash budget shows the pattern of short-term, "self-liquidating" financing. Seasonal peaks often result in heavy drains on cash—for merchandise purchases and operating expenses—before the company makes sales and collects cash from customers. The resulting loan is "self-liquidating"—that is, the company uses borrowed money to acquire merchandise for sale, and uses the proceeds from sales to repay the loan. This "working capital cycle" moves from cash to inventory to receivables and back to cash.

STEP 3C: BUDGETED BALANCE SHEET The final step in preparing the master budget is to construct the budgeted balance sheet (Exhibit 6-6) that projects each balance sheet item in accordance with the business plan as expressed in the previous schedules. Specifically, the

Exhibit 6-6

The Cooking Hut Company
Budgeted Balance Sheet
June 30, 20X1

Assets

Current Assets		
Cash (Exhibit 6-5)	$10,990	
Accounts receivable, net (.4 × June sales of $60,000)	24,000	
Inventory (Schedule c)	48,000	
Unexpired insurance (for July–December)	1,200	$ 84,190
Plant Assets		
Equipment, fixtures, and other ($37,000 + $3,000)	$40,000	
Accumulated Depreciation ($12,800 + $1,500)	(14,300)	25,700
Total assets		$109,890

Liabilities and Owners' Equity

Current liabilities		
Accounts payable (.5 × June purchases of $36,400)	$18,200	
Short-term bank loan	4,000	
Accrued wages and commissions payable (.5 × 11,500)	5,750	$ 27,950
Owners' equity (78,950 × 2,990 net income)		81,940
Total liabilities and owners' equity		$109,890

Note: March 31, 20X1 beginning balances are used for computations of unexpired insurance, plant assets, and owners' equity.

Business Plans and Budgets

Start-up companies in a variety of industries have mushroomed into multibillion-dollar companies. How do these companies get started? An essential component in securing initial funding for a start-up is the development of a business plan. The federal government's Small Business Administration recommends a business plan with three sections:

1. The Business—includes a description of the business, a marketing plan, an assessment of the competition, a list of operating procedures, and a roster of personnel
2. Financial Data—includes the following items:
   Loan applications
   Capital equipment and supply list
   Pro forma balance sheet
   Break-even analysis
   Pro forma income projections (income statements):
     Three-year summary
     Detail by month, first year
     Detail by quarters, second and third years
     Assumptions upon which projections were based
     Pro forma cash flow statements
3. Supporting Documents—includes a variety of legal documents and information about the principals involved, suppliers, customers, etc.

Financial data are an important part of a business plan, the centerpiece of which is the master budget. The budgeted income statement and budgeted cash flow statement are essential to predicting the future prospects of any business. They are especially critical to assessing the prospects of a new company that has little history to analyze.

The importance of a budget to a start-up company was emphasized by Jim Rowan, former senior vice president of SunAmerica, who left to form a new company, EncrypTix. He raised $36 million in investment funding to spin EncrypTix off from Stamps.com. The company focuses on Internet delivery and storage of tickets, coupons, and vouchers. Rowan stated, "The key thing for a start-up is to develop a budget and put it like a stake in the ground, so you can measure against it. It's not a ceiling, it's not carved in stone, but you have to have something that's a benchmark."

Budgeting is often not the most exciting task for entrepreneurs. However, lack of a credible budget is one of the main reasons venture capitalists cite when they refuse funding for a start-up. Further, a cash shortage is one of the main causes of failure among start-up companies. Anyone wanting to be an entrepreneur would be well-advised to study budgeting and learn how it can be a powerful tool both for managing the company and for promoting the company to potential investors.

Sources: Adapted from Small Business Administration, *The Business Plan: Roadmap to Success* (www.sba.gov/starting/indexbusplans.html); and K. Klein, "Budgeting Helps Secure Longevity," *Los Angeles Times*, August 2, 2000, p. C6.

beginning balances at March 31 would be increased or decreased in light of the expected cash receipts and cash disbursements in Exhibit 6-5 and in light of the effects of noncash items appearing on the income statement in Exhibit 6-4. For example, unexpired insurance is a noncash item that would decrease from its balance of $1,800 on March 31 to $1,200 on June 30.

Strategy and the Master Budget

The master budget is an important management tool for evaluating and revising strategy. For example, the initial formulation of the budgeted financial statements may prompt management to consider new sales strategies to generate more demand. Alternatively, management may explore the effects of various adjustments in the timing of cash receipts and disbursements. The large cash deficiency in April, for example, may lead to an emphasis on cash sales or an attempt to speed up collection of accounts receivable. In any event, the first draft of the master budget is rarely the final draft. As managers revise strategy, the budgeting process becomes an integral part of the management process itself—budgeting is planning and communicating. The Business First box above describes the important role of budgets in start-up companies.

Making Managerial Decisions

Some managers focus on the operating budget, while others are more concerned with the financial budget. How does the operating budget differ from the financial budget?

Answer

The operating budget focuses on the income statement, which uses accrual accounting. It measures revenues and expenses. Line operating managers usually prepare and use the operating budget. In contrast, the financial budget focuses primarily on cash flow. It measures the receipts and disbursements of cash. Financial managers, such as controllers and treasurers, focus on the financial budget. The operating budget is a better measure of long-run performance, but the financial budget is essential to plan for short-term cash needs and manage cash balances. A shortage of cash can get a company into financial trouble even when operating performance appears to be okay. Thus, both operating and financial budgets are important to an organization.

Summary Problem for Your Review

Be sure you understand every step of the CHC example before you tackle this review problem.

PROBLEM

The Country Store is a retail outlet for a variety of hardware and housewares. The owner is eager to prepare a budget and is especially concerned with her cash position. The company will have to borrow in order to finance purchases made in preparation for high expected sales during the busy last quarter of the year. When the company needs cash, borrowing occurs at the end of a month. When cash is available for repayments, the repayment occurs at the end of a month. The company pays interest in cash at the end of every month at a monthly rate of 1% on the amount outstanding during that month.

Review the structure of the example in the chapter and then prepare the Country Store's master budget for the months of October, November, and December. The owner has gathered the data shown in Exhibit 6-7 to prepare the simplified budget. In addition, she will purchase equipment in October for $19,750 cash and pay dividends of $4,000 in December.

Balance Sheet as of September 30, 20X1

Assets
Cash	$ 9,000
Accounts receivable	48,000
Inventory	12,600
Plant and equipment (net)	200,000
Total assets	$269,600

Liabilities and stockholders' equity
Interest payable	0
Note payable	0
Accounts payable	18,300
Capital stock	180,000
Retained earnings	71,300
Total liabilities and stockholders' equity	$269,600

Budgeted expenses (per month):
Salaries and wages	$ 7,500
Freight out as a percent of sales	6%
Advertising	$ 6,000
Depreciation	$ 2,000
Other expense as a percent of sales	4%
Minimum inventory policy as a percent of next month's cost of goods sold	30%

Budgeted sales:
September (actual)	$60,000
October	70,000
November	85,000
December	90,000
January 20X2	50,000

Other data:
Required minimum cash balance	$ 8,000
Sales mix, cash/credit	
Cash sales	20%
Credit sales (collected the following month)	80%
Gross profit rate	40%
Loan interest rate (interest paid in cash monthly)	12%
Inventory paid for in	
Month purchased	50%
Month after purchase	50%
Salaries and wages, freight-out, advertising, and other expenses are paid in cash in the month incurred.	

Exhibit 6-7
The Country Store
Budget Data

SOLUTION

Schedule a: Sales budget

	October	November	December	Total
Credit sales, 80%	$56,000	$68,000	$72,000	$196,000
Cash sales, 20%	14,000	17,000	18,000	49,000
Total sales	$70,000	$85,000	$90,000	$245,000

Schedule b: Cash collections from customers

	October	November	December	Total
Cash sales	$14,000	$17,000	$18,000	$ 49,000
Collections from prior month	48,000	56,000	68,000	172,000
Total collections	$62,000	$73,000	$86,000	$221,000

Schedule c: Purchases budget

	October	November	December	Total
Desired ending inventory	$15,300	$16,200	$ 9,000	$ 40,500
Plus cost of goods sold	42,000	51,000	54,000	147,000
Total needed	$57,300	$67,200	$63,000	$187,500
Less: Beginning inventory	12,600	15,300	16,200	44,100
Total purchases	$44,700	$51,900	$46,800	$143,400

Schedule d: Cash disbursements for purchases

	October	November	December	Total
For September*	$18,300			$ 18,300
For October	22,350	$22,350		44,700
For November		25,950	$25,950	51,900
For December			23,400	23,400
Total disbursements	$40,650	$48,300	$49,350	$138,300

*The amount payable on the September 30, 20X1, balance sheet.

Schedules e and f: Operating expenses and disbursements for expenses (except interest)

	October	November	December	Total
Cash expenses:				
Salaries and wages	$ 7,500	$ 7,500	$ 7,500	$22,500
Freight-out	4,200	5,100	5,400	14,700
Advertising	6,000	6,000	6,000	18,000
Other expenses	2,800	3,400	3,600	9,800
Total disbursements for expenses	$20,500	$22,000	$22,500	$65,000
Noncash expenses:				
Depreciation	2,000	2,000	2,000	6,000
Total expenses	$22,500	$24,000	$24,500	$71,000

The Country Store
Cash Budget for the Months of October–December, 20X1

	October	November	December
Beginning cash balance	$ 9,000	$ 8,000	$ 8,000
Minimum cash balance desired	8,000	8,000	8,000
Available cash balance	1,000	0	0
Cash receipts and disbursements:			
Collections from customers	62,000	73,000	86,000
Payments for merchandise	(40,650)	(48,300)	(49,350)
Operating expenses	(20,500)	(22,000)	(22,500)
Equipment purchases	(19,750)	0	0
Dividends	0	0	(4,000)
Interest*	0	(179)	(154)
Net cash receipts and disbursements	(18,900)	2,521	9,996
Excess (deficiency) of cash before financing	$ (17,900)	$ 2,521	$ 9,996
Financing:			
Borrowing†	$ 17,900	$ 0	$ 0
Repayments	0	(2,521)	(9,996)
Total cash from financing	17,900	(2,521)	(9,996)
Ending cash balance	$ 8,000	$ 8,000	$ 8,000

*Interest is paid on the loan amounts outstanding during the month. November: $(.01) \times (\$17,900) = \$179$; December: $(.01) \times (\$17,900 - \$2,521) = \$154$.

†Borrowings are at the end of the month in the amounts needed. Repayments also are made at the end of the month in the amount that excess cash permits.

The Country Store
Budgeted Income Statement for October–December, 20X1

	October	November	December	October–December Total
Sales	$70,000	$85,000	$90,000	$245,000
Cost of goods sold	42,000	51,000	54,000	147,000
Gross margin	28,000	34,000	36,000	98,000
Operating expenses				
Salaries and wages	7,500	7,500	7,500	22,500
Freight-out	4,200	5,100	5,400	14,700
Advertising	6,000	6,000	6,000	18,000
Other	2,800	3,400	3,600	9,800
Interest*	—	179	154	333
Depreciation	2,000	2,000	2,000	6,000
Total operating expense	$22,500	$24,179	$24,654	$ 71,333
Net operating income	$ 5,500	$ 9,821	$11,346	$ 26,667

*Interest expense is the monthly interest rate times the borrowed amount held for the month. November: $(.01) \times \$17,900 = \$179$; December: $(.01) \times \$15,379 = \$154$.

The Country Store
Budgeted Balance Sheets as of the Ends of October–December, 20X1

Assets	October	November	December*
Current assets			
Cash	$ 8,000	$ 8,000	$ 8,000
Accounts receivable	56,000	68,000	72,000
Inventory	15,300	16,200	9,000
Total current assets	79,300	92,200	89,000
Plant, less accumulated depreciation†	217,750	215,750	213,750
Total assets	$297,050	$307,950	$302,750
Liabilities and Stockholders' Equities			
Liabilities			
Accounts payable	$ 22,350	$ 25,950	$ 23,400
Notes payable	17,900	15,379	5,383
Total liabilities	40,250	41,329	28,783
Stockholders' equity			
Capital stock	180,000	180,000	180,000
Retained earnings	76,800	86,621	93,967
Total stockholders' equities	256,800	266,621	273,967
Total liabilities and stockholders' equities	$297,050	$307,950	$302,750

*The December 30, 20X1, balance sheet is the ending balance sheet for the quarter.

†October ending balance in Plant = beginning balance + equipment purchases − depreciation = $200,000 + $19,750 − $2,000 = $217,750.

Activity-Based Master Budgets

The budget process we have described thus far in this chapter can be called **functional budgeting** because the focus is on preparing budgets by function, such as production, selling, and administrative support. Organizations that have implemented activity-based cost accounting systems often use these systems as a vehicle to prepare an **activity-based budget (ABB)**—a budget that focuses on the budgeted cost of activities required to produce and sell products and services.

An activity-based budgetary system emphasizes the planning and control purpose of cost management. Our discussion of activity-based costing (ABC) focused on designing cost accounting and cost allocation systems that provided more accurate product and service costs. However, once a company has designed and implemented an ABC system, it can use the same framework for its budgetary system. Exhibit 6-8 highlights the main concepts and differences between ABC allocation of resource costs to activities and products, and ABB.

Just as in functional budgeting (see Exhibit 6-2), ABB begins with the forecasted demand for products or services—the sales budget. In functional budgeting, the next steps are to determine the ending-inventory budget, the material purchases budget, and the cost-of-goods-sold budget. In ABB, the focus is on estimating the demand for each activity's output as measured by its cost driver. Then, we use the rate at which activities consume resources to estimate or budget the resources needed. As we can see from comparing Exhibits 6-2 and 6-8, functional budgeting determines the resources needed directly from the predicted sales of products or services, while ABB uses the sales predictions to estimate the activities required, which in turn determines the resources needed. Because of the emphasis on activities and their consumption of resources, some managers believe that ABB is more useful for controlling waste and improving efficiency—a primary objective of budgeting.

functional budgeting
Budgeting process that focuses on preparing budgets for various functions, such as production, selling, and administrative support.

activity-based budget (ABB)
A budget that focuses on the budgeted cost of activities required to produce and sell products and services.

Exhibit 6-8
ABC and ABB Compared

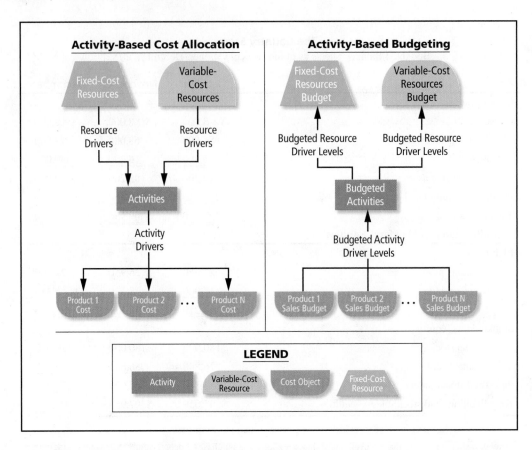

Most companies do not realize the full benefits of ABC until they also integrate it into their budgeting system. Often accountants "own" the costing system of a company, but the budgeting system "belongs" to managers. ABB requires managers to focus on managing activities as they prepare their budgets using the same framework used by the ABC system. For example, when **Dow Chemical** integrated its new ABC system with its budgeting process, it undertook a massive training effort for "controllers, accountants, work process subject matter experts, cost center owners, business manufacturing leaders, and site general managers." By creating budgets consistent with cost reports, Dow gained much greater benefit from its ABB system.

Government organizations such as the U.S. Small Business Administration (SBA) also use ABB. The SBA is one of the five largest federal credit agencies with over $50 billion in loans. An article published by the SBA touted its use of ABB:

> Our goal is to clearly identify the activities that must be performed to produce critical outputs and then determine the level of resources that must be committed to successfully complete the activity. Once this is done, we can determine how various funding levels affect the outputs produced by the SBA. The ABB process provides SBA management the quality information necessary for sound decision making.

Budgets as Financial Planning Models

financial planning model

A mathematical model of the master budget that can incorporate any set of assumptions about sales, costs, or product mix.

A well-made master budget that considers all aspects of the company (the entire value chain) provides the basis for an effective **financial planning model**, a mathematical model that can incorporate the effects of alternative assumptions about sales, costs, or product mix. Today, many large companies have developed large-scale financial planning models based on the master budget to predict how various decisions might affect the company. For example, a manager might want to predict the consequences of changing the mix of products offered for sale to emphasize several products with the highest prospects for growth. A financial planning model would provide operational and financial budgets under alternative assumptions about the product mix, sales levels, production constraints, quality levels, scheduling, and so on. Most importantly, managers can get answers to what-if questions, such as "What if sales are 10% below forecasts? What if material prices increase 8% instead of 4% as expected? What if the new union contract grants a 6% raise in consideration for productivity improvements?"

Using the master budget in this way is a step-by-step process in which managers revise their tentative plans as they exchange views on various aspects of expected activities. For instance, Dow Chemical's model uses 140 separate, constantly revised cost inputs that are based on several different cost drivers. By mathematically describing the relationships among all the operating and financial activities and among the other major internal and external factors that affect the results of management decisions, financial planning models allow managers to assess the predicted impacts of various alternatives before they make final decisions.

Financial planning models have shortened managers' reaction times dramatically. We can prepare in minutes (or even seconds) a revised plan for a large company that once took many accountants many days to prepare by hand. For example, Public Service Enterprise Group, a New Jersey utility company, can revise its total master budget several times a day, if necessary.

Spreadsheet software has put financial planning models within reach of even the smallest organizations. Appendix 7 illustrates how to use a spreadsheet model for planning. Ready access to powerful modeling, however, does not guarantee plausible or reliable results. Financial planning models are only as good as the assumptions and the inputs used to build and manipulate them—what computer specialists call GIGO (garbage in, garbage out). Nearly every CFO has a horror story to tell about following the bad advice generated from a financial planning model with accurate calculations but faulty assumptions or inputs.

Highlights to Remember

1. **Explain how budgets facilitate planning and coordination.** A budget expresses, in quantitative terms, an organization's objectives and possible steps for achieving them. Thus, a budget is a tool that helps managers in both their planning and control functions. Budgets provide a mechanism for communication between units and across levels of the organization. In an environment that encourages open communication of the opportunities and challenges facing the organization, the budget process allows managers to coordinate ongoing activities and plan for the future.

2. **Anticipate possible human relations problems caused by budgets.** The success of a budget depends heavily on employee reaction to it. Negative attitudes toward budgets often prevent realization of many of the potential benefits. Such attitudes are usually caused by managers who use budgets only to limit spending or to punish employees. Budgets generally are more useful when all affected parties participate in their preparation.

3. **Explain potentially dysfunctional incentives in the budget process.** When managers want to increase the resources allocated to their unit or when managers are evaluated based on performance relative to budgeted amounts, there are incentives to bias the information that goes into their budgets, making budget information less useful. When managers are compensated using typical bonus schemes, there may be pressure to report inflated results and incentives to make short-run decisions that are not in the best long-run interests of the organization. Not only do such incentives lead managers to make poor decisions, they undercut efforts to maintain high ethical standards in the organization.

4. **Explain the difficulties of sales forecasting.** Sales forecasting combines various techniques as well as opinions of sales staff and management. Sales forecasters must consider many factors, such as past patterns of sales, economic conditions, and competitors' actions. Sales forecasting is difficult because of its complexity and the rapid changes in the business environment in which most companies operate.

5. **Explain the major features and advantages of a master budget.** The two major parts of a master budget are the operating budget and the financial budget. Advantages of budgets include formalization of planning, providing a framework for judging performance, and aiding managers in communicating and coordinating their efforts.

6. **Follow the principal steps in preparing a master budget.** Master budgets typically cover relatively short periods—usually 1 month to 1 year. The steps involved in preparing the master budget vary across organizations but follow the general outline given on pages 223–227. Invariably, the first step is to forecast sales or service levels. The next step should be to forecast cost-driver activity levels, given expected sales and service. Using these forecasts and knowledge of cost behavior, collection patterns, and so on, managers can prepare the operating and financing budgets.

7. **Prepare the operating budget and the supporting schedules.** The operating budget includes the income statement for the budget period. Managers prepare it using the following supporting schedules: sales budget, purchases budget, and operating expense budget.

8. **Prepare the financial budget.** The second major part of the master budget is the financial budget. The financial budget consists of a cash budget, capital budget, and a budgeted balance sheet. Managers prepare the cash budget from the following supporting schedules: cash collections, disbursements for purchases, disbursements for operating expenses, and other disbursements.

Appendix 6: Use of Spreadsheet Models for Sensitivity Analysis

Spreadsheet software is a powerful and flexible tool for budgeting. An obvious advantage of a spreadsheet is that arithmetic errors are virtually nonexistent. More importantly, managers can use spreadsheets to make a mathematical model (a financial planning model) of the organization. At very low cost, they can apply this model with a variety of assumptions that reflect possible changes in expected sales, cost drivers, cost functions, and so on. The objective of this appendix is to illustrate how to use a spreadsheet model for sensitivity analysis.

Recall the chapter's Cooking Hut Company (CHC) example. Suppose CHC has prepared its master budget using spreadsheet software. To simplify making changes to the budget, we have placed the relevant forecasts and other budgeting details in Exhibit 6-9. Note that for simplification, we have included only the data necessary for the purchases budget. The full master budget would require a larger table that includes all the data given in the chapter.

Each cell of the spreadsheet is referenced by its column (a letter) and its row (a number). For example, the beginning inventory for the budget period is in "D4," which is shown as $48,000. By referencing the budget data's cell addresses, you can generate the purchases budget (Exhibit 6-11) within the same spreadsheet by entering formulas instead of numbers into the schedule. Consider Exhibit 6-10. Instead of retyping $48,000, April's beginning inventory in the purchases budget, in cell D17, type a formula with the cell address for the April beginning inventory from the preceding table, =D4 (the cell address preceded by an "=" sign—the common spreadsheet indicator for a formula). Likewise, all the cells of the purchases budget will contain formulas that include cell addresses instead of numbers. The total inventory needed in April (cell D16) is =D13 + D14, and budgeted purchases in April (cell D19) are =D16 – D17. We can compute the figures for May and June similarly within the respective columns. This approach gives the spreadsheet the most flexibility because you can change any number in the budget data in Exhibit 6-9 (for example, a sales forecast), and the software automatically recalculates the numbers in the entire purchases budget. Exhibit 6-10 shows the formulas used for the purchases budget. Exhibit 6-11 is the purchases budget displaying the numbers generated by the formulas in Exhibit 6-10 using the input data in Exhibit 6-9.

Exhibit 6-9

The Cooking Hut Company
Budget Data (Column and row labels are given by the spreadsheet.)

	A	B	C	D	E	F
1	Budgeted data					
2	Sales forecasts		Other information			
3						
4	March (actual)	$40,000	Beginning inventory	$48,000		
5	April	50,000	Desired ending inventory: Base amount	$20,000		
6	May	80,000	Plus percent of next			
7	June	60,000	month's cost of			
8	July	50,000	goods sold	80%		
9			Cost of goods sold			
10			as percent of sales	70%		

Exhibit 6-10
The Cooking Hut Company
Purchases Budget Formulas

	A	B	C	D	E	F
11	Schedule c					
12	Purchases budget			April	May	June
13	Desired ending inventory			= D5 + D8* (D10*B6)	= D5 + D8* (D10*B7)	= D5 + D8* (D10*B8)
14	Plus cost of goods sold			= D10*B5	= D10*B6	= D10*B7
15						
16	Total needed			= D13 + D14	= E13 + E14	= F13 + F14
17	Less beginning inventory			= D4	= D13	= E13
18						
19	Purchases			= D16 − D17	= E16 − E17	= F16 − F17

Now, what if you want to know the effect on budgeted purchases if the sales forecast is revised upward by 10%? By changing the sales forecasts in spreadsheet Exhibit 6-9, you obtain a nearly instantaneous revision of the purchases budget. Exhibit 6-12 shows the revised budget based on these alternative sales forecasts. The revised sales forecasts are shown in red type and the revised purchases budget is shown in blue type. We can alter any piece of budget data in the table, and easily view or print out the effects on purchases. This sort of analysis, assessing the effects of varying one of the budget inputs, up or down, is an example of **sensitivity analysis**—the systematic varying of decision input assumptions to examine the effect on the decision. This is one of the most powerful uses of spreadsheets for financial planning models. Note that while you can vary more than one type of budget input at a time, it becomes more difficult to isolate the effects of individual changes once you start making multiple changes simultaneously.

sensitivity analysis
The systematic varying of decision input assumptions to examine the effect on a decision.

We can prepare every schedule, operating budget, and financial budget of the master budget on a spreadsheet, linking the various schedules using the appropriate cell addresses just as we linked the budget input data (Exhibit 6-9) to the purchases budget (Exhibits 6-10 and 6-11). As in the purchases budget, ideally all cells in the master budget are formulas, not numbers. That way, every budget input can be the subject of sensitivity analysis by simply changing the budget data in Exhibit 6-9.

Preparing the master budget on a spreadsheet is time-consuming the first time. However, once the spreadsheet is prepared, relatively little additional time is required to update the budget in subsequent periods, and the benefits from increased planning and sensitivity analysis capabilities are enormous. In order to obtain these benefits, it is essential for the master budget model to be well documented, with all assumptions described either within the spreadsheet or in a separate document that is readily available to subsequent users.

Exhibit 6-11
The Cooking Hut Company
Purchases Budget

	A	B	C	D	E	F
11	Schedule c					
12	Purchases budget			April	May	June
13	Desired ending inventory			$64,800	$53,600	$48,000
14	Plus cost of goods sold			35,000	56,000	42,000
15						
16	Total needed			99,800	109,600	90,000
17	Less beginning inventory			48,000	64,800	53,600
18						
19	Purchases			$51,800	$44,800	$36,400

	A	B	C	D	E	F
1	Budgeted data					
2	Sales forecasts		Other information			
3						
4	March (actual)	$40,000	Beginning inventory	$48,000		
5	April	55,000	Desired ending inventory:			
			Base amount	$20,000		
6	May	88,000	Plus percent of next			
7	June	66,000	month's cost of			
8	July	55,000	goods sold	80%		
9			Cost of goods sold			
10			as percent of sales	70%		
11	Schedule c					
12	Purchases budget			April	May	June
13	Desired ending inventory			$ 69,280	$ 56,960	$50,800
14	Plus cost of goods sold			38,500	61,600	46,200
15						
16	Total needed			107,780	118,560	97,000
17	Less beginning inventory			48,000	69,280	56,960
18						
19	Purchases			$ 59,780	$ 49,280	$40,040

Exhibit 6-12
The Cooking Hut Company
Purchases Budget

Accounting Vocabulary

activity-based budget (ABB), p. 231
budget padding, p. 216
budgetary slack, p. 216
capital budget, p. 219
cash budget, p. 225
continuous budget, p. 219

financial budget, p. 219
financial planning model, p. 232
functional budgeting, p. 231
long-range plan, p. 219
master budget, p. 219
operating budget, p. 219
participative budgeting, p. 216

profit plan, p. 219
rolling budget, p. 219
sales budget, p. 218
sales forecast, p. 218
sensitivity analysis, p. 235
strategic plan, p. 219
zero-base budget, p. 214

MyAccountingLab # Fundamental Assignment Material

Special note: Problems 6-A1 and Problems 6-B1 provide single-problem reviews of most of the chapter topics. Those readers who prefer to concentrate on the fundamentals in smaller chunks should consider any of the other problems.

6-A1 Prepare Master Budget

You are the new manager of the local GreatBuy Electronics store. Top management of GreatBuy Electronics is convinced that management training should include the active participation of store managers in the budgeting process. You have been asked to prepare a complete master budget for your store for June, July, and August. All accounting is done centrally so you have no expert help on the premises. In addition, tomorrow the branch manager and the assistant controller will be here to examine your work; at that time, they will assist you in formulating the final budget document. The idea is to have you prepare the initial budget on your own so that you gain more confidence about accounting matters. You want to make a favorable impression on your superiors, so you gather the financial statement and sales data as of May 31, 20X8, on the top of the next page.

Credit sales are 70% of total sales. Seventy percent of each credit account is collected in the month following the sale and the remaining 30% is collected in the subsequent month. Assume that bad debts are negligible and can be ignored. The accounts receivable on May 31 are the result of the credit sales for April and May:

$$(.30 \times .70 \times \$130,000) + (1.0 \times .70 \times \$130,000) = \$118,300.$$

Cash	$ 6,600	Recent and Projected Sales	
Inventory	151,200	April	$130,000
Accounts receivable	118,300	May	130,000
Net furniture and fixtures	·52,000	June	240,000
Total assets	$328,100	July	170,000
Accounts payable	$156,200	August	170,000
Owners' equity	171,900	September	120,000
Total liabilities and owners' equities	$328,100		

The policy is to acquire enough inventory each month to equal the following month's projected cost of goods sold. All purchases are paid for in the month following purchase.

The average gross profit on sales is 37%. Salaries, wages, and commissions average 24% of sales; all other variable expenses are 3% of sales. Fixed expenses for rent, property taxes, and miscellaneous payroll and other items are $9,000 monthly. Assume that these variable and fixed expenses require cash disbursements each month. Depreciation is $1,000 monthly.

In June, $5,000 is going to be disbursed for fixtures acquired and recorded in furniture and fixtures in May. The May 31 balance of accounts payable includes this amount.

Assume that a minimum cash balance of $4,000 is to be maintained. Also assume that all borrowings are effective at the beginning of the month and all repayments are made at the end of the month of repayment. Interest is compounded and added to the outstanding balance each month, but interest is paid only at the ends of months when principal is repaid. The interest rate is 9% per year; round interest computations and interest payments to the nearest dollar. Interest payments may be any dollar amount, but all borrowing and repayments of principal are made in multiples of $1,000.

1. Prepare a budgeted income statement for the coming June–August quarter, a cash budget for each of the 3 months, and a budgeted balance sheet for August 31, 20X8. All operations are evaluated on a before-income-tax basis, so income taxes may be ignored here.
2. Explain why there is a need for a bank loan and what operating sources supply cash for repaying the bank loan.

6-B1 Prepare Master Budget

Flying Fish Kite Company, a small Woy Woy, Australia, firm that sells kites on the Web, wants a master budget for the 3 months beginning January 1, 20X2. It desires an ending minimum cash balance of $15,000 each month. Sales are forecasted at an average wholesale selling price of $14 per kite. Merchandise costs average $5 per kite. All sales are on credit, payable within 30 days, but experience has shown that 40% of current sales are collected in the current month, 10% in the next month, and 50% in the month thereafter. Bad debts are negligible.

In January, Flying Fish Kite is beginning just-in-time (JIT) deliveries from suppliers, which means that purchases will equal expected sales. On January 1, purchases will cease until inventory decreases to $22,000, after which time purchases will equal sales. Purchases during any given month are paid in full during the following month.

Monthly operating expenses are as follows:

Wages and salaries	$80,000
Insurance expired	450
Depreciation	900
Miscellaneous	4,000
Rent	$500/month + 5% of quarterly sales over $50,000

Cash dividends of $2,400 are to be paid quarterly, beginning January 15, and are declared on the fifteenth of the previous month. All operating expenses are paid as incurred, except insurance, depreciation, and rent. Rent of $500 is paid at the beginning of each month, and the additional 5% of sales is settled quarterly on the tenth of the month following the end of the quarter. The next rent settlement date is January 10.

The company plans to buy some new fixtures for $4,000 cash in March.

Money can be borrowed and repaid in multiples of $2,000. Management wants to minimize borrowing and repay rapidly. Simple interest of 9% per annum is computed monthly but paid when the principal is repaid. Assume that borrowing occurs at the beginning, and repayments at the end, of the months in question. Compute interest to the nearest dollar.

Assets as of December 31, 20X1		Liabilities and Owners' Equities as of December 31, 20X1	
Cash	$ 30,000	Accounts payable	$151,500
Accounts receivable	180,600	(merchandise)	
Inventory*	153,000	Dividends payable	2,400
Unexpired insurance	5,400	Rent payable	27,950
Fixed assets, net	62,000	Owners' equity	249,150
	$431,000		$431,000

*November 30 inventory balance = $59,000.

Recent and forecasted sales:

October	$280,000	December	$161,000	February	$413,000	April	$280,000
November	168,000	January	378,000	March	273,000		

1. Prepare a master budget including a budgeted income statement, balance sheet, cash budget, and supporting schedules for the months January–March 20X2.
2. Explain why there is a need for a bank loan and what operating sources provide the cash for the repayment of the bank loan.

MyAccountingLab # Additional Assignment Material

QUESTIONS

6-1 What are the major benefits of budgeting?

6-2 Is budgeting used primarily for scorekeeping, attention directing, or problem solving?

6-3 How do strategic planning, long-range planning, and budgeting differ?

6-4 "I oppose continuous budgets because they provide a moving target. Managers never know at what to aim." Discuss.

6-5 Why is it important to align performance goals of the company and the system used to evaluate and reward employees?

6-6 Explain the cycle of bias by lower-level managers and bias-adjustment by upper-level managers that can spiral out of control and result in meaningless budgets.

6-7 What are the incentives for inappropriate behaviors to *increase* reported profit when it appears that profits are likely to fall just short of a manager's bonus target?

6-8 Why is there an incentive for a manager to inappropriately *reduce* reported profit when it appears that profits are likely to be above the upper limit of a manager's bonus range?

6-9 Why is budgeted performance better than past performance as a basis for judging actual results?

6-10 "Budgets are okay in relatively certain environments. But everything changes so quickly in the electronics industry that budgeting is a waste of time." Comment on this statement.

6-11 "Budgeting is an unnecessary burden on many managers. It takes time away from important day-to-day problems." Do you agree? Explain.

6-12 Why is the sales forecast the starting point for budgeting?

6-13 What factors influence the sales forecast?

6-14 Differentiate between an operating budget and a financial budget.

6-15 Distinguish between operating expenses and disbursements for operating expenses.

6-16 What is the principal objective of a cash budget?

6-17 "Education and salesmanship are key features of budgeting." Explain.

6-18 What are the main differences between functional and activity-based budgets?

6-19 "Financial planning models guide managers through the budget process so that managers do not really need to understand budgeting." Do you agree? Explain.

6-20 Study Appendix 6. "I cannot be bothered with setting up my monthly budget on a spreadsheet. It just takes too long to be worth the effort." Comment.

6-21 Study Appendix 6. How do spreadsheets aid the application of sensitivity analysis?

CRITICAL THINKING EXERCISES

6-22 Budgets as Limitations on Spending
Many nonprofit organizations use budgets primarily to limit spending. Why does this limit the effectiveness of budgets?

6-23 Sales Personnel and Budgeting
The sales budget is the foundation of the entire master budget. How do sales personnel help formulate the budget? Compare the role of sales personnel to that of a central staff function, such as market research.

6-24 Master Budgets for Research and Development
The text focuses on budgets for organizations that have revenues and expenses. Suppose you were the manager of a research and development division of a biotech company that has no revenue. How would budgets be helpful to you?

6-25 Production Budgets and Performance Evaluation
The Akron plant of American Tire Company prepares an annual master budget each November for the following year. At the end of each year, it compares the actual costs incurred to the budgeted costs. How can American Tire get employees to accept the budget and strive to meet or beat the budgeted costs?

EXERCISES

6-26 Fill In the Blanks
Enter the word or phrase that best completes each sentence.

1. The financial budget process includes the following budgets:
   a. _____
   b. _____
   c. _____
2. The master budget process usually begins with the _____ budget.
3. A(n) _____ budget is a plan that is revised monthly or quarterly, dropping one period and adding another.
4. Strategic planning sets the _____.

6-27 Cash Budgeting
Blake and Anna Carlson are preparing a plan to submit to venture capitalists to fund their business, Music Masters. The company plans to spend $380,000 on equipment in the first quarter of 20X7. Salaries and other operating expenses (paid as incurred) will be $35,000 per month beginning in January 20X7 and will continue at that level thereafter. The company will receive its first revenues in January 20X8, with cash collections averaging $30,000 per month for all of 20X8. In January 20X9, cash collections are expected to increase to $100,000 per month and continue at that level thereafter.

Assume that the company needs enough funding to cover all its cash needs until cash receipts start exceeding cash disbursements. How much venture capital funding should Blake and Anna seek?

6-28 Purchases and Cost of Goods Sold
Popeil Products, a wholesaler of fishing equipment, budgeted the following sales for the indicated months:

	June 20X8	July 20X8	August 20X8
Sales on account	$1,850,000	$1,920,000	$1,910,000
Cash sales	130,000	156,000	274,000
Total sales	$1,980,000	$2,076,000	$2,184,000

All merchandise is marked up to sell at its invoice cost plus 20%. Target merchandise inventories at the beginning of each month are 25% of that month's projected cost of goods sold.

1. Compute the budgeted cost of goods sold for the month of June 20X8.
2. Compute the budgeted merchandise purchases for July 20X8.

6-29 Purchases and Sales Budgets
All sales of Tracy's Jeans and Uniforms (TJU) are made on credit. Sales are billed twice monthly, on the fifth of the month for the last half of the prior month's sales and on the twentieth of the month for the first half of the current month's sales. For accounts paid within the first 10 days after the billing date, TJU gives customers a 2% discount; otherwise the full amount is due within 30 days of the

billing date, and customers that do not pay within the 10-day discount period generally wait the full 30 days before making payment. Based on past experience, the collection experience of accounts receivable is as follows:

Within the 10-day discount period	70%
At 30 days after billing	28%
Uncollectible	2%

Sales for May 20X8 were $790,000. The forecast sales for the next 4 months are as follows:

June	$810,000
July	990,000
August	940,000
September	660,000

TJU's average markup on its products is 40% of the sales price.

TJU purchases merchandise for resale to meet the current month's sales demand and to maintain a desired monthly ending inventory of 25% of the next month's cost of goods sold. All purchases are on credit. TJU pays for one-half of a month's purchases in the month of purchase and the other half in the month following the purchase.

All sales and purchases occur uniformly throughout the month.

1. How much cash can TJU plan to collect from accounts receivable collections during July 20X8?
2. Compute the budgeted dollar value of TJU inventory on May 31, 20X8.
3. How much merchandise should TJU plan to purchase during June 20X8?
4. How much should TJU budget in August 20X8 for cash payments for merchandise purchased?

6-30 Sales Budget

Suppose a lumber yard has the following data:

- Accounts receivable, May 31: $(.2 \times$ May sales of $360,000) = $72,000$
- Monthly forecasted sales: June, $437,000; July, $441,000; August, $502,000; September, $531,000

Sales consist of 80% cash and 20% credit. All credit accounts are collected in the month following the sales. Uncollectible accounts are negligible and may be ignored.

Prepare a sales budget schedule and a cash collections budget schedule for June, July, and August.

6-31 Sales Budget

A Sendai clothing wholesaler was preparing its sales budget for the first quarter of 20X8. Forecast sales are as follows (All values are in thousands of yen).

January	¥203,000
February	¥227,000
March	¥248,000

Sales are 40% cash and 60% on credit. Fifty-five percent of the credit accounts are collected in the month of sale, 35% in the month following the sale, and 10% in the following month. No uncollectible accounts are anticipated. Accounts receivable at the beginning of 20X8 are ¥82,950 (10% of November credit sales of ¥150,000 and 45% of December credit sales of ¥151,000).

Prepare a schedule showing sales and cash collections for January, February, and March, 20X8.

6-32 Cash Collection Budget

Northwest Equipment offers a 3% discount to customers who pay cash at the time of sale and a 2% discount to customers who pay within the first 10 days of the month after sale. Past experience shows that cash collections from customers tend to occur in the following pattern:

Cash collected at time of sale	55%
Collected within cash discount period in first 10 days of month after sale	15
Collected after cash discount period in first month after month of sale	10
Collected after cash discount period in second month after month of sale	15
Never collected	5

Compute the total cash budgeted to be collected in March if sales forecasts are $370,000 for January, $420,000 for February, and $460,000 for March.

6-33 Purchases Budget

Green Lighting Supply plans inventory levels (at cost) at the end of each month as follows: May, $271,000; June, $226,000; July, $209,000; and August, $241,000.

Sales are expected to be June, $449,000; July, $359,000; and August, $306,000. Cost of goods sold is 65% of sales.

Purchases in April were $258,000 and in May they were $188,000. Payments for each month's purchases are made as follows: 15% during that month, 70% the next month, and the final 15% the next month.

Prepare budget schedules for June, July, and August for purchases and for disbursements for purchases.

6-34 Purchases Budget

Leimersheim GmbH has adopted the following policies regarding merchandise purchases and inventory. At the end of any month, the inventory should be €15,000 plus 90% of the cost of goods to be sold during the following month. The cost of merchandise sold averages 60% of sales. Purchase terms are generally net, 30 days. A given month's purchases are paid as follows: 20% during that month and 80% during the following month.

Purchases in May had been €150,000 and the inventory on May 31 was higher than planned at €230,000. The manager was upset because the inventory was too high. Sales are expected to be June, €300,000; July, €290,000; August, €340,000; and September, €400,000.

1. Compute the amount by which the inventory on May 31 exceeded the company's policies.
2. Prepare budget schedules for June, July, and August for purchases and for disbursements for purchases.

6-35 Cash Budget

Consider the budgeted income statement for Carlson Company for June 20X4 in Exhibit 6-13.

The cash balance, May 31, 20X4, is $15,000.

Sales proceeds are collected as follows: 80% the month of sale, 10% the second month, and 10% the third month.

Accounts receivable are $44,000 on May 31, 20X4, consisting of $20,000 from April sales and $24,000 from May sales.

Accounts payable on May 31, 20X4, are $145,000.

Carlson Company pays 25% of purchases during the month of purchase and the remainder during the following month.

All operating expenses requiring cash are paid during the month of recognition, except that insurance and property taxes are paid annually in December for the forthcoming year.

Prepare a cash budget for June. Confine your analysis to the given data. Ignore income taxes.

Exhibit 6-13

Carlson Company
Budgeted Income Statement for the Month Ended June 30, 20X4 (in thousands)

Sales		$290
Inventory, May 31	$ 50	
Purchases	192	
Available for sale	242	
Inventory, June 30	40	
Cost of goods sold		202
Gross margin		$ 88
Operating expenses		
Wages	$ 36	
Utilities	5	
Advertising	10	
Depreciation	1	
Office expenses	4	
Insurance and property taxes	3	59
Operating income		$ 29

PROBLEMS

6-36 Cash Budget

Daniel Merrill is the manager of an airport gift shop, Merrill News and Gifts. From the following data, Mr. Merrill wants a cash budget showing expected cash receipts and disbursements for the month of April, and the cash balance expected as of April 30, 20X7.

- Planned cash balance, March 31, 20X7: $100,000
- Customer receivables as of March 31: $530,000 total, $80,000 from February sales, $450,000 from March sales
- Accounts payable, March 31: $460,000
- Merchandise purchases for April: $450,000, 40% paid in month of purchase, 60% paid in next month
- Payrolls due in April: $90,000
- Other expenses for April, payable in April: $45,000
- Accrued taxes for April, payable in June: $7,500
- Bank note due April 10: $90,000 plus $7,200 interest
- Depreciation for April: $2,100
- Two-year insurance policy due April 14 for renewal: $1,500, to be paid in cash
- Sales for April: $1,000,000, half collected in month of sale, 40% in next month, 10% in third month

Prepare the cash budget for the month ending April 30, 20X7.

6-37 Cash Budget

Prepare a statement of estimated cash receipts and disbursements for October 20X7 for the Herbal Magic Company, which sells one product, herbal soap, by the case. On October 1, 20X7, part of the trial balance showed the following:

	DR	CR
Cash	$ 5,000	
Accounts receivable	15,620	
Allowance for bad debts		$2,100
Merchandise inventory	12,240	
Accounts payable, merchandise		7,280

The company pays for its purchases within 10 days of purchase, so assume that one-third of the purchases of any month are due and paid for in the following month.

The cost of the merchandise purchased is $12 per case. At the end of each month, it is desired to have an inventory equal in units to 60% of the following month's sales in units.

Sales terms include a 3% discount if payment is made by the end of the calendar month. Past experience indicates that 70% of sales will be collected during the month of the sale, 20% in the following calendar month, 5% in the next following calendar month, and the remaining 5% will be uncollectible. The company's fiscal year begins August 1.

Unit selling price	$	22
August actual sales	$	8,800
September actual sales		44,000
October estimated sales		37,400
November estimated sales		19,800
Total sales expected in the fiscal year		$528,000

Exclusive of bad debts, total budgeted selling and general administrative expenses for the fiscal year are estimated at $84,600, of which $27,000 is fixed expense (which includes a $12,900 annual depreciation charge). The Herbal Magic Company incurs these fixed expenses uniformly throughout the year. The balance of the selling and general administrative expenses varies with sales. Expenses are paid as incurred.

6-38 Budgeting at Intercontinental

Intercontinental has several hotels and resorts in the South Pacific. For one of these hotels, management expects occupancy rates to be 95% in December, January, and February; 85% in November, March, and April; and 70% the rest of the year. This hotel has 300 rooms and the average room rental is $250 per night. Of this, on average 10% is received as a deposit the month before the stay, 60% is received in the month of the stay, and 28% is collected the month after. The remaining 2% is never collected.

Most of the costs of running the hotel are fixed. The variable costs are only $30 per occupied room per night. Fixed salaries (including benefits) run $400,000 per month, depreciation is $350,000 a month, other fixed operating costs are $120,000 per month, and interest expense is $600,000 per month. Variable costs and salaries are paid in the month they are incurred, depreciation is recorded at the end of each quarter, other fixed operating costs are paid as incurred, and interest is paid semi-annually each June and December.

1. Prepare a monthly cash budget for this Intercontinental hotel for the entire year. For simplicity, assume that there are 30 days in each month.
2. How much would the hotel's annual profit increase if occupancy rates increased by 5% during the off-season (that is, from 70% to 75% in each of the months from May–October)?

6-39 Activity-Based Budgeting

A recent directive from Laura Jensen, CEO of Hermantown Manufacturing, had instructed each department to cut its costs by 15%. The traditional functional budget for the shipping and receiving department was as follows:

Salaries, four employees at $63,000	$252,000
Benefits at 10%	50,400
Depreciation, straight-line basis	114,000
Supplies	65,100
Overhead at 35% of above costs	168,525
Total	$650,025

Therefore, the shipping and receiving department needed to find $97,504 to cut.

Janice Starke, a recent MBA graduate, was asked to pare $97,504 from the shipping and receiving department's budget. As a first step, she recast the traditional budget into an activity-based budget.

Receiving, 620,000 pounds	$139,500
Shipping, 404,000 boxes	303,000
Handling, 11,200 moves	168,000
Record keeping, 65,000 transactions	39,525
Total	$650,025

1. What actions might Starke suggest to attain a $97,504 budget cut? Why would these be the best actions to pursue?
2. Which budget helped you most in answering number 1? Explain.

6-40 Budgeting, Behavior, and Ethics

Mathew Philp, president of North Idaho Mining, Ltd., has made budgets a major focus for managers. Making budgets was such an important goal that the only two managers who had missed their budgets in 20X7 (by 2% and 4%, respectively) had been summarily fired. This caused all managers to be wary when setting their 20X8 budgets.

The Red Mountain division of North Idaho Mining had the following results for 20X7:

Sales, 1.6 million pounds at $.95/pound	$1,520,000
Variable costs	880,000
Fixed costs, primarily depreciation	450,000
Pretax profit	$ 190,000

Molly Stark, general manager of Red Mountain, received a memo from Philp that contained the following:

We expect your profit for 20X8 to be at least $209,000. Prepare a budget showing how you plan to accomplish this.

Stark was concerned because the market had recently softened. Her market research staff forecast that sales would be at or below the 20X7 level, and prices would likely be between $.92 and $.94 per pound. Her manufacturing manager reported that most of the fixed costs were committed and there were few efficiencies to be gained in the variable costs. He indicated that perhaps a 2% savings in variable costs might be achievable but certainly no more.

1. Prepare a budget for Stark to submit to headquarters. What dilemmas does Stark face in preparing this budget?
2. What problems do you see in the budgeting process at North Idaho Mining?
3. Suppose Stark submitted a budget showing a $209,000 profit. It is now late in 20X8, and she has had a good year. Despite an industry-wide decline in sales, Red Mountain's sales matched last year's 1.6 million pounds, and the average price per pound was $.945, nearly at last year's level and well above that forecast. Variable costs were cut by 2% through extensive efforts. Still, profit projections were more than $9,000 below budget. Stark was concerned for her job so she approached the controller and requested that depreciation schedules be changed. By extending the lives of some equipment for 2 years, depreciation in 20X8 would be reduced by $15,000. Estimating the economic lives of equipment is difficult, and it would be hard to prove that the old lives were better than the new proposed lives. What should the controller do? What ethical issues does this proposal raise?

6-41 Spreadsheets and Sensitivity Analysis of Income Statement

Study Appendix 7. A Speedy-Mart Store in Northcenter Mall has the following budgeted sales, which are uniform throughout the month:

May	$450,000
June	375,000
July	330,000
August	420,000

Cost of goods sold averages 70% of sales, and merchandise is purchased and paid for essentially as needed. Employees earn fixed salaries of $22,000 monthly and commissions of 10% of the current month's sales, paid as earned. Other expenses are rent, $6,000, paid on the first of each month for that month's occupancy; miscellaneous expenses, 6% of sales, paid as incurred; insurance, $450 per month, from a 1-year policy that was paid for on January 2; and depreciation, $2,850 per month.

1. Using spreadsheet software, prepare a table of budget data for the Speedy-Mart Store.
2. Continue the spreadsheet in number 1 to prepare budget schedules for (a) disbursements for operating expenses and (b) operating income for June, July, and August.
3. Adjust the budget data appropriately for each of the following scenarios independently and recompute operating income using the spreadsheet:
   a. A sales promotion that will cost $30,000 in May could increase sales in each of the following 3 months by 5%.
   b. Eliminating the sales commissions and increasing employees' salaries to $52,500 per month could decrease sales thereafter by a net of 2%.

6-42 Spreadsheets and Sensitivity Analysis of Operating Expenses

Study Appendix 6. The high definition LCD division (HDLD) of Fisher Displays produces LCD TV displays. The displays are assembled from purchased components. The costs (value) added by HDLD are indirect costs, which include assembly labor, packaging, and shipping. HDLD produces two sizes of displays: 42 and 50″. Cost behavior of HDLD is as follows:

	Fixed Cost/Month	Variable Cost
Purchased components		
50″ Displays		$80 per component
42″ Displays		55 per component
Assembly labor	$40,000	16 per component
Packaging	8,000	4 per display
Shipping	5,000	2 per display

Both displays require three components per display. Therefore, the total cost of components for 50″ displays is $240 and for 42″ displays is $165. HDLD uses a 6-month continuous budget that is revised monthly. Sales forecasts reflect the expectation that unit sales of 42″ displays will be 25% higher than unit sales of 50″ displays. Sales forecasts for the next 8 months are as follows:

	50″ Displays	42″ Displays
October	3,200 units	4,000 units
November	2,400	3,000
December	5,600	7,000
January	3,200	4,000
February	3,200	4,000
March	2,400	3,000
April	2,400	3,000
May	2,800	3,500

Treat each of the following events in succession.

1. Use spreadsheet software to prepare a table of budgeting information and an operating expense budget for HDLD for October–March. Prepare a spreadsheet that can be revised easily for succeeding months in parts 2 and 3.
2. October's actual sales were 2,800 50″ displays and 3,600 42″displays. This outcome has caused HDLD to revise its sales forecasts downward by 10%. Revise the operating expense budget for November–April.
3. At the end of November, HDLD decides that the proportion of 50″ to 42″ displays is changing. Unit sales of 42″ displays are expected to be 50% higher than unit sales of 50″ displays sales. Expected sales of 50″ displays are unchanged from number 2. Revise the operating expense budget for December–May.

CASES

6-43 Comprehensive Cash Budgeting

Christine Morrison, treasurer of Salt Lake Light Opera (SLLO), was preparing a loan request to the South Utah National Bank in December 20X4. The loan was necessary to meet the cash needs of the SLLO for year 20X5. In a few short years, the SLLO had established itself as a premier opera company. In addition to its regular subscription series, it started a series for new composers and offered a very popular holiday production. The holiday production was the most financially successful of the SLLO's activities, providing a base to support innovative productions that were artistically important to the SLLO but did not usually succeed financially.

Exhibit 6-14

Salt Lake Light Opera

Balance Sheets as of December 31 (in thousands of dollars)

	20X2	20X3	20X4
Assets			
Cash	$2,688	$ 229	$ 208
Accounts receivable	2,942	3,372	4,440
Supplies inventory	700	700	500
Total current assets	$6,330	$4,301	$ 5,148
Plant and equipment	2,643	4,838	5,809
Total assets	$8,973	$9,139	$10,957
Liabilities and Equities			
Bank loan	$ 0	$ 0	$ 1,620*
Accounts payable	420	720	780
Accrued payroll expenses	472	583	646
Mortgage, current	250	250	250
Total current liabilities	$1,142	$1,553	$ 3,296
Other payables	270		
Mortgage payable, long-term	3,750	3,500	3,250
Net assets†	3,811	4,086	4,411
Total liabilities and equities	$8,973	$9,139	$10,957

*Includes $32,000 of accrued interest.

†The "Net assets" account for a nonprofit organization is similar to "Stockholders' equity" for a corporation.

Exhibit 6-15

Salt Lake Light Opera

Income Statements for the
Year Ended December 31
(in thousands of dollars)

	20X2	20X3	20X4
Ticket sales	$3,303	$4,060	$5,263
Contributions	1,041	1,412	1,702
Grants and other revenues	1,202	1,361	1,874
Total revenues	$5,546	$6,833	$8,839
Expenses*			
Production	$4,071	$4,805	$6,307
Operations	271	332	473
Public relations and			
community development	1,082	1,421	1,734
Total expenses	$5,424	$6,558	$8,514
Excess of revenues over expenses	$ 122	$ 275	$ 325

*Expenses include depreciation of $355, $370, and $470 and general and administrative expenses of $1,549, $1,688, and $2,142 in the years 20X2, 20X3, and 20X4, respectively.

In total, the SLLO had done well financially, as shown in Exhibits 6-14 and 6-15. Its profitable operations had enabled it to build its own building and generally acquire a large number of assets. It had at least broken even every year since its incorporation, and management anticipates continued profitable operations. The Corporate Community for the Arts in Salt Lake and several private foundations had made many grants to the SLLO, and such grants are expected to continue. Most recently, the largest bank in town had agreed to sponsor the production of a new opera by a local composer. The SLLO's director of development, Harlan Wayne, expected such corporate sponsorships to increase in the future.

To provide facilities for the Opera's anticipated growth, SLLO began work on an addition to its building 2 years ago. The new facilities are intended primarily to support the experimental offerings that were becoming more numerous. The capital expansion was to be completed in 20X5; all that remained was acquisition and installation of lighting, sound equipment, and other new equipment to be purchased in 20X5.

SLLO had borrowed working capital from South Utah National Bank for the past several years. To qualify for the loans, the SLLO had to agree to the following:

1. Completely pay off the loan for 1 month during the course of the year.
2. Maintain cash and accounts receivable balances equal to (or greater than) 120% of the loan.
3. Maintain a compensating cash balance of $200,000 at all times.

In the past, the SLLO has had no problem meeting these requirements. However, in 20X4 the SLLO had been unable to reduce the loan to zero for an entire month. Although South Utah continued to extend the needed credit, the loan manager expressed concern over the situation. She asked for a quarterly cash budget to justify the financing needed for 20X5. Ms. Morrison began to assemble the data needed to prepare such a budget.

SLLO received revenue from three main sources: ticket sales, contributions, and grants. Ms. Morrison formed Exhibit 6-16 to calculate the accounts receivable balance for each of these sources for 20X5. She assumed that SLLO would continue its normal practices for collecting pledges and grant revenues.

	Ticket Sales		Contributions		Grants	
	Revenues	End of Quarter Receivables	Revenues	End of Quarter Receivables	Revenues	End of Quarter Receivables
First Quarter	$ 852	$2,795	$ 75	$ 794	$ 132	$ 1,027
Second Quarter	1,584	3,100	363	888	448	1,130
Third Quarter	2,617	3,407	1,203	1,083	1,296	1,240
Fourth Quarter	1,519	3,683	442	1,170	528	1,342

Exhibit 6-16

Salt Lake Light Opera

Estimated Quarterly Revenues and End of Quarter Receivables for the Year Ended December 31, 20X5
(in thousands of dollars)

Most expenses were constant from month to month. An exception was supplies, which were purchased twice a year in December and June. In 20X5, SLLO expects to purchase $200,000 of supplies in June and $700,000 in December on terms of net, 30 days. The supplies inventory at the end of December was expected to be $600,000. Depreciation expense of $500,000 was planned for 20X5, and other expenses were expected to run at a steady rate of $710,000 a month throughout the year, of which $700,000 was payroll costs. Salaries and wages were paid on the Monday of the first week following the end of the month. The remaining $10,000 of other expenses were paid as incurred.

The major portion of the new equipment to be installed in 20X5 was to be delivered in September; payments totaling $400,000 would be made in four equal monthly installments beginning in September. In addition, small equipment purchases are expected to run $20,000 per month throughout the year. They will be paid for on delivery.

In late 20X2, SLLO had borrowed $4 million (classified as a mortgage payable) from Farmers' Life Insurance Company. The SLLO is repaying the loan over 16 years, in equal principal payments in June and December of each year. Interest at 8% annually is also paid on the unpaid balance on each of these dates. Total interest payments for 20X5, according to Ms. Morrison's calculations, would be $275,000.

Interest on the working capital loan from South Utah National Bank was at an annual rate of 10%. Interest is accrued quarterly but paid annually; payment for 20X4's interest would be made on January 10, 20X5, and that for 20X5's interest would be made on January 10, 20X6. Working capital loans are taken out on the first day of the quarter that funds are needed, and they are repaid on the last day of the quarter when extra funds are generated. SLLO has tried to keep a minimum cash balance of $200,000 at all times, even if loan requirements do not require it.

1. Compute the cash inflows and outflows for each quarter of 20X5. What are SLLO's loan requirements each quarter?
2. Prepare a projected income statement and balance sheet for SLLO for 20X5.
3. What financing strategy would you recommend for SLLO?

6-44 Cash Budgeting for a Hospital

Highline Hospital provides a wide range of health services in its community. Highline's board of directors has authorized the following capital expenditures:

Intra-aortic balloon pump	$1,400,000
Computed tomography scanner	850,000
X-ray equipment	550,000
Laboratory equipment	1,200,000
Total	$4,000,000

The expenditures are planned for October 1, 20X7, and the board wishes to know the amount of borrowing, if any, necessary on that date. Rebecca Singer, hospital controller, has gathered the following information to be used in preparing an analysis of future cash flows.

Billings, made in the month of service, for 20X7 are shown next, with actual amounts for January–June and estimated amounts for July–December:

Month	Amount Billed
January	$5,300,000
February	5,300,000
March	5,400,000
April	5,400,000
May	5,700,000
June	6,000,000
July (estimated)	5,800,000
August (estimated)	6,200,000
September (estimated)	6,600,000
October (estimated)	6,800,000
November (estimated)	7,000,000
December (estimated)	6,600,000

Ninety percent of Highline billings are made to third parties, such as **BlueCross**, federal or state governments, and private insurance companies. The remaining 10% of the billings are made directly to patients. Historical patterns of billing collections are as follows:

	Third-Party Billings	Direct-Patient Billings
Month of service	20%	10%
Month following service	50	40
Second month following service	20	40
Uncollectible	10	10

Singer expects the same billing and collection patterns that have been experienced during the first 6 months of 20X7 to continue during the last 6 months of the year. The following schedule presents the purchases that have been made during the past 3 months and the planned purchases for the last 6 months of 20X7.

Month	Amount
April	$1,300,000
May	1,450,000
June	1,450,000
July	1,500,000
August	1,800,000
September	2,200,000
October	2,350,000
November	2,700,000
December	2,100,000

All purchases are made on account, and accounts payable are remitted in the month following the purchase.

- Salaries for each month during the remainder of 20X7 are expected to be $1,800,000 per month plus 20% of that month's billings. Salaries are paid in the month of service.
- Highline's monthly depreciation charges are $150,000.
- Highline incurs interest expenses of $180,000 per month and makes interest payments of $540,000 on the last day of each calendar quarter.
- Endowment fund income is expected to continue to total $210,000 per month.
- Highline has a cash balance of $350,000 on July 1, 20X7, and has a policy of maintaining a minimum end-of-month cash balance of 10% of the current month's purchases.
- Highline Hospital employs a calendar-year reporting period.

1. Prepare a schedule of budgeted cash receipts by month for the third quarter of 20X7.
2. Prepare a schedule of budgeted cash disbursements by month for the third quarter of 20X7.
3. Determine the amount of borrowing, if any, necessary on October 1, 20X7, to acquire the capital items totaling $4,000,000.

6-45 Comprehensive Budgeting for a University

Suppose you are the controller of Nebraska State University. The university president, Lisa Larsson, is preparing for her annual fund-raising campaign for 20X7–20X8. To set an appropriate target, she has asked you to prepare a budget for the academic year. You have collected the following data for the current year (20X6–20X7):

	Undergraduate Division	Graduate Division
Average salary of faculty member	$58,000	$58,000
Average faculty teaching load in semester credit-hours per year (eight undergraduate or six graduate courses)	24	18
Average number of students per class	30	20
Total enrollment (full-time and part-time students)	3,600	1,800
Average number of semester credit-hours carried each year per student	25	20
Full-time load, semester hours per year	30	24

For 20X7–20X8, all faculty and staff will receive a 6% salary increase. Undergraduate enrollment is expected to decline by 2%, but graduate enrollment is expected to increase by 5%.

- The 20X6–20X7 budget for operation and maintenance of facilities was $500,000, which includes $240,000 for salaries and wages. Experience so far this year indicates that the budget is accurate. Salaries and wages will increase by 6% and other operating costs will increase by $12,000 in 20X7–20X8.
- The 20X6–20X7 and 20X7–20X8 budgets for the remaining expenditures are as follows:

	20X6–20X7	20X7–20X8
General administrative	$500,000	$525,000
Library		
Acquisitions	150,000	155,000
Operations	190,000	200,000
Health services	48,000	50,000
Intramural athletics	56,000	60,000
Intercollegiate athletics	240,000	245,000
Insurance and retirement	520,000	560,000
Interest	75,000	75,000

- Tuition is $92 per credit hour. In addition, the state legislature provides $780 per full-time-equivalent student. (A full-time equivalent is 30 undergraduate hours or 24 graduate hours.) Full-tuition scholarships are given to 30 full-time undergraduates and 50 full-time graduate students.
- Revenues other than tuition and the legislative apportionment are as follows:

	20X6–20X7	20X7–20X8
Endowment income	$200,000	$210,000
Net income from auxiliary services	325,000	335,000
Intercollegiate athletic receipts	290,000	300,000

- The chemistry/physics classroom building needs remodeling during the 20X7–20X8 period. Projected cost is $575,000.

1. Prepare a schedule for 20X7–20X8 that shows, by division, (a) expected enrollment, (b) total credit hours, (c) full-time-equivalent enrollment, and (d) number of faculty members needed.
2. Calculate the budget for faculty salaries for 20X7–20X8 by division.
3. Calculate the budget for tuition revenue and legislative apportionment for 20X7–20X8 by division.
4. Prepare a schedule for President Larsson showing the amount that must be raised by the annual fund-raising campaign.

NIKE 10-K PROBLEM

6-46 Budgeting Assumptions at Nike

Examine **Nike**'s 2011 10-K presented. Find the section of the 10-K titled "Results of Operations" showing a condensed income statement for fiscal years 2009, 2010, and 2011. Use the condensed income statement to calculate budgeted net income for fiscal 2012 under the following alternative sets of assumptions. Round amounts to the nearest million dollars.

1. Note that Nike's revenues increased by about 10% last year. Assume cost of sales is 55% of revenue, selling and administrative expense is 32% of revenue, and income tax expense is 25% of income before income taxes. Assume that all costs are variable.
   a. Calculate budgeted net income if revenue increases by 10%.
   b. Calculate budgeted net income if revenue decreases by 10%.

2. Now assume that selling and administrative expense is fixed at the dollar amount shown in the 2011 10-K, but continue to assume cost of sales is 55% of revenue and income tax expense is 25% of income before income taxes.
   a. Calculate budgeted net income if revenue increases by 10%.
   b. Calculate budgeted net income if revenue decreases by 10%.

3. Note that Nike's gross margin was about 45% in fiscal 2011 but was about 1% higher in 2010 and about 1% lower in 2009. Assume revenue for 2012 will be the same as in 2011, selling and administrative expense is a fixed cost equal to the dollar amount shown in the 2011 10-K, and income tax expense is 25% of income before income taxes.
   a. Calculate budgeted net income if the gross margin increases to 46%.
   b. Calculate budgeted net income if the gross margin decreases to 44%.

EXCEL APPLICATION EXERCISE

6-47 Preparing a Cash Budget to Assist Long-Range Planning

Goal: Create an Excel spreadsheet to prepare a cash budget to assist with long-range planning. Use the results to answer questions about your findings.

Scenario: Music Masters has asked you to prepare an analysis of its cash requirements until such time as its forecasted cash receipts begin to exceed its forecasted cash disbursements. The company will use your analysis to determine venture capital funding requests. Additional background information for your spreadsheet appears in Exercise 6-27 on page 239.

When you have completed your spreadsheet, answer the following questions:

1. Based on its stated objective of stopping venture capital funding when cash receipts begin to exceed cash disbursements, in what month/year should Music Masters no longer require venture capital funding? Why?
2. What is the total amount of expenditures Music Masters will incur before its cash receipts begin to exceed its cash disbursements? What is the total amount of venture capital funding that Music Masters should request?
3. Is the amount of venture capital funding that Music Masters should request equal to its total expenditures? If not, why are the amounts different?

Step-by-Step:

1. Open a new Excel spreadsheet.
2. In column A, create a bold-faced heading that contains the following:
   Row 1: Chapter 6 Decision Guideline
   Row 2: Music Masters
   Row 3: Cash Budget for Venture Capital Requirements
   Row 4: Today's Date
3. Merge and center the four heading rows across columns A–F.
4. In row 7, create the following bold-faced, center-justified column headings with a column width of 10.57:
   Column B: 20X7
   Column C: 20X8
   Column D: 20X9
   Column E: 20Y0
   Column F: Total
5. In column A, create the following row headings:
   Row 8: Equipment Purchase
   Row 9: Salaries and Other Operating Expenses
   Row 10: Revenues
   Row 11: Net Cash Requirements

   Note: Adjust column width as necessary.

6. Use data from Exercise 6-27 to enter the amounts for the yearly cash requirements for the three income/expense categories. Use formulas to calculate the appropriate yearly amounts within each category when necessary.

   Hint: Use different signs for the cash receipt (revenue) and cash disbursement (expense) amounts.

7. Use the SUM function to calculate totals for each column in row 11 and for each row in column F.

8. Format amounts in rows 8 and 11 as follows:

> **Number tab:**   Category:
>
> Decimal: 0
>
> Symbol: $

9. Format amounts in Rows 9 and 10 as follows:

> **Number tab:**   Category:
>
> Decimal: 0
>
> Symbol: None

10. Apply top and bottom borders to the amounts in row 11 by clicking the drop-down indicator on the Borders icon from the toolbar. Select the "Top and Double Bottom Border."

11. Save your work, and print a copy for your files.

COLLABORATIVE LEARNING EXERCISE

6-48 Personal Budgeting

Budgeting is useful to many different types of entities, including the individual. Consider an entity that you know well, the college or university student. Form a group of two to six students, and pool the information that you have about what it costs to spend a year as a full-time student.

Prepare a revenue and expense budget for an average prospective full-time student at your college or university. Identify possible sources of revenue and the amount to be received from each. Identify the costs a student is likely to incur during the year. To simplify your analysis, assume that cash disbursements are made immediately for all expenses so the budgeted income statement and cash budget are identical.

When all groups have completed their budgets, compare those budgets. What are the differences? What assumptions led to the differences?

INTERNET EXERCISES

6-49 Carnival Corporation

The budgeting process helps firms to identify sources of revenues and expenses as well as the timing of cash flows. While many parts of the budgeting process are confidential, there are some things that may be identifiable by someone outside the firm who would like to make some potential budget projections for the following year. Consider **Carnival Corporation**, the cruise ship firm. Go to the Carnival Web site at www.carnivalcorp.com.

1. Look at the list of Carnival Corporation's global brands. How many different brand lines operate under the corporation shell? What are they? Visit a couple of the links. Do the brands each offer exactly the same services? Why might the firm have different names for the cruise lines serving different areas?

2. The sales figure is one of the most important pieces of information the firm uses in beginning the planning process. Carnival's sales figure is made up primarily of two parts—the number of passenger cruise days and the price charged for each passenger cruise day. Go to "Investor Relations" and then "Financial Reports." From the list of Annual Reports, open Carnival's annual report (10-K) for the most recent year. Notice the total revenues for the year and then find information about passenger capacity. What is the occupancy percentage?

3. Find the information provided by management about the expected increase in passenger capacity during the coming years. Assuming revenue increases in proportion to passenger capacity, what would be the expected revenue for 2012? Should the firm expect an increase in costs associated with the increase in capacity? When budgeting for these costs, would the costs be proportional to the increase in revenues? Why or why not?

4. The other component in revenue is how much the passenger pays for the cruise. Select one of the cruise line links from the main page. Find the subsequent link that takes you to information about cruise prices. Are prices for the same length cruise always the same? Look at the fine print with respect to the cruise pricing. What does it tell about how the price is determined? Why might the capacity level of the cruise determine the price that is charged for the cruise?

Flexible Budgets and Variance Analysis

LEARNING OBJECTIVES

When you have finished studying this chapter, you should be able to:

1. Identify variances and label them as favorable or unfavorable.

2. Distinguish between flexible budgets and static budgets.

3. Use flexible-budget formulas to construct a flexible budget.

4. Compute and interpret static-budget variances, flexible-budget variances, and sales-activity variances.

5. Understand how the setting of standards affects the computation and interpretation of variances.

6. Compute and interpret price and quantity variances for materials and labor.

7. Compute variable overhead spending and efficiency variances.

8. Compute the fixed-overhead spending variance.

▶ MCDONALD'S

McDonald's is consistently ranked among the world's best-known brands in *BusinessWeek*'s annual ranking of global brands. You can eat a Big Mac under the Golden Arches in more than 115 countries.

With total sales of more than $65 billion, the challenge is to ensure that the taste of each Big Mac is the same at each of the more than 33,000 company-owned, franchised, or affiliated restaurants. How does McDonald's maintain cost and quality control? How does it ensure that each of the nearly 68 million customers it serves daily receives the same quality product? It uses standards, budgets, and variance analysis. For example, the standards for material are the same for hamburgers wherever they are sold—1 bun, 1 hamburger patty, 1 pickle slice, 1/8 tablespoon of dehydrated onion, 1/4 tablespoon mustard, and 1/2 ounce of ketchup. For each of these ingredients management determines variances—differences between the amount actually used and what should have been used given the number and types of sandwiches produced.

McDonald's managers budget sales for each hour during the day. Based on the sales budgeted, they construct a budget for each of the materials that make up their menu. They use the budget for planning (to make sure materials will be available when needed) and control (to evaluate the use of materials). McDonald's applies these planning and control concepts not just to material costs, but also to labor and overhead costs. Further, McDonald's uses budgets for planning and control of revenues, as well as costs. Understanding what went wrong and what went right helps managers plan and manage more effectively in future periods.

McDonald's also uses nonfinancial standards to meet its quality and service goals. Here are three examples: (1) The standard time for a drive-through customer is 310 seconds, from pulling up to the menu board to driving away; (2) employees must destroy cooked meat that is not used in a sandwich within

30 minutes; and (3) once employees make a sandwich and place it in the transfer bin, they must sell it within 10 minutes or throw it away.

This chapter focuses on flexible budgets and variances. Flexible budgets extend the budget developed in Chapter 6 for a single level of activity. Flexible budgets help managers plan and evaluate results for levels of activity other than the level originally planned. Variances are deviations of actual results from expected (or planned) results. Each variance should cause a manager to ask, "Why did results differ from the plan?" Variances are an important evaluation tool that directs management to areas that deserve attention and helps managers identify ways to improve future decisions and results. (For more background on how managers use variances, you might want to review the discussion of management by exception in Chapter 3, page 96.) ■

© China Foto Press/ZUMA Press/Newscom

Using Budgets and Variances to Evaluate Results

To illustrate how companies use budgets and variances, consider the Dominion Company, a firm in Toronto that manufactures a wheeled, collapsible suitcase carrier popular with airline flight crews. Assume for simplicity that the company produces a single product, sales are equal to production, and inventory levels are zero. Exhibit 7-1 shows the actual results for sales volume of 7,000 units in June 20X1 in column (1); the budgeted amounts for sales volume of 9,000 units in column (2); and the variances, the differences between the first two columns, in column (3).

Using flexible budgets to analyze performance is important to individual McDonald's restaurants, such as this one in Asia, as well as to the company as a whole.

Objective 1

Identify variances and label them as favorable or unfavorable.

Favorable and Unfavorable Variances

Recall from Chapter 3 that variances are deviations from plans. In this chapter we focus on deviations of profits, revenues, and costs from budgeted amounts. We label profit, revenue, and cost variances as favorable or unfavorable depending on the direction of the effect on profitability. **Favorable profit variances** arise when actual profits exceed budgeted profits.

favorable profit variance
A variance that occurs when actual profit exceeds budgeted profit.

	Actual (1)	Budget @ 9,000 units (2)	Variances (3)
Units	7,000	9,000	2,000 U
Sales	$217,000	$279,000	$62,000 U
Variable costs			
Variable manufacturing costs	$151,270	$189,000	$37,730 F
Shipping costs (selling)	5,000	5,400	400 F
Administrative costs	2,000	1,800	200 U
Total variable costs	$158,270	$196,200	$37,930 F
Contribution margin	$ 58,730	$ 82,800	$24,070 U
Fixed expenses			
Fixed manufacturing costs	$ 37,300	$ 37,000	$ 300 U
Fixed selling and administrative costs	33,000	33,000	—
Total fixed costs	$ 70,300	$ 70,000	$ 300 U
Operating income (loss)	$(11,570)	$ 12,800	$24,370 U

U = Unfavorable cost variances occur when actual costs are more than budgeted costs. Unfavorable revenue (or profit) variances occur when actual revenues (or profits) are less than budgeted.

F = Favorable cost variances occur when actual costs are less than budgeted costs. Favorable revenue (or profit) variances occur when actual revenues (or profits) are more than budgeted.

Exhibit 7-1

Dominion Company
Performance Report Using a Static Budget for the Month Ended June 30, 20X1

unfavorable profit variance

A variance that occurs when actual profit falls below budgeted profit.

favorable revenue variance

A variance that occurs when actual revenue exceeds budgeted revenue.

unfavorable revenue variance

A variance that occurs when actual revenue falls below budgeted revenue.

unfavorable cost variance

A variance that occurs when actual costs exceed budgeted costs.

favorable cost variance

A variance that occurs when actual costs are less than budgeted costs.

Unfavorable profit variances arise when actual profits fall below budgeted profits. Because increases in revenues increase profits, revenue variances work in exactly the same way: Actual revenues that exceed budgeted revenues result in **favorable revenue variances**, and actual revenues that fall short of budgeted revenues result in **unfavorable revenue variances**. However, cost variances work in the opposite way because increases in costs decrease profitability: When actual costs exceed budgeted costs, we have **unfavorable cost variances**; when actual costs are less than budgeted costs, we have **favorable cost variances**. The following chart summarizes these relationships using the abbreviations that we will use for favorable (F) and unfavorable (U) variances.

Favorable (F) Versus Unfavorable (U) Variances

	Profits	Revenues	Costs
Actual > Expected	F	F	U
Actual < Expected	U	U	F

The favorable and unfavorable labels indicate only the directional relationships summarized in the chart above—they do not indicate that the explanation for the variance is necessarily good or bad. For example, spending less than budgeted for maintenance expenditures will create a favorable variance but may nonetheless have adverse effects, especially in later periods when the effects of too-low maintenance began to materialize. As another example, spending less than budgeted on research and development will create a favorable variance but might mean that research expenditures were lower than the optimal level. The important point is that the favorable and unfavorable labels do not, by themselves, indicate whether decisions were good or bad. Rather than basing evaluation of variances only on these labels, managers should determine the explanation for the direction of the relation between actual and expected results and then carefully evaluate the implications of the explanation.

Static Budgets Versus Flexible Budgets

Objective 2

Distinguish between flexible budgets and static budgets.

static budget

A budget that is prepared for only one expected level of activity.

Let's consider two ways to prepare a budget. A budget prepared for only one level of activity is a **static budget**. A budget that adjusts to different levels of activity is a **flexible budget** (sometimes called a **variable budget**). To illustrate these concepts, suppose Dominion Company expects to sell 9,000 units in 20X1. The static budget consists of the revenues, costs, and profits expected at a volume of 9,000 units. However, to prepare for the possibility that volume might be lower than 9,000 units, Dominion Company could prepare a flexible budget that predicts revenues, costs, and profits at lower volumes, say, volumes of 7,000 and 8,000 units. Flexible budgets show the revenues, costs, and profits expected at alternative volumes.

Flexible-Budget Formulas

Objective 3

Use flexible-budget formulas to construct a flexible budget.

To develop a flexible budget, managers use flexible-budget formulas that describe revenue and cost behavior with respect to appropriate cost drivers. The cost functions that we introduced in Chapter 4 and estimated in Chapter 5 are examples of flexible-budget formulas. Exhibit 7-2 shows a graphical version of the flexible-budget formula for Dominion Company based on a

Exhibit 7-2

Dominion Company
Graph of Flexible Budget of Costs

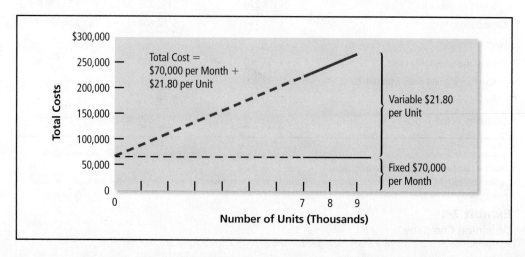

single cost driver, units of output. The solid line between 7,000 and 9,000 units indicates that the relevant range for these flexible-budget formulas is 7,000 to 9,000 units. Within this range, we expect fixed costs to be constant at $70,000 per month, the point where the line meets the vertical axis, and variable costs to be $21.80 per unit, the slope of the line. The dashed line below 7,000 units indicates that this portion of the flexible-budget line is outside the relevant range.

Exhibit 7-3 shows flexible budgets for output levels of 7,000, 8,000, and 9,000 units, respectively. The flexible budgets incorporate effects of changes in activity on each revenue and cost. Note that the static budget is just the flexible budget for the original planned level of activity. Thus, the amounts shown in the budget column in Exhibit 7-1 for sales of 9,000 unit, the static budget, are exactly the same as the amounts in the far right column of Exhibit 7-3, the flexible budget for sales of 9,000 units.

How does the master budget introduced in Chapter 6 relate to static and flexible budgets? The modifier "master" refers to the scope of the budget, not to whether it is static or flexible. Master budgets are comprehensive, encompassing all the components shown in Exhibit 7-2. Flexible budgets can also be comprehensive, although often they are more narrowly focused. The master budgets used in Chapter 6 were static master budgets that assumed one fixed level of volume. However, there is no reason that a company could not prepare a flexible master budget.

Activity-Based Flexible Budgets

Dominion Company's flexible budget in Exhibit 7-3 is based on a single cost driver—units of output. This is an appropriate approach when "units of output" is a plausible and reliable cost driver for all of a company's costs. But what if some of a company's costs are driven by activities such as order processing or setting up for production? A company that has an activity-based costing system with multiple cost drivers, such as the systems will prepare an **activity-based flexible budget** by budgeting costs for each activity using the related cost driver.

Exhibit 7-4 shows an activity-based flexible budget for the Dominion Company. There are four activities: processing, setup, marketing, and administration. For each activity, costs depend on a different cost driver. For example, in Exhibit 7-4 we assume that setup costs are variable with respect to the "number of setups," whereas in Exhibit 7-3 we assumed that the $12,000 of setup costs included in the manufacturing costs of $37,000 are fixed with respect to "units of output." To see why setup costs might vary with respect to the number of setups but not with respect to the number of units, consider the example of setup supplies. Each time employees set up a production run, they use a batch of setup supplies. However, once the run is set up, production of additional units uses no additional setup supplies. Thus, the cost of supplies varies directly with the number of setups (at a cost of $500 per setup) but does not vary directly with the number of units produced.

Compare the traditional flexible budgets (Exhibit 7-3) and the activity-based flexible budgets (Exhibit 7-4). Note that assumptions about fixed and variable costs differ in the two exhibits. Because of differing assumptions about cost behavior, the calculated cost using a single cost driver differs from the calculated cost using multiple activity-based cost drivers.

flexible budget (variable budget)
A budget that adjusts to different levels of activity.

activity-based flexible budget
A budget based on budgeted costs for each activity using the related cost driver.

Exhibit 7-3
Dominion Company
Flexible Budgets

	Flexible-Budget Formula	Flexible Budgets for Various Levels of Sales/Production Activity		
Units		7,000	8,000	9,000
Sales	$ 31.00	$217,000	$248,000	$279,000
Variable costs				
Variable manufacturing costs	$ 21.00	$147,000	$168,000	$189,000
Shipping costs (selling)	.60	4,200	4,800	5,400
Administrative costs	.20	1,400	1,600	1,800
Total variable costs	$ 21.80	$152,600	$174,400	$196,200
Contribution margin	$ 9.20	$ 64,400	$ 73,600	$ 82,800
Fixed costs per month				
Fixed manufacturing costs	$37,000	$ 37,000	$ 37,000	$ 37,000
Fixed selling and administrative costs	33,000	33,000	33,000	33,000
Total fixed costs	$70,000	$ 70,000	$ 70,000	$ 70,000
Operating income (loss)		$ (5,600)	$ 3,600	$ 12,800

Exhibit 7-4
Dominion Company
Activity-Based Flexible Budget for the Month Ended June 30, 20X1

	Budget Formula			
		Units		
Sales in units		7,000	8,000	9,000
Sales in dollars	$31.00/unit	$217,000	$248,000	$279,000
ACTIVITY				
Processing	Cost Driver: Number of Machine Hours (MH)			
Cost-driver level		14,000	16,000	18,000
Variable costs	$10.50/MH	$147,000	$168,000	$189,000
Fixed costs	$13,000	$ 13,000	$ 13,000	$ 13,000
Total costs of processing activity		$160,000	$181,000	$202,000
Setup	Cost Driver: Number of Setups			
Cost-driver level		20	22	24
Variable costs	$500/setup	$ 10,000	$ 11,000	$ 12,000
Fixed costs	$12,000	$ 12,000	$ 12,000	$ 12,000
Total costs of setup activity		$ 22,000	$ 23,000	$ 24,000
Marketing	Cost Driver: Number of Orders			
Cost-driver level		350	400	450
Variable costs	$12.00/order	$ 4,200	$ 4,800	$ 5,400
Fixed costs	$15,000	$ 15,000	$ 15,000	$ 15,000
Total costs of marketing activity		$ 19,200	$ 19,800	$ 20,400
Administration	Cost Driver: Number of Units			
Cost-driver level		7,000	8,000	9,000
Variable costs	$.20/unit	$ 1,400	$ 1,600	$ 1,800
Fixed costs	$18,000	$ 18,000	$ 18,000	$ 18,000
Total costs of administration activity		$ 19,400	$ 19,600	$ 19,800
Total costs		$220,600	$243,400	$266,200
Operating income (loss)		$ (3,600)	$ 4,600	$ 12,800

When should a company use a more sophisticated activity-based flexible budget with multiple cost drivers rather than a simple flexible budget with a single cost driver, such as units of output? When a significant portion of its costs vary with cost drivers other than units of output. For the remainder of this chapter, we return to a simpler flexible budget based on a single cost driver: units of output.

Static-Budget Variances and Flexible-Budget Variances

How should we evaluate the performance of Dominion Company for June 20X1? We can examine variances, which compare actual amounts with budgeted amounts. However, we now have two candidates for "the" budgeted amount: The static budget for the original expected level of output or the flexible budget for the achieved level of output.

STATIC-BUDGET VARIANCE Let's begin by comparing Dominion Company's actual results with the static budget for a projected sales volume of 9,000 units. Differences between actual results and the static budget for the original planned level of output are **static-budget variances**. Column 2 of Exhibit 7-1 is the static budget for projected sales of 9,000 units. Column 3 shows the static-budget variances. Exhibit 7-1 shows the difference between the actual operating loss of $11,570 and budgeted operating income of $12,800 is a $24,370 U static-budget income variance.

The static-budget variance shows the difference between actual results and the original budgeted amounts for sales of 9,000 units, but does not take into account that the actual level of sales was only

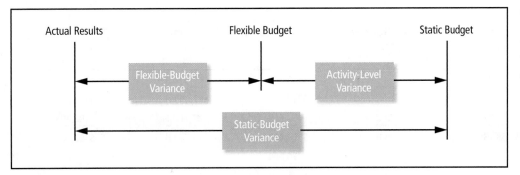

7,000 units. When you produce only 7,000 units wouldn't you expect income to be lower than in the static budget for production of 9,000 units? Of course! Therefore, we introduce flexible-budget variances to compare actual results with budgeted results adjusted to reflect the actual volume achieved.

FLEXIBLE-BUDGET VARIANCE   Differences between actual results and the flexible budget for the actual level of output achieved are **flexible-budget variances**. Flexible budget variances reflect how actual results deviate from what was expected given the achieved level of activity. The flexible-budget approach says, "Give me any achieved activity level, and I'll provide a budget tailored to that particular level." For example, when Dominion's sales turn out to be 7,000 units instead of 9,000, the flexible budget shows what income to expect based on the achieved sales level of 7,000 units. Many companies routinely "flex" their budgets to provide a better benchmark for evaluating performance.

flexible-budget variance
The difference between actual results and the flexible budget for the actual level of output achieved.

Integrating Static-Budget, Flexible-Budget, and Sales-Activity Variances

We saw earlier that a static-budget variance is the difference between actual results and the original plan, the static budget. Exhibit 7-5 shows that the static-budget variance is the sum of (1) the difference between actual results and the flexible budget (the flexible-budget variance discussed previously), and (2) the difference between the flexible budget and the static budget—the **activity-level variance**. The activity-level variance describes the budgeted effect of operating at an actual level of activity that is different than the level of activity used to determine the static budget. Therefore, if the actual level of activity is the same as the level in the original, static budget, the activity-level variance will be zero. The flexible-budget variance is the difference between actual results and planned results in the flexible budget for the actual level of activity.

activity-level variances
The differences between the static budget amounts and the amounts in the flexible budget.

The division of static-budget variances into flexible-budget variances and activity-level variances is illustrated for Dominion Company in Exhibit 7-6. The activity-level variances here are **sales-activity variances** because sales is used as the measure of activity level. The flexible budget (column 3) for sales-activity of 7,000 units taken from Exhibit 7-3 (and simplified) provides an explanatory bridge between the static budget (column 5) for sales-activity of 9,000 units and the actual results (column 1). The bottom lines of Exhibit 7-6 summarize the income variances. Note that the sum of the activity-level variance and the flexible-budget variance equals the static-budget variance: $18,400 U + $5,970 U = $24,370 U.

sales-activity variances
The activity-level variances when sales is used as the cost driver.

Making Managerial Decisions

Consider a company that plans to sell 1,000 units for $3 per unit. Budgeted variable costs are $2 per unit, budgeted fixed costs are $700, and the static-budget profit is $300. Suppose the company actually sells 800 units and income is $110. Compute and interpret the static-budget income variance, the sales-activity income variance, and the flexible-budget income variance.

Answer
There is a $190 unfavorable static-budget income variance, the difference between static budgeted profit of $300 and the actual profit of $110. The static-budget variance is the

sum of two components: the sales-activity variance and the flexible-budget variance. The sales-activity income variance is the difference between the static-budgeted profit of $300 for planned production of 1,000 units versus the flexible-budgeted profit of $100 for production of 800 units, a $200 unfavorable variance that indicates the budgeted effect of failing to achieve the original planned level of sales. The flexible-budget income variance is the difference between the flexible-budgeted profit of $100 versus the actual profit of $110, a favorable variance of $10 that indicates that, given the achieved level of sales, the operation was efficient.

	Actual Results at Actual Activity Level* (1)	Flexible-Budget Variances † (2) = (1) − (3)	Flexible Budget For Actual Sales Activity ‡ (3)	Sales-Activity Variances (4) = (3) − (5)	Static Budget* (5)
Units	7,000	—	7,000	2,000 U	9,000
Sales	$ 217,000	—	$217,000	$62,000 U	$279,000
Variable costs	158,270	5,670 U	152,600	43,600 F	196,200
Contribution margin	$ 58,730	$5,670 U	$ 64,400	$18,400 U	$ 82,800
Fixed costs	70,300	300 U	70,000	—	70,000
Operating income	$ (11,570)	$5,970 U	$ (5,600)	$18,400 U	$ 12,800

Total flexible-budget variances
$5,970 U

Total sales-activity variances
$18,400 U

Total static budget variances, $24,370 U

U = Unfavorable. F = Favorable.

*Figures are from Exhibit 7-1.

†Figures are shown in more detail in Exhibit 7-7.

‡Figures are from the 7,000-unit column in Exhibit 7-3.

Exhibit 7-6

Dominion Company

Summary of Performance for the Month Ended June 30, 20X1

Revenue and Cost Variances

Because income is the sum of revenues less costs, we can describe any income variance as the sum of revenue and cost variances. For example, a static-budget income variance can be described as the sum of the static-budget revenue variance and the static-budget cost variances. Similarly, a flexible-budget income variance is the sum of the flexible-budget revenue variance and the flexible-budget cost variances, and an activity-level income variance is the sum of the activity-level revenue variance and the activity-level cost variances.

Sales-Activity Variances

For Dominion Company, we assume that the driver for variable costs in the flexible budget is unit sales volume, so the activity-level variances are sales-activity variances. Dominion Company's sales activity fell 2,000 units short of the planned level. The sales-activity variances (totaling $18,400 U) in the final three columns of Exhibit 7-6 measure the budgeted effect of falling short of the original sales objective. Falling short of the sales target by 2,000 units explains $18,400 of the income shortfall relative to the amount initially budgeted (a $5,600 flexible-budget loss instead of a $12,800 static-budget profit). Figure 7-6 also shows that we can express the sales-activity income variance as the sum of the sales-activity revenue variance and sales-activity cost variances:

$$\text{Sales-activity income variance} = \text{Sales-activity revenue variance}$$
$$+ \text{Sales-activity variable-cost variance}$$
$$+ \text{Sales-activity fixed-cost variance}$$
$$= \$62,000 \text{ U} + \$43,600 \text{ F} + \$0$$
$$= \$18,400 \text{ U}$$

Alternatively, we can also derive this $18,400 sales-activity income variance as the shortfall of 2,000 units multiplied by the budgeted contribution margin of $9.20 per unit (from the first column of Exhibit 7-3):

$$\text{Sales-activity income variance} = (\text{Actual units} - \text{Static budget units}) \times \text{Budgeted contribution per unit}$$
$$= (7,000 - 9,000) \times \$9.20$$
$$= \$18,400 \text{ unfavorable}$$

Who has responsibility for the sales-activity income variance? Marketing managers usually have the primary responsibility for reaching the sales level specified in the static budget. Many factors can cause variations in sales, including poor production quality and missed delivery schedules. Nevertheless, marketing managers are typically in the best position to explain why actual sales levels differed from plans.

Note that changes in unit prices or unit variable costs do not affect activity-level variances. Why? Only the unit sales volume affects the sales-activity variances because the flexible budget and the static budget use the same budgeted unit prices, unit variable costs, and total fixed costs. The static and flexible budgets differ only due to different assumed levels of activity. Also note that there can never be a sales-activity variance for fixed costs, as long as the budgeted activity levels remain within the relevant range. Why? Because for fixed costs, the total budgeted amounts are the same in the flexible budget and the static budget.

Flexible-Budget Variances

Exhibit 7-6 shows income variances as the sum of revenue and cost variances. The flexible-budget variances are shown in column (2), the difference between actual results in column (1) and the flexible-budget amounts for the actual sales activity in column (3). The flexible-budget income variance is as follows:

Flexible-budget income variance = Actual income − Flexible-budget income (at actual sales level)

$$= (-\$11,570) - (-\$5,600)$$
$$= \$5,970 \text{ U}$$

Column (2) of Exhibit 7-6 shows the $5,970 U flexible-budget income variance is the sum of three variances, the flexible-budget revenue variance (which in this example is $0 because there is no difference between the actual sales price and the flexible-budgeted sales price), a $5,670 U flexible-budget variable-cost variance, and a $300 U flexible-budget fixed-cost variance.

Note that Exhibit 7-1 showed a favorable total variable-cost static-budget variance, yet there is an unfavorable variable-cost flexible-budget variance in Exhibit 7-6. Why is this? Sales fell far short of the static-budget volume of 9,000 units. The favorable static-budget variance of $37,930 in Exhibit 7-1 occurs because actual variable costs to produce 7,000 units were lower than the budgeted costs to produce 9,000 units, the volume projected in the static budget. However, the variable-cost static-budget variance combines two effects, the expected effect of producing fewer units (measured by the activity-level variable-cost variance $43,600 F) and the difference between actual variable costs and the expected costs from the flexible budget for the achieved level of output (measured by the flexible-budget variable-cost variance $5,670 U).

Exhibit 7-7 provides flexible-budget cost variances in even more detail, showing flexible-budget variances for individual variable and fixed manufacturing costs. For example, the $5,670 U variable-cost flexible-budget variance in Exhibit 7-6 is the sum of eight individual variable-cost variances. These eight individual variances net to the overall variance of $5,670 U.

The last column of Exhibit 7-7 provides examples of some possible explanations for Dominion Company's variances. These explanations illustrate our earlier point that you should not assume that the "favorable" and "unfavorable" labels tell you everything you need to know. Instead, always ask questions and look for underlying explanations to be sure you understand why variances occurred and who is responsible. For example, the $400 U variance due to higher than budgeted cleanup costs does not indicate poor performance by the person responsible for cleaning—once the spill had occurred, the decision to clean up the spilled solvent was undoubtedly a good decision. Instead, this variance should be attributed to the person responsible for the spill. Similarly, it is not clear that the $800 U variance due to the use of airfreight is the responsibility of the shipping manager. Could the need for airfreight delivery have been avoided with additional planning and coordination by sales staff? Or by production? Evaluation of management's decisions and who is responsible depends on the answers to questions such as these.

	Actual Costs Incurred	Flexible Budget*	Flexible-Budget Variances†	Possible Explanation
Units	7,000	7,000	—	
Variable costs				
Direct materials	$ 69,920	$ 70,000	$ 80 F	Lower prices but higher usage
Direct labor	61,500	56,000	5,500 U	Higher wage rates and higher usage
Indirect labor	9,100	11,900	2,800 F	Decreased setup time
Idle time	3,550	2,800	750 U	Excessive machine breakdowns
Cleanup time	2,500	2,100	400 U	Cleanup of spilled solvent
Supplies	4,700	4,200	500 U	Higher prices and higher usage
Variable manufacturing costs	$151,270	$147,000	$4,270 U	
Shipping	5,000	4,200	800 U	Use of air freight to meet delivery
Administration	2,000	1,400	600 U	Excessive copying and long-distance calls
Total variable costs	$158,270	$152,600	$5,670 U	
Fixed costs				
Factory supervision	$ 14,700	$ 14,400	$ 300 U	Salary increase
Factory rent	5,000	5,000	—	
Equipment depreciation	15,000	15,000	—	
Other fixed factory costs	2,600	2,600	—	
Fixed manufacturing costs	$ 37,300	$ 37,000	$ 300 U	
Fixed selling and administrative costs	33,000	33,000	—	
Total fixed costs	$ 70,300	$ 70,000	$ 300 U	
Total variable and fixed costs	$228,570	$222,600	$5,970 U	

*From 7,000-unit column of Exhibit 7-3.
†This is a line-by-line breakout of the variances in column 2 of Exhibit 7-6.

Exhibit 7-7
Dominion Company
Cost-Control Performance Report for the Month Ended June 30, 20X1

The Role of Standards in Determining Variances

Objective 5

Understand how the setting of standards affects the computation and interpretation of variances.

standard cost
A cost that should be achieved.

expected cost
The cost most likely to be attained.

currently attainable standards
Levels of performance that managers can achieve by realistic levels of effort.

perfection standards (ideal standards)
Expressions of the most efficient performance possible under the best conceivable conditions, using existing specifications and equipment.

Both static-budget variances and flexible-budget variances depend on the costs used in the budget formulas. Budget formula costs are **standard costs**—costs that should be achieved. However, standard costs are defined in different ways by different companies. Many companies set standard cost equal to **expected cost**, the cost that is most likely to be attained. However, other companies use a definition based on **currently attainable standards**—levels of performance that managers can achieve by realistic levels of effort, including allowances for normal defectives, spoilage, waste, and nonproductive time. However, depending on what is considered a "realistic" level of effort and what are "normal" allowances, currently attainable standards can range from easily attainable to extremely difficult to attain. The level at which standards are set will affect the variances generated and the incentives created.

Easily attainable standards will generally lead to favorable variances and, because employees can attain them with little effort, they may not provide much motivation. Extremely difficult-to-attain standards will generally lead to unfavorable variances and also may not motivate employees. The most difficult-to-attain standards are **perfection standards** (also called **ideal standards**). Perfection standards represent the most efficient performance possible under the best conceivable conditions, using existing specifications and equipment. Perfection standards make no provision for waste, spoilage, machine breakdowns, or other inefficiencies inherent in a normal system. Those who favor using perfection standards maintain that the generally unfavorable variances will constantly remind personnel of the need for continuous improvement in all phases of operations. Although concern for continuous improvement is widespread, perfection standards are not widely used because of their adverse effect on employee motivation. Employees tend to ignore goals that they know cannot be reached.

Business First

The Need to Adapt Standard Cost Approaches

Critics of standard costs and variance analysis maintain that predetermined standards do not work well in today's dynamic, fast-paced, just-in-time environment. Nonetheless, companies continue to use standards and to measure performance against them. Surveys in nine different countries have shown that between 56% and 92% of manufacturing companies use standard costs. Companies have apparently adapted the approach to fit their environment.

To apply standards in a dynamic environment, how should managers measure and report variances? First, they should continually evaluate their standards. If a company is in a state of continuous improvement, it must continually revise its standards. Second, standards and variances should measure key strategic variables. The concept of setting a benchmark, comparing actual results to the benchmark, and identifying causes for any differences is universal. We can apply it to many types of measures, such as production quantity or quality, as well as to costs. Finally, variances should not lead to affixing blame. Standards are plans, and things do not always go according to plan—often with no one being at fault.

One company that has adapted standard costs to meet its particular needs is the Brass Products Division (BPD) at **Parker Hannifin Corporation**, a $13 billion company that produces motion and control technologies and systems. BPD uses standard costs and variances to pinpoint problem areas that need attention if the division is to meet its goal of continuous improvement. Among the changes that have increased the value of the standard cost information are more timely product cost information, variances computed at more detailed levels, and regular meetings to help employees understand their impact on the variances.

Managers and accountants adapt the standard cost concept to fit the particular needs of a company. For example, BPD created three new variances: (1) The standard run quantity variance examines the effect of actual compared to optimal batch size for production runs; (2) the material substitution variance compares material costs to the costs of alternative materials; and (3) the method variance measures costs using actual machines compared to costs using alternative machines. All three variances use the concept of setting a standard and comparing actual results to the standard, but they do not apply the traditional standard cost-variance formulas.

Sources: Adapted from D. Johnsen and P. Sopariwala, "Standard Costing Is Alive and Well at Parker Brass," *Management Accounting Quarterly*, Winter 2000, pp. 12–20; C. B. Cheatham and L. R. Cheatham, "Redesigning Cost Systems: Is Standard Costing Obsolete?" *Accounting Horizons*, December 1996, pp. 23–31; C. Horngren, G. Foster, and S. Datar, *Cost Accounting: A Managerial Emphasis*, 12th ed. (Upper Saddle River, NJ: Prentice Hall, 2006), p. 229; and Parker Hannifin Corp., *Parker Hannifin 2012 Annual Report*.

Many companies set standards somewhere between easily-attained and extremely difficult-to-attain. The resulting variances reflect performance relative to an achievable standard so employees regard their attainment as probable if they apply normal effort and diligence. The major advantages of this approach to setting standards are as follows:

1. The resulting standards lead to variances that indicate a departure from what is normally expected and are more useful for management by exception. In contrast, perfection standards tend to lead to large unfavorable variances in every period because perfection is not attainable.
2. The standards represent what is expected under normal conditions, so companies can use the same standard costs for financial budgeting and inventory valuation. In contrast, they cannot use perfection standards for inventory valuation or financial budgeting because they know that the resulting standard costs are unrealistically low.
3. Reasonable standards have a desirable motivational impact on employees, especially when combined with incentives for continuous improvement. Employees accept the standards as reasonable performance goals.

What standards should a company use? Should a standard be so strict that the company rarely, if ever, meets it? Should the company attain the standard about 50% of the time? 90%? 20%? Individuals who have worked a lifetime setting and evaluating standards for budgeting disagree on this question, so there are no universal answers. As described in the Business First box above, companies are adapting standards to fit their particular needs.

Finding Explanations for Variances

When evaluating performance, managers distinguish between **effectiveness**—the degree to which an organization meets an objective—and **efficiency**—the degree to which an organization minimizes the resources used to achieve an objective. Performance may be effective, efficient, both, or neither.

effectiveness
The degree to which an organization meets an objective.

efficiency
The degree to which an organization minimizes the resources used to achieve an objective.

For example, Dominion Company set a static-budget objective of manufacturing and selling 9,000 units. It actually made and sold only 7,000 units. Was Dominion effective in meeting its sales objective? No. Performance was ineffective, as measured by the sales-activity variance. Was Dominion's performance efficient? Managers judge the degree of efficiency by comparing actual inputs used (such as the costs of direct materials and direct labor) to budgeted inputs for the level of output achieved (7,000 units). The less input used to produce a given output, the more efficient the operation. Dominion was inefficient because the actual cost of its inputs exceeded the cost expected for the actual level of output, as measured by the unfavorable flexible-budget variances.

A **McDonald's** restaurant could use a similar analysis to examine efficiency—the difference between actual costs and the flexible budget costs expected for the level of sales actually attained. Suppose the restaurant expects to sell 1 million Big Macs and prepares the static budget showing budgeted cost of $100,000 for buns at $.10 per bun. If the restaurant sells only 900,000 Big Macs and pays $94,000 for buns, the static-budget cost variance is $100,000 − $94,000 = $6,000 F. However, the static-budget variance doesn't adjust for the expected decrease in costs due to the decrease in sales volume. Buns for 900,000 Big Macs should cost only $90,000, the flexible budget expected cost for the achieved sales of 900,000 Big Macs. Therefore, the sales-activity cost variance is $100,000 − $90,000 = $10,000 F. The efficiency is measured by the flexible-budget cost variance of $94,000 − $90,000 = $4,000 U, which shows the inefficiency of spending $4,000 more for buns than expected given the lower actual sales level of 900,000 Big Macs.

Trade-Offs Among Variances

Because the various activities of an organization are interrelated, the level of performance in one area will often affect performance in other areas. Often there are trade-offs among costs. For example, McDonald's may generate favorable labor variances by hiring less-skilled and lower-paid employees, but this might also lead to more waste because substandard products need to be scrapped, resulting in unfavorable materials variances. As another example, **Ford** may experience unfavorable materials variances by purchasing higher-quality materials at a higher than planned price, but this may be more than offset by other favorable variances due to lower waste, fewer inspections, reduced labor time, and higher-quality products.

Because of the many interdependencies among activities, an "unfavorable" or "favorable" label should not lead a manager to jump to conclusions. By themselves, variances merely raise questions and provide clues to the causes of performance. Variances are attention directors, not problem solvers. Furthermore, because variances depend on standards as well as on actual results, the cause of unfavorable variances might be unrealistically high standards rather than poor execution by managers. One of the first questions a manager should consider when investigating a large variance is whether standards represented reasonable expectations.

When to Investigate Variances

When should management investigate a variance? For some critical items, any deviation may prompt a follow-up. However, for most items, managers recognize that, even if everything operates normally, variances are unlikely to be exactly zero. For these items, managers specify a range of "acceptable" variances based on economic analysis of how big a variance must be before investigation would be worth the effort. While the acceptable range is sometimes stated in percentage terms, it is important to also consider the dollar deviation from budget. For example, a 4% variance in a $1 million material cost may deserve more attention than a 20% variance in a $1,000 repair cost. Because knowing exactly when to investigate is difficult, many organizations have developed rules of thumb that incorporate both absolute and relative size measures such as "Investigate all variances exceeding either $5,000 or 15% of expected cost."

Comparisons with Prior Period's Results

Some organizations compare actual results with last year's results for the same period rather than using flexible-budget benchmarks. For example, an organization might compare March 2013's actual results to March 2012's actual results. However, simplistic comparisons with prior period results should always be used cautiously. In general, a carefully developed flexible budget provides a better benchmark than prior period results for evaluating performance. Why? First, using actual results from the prior year as a benchmark assumes that prior year values are what we aspire to achieve and don't contain any inefficiencies or substandard results. Second, many changes occur in the environment and in the organization, and these changes can make a comparison to the prior year invalid. Few organizations and environments are so stable that the only difference between now and a year ago is merely the passage of time. For example, the turmoil in the stock market in 2008 and 2009 led many financial institutions to make sweeping changes in operations. Comparisons of operating results in these years to previous years would not have been meaningful because the economic climate was so different. Even comparisons with the prior month's actual results may not be as useful as comparisons with an up-to-date flexible budget. Comparisons with previous years may be useful for analyzing trends in such key variables as sales volume, market share, and product mix, but they do not help answer questions such as Dominion Company's "Why did we have a loss of $11,570 in June, when we expected a profit of $12,800?"

Summary Problem for Your Review

PROBLEM

Refer to the data in Exhibits 7-1 and 7-3. Suppose actual production and sales were 8,500 units instead of 7,000 units; actual variable costs were $188,800; and actual fixed costs were $71,200. The selling price remained at $31 per unit.

1. Compute the static-budget income variance. What does this tell you about the efficiency of operations? The effectiveness of operations?

2. Compute the sales-activity income variance. Is the performance of the marketing function the sole explanation for this variance? Why?

3. Using a flexible budget at the actual activity level, compute the budgeted contribution margin, budgeted income, and flexible-budget income variance. What do you learn from this variance?

SOLUTION

1. Actual operating income = (8,500 × $31) − $188,800 − $71,200 = $3,500

    Static-budget operating income = $12,800 (from Exhibit 7-1)

    Static-budget variance = $12,800 − $3,500 = $9,300 U

    Three factors affect the static-budget variance: sales activity, efficiency, and price changes. There is no way to tell from the static-budget variance alone how much of the $9,300 U was caused by each of these factors.

2. Sales-activity variance = Budgeted unit contribution margin × Difference between the
   actual unit sales and the static budget unit sales

   = $9.20 per unit CM × (8,500 − 9,000)

   = $4,600 U

   The sales-activity income variance quantifies the impact of the deviation from an original sales target while holding price and efficiency factors constant. This is a measure of the effectiveness of Dominion in meeting its sales objective. Management might attribute the failure to reach target sales to ineffectiveness of marketing personnel or to causes beyond the control of marketing personnel, such as material shortages, factory breakdowns, delivery problems, and so on.

3. The budget formulas in Exhibit 7-3 are the basis for the following answers:

   Flexible-budget contribution margin = $9.20 × 8,500 = $78,200

   Flexible-budget operating income = $78,200 − $70,000 fixed costs = $8,200

   Actual operating income = $3,500 (from number 1)

   Flexible-budget income variance = $8,200 − $3,500 = $4,700 U

   The flexible-budget variance shows that the company spent $4,700 more to produce and sell the 8,500 units than it should have spent if operations had been efficient. Note that this $4,700 U flexible-budget variance plus the $4,600 U sales-activity variance total to the $9,300 U static-budget variance.

More Detailed Analysis of Flexible-Budget Variances

The remainder of this chapter explains how to further analyze flexible-budget variances by dividing them into component variances. Previously, we explained how to divide the static-budget variance into activity-level and flexible-budget variances. In this section, we describe how to divide the flexible-budget variance into price and quantity variances (for material or labor) and into spending and efficiency variances (for variable overhead).

We begin with material and labor variances. Exhibit 7-8 shows how price and quantity variances fit in the framework depicted in Exhibit 7-5 and specifically how the sum of price and quantity variances equals the flexible-budget variance. Exhibit 7-8 provides only a broad conceptual overview—actual calculations are illustrated in Exhibit 7-9 after we introduce some additional required information.

Variances for Direct Material and Direct Labor

Let's consider the components of the flexible-budget variances for the Dominion Company. As shown in Exhibit 7-7, the flexible-budget variances for material and labor are $80 F and $5,500 U, respectively:

	Actual Cost Incurred	Flexible Budget	Flexible-Budget Variance
Direct materials	$69,920	$70,000	$ 80 F
Direct labor	61,500	56,000	5,500 U

To further analyze the flexible-budget variances, we need more information. First, we need information about the standard prices and standard quantities used in the flexible budget formulas. Dominion Company's flexible budget is the amount that Dominion expected to incur based on standard quantities and standard prices for direct materials and direct labor to produce the output achieved, computed as follows:

$$\text{Flexible budget} = \text{Units of actual output achieved} \times \text{Standard input allowed per unit of output achieved} \times \text{Standard price per unit of input}$$

Note that the flexible budget is constructed for the level of actual output achieved. We will refer to the flexible budget for the actual output achieved as "standard cost allowed."

Let's assume the flexible-budget amounts in Exhibit 7-7 were based on $10 per unit of output for direct materials and $8 per unit of output for direct labor. Further assume these

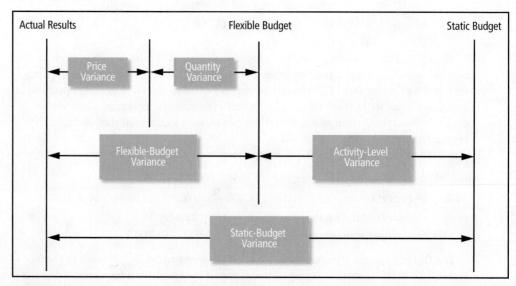

Exhibit 7-8

Relationship Between the Flexible-Budget Variance and the Price and Quantity Variances

amounts were the product of the standard quantities and the standard prices shown in the following table:

| | Standards | | |
	Standard Quantity of Input Allowed per Unit of Output	Standard Price per Unit of Input	Flexible Budget Formula per Unit of Output
Direct materials	5 pounds	$2/pound	$10
Direct labor	$\frac{1}{2}$ hour	$16/hour	8

For the 7,000 units of output achieved by Dominion, these standards translate into the budgeted standard costs allowed shown in Exhibit 7-7:

Direct-materials cost allowed = 7,000 units × 5 pounds × $2.00 per pound = $70,000

Direct-labor cost allowed = 7,000 units × $\frac{1}{2}$ hour × $16.00 per hour = $56,000

We next introduce additional information about the actual quantities of material or labor used and the actual prices per unit of material or labor. Let's assume the following actual prices and quantities explain the actual direct material and direct labor costs shown in Exhibit 7-7:

- Direct materials: Dominion purchased and used 36,800 pounds of material at an actual unit price of $1.90 for a total actual cost of 36,800 × $1.90 = $69,920.
- Direct labor: Dominion used 3,750 hours of labor at an actual hourly price (rate) of $16.40, for a total cost of 3,750 × $16.40 = $61,500.

Computing Price and Quantity Variances

The flexible-budget variance (the difference between actual cost incurred and the flexible-budget cost) can be divided into 1) a quantity variance, attributable to the difference between actual quantity used and standard quantity allowed, and 2) a price variance, attributable to the difference between actual price per unit and standard price per unit. The **price variance** indicates whether the actual price paid was more or less than the standard price:

Price variance = (Actual price − Standard price) × Actual quantity used

The **quantity variance** indicates whether the actual quantity used was more or less than the standard quantity allowed for the output achieved:

Quantity variance = (Actual quantity used − Standard quantity allowed for actual output) × Standard price

Exhibit 7-9 shows the calculation of price and quantity variances for materials and labor for Dominion Company. Although the exhibit may seem complex at first, studying it will solidify your understanding of variance analysis.

Column A of Exhibit 7-9 contains the actual costs incurred based on the actual quantities used at actual prices. Column C is the flexible-budget amount based on standard input quantities allowed for the outputs achieved multiplied by standard prices. We insert column B, the actual input quantities used multiplied by standard prices, between A and C to separate price and quantity effects. The difference between columns A and B is the price variance, due to the difference between actual versus standard prices. The difference between columns B and C is the quantity variance, due to the difference between actual versus standard quantities.

The price and quantity variances corresponding to Dominion Company's flexible-budget variances for material and labor are as follows:

Materials price variance = (Actual price − Standard price) × Actual quantity

= ($1.90 − $2.00) per pound × 36,800 pounds

= $3,680 Favorable

Labor price variance = (Actual price − Standard price) × Actual quantity

= ($16.40 − $16.00) per hour × 3,750 hours

= $1,500 Unfavorable

Objective 6

Compute and interpret price and quantity variances for materials and labor.

price variance
The difference between actual input prices and standard input prices multiplied by the actual quantity of inputs used.

quantity variance
The difference between the actual quantity of inputs used and the standard quantity allowed for the good output achieved multiplied by the standard price of the input.

The quantity (or usage) variances are as follows:

Materials quantity variance = (Actual quantity − Standard quantity) × Standard price

= [36,800 − (7,000 × 5)] pounds × $2.00 per pound

= [36,800 − 35,000] pounds × $2.00 per pounds

= $3,600 Unfavorable

Labor quantity variance = (Actual quantity − Standard quantity) × Standard price

= [3,750 − (7,000 × 1/2)] hours × $16.00 per hour

= [3,750 − 3,500] hours × $16.00 per hour

= $4,000 Unfavorable

By definition, the sum of the direct-materials price and quantity variances equals the total direct-materials flexible-budget variance. Similarly, the sum of the direct-labor price and quantity variances equals the direct-labor flexible-budget variance.

Materials flexible-budget variance = $3,680 Favorable + $3,600 Unfavorable

= $80 Favorable

Labor flexible-budget variance = $1,500 Unfavorable + $4,000 Unfavorable

= $5,500 Unfavorable

Note that the flexible budget quantities used in computing price and quantity variance are quantities of inputs, which are related to, but different than, the quantity of output achieved. For Dominion Company, a single-product firm, standard inputs allowed is simply units of

Exhibit 7-9

General Approach to
Analysis of Direct-Labor and
Direct-Materials Variances

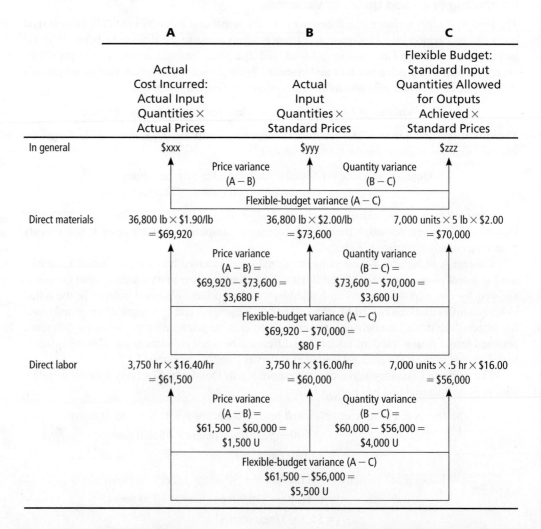

output multiplied by the standard quantity of input per unit. For more complex companies that manufacture a variety of products, there are standard inputs allowed for the output achieved for each product. For example, consider a furniture manufacturer that produced 12,000 chairs and 3,000 sofas. If each chair requires 1 standard labor hour and each sofa requires 2 standard labor hours, standard hours allowed for outputs achieved is $(12,000 \times 1) + (3,000 \times 2) = 18,000$. Standard hours allowed for output achieved is the result of translating disparate output units (chairs and sofas) into a common standard measure of activity (standard labor hours allowed for output achieved).

Exhibit 7-10 provides a graphical overview of the computation of price and quantity variances. Panels A and B show the simple cases where there is either a quantity or a price variance but not both, so there is no interaction between the price and quantity variances. In both panels, the flexible budget is the standard quantity allowed multiplied by the standard price—the rectangle shaded blue. The variances depend on the difference between standard and actual price and the difference between standard and actual quantity. In Panel A, the variance is the quantity used in excess of the standard quantity times the standard price—the rectangle shaded orange. In Panel B, the variance is the price paid in excess of the standard price times the standard quantity—the rectangle shaded purple.

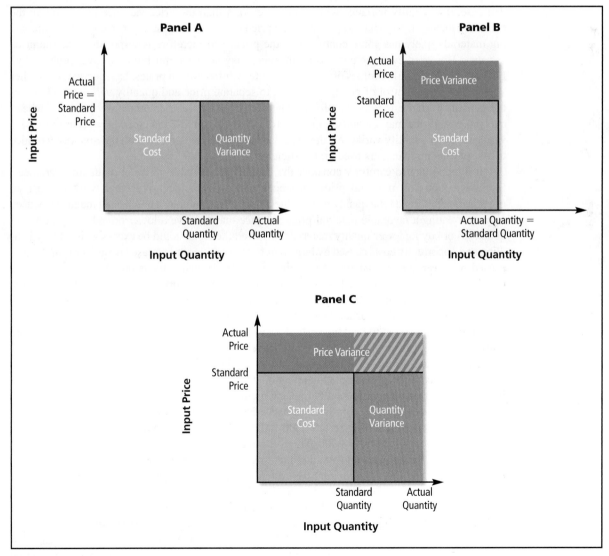

Exhibit 7-10
Graphical Representation of Quantity and Price Variances

Panel C illustrates the situation where both quantity and price variances exist. The interaction of the two variances is represented by the cross-hatched purple region. In concept, this joint effect could be defined to be a separate, third variance. In practice, most companies include this joint effect as part of the price variance, as in the calculations shown in Exhibit 7-9. This means the price variance is the result of multiplying the difference between actual and standard price by the total actual quantity used. This definition includes the joint effect represented by the purple cross-hatched area as part of the price variance. The quantity variance is then the difference between actual and standard quantity multiplied by the standard price.

You are likely to encounter various terms used for price and quantity variances in practice. For example, many companies call a price variance applied to labor a **rate variance**, and many refer to quantity variances as **usage** or **efficiency variances**. Moreover, you may encounter new variance definitions such as those created by the Brass Products Division in the Business First box on page 216 or in the Making Managerial Decisions section on page 257. Because there is so much variation in definitions and terminology, be sure to ask whatever questions are necessary to be sure that you understand the exact definition of any variance that you encounter.

rate variance
An alternative name for the price variance applied to labor.

usage variance (efficiency variance)
Alternative names for the quantity variance.

Interpreting Price and Quantity Variances

By dividing flexible-budget variances into price and quantity variances, we can better evaluate managers on variances that they can control. Consider an operating manager who has control over the quantity of materials used in the production process but little control over the price. In that case, the quantity variance will be more relevant than the price variance in evaluating the operating manager. Who has control over the price variance? The manager in charge of purchasing materials likely has some control over the price, and therefore is responsible for the price variance. However, even the purchasing manager may not have much control over price. Why? Because external market forces often are the primary influence on prices. Irrespective of whether any manager has control of price, it is useful to separate price and quantity variances whenever the quantity variance is important for evaluation. For example, the commodity prices of wheat, oats, corn, and rice may be outside the control of General Mills managers. By separating price variances from quantity variances, the breakfast cereal maker can focus on the quantity variance to assess whether managers used grain efficiently.

It is important to carefully consider the incentives created by price and quantity variances. Exclusive focus on material price variances can provide incentives that work against an organization's JIT and total quality management goals. For example, a purchasing manager focused only on creating a favorable material price variance may achieve a lower price by buying larger quantities or buying lower-quality material. However, the result could be excessive inventory handling and opportunity costs caused by large purchase quantities or increased manufacturing defects caused by lower-quality material. As another example, exclusive focus on labor price variances could motivate managers to use lower-cost (and lower-skilled) workers or to rush workers through critical tasks. In either case, the result could impair quality of products and services.

Companies that use variances primarily to fix blame often find that managers resort to cheating and subversion to beat the system. Lower-level operations managers usually have more information about their operations than higher-level managers. If supervisors use that information against them, lower-level managers might withhold or misstate valuable information for their own protection. For example, one manufacturing firm actually followed a policy of reducing the next period's departmental budget by the amount of the department's unfavorable variances in the current period. If a division had a $50,000 expense budget for labor and $52,000 of actual labor costs resulting in a $2,000 unfavorable labor variance, the following period's budget would be reduced to $48,000. This system led managers to cheat and to falsify reports to avoid unfavorable variances and avoid reductions in their budgets. We can criticize departmental managers' ethics in this situation, but the system design was also at fault.

Variances by themselves cannot provide the complete picture of why the company achieved or failed to achieve the budgeted results. For instance, one possible explanation for Dominion's set of variances is that a manager made a trade-off. Perhaps the manager purchased substandard-quality materials at a favorable price, saving $3,680 (the favorable materials price variance) knowing that the substandard material would lead to extra waste of materials (the $3,600 unfavorable material quantity variance). In this case, the material price variance more than offsets the material quantity variance, as indicated by the net materials flexible-budget variance of $80 favorable.

Of course, to fully understand the effect of the decision to purchase substandard materials, still more investigation and analysis might be required. For example, the material waste due to substandard materials might also have caused excess use of direct labor. Why? Perhaps Dominion used direct labor time working on units that ended up being defective, thus wasting that time. Suppose the labor wasted on the defective units was more than the $80 favorable materials flexible budget variance described in the previous paragraph. Then, the decision to purchase substandard material was not successful because the labor cost inefficiencies caused by using substandard materials exceeded the materials cost savings from the favorable price. The important point again is that variances are useful tools that provide clues and direct attention to problems, but variances are only the starting point of the search for answers to the complex question of why actual results differ from expectations.

Making Managerial Decisions

Managers can apply the concepts of variance analysis to construct new variance definitions to fit new situations. For example, consider a production plant that plans to produce 50 units per hour and work 8 hours per day for a total planned production of 400 units each day. On March 23, the plant produced just 276 units for a total unfavorable production variance of 124 units. Because of machine breakdowns, the plant operated for only 6 hours that day. Using a three-column framework like that used in Exhibit 7-9, define variances that separate how much of the 124 unit shortfall in production was caused by operating only 6 hours versus how much was caused by low production efficiency during the 6 hours of actual operation.

Answer

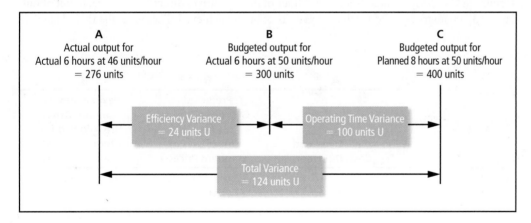

Column A shows actual production of 276 units over 6 actual operating hours equates to 46 units per hour. Column C shows standard production of 8 hours per day × 50 units per hour = 400 units per day. Column B shows standard production rates for actual operating hours, 6 hours of production × 50 units per hour = 300 units. The difference between columns B and C is the production shortfall caused by loss of 2 hours of operating time due to the machine breakdowns, 2 hours × 50 units per hour = 100 unit unfavorable variance. The difference between columns A and B is the shortfall caused by an actual rate of production (276 ÷ 6 = 46 units per hour) lower than the standard rate of 50 units per hour. This difference is the rate shortfall (4 units per hour) multiplied by the actual hours worked for the day (6 hours) = 24 unit unfavorable variance. The total variance, 100 units + 24 units = 124 units, is the difference between columns A and C.

Overhead Variances

The evaluation of overhead variances is different from the evaluation of direct materials and direct labor because overhead costs are generally indirect costs that companies allocate rather than trace to output. In this section, we outline the framework used to construct variable overhead variances and then briefly discuss variances for fixed overhead.

Objective 7

Compute variable overhead spending and efficiency variances.

Variable Overhead Variances

Companies allocate variable overhead to output based on some cost driver. For example, the variable-overhead cost driver for Dominion Company is direct-labor hours. The variable-overhead flexible-budget variance can be divided into two variances. When actual cost-driver activity differs from the standard amount allowed for the actual output achieved, we have a **variable-overhead efficiency variance**, calculated as follows:

variable-overhead efficiency variance
The difference between actual cost-driver activity and the standard amount allowed for the actual output achieved multiplied by the standard variable-overhead rate per cost-driver unit.

$$\text{Variable-overhead efficiency variance} = \left(\begin{array}{c}\text{Actual cost-} \\ \text{driver activity}\end{array} - \begin{array}{c}\text{Standard cost-driver} \\ \text{activity allowed}\end{array}\right) \times \begin{array}{c}\text{Standard variable-overhead} \\ \text{rate per cost-driver unit}\end{array}$$

The variable-overhead efficiency variance depends entirely on whether the quantity of the cost driver used is more or less than the quantity allowed for the actual output achieved. It measures how control of the cost driver activity affected variable overhead costs.

The **variable-overhead spending variance** arises when actual variable overhead costs differ from the amount predicted for the actual cost-driver activity:

variable-overhead spending variance
The difference between the actual variable overhead cost and the amount predicted for the actual level of cost-driver activity.

$$\begin{array}{c}\text{Variable-overhead spending} \\ \text{variance}\end{array} = \begin{array}{c}\text{Actual variable} \\ \text{overhead}\end{array} - \left(\begin{array}{c}\text{Standard variable} \\ \text{overhead rate per} \\ \text{unit of cost-driver}\end{array} \times \begin{array}{c}\text{Actual cost-driver} \\ \text{activity used}\end{array}\right)$$

This variance combines price and quantity effects and tells us how the actual variable overhead cost compares to the predicted amount for the actual level of cost-driver activity.

Exhibit 7-11 illustrates the calculation of variable and fixed overhead variances for Dominion Company. The exhibit breaks the $500 unfavorable flexible-budget variable overhead variance for supplies into spending and efficiency variances. We compute the efficiency variance by multiplying the standard variable overhead rate times the difference between the quantity of the cost driver used and the quantity of the cost driver allowed for the output achieved. For Dominion Company, standards allow 1/2 hour of the cost driver direct labor for each unit of output, or 3,500 hours allowed for the 7,000 units of output achieved. Therefore, the flexible budget

Exhibit 7-11
General Approach to Analysis of Overhead Variances

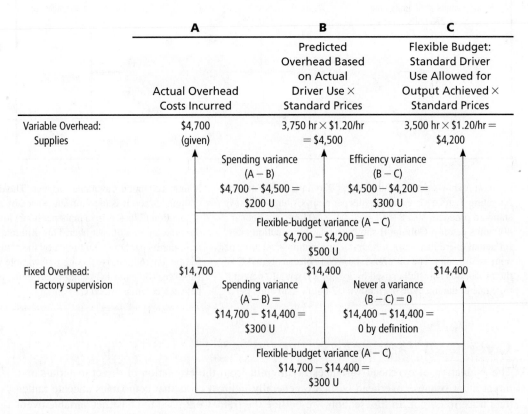

	A	B	C
	Actual Overhead Costs Incurred	Predicted Overhead Based on Actual Driver Use × Standard Prices	Flexible Budget: Standard Driver Use Allowed for Output Achieved × Standard Prices
Variable Overhead: Supplies	$4,700 (given)	3,750 hr × $1.20/hr = $4,500	3,500 hr × $1.20/hr = $4,200

Spending variance (A − B) $4,700 − $4,500 = $200 U

Efficiency variance (B − C) $4,500 − $4,200 = $300 U

Flexible-budget variance (A − C) $4,700 − $4,200 = $500 U

| Fixed Overhead: Factory supervision | $14,700 | $14,400 | $14,400 |

Spending variance (A − B) = $14,700 − $14,400 = $300 U

Never a variance (B − C) = 0 $14,400 − $14,400 = 0 by definition

Flexible-budget variance (A − C) $14,700 − $14,400 = $300 U

amount of \$4,200 for supplies in Exhibit 7-7 translates to \$4,200 ÷ 3,500 hours = \$1.20 per direct-labor hour allowed for output achieved. Because Dominion Company used 3,750 labor hours when the standard for production of 7,000 units is 1/2 hour/unit × 7,000 units = 3,500 standard hours allowed, it used an excess of 250 labor hours. Each labor hour drives \$1.20 of variable overhead, so the excess labor hours drive 250 units × \$1.20/unit = \$300 of extra variable overhead costs.

$$
\begin{aligned}
\text{Variable-overhead efficiency} \atop \text{variance of supplies} &= \left({\text{Actual direct-} \atop \text{labor hours}} - {\text{Standard direct-labor} \atop \text{hours allowed}} \right) \times {\text{Standard variable-} \atop \text{overhead rates per hour}} \\
&= \left({\text{3,750 Actual} \atop \text{hours}} - {\text{3,500 Standard} \atop \text{hours allowed}} \right) \times \quad \$1.20 \text{ per hour} \\
&= (250 \text{ excess hours}) \times \$1.20 \text{ per hour} \\
&= \$300 \text{ Unfavorable}
\end{aligned}
$$

This example illustrates a general principle: When actual cost-driver activity exceeds the activity allowed for the actual output achieved, variable-overhead efficiency variances are unfavorable and vice versa. In essence, the variable-overhead efficiency variance tells management how much variable overhead cost it wastes if the variance is unfavorable (or saves, if the variance is favorable) due to cost-driver activity.

The other component of the flexible-budget variance measures control of overhead spending given actual cost-driver activity. The variable-overhead spending variance is the difference between the actual variable overhead and the amount of variable overhead predicted when using 3,750 actual direct-labor hours:

$$
\begin{aligned}
\text{Variable-overhead spending} \atop \text{variance of supplies} &= {\text{Actual variable} \atop \text{overhead}} - \left({\text{Standard variable} \atop \text{overhead rate}} \times {\text{Actual direct-} \atop \text{labor hours used}} \right) \\
&= \$4,700 \quad - (\$1.20 \times 3,750) \\
&= \$4,700 \quad - \$4,500 \\
&= \$200 \text{ Unfavorable}
\end{aligned}
$$

Like other variances, a variable-overhead variance does not by itself identify the causes of results that differ from the static and flexible budgets. The distinction between efficiency and spending variances for variable overhead provides a springboard for more investigation, but the only way for management to discover why overhead performance did not agree with the budget is to investigate possible causes.

Fixed Overhead Variances

The framework for analysis of fixed overhead variances differs from the framework for variable cost variances. Consider factory supervision, a fixed cost, shown at the bottom of Exhibit 7-11. The flexible budget in column B based on actual use of the cost driver and the flexible budget in column C based on standard use of the cost driver are always the same. Why? Because fixed overhead does not vary with the level of use of the cost driver. Because there is no difference between columns B and C, the entire fixed overhead flexible-budget variance in Exhibit 7-11 is due to the difference between columns A and B. This difference between the actual fixed-overhead cost in column A and the budgeted cost in columns B and C is the **fixed-overhead spending variance**. For example, Dominion Company's factory supervision fixed-overhead spending variance is the flexible-budget variance of \$14,700 − \$14,400 = \$300 unfavorable, the difference between the actual cost of factory supervision and the budgeted fixed amount.

You will encounter a second type of fixed-overhead variance, the production-volume variance. Because this second type of variance does not involve the control of costs, we consider only the fixed-overhead spending variance in this chapter.

Objective 8

Compute the fixed-overhead spending variance.

fixed-overhead spending variance
The difference between actual fixed overhead and budgeted fixed overhead.

Summary Problem for Your Review

PROBLEM

The following questions are based on standards for the Dominion Company in this chapter.

- Direct materials: standard, 5 pounds per unit at $2 per pound
- Direct labor: standard, 1/2 hour at $16 per hour

Earlier we computed variances based on actual results for production of 7,000 units. Suppose now we have actual results for production of 8,500 units:

- Direct materials: Dominion purchased and used 46,000 pounds at an actual unit price of $1.85 per pound, for an actual total cost of $85,100.
- Direct labor: Dominion used 4,125 hours of labor at an actual hourly rate of $16.80, for a total actual cost of $69,300.

1. Compute the flexible-budget variance and the price and quantity variances for direct labor and direct material.

2. In requirement 1, you should have computed a direct-materials price variance of $6,900 favorable. Is this a good outcome? Explain.

SOLUTION

1. The variances are as follows:

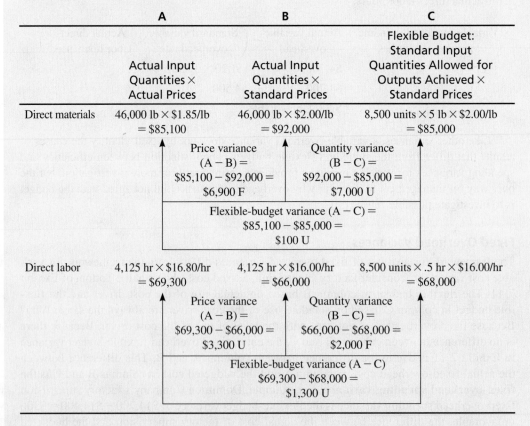

	A	B	C
	Actual Input Quantities × Actual Prices	Actual Input Quantities × Standard Prices	Flexible Budget: Standard Input Quantities Allowed for Outputs Achieved × Standard Prices
Direct materials	46,000 lb × $1.85/lb = $85,100	46,000 lb × $2.00/lb = $92,000	8,500 units × 5 lb × $2.00/lb = $85,000

Price variance
(A − B) =
$85,100 − $92,000 =
$6,900 F

Quantity variance
(B − C) =
$92,000 − $85,000 =
$7,000 U

Flexible-budget variance (A − C) =
$85,100 − $85,000 =
$100 U

| Direct labor | 4,125 hr × $16.80/hr = $69,300 | 4,125 hr × $16.00/hr = $66,000 | 8,500 units × .5 hr × $16.00/hr = $68,000 |

Price variance
(A − B) =
$69,300 − $66,000 =
$3,300 U

Quantity variance
(B − C) =
$66,000 − $68,000 =
$2,000 F

Flexible-budget variance (A − C) =
$69,300 − $68,000 =
$1,300 U

2. The favorable price variance may not be a good outcome. When prices are low, it may motivate Dominion Company managers to buy extra inventory in excess of its immediate needs, causing extra storage and handling costs. The favorable price variance may also mean that lower quality material has been purchased. The favorable materials price variance is a good outcome only if it exceeds any unfavorable material, labor, and overhead variances caused by the volume and quality of materials purchased.

Highlights to Remember

1. **Identify variances and label them as favorable or unfavorable.** Variances are differences between actual and budgeted results. When the direction of the difference corresponds to actual profit greater than budgeted, the variance is labeled as favorable. When the direction corresponds to actual profit less than budgeted, the variance is unfavorable.

2. **Distinguish between flexible budgets and static budgets.** Flexible budgets are geared to changing levels of cost-driver activity rather than to the single level of the static budget. Organizations tailor flexible budgets to particular levels of sales or cost-driver activity—before or after the fact. Flexible budgets tell how much revenue and cost to expect for any level of activity.

3. **Use flexible-budget formulas to construct a flexible budget.** Cost functions, or flexible-budget formulas, reflect fixed- and variable-cost behavior and allow managers to compute budgets for any volume of output achieved. We compute the flexible-budget amounts for variable costs by multiplying the variable cost per unit of output times the level of output. The flexible-budgeted fixed cost is a lump sum, independent of the level of output (within the relevant range).

4. **Compute and interpret static-budget variances, flexible-budget variances, and sales-activity variances.** Static-budget variances are differences between actual results and the budgeted amounts for the level of activity assumed in the static budget. Sales-activity variances are the budgeted effects of operating at the actual achieved level of activity rather than the level of activity assumed in the static budget. Flexible-budget variances are the deviations of actual results from the flexible budget amounts for the achieved level of activity.

5. **Understand how the setting of standards affects the computation and interpretation of variances.** Because variances are the difference between budgeted and actual amounts, they depend on the standards used to construct the budget. Most companies set standards that are neither too easy nor too hard to attain.

6. **Compute and interpret price and quantity variances for materials and labor.** Managers often find it useful to subdivide flexible-budget variances for variable inputs into price and quantity variances. Price variances (also referred to as rate variances) reflect the effects of changing input prices, holding inputs constant at actual input use. Quantity variances (also referred to as usage variances or efficiency variances) reflect the effects of different levels of input usage, holding prices constant at standard prices.

7. **Compute variable overhead spending and efficiency variances.** The variable-overhead spending variance is the difference between the actual variable overhead and the amount of variable overhead budgeted for the actual level of cost-driver activity. The variable-overhead efficiency variance is the difference between the actual cost-driver activity and the amount of cost-driver activity allowed for the actual output achieved, costed at the standard variable-overhead rate.

8. **Compute the fixed-overhead spending variance.** The fixed-overhead spending variance is the difference between the actual fixed overhead expenditures and the budgeted amount of fixed overhead.

Accounting Vocabulary

MyAccountingLab **Fundamental Assignment Material**

7-A1 Flexible and Static Budgets

Walcker Transportation Company's general manager reports quarterly to the company president on the firm's operating performance. The company uses a budget based on detailed expectations for the forthcoming quarter. The general manager has just received the condensed quarterly performance report shown in Exhibit 7-12.

Although the general manager was upset about not obtaining enough revenue, she was happy that her cost performance was favorable; otherwise, her net income would be even worse.

The president was not satisfied with the performance report and remarked, "I can see some merit in comparing actual performance with budgeted performance because we can see whether actual revenue coincided with our best guess for budget purposes. But I can't see how this performance report helps me evaluate cost-control performance."

1. Prepare a columnar flexible budget for Walcker Transportation at revenue levels of $12,600,000, $13,000,000, and $13,400,000. Use the format of the last three columns of Exhibit 7-3, page 255. Assume that the prices and mix of products sold are equal to the budgeted prices and mix.
2. Write out the flexible budget formula for costs as a function of revenue.
3. Prepare a condensed table showing the static budget variance, the sales-activity variance, and the flexible-budget variance. Use the format of Exhibit 7-6, page 258.

7-A2 Activity Level Variances

The systems consulting department of Gullickson Golf Products designs systems for data collection, encoding, and reporting to fit the needs of other departments within the company. The cost driver for costs in the systems consulting department is the number of requests made to the department. The expected variable cost of handling a request was $500, and the number of requests expected for June 20X1 was 75. Gullickson budgeted its monthly fixed costs for the department (salaries, equipment depreciation, space costs) at $65,000.

The actual number of requests serviced by systems consulting in June 20X1 was 90, and the total costs incurred by the department was $124,000. Of that amount, $78,000 was for fixed costs.

Compute the static budget variances and the flexible-budget variances for variable and fixed costs for the systems consulting department for June 20X1.

Exhibit 7-12

Walcker Transportation
Operating Performance
Report

Second Quarter, 20X1

	Budget	Actual	Variance
Net revenue	$13,000,000	$12,700,000	$300,000 U
Variable Costs			
Fuel	$ 520,000	$ 516,000	$ 4,000 F
Repairs and maintenance	390,000	398,000	8,000 U
Supplies and miscellaneous	2,080,000	2,070,000	10,000 F
Variable payroll	8,060,000	7,940,000	120,000 F
Total variable costs*	$11,050,000	$10,924,000	$126,000 F
Fixed Costs			
Supervision	$ 160,000	$ 177,000	$ 17,000 U
Rent	200,000	200,000	—
Depreciation	460,000	460,000	—
Other fixed costs	170,000	163,000	7,000 F
Total fixed costs	990,000	1,000,000	$ 10,000 U
Total fixed and variable costs	$12,040,000	$11,924,000	$116,000 F
Operating income	$ 960,000	$ 776,000	$184,000 U

U = Unfavorable. F = Favorable.

*For purposes of this analysis, assume that all of these costs are totally variable with respect to sales revenue. In practice, many are mixed and would have to be subdivided into variable and fixed components before a meaningful analysis could be made. Also, assume that the prices and mix of services sold remain unchanged.

7-A3 Direct-Material and Direct-Labor Variances

Hill Fine Instruments manufactures trumpets, trombones, tubas, and other brass instruments. The following standards were developed for a line of trumpets:

	Standard Inputs Expected for Each Unit of Output Achieved	Standard Price per Unit of Input
Direct materials	5 pounds	$10 per pound
Direct labor	10 hours	$25 per hour

During April, Hill scheduled 550 trumpets for production. However, the company produced only 525.

Hill purchased and used 3,100 pounds of direct materials at a unit price of $9.00 per pound. It used 5,500 hours of direct labor at an actual rate of $26.00 per hour.

1. Compute the standard cost per trumpet for direct materials and direct labor.
2. Compute the price variances and quantity variances for direct materials and direct labor.
3. Based on these sketchy data, what clues for investigation are provided by the variances?

7-B1 Summary Performance Reports

Consider the following data for Robert Campbell Tax Services:

- Static budget data: sales, 3,500 clients at $350 each; variable costs, $300 per client; fixed costs, $150,000
- Actual results at actual prices: sales, 3,000 clients at $360 per client; variable costs, $920,000; fixed costs, $159,500

1. Prepare a summary performance report similar to Exhibit 7-6, page 258.
2. Fill in the blanks:

Static-budget income		$ —
Variances		
Sales-activity variances	$ —	
Flexible-budget variances	—	—
Actual income		$

7-B2 Material and Labor Variances

Consider the following data for Tripp Manufacturing:

	Direct Materials	Direct Labor
Actual price per unit of input (lb and hr)	$ 7.50	$ 12.00
Standard price per unit of input	$ 7.00	$ 14.00
Standard inputs allowed per unit of output	10	2
Actual units of input	116,000	29,000
Actual units of output (product)	14,400	14,400

1. Compute the price, quantity, and flexible-budget variances for direct materials and direct labor. Use U or F to indicate whether the variances are unfavorable or favorable.
2. Prepare a plausible explanation for the performance.

7-B3 Variable-Overhead Variances

You have been asked to prepare an analysis of the overhead costs in the order processing department of a mail-order company like Eddie Bauer. As an initial step, you prepare a summary of some events that bear on overhead for the most recent period. Variable overhead is applied based on hours of processing-clerk labor. The standard variable-overhead rate per order was $.06. The rate of 10 orders per hour is regarded as standard productivity per clerk. The total overhead incurred was $204,000, of which $138,000 was fixed. The fixed-overhead spending variance was $2,500 unfavorable. The variable-overhead flexible-budget variance was $6,000 unfavorable. The variable-overhead spending variance was $3,600 favorable.

Find the following:

1. Variable-overhead efficiency variance
2. Actual hours of input
3. Standard hours of input allowed for output achieved
4. Budgeted-fixed overhead

MyAccountingLab # Additional Assignment Material

QUESTIONS

7-1 Distinguish between favorable and unfavorable cost (and revenue) variances.

7-2 "The flex in the flexible budget relates solely to variable costs." Do you agree? Explain.

7-3 "We want a flexible budget because costs are difficult to predict. We need the flexibility to change budgeted costs as input prices change." Does a flexible budget serve this purpose? Explain.

7-4 Explain the role of understanding cost behavior and cost-driver activities for flexible budgeting.

7-5 "An activity-based flexible budget has a 'flex' for every activity." Do you agree? Explain.

7-6 "Effectiveness and efficiency go hand in hand. You can't have one without the other." Do you agree? Explain.

7-7 Differentiate between a static-budget variance and a flexible-budget variance.

7-8 "Managers should be rewarded for favorable variances and punished for unfavorable variances." Do you agree? Explain.

7-9 "A good control system places the blame for every unfavorable variance on someone in the organization. Without affixing blame, no one will take responsibility for cost control." Do you agree? Explain.

7-10 Who is usually responsible for sales-activity variances? Why?

7-11 Differentiate between perfection standards and currently attainable standards.

7-12 What are two possible approaches to setting "currently attainable standards"?

7-13 "A standard is one point in a band or range of acceptable outcomes." Evaluate this statement.

7-14 "Price variances should be computed even if prices are regarded as being outside of company control." Do you agree? Explain.

7-15 What are some common causes of unfavorable quantity variances?

7-16 "Failure to meet price standards is the responsibility of the purchasing officer." Do you agree? Explain.

7-17 "The variable-overhead efficiency variance is not really an overhead variance." Evaluate this statement.

7-18 Why do the techniques for controlling overhead differ from those for controlling direct materials?

CRITICAL THINKING EXERCISES

7-19 Interpretation of Favorable and Unfavorable Variances

A division budgeted an operating profit of $3,000 on sales of $8,000 and costs of $5,000. However, at the beginning of the period one of the division's machines broke down and could not be fixed until the end of the period. When the machine broke, the division manager determined that there were two feasible alternatives: First, production and sales could be cut back by 25%, reducing sales to $6,000 and costs to $4,000. (Note that costs are not reduced by 25% because some of the costs are fixed.) Second, a replacement machine could be obtained and installed, allowing sales to be maintained at $8,000 but increasing costs to $6,500. The division manager analyzed the alternatives and concluded that revenues less costs would be greater if sales were reduced ($6,000 less $4,000 = $2,000 operating profit) than if the replacement machine was obtained ($8,000 less $6,500 = $1,500 operating profit). The manager, therefore, chose not to replace the machine. However, because revenue was lower than planned by $2,000, there is an unfavorable revenue variance of $2,000. Comment on how the unfavorable revenue variance should be interpreted in evaluating the performance of the manager.

7-20 Marketing Responsibility for Sales-Activity Variances

Suppose a company budgeted an operating profit of $100 on sales of $1,000. Actual sales were $900. The marketing department claimed that because sales were down 10%, it was responsible for only 10% of $100 or $10 of any drop in profit. Any further shortfall must be someone else's responsibility. Comment on this claim.

7-21 Production Responsibility for Flexible-Budget Variances

Suppose a plant manager planned to produce 100 units of product at a total cost of $1,000. Instead, actual production was 10% higher at 110 units. When costs came in at less than a 10% increase in costs or $1,100, the plant manager claimed that she should get credit for a favorable variance equal to the amount by which the actual costs fell short of $1,100. Comment on this claim.

7-22 Responsibility of Purchasing Manager
A company's purchasing manager bought 5,000 pounds of material for $5.50 per pound instead of the budgeted $6.00 per pound, resulting in a favorable variance of $2,500. The company has a policy of rewarding employees with 20% of any cost savings they generate. Before awarding a $500 bonus to the purchasing manager, what other variances would you look at to determine the total effect of the purchasing decision? Explain.

7-23 Variable-Overhead Efficiency Variance
Birmingham Company had a $1,000 U variable-overhead efficiency variance. Neither the plant manager, who was responsible primarily for labor scheduling, nor the administrative manager, who was responsible for most support services, felt responsible for the variance. Who should be held responsible? Why?

EXERCISES

7-24 Flexible Budget
Coppins Sports Equipment Company made 44,000 basketballs in a given year. Its manufacturing costs were $294,800 variable and $9,100 fixed. Assume that no price changes will occur in the following year and that no changes in production methods are applicable. Compute the budgeted cost for producing 52,000 basketballs in the following year.

7-25 Basic Flexible Budget
The superintendent of police of Fargo is attempting to predict the costs of operating a fleet of police cars. Among the items of concern are fuel, $.22 per mile, and depreciation, $6,600 per car per year.

The manager is preparing a flexible budget for the coming year. Prepare the flexible-budget amounts for fuel and depreciation for each car at a level of 40,000, 50,000, and 60,000 miles.

7-26 Flexible Budget
Pohle Designs has a department that makes high-quality leather cases for iPads. Consider the following data for a recent month:

	Budget Formula per Unit	Various Levels of Output		
Units		10,000	11,000	12,000
Sales	$19	$?	$?	$?
Variable costs				
Direct materials	?	65,000	?	?
Hand labor	4.40	?	?	?
Fixed costs				
Depreciation		?	18,000	?
Salaries		?	?	33,000

Fill in the unknowns.

7-27 Basic Flexible Budget
The budgeted prices for materials and direct labor per unit of finished product are $8 and $7, respectively. The production manager is delighted about the following data:

	Static Budget	Actual Costs	Variance
Direct materials	$59,200	$49,900	$9,300 F
Direct labor	51,800	39,200	12,600 F

Is the manager's happiness justified? Prepare a report that might provide a more detailed explanation of why the static budget was not achieved. Good output was 5,300 units.

7-28 Activity-Level Variances
Materials-support costs for the Pittsburgh Steel Company (PSC) are variable costs that depend on the weight of material (plate steel, castings, etc.) moved. For the current budget period and based on scheduled production, PSC expected to move 750,000 pounds of material at a cost of $.25 per pound. Several orders were canceled by customers, and PSC moved only 650,000 pounds of material. Total materials support costs for the period were $177,000.

Compare actual support costs to the static-budget support costs by computing static budget, activity-level, and flexible-budget variances for materials-support costs.

7-29 Direct-Material Variances

Nakhon Custom Shirt Company uses a special fabric in the production of dress shirts. During August, Nakhon Custom Shirt purchased and used 4,100 square yards in the production of 3,700 shirts at a total cost of B2,812,600. (B stands for the Thai baht. There are roughly 30 bahts to a U.S. dollar.) The standard allows one yard at B680 per yard for each shirt.

Calculate the material price variance and the material quantity variance.

7-30 Labor Variances

Ellen Chenoweth, the manager of the city of St. Paul road maintenance shop, uses standards to judge performance. Because a clerk mistakenly discarded some labor records, however, Ellen has only partial data for April. She knows that the total direct-labor flexible-budget variance was $1,643 favorable. Moreover, a recent pay raise produced an unfavorable labor price variance for April of $1,157. The actual hours of input were 1,780 and the standard labor price was $20 per hour.

1. Find the actual labor rate per hour.
2. Determine the standard hours allowed for the output achieved.

7-31 Quantity Variances

Lindsey Toy Company produced 13,000 stuffed bears. The standard direct-material allowance is 1.5 kilograms per bear, at a cost per kilo of $3.20. Actually, 18,700 kilos of materials (input) were used to produce the 13,000 bears (output).

Similarly, the standard allowance for direct labor is 5.1 hours to produce one bear, and the standard hourly labor cost is $6. But 67,100 hours (input) were used to produce the 13,000 bears.

Compute the quantity variances for direct materials and direct labor.

7-32 Labor and Material Variances

Standard direct-labor rate	$ 15.00
Actual direct-labor rate	$ 11.50
Standard direct-labor hours	10,000
Direct-labor quantity variance—unfavorable	$ 9,000
Standard unit price of materials	$ 4.60
Actual quantity purchased and used	2,500
Standard quantity allowed for actual production	1,850
Materials purchase price variance—favorable	$ 500

1. Compute the actual hours worked, rounded to the nearest hour.
2. Compute the actual purchase price per unit of materials, rounded to the nearest penny.

7-33 Material and Labor Variances

Consider the following data:

	Direct Materials	Direct Labor
Costs incurred: actual inputs × actual prices incurred	$120,495	$101,255
Actual inputs × expected prices	127,155	96,250
Standard inputs allowed for actual outputs achieved × expected prices	130,200	92,500

Compute the price, quantity, and flexible-budget variances for direct materials and direct labor. Use U or F to indicate whether the variances are unfavorable or favorable.

PROBLEMS

7-34 National Park Service

The National Park Service prepared the following budget for one of its national parks for 20X1:

Revenue from fees	$5,000,000
Variable costs (miscellaneous)	500,000
Contribution margin	$4,500,000
Fixed costs (miscellaneous)	4,500,000
Income	$ 0

The fees were based on an average of 25,000 vehicle-admission days (vehicles multiplied by number of days in parks) per week for the 20-week season, multiplied by average entry and other fees of $10 per vehicle-admission day.

The season was booming for the first 4 weeks. During the fifth week, however, there were major forest fires. A large percentage of the park was scarred by the fires. As a result, the number of visitors to the park dropped sharply during the remainder of the season.

Total revenues fell $1.2 million short of the original budget. Variable costs fell as expected, and fixed costs were unaffected except for hiring extra firefighters at a cost of $300,000.

Prepare a columnar summary of performance, showing the original (static) budget, sales-activity variances, flexible budget, flexible-budget variances, and actual results.

7-35 Flexible and Static Budgets

Beta Gamma Sigma, the business honor society, recently held a dinner dance. The original (static) budget and actual results were as follows:

	Static Budget	Actual	Variance
Attendees	75	90	
Revenue	$2,625	$3,255	$630 F
Chicken dinners at $19.00	1,425	1,767	342 U
Beverages, $6 per person	450	466	16 U
Club rental, $75 plus 8% tax	81	81	0
Music, 3 hours at $250 per hour	750	875	125 U
Profit	$ (81)	$ 66	$147 F

1. Subdivide each variance into a sales-activity variance portion and a flexible-budget variance portion. Use the format of Exhibit 7-6, page 258.
2. Provide possible explanations for the variances.

7-36 Summary Explanation

Higgins Company produced 50,000 units, 10,000 more than budgeted. Production data are as follows. Except for physical units, all quantities are in dollars.

	Actual Results at Actual Prices	Flexible-Budget Variances	Flexible Budget	Sales-Activity Variances	Static Budget
Physical units	50,000	—	?	?	40,000
Sales	?	5,500 F	?	?	520,000
Variable costs	315,000	?	300,000	?	?
Contribution margin	?	?	?	?	?
Fixed costs	?	8,000 U	?	?	60,000
Income	?	?	?	?	?

1. Fill in the unknowns.
2. Give a brief summary explanation of why the original target income was not attained.

7-37 Explanation of Variance in Income

Damerow Credit Services produces reports for consumers about their credit ratings. The company's standard contribution margins average 70% of dollar sales, and average selling prices are $50 per report. Average productivity is four reports per hour. Some employees work for sales commissions and others for an hourly rate. The static budget for 20X1 had predicted processing 800,000 reports, but Damerow processed only 700,000 reports.

Fixed costs of rent, supervision, advertising, and other items were budgeted at $22 million, but the budget was exceeded by $600,000 because of extra advertising in an attempt to boost revenue. There were no variances from the average selling prices, but the actual commissions paid to preparers and the actual productivity per hour resulted in flexible-budget variances (i.e., total price and quantity variances) for variable costs of $900,000 unfavorable.

The president of Damerow was unhappy because the budgeted income of $6 million was not achieved. He said, "Sure, we had unfavorable variable-cost variances, but our income was down far more than that. Please explain why."

Explain why the budgeted income was not attained. Use a presentation similar to Exhibit 7-6, page 258. Enough data have been given to permit you to construct the complete exhibit by filling in the known items and then computing the unknowns. Complete your explanation by summarizing what happened, using no more than three sentences.

7-38 Activity and Flexible-Budget Variances at KFC

Suppose a chain of **KFC** franchises in Shanghai had budgeted sales for 2012 of RMB 7.8 million (where RMB stands for the Chinese unit of currency, officially the renminbi, also called the yuan). Cost of goods sold and other variable costs were expected to be 55% of sales. Budgeted annual fixed costs were RMB 2.1 million. A strong Chinese economy caused actual 2012 sales to rise to RMB 10 million and actual profits to increase to RMB 2,050,000. Fixed costs in 2012 were as budgeted. The franchisee was pleased with the increase in profit.

1. Compute the sales-activity variance and the flexible-budget variance for income for 2012. What can the franchisee learn from these variances?
2. Suppose that in 2013 the Chinese economy weakened, and the franchise's sales fell back to the RMB 7.8 million level. Given what happened in 2012, what do you expect to happen to profits in 2013?

7-39 Summary of Airline Performance

The performance (in thousands of dollars) of Sandpiper Airlines for the most recent year is shown in the following table:

	Actual Results at Actual Prices	Static Budget	Variance
Revenue	$?	$385,000	$?
Variable expenses	285,800	250,250*	35,550 U
Contribution margin	?	134,750	?
Fixed expenses	95,300	88,000	7,300 U
Income	$?	$ 46,750	$?

*Includes jet fuel of $55,000.

The static budget had been based on a budget of $.35 revenue per passenger mile. A passenger mile is one paying passenger flown one mile. An average airfare decrease of 6% had helped generate an increase in passenger miles flown that was 20% in excess of the static budget for the year.

The price per gallon of jet fuel rose above the price used to formulate the static budget. The average jet fuel price increase for the year was 20%.

1. Prepare a summary report similar to Exhibit 7-6, page 258, to help the president understand performance for the most recent year.
2. Assume that jet fuel costs are purely variable, and the quantity of fuel used was at the same level of efficiency as predicted in the static budget. What part of the flexible-budget variance for variable expenses is attributable to jet fuel expenses? Explain.

7-40 Hospital Costs and Explanation of Variances

The emergency room at Rochester General Hospital uses a flexible budget based on patients seen as the measure of activity. The hospital must maintain an adequate staff of attending and on-call physicians at all times, so patient activity does not affect physician scheduling. Nurse scheduling varies as volume changes, however. A standard of .5 nurse hours per patient visit was set. Hourly pay for nurses ranges from $9 to $18 per hour, and the average pay rate is $15 per hour. The hospital considers all materials to be supplies, a part of overhead; there are no direct materials. A statistical study showed that the cost of supplies and other variable overhead is more closely associated with nurse hours than with patient visits. The standard for supplies and other variable overhead is $10 per nurse hour.

The head physician of the emergency room unit, Brad Narr, is responsible for control of costs. During October the emergency room unit treated 4,000 patients. The budget and actual costs were as follows:

	Budget	Actual	Variance
Patient visits	3,800	4,000	200
Nurse hours	1,900	2,080	180
Nursing cost	$ 28,500	$ 33,180	$4,680
Supplies and other variable overhead	19,000	20,340	1,340
Fixed costs	92,600	92,600	0
Total cost	$140,100	$146,120	$6,020

1. Calculate price and quantity variances for nursing costs.
2. Calculate spending and efficiency variances for supplies and other variable overhead.
3. The hospital's chief administrator has asked Dr. Narr to explain the variances. Provide possible explanations.

7-41 Flexible Budgeting

For the convenience of its reporters and staff based in London, CNN operates a motor pool. The motor pool operated with 25 vehicles until February of this year, when it acquired an additional automobile. The motor pool furnishes petrol (gasoline), oil, and other supplies for the cars and hires one mechanic who does routine maintenance and minor repairs. Major repairs are done at a nearby commercial garage. A supervisor manages the operations.

Each year the supervisor prepares an operating budget, informing CNN management of the funds needed to operate the pool. Depreciation on the automobiles is recorded in the budget in order to determine the cost per mile.

The following schedule presents the annual budget approved by the news division. The actual costs for March are compared with one-twelfth of the annual budget.

CNN London Motor Pool				
Budget Report for March 20X1				
	Annual Budget	One-Month Budget	March Actual	Over (Under)
Petrol (gasoline)	£ 82,500	£ 6,875	£ 8,200	£1,325
Oil, minor repairs, parts, and supplies	30,000	2,500	2,540	40
Outside repairs	2,700	225	50	(175)
Insurance	4,800	400	416	16
Salaries and benefits	21,600	1,800	1,800	—
Depreciation	22,800	1,900	1,976	76
Total costs	£164,400	£13,700	£14,982	£1,282
Total kilometers	1,500,000	125,000	140,000	
Cost per kilometer	£ .1096	£ .1096	£ .1070	
Number of automobiles	25	25	26	

The annual budget was constructed based on the following assumptions:

1. 25 automobiles in the pool
2. 60,000 kilometers per year per automobile
3. 8 kilometers per liter of petrol for each automobile
4. £.44 per liter of petrol
5. £.02 per kilometer for oil, minor repairs, parts, and supplies
6. £108 per automobile in outside repairs

The supervisor is unhappy with the monthly report comparing budget and actual costs for March; she claims it presents her performance unfairly. Her previous employer used flexible budgeting to compare actual costs with budgeted amounts.

1. Employing flexible-budgeting techniques, prepare a report that shows budgeted amounts, actual costs, and monthly variation for March.
2. Explain briefly the basis of your budget figure for outside repairs.

7-42 Activity-Based Flexible Budget

Cost behavior analysis for the four activity centers in the billing department of Fargo Power Company is given next.

	Traceable Costs		
Activity Center	**Variable**	**Fixed**	**Cost-Driver Activity**
Account inquiry	$ 79,910	$156,380	3,300 labor hours
Correspondence	9,800	25,584	2,800 letters
Account billing	154,377	81,400	2,440,000 lines
Bill verification	10,797	78,050	20,000 accounts

The billing department constructs a flexible budget for each activity center based on the following ranges of cost-driver activity.

Activity Center	**Cost Driver**	**Relevant Range**	
Account inquiry	Labor hours	3,000	5,000
Correspondence	Letters	2,500	3,500
Account billing	Lines	2,000,000	3,000,000
Bill verification	Accounts	15,000	25,000

1. Develop flexible-budget formulas for each of the four activity centers.
2. Compute the budgeted total cost in each activity center for each of these levels of cost-driver activity: (a) the smallest activity in the relevant range, (b) the midpoint of the relevant range, and (c) the highest activity in the relevant range.
3. Determine the total cost function for the billing department.
4. The following table gives the actual results for the billing department. Prepare a cost-control performance report comparing the flexible budget to actual results for each activity center. Compute flexible-budget variances.

Activity Center	**Actual Cost-Driver Level**	**Actual Cost**
Account inquiry	4,300 labor hours	$235,400
Correspondence	3,200 letters	38,020
Account billing	2,950,000 lines	285,000
Bill verification	23,000 accounts	105,320

7-43 Straightforward Variance Analysis

Crescent Tool Works uses a standard cost system. The month's data regarding its iron castings follow:

- Materials purchased and used, 3,300 pounds
- Direct-labor costs incurred, 5,500 hours, $42,350
- Variable-overhead costs incurred, $4,620
- Finished units produced, 1,000
- Actual materials cost, $.97 per pound
- Standard variable-overhead rate, $.80 per direct-labor hour
- Standard direct-labor cost, $8 per hour
- Standard materials cost, $1 per pound
- Standard pounds of material in a finished unit, 3
- Standard direct-labor hours per finished unit, 5

Prepare schedules of all variances, using the formats of Exhibits 7-9 and 7-11 on pages 266 and 270.

7-44 Variance Analysis

The Lucerne Chocolate Company uses standard costs and a flexible budget to control its manufacture of fine chocolates. The purchasing agent is responsible for material price variances, and the production manager is responsible for all other variances. Operating data for the past week are summarized as follows:

1. Finished units produced: 2,900 boxes of chocolates.
2. Direct materials: Purchased and used, 3,400 pounds of chocolate at 17.3 Swiss francs (CHF) per pound; standard price is CHF 18 per pound. Standard allowed per box produced is 1 pound.
3. Direct labor: Actual costs, 3,925 hours at CHF 38.6, or CHF 151,505. Standard allowed per box produced is 1.25 hours. Standard price per direct-labor hour is CHF 38.
4. Variable manufacturing overhead: Actual costs, CHF 46,675. Budget formula is CHF 11 per standard direct-labor hour.

Compute the following:
1. a. Materials purchase-price variance
   b. Materials quantity variance
   c. Direct-labor price variance
   d. Direct-labor quantity variance
   e. Variable manufacturing-overhead spending variance
   f. Variable manufacturing-overhead efficiency variance
   (Hint: For format, see the solution to the Summary Problem for Your Review, page 272.)
2. a. What is the budget allowance for direct labor?
   b. Would it be any different if production were 3,900 boxes?

7-45 Similarity of Direct-Labor and Variable-Overhead Variances

The Koh Company has had great difficulty controlling costs in Singapore during the past 3 years. Last month, the company installed a standard-cost and flexible-budget system. A condensation of results for a department follows:

	Expected Cost per Standard Direct-Labor Hour	Flexible-Budget Variance
Lubricants	$ .60	$330 F
Other supplies	.30	225 U
Rework	.60	450 U
Other indirect labor	1.50	450 U
Total variable overhead	$3.00	$795 U

F = Favorable. U = Unfavorable.

The department had initially planned to manufacture 9,000 audio speaker assemblies in 6,000 standard direct-labor hours allowed. Material shortages and a heat wave resulted in the production of 8,100 units in 5,800 actual direct-labor hours. The standard wage rate is $5.25 per hour, which was $.15 higher than the actual average hourly rate.

1. Prepare a detailed performance report with two major sections: direct labor and variable overhead.
2. Prepare a summary analysis of price and quantity variances for direct labor and spending and efficiency variances for variable overhead.
3. Explain the similarities and differences between the direct-labor and variable-overhead variances. What are some of the likely causes of the overhead variances?

7-46 Material, Labor, and Overhead Variances

Poulsbo Kayak Company makes molded plastic kayaks. Standard costs for an entry-level whitewater kayak are as follows:

Direct materials, 60 lb at $5.50/lb	$330
Direct labor, 1.5 hr at $16/hr	24
Overhead, at $12 per kayak	12
Total	$366

The overhead rate assumes production of 450 kayaks per month. The overhead cost function is $2,808 + ($5.76 × number of kayaks).

During March, Poulsbo produced 430 kayaks and had the following actual results:

Direct materials purchased and used	27,000 pounds at $5.30/lb
Direct labor	670 hours at $15.90/hr
Actual overhead	$5,335

1. Compute material, labor, and overhead variances.
2. Interpret the variances.
3. Suppose the cost function for variable overhead was $3.84 per labor hour instead of $5.76 per kayak. Compute the variable-overhead efficiency variance and the total overhead spending variance. Would these variances lead you to a different interpretation of the overhead variances from the interpretation in requirement 2? Explain.

7-47 Automation and Direct Labor as Overhead

Kilgore Precision Machining (KPM) has a highly automated manufacturing process for producing a variety of auto parts. Through the use of computer-aided manufacturing and robotics, the company has reduced its labor costs to only 5% of total manufacturing costs. Consequently, the company does not account for labor as a separate item but instead accounts for labor as part of overhead.

Consider a part used in antilock braking systems. The static budget for producing 750 units in March 20X1 is as follows:

Direct materials	$18,000*
Overhead	
Supplies	1,875
Power	1,310
Rent and other building services	2,815
Factory labor	1,500
Depreciation	4,500
Total manufacturing costs	$30,000

*3 lb/unit * $8/lb * 750 units.

Supplies and power are variable, and the other overhead items are fixed costs.
Actual costs in March 20X1 for producing 900 units of the brake part were as follows:

Direct materials	$21,840*
Overhead	
Supplies	2,132
Power	1,612
Rent and other building services	2,775
Factory labor	1,618
Depreciation	4,500
Total manufacturing costs	$34,477

*KPM purchased and used 2,800 pounds of materials at $7.80 per pound.

1. Compute (a) the direct-materials price and quantity variances and (b) the flexible-budget variance for each overhead item.
2. Comment on the way KPM accounts for and controls factory labor.

7-48 Standard Material Allowances

Chesapeake Chemical Company supplies primarily industrial users. Your superior has asked you to develop a standard product cost for a new solution the company plans to introduce.

The new chemical solution is made by combining altium and bollium, boiling the mixture, adding credix, and bottling the resulting solution in 20-liter containers. The initial mix, which is 20 liters in volume, consists of 24 kilograms of altium and 19.2 liters of bollium. A 20% reduction in volume occurs during the boiling process. The solution is then cooled slightly before adding 10 kilograms of credix to each 20-liter container; the addition of credix does not affect the total liquid volume.

The purchase prices of the raw materials used in the manufacture of this new chemical solution are as follows:

Altium	$2.20 per kilogram
Bollium	$4.60 per liter
Credix	$3.20 per kilogram

Determine the standard quantity for each of the raw materials needed to produce 20 liters of Chesapeake Chemical Company's new chemical solution and the total standard materials cost of 20 liters of the new product.

7-49 Role of Defective Units and Nonproductive Time in Setting Standards

Haig McNamee owns and operates McNamee Machining, a subcontractor to several aerospace industry contractors. When Mr. McNamee wins a bid to produce a piece of equipment, he sets standard costs for the production of the item. He then compares actual manufacturing costs with the standards to judge the efficiency of production.

In April 20X1, McNamee won a bid to produce 15,000 units of a shielded component used in a navigation device. Specifications for the component were very tight, and Mr. McNamee expected that on average 1 out of every 6 finished components would fail his final inspection, even if employees exercise every care in production. There was no way to identify defective items before production was complete. Therefore, the company had to produce 18,000 units to get 15,000 good components. The company set standards to include an allowance for the expected number of defective items.

Each final component contained 3.2 pounds of direct materials, and the company expected normal scrap from production to average an additional .4 pounds per unit. It expected the direct material to cost $11.40 per pound plus $.80 per pound for shipping and handling.

Machining of the components required close attention by skilled machinists. Each component required 4 hours of machining time. McNamee paid the machinists $20 per hour, and they worked 40-hour weeks. Of the 40 hours, employees spent an average of 32 hours directly on production. The other 8 hours consisted of time for breaks and waiting time when machines were broken down or there was no work to be done. Nevertheless, the company considered all payments to machinists to be direct labor, whether or not they represented time spent directly on production. In addition to the basic wage rate, McNamee paid fringe benefits averaging $6 per hour and payroll taxes of 10% of the basic wages.

Determine the standard cost of direct materials and direct labor for each good unit of output.

7-50 Review of Major Points in This Chapter

The following questions are based on the Dominion Company data contained in Exhibit 7-1 (page 253) and in the table showing Dominion's direct material and direct labor price and quantity standards on page 260.

1. Suppose actual production and sales were 8,000 units instead of 7,000 units. (a) Compute the sales-activity variance. Is the performance of the marketing function the sole explanation for this variance? Why? (b) Using a flexible budget, compute the budgeted contribution margin, the budgeted income, budgeted direct material, and budgeted direct labor.

2. Suppose the following were the actual results for the production of 8,000 units.

   Direct materials: 42,000 pounds were used at an actual unit price of $1.86, for a total actual cost of $78,120.

   Direct labor: 4,140 hours were used at an actual hourly rate of $16.40, for a total actual cost of $67,896.

   Compute the flexible-budget variance and the price and quantity variances for direct materials and direct labor. Present your answers in the form shown in Exhibit 7-9, page 266.

3. Evaluate Dominion Company's performance based on the variances you calculated in numbers 1 and 2.

7-51 Review Problem on Standards and Flexible Budgets; Answers Are Provided

The Des Moines Leather Company makes a variety of leather goods. It uses standard costs and a flexible budget to aid planning and control. Budgeted variable overhead at a 45,000-direct-labor-hour level is $81,000.

During April, the company had a favorable variable-overhead efficiency variance of $2,970. Material purchases were $241,900. Actual direct-labor costs incurred were $422,100. The direct-labor quantity variance was $15,300 unfavorable. The actual average wage rate was $.60 lower than the standard average wage rate.

The company uses a variable-overhead rate of 20% of standard direct-labor cost for flexible-budgeting purposes. Actual variable overhead for the month was $92,250.

Compute the following amounts; use U or F to indicate whether variances are unfavorable or favorable.

1. Standard direct-labor cost per hour
2. Actual direct-labor hours worked
3. Total direct-labor price variance
4. Total flexible budget for direct-labor costs
5. Total direct-labor flexible-budget variance
6. Variable-overhead spending variance in total

7-51 Answers to Problem 7-51

1. $9. The variable-overhead rate is $1.80, obtained by dividing $81,000 by 45,000 hours. Therefore, the direct-labor rate must be $1.80 ÷ .20 = $9.
2. 50,250 hours. Actual costs, $422,100 ÷ ($9 − $.60) = 50,250 hours.
3. $30,150 F. 50,250 actual hours × $.60 = $30,150.
4. $436,950. Quantity variance was $15,300 U. Therefore, excess hours must have been $15,300 ÷ $9 = 1,700. Consequently, standard hours allowed must be 50,250 − 1,700 = 48,550. Flexible budget = 48,550 × $9 = $436,950.
5. $14,850 F. $436,950 − $422,100 = $14,850 F; or $30,150 F − $15,300 U = $14,850 F.
6. $7,830 U. Flexible budget = 48,550 × 1.80 = $87,390. Total variance = $92,250 − $87,390 = $4,860 U. Spending variance = Total variance − Efficiency variance = $4,860 + $2,970 = $7,830 U. Check: $92,250 − (.20 × $422,100) = $7,830.

CASES

7-52 Activity and Flexible-Budget Variances

Several years ago, Methodist Hospital initiated its substance abuse program, which focused on counseling current and potential substance abusers. The program was funded by a grant from the state department of health that paid $76 per visit for counseling. Pat Leizinger, CFO of Methodist Hospital, was concerned about the substance abuse program. It had never broken even and, thus, was subsidized by the other patients in the hospital. Mr. Leizinger was preparing the hospital's budget for 20X8, and he did not like the substance abuse program's financial situation. The results for 20X7 are shown below:

Revenues ($76 per visit; 17,000 visits)	$1,292,000
Cost of services:	
Supplies	$ 114,750
Physician salaries	204,000
Nurse salaries	153,000
Overhead	676,200
Total direct cost of services	1,147,950
General and administrative expenses	194,250
Total expenses	1,342,200
Net loss	$ (50,200)

Substance Abuse Program
20X7 Results

A recent cost analysis had determined the following facts about the behavior of costs in the substance abuse program:

a. Supplies and physician and nurse salaries were totally variable with respect to number of visits within the range of 15,000–30,000.

b. Variable overhead was equal to 20% of labor costs in 20X7; the remainder of the overhead was fixed.

c. $181,500 of the general and administrative cost was fixed; the remainder varied with number of visits.

d. Costs in 20X8 are expected to behave the same as those in 20X7, except that variable-overhead costs will be 21% of labor costs in 20X8 compared to only 20% of labor costs in 20X7. (Fixed overhead costs will remain the same in 20X8 as in 20X7.)

Leizinger had been pressuring the director of the substance abuse program, Jody Lee, for the last couple of years to try to get her costs under control. Ms. Lee responded that it was a very important program for the community. Besides, the program was so close to breaking even that all it needed was a little more time and the results would be better. She predicted 18,000 visits in 20X8, an increase of nearly 6%, which would certainly make the financial picture brighter.

Leizinger agreed on the importance of the program, but he also said that pressures were building from others in Methodist Hospital to eliminate programs that were a drain on the hospital's resources. Thus, he believed that if the substance abuse program was not at least at a break-even point in 20X8, the program would be in jeopardy. He doesn't believe that even the increase of 1,000 visits would be enough to break even.

1. Compute the cost function for the substance abuse program for use in budgeting for 20X8. That is, compute the variable cost per visit and the total annual fixed cost based on the cost analysis that Leizinger conducted.

2. Compute the budgeted profit (loss) for 20X8, assuming that there will be 18,000 visits at $76 each and the costs behave as expected.

3. Suppose that Methodist Hospital accepted the budget for the substance abuse program that you computed in number 2. At the end of 20X8, the actual loss for the program was $15,500 and the actual number of visits was 18,400. Explain the difference between the amount of loss you budgeted in number 2 and the actual loss of $15,500 in as much detail as you can, given the information you have. Based on this, give a one-sentence answer to each of the following questions:
    a. What was the financial impact of the extra 400 visits?
    b. How well did the substance abuse program control its costs in 20X8?

7-53 Activity-Based Costing and Flexible Budgeting

A new printing department provides printing services to the other departments of Farmers & Mechanics Insurance Company (FMIC). Before the establishment of the in-house printing department, the departments contracted with external printers for their printing work. FMIC's printing policy is to charge departments for the variable printing costs on the basis of number of pages printed. The company recovers fixed costs in pricing of external jobs.

The first year's budget for the printing department was based on the department's expected total costs divided by the planned number of pages to be printed.

Most external government accounts and all internal jobs were expected to use only single-color printing. External commercial accounts use primarily four-color printing. FMIC estimated its variable costs based on the typical mix of single-color versus four-color printing and the average variable cost of printing a four-color page that is one-fourth graphics and three-fourths text. The expected annual costs for each division were as follows:

Department	Planned Pages Printed	Budgeted Charges	Estimated Cost per Page
Government accounts	120,000	$ 90,000	
Commercial accounts	250,000	300,000	
Internal departments	50,000	30,000	
Total	420,00 0	$420,000	$1

After the first month of operations, the printing department announced that its variable cost estimate of $1 per page was too low. The first month's actual costs were $51,000 to print 40,000 pages.

Government accounts	9,000 pages
Commercial accounts	27,500
Central administration	3,500

Two reasons were cited for higher-than-expected costs: All departments were using more printing services than planned, and government and internal jobs were using more four-color printing and more graphics than anticipated in the original variable cost projections. The printing department also argued that it would have to purchase additional four-color printing equipment if demand for four-color printing continued to grow.

1. Compare the printing department actual results, static budget, and flexible budget for the month just completed.
2. Discuss possible reasons why the printing department static budget was inaccurate.
3. An ABC study completed by a consultant indicated that printing costs are driven by number of pages (at $.35 per page), and use of colors (at $1 extra per page for color).
   a. Discuss the likely effects of using the ABC results for budgeting and control of printing department use.
   b. Discuss the assumptions regarding cost behavior implied in the ABC study results.
   c. All commercial accounts during the first month (27,500 pages) used four colors per page. Compare the cost of commercial accounts under the old and the proposed ABC system.

7-54 Analyzing Performance

Hopkins Community Hospital operates an outpatient clinic in a town several miles from the main hospital. For several years the clinic has struggled just to break even. The clinic's financial budget for 20X7 is shown below:

20X7 Budget

		Total	Per Patient
Revenues (4,000 patients at $180 each)		$ 720,000	$180
Cost of services			
Physicians	$240,000		
Nurses and technicians	180,000		
Supplies	60,000		
Overhead	252,000	732,000	183
Net loss		$ (12,000)	$ (3)

On the average, billings for each patient-visit are expected to be $180. Costs in 20X7 are expected to average $183 per patient-visit, as follows:

Physician time	$ 60
Nurse and technician time	45
Supplies	15
Overhead	63
Total	$183

The clinic is generally staffed by one physician who must be present whether or not there is a patient to see. Currently, about 10% of the physician's time is idle. The clinic employs nurses and technicians to meet the actual workload necessitated by patient appointments. Their cost averages $30 per hour, and usage varies proportionately with the number of patient-visits. Supplies cost is also variable with respect to patient-visits. Fixed overhead in 20X7 was expected to be $180,000; the remaining $72,000 of overhead varies with respect to patient visits. Included in the fixed overhead was $30,000 of hospital-wide administrative costs that the hospital allocates to the clinic and $37,500 of depreciation on the clinic's property and equipment.

Cindy Ryden, controller of Hopkins Community Hospital, reported the actual loss of $20,200 in 20X7 shown next. This represented the fifth straight year of losses. She does not feel it is right for patients in the main hospital to subsidize those using the clinic. Therefore, she suggested that unless the situation could be changed, the clinic should be closed. Brett Johnson, administrative vice president of the hospital, charged with oversight of the clinic, disagreed: "We provide a valuable service to the community with the clinic. Even if we are losing money, it is worthwhile to keep it open."

At the end of 20X7, the clinic's actual results for the year were as follows:

		Total
Revenues (3,800 patients at $180)		$ 684,000
Cost of services		
Physicians	$231,000	
Nurses and technicians (5,800 hours)	182,700	
Supplies	58,500	
Overhead	232,000	704,200
Net loss		$ (20,200)

1. Would Hopkins Community Hospital have saved money in 20X7 if the outpatient clinic was closed? Explain.
2. Explain the difference between the budgeted loss of $12,000 and the actual loss of $20,200 (that is, the static-budget variance of $8,200) in as much detail as possible. From the analysis of the 20X7 results, what actions would you suggest to avoid a loss in 20X8?

7-55 Complete Variance Analysis

Gates Video Games manufactures video game machines. Market saturation and technological innovations have caused pricing pressures that have resulted in declining profits. To stem the slide in profits until the company can introduce new products, top management has turned its attention to both manufacturing economies and increased production. To realize these objectives, management developed an incentive program to reward production managers who contribute to an increase in the number of units produced and achieve cost reductions. In addition, the company instituted a JIT purchasing program so that it purchases raw materials on an as-needed basis.

The production managers have responded to the pressure to improve manufacturing performance in several ways that have resulted in an increase over normal production levels. The video game machines put together by the assembly group require parts from both the printed circuit boards (PCB) and the reading heads (RH) departments. To attain increased production levels, the PCB and RH departments started rejecting parts from suppliers that previously would have been tested and modified to meet manufacturing standards. Preventive maintenance on machines used in the production of these parts has been postponed with only emergency repair work being performed to keep production lines moving. The maintenance staff is concerned that there will be serious breakdowns and unsafe operating conditions.

The more aggressive assembly group production supervisors have pressured maintenance personnel to attend to their machines at the expense of other groups. This has resulted in machine downtime in the PCB and RH departments which, when coupled with demands for accelerated parts delivery by the assembly department, has led to more frequent parts rejections and increased friction among departments. Gates Video Games operates under a standard-costing system. The standard costs at a production level of 24,000 units per year are in part A of Exhibit 7-13.

Exhibit 7-13
Gates Video Games

	Standard Cost per Unit		
	Quantity	Cost	Total
A. Standard Cost Report			
Direct materials:			
Housing unit	1 unit	$ 20	$ 20
Printed circuit boards (PCB)	2 boards	15	30
Reading heads (RH)	4 heads	10	40
Direct labor:			
Assembly department	2.0 hours	8	$ 16
PCB department	1.0 hour	9	9
RH department	1.5 hours	10	15
Overhead:			
Variable	4.5 hours	$ 2	$ 9
Fixed	4.5 hours	4	18
Total manufacturing cost per unit			$157
Selling and administrative:			
Fixed		$ 12	$ 12
Total standard cost per unit			$169
B. Income Statement for May			
Revenues (2,200 units)		$440,000	
Variable costs:			
Direct materials	220,400		
Direct labor	93,460		
Variable overhead	18,800		
Fixed costs:			
Overhead	37,600		
Selling and administrative	22,000		
Total costs		392,260	
Income before taxes		$ 47,740	

C. Usage Report for May

Cost Item	Actual Quantity	Actual Cost
Direct materials:		
Housing units	2,200 units	$ 44,000
Printed circuit boards	4,700 boards	75,200
Reading heads	9,200 heads	101,200
Direct labor:		
Assembly department	3,900 hours	31,200
PCB department	2,400 hours	23,760
RH department	3,500 hours	38,500
Overhead:		
Variable		18,800
Fixed		37,600
Total manufacturing costs		$370,260

Gates Video Games prepares monthly income statements based on actual expenses. Part B of Exhibit 7-13 shows the statement for May, when production and sales both reached 2,200 units. The budgeted sales price was $200 per unit, and budgeted (normal) production and sales were 24,000 units per year. Top management was surprised by the low profit in spite of increased sales for May. The original budget had called for income before taxes of $62,000, and with the added sales, the president had expected at least $68,200 of income ($6,200 more income; 200 extra units × $31 per unit).

The president called on Michelle Barber, director of cost management, to report on the reasons for the shortfall in income. After a thorough review of the data, Barber prepared the report in part C of Exhibit 7-13.

1. Prepare a budgeted income statement in contribution margin format for Gates Video Games showing why the company expected income before taxes to be $62,000.
2. Assume that you have been given Michelle Barber's task. Prepare a complete analysis explaining the reason for the difference between the original projected income before taxes of $62,000 and the actual of $47,740. Compute all the variances that are helpful in explaining this difference, and explain what you learn from the variances.

NIKE 10-K PROBLEM

7-56 Performance Standards

Examine Nike's income statement shown in condensed form as "Results of Operations" for fiscal years 2009, 2010, and 2011. Suppose that Nike used results for 2010 to set standards for 2011. Assume that cost of sales is a variable cost and that selling and administrative costs are fixed costs and that income is simply revenue − cost of sales − selling and administrative costs. Prepare a static budget based on the assumption that sales and cost of sales (variable costs) will grow by 10%. Prepare a flexible budget based on the sales level achieved for 2011. Using the actual results for 2011, determine the static-budget variances, the sales-activity variances, and the flexible-budget variances for sales, cost of sales, selling and administrative costs, and income.

EXCEL APPLICATION EXERCISE

7-57 Flexible-Budget and Sales-Activity Variances

Goal: Create an Excel spreadsheet to prepare a summary performance report that identifies flexible-budget and sales-activity variances. Use the results to answer questions about your findings.

Scenario: David Campbell Tax Services has asked you to prepare a summary performance report identifying its flexible-budget and sales-activity variances. The background data for the summary performance report appears in the Fundamental Assignment Material 7-B1. Prepare the summary performance report using a format similar to Exhibit 7-6.

When you have completed your spreadsheet, answer the following questions:

1. What caused the flexible-budget variance for sales?
2. What was the change in actual income compared to the income calculated in the static budget?
3. Can the amount in question 2 be explained by the flexible-budget and sales-activity variances? Explain.

Step-by-Step:

1. Open a new Excel spreadsheet.
2. In column A, create a bold-faced heading that contains the following:
   Row 1: Chapter 7 Decision Guideline
   Row 2: Campbell Tax Services
   Row 3: Summary Performance Report
   Row 4: Today's Date
3. Merge and center the four heading rows across columns A–H.
4. In column A, create the following row headings:
   Row 8: Clients
   Skip a row.
   Row 10: Sales
   Row 11: Variable Costs
   Row 12: Contribution Margin
   Row 13: Fixed Costs
   Skip a row.
   Row 15: Operating Income
5. Change the format of Contribution margin (row 12) and Operating income (row 15) to boldfaced headings.
   Note: Adjust width of column A to accommodate row headings.
6. In row 7, create the following bold-faced, center-justified column headings:
   Column B: Actual Results at Actual Activity
   Column C: Flexible-Budget Variances

Skip a column.
Column E: Flexible Budget at Actual Activity
Column F: Sales-Activity Variances
Skip a column.
Column H: Static Budget

7. Change the format of the column headings in row 7 to permit the titles to be displayed on multiple lines within a single cell.

| **Alignment tab:** | Wrap Text: | Checked |

Note: Adjust column widths so that headings use only two lines. Adjust row height to ensure that row is same height as adjusted headings.

8. Change format of the column width of columns D and G to a size of 2.

9. Use the scenario data to fill in client and fixed cost amounts for actual, flexible-budget, and static-budget columns as well as variable costs for the actual column.

10. Calculate variable costs for flexible-budget and static budget columns. Use appropriate formulas to calculate sales, contribution margin, and operating income amounts for actual, flexible-budget, and static-budget columns.

11. Use appropriate formulas to calculate flexible-budget variances as actual − flexible budget and sales-activity variances as flexible budget − static budget and display as absolute values.
= ABS(*variance formula*)

12. To indicate whether variances are favorable (F) or unfavorable (U), use one of the following formula templates:
For sales, margin and income variances and for client variances,
= IF(*variance formula* > 0,"F",IF(*variance formula* < 0,"U","−"))
For clients, variable and fixed cost variances,
= IF(*variance formula* < 0,"F",IF(*variance formula* > 0,"U","−"))

(Hint: Go to the "Help" text and type "copy formulas" in the search area to obtain instructions for copying formulas from one cell to another. If done correctly, you should have to type in each of the formula templates only once.)

13. Format all amounts as follows:

Number:	Category:	
	Decimal places:	0
	Symbol:	None
	Negative numbers:	Red with parentheses

14. Change the format of the amounts for sales, contribution margin, and operating income to display a dollar symbol.

15. Change the format of the operating income amounts for actual, flexible budget, and static budget to display as bold.

16. Change the format of the row headings for contribution margin and operating income to display as indented.

| **Alignment tab:** | Horizontal: | Left (Indent) |
| | Indent: | 1 |

Note: Adjust width of column A to accommodate row headings.

17. Save your work, and print a copy for your files.

Note: Print your spreadsheet using landscape format in order to ensure that all columns appear on one page.

COLLABORATIVE LEARNING EXERCISE

7-58 Setting Standards

Form groups of two to six persons each. The groups should each select a simple product or service. Be creative, but do not pick a product or service that is too complex. For those having difficulty choosing a product or service, some possibilities are as follows:

- One dozen chocolate-chip cookies
- A 10-mile taxi ride
- One copy of a 100-page course syllabus
- A machine-knit wool sweater
- A hand-knit wool sweater
- One hour of lawn mowing and fertilizing
- A hammer

1. Each student should individually estimate the direct materials and direct labor inputs needed to produce the product or service. For each type of direct material and direct labor, determine the standard quantity and standard price. Also, identify the overhead support needed, and determine the standard overhead cost of the product or service. The result should be a total standard cost for the product or service.
2. Each group should compare the estimates of its members. Where estimates differ, determine why there were differences. Did assumptions differ? Did some members have more knowledge about the product or service than others? Form a group estimate of the standard cost of the product or service.
3. After the group has agreed on a standard cost, discuss the process used to arrive at the cost. What assumptions did the group make? Is the standard cost an "ideal" standard or a "currently attainable" standard? Note how widely standard costs can vary depending on assumptions and knowledge of the production process.

INTERNET EXERCISE

7-59 Flexible Budgets at Hershey Food Corporation

This chapter focused on flexible budgets and variance analysis. While the information used to determine both of these is generally for internal purposes only and not available to an outsider, it is possible to look at what information a firm reports and, based on that information, to make some judgments about what occurred.

1. Look at the Hershey Company home page at www.hersheys.com. Who is Hershey's home page directed to? What are the most prominent items on the page? Where do you find financial information?
2. Click on "Corporate Information," then on "Investors," and then "Financial Reports." Examine Hershey's income statement from its most recent 10-K in "SEC Filings." Prepare a static budget for income before income taxes based on the assumption that net sales and variable costs are expected to increase by 4% for the next fiscal year. Assume that cost of sales is the only variable cost and that all other costs are fixed costs. (The assumption that all other costs—including items such as realignment and impairment charges, gains on sales of businesses, and other such one-time charges—are fixed costs, is a simplification. A more realistic assumption might be that these are nonrecurring costs.)
3. Now, suppose that selling prices were exactly as budgeted in question 2, but sales and variable costs actually increased by 6% and fixed costs increased by 1%. Determine the static-budget variance, the sales-activity variance, and the flexible-budget variance for operating income.

Management Control Systems and Responsibility Accounting

LEARNING OBJECTIVES

When you have finished studying this chapter, you should be able to:

1. Describe the relationship of management control systems to organizational goals.

2. Explain the importance of evaluating performance and describe how it impacts motivation, goal congruence, and employee effort.

3. Develop performance measures and use them to monitor the achievements of an organization.

4. Use responsibility accounting to define an organizational subunit as a cost center, a profit center, or an investment center.

5. Prepare segment income statements for evaluating profit and investment centers using the contribution margin and controllable-cost concepts.

6. Measure performance against nonfinancial performance measures such as quality, cycle time, and productivity.

7. Use a balanced scorecard to integrate financial and nonfinancial measures of performance.

8. Describe the difficulties of management control in service and nonprofit organizations.

▶ HEALTH NET

It's 2:30 AM. You don't feel well. Should you call your doctor? Go to the emergency room? Is what you're feeling really something to worry about? What you need is good quality health care and you need it now, not tomorrow morning, and you do not want to worry about its cost. Sound familiar? This is a dilemma that we have all faced at some time. One health-care organization that has a solution is **Health Net**, one of the largest managed health-care organizations in the United States. With approximately 7,500 employees and 2011 revenues of about $12 billion, it provides coverage to 5.6 million health plan members.

Health-care organizations must compete just as any other business, offering high-quality health care at an affordable cost. To maintain its competitive advantage, Health Net undertook a major information systems development program called "fourth generation medical management." According to Dr. Malik Hasan, former chairman and CEO, Health Net created this new management control system "because the greatest opportunity for increasing overall quality and decreasing the cost of health care lies in managing patient care by seamlessly linking the entire health care delivery system electronically." The system "gives physicians and health care providers instant, user-friendly electronic access to comprehensive information about a patient's medical history and the best clinical treatments recommended."

The result? A fast and preapproved referral to the best clinical resource, whether it be a specialist, the emergency room or urgent care center, your regular physician, or safe self-care. In other words, a satisfied customer! And as a bonus, costs are reduced. As Medical Director John Danaher, MD, explains, "Paper charting and duplicative lab and radiology tests are eliminated."

This chapter builds on concepts developed in previous chapters to explore how managers blend the individual tools of management accounting to help achieve organizational goals. Tools such as activity-based costing, relevant costing, budgeting, and variance analysis are useful by themselves. They are most useful, however, when they are parts of an integrated system—a comprehensive plan to coordinate and evaluate all the activities of the organization's value chain. Just as in the case of Health Net, managers of most organizations today realize that long-run success requires a focus on cost, quality, and service—the three components of the competitive edge. This chapter considers how the management control system helps managers achieve such a focus. As you will see, no single management control system is inherently superior to another. The "best" system for any organization is the one that most consistently leads to actions that meet the organization's goals and objectives. ■

© Stockbroker/Alamy

Management Control Systems

A **management control system** is an integrated set of techniques for gathering and using information to make planning and control decisions, for motivating employee behavior, and for evaluating performance. A well-designed management control system supports and coordinates the decision-making process and motivates individuals throughout the organization to act in concert. It also facilitates forecasting and budgeting. An effective management control system should

- clearly define and communicate the organization's goals,
- ensure that managers and employees understand the specific actions required to achieve organizational goals,
- communicate results of actions across the organization, and
- motivate managers and employees to achieve the organization's goals.

Exhibit 8-1 describes elements of the planning and control processes. As we pointed out in Chapter 3, planning and control are so strongly interrelated that it is somewhat artificial to separate them in practice. To the extent we can separate them, planning includes defining goals (A) and establishing and carrying out plans to achieve the goals (B). Control includes measuring and reporting results (C) and performance evaluation (D). The clockwise ordering of the elements represents the order that managers would naturally follow when designing and evaluating the management control system. However, once an organization has implemented the control system, it continues to adapt and revise the interrelated elements through feedback and learning. For example, the organization may revise the measures used to monitor and report in C to better fit with the goals in A. Similarly, it might realign the performance evaluation system in D to better fit with the specific plans and objectives in B. We will refer to Exhibit 8-1 often as we consider the design and operation of management control systems.

Doctors and managers at Health Net use a state-of-the-art medical management system and management control system to offer high-quality health care at an affordable price.

management control system
An integrated set of techniques for gathering and using information to make planning and control decisions, for motivating employee behavior, and for evaluating performance.

Management Control Systems and Organizational Goals

The first and most basic component in a management control system is the organization's goals. Top managers set organization-wide goals, performance measures, and targets. These goals provide a long-term framework around which an organization will form its comprehensive plan for positioning itself in the market. Goals address the question in Exhibit 8-1, "What do we want to achieve?" However, goals without performance measures do not motivate managers.

A basic adage of management control is that "you get what you measure." Because measures of performance set direction and motivate managers' decisions, every performance measure should be consistent with organizational goals. Otherwise, managers who achieve high performance measures may not create value for the company and its owners. An ideal management control system should include at least one performance measure related to every goal. The book *Cracking the Value Code* states this succinctly when it says that we tend to "value what we measure but we do not always measure what we value."

Exhibit 8-1
The Management Control System

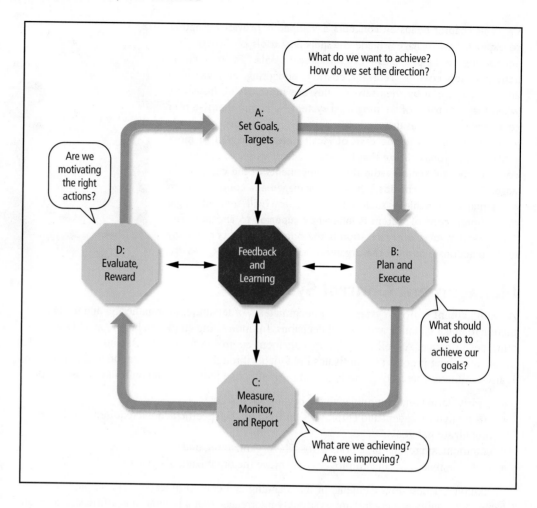

To illustrate, suppose a hotel such as Arizona-based Scottsdale Luxury Suites has the following organizational goals and related performance measures:

Organizational Goals	Performance Measures
Exceed guest expectations	• Customer satisfaction index • Number of repeat stays
Maximize revenue yield	• Occupancy rate • Average room rate • Income before fixed costs
Focus on innovation	• New products/services implemented per year • Number of employee suggestions

The company sets quantifiable targets for each of the measures. For example, the target for occupancy rate might be "at least 70%." Note that every goal has at least one performance measure, and every measure is related to at least one goal.

Exhibit 8-2 illustrates how managers set goals and objectives and develop related performance measures for the organization. Performance measures become more specific as we move to lower levels of the organization. For example, higher-level managers work with subordinates within each business unit to select specific short-term actions (or activities) that managers can carry out, along with observable performance measures. One approach to selecting these actions and measures is for top managers to identify **key success factors**—characteristics or attributes that managers must achieve in order to drive the organization toward its goals. For example, at Scottsdale Luxury Suites, a key success factor for the goal to exceed guest expectations might be timeliness. This key success factor suggests that Scottsdale Luxury Suites should consider

key success factors

Characteristics or attributes that managers must achieve in order to drive the organization toward its goals.

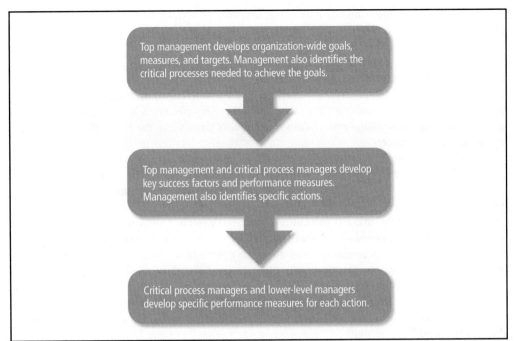

Exhibit 8-2
Translating Goals and Objectives into Performance Measures

specific actions, such as implementing an express check-in system. In addition, it should measure timeliness by using performance measures, such as time to check in, time to check out, and response time to guest requests (for example, number of rings before someone at the front desk answers the telephone).

Balancing various goals is an important part of designing a management control system. Managers often face trade-offs. For example, a manager may meet a goal of increased customer satisfaction by establishing a more generous policy for accepting returned merchandise. However, this policy will also impose additional costs that decrease short-term profitability. Choosing the best trade-off between short-term profitability and long-term customer satisfaction is often difficult, especially when the long-term benefits of increased customer satisfaction are hard to predict.

Designing Management Control Systems

To design a management control system that meets the organization's needs, managers must identify what motivates employees, develop performance measures based on these motivations, and establish a monitoring and reporting structure for these measures. Let's look at each of these.

Motivating Employees

An important goal of the management control system is to motivate employees to work in the best interests of the organization. A good management control system fosters both goal congruence and managerial effort. A system fosters **goal congruence** when employees, responding to the incentives created by the control system, make decisions that help meet the overall goals of the organization. To be effective, goal congruence must be accompanied by **managerial effort**— exertion toward a goal or objective—including not only working harder or faster but also working smarter. It includes all conscious actions (such as supervising, planning, and analysis) that result in more efficiency and effectiveness.

As we saw in Exhibit 8-1, the challenge of management control system design is to induce (or at least not discourage) employee decisions that achieve organizational goals. For example, an organization may identify continuous improvement in employee efficiency and effectiveness as one of its goals. Employees, however, might perceive that continuous improvements will result in tighter standards, faster pace of work, and loss of jobs. Even though they may agree with management that continuous improvements are competitively necessary, management should not expect them to exert effort for continuous improvements unless rewards are in place to make this effort in their own best interests.

Objective 2

Explain the importance of evaluating performance and describe how it impacts motivation, goal congruence, and employee effort.

goal congruence

A condition where employees, responding to the incentives created by the control system, make decisions that help meet the overall goals of the organization.

managerial effort

Exertion toward a goal or objective, including all conscious actions (such as supervising, planning, and thinking) that result in more efficiency and effectiveness.

As another example, students may enroll in a college course because their goal is to learn about management accounting. The faculty and the students share the same goal, but goal congruence is not enough. Faculty also introduce a grading system to reward student effort. Grading is a form of performance evaluation, similar to organizations using management control reports for raises, promotions, and other forms of rewards. Performance evaluation improves effort because most individuals tend to perform better when performance reports lead directly to personal rewards. Thus, manufacturers that set quality improvements as critical organizational goals, such as **Allen-Bradley** and **Corning**, put quality targets into the bonus plans of top managers and factory workers.

motivation

The drive that creates effort and action toward a goal.

Motivation—the drive that creates effort and action toward a goal—is key to management control. Yet employees differ widely in their motivations. This makes the system designer's task complex and ill-structured. Each system must fit the specific organizational environment and behavioral characteristics of the employees. The system designer must align individuals' self-interests with the goals of the organization. Thus, the designer must predict the motivational impact of a particular system—how it will cause people to respond—and compare it to the motivational impact of other potential systems. Designing performance measures is not a back-office accounting task. It requires direction from top management and the direct involvement of those affected. Stephen Kaufman, former chairman of the board of **Arrow Electronics** put it this way: "It's very difficult to define the right metric and anticipate exactly how your people will react to it. Your best chance of knowing whether it will have the intended effect is to talk to the people directly involved."

All management control tools, such as budgets and variances, should constructively influence behavior. These tools are most effective when managers use them positively to encourage employees to improve performance, rather than negatively to punish, place blame, or find fault. Used negatively, these tools pose a threat to employees, who will resist the use of such techniques. Critics have pointed to **Enron**'s management control system as a major cause of the company's problems. Employees were heavily rewarded for good performance. More importantly, the employees who were ranked lowest at each evaluation were fired. This created intense competition, which at first seemed to create exceptional performance levels for the company. Later, it became clear that the pressure for good performance caused some employees to use unethical methods to increase their performance measures, which eventually led to the demise of the company.

Developing Performance Measures

Objective 3

Develop performance measures and use them to monitor the achievements of an organization.

For most organizations, an effective management control system requires multiple performance measures, including both financial and nonfinancial measures, where the measures have the following characteristics:

1. Reflect key actions and activities that relate to the goals of the organization
2. Affected by actions of managers and employees
3. Readily understood by employees
4. Reasonably objective and easily measured
5. Used consistently and regularly in evaluating and rewarding managers and employees
6. Balance long-term and short-term concerns

Sometimes accountants and managers focus too much on financial measures—such as operating budgets, profit targets, or required return on investment—because the accounting system readily produces such measures. Further, it is often difficult to construct performance measures for nonfinancial goals such as customer satisfaction, improvements in quality, environmental stewardship, social responsibility, and organizational learning, which many companies list as key goals. However, well-designed management control systems develop and report both financial and nonfinancial measures of performance because "You can't manage something you can't measure."

Nonfinancial measures often motivate employees toward achieving important performance goals. For example, **AT&T Universal Card Services**, which received the prestigious Baldrige National Quality Award (presented by the U.S. Department of Commerce), used 18 performance measures for its customer inquiries process. These measures include average speed of

Business First

Performance Measures in Practice

An organization's performance measures depend on its goals and objectives. For example, a software company and an auto manufacturer have different goals and objectives and therefore have different performance measures. The measures also must span a variety of key success factors for the organization. Performance measures too focused on one aspect of performance may foster neglect of other important factors.

Let's look at a classic management control system, the one developed by General Electric in the 1950s. The system focused on eight "key result areas," as GE called them:

Financial Key Result Areas
1. Profitability
2. Productivity
3. Market position

Nonfinancial Key Result Areas
4. Product leadership
5. Personnel development
6. Employee attitudes
7. Public responsibility
8. Balance between short-run and long-range goals

Measures in each of these eight areas are just as relevant today as in the 1950s. These are clearly long-run strategic goals. Measures might change as an organization adapts the means of achieving the goals, but the basic framework of a management control system does not need to change as management fads come and go.

A more recent example is Southwest Airlines. The mission of Southwest Airlines is "dedication to the highest quality of customer service delivered with a sense of warmth, friendliness, individual pride, and company spirit." Yet, until recently, the company focused mainly on financial measures in evaluating managers. Recently, Southwest introduced nonfinancial measures into the mix, including the following:

- Load factor (percentage of seats occupied)
- Utilization factors on aircraft and personnel
- On-time performance
- Available seat miles
- Denied boarding rate
- Lost bag reports per 10,000 passengers
- Flight cancellation rate
- Employee head count
- Customer complaints per 10,000 passengers

By including nonfinancial measures, Southwest focuses managers' attention on the key success factors that relate most closely to Southwest's mission and goals.

Sources: David Solomons, *Divisional Performance: Measurement and Control* (Homewood, IL: Irwin, 1965); and Southwest Airlines Web site (www.southwest.com).

---

answer, abandon rate, and application processing time (3 days compared to the industry average of 34 days).

Financial measures often are lagging indicators that arrive too late to help prevent problems and ensure the organization's health. The effects of poor nonfinancial performance (for example, lack of organizational learning and low customer satisfaction) may not show up in the financial measures until the company has lost considerable ground. Many companies now stress management of the activities that drive revenues and costs, rather than waiting to explain the revenues or costs themselves. Superior financial performance usually follows from superior nonfinancial performance. Examples of both financial and nonfinancial measures are in the accompanying Business First box.

Monitoring and Reporting Results

Notice that Exhibit 8-1 has feedback and learning at the center of the management control system. Organization-wide learning is fundamental to gaining and maintaining financial strength. Some management experts have said that the only sustainable competitive advantage is the rate at which a company's managers learn. Harley-Davidson, a company with 2011 sales of about $5.3 billion, emphasizes learning for operational excellence—eliminating waste, improving quality, and helping drive customer satisfaction.

Once a company has superior intellectual capital, how can it best maintain its leadership? Exhibit 8-3 shows how organizational learning leads to financial strength. Measures such as training time, employee turnover, and staff satisfaction scores on employee surveys monitor organizational learning. The result of learning is continuous process improvement. Measures such as lead time, number of defects (quality), and activity costs can assess improvement. Customers will value improved response time, higher quality, and lower prices and will increase their demand for products and services. Increased demand, combined with lower costs to make and deliver products and services, results in improved product profitability and earnings.

Exhibit 8-3

The Components of a
Successful Organization and
Measures of Achievement

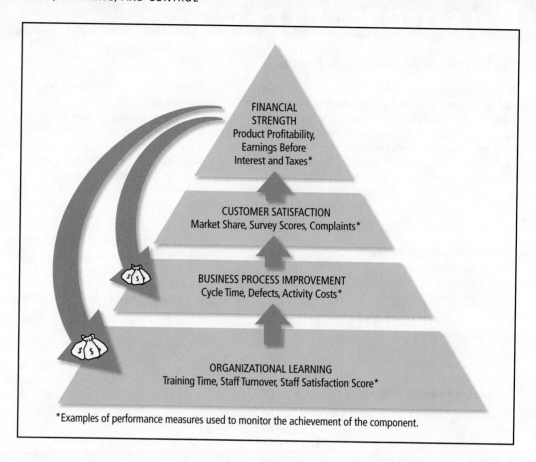

*Examples of performance measures used to monitor the achievement of the component.

Successful organizations continuously repeat this cycle, where learning leads to process improvements, which lead to increased customer satisfaction, which leads to improved financial strength, which provides the financial resources required to begin a new cycle of learning and process improvements.

There are no guarantees that each of the components automatically follows from success at the previous component. If efforts are not coordinated throughout the value chain, the cause-effect links can be broken. For example, new and improved products or services may fail if marketing and distribution techniques do not place them at the location desired by the customer. As another example, development of a great Web site does no good if customers never visit the site. The point is that improvement in business processes must be coordinated across all parts of the value chain.

Another message from Exhibit 8-3 is that a key driver of enterprise performance is the culture within the company that fosters continual learning and growth at all levels of management. It is not sufficient to use money to train managers without making sure that the resulting learning translates into improved processes, products, and services. This requires a culture of learning that motivates managers to translate learning into growth.

General Electric provides a good example of the application of the enterprise learning culture. With sales of nearly $150 billion, GE has demonstrated a remarkable ability to generate formidable profits with products ranging from aircraft engines to medical imaging to business and consumer financing. GE employs more than 300,000 people worldwide. In 2012, GE was fifteenth on *Fortune* magazine's "Most Admired Company in America," and has consistently been at or near the top of the list throughout the last decade. Many of the company's divisions dominate their markets.

Just before he retired, former CEO John Welch attributed GE's success to

> *. . . .a General Electric culture that values the contributions of every individual, thrives on learning, thirsts for the better idea, and has the flexibility and speed to put the better idea into action every day. We are a learning company, a company that studies its own successes and failures and those of others—a company that has the self-confidence and the resources to take big swings and pursue numerous opportunities based on winning ideas*

and insights, regardless of their source. That appetite for learning, and the ability to act quickly on that learning, will provide GE with what we believe is an insurmountable and sustainable competitive advantage.

Exactly what did John Welch mean by the "ability to act quickly on that learning"? According to Welch, GE "opened [its] culture up to ideas from everyone, everywhere, killed NIH (Not Invented Here) thinking, decimated the bureaucracy, and made boundaryless behavior a reflexive and natural part of our culture, thereby creating the learning culture." His successor, Jeff Immelt, points out another important part of the GE learning culture—openness to dropping old management approaches in favor of new and better techniques: "Most people inside GE learn from the past but have a healthy disrespect for history. They have an ability to live in the moment and not be burdened by the past, which is extremely important."

Weighing Costs and Benefits

The designer of a management control system must always weigh the costs and benefits of various alternatives. Benefits and costs of management control systems are often difficult to measure, and both may become apparent only after implementation. For example, the director of accounting policy of **Citicorp** stated that, after using a very detailed management control system for several years, the system proved to be too costly to administer relative to the perceived benefits. Accordingly, Citicorp returned to a simpler, less costly—though less detailed—management control system. In contrast, **Home Depot** added detail in the form of additional metrics to its management control system. When employees asked then-CEO Bob Nardelli why they should use the new metrics, he compared the metrics to gauges in a car: "Why do you need a gas gauge? Why do you need a speedometer?" He believed the metrics were worth the cost because they help top management know what is occurring throughout the company.

Summary Problem for Your Review

PROBLEM

The Blue Harbor Inn is developing performance measures for each of its major goals. Top management established an organization-wide goal to "exceed guest expectations." Among the key success factors are timeliness of customer service and quality of personalized service. Patty Bowen, vice president of sales, is the manager responsible for the actions required to meet the goal of exceeding guest expectations. She has already identified one action (objective) for the coming year—upgrade customer service department capabilities.

1. Identify several possible performance measures for the quality-of-personalized-service key success factor.
2. Recommend several specific actions or activities associated with upgrading customer service department capabilities that would drive Luxury Suites toward its goal of exceeding customer expectations.

SOLUTION

1. Performance measures for the quality of personalized service might include the number of changes to registration, rating on the "friendly, knowledgeable staff" question on the guest survey, number of complaints, percentage of return guests, and percentage of customers with completed customer profile (which profiles the special needs of customers).
2. Specific actions or activities might include training employees, implementing a call checklist (list of services and options available to the guest) and monitoring compliance with the list, developing a customer satisfaction survey, and reengineering the guest registration and reservation processes.

Controllability and Measurement of Financial Performance

Management control systems often distinguish between controllable and uncontrollable events and between controllable and uncontrollable costs. These terms refer to relative rather than absolute controllability—no cost is completely under the control of a manager. A **controllable cost** is one that a manager's decisions and actions can influence to a reasonable extent. An **uncontrollable cost** is any cost that management cannot reasonably affect within a given time span. For example, Dow Chemical is likely to consider the cost of the crude oil used to make various chemicals as uncontrollable by the manager of a chemical factory because the manager cannot control the market price of crude oil. On the other hand, Dow Chemical is likely to consider labor costs as controllable by the factory manager even though there are some aspects of labor costs that are not controlled by the manager, such as the effects of union contracts on pay rates and labor usage.

The distinction between controllable and uncontrollable costs is used in evaluating the performance of a manager. Costs that are completely uncontrollable provide no insight into a manager's decisions and actions because, by definition, manager actions will not affect uncontrollable costs. In contrast, controllable costs provide evidence about costs that are affected by the manager's decisions.

controllable cost

Any cost that a manager's decisions and actions can influence.

uncontrollable cost

Any cost that the management of a responsibility center cannot affect within a given time span.

Identifying Responsibility Centers

Designers of management control systems identify the responsibilities of each manager by establishing responsibility centers based on what a manager can control. A **responsibility center** is a set of activities and resources assigned to a manager, a group of managers, or other employees. A set of machines and machining activities, for example, may be a responsibility center for a production supervisor. The full production department may be a responsibility center for the department head. Finally, the entire organization may be a responsibility center for the president. In some organizations, groups of employees share management responsibility to create wide "ownership" of management decisions, to allow creative decision making, and to prevent one person's concern (or lack of concern) over risk from dominating decisions.

An effective management control system gives each manager responsibility for a group of activities and actions and then, as Exhibit 8-1 shows, monitors and reports on (1) the results of the activities and (2) the manager's influence on those results. Such a system has intrinsic appeal for most top managers (because it helps them delegate decision making and frees them to focus on more strategic issues) and lower-level managers (who value the decision-making autonomy they inherit). Thus, system designers apply **responsibility accounting** to identify what parts of the organization have primary responsibility for each action, develop performance measures and targets, and design reports of these measures by responsibility center. Responsibility centers usually have multiple goals and actions that the management control system monitors. We classify responsibility centers as cost centers, profit centers, or investment centers based on their managers' primary financial responsibilities.

COST, PROFIT, AND INVESTMENT CENTERS   In a **cost center**, managers are responsible for costs only. A cost center may encompass an entire department, or a department may contain several cost centers. For example, although one manager may supervise an assembly department, the department may contain several assembly lines and each assembly line may be considered a separate cost center. Likewise, within each line, each separate machine may be its own cost center. The determination of the number of cost centers depends on cost-benefit considerations—do the benefits (for planning, control, and evaluation) of smaller, more numerous cost centers exceed the higher costs of reporting?

In a **profit center** managers are responsible for controlling revenues as well as costs—that is, profitability. Despite the name, a profit center can exist in nonprofit organizations (though it might not be referred to as such) when a responsibility center receives revenues for its services. For example, the Western Area Power Authority (WAPA) is charged with recovering its costs of operations through sales of power to electric utilities in the western United States. Therefore, WAPA is a profit center responsible for both revenues and costs, though its objective is not to maximize profits but rather to break even.

responsibility center

A set of activities and resources assigned to a manager, a group of managers, or other employees.

responsibility accounting

Identifying what parts of the organization have primary responsibility for each action, developing performance measures and targets, and designing reports of these measures by responsibility center.

cost center

A responsibility center in which managers are responsible for costs only.

profit center

A responsibility center in which managers are responsible for revenues as well as costs—that is, profitability.

An **investment center** adds responsibility for investment to profit-center responsibilities. Investment-center success depends on both income and invested capital, measured by relating income generated to the value of the capital employed.

Systems designers must understand operating processes and cost behavior to help identify responsibility for controllable costs. For example, by isolating activities and related cost drivers, activity-based costing can help to point out controllable costs. Procter & Gamble credited its activity-based management control system with identifying controllable costs in one of its detergent divisions, which led to major strategic changes.

Responsibility center managers are often able to explain their center's uncontrollable costs, even in situations where they are not held responsible for these uncontrollable costs. For example, an importer of grapes from Chile to the United States suffered a sudden loss of sales several years ago after a few grapes were found to contain poisonous cyanide. Because the tampering was beyond the import manager's control, the manager was responsible for efficiency (the flexible-budget variance [see Chapter 8]) but not for the effects of activity volume (the sales-activity variance). Even though he was not held responsible for the sales-activity variance, the manager was in the best position to provide an explanation for the variance because he had the best information about the reasons for the decline in sales.

Contribution Margin

Many organizations combine the contribution approach to measuring income with responsibility accounting—that is, they report by cost behavior as well as by degrees of controllability. Exhibit 8-4 is an organization chart showing selected units of a retail grocery company like Safeway, Kroger, or SuperValu. Exhibit 8-5 illustrates the contribution approach to measuring financial performance of the various units shown on the organization chart. **Segments** are responsibility centers for which a company develops separate measures of revenues and costs. Exhibit 8-5 provides perspective on how a management-control system report can stress cost behavior, controllability, manager performance, and responsibility center performance simultaneously.

Line (a) in Exhibit 8-5 shows the contribution margin, sales revenues less variable expenses. The contribution margin ratio, defined as the ratio of contribution margin to sales, is especially helpful for predicting the impact on income of short-run changes in sales volume. Managers may quickly calculate expected changes in income by multiplying the contribution margin ratio by the expected change in dollar sales. For example, the contribution margin ratio for meats in the West Division is $180 \div \$900 = .20$. A $1,000 increase in sales of meats in the West Division should produce a $200 increase in contribution margin and income ($.20 \times \$1,000 = \$200$) if there are no changes in selling prices, variable operating expenses per unit, fixed costs, or mix of sales.

investment center
A responsibility center where managers are responsible for investment as well as profits.

segments
Responsibility centers for which a company develops separate measures of revenues and costs.

Exhibit 8-4
Retail Grocery Company Organization Chart

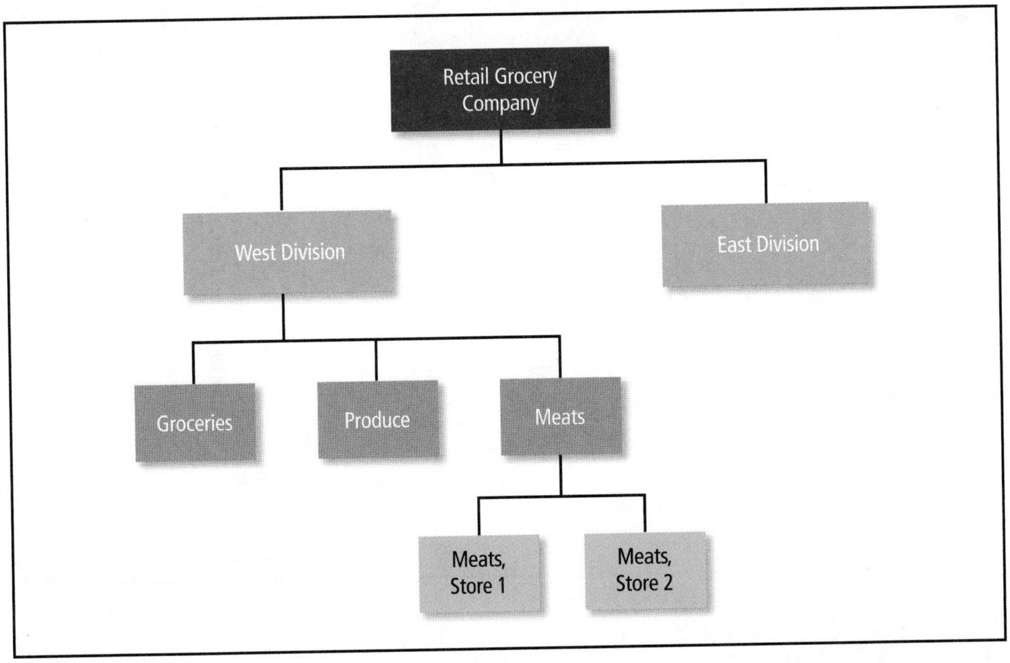

	Company as a Whole	Company Breakdown into Two Divisions		Breakdown of West Division Only				Breakdown of West Division, Meats Only		
		East Division	West Division	Not Allocated†	Groceries	Produce	Meats	Not Allocated†	Store 1	Store 2
Net sales	$4,000	$1,500	$2,500	—	$1,300	$300	$900	—	$600	$300
Variable costs										
Cost of merchandise sold	$3,000	$1,100	$1,900	—	$1,000	$230	$670	—	$450	$220
Variable operating costs‡	260	100	160	—	100	10	50	—	35	15
Total variable costs	$3,260	$1,200	$2,060	—	$1,100	$240	$720	—	$485	$235
(a) Contribution margin	$740	$300	$440	—	$200	$60	$180	—	$115	$65
Less: Fixed costs controllable by segment managers§	260	100	160	$20	40	10	90	$30	35	25
(b) Contribution controllable by segment managers	$480	$200	$280	$(20)	$160	$50	$90	$(30)	$80	$40
Less: Fixed costs controllable by others¶	200	90	110	20	40	10	40	10	22	8
(c) Contribution by segments	$280	$110	$170	$(40)	$120	$40	$50	$(40)	$58	$32
Less: Unallocated costs‖	100									
(d) Income before income taxes	$180									

*Three different types of segments are illustrated here: divisions, product lines, and stores. As you read across, note that the focus becomes narrower; from East and West divisions to West Division only, to meats in West Division only.

†Only those costs clearly identifiable to a product line or store should be allocated.

‡Principally wages and payroll-related costs.

§Examples are certain advertising, sales promotions, salespersons' salaries, management consulting, training, and supervision costs.

¶Examples are depreciation, property taxes, insurance, and perhaps the segment manager's salary.

‖These costs are not clearly or practically allocable to any segment except by some highly questionable allocation base.

Exhibit 8-5
Retail Grocery Store
Contribution Approach: Model Income Statement by Segments *(thousands of dollars)*

Contribution Controllable by Segment Managers

Designers of management control systems distinguish between the segment as an economic investment and the manager as a decision maker. For instance, an extended period of drought coupled with an aging population may adversely affect the desirability of continued economic investment in a ski resort, but the resort manager may nonetheless be doing an excellent job under these adverse circumstances.

Objective 5

Prepare segment income statements for evaluating profit and investment centers using the contribution margin and controllable-cost concepts.

Exhibit 8-5 separates costs by controllability. The manager of meats at Store 1 may have influence over some local advertising but not other advertising, some fixed salaries but not other salaries, and so forth. Moreover, the meat manager at both the division and store levels may have zero influence over store depreciation or the president's salary. Managers on all levels help explain the total segment contribution, but they are responsible only for the controllable contribution. Note that we deduct the fixed costs controllable by the segment managers from the contribution margin to obtain the contribution controllable by segment managers. These controllable costs are usually discretionary fixed costs such as local advertising and some salaries.

As we move to the right in Exhibit 8-5, we see allocations of only part of the fixed costs to lower levels in the organization. For example, consider the line with fixed costs controllable by segment managers. Of the $160,000 fixed costs that the West Division manager controls, groceries, produce, and meat departments control only $140,000. We do not allocate the remaining $20,000 of West Division fixed costs because they are not controllable farther down in the organization chart. That is, the West Division manager controls all $160,000 of fixed costs, but subordinates (grocery, produce, and meat managers) control only $140,000. Similarly, the meats manager controls $90,000 of fixed costs, but subordinates at stores 1 and 2 control only $35,000 and $25,000, respectively.

Contribution by Segments

The contribution by segments, line (c) in Exhibit 8-5, is an attempt to approximate the financial performance of the segment, as distinguished from the financial performance of its manager, which we measure in line (b). The "fixed costs controllable by others" typically include committed costs (such as depreciation and property taxes) and discretionary costs (such as the segment manager's salary). Although the segment manager does not control these costs, they are necessary for the operation of the segment.

Unallocated Costs

Exhibit 8-5 shows "unallocated costs" immediately before line (d). These costs might include central corporate costs, such as the costs of top management and some corporate-level services (for example, legal and taxation). When an organization cannot find a persuasive cause-and-effect or activity-based justification for allocating such costs, it generally should not allocate them to segments.

Summary

The correct classification of costs as illustrated in Exhibit 8-5 is sometimes ambiguous. Determining controllability is a problem when a company allocates service department costs to other departments. Should a store manager bear a part of the division headquarters' costs? If so, how much and on what basis? How much, if any, store depreciation or lease expenses should we deduct in computing the controllable contribution? There are no universally correct answers to these questions. Each organization makes choices that balance costs and benefits. (This differs from the situation in external accounting systems, where tax or financial reporting regulations usually specify the required classification of costs.)

Because of the subjectivity involved in classification of costs, measures of financial performance such as those illustrated in Exhibit 8-5 are subjective. The calculation of the contribution margin near the top of the report tends to be the most objective, because managers can usually objectively identify and assign variable costs. As you read downward in the report, the allocations become increasingly subjective, and the resulting measures of contributions become more subject to dispute. Nonetheless, many organizations find that allocation of costs to units makes managers more aware of the costs of the entire organization and leads to better organizational cost control.

Making Managerial Decisions

Managers should try to distinguish between controllable and uncontrollable costs when designing segment financial reports. For each of the following costs of a suburban **Wal-Mart** store, indicate whether it is a variable cost, fixed cost controllable by segment managers, fixed cost controllable by someone other than the segment manager, or a cost the company normally does not allocate:

Property taxes
Supervision of local sales staff
Depreciation of store
Cost of goods sold
Local store advertising
Corporate-level advertising
Corporate-level public relations
Temporary sales labor

Answer

Variable costs are generally controllable by the store manager. Cost of goods sold and temporary sales labor are examples.

Fixed costs controllable by the segment (store) manager include local store advertising and supervision of the local sales staff. The store manager usually decides the appropriate level for these costs.

Fixed costs controllable by those other than the store manager include property taxes and depreciation of the store. These costs relate directly to the store, but the store manager cannot change them.

Unallocated costs include corporate-level advertising and public relations. These costs have a tenuous link to the store.

Summary Problem for Your Review

PROBLEM

The Book & Game Company has two bookstores: Auntie's and Merlin's. Each store has managers who have a great deal of decision authority over their store. Advertising, market research, acquisition of books, legal services, and other staff functions, however, are handled by a central office. The Book & Game Company's current accounting system allocates all costs to the stores. Results for 20X1 were as follows:

Item	Total Company	Auntie's	Merlin's
Sales revenue	$ 700,000	$ 350,000	$ 350,000
Cost of merchandise sold	450,000	225,000	225,000
Gross margin	250,000	125,000	125,000
Operating expenses			
Salaries and wages	63,000	30,000	33,000
Supplies	45,000	22,500	22,500
Rent and utilities	60,000	40,000	20,000
Depreciation	15,000	7,000	8,000
Allocated staff costs	60,000	30,000	30,000
Total operating expenses	243,000	129,500	113,500
Operating income (loss)	$ 7,000	$ (4,500)	$ 11,500

Each bookstore manager makes decisions that affect salaries and wages, supplies, and depreciation. In contrast, rent and utilities are beyond the managers' control because the managers did not choose the location or the size of the store.

Supplies are variable costs. Variable salaries and wages are equal to 8% of the cost of merchandise sold; the remainder of salaries and wages is a fixed cost. Rent, utilities, and depreciation also are fixed costs. Staff costs represent the cost of activities performed by the central office. Events at the individual bookstores do not affect staff costs; nevertheless, Book & Game Company allocates staff costs as a proportion of sales revenue.

1. Using the contribution approach, prepare a performance report that distinguishes the performance of each bookstore from that of the bookstore manager.
2. Evaluate the financial performance of each bookstore.
3. Evaluate the financial performance of each manager.

SOLUTION

1. See Exhibit 8-6.
2. We can evaluate the financial performances of the bookstores (that is, segments of the company) using the line "contribution by bookstore." Merlin's has a substantially higher contribution, despite equal levels of sales revenues in the two stores. The major reason for this advantage is that Merlin's pays less for rent and utilities.
3. We can evaluate the financial performance of the managers using the line "contribution controllable by managers." By this measure, the performance of Auntie's manager is better than that of Merlin's. The contribution margin is the same for each store, but Merlin's manager paid $4,000 more in controllable fixed costs than did Auntie's manager. Note that the additional fixed costs could be beneficial in the long run. What is missing from each of these segment reports is the year's master budget and a flexible budget, which would be the best benchmark for evaluating both bookstores and bookstore managers.

Item	Total Company	Auntie's	Merlin's
Sales revenue	$700,000	$350,000	$350,000
Variable costs			
Cost of merchandise sold	450,000	225,000	225,000
Salaries and wages—variable portion	36,000	18,000	18,000
Supplies	45,000	22,500	22,500
Total variable costs	531,000	265,500	265,500
Contribution margin by bookstore	169,000	84,500	84,500
Less: Fixed costs controllable by bookstore managers			
Salaries and wages—fixed portion	27,000	12,000	15,000
Depreciation	15,000	7,000	8,000
Total controllable fixed costs	42,000	19,000	23,000
Contribution controllable by managers	127,000	65,500	61,500
Less: Fixed costs controllable by others			
Rent and utilities	60,000	40,000	20,000
Contribution by bookstore	67,000	$ 25,500	$ 41,500
Unallocated staff costs	60,000		
Operating income	$ 7,000		

Exhibit 8-6
The Book & Game Company
Performance Report

Measurement of Nonfinancial Performance

In recent years, many organizations have developed a new awareness of the importance of controlling aspects of nonfinancial performance. For example, sales organizations follow up on customers to ensure their satisfaction, and manufacturers track manufacturing defects and product performance. We first examine individual examples of nonfinancial performance measures such as quality, cycle time, and productivity. Then, we discuss the balanced scorecard, a popular approach that integrates financial and nonfinancial performance measures tied to the organization's fundamental strategy.

Objective 6

Measure performance against nonfinancial performance measures such as quality, cycle time, and productivity.

Control of Quality

Many companies use performance metrics that measure the quality of their products or services. **Quality control** is the effort to ensure that products and services perform to customer requirements. Customer needs define quality. For example, customers judge the quality of an automobile

quality control
The effort to ensure that products and services perform to customer requirements.

relative to their needs for reliability, performance, styling, safety, image, and other attributes. Defining quality in terms of customer requirements is only half the battle. There remains the problem of reaching and maintaining the desired level of quality.

The traditional approach to controlling quality in the United States was to inspect products after completing them and reject or rework those that failed the inspections. Because testing is expensive, companies often inspected only a sample of products. They judged the process to be in control as long as the number of defective products did not exceed an acceptable quality level. This meant that some defective products could still make their way to customers. When a company does not discover defects until the product reaches the customer, it is costly to repair products already in use by a customer or to win back a dissatisfied customer. IBM's former CEO John Akers was quoted in the *Wall Street Journal* as saying, "I am sick and tired of visiting plants to hear nothing but great things about quality and cycle time—and then to visit customers who tell me of problems."

cost of quality report
A report that displays the financial impact of quality.

A **cost of quality report** displays the financial impact of quality. The quality cost report shown in Exhibit 8-7 measures four categories of quality costs:

1. Prevention—costs incurred to prevent the production of defective products or delivery of substandard services including engineering analyses to improve product design for better manufacturing, improvements in production processes, increased quality of material inputs, and programs to train personnel
2. Appraisal—costs incurred to identify defective products or services including inspection and testing
3. Internal failure—costs of defective components and final products or services that are scrapped or reworked; also costs of delays caused by defective products or services
4. External failure—costs caused by delivery of defective products or services to customers, such as field repairs, returns, and warranty expenses

Exhibit 8-7 shows that internal or external failures caused most of the costs incurred by Eastside Manufacturing Company. These costs almost certainly are understated, however, because they omit opportunity costs of internal delays and lost sales. For example, quality problems in American-built automobiles in the 1980s caused sales to drop for many years. The opportunity cost of these lost future sales were much more significant than the immediate tangible costs measured in any quality cost report.

In recent years, more U.S. companies have moved away from the traditional approach to achieve quality by "inspecting it in." Many companies have discovered that it is more cost effective to prevent defects rather than inspect and correct them. The resources consumed to detect defective products do not add value. Further, if the company must scrap the defective product, it wastes the resources that were consumed to produce it. Even when the company can correct the product defects, it wastes the resources required for rework.

total quality management (TQM)
An approach to quality that focuses on prevention of defects and on customer satisfaction.

Many companies have adopted an approach first espoused by an American, W. Edwards Deming, and embraced by Japanese companies decades ago: **total quality management (TQM)**. Following the old adage "an ounce of prevention is worth a pound of cure," it focuses on prevention of defects and on achievement of customer satisfaction. The TQM approach builds on the assumption that an organization minimizes the cost of quality when it achieves high quality levels. TQM is the application of quality principles to all of the organization's endeavors to satisfy customers. TQM has significant implications for organization goals, structure, and management control systems.

quality-control chart
The statistical plot of measures of various product quality dimensions or attributes.

To implement TQM, an organization trains employees to prepare, interpret, and act on quality-control charts, such as that shown in Exhibit 8-8. The **quality-control chart** is a statistical plot of measures of various product quality dimensions or attributes. This plot helps detect process deviations and identify excessive variation in product dimensions or attributes that process or design engineers should address. The chart in Exhibit 8-8 shows that, except for a brief period near the end of April, the Eastside Manufacturing Company generally is not meeting its defects objective of .6% defects. Managers looking at this chart would know that they should take corrective action.

The most recent trend in quality control is Six Sigma, defined in Chapter 3 as a data-driven approach to eliminating defects and improving quality. The name Six Sigma comes from the idea of an extremely low defect rate of fewer than 3.4 defects per million (far lower than the objective

Month			Quality Cost Area	Year to Date		
Actual	Plan	Variance		Actual	Plan	Variance
			1. Prevention Cost			
3	2	1	A. Quality—administration	5	4	1
16	18	(2)	B. Quality—engineering	37	38	(1)
7	6	1	C. Quality—planning by others	14	12	2
5	7	(2)	D. Supplier assurance	13	14	(1)
31	33	(2)	Total prevention cost	69	68	1
5.5%	6.1%		Percentage of total quality cost	6.2%	6.3%	
			2. Appraisal cost			
31	26	5	A. Inspection	55	52	3
12	14	(2)	B. Test	24	28	(4)
7	6	1	C. Inspection & test of purchased materials	15	12	3
11	11	0	D. Product quality audits	23	22	1
3	2	1	E. Maintenance of inspection & test equipment	4	4	0
2	2	0	F. Materials consumed in inspection & testing	5	4	1
66	61	5	Total appraisal cost	126	122	4
11.8%	11.3%		Percentage of total quality cost	11.4%	11.3%	
			3. Internal failure cost			
144	140	4	A. Scrap & rework—manufacturing	295	280	15
55	53	2	B. Scrap & rework—engineering	103	106	(3)
28	30	(2)	C. Scrap & rework—supplier	55	60	(5)
21	22	(1)	D. Failure investigation	44	44	0
248	245	3	Total internal failure cost	497	490	7
44.3%	45.4%		Percentage of total quality cost	44.9%	45.3%	
345	339	6	Total internal quality cost (1 + 2 + 3)	692	680	12
61.6%	62.8%		Percentage of total quality cost	62.6%	62.8%	
			4. External failure quality cost			
75	66	9	A. Warranty expense—manufacturing	141	132	9
41	40	1	B. Warranty expense—engineering	84	80	4
35	35	0	C. Warranty expense—sales	69	70	(1)
46	40	6	D. Field warranty cost	83	80	3
18	20	(2)	E. Failure investigation	37	40	(3)
215	201	14	Total external failure cost	414	402	12
38.4%	37.2%		Percentage of total quality cost	37.4%	37.2%	
560	540	20	Total quality cost	1,106	1,082	24
9,872	9,800		Total product cost	20,170	19,600	
5.7%	5.5%		Total quality cost as percentage of total production cost	5.5%	5.5%	

*Adapted from Allen H. Seed III, *Adapting Management Accounting Practice to an Advanced Manufacturing Environment* (Montvale, NJ: National Association of Accountants, 1988), Table 5-2, p. 76.

Exhibit 8-7
Eastside Manufacturing Company
Quality Cost Report (thousands of dollars)*

of less than 6 defects per thousand in the Eastside Manufacturing example). However, the Six Sigma approach has broadened into a general approach to defining, measuring, analyzing, and improving a production process to minimize errors. The focus is on measuring how many defects a company has in its process because, once a company measures the defects, it can take steps to eliminate them. Developed by Motorola, Six Sigma is making large impacts at companies such as General Electric, Dow Chemical, and 3M. At Dow, each Six Sigma project has created an average of $500,000 in savings.

Control of Cycle Time

Reducing cycle time is a key to improving quality. **Cycle time**, or **throughput time**, is the time it takes to complete a product or service. It is a summary measure of efficiency and effectiveness and is also an important cost driver. You may find it surprising that faster cycle times often lead to higher quality and lower defect rates. A faster cycle time requires smooth-running processes and high quality. It also creates increased flexibility and brings products or services to customers more quickly, which increases customer satisfaction.

cycle time (throughput time)

The time taken to complete a product or service.

Exhibit 8-8

Eastside Manufacturing Company
Quality-Control Chart

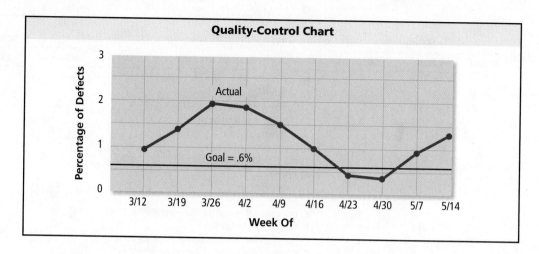

One way to measure cycle time is to attach an identifier such as a bar code or RFID (radio-frequency identification) tag to each component or product and use a scanner to read the code at the end of each stage of completion. Cycle time for each stage is the time between readings of the identifier tag. Tagging also permits effective tracking of materials and products for inventories, scheduling, and delivery.

Exhibit 8-9 is a sample cycle-time report showing that Eastside Manufacturing Company is meeting its cycle-time objectives at two of its five production process stages. This report is similar to the flexible budget reports of Chapter 7, but note that the variances here are measured in units of time, rather than in dollars of revenue or cost. Explanations for the variances in the right column indicate that poor-quality materials and poor design led to extensive rework and retesting.

Control of Productivity

productivity

A measure of outputs divided by inputs.

More than half the companies in the United States measure and manage productivity as part of the effort to improve their competitiveness. **Productivity** is a measure of outputs divided by inputs. The fewer inputs needed to produce a given output, the more productive the organization. This simple definition, however, raises difficult measurement questions. How should the company measure outputs and inputs? Specific management control issues usually determine the most appropriate measures. Labor-intensive organizations, especially service organizations, focus on increasing the productivity of labor, so labor-based measures are appropriate. Highly automated companies focus on machine use and productivity of capital investments, so capacity-based measures, such as the percentage of time machines are available, may be most important to them. Manufacturing companies, in general, monitor the efficient use of materials. For them, measures of material yield (a ratio of material outputs over material inputs) may be useful indicators of productivity.

Exhibit 8-10 shows 12 examples of productivity measures. As you can see from these examples, measures vary widely according to the type of resource that management wishes

Exhibit 8-9

Eastside Manufacturing Company
Cycle Time Report for the Second Week of May

Process Stage	Actual Cycle Time*	Standard Cycle Time	Variance	Explanation
Materials processing	2.1	2.5	0.4 F	
Circuit board assembly	44.7	28.8	15.9 U	Poor-quality materials caused rework
Power unit assembly	59.6	36.2	23.4 U	Engineering change required rebuilding all power units
Product assembly	14.6	14.7	0.1 F	
Functional and environmental test	53.3	32.0	21.3 U	Software failure in test procedures required retesting

F = Favorable. U = Unfavorable.
*Average time per stage over the week.

Exhibit 8-10
Measures of Productivity

Resource	Possible Outputs (Numerator)		Possible Inputs (Denominator)
Labor	Standard direct-labor hours allowed for good output	÷	Actual direct-labor hours used
	Sales revenue	÷	Number of employees
	Sales revenue	÷	Direct-labor costs
	Bank deposit/loan activity (by a bank)	÷	Number of employees
	Service calls	÷	Number of employees
	Customer orders	÷	Number of employees
Materials	Weight of output	÷	Weight of input
	Number of good units	÷	Total number of units
Equipment, capital, physical capacity	Time (e.g., hours) used	÷	Time available for use
	Time available for use	÷	Time (e.g., 24 hours per day)
	Expected machine hours for good output	÷	Actual machine hours
	Sales revenue	÷	Direct-labor cost

to use efficiently. In all cases, a measure of the resource that management wishes to control is in the denominator (the input) and a measure of the objective of using the resource is in the numerator (the output).

Choice of Productivity Measures

Which productivity measures should a company choose to manage? The choice determines the incentives created by the management control system. For example, if top management evaluates subordinates' performance based on direct-labor productivity, lower-level managers will focus on improving that specific measure.

The challenge in choosing productivity measures is to avoid motivating decisions that improve one dimension of performance but hurt another dimension. For example, measuring and rewarding productivity per machine would provide incentives for longer production runs. However, longer production runs might result in excessive inventory handling and holding costs. As another example, measuring labor productivity might motivate workers to produce more units per hour. However, spending less time on each unit produced may cause a higher rate of product defects.

Use of a single measure of productivity is unlikely to result in overall improvements in performance. The choice of performance measures requires anticipating the trade-offs that employees will make. Many organizations implement management controls for all of the most important activities, including nonfinancial measures such as quality and customer satisfaction, and use multiple measures to monitor the actual benefits of improvements in these activities.

Productivity Measures Over Time

Be careful when comparing productivity measures over time. Changes in the process or in the rate of inflation can make results misleading. For example, consider labor productivity at Adobe Systems. One measure of productivity is sales revenue per employee.

	2001	2011	Percent Change
Total revenue (millions)	$ 1,230	$ 4,216	243%
Employees	÷ 3,043	÷ 9,925	226%
Revenue per employee (unadjusted for inflation)	$404,206	$424,786	5%

By this measure, Adobe appears to have achieved a 5% increase in the productivity of labor because the number of employees grew more slowly than total revenue. However, total revenue has not been adjusted for the effects of inflation. Because of inflation, each 2001 dollar was equivalent to 1.27 dollars in 2011. Therefore, Adobe's 2001 sales revenue, expressed in 2011

Business First

Balanced Scorecard Hall of Fame

Robert Kaplan and David Norton created the balanced scorecard (BSC) in 1992. The Balanced Scorecard Hall of Fame honors organizations that have achieved execution excellence through the use of the BSC. To be selected for the Hall of Fame, a company must apply one or more of the following five principles to create a strategy-focused organization: "mobilize change through executive leadership; translate the strategy into operational terms; align the organization around its strategy; make strategy everyone's job; and make strategy a continual process." By the end of 2011, the Balanced Scorecard Collaborative had recognized a total of 167 Hall of Fame organizations. Past inductees include Army and Air Force Exchange Service (AAFES), the City of Corpus Christi, BMW Financial Services, and Wendy's International.

AAFES is a $9.9 billion global retailer with 43,000 employees serving military customers in 3,100 stores in 30 countries. AAFES adopted the BSC to prepare the organization to meet growing and diverse demands of its increasingly mobile customers. The BSC helps create alignment, drive accountability, optimize resource allocation, and link strategy to operations. In 4 years revenue increased by 11%, dividends 19%, employee satisfaction 16%, and customer satisfaction 17%. Inventory was reduced by about $108 million. Michael Howard, AAFES chief operating officer, observed the following: "The BSC has given us the ability to look beyond traditional financial measures to drive long-term sustainability that focuses on employee optimization. The BSC aligns corporate resources and energies to drive performance that ensure AAFES continues to provide a valued benefit to the military market."

The City of Corpus Christi is the largest coastal city in Texas and the nation's sixth largest port. The city employs about 3,000, serving a population of 305,000. The city adopted the BSC to clarify and communicate its strategy; align departments, divisions, and employees; and make more timely and better informed decisions that impact citizens' lives. Constituent satisfaction increased 16%, workforce retention was up, and citizen/customer wait time down. The city's bond rating improved, fueled in part by the BSC management system. Angel R. Escobar, interim city manager commented, "Now, with the BSC, we know what we are great at and what we need to improve upon...our monthly BSC meetings unify departmental directors to collectively focus on and discuss solutions to real issues."

BMW Financial Services was established in 1993 to support the sales and marketing efforts of BMW North America. The company has more than $24 billion in managed assets and offers customers flexible lease and retail financing options. BMW Financial Services adopted the BSC in 1998 and has seen remarkable growth in annual sales and number of customer accounts. The company uses the scorecard to link objectives, initiatives, and metrics to its strategy and communicate these links throughout the company.

Wendy's International is one of the world's largest restaurant operating and franchising companies, with about 6,600 restaurants and 2011 revenue of $2.4 billion. The company implemented the BSC to get a better handle on intangible assets, such as intellectual capital and customer focus. CEO Jack Schuessler lauded the BSC's success in "establishing targets and measuring our progress in key dimensions ranging from employee retention at the restaurant level, to restaurant evaluation scores, to business processes, to total revenue growth. They are all vitally important, not just the financial measures." The BSC provides a framework for balancing financial and nonfinancial measures.

The BSC has helped these and other award-winning organizations in many different ways. It has gained wide acceptance and successful implementation in many companies since its introduction more than 15 years ago.

Sources: AAFES Web site (www.shopmyexchange.com); City of Corpus Christi Web site (cctexaswww.cctexas); BMW of North America Web site (www.bmwusa.com); The Wendy's Company 2011 Annual Report; Palladium Group Web site (www.thepalladiumgroup.com).

---

dollars (so we can compare it with 2011 sales revenue), is $1,230 \times 1.27 = $1,562$. The adjusted 2001 sales revenue per employee is as follows:

	2001 (adjusted)	2011	Percent Change
Total revenue (millions)	$ 1,562	$ 4,216	170%
Employees	÷ 3,043	÷ 9,925	226%
Revenue per employee (adjusted for inflation)	$513,309	$424,786	−17%

Adjusting for the effects of inflation reveals that Adobe's labor productivity has actually decreased by 17% rather than increased by 5%.

The Balanced Scorecard

Objective 7

Use a balanced scorecard to integrate financial and nonfinancial measures of performance.

A **balanced scorecard (BSC)** is a system that strikes a balance between financial and nonfinancial measures in the performance measurement process, links performance to rewards, and gives explicit recognition to the link between performance measurement and organizational goals and objectives. The balanced scorecard focuses management attention on measures that drive an organization to achieve its goals. About 50% of the 1,000 largest U.S. firms use some version of the

Exhibit 8-11
Performance Indicators for
Philips Electronics' Balanced
Scorecard

Financial	Processes
Economic profit realized	Percentage reduction in process cycle time
Income from operations	Number of engineering changes
Working capital	Capacity utilization
Operational cash flow	Order response time
Inventory turns	Process capability
Customers	**Competence**
Rank in customer survey	Leadership competence
Market share	Percentage of patent-protected turnover
Repeat order rate	Training days per employee
Complaints	Quality improvement team participation
Brand index	

balanced scorecard, including **Microsoft, American Express, ExxonMobil, Allstate**, and **Apple Computer**. Government and nonprofit agencies, such as the U.S. Department of Transportation and the United Way of America, also use the balanced scorecard. We describe some of the more successful organizations that use the balanced scorecard in the Business First box on page 312.

The balanced scorecard helps line managers understand the relationship between nonfinancial measures and organizational goals. The balanced scorecard identifies performance measures from each of the four components of the successful organization shown in Exhibit 8-3 on page 300. Links between the measures and organizational objectives help managers throughout the organization understand how their actions support the organization's goals.

What does a balanced scorecard look like? The classic balanced scorecard developed by Robert Kaplan and David Norton includes **key performance indicators**—measures that drive the organization to meet its goals—grouped into four categories: (1) financial, (2) customers, (3) internal business processes, and (4) innovation and learning. Some companies use other terminology and some include additional categories—the most common are additional categories for employees or other stakeholders.

All balanced scorecards develop performance measures for each objective within each category. For example, **Philips Electronics** uses the categories and performance indicators in Exhibit 8-11. Most companies that use a balanced scorecard specify the categories that each business segment will use but allow the segments to choose the relevant performance measures for each category. For example, every Microsoft division has measures for financial, customer, internal processes, and learning perspectives, but the Latin American division has different measures in each category than does the Seattle headquarters. The balanced scorecard should not be a straightjacket; rather it is a flexible framework for motivating and measuring performance.

balanced scorecard (BSC)
A performance measurement and reporting system that strikes a balance between financial and nonfinancial measures, links performance to rewards, and gives explicit recognition to the link between performance measurement and organizational goals and objectives.

key performance indicators
Measures that drive the organization to achieve its goals.

Making Managerial Decisions

The balanced scorecard emphasizes the connections between performance measures and financial and nonfinancial goals. Indicate where each of the following goals of **Whirlpool** fits with the four components of a successful organization shown in Exhibit 8-3 on page 300, and explain how these components relate to one another:

 People commitment
 Total quality
 Customer satisfaction
 Financial performance
 Growth and innovation

Answer

The components listed in Exhibit 8-3 depict the causal links from organizational learning to business process improvement,

to customer satisfaction, and finally to financial strength. The five goals set by top managers at Whirlpool suggest the following links among the goals:

If Whirlpool makes a solid commitment to its people and invests in growth and innovation, the company will make progress in organizational learning. This will lead to business process improvements that decrease costs, increase efficiency, and increase the total quality of its products, which will then lead to increased customer satisfaction. The ultimate result of satisfied customers is improved financial performance. Sustainable financial strength should allow Whirlpool to repeat the cycle and continue to invest in both organizational learning and internal business processes.

Management Control Systems in Service, Government, and Nonprofit Organizations

Many service organizations face substantial difficulty implementing management control systems. Why? Because the outputs of service organizations are difficult to measure. For example, what is a good measure of output for a bank's call center (where service representatives answer customers' questions)? Number of calls or total time spent on calls? The measure "number of calls" might motivate many short calls that do not provide thorough answers to customers. The measure "total time spent on calls" might motivate long, time-wasting calls. It is often difficult to know the quality, or sometimes even the quantity, of the service provided until long after the organization delivers the service. When quality and quantity of output are hard to measure, developing timely measures of input/output relationships is nearly impossible.

The keys to successful management control in any organization are proper training and motivation of employees to achieve the organization's strategic objectives, accompanied by consistent monitoring of measures chosen to fit with these objectives. These keys are equally important in service-oriented organizations. **MBNA America**, a large issuer of bank credit cards, works hard to measure the amount and quality of its service. It identifies customer retention as its most important key success factor. MBNA trains its customer representatives carefully. Each day it measures and reports performance on 14 objectives consistent with customer retention, and it rewards every employee based on those 14 objectives. Measures include answering every call by the second ring, keeping the computer up 100% of the time, and processing credit-line requests within 1 hour. Employees earn bonuses as high as 20% of their annual salaries by meeting those objectives.

Government and nonprofit organizations face additional difficulties. When for-profit organizations confront conflicting goals, the appropriate trade-off is determined by the net effect on the financial "bottom line." When government and nonprofit organizations face conflicting goals as to when, where, and to whom they will provide services, the relevant trade-offs are often unclear. Because they have no precisely defined objective function that specifies how to make these trade-offs, it is difficult to determine the "right" incentives to be incorporated in the management control system.

Further, the design of management control systems in nonprofit organizations is complicated by the fact that many people in these organizations seek primarily nonmonetary rewards. For example, volunteers in the **Peace Corps** receive little pay but derive much satisfaction from helping to improve conditions in underdeveloped countries. **AmeriCorps** volunteers have similar objectives domestically. Thus, monetary incentives are generally less effective in nonprofit organizations.

In summary, management control systems in nonprofit organizations probably will never be as highly developed as are those in profit-seeking firms because of the following:

1. Organizational goals and objectives are less clear. Moreover, there are often multiple goals and objectives, requiring difficult trade-offs.
2. Professionals (for example, teachers, attorneys, physicians, scientists, economists) tend to dominate nonprofit organizations. Because of their perceived professional status, they are often less receptive to the installation of formal control systems.
3. Measurements are more difficult because
   a. there is no profit measure, and
   b. there are heavy amounts of discretionary fixed costs, which make the relationships of inputs to outputs difficult to specify and measure.
4. There is less competitive pressure from other organizations or "owners" to improve management control systems. As a result, many cities in the United States are "privatizing" some essential services, such as sanitation, by contracting with private firms.
5. The role of budgeting, instead of being a rigorous planning process, is often more a matter of playing bargaining games with sources of funding to get the largest possible authorization.
6. Motivations and incentives of employees may differ from those in for-profit organizations.

Making Managerial Decisions

Study Exhibit 8-3 again. Use the same four general components, but rearrange them to reflect a framework that might help managers of a successful governmental or nonprofit organization.

Answer

For governmental and nonprofit organizations, the ultimate objective is not to focus on financial results but to deliver the maximum benefits to customers (or citizens) based on an available pool of financial resources. Thus, the causal relationships might be as follows:

Organizational learning → process improvements in delivering programs → improved fiscal or financial strength → greater program benefits for citizens or clients

Future of Management Control Systems

As organizations mature and as environments change, managers expand and refine their management control tools. The management control techniques that were satisfactory 10 or 20 years ago are not adequate for many organizations today.

A changing environment often means that organizations adjust their goals or key success factors. New goals require different benchmarks for evaluating performance. The management control system must evolve, too, or the organization may not manage its resources effectively or efficiently. A summary of management control principles that will always be important and can guide the redesign of systems follows:

1. Always expect that individuals will be pulled in the direction of their own self-interest. You may be pleasantly surprised that some individuals will act selflessly, but management control systems should be designed to take advantage of more typical human behavior. Also, be aware that managers in different cultures may perceive self-interest differently.

2. Design incentives so that individuals who pursue their own self-interest also achieve the organization's objectives. Because there are usually multiple objectives, multiple incentives are appropriate. Do not underestimate the difficulty of balancing multiple incentives.

3. Evaluate actual performance relative to planned performance. Where appropriate, revise planned performance to reflect actual output achieved. You can apply the concept of flexible budgeting to many goals and actions, both financial and nonfinancial.

4. Consider nonfinancial performance to be an important determinant of long-term success. In the short run, a manager may be able to generate good financial performance while neglecting nonfinancial performance, but it is not likely over the long haul.

5. Array performance measures across the entire value chain of the company to ensure that the management control system incorporates all activities that are critical to the long-run success of the company.

6. Periodically review the success of the management control system. Is the organization achieving its overall goals? Do the actions motivated by the management control system lead to goal achievement? Do individuals understand the management control system and effectively use the information it provides?

7. Learn from the management control successes (and failures) of competitors around the world. Despite cultural differences, human behavior is remarkably similar. Managers can learn from successful applications of new technology and management controls by reading books or attending courses that describe management control systems at other companies.

Highlights to Remember

1. **Describe the relationship of management control systems to organizational goals.** The starting point for designing and evaluating a management control system is the identification of organizational goals as specified by top management.

2. **Explain the importance of evaluating performance and describe how it impacts motivation, goal congruence, and employee effort.** The way an organization measures and evaluates performance affects individuals' behavior. The more that it ties rewards to performance measures, the more incentive there is to improve the measures. Poorly designed measures may actually work against the organization's goals.

3. **Develop performance measures and use them to monitor the achievements of an organization.** A well-designed management control system measures both financial and nonfinancial performance. Superior nonfinancial performance usually leads to superior financial performance in time. The performance measures should tell managers how well they are meeting the organization's goals.

4. **Use responsibility accounting to define an organizational subunit as a cost center, a profit center, or an investment center.** Responsibility accounting assigns revenue and cost objectives to the management of the subunit that has the greatest influence over them. Cost centers focus on costs only, profit centers on both revenues and costs, and investment centers on profits relative to the amount invested.

5. **Prepare segment income statements for evaluating profit and investment centers using the contribution margin and controllable-cost concepts.** The contribution approach to measuring a segment's income aids performance evaluation by separating a segment's costs into those controllable by the segment management and those beyond management's control. It allows separate evaluation of a segment as an economic investment and the performance of the segment's manager.

6. **Measure performance against nonfinancial performance measures such as quality, cycle time, and productivity.** Measuring performance in areas such as quality, cycle time, and productivity causes employees to direct attention to those areas. Achieving goals in these nonfinancial measures can help meet long-run financial objectives.

7. **Use a balanced scorecard to integrate financial and nonfinancial measures of performance.** The balanced scorecard helps managers monitor actions that are designed to meet the various goals of the organization. It integrates key performance indicators that measure how well the organization is meeting its goals.

8. **Describe the difficulties of management control in service and nonprofit organizations.** Management control in service and nonprofit organizations is difficult because of a number of factors, including a relative lack of clearly observable outcomes and, for many nonprofit organizations, the lack of a clearly defined objective function.

Accounting Vocabulary

balanced scorecard (BSC), p. 313
controllable cost, p. 302
cost center, p. 302
cost of quality report, p. 308
cycle time, p. 309
goal congruence, p. 297
investment center, p. 303
key performance indicators, p. 313

key success factor, p. 296
management control system, p. 295
managerial effort, p. 297
motivation, p. 298
productivity, p. 310
profit center, p. 302
quality control, p. 307
quality-control chart, p. 308

responsibility accounting, p. 302
responsibility center, p. 302
segments, p. 303
throughput time, p. 309
total quality management (TQM), p. 308
uncontrollable cost, p. 302

Fundamental Assignment Material

MyAccountingLab

8-A1 Responsibility of Purchasing Agent

Excel Electronics Company, a privately held enterprise, has a subcontract from a large aerospace company in Chicago. Although Excel was a low bidder, the aerospace company was reluctant to award the business to the company because it was a newcomer to this kind of activity. Consequently, Excel assured the aerospace company of its financial strength by submitting its audited financial statements. Moreover, Excel agreed to a pay a penalty of $5,000 per day for each day of late delivery for whatever cause.

Amy Greer, the Excel purchasing agent, is responsible for acquiring materials and parts in time to meet production schedules. She placed an order with an Excel supplier for a critical manufactured component. The supplier, who had a reliable record for meeting schedules, gave Greer an acceptable delivery date. Greer checked up several times and was assured that the component would arrive at Excel on schedule.

On the date specified by the supplier for shipment to Excel, Greer was informed that the component had been damaged during final inspection. It was delivered 10 days late. Greer had allowed 4 extra days for possible delays, but Excel was 6 days late in delivering to the aerospace company and so had to pay a penalty of $30,000.

What department should bear the penalty? Why?

8-A2 Contribution Approach to Responsibility Accounting

Joe Albright owns and operates a small chain of convenience stores in Waterloo and Cedar Rapids. The company has five stores including a downtown store and a Sumner store in the Waterloo division, and a downtown store, a Solon store, and an airport store in the Cedar Rapids division. There is also a separate administrative staff that provides market research, personnel, and accounting and finance services.

The company had the following financial results for 20X1 (in thousands):

Sales revenue	$8,000
Cost of merchandise sold	3,500
Gross margin	4,500
Operating expenses	2,200
Income before income taxes	$2,300

The following data about 20X1 operations were also available:

1. All five stores used the same pricing formula; therefore, all had the same gross margin percentage.
2. Sales were largest in the two downtown stores, with 30% of the total sales volume in each. The Solon and airport stores each provided 15% of total sales volume, and the Sumner store provided 10%.
3. Variable operating costs at the stores were 10% of revenue for the downtown stores. The other stores had lower variable and higher fixed costs. Their variable operating costs were only 5% of sales revenue.
4. The fixed costs over which the store managers had control were $125,000 in each of the downtown stores, $180,000 at Solon and airport, and $40,000 at Sumner.
5. The remaining $910,000 of operating costs consisted of
   a. $210,000 controllable by the Cedar Rapids division manager but not by individual stores,
   b. $100,000 controllable by the Waterloo division manager but not by individual stores, and
   c. $600,000 controllable by the administrative staff.
6. Of the $600,000 spent by the administrative staff, $350,000 directly supported the Cedar Rapids division, with 20% for the downtown store, 30% for each of the Solon and airport stores, and 20% for Cedar Rapids operations in general. Another $140,000 supported the Waterloo division, 50% for the downtown store, 25% for the Sumner store, and 25% supporting Waterloo operations in general. The other $110,000 was for general corporate expenses.

Prepare an income statement by segments using the contribution approach to responsibility accounting. Use the format of Exhibit 8-4, page 303. Column headings should be as follows:

	Breakdown into Two Divisions		Breakdown of Waterloo Division			Breakdown of Cedar Rapids Division			
Company as a whole	Waterloo	Cedar Rapids	Not allocated	Downtown	Sumner	Not allocated	Downtown	Solon	Airport

8-A3 Comparison of Productivity

Forsythe and Sorteberg are manufacturing companies. Comparative data for 20X1 and 20X7 are as follows:

		Forsythe	Sorteberg
Sales revenue	20X1	$4,720,000,000	$7,997,000,000
	20X7	$6,500,000,000	$9,007,000,000
Number of employees	20X1	53,600	77,900
	20X7	57,800	78,200

Assume that inflation has totaled 18% during these 6 years so that each 20X1 dollar is equivalent to 1.18 dollars in 20X7, due to inflation.

1. Compute 20X1 and 20X7 productivity measures in terms of revenue per employee for Forsythe and Sorteberg.
2. Compare the change in productivity between 20X1 and 20X7 for Forsythe with that for Sorteberg.

8-B1 Responsibility Accounting

The Kephart Company produces precision machine parts. Kephart uses a standard cost system, calculates standard cost variances for each department, and reports them to department managers. Managers use the information to improve their operations. Superiors use the same information to evaluate managers' performance.

Liz Elder was recently appointed manager of the assembly department of the company. She has complained that the system as designed is disadvantageous to her department. Included among the variances charged to the departments is one for rejected units. The inspection occurs at the end of the assembly department. The inspectors attempt to identify the cause of the rejection so that the department where the error occurred can be charged with it. Not all errors can be easily identified with a department, however. The nonidentified units are totaled and apportioned to the departments according to the number of identified errors. The variance for rejected units in each department is a combination of the errors caused by the department plus a portion of the unidentified causes of rejects.

1. Is Elder's complaint valid? Explain the reason(s) for your answer.
2. What would you recommend that the company do to solve its problem with Elder and her complaint?

8-B2 Divisional Contribution, Performance, and Segment Margins

The president of Reading Railroad wants to obtain an overview of the company's operations, particularly with respect to comparing freight and passenger business. He has heard about "contribution" approaches to cost allocations that emphasize cost behavior patterns and contribution margins, contributions controllable by segment managers, and contributions by segments. The president has hired you as a consultant to help him. He has given you the following information.

Total revenue in 20X3 was $80 million, of which $72 million was freight traffic and $8 million was passenger traffic. Forty percent of the passenger revenue was generated by division 1, 50% by division 2, and 10% by division 3.

Total variable costs were $40 million, of which $36 million was caused by freight traffic. Of the $4 million allocable to passenger traffic, $2.1, $1.6, and $.3 million could be allocated to divisions 1, 2, and 3, respectively.

Total separable discretionary fixed costs were $8 million, of which $7.6 million applied to freight traffic. For the remaining $400,000 applicable to passenger traffic, $80,000 could not be allocated to specific divisions, while $200,000, $100,000, and $20,000, were allocable to divisions 1, 2, and 3, respectively.

Total separable committed costs, which were not regarded as being controllable by segment managers, were $25 million, of which 80% was allocable to freight traffic. Of the 20% traceable to passenger traffic, divisions 1, 2, and 3 should be allocated $3 million, $700,000, and $300,000, respectively; the balance was unallocable to a specific division.

The common fixed costs not clearly allocable to any part of the company amounted to $800,000.

1. The president asks you to prepare statements, dividing the data for the company as a whole between the freight and passenger traffic and then subdividing the passenger traffic into three divisions.
2. Some competing railroads actively promote a series of one-day sightseeing tours on summer weekends. Most often, these tours are timed so that the cars with the tourists are hitched on with regularly scheduled passenger trains. What costs are relevant for making decisions to run such

tours? Other railroads, facing the same general cost structure, refuse to conduct such sightseeing tours. Why?

3. Suppose that the railroad has petitioned government authorities for permission to drop division 1. What would be the effect on overall company net income for 20X4, assuming that the figures are accurate and that 20X4 operations are expected to be in all respects a duplication of 20X3 operations?

8-B3 Balanced Scorecard for a Law Firm

Young, Martinez, and Cheung (YMC) is a law firm in Chicago. The firm has had a very loose and relaxed management style that has served it well in the past. However, more aggressive law firms have been winning new clients faster than YMC has. Thus, the managing partner, Jerry Martinez, recently attended an ABA seminar on performance measurement in law firms, where he learned about the balanced scorecard. He thought it might be a good tool for YMC, one that would allow the firm to keep its culture yet still more aggressively seek new clients.

Martinez identified the following strategic objectives that fit with the firm's core values and provide a framework for assessing progress toward the firm's goals:

Financial

    a. Steadily increase the firm's revenues and profits.

Customer

    a. Understand the firm's customers and their needs.

    b. Value customer service over self-interest.

Internal Business Process

    a. Encourage knowledge sharing among the legal staff.

    b. Communicate with each other openly, honestly, and often.

    c. Empower staff to make decisions that benefit clients.

Organizational Learning

    a. Maintain an open and collaborative environment that attracts and retains the best legal staff.

    b. Seek staff diversity.

1. Develop at least one measure for each of the strategic objectives listed.
2. Explain how YMC can use this balanced scorecard to evaluate staff performance.
3. Should staff compensation be tied to the scorecard performance measures? Why or why not?

Additional Assignment Material

MyAccountingLab

QUESTIONS

8-1 What is a management control system?

8-2 What are the purposes of a management control system?

8-3 What are the major components of a management control system?

8-4 What is a key success factor?

8-5 "Goals are useless without performance measures." Do you agree? Explain.

8-6 "There are corporate goals other than to improve profit." Name three.

8-7 How does management determine its key success factors?

8-8 Give three examples of how managers may improve short-run performance to the detriment of long-run results.

8-9 Name three kinds of responsibility centers.

8-10 How do profit centers and investment centers differ?

8-11 List five characteristics of a good performance measure.

8-12 List four nonfinancial measures of performance that managers find useful.

8-13 "Performance evaluation seeks to achieve goal congruence and managerial effort." Explain what is meant by this statement.

8-14 "Managers of profit centers should be held responsible for the center's entire profit. They are responsible for profit even if they cannot control all factors affecting it." Discuss.

8-15 "Variable costs are controllable and fixed costs are uncontrollable." Do you agree? Explain.

8-16 "The contribution margin is the best measure of short-run performance." Do you agree? Explain.

8-17 Give four examples of segments.

8-18 "Always try to distinguish between the performance of a segment and its manager." Why?

8-19 "The contribution margin approach to performance evaluation is flawed because focusing on only the contribution margin ignores important aspects of performance." Do you agree? Explain.

8-20 What is a balanced scorecard and why are more companies using one?

8-21 What are key performance indicators?

8-22 There are four categories of cost in the quality cost report; explain them.

8-23 Why are companies increasing their quality control emphasis on the prevention of defects?

8-24 "Nonfinancial measures of performance can be controlled just like financial measures." Do you agree? Explain.

8-25 Identify three measures of labor productivity, (a) one using all physical measures, (b) one using all financial measures, and (c) one that mixes physical and financial measures.

8-26 Discuss the difficulties of comparing productivity measures over time.

8-27 "Control systems in nonprofit organizations will never be as highly developed as in profit-seeking organizations." Do you agree? Explain.

CRITICAL THINKING EXERCISES

8-28 Management Control Systems and Innovation

The president of a fast-growing, high-technology firm remarked, "Developing budgets and comparing performance with the budgets may be fine for some firms. But we want to encourage innovation and entrepreneurship. Budgets go with bureaucracy, not innovation." Do you agree? How can a management control system encourage innovation and entrepreneurship?

8-29 Municipal Responsibility Accounting

After barely avoiding bankruptcy, New York City established one of the most sophisticated budgeting and reporting systems of any municipality. The Integrated Financial Management System (IFMS) "clearly identifies managers in line agencies and correlates allocations and expenditures with organizational structure. . . . In addition, managers have more time to take corrective measures when variances between budgeted and actual expenditures start to develop." (*FE—The Magazine for Financial Executives*, 1, no. 8, p. 26.)

Discuss how a responsibility accounting system such as IFMS can help manage a municipality such as New York City.

8-30 Control Systems and Customer Service Function of the Value Chain

Companies increasingly use nonfinancial measures to supplement financial measures of performance. One of the most important areas of nonfinancial performance is customer service. The last decade has brought an increased focus on the customer, and this focus is reflected in many companies' management control systems, where companies use "customer-value metrics." That is, they develop measures that monitor how well the company is meeting its customers' interests. What customer-value metrics might a company such as **Volvo**, the Swedish automobile company, use in its management control system?

8-31 Control Systems and the Production Function of the Value Chain

In recent years, many organizations have focused on the value of controlling nonfinancial performance as a key to improved productivity. In particular, to gain and maintain a competitive edge, companies focus on quality and cycle time. Discuss how quality, cycle time, and productivity are related.

8-32 Key Performance Indicators

Research on performance management suggests that organizations can compete most effectively by identifying and monitoring those elements that are most closely linked to organizational success. A key performance indicator can be thought of as a measure that drives organizational success. For each of the following companies or organizations, identify two possible key performance indicators.

1. **Delta Airlines**
2. **Wal-Mart**
3. **Hewlett Packard**
4. **New York Department of Motor Vehicles**

EXERCISES

8-33 Responsibility for Stable Employment Policy

The Mid-Atlantic Metal Fabricating Company has been manufacturing machine tools for a number of years and has had an industry-wide reputation for doing high-quality work. The company has been faced with fluctuations in demand over the years. It has been company policy to lay off welders as soon as there was insufficient work to keep them busy and to rehire them when demand warranted. Because of this lay-off policy, the company now has poor labor relations and finds it difficult to hire good welders. Consequently, the quality of the products has been declining steadily.

The plant manager has proposed that welders, who earn $20 per hour, be retained during slow periods to do menial plant maintenance work that is normally performed by workers earning $14 per hour in the plant maintenance department.

You, as controller, must decide the most appropriate accounting procedure to handle the wages of the welders doing plant maintenance work. What department(s) should be charged with this work, and at what rate? Discuss the implications of your plan.

8-34 Salesclerk's Compensation Plan

You are the manager of a department store in Tokyo. Sales are subject to month-to-month variations, depending on the individual salesclerk's efforts and other factors. A new salary-plus-bonus plan has been in effect for 4 months, and you are reviewing a sales performance report. The plan provides for a base salary of ¥50,000 per month, a ¥68,000 bonus each month if the salesclerk meets the monthly sales quota, and an additional commission of 5% of all sales over the monthly quota. Each month, the quota is reset at approximately 3% above the previous month's sales to motivate clerks to continually increase sales. The monthly quotas and actual amounts for the first 4 months of the plan are shown in the following sales report (in thousands):

		Salesclerk A	Salesclerk B	Salesclerk C
January	Quota	¥4,500	¥1,500	¥7,500
	Actual	1,500	1,500	9,000
February	Quota	¥1,545	¥1,545	¥9,270
	Actual	3,000	1,545	3,000
March	Quota	¥3,090	¥1,590	¥3,090
	Actual	5,250	750	9,000
April	Quota	¥5,400	¥ 775	¥9,270
	Actual	1,500	780	4,050

1. Compute the compensation for each salesclerk for each month.
2. Evaluate the compensation plan. Be specific. What changes would you recommend?

8-35 Common Measures on a Balanced Scorecard

Listed next are common performance measures appearing on balanced scorecards. Indicate whether the listed measure is primarily associated with the financial, customer, internal process, or learning and growth perspective. (Note that some measures might reasonably be associated with more than one perspective.)

- Return on sales
- Retention of target customers
- Net cash flow
- Training hours
- Employee turnover rate
- Materials handling cost per unit
- Market share
- Product-development cycle time
- Revenue growth in segments
- Occupational injuries and illness
- Day's sales in inventory
- Average cost per invoice

8-36 Goals and Objectives at Health Net

Health Net provides health care to more than 5.6 million members. As a managed health-care organization, the company strives to provide high-quality health care at a reasonable cost. Many stakeholders have an interest in Health Net's operations, including doctors and other medical personnel, patients, insurance companies, government regulators, and the general public.

Prepare a goal and one measure for assessing achievement of that goal for each of the following key areas:

Customer satisfaction
Efficient use of lab tests
Usage of physician time
Maintenance of state-of-the-art facilities
Overall financial performance

8-37 **Performance Evaluation**

Daniel Merrill & Co. is a stock brokerage firm that evaluates its employees on sales activity generated. Recently, the firm also began evaluating its stockbrokers on the number of new accounts generated.

Discuss how these two performance measures are consistent and how they may conflict. Do you believe that these measures are appropriate for the long-term goal of profitability?

8-38 **Simple Controllable Costs**

Shortline Espresso is a gourmet dessert restaurant in Seattle. Margie McMahon, the sole proprietor, expanded to a second location in Bellingham 3 years ago. Recently, McMahon decided to enroll in a PhD program and retire from active management of the individual restaurants but continues to oversee the entire company. She hired a manager for each restaurant. In 20X3, each had sales of $1,200,000. The Bellingham restaurant is still pricing lower than the Seattle restaurant to establish a customer base. Variable expenses run 70% of sales for the Seattle restaurant and 75% of sales for the Bellingham restaurant.

Each manager is responsible for the rent and some other fixed costs for his or her restaurant. These costs amounted to $110,000 for the Seattle restaurant and $75,000 for the one in Bellingham. The difference is primarily due to lower rent in Bellingham. In addition, several costs, such as advertising, legal services, accounting, and personnel services, were centralized. The managers had no control of these expenses, but some of them directly benefited the individual restaurants. Of the $345,000 cost in this category, $100,000 related to Seattle and $185,000 to Bellingham, where most of the additional cost in Bellingham is due to the cost of extra advertising to build up its customer base. The remaining $60,000 was general corporate overhead.

1. Prepare income statements for each restaurant and for the company as a whole. Use a format that allows easy assessment of each manager's performance and each restaurant's economic performance.
2. Using only the information given in this exercise, do the following:
   a. Evaluate each restaurant as an economic investment.
   b. Evaluate each manager.

8-39 **Quality Theories Compared**

Examine the following two graphs. Compare the total quality management approach to the traditional theory of quality. Which theory do you believe represents the current realities of today's global competitive environment? Explain.

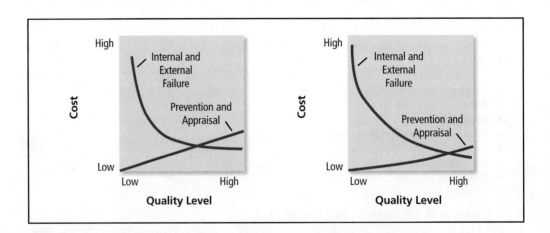

8-40 **Quality-Control Chart**

San Angelo Manufacturing Company was concerned about a growing number of defective units being produced. At one time, the company had the percentage of defective units down to less than five per thousand, but recently rates of defects have been near, or even above, 1%. The company decided to graph its defects for the last 8 weeks (40 working days), beginning Monday, September 1 through Friday, October 24. The graph is shown in Exhibit 8-12.

1. Identify two important trends evident in the quality-control chart.
2. What might management of San Angelo do to deal with each trend?

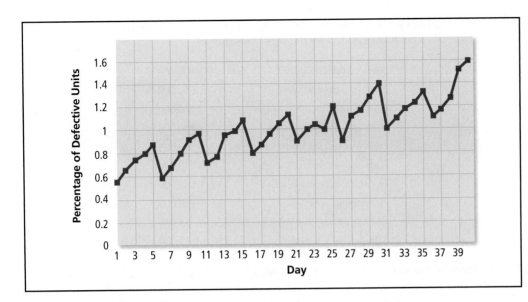

Exhibit 8-12
San Angelo Manufacturing Company
Quality-Control Chart for September 1 Through October 24

8-41 Cycle-Time Reporting

The Pierre plant of Global Electronics produces computers. The plant monitors its cycle time closely to prevent schedule delays and excessive costs. The standard cycle time for the manufacture of printed circuit boards for one of its computers is 26 hours. Consider the following cycle-time data from the past 6 weeks of circuit board production:

Week	Units Completed	Total Cycle Time
1	564	14,108 hours
2	544	14,592
3	553	15,152
4	571	16,598
5	547	17,104
6	552	16,673

Analyze circuit board cycle time performance in light of the 26-hour objective.

PROBLEMS

8-42 Multiple Goals and Profitability

The following multiple goals were identified by **General Electric**:

> Profitability
> Market position
> Productivity
> Product leadership
> Personnel development
> Employee attitudes
> Public responsibility
> Balance between short-range and long-range goals

General Electric is a huge, highly decentralized corporation. At the time it developed these goals, GE had approximately 170 responsibility centers called departments, but that is a deceptive term. In most other companies, these departments would be called divisions. For example, some GE departments had sales of more than $500 million.

Each department manager's performance was evaluated annually in relation to the specified multiple goals. A special measurements group was set up to devise ways of quantifying accomplishments in each of the areas. In this way, the evaluation of performance would become more objective as the various measures were developed and improved.

1. How would you measure performance in each of these areas? Be specific.
2. Can the other goals be encompassed as ingredients of a formal measure of profitability? In other words, can profitability per se be defined to include the other goals?

8-43 Responsibility Accounting, Profit Centers, and Contribution Approach

Richfield Honda had the following data for the year's operations:

Sales of vehicles	$3,100,000
Sales of parts and service	500,000
Cost of vehicle sales	2,480,000
Parts and service materials	100,000
Parts and service labor	200,000
Parts and service overhead	40,000
General dealership overhead	180,000
Advertising of vehicles	100,000
Sales commissions, vehicles	155,000
Sales salaries, vehicles	88,000

The president of the dealership has long regarded the markup on material and labor for the parts and service activity as the amount that is supposed to cover all parts and service overhead plus some general overhead of the dealership. In other words, the parts and service department is viewed as a cost-recovery operation, while the sales of vehicles is viewed as the income-producing activity.

1. Prepare a departmentalized operating statement that harmonizes with the views of the president.
2. Prepare an alternative operating statement that would reflect a different view of the dealership operations. Assume that $30,000 and $89,000 of the $180,000 general overhead can be allocated with confidence to the parts and service department and to sales of vehicles, respectively. The remaining $61,000 cannot be allocated except in some highly arbitrary manner.
3. Comment on the relative merits of numbers 1 and 2.

8-44 Incentives in Planned Economies

Often government-owned companies in planned economies reward managers based on nonfinancial measures. For example, the government might give managers a bonus for exceeding a 5-year-planned target for production quantities. A problem with this method is that managers tend to predict low volumes so that officials will set the targets low. This makes it easier for the managers to meet the targets, but it severely hinders planning because managers do not provide accurate information about production possibilities.

The former Soviet Union developed an alternative performance measurement and reward system. Suppose F is the forecast of production, A is actual production, and X, Y, and Z are positive constants set by top officials, with X, Y, $Z > 0$. The following performance measure was designed to motivate both high production and accurate forecasts.

$$\text{performance measure} = (Y \times F) + [X \times (A - F)] \text{ if } F \leq A$$
$$(Y \times F) - [Z \times (F - A)] \text{ if } F > A$$

Assume that Cuba adopted this measure at a time when Soviet influence was great. Consider the Havana Television Manufacturing Company (HTMC). During 19X3, the factory manager, Che Chavez, had to predict the number of TVs that HTMC could produce during the next year. He was confident that at least 700,000 TVs could be produced in 19X4, and most likely they could produce 800,000 TVs. With good luck, they might even produce 900,000. Government officials told him that the new performance evaluation measure would be used, and that $X = .50$, $Y = .80$, and $Z = 1.00$ for 19X4 and 19X5.

1. Suppose Chavez predicted production of 800,000 TVs and HTMC actually produced 800,000. Calculate the performance measure.
2. Suppose again that HTMC produced 800,000 TVs. Calculate the performance measure if Chavez had been conservative and predicted only 700,000 TVs. Also calculate the performance measure if he had predicted 900,000 TVs.
3. Now suppose it is November 19X4, and it is clear that HTMC cannot achieve the 800,000 target. Does the performance measure motivate continued efforts to increase production? Suppose it is clear that HTMC will easily meet the 800,000 target. Will the system motivate continued efforts to increase production?

8-45 Balanced Scorecard

Indianapolis Pharmaceuticals Company (IPC) recently revised its performance evaluation system. The company identified four major goals and several objectives required to meet each goal. Kris Nordmark, controller of IPC, suggested that a balanced scorecard be used to report on progress toward meeting the objectives. At a recent meeting, she told the managers of IPC that listing the objectives was only the first step in installing a new performance measurement system. Each objective has to be accompanied by one or more measures to monitor progress toward achieving the objectives. She asked the help of the managers in identifying appropriate measures.

The goals and objectives determined by the top management of IPC are as follows:

1. Maintain strong financial health.
   a. Keep sufficient cash balances to assure financial survival.
   b. Achieve consistent growth in sales and income.
   c. Provide excellent returns to shareholders.
2. Provide excellent service to customers.
   a. Provide products that meet the needs of customers.
   b. Meet customer needs on a timely basis.
   c. Meet customer quality requirements.
   d. Be the preferred supplier to customers.
3. Be among the industry leaders in product and process innovations.
   a. Bring new products to market before competition.
   b. Lead competition in production process innovation.
4. Develop and maintain efficient, state-of-the-art production processes.
   a. Excel in manufacturing efficiency.
   b. Meet or beat product introduction schedules.

Propose at least one measure of performance for each of the objectives of IPC.

8-46 Quality Cost Report

The manufacturing division of Red Lake Enterprises makes a variety of home furnishings. The company prepares monthly reports on quality costs. In early 20X7, Red Lake's president asked you, the controller, to compare quality costs in 20X6 to those in 20X4. He wanted to see only total annual numbers for 20X6 compared with 20X4. You have prepared the report shown in Exhibit 8-13.

1. For each of the four quality cost areas, explain what types of costs are included and how those costs have changed between 20X4 and 20X6.
2. Assess overall quality performance in 20X6 compared with 20X4. What do you suppose has caused the changes observed in quality costs?

8-47 Six Sigma, Mean, and Variance

A major objective of Six Sigma quality-control programs is to better meet customers' needs. One place companies have applied Six Sigma is to order delivery times. They have directed efforts at reducing both the mean (average) time to delivery and the variance or standard deviation (dispersion) of the delivery times. Customers want to get their products sooner, as reflected in the mean. But they also want assurance that the product will arrive when promised. This requires delivery schedules to have little random variance.

Exhibit 8-13

Red Lake Enterprises
Quality Cost Report (thousands of dollars)

Quality Cost Area	20X4 Cost	20X6 Cost
1. Prevention cost	45	107
Percentage of total quality cost	3.3%	12.4%
2. Appraisal cost	124	132
Percentage of total quality cost	9.1%	15.2%
3. Internal failure cost	503	368
Percentage of total quality cost	36.9%	42.5%
Total internal quality cost (1 + 2 + 3)	672	607
Percentage of total quality cost	49.3%	70.1%
4. External failure cost	691	259
Percentage of total quality cost	50.7%	29.9%
Total quality cost	1,363	866
Total product cost	22,168	23,462

Consider the following experience with the implementation of Six Sigma at a major manufacturing company:

Order Delivery Times (Days)	
Before Six Sigma	**After Six Sigma**
28	16
10	21
13	12
7	7
24	16
21	4
22	5
24	16
28	11
43	2

Compute the mean and standard deviation of order-delivery time before and after implementation of Six Sigma. From a customer's perspective, how would you view the results of this application of Six Sigma?

8-48 Productivity

In early 20X1, SpaceTel Communications, a U.S.-based international telephone communications company, purchased the controlling interest in Sofia Telecom, Ltd. (STL) in Bulgaria. A key productivity measure monitored by SpaceTel is the number of customer telephone lines per employee. Consider the following data for SpaceTel:

	20X1 without STL	**20X1 with STL**	**20X0**
Customer lines	15,370,000	21,460,000	14,787,000
Employees	72,500	116,000	69,750
Lines per employee	212	185	212

1. What are SpaceTel's 20X0 productivity and 20X1 productivity without STL?
2. What are STL's 20X1 productivity and SpaceTel's 20X1 productivity with STL?
3. What difficulties do you foresee if SpaceTel brings STL's productivity in line?

8-49 Productivity Measurement

Morrison's Laundry had the following results in 20X1 and 20X3:

	20X1	**20X3**
Pounds of laundry processed	1,420,000 pounds	1,505,000 pounds
Sales revenue	$690,000	$1,024,000
Direct-labor hours worked	44,500 hours	46,450 hours
Direct-labor cost	$318,000	$400,000

The laundry used the same facilities in 20X3 as in 20X1. During the past 3 years, however, the company put more effort into training its employees. The manager of Morrison's was curious about whether the training had increased labor productivity.

1. Compute a measure of labor productivity for 20X3 based entirely on physical measures. Do the same for 20X1. That is, from the data given, choose measures of physical output and physical input, and use them to compare the physical productivity of labor in 20X3 with that in 20X1.
2. Compute a measure of labor productivity for 20X3 based entirely on financial measures. Do the same for 20X1. That is, from the data given, choose measures of financial output and financial input, and use them to compare the financial productivity of labor in 20X3 with that in 20X1.

3. Suppose the following productivity measure was used:

$$\text{Productivity} = \frac{\text{sales revenue}}{\text{direct-labor hours worked}}$$

Because of inflation, each 20X1 dollar is equivalent to 1.13 dollars in 20X3. Compute appropriate productivity numbers for comparing 20X3 productivity with 20X1 productivity.

CASES

8-50 Trade-Offs Among Objectives

Computer Data Services (CDS) performs routine and custom information systems services for many companies in a large midwestern metropolitan area. CDS has built a reputation for high-quality customer service and job security for its employees. Quality service and customer satisfaction have been CDS's primary subgoals—retaining a skilled and motivated workforce has been an important factor in achieving those goals. In the past, temporary downturns in business did not mean layoffs of employees, though some employees were required to perform other than their usual tasks. In anticipation of growth in business, CDS leased new equipment that, beginning in August, added $10,000 per month in operating costs. Three months ago, however, a new competitor began offering the same services to CDS customers at prices averaging 19% lower than those of CDS. Rico Estrada, the company founder and president, believes that a significant price reduction is necessary to maintain the company's market share and avoid financial ruin, but he is puzzled about how to achieve it without compromising quality, service, and the goodwill of his workforce.

    CDS has a productivity objective of 20 accounts per employee. Estrada does not think that he can increase this productivity and still maintain both quality and flexibility to customer needs. CDS also monitors average cost per account and the number of customer satisfaction adjustments (resolutions of complaints). The average billing markup rate is 25% of cost. Consider the following data from the past 6 months:

	June	July	August	September	October	November
Number of accounts	797	803	869	784	723	680
Number of employees	40	41	44	43	43	41
Average cost per account	$ 153	$ 153	$ 158	$ 173	$ 187	$ 191
Average salary per employee	$3,000	$3,000	$3,000	$3,000	$3,000	$3,000

1. Discuss the trade-offs facing Rico Estrada.
2. Can you suggest solutions to his trade-off dilemma?

8-51 Six Sigma

The chapter mentions four companies that use Six Sigma for measuring and controlling quality: **Motorola, General Electric, 3M**, and **Dow Chemical**. Go to the Web site for each of these companies and find what each says about its Six Sigma efforts.

8-52 Review of Chapters 3–8

William Whitebear, general manager of the Kamloops Division of Canada Enterprises, is preparing for a management meeting. His divisional controller provided the following information:

1. The master budget for the fiscal year ended June 30, 20X4, follows:

Sales (50,000 units of A and 70,000 units of B)	$870,000
Manufacturing cost of goods sold	740,000
Manufacturing margin	$130,000
Selling and administrative expenses	120,000
Operating income	$ 10,000

2. The standard variable manufacturing cost per unit follows:

	Product A		Product B	
Direct materials	10 pieces at $.25	$2.50	5 pounds at $.30	$1.50
Direct labor	1 hour at $3.00	3.00	.3 hour at $2.50	.75
Variable overhead	1 hour at $2.00	2.00	.3 hour at $2.50	.75
Total		$7.50		$3.00

3. All budgeted selling and administrative expenses are common, fixed expenses; 60% are discretionary expenses.

4. The actual income statement for the fiscal year ended June 30, 20X4, follows:

Sales (53,000 units of A and 64,000 units of B)	$861,000
Manufacturing cost of goods sold	749,200
Manufacturing margin	$111,800
Selling and administrative expenses	116,000
Operating income	$ (4,200)

5. The budgeted sales prices for products A and B were $9 and $6, respectively. Actual sales prices equaled budgeted sales prices.

6. The schedule of the actual variable manufacturing cost of goods sold by product follows (actual quantities in parentheses):

Product A:	Materials	$134,500	(538,000 pieces)
	Labor	156,350	(53,000 hours)
	Overhead	108,650	(53,000 hours)
Product B:	Materials	102,400	(320,000 pounds)
	Labor	50,000	(20,000 hours)
	Overhead	50,000	(20,000 hours)
Total		$601,900	

7. Products A and B are manufactured in separate facilities. Of the budgeted fixed manufacturing cost, $130,000 is separable as follows: $45,000 to product A and $85,000 to product B. Ten percent of these separate costs are discretionary. All other budgeted fixed manufacturing expenses, separable and common, are committed.

8. There are no beginning or ending inventories.

During the upcoming management meeting, it is quite likely that some of the information from the controller will be discussed. In anticipation you set out to prepare answers to possible questions.

1. Determine the firm's budgeted break-even point in dollars, overall contribution-margin ratio, and contribution margins per unit by product. Assume no change in product mix.
2. Considering products A and B as segments of the firm, find the budgeted "contribution by segments" for each.
3. It is decided to allocate the budgeted selling and administrative expenses to the segments (in number 2) as follows: committed costs on the basis of budgeted unit sales mix and discretionary costs on the basis of actual unit sales mix. What are the final expense allocations? Briefly appraise the allocation method.
4. How would you respond to a proposal to base commissions to salespersons on the sales (revenue) value of orders received? Assume all salespersons have the opportunity to sell both products.
5. Determine the firm's actual "contribution margin" and "contribution controllable by segment managers" for the fiscal year ended June 30, 20X4. Assume no variances in committed fixed costs.
6. Determine the "sales-activity variance" for each product for the fiscal year ended June 30, 20X4.
7. Determine and identify all variances in variable manufacturing costs by product for the fiscal year ended June 30, 20X4.

NIKE 10-K PROBLEM

8-53 Strategy at Nike

Find "Item 7 Management's Discussion and Analysis of Financial Condition and Results of Operations" near the beginning of the **Nike** 10-K report.

1. Outline Nike's strategy to convert revenue growth to shareholder value in five key areas.
2. What are four long-term financial goals?
3. How well have these financial goals been met?
4. List some nonfinancial goals that Nike might use in a BSC.

EXCEL APPLICATION EXERCISE

8-54 Wages for New Salary-Plus-Bonus Plan

Goal: Create an Excel spreadsheet to calculate the impact on employee wages of a new salary-plus-bonus plan established to motivate salesclerks to increase sales. Use the results to answer questions about your findings.

Scenario: As the department store manager, you must determine if the new plan is the best way to motivate salesclerks and meet the objective of increasing sales. The background data for the compensation plan appear in Exercise 8-34. Use only data for salesclerk A and salesclerk B to prepare your spreadsheet.

When you have completed your spreadsheet, answer the following questions:

1. Which salesclerk has the highest average total salary over the four-month period?
2. What part of the compensation plan had the most impact on the salesclerks' salaries? The least impact?
3. Do you see any problems with this compensation plan? Explain.

Step-by-Step:

1. Open a new Excel spreadsheet.
2. In column A, create a bold-faced heading that contains the following:
   Row 1: Chapter 8 Decision Guideline
   Row 2: Tokyo Department Store
   Row 3: Salary-Plus-Bonus Plan Analysis
   Row 4: Today's Date
3. Merge and center the four heading rows across columns A–H.
4. In column A, create the following row headings:
   Row 7: Salesclerk A
   Row 8: Month
   Row 9: January
   Row 10: February
   Row 11: March
   Row 12: April
   Skip three rows.
   Row 16: Salesclerk B
   Row 17: Month
   Row 18: January
   Row 19: February
   Row 20: March
   Row 21: April
5. Change the format of salesclerk names (rows 7, 16) to bold-faced, underlined headings.
6. Change the format of month (rows 8, 17) to bold-faced headings.
7. In rows 8 and 17, create the following bold-faced, right-justified column headings:
   Column B: Quota
   Column C: Sales
   Column D: Over Quota
   Column E: Base Salary
   Column F: Quota Bonus
   Column G: Commission
   Column H: Total Salary

Note: Adjust column widths as necessary.

8. In column G, create the following right-justified cell headings:
   Row 14: Average:
   Row 23: Average:

9. Use the scenario data to fill in quota, sales, and base salary amounts from January–April for each salesclerk.

10. Use the appropriate IF statements to calculate over quota and quota bonus amounts when the salesclerks' sales met or exceeded their respective quotas (negative commissions should not be calculated).

$$= IF (formula > 0, formula, 0)$$
For Over Quota only.

$$= IF (formula < 0, 0, 68000) \text{ OR } = IF (formula > 0, 68000, 0)$$
For Quota Bonus only.

Hint: Go to the "Help" text and type "copy formulas" in the search area to obtain instructions for copying formulas from one cell to another. If done correctly, you should have to type in each of the formulas only once.

11. Use appropriate formulas to calculate commission and total salary amounts for each month, as well as an average amount for the January–April period for each salesclerk.

12. Format all amounts as follows:

Number tab:	Category:	Currency
	Decimal places:	0
	Symbol:	None
	Negative numbers:	Black with parentheses

13. To format specific amounts to display with a yen symbol, do the following:
   a. In an empty cell, hold down the Alt key and enter 0165 from the numeric keypad. When you stop holding the Alt key down, a yen sign will be displayed.

   Note: If your keyboard does not have a numeric keypad, use the shift and NumLk keys to activate the imbedded numeric keypad. Then, follow the instructions in part a. Use the shift and NumLk keys to turn the feature off.

   b. Highlight the yen character you have just created, select Edit, Cut. This will paste the yen sign to the clipboard. To see the clipboard, select View, Toolbars, Clipboard.
   c. Select the average amount for salesclerk A and open the Format, Cells. . . . dialog box.
   d. Select the custom category on the number tab. Scroll down toward the bottom of the type list and highlight the type shown next.

   Type: ($*#, ##0); ($*#, ##0); ($*" – "); (@)

   Change the data between the quotation marks in the third grouping from "–" to "0."
   Paste the yen sign over EACH occurrence of the dollar sign.

   Hint: Highlight the $ sign; press "Ctrl" and "V." This will paste the yen sign from the clipboard over the $ sign that has been highlighted in the Type field.

   e. Click the OK button.
   f. Utilize the custom format, which should now be at the bottom of the type list, to print the yen sign for all January amounts for both clerks and the average amount for salesclerk B.

14. Save your work, and print a copy for your files.

Note: Print your spreadsheet using landscape in order to ensure that all columns appear on one page.

COLLABORATIVE LEARNING EXERCISE

8-55 Goals, Objectives, and Performance Measures

There is increasing pressure on colleges and universities to develop measures of accountability. The objective is to specify goals and objectives and to develop performance measures to assess the achievement of those goals and objectives.

Form a group of four to six students to be a consulting team to the accounting department at your college or university. (If you are not using this book as part of a course in an accounting department, select any department at your college or university.) Based on your collective knowledge of the department, its mission, and its activities, formulate a statement of goals for the department. From that statement, develop several specific objectives, each of which can be measured. Then, develop at least one measure of performance for each objective.

An optional second step in this exercise is to meet with a faculty member from the department, and ask him or her to critique your objectives and performance measures. To the department member, do the objectives make sense? Are the proposed measures feasible, and will they correctly measure attainment of the objectives? Will they provide proper incentives to the faculty? If the department has created objectives and performance measures, compare them to those your group developed.

INTERNET EXERCISE

8-56 Management Control System at Procter & Gamble

Setting up management control systems and determining measurement methods and who should be responsible for particular revenues, costs, and information can be a large task. The structure of the organization plays a part in how well a particular measure is likely to work. Ensuring that the goals of the organization are in concert with the management control system is also an important factor. It is not possible to evaluate a company's management control system from an Internet site. What we can do, however, is to use a site as an example and apply some of the concepts of the chapter to measures and tools that would be possibilities for a firm.

1. A well-known and well-established company with worldwide acceptance is **Procter & Gamble (P&G)**. Log on to the company's Web site at www.pg.com. Locate the most recent annual report by following the links under the "Investor/Shareholder Relations" tab to "Financial Reporting." Examine the "Letter to Shareholders" section of the annual report. What does P&G consider to be the most important factors that drive their growth strategy? How does P&G ensure that managers meet the company's objectives?

2. The company has numerous products, and the Web site divides them into different categories and brands to help customers find relevant product information. Click on "Brands and Innovation." What are the major categories of brands listed on the Web site? Click on the "Household Care" category. What are some of the brands in this category that you are familiar with? How could a system be set up to help measure the success of the firm's goal to build brands in the "Household Care" category? What would be three possible financial measures? What about three nonfinancial measures?

Management Control in Decentralized Organizations

LEARNING OBJECTIVES

When you have finished studying this chapter, you should be able to:

1. Define *decentralization* and identify its expected benefits and costs.

2. Distinguish between responsibility centers and decentralization.

3. Explain how the linking of rewards to responsibility-center performance metrics affects incentives and risk.

4. Compute return on investment (ROI), economic profit, and economic value added (EVA).

5. Compare the incentives created by income, ROI, and economic profit (or EVA) performance measures.

6. Define *transfer prices* and identify their purpose.

7. State the general rule for transfer pricing and use it to assess alternative transfer prices based on total costs, variable costs, or market prices.

8. Identify the factors affecting multinational transfer prices.

9. Explain how controllability and management by objectives (MBO) aid the implementation of management control systems.

▶ **NIKE**

In a little more than 30 years, Nike has become the largest sports and fitness company in the world. It has grown from a small Beaverton, Oregon, company into a global giant with a presence in many different sports. For example, in the world of soccer, Nike was only a minor factor 10 years ago. Now Nike has placed itself at the center of attention for soccer fans worldwide. Nike has endorsement arrangements with the Italian and French national teams, as well as Manchester United, FC Barcelona, Inter Milan, and PSV Eindhoven. Further, its visibility continues to grow. Nike was the official sponsor and supplier for Chinese athletes for the 2008 Beijing Olympic Games.

From 1986 to 2011, Nike's revenues increased from $1 billion to almost $21 billion. During this same period, the percentage of non-U.S. revenues increased from 25% to 57%. Nike now has more stores outside the United States than inside. While footwear still accounts for more than half of Nike's sales, apparel sales now account for nearly one-third. A sampling of endorsements (promotional contracts with famous sports teams, individuals, and organizations) in addition to the soccer teams previously listed gives another perspective on the company's global presence. Tennis stars Roger Federer, Rafael Nadal, Maria Sharapova, Serena Williams; basketball stars Kobe Bryant, LeBron James, and Kevin Durant; and golf's Trevor Immelman, Anthony Kim, and Paul Casey all have endorsement deals with Nike. Watch almost any sports event on television, and you are likely to see the Nike "swoosh" logo.

Nike made a conscious decision to go global—a process that has generated substantial financial rewards. What are some of the keys to success when a company like Nike decides to significantly expand its operations abroad? To manage and coordinate widely dispersed operations, Nike needs information. Increasing sophistication of communications—Internet, e-mail, and worldwide cellular phone coverage—means that geographical separation no longer implies lack of access to information. While communications technology can help Nike and others get information quickly, the information they receive is determined by their management control system.

This chapter focuses on the role of management control systems in decentralized organizations such as Nike. We discuss how companies use performance metrics to motivate managers of separate units, including various ways of measuring performance to encourage actions by managers that are in the company's best interests. Finally, we address the special problems created when one segment of an organization charges another for providing goods or services. ■

© Interfoto/Alamy

Nike is a globally decentralized company. Customers throughout the world recognize its "swoosh" trademark. Achieving the appropriate balance between autonomy at the local level and efficiencies at the corporate level is a challenge when designing Nike's management control system.

Centralization Versus Decentralization

As organizations grow and undertake more diverse and complex activities, they face decisions about how much decision-making authority to delegate to lower levels of the organization. Concentration of decision-making authority only at the highest levels of the organization is **centralization**. Delegation of decision-making authority to lower levels is **decentralization**. Note that centralization or decentralization is a matter of degree, depicted as a choice along the continuum shown in Exhibit 9-1. The lower in the organization that authority is delegated, the greater the decentralization.

Nike has delegated a great deal of decision-making authority to the local-market level. For example, local Nike managers in Germany made the decision to sign an endorsement contract with world-champion racecar driver Michael Schumacher. According to CEO Philip Knight, "[Previously] it would have taken a move from within the company headquarters to strike such a deal. . . . But this time it was a decision made in country." The local German manager knew that Schumacher was extremely relevant to the German market and that this would be a "profit driven, culturally significant, and brand enhancing move." Knight credits this move toward decentralization for Nike's rapid increase in international sales: "It is a great example of what we are trying to do: Make decisions on the ground in faraway places."

The best choice along the continuum between centralization and decentralization is seldom obvious. In fact, organizations and industries seem to cycle from increasing decentralization to increasing centralization, and back again. For example, a decade or so ago most airlines, such as South China Airlines, Iberia Airlines, and Air France, decentralized. In contrast, at the same time, Sabena, Belgium's state-owned airline until its bankruptcy in 2001, undertook a centralization effort. In the insurance industry, Aetna decentralized at the same time AXA Equitable was centralizing. Let's take a look at some of the factors companies consider as they choose their position along the centralization/decentralization continuum.

Objective 1

Define *decentralization* and identify its expected benefits and costs.

centralization
Concentration of decision-making authority only at the highest levels of an organization.

decentralization
The delegation of decision-making authority to lower levels of the organization. The lower in the organization that authority is delegated, the greater the decentralization.

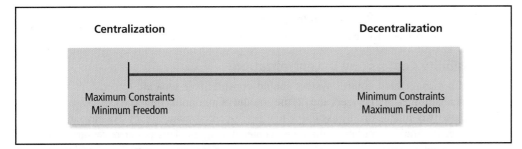

Exhibit 9-1
Centralization Versus Decentralization

Costs and Benefits of Decentralization

Most organizations realize benefits from some level of decentralization. Managers of lower-level units (which we will refer to as "local" managers), often have the best information concerning local conditions and, therefore, are able to make faster and better decisions on local issues than higher-level managers (which we will refer to as "central" managers). By delegating decision-making authority to local managers, central managers free up time to deal with larger issues and fundamental strategy. In addition, decentralization gives local managers an opportunity to develop their decision-making ability and other management skills, ensuring that the organization develops future leaders. Finally, local managers who are given more authority often have greater motivation and job satisfaction.

Decentralization also has its costs. Local managers may make decisions that are not in the organization's best interests. Why? Either because they act to improve their own segment's performance at the expense of the organization or because they do not fully understand the effects of their decisions on other segments and the organization as a whole. In a decentralized organization, innovative ideas to improve performance are less likely to be shared across units. Local managers in decentralized organizations also tend to duplicate services that might be less expensive if centralized (e.g., accounting, advertising, and personnel). Furthermore, costs of accumulating and processing information frequently rise under decentralization because top management needs additional accounting reports to learn about and evaluate decentralized units and their managers. Finally, managers in decentralized units may waste time negotiating with other units about goods or services that are being transferred between units. You can see some of the costs and benefits of decentralization in the Business First box on page 335.

Decentralization is more popular in profit-seeking organizations (where accountants can more easily measure outputs and inputs) than in nonprofit organizations (where it is more difficult to find reliable performance measures, so granting managers freedom is more risky). Central management can give local managers more freedom when it can more easily measure the results of their decisions and thereby hold local managers accountable for the results. In a profit-seeking firm, poor decisions become apparent from the inadequate profit generated.

Middle Ground

The optimal choice along the centralization/decentralization continuum is likely to differ from one company to the next. For every Nike that finds the benefits of increased decentralization exceeding the costs, another company finds the costs exceeding the benefits. In fact, the optimal choice for one part of the organization may differ from the optimal choice for another part. For example, many companies decentralize much of the controller's problem-solving and attention-directing functions and handle them at lower levels. In contrast, they generally centralize income tax planning and mass scorekeeping functions such as accounting for payroll.

Decentralization is more successful when an organization's segments are relatively independent of one another—that is, when the decisions of a manager in one segment will not affect other segments. When segments do much internal buying or selling, much buying from the same outside suppliers, or much selling to the same outside markets, they are candidates for more centralization.

In Chapter 9, we stressed that managers should consider cost-benefit tests, goal congruence, and managerial effort when designing a management control system. If management has decided in favor of heavy decentralization, then **segment autonomy**—the delegation of decision-making power to managers of segments of an organization—is also crucial. For decentralization to work, however, this autonomy must be real, not just "lip service." Top managers must be willing to abide by decisions made by segment managers in most circumstances.

segment autonomy

The delegation of decision-making power to managers of segments in an organization.

Responsibility Centers and Decentralization

Objective 2

Distinguish between responsibility centers and decentralization.

Design of a management control system should consider two separate dimensions of control: (1) the responsibilities of managers and (2) the amount of autonomy they possess. Some managers confuse these two dimensions by assuming that profit-center managers always have more decentralized decision-making authority than cost-center managers. This is not necessarily the case. Some profit-center managers, such as those at General Electric, possess vast freedom to make decisions concerning labor contracts, supplier choices, equipment purchases, personnel decisions, and so on. In contrast, profit-center managers at other companies need top-management

Business First

Benefits and Costs of Decentralization

Many companies believe that decentralization is important to their success, including **PepsiCo**, **DuPont**, and **Procter & Gamble**. But one company stands out from the others in its efforts to decentralize: **Johnson & Johnson**. Johnson & Johnson (with 2011 sales of $65 billion, 118,000 employees, and more than 250 companies operating in 60 countries) is the maker of products such as Tylenol, Listerine, Johnson's Baby Powder, Neutrogena, and Neosporin. The company has a long history of decentralization, beginning in the 1930s. Its 2011 annual report states ". . . the Company views its principle of decentralized management as an asset and fundamental to the success of a broadly based business. It also fosters an entrepreneurial spirit, combining the extensive resources of a large organization with the ability to anticipate and react quickly to local market changes and challenges."

Under the company's management structure, each of its operating companies functions autonomously. One benefit is that decisions are made by executives who are closer to the marketplace. One disadvantage is the additional expense because many of the operating companies duplicate many overhead costs. Although ultimately accountable to executives at Johnson & Johnson headquarters in New Brunswick, New Jersey, some segment presidents see their bosses as few as four times a year. Bill Weldon, Johnson & Johnson chairman of the board and former CEO, extols the virtues of decentralization: "Johnson & Johnson has maintained a significant and well-established presence in these markets for decades, utilizing our decentralized operating model to stay close to patients, consumers and health care providers with local market insights, products, and strategies." He believes the structure has been essential to its strategy of developing executives from within because young managers can be given responsibility for running whole companies. "This allows people to be entrepreneurial," he said, "and to grow."

BusinessWeek summarized Weldon's approach as follows: "[Johnson & Johnson's] success has hinged on its unique culture and structure.... Each of its far-flung units operates pretty much as an independent enterprise. Businesses set their own strategies; they have their own finance and human resources departments, for example. While this degree of decentralization makes for relatively high overhead costs, no chief executive, Weldon included, has thought that too high a price to pay."

As you can see, decentralization has benefits and costs. Some companies have vacillated between decentralization and centralization, sometimes believing that the benefits of centralizing common activities dominate the benefits of decentralization, while at other times seeking the decision-making advantages of decentralization. In contrast, Johnson & Johnson has continued its policy of decentralization in good times and bad, through a long succession of top management leadership. The company has a long-term credo that mandates decentralization. It would take a brave (or foolhardy) leader to change Johnson & Johnson's philosophy of decentralization.

Sources: Adapted from *Johnson & Johnson 2011 Annual Report*; M. Petersen, "From the Ranks, Unassumingly," *New York Times*, February 24, 2002, Section 3, page 2; and A. Barrett, "Staying on Top," *BusinessWeek*, May 5, 2003.

approval for almost all the decisions just mentioned. Similarly, cost centers may be more heavily decentralized than profit centers. The fundamental question in deciding between using a cost center or a profit center for a given segment is not whether heavy decentralization exists. Instead, the fundamental question is, for whatever level of decentralization that exists, "Will a profit center or a cost center better solve the problems of goal congruence and management effort?"

The management control system should be designed to achieve the best possible alignment between local manager decisions and the actions central management seeks. For example, a plant may seem to be a "natural" cost center because the plant manager has no influence over decisions concerning the marketing of its products. Nevertheless, some companies insist on evaluating a plant manager by the plant's profitability. Why? Because they believe this broader evaluation base will positively affect the plant manager's behavior. Instead of being concerned solely with running an efficient cost center, the system motivates the plant manager to consider quality control more carefully and react to customers' special requests more sympathetically. In designing accounting control systems, top managers must consider the system's impact on behavior desired by the organization.

Performance Metrics and Management Control

A major factor in designing decentralized management control systems is how the system's performance metrics affect managers' incentives. **Incentives** are the rewards, both implicit and explicit, for managerial effort and actions. A **performance metric** is a specific measure of management accomplishment. Organizations should choose performance metrics that improve the alignment of manager incentives with organizational objectives. The organization wants managers to use decision-making autonomy to meet the company's objectives, not to pursue

Objective 3

Explain how the linking of rewards to responsibility-center performance metrics affects incentives and risk.

incentives

Rewards, both implicit and explicit, for managerial effort and actions.

performance metric

A specific measure of management accomplishment.

agency theory

A theory that deals with relationships where one party (the principal) delegates decision-making authority to another party (the agent).

other goals. For example, Nike executives wanted the company's manager of German operations to sign auto-racer Michael Schumacher to a contract only if it would create additional profits for Nike, not to provide an entree for the manager into the inner circles of auto racing.

Agency Theory, Performance, and Rewards

Agency theory provides a model to analyze relationships where one party (the principal) delegates decision-making authority to another party (the agent). Agency theory is useful to analyze situations where there is imperfect alignment between the principal's and agent's 1) information and 2) objectives. As discussed earlier, it is common for local managers to have better information about their units than do higher-level central managers. Because the local managers have different information than central managers, they make different decisions. Similarly, as discussed in Chapter 8, it is common for the objectives of local managers to differ from central organizational objectives. Agency theory provides a framework to analyze these differences in designing a management control system.

Exhibit 9-2 shows how the design of a management control system affects the actions of managers. Managers have beliefs about how alternative action choices will lead to outcomes for their unit, and the management control system specifies how outcomes translate into unit performance metrics and into both explicit and implicit rewards. Managers' preferences motivate them to select actions that generate outcomes measured and rewarded by a company's management control system. The manager's understanding of how the control system links outcomes, performance metrics, and rewards influences the manager's choice of actions. Thus, the right metrics and rewards motivate actions that are in the company's best interests.

The links between outcomes and performance metrics and rewards are critical features of the management control system. While the importance of explicit links is clear, implicit links may also be important. For example, the management control system might include an explicit link that specifies the amount of bonus that will be paid for different levels of profit, but there may be an additional implicit link between performance and promotions. Similarly, it is important to recognize that rewards may be monetary or nonmonetary. Examples of monetary rewards include pay raises and bonuses. Examples of nonmonetary rewards include praise, better offices, and other perquisites. Thus, while we often focus on explicit monetary rewards, remember that implicit and nonmonetary rewards associated with outcomes and metrics play important roles in the management control system.

One important rule for performance measurement is clear: *You get what you measure.* Managers focus on areas where an organization measures managerial performance, even when the management control system does not include explicit rewards tied to the measures. Therefore, it is important to choose accounting measures that provide objective and easy-to-understand evaluations of performance, where managers believe there is a clear connection between their action choices and the performance metric.

Agency Theory and Risk

Ideally, companies should reward managers based on their individual performance, but often an organization cannot directly measure a manager's performance. For example, a company may not be able to separate the manager's effect on responsibility-center results from the effect of other factors beyond a manager's control. The greater the influence of noncontrollable factors

Exhibit 9-2
Design of a Management Control System

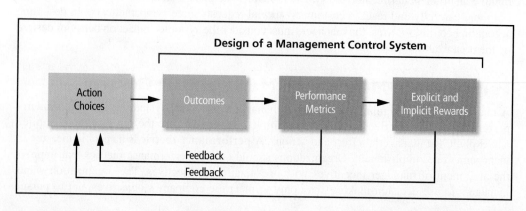

on responsibility-center results, the more problems there are in using the results to measure and reward a manager's performance.

Consider a particular Niketown store. Suppose its profits increased dramatically. The following factors all contributed to the increase in profits:

- A lengthy strike by employees of a competitor resulted in many customers switching to Nike.
- The store implemented a new cost management system resulting in a significant reduction in the costs of handling merchandise.
- Overall population growth in the store's region has been much higher than in other Niketown locations.
- Labor costs in the region have not increased as much as in most Niketown locations.
- Employee turnover is lower than the system average. Employees cite their excellent relationship with fellow employees and management as the reason for their high level of job satisfaction.

From the factors listed, it is likely that a significant portion of the store's profit increase was due to factors the store manager could not control (the competitor's strike, population growth, and regional labor costs). Nonetheless, it is also likely that a portion of the profit increase was due to factors the manager could control (adopting the cost-management system and creating a productive working environment for all employees). How should Nike evaluate the performance of the store manager? Should it measure the manager's performance by comparing profit across other Niketown stores? What other measures could Nike use?

An ideal performance metric would measure and reward the manager for controllable factors and neither reward nor punish the manager for uncontrollable factors. Although this ideal is hard to achieve, agency theory can guide the design of a system to link performance metrics and rewards. When an organization hires a manager, the employment contract details performance metrics and how they will affect rewards. However, not all rewards are explicitly specified. For example, a company can reward a manager with a promotion, but the contract will probably not explicitly specify the requirements for promotion.

According to agency theory, employment contracts must balance three factors:

1. Incentive: The more a manager's reward depends on a performance metric, the more incentive the manager has to take actions that maximize that measure. Top management should define the performance metric to promote goal congruence and base enough reward on it to achieve managerial effort.
2. Risk: The more uncontrollable factors affect a manager's reward, the more risk the manager bears. People generally avoid risk, so a company must pay managers more if it expects them to bear more risk. Creating incentive by linking rewards to responsibility-center results, which is generally desirable, has the undesirable side effect of imposing risk on managers if noncontrollable factors affect some part of the center's results.
3. Cost of measuring performance: The incentive versus risk trade-off is not necessary if a manager's controllable performance can be perfectly measured. Why? Because managers completely control their own performance, perfect measurement of controllable performance would eliminate risk to the manager. With perfect performance measurement, a manager could be paid a fixed amount if he or she performs as agreed, and nothing otherwise. But perfectly measuring controllable performance is usually inordinately expensive if not outright impossible. The cost-benefit criterion therefore leads companies to rely on imperfect but low-cost measures. Unfortunately, these measures frequently confound the manager's controllable performance with uncontrollable factors.

Consider the example of a promoter hired by a group of investors to promote and administer an outdoor concert. Suppose the investors offer the promoter a contract with part guaranteed pay and part bonus based on total attendance. A larger bonus portion compared with the guaranteed portion creates more incentive, but it also creates more risk for the promoter. For example, what happens if it rains? The promoter could do an outstanding job promoting the concert but the weather might keep fans away. To compensate the promoter for added risk, the expected total payment to the promoter will have to be higher for a contract where a higher portion of the total payment is based on attendance. The investors must decide on the optimal trade-off between the benefit from the added incentive created by a larger bonus and the extra total payment necessary to compensate for the added risk. Note that these contracting issues would not arise if the investors could directly measure the promoter's effort and judgment, rather than basing the bonus on attendance at the concert, a low-cost and readily-available measure that unfortunately is also influenced by factors outside the control of the promoter.

Measures of Segment Performance

Objective 4

Compute return on investment (ROI), economic profit, and economic value added (EVA).

It is hard to find a company that does not include some measure of profitability among its segment performance metrics. For example, companies that use performance measurement systems such as the balanced scorecard (discussed in Chapter 8) almost always include a profitability measure among their multiple metrics. The trouble is that there are many ways to measure profitability, and it is not clear which is the best measure. Is it income? Is it income before or after interest and taxes? Is it an absolute amount? A percentage? If a percentage, is it a percentage of revenue or of investment? In this section, we consider how alternative profitability measures affect managers' incentives.

Income Measures

Measures of income are readily available from the financial reporting system at any level of the organization for which a company can identify revenues and expenses, such as a subsidiary, a division, or a business unit. Moreover, accountants can easily customize income measures to exclude factors that the company considers to be outside the control of the manager. For example, earnings before interest and taxes (EBIT) excludes the effects of interest and taxes, while earnings before interest, taxes, depreciation, and amortization (EBITDA) also excludes the effects of depreciation and amortization.

However, income measures can create incentives to focus too narrowly on income without considering the resources required to generate income. For example, suppose a manager is considering an investment that will generate $1,000 of income. If the manager is evaluated only on income, the incentive is to make this investment, whether the required investment is $5,000 or $500,000. Thus, performance evaluation based on income measures can lead managers to focus only on income and ignore the investment required to generate that income.

Similarly, income measures can provide misleading performance comparisons. Suppose a company has two divisions, A, with operating income of $200,000, and B, with operating income of $150,000. Further suppose the investment in division A is $20 million while the investment in division B is $1 million. The operating income measure obviously provides an incomplete comparison of the performance of the two divisions. Although division A is generating slightly higher operating income than division B, division A requires a far larger investment. Division B is generating much higher income relative to the resources used to generate the income—$150,000 of income using $1 million of investment is far better performance than $200,000 of income using $20 million of investment.

Return on Investment (ROI)

return on investment (ROI)

A measure of income divided by the investment required to obtain that income.

A more comprehensive measure of profitability that takes into account the investment required to generate income is the **return on investment (ROI)**. ROI is income divided by the investment required to generate that income. For a given amount of investment (and holding risk constant), the investor wants the maximum income.

ROI facilitates the comparison of a unit's performance with other segments within the company or with similar units outside the company. Why? Because, unlike income alone, ROI takes into account the investment required to generate the income. Further, ROI is a return per unit of investment and does not depend on the size of the segments being compared. In the preceding example, division A has a much lower ROI than division B:

$$\text{ROI} = \frac{\text{income}}{\text{investment}}$$

$$\text{ROI division A} = \frac{\$200,000}{\$20,000,000} = 1\%$$

$$\text{ROI division B} = \frac{\$150,000}{\$1,000,000} = 15\%$$

	ROI	Income / Invested Capital	=	Income / Revenue	×	Revenue / Invested Capital
Present Outlook	20%	$\frac{16}{80}$	=	$\frac{16}{100}$	×	$\frac{100}{80}$
Alternative: 1. Increase return on sales by reducing expenses relative to sales.	25%	$\frac{20}{80}$	=	$\frac{20}{100}$	×	$\frac{100}{80}$
Alternative: 2. Increase capital turnover by decreasing investment.	25%	$\frac{16}{64}$	=	$\frac{16}{100}$	×	$\frac{100}{64}$

Exhibit 9-3
Return on Investment as the Product of Return on Sales and Capital Turnover

Every dollar invested in division B is generating income of $.15, compared to the $.01 generated by every dollar invested in division A.

ROI as the Product of Return on Sales and Investment Turnover

As shown in the following equations, we can write ROI as the product of two items: **return on sales** (income divided by revenue) and **capital turnover** (revenue divided by invested capital).

$$\text{return on investment} = \frac{\text{income}}{\text{invested capital}}$$

$$= \frac{\text{income}}{\text{revenue}} \times \frac{\text{revenue}}{\text{invested capital}}$$

$$= \text{return on sales} \times \text{capital turnover}$$

return on sales
Income divided by revenue.

capital turnover
Revenue divided by invested capital.

This expression shows that increasing either return on sales or capital turnover will increase ROI. Exhibit 9-3 shows an example where either of two alternatives could increase ROI to 25% from its current value of 20%. Alternative 1 improves return on sales by decreasing expenses relative to sales without increasing investment. Alternative 2 increases capital turnover by decreasing investment without reducing sales. Increasing capital turnover by decreasing investment means using fewer assets, such as cash, receivables, inventories, or equipment, for each dollar of revenue generated.

Increasing turnover is one of the advantages of implementing the just-in-time (JIT) philosophy (see Chapter 3). Many companies implementing JIT purchasing and production systems are able to lower inventory levels while maintaining the return on sales, resulting in dramatic improvements in ROI.

Measuring Investment

To understand what an ROI measure implies for a particular company, you must first determine how the company defines its components: income and investment. We discussed alternative definitions of segment income in Chapter 8, pages 302–305, so we will not repeat them here. In this section, we discuss alternative definitions of investment.

Definitions of Investment

Consider the following balance sheet:

Current assets	$ 400,000	Current liabilities	$ 200,000
Property, plant, and equipment, net	900,000	Long-term liabilities	400,000
		Stockholders' equity	700,000
Total assets	$1,300,000	Total liabilities and stockholders' equity	$1,300,000

Possible definitions of investment in this example are as follows:

1. Stockholders' equity: This definition considers only the investment by the stockholders, $700,000.
2. Stockholders' equity and long-term liabilities, $700,000 + $400,000 = $1,100,000. This definition encompasses not only the investment by stockholders but also the investment by debt investors. The combination of stockholders' equity and long-term liabilities is sometimes described as long-term invested capital. Note that because of the accounting identity total assets = short-term liabilities + long-term liabilities + stockholders' equity, this can alternatively be computed as total assets less short-term liabilities, $1,300,000 − $200,000 = $1,100,000.
3. Stockholders' equity, long-term liabilities, and current liabilities, $1,300,000: This definition encompasses all sources of financing for the firm. Because of the accounting identity, this is also equal to total assets.

Each of these alternative measures of investment paired with a measure of income yields a specific ROI measure. For example, net income divided by the first measure, investment by stockholders, is return on equity (ROE) while net income divided by the third measure, total assets, is return on assets (ROA).

For measuring segment performance, firms usually rely on ROA because it is impossible to measure investment by stockholders separately for segments. Further, ROA focuses on how well the division manager is using assets without regard to how they were financed.

Valuation of Assets

gross book value
The original cost of an asset before deducting accumulated depreciation.

net book value
The original cost of an asset less any accumulated depreciation.

When firms use ROA measures, two additional issues arise related to the valuation of total assets. First, companies could value assets contained in the investment base at either **gross book value** (the original cost of an asset) or **net book value** (the original cost of an asset less any accumulated depreciation). Second, they could value assets at either historical cost or some version of current cost. Practice is overwhelmingly in favor of using net book value based on historical costs, which are measures consistent with the numbers reported in the financial statements. However, the following three sections explain when gross book value or current cost might provide a better measure of performance to achieve desired incentives, and how to decide whether to measure assets at beginning-of-the-period values, end-of-the-period values, or at the average value duing the period.

HISTORICAL OR CURRENT COST?   Most companies favor historical cost over any measure of current cost such as replacement cost or liquidation values. Yet, critics maintain that historical cost provides a faulty basis for decision making and performance evaluation. Historical costs may be far from what a company might pay to purchase the asset today or the amount it could get from selling it—the values relevant to decisions affecting the asset. Despite these criticisms, managers have been slow to depart from historical cost.

Why is historical cost so widely used? Some critics would say that sheer ignorance is the explanation. But a more persuasive answer comes from cost-benefit analysis. Accounting systems are costly. Companies must keep historical records for many legal purposes, so historical records are already in place. A company spends no additional money evaluating performance based on historical costs. Many top managers believe that improvements in collective operating decisions that would result from using current cost are not large enough to warrant the added expense.

PLANT AND EQUIPMENT: GROSS OR NET?   In valuing assets, we need to distinguish between net and gross book values. Most companies use net book value in calculating their investment base. However, a significant minority uses gross book value. The proponents of gross book value maintain that it facilitates comparisons between years and between plants or divisions. Under gross values, performance evaluations depend only on what assets are in use, not on the depreciation assumptions or how old the assets are.

Consider an example of a $600,000 piece of equipment with a 3-year life and no residual value.

Year	Operating Income Before Depreciation	Depreciation	Operating Income	Average Net Book Value*	Net BV Rate of Return	Gross Book Value	Gross BV Rate of Return
1	$260,000	$200,000	$60,000	$500,000	12%	$600,000	10%
2	260,000	200,000	60,000	300,000	20	600,000	10
3	260,000	200,000	60,000	100,000	60	600,000	10

*($600,000 + $400,000) ÷ 2; ($400,000 + $200,000) ÷ 2; and so on.

Notice that operating income does not change in the example, yet the rate of return on net book value increases as the equipment ages. In contrast, the rate of return on gross book value is unchanged. Proponents of using gross book value for performance evaluation maintain that a performance metric should not improve simply because assets are getting older. On the other hand, advocates maintain that using net book value is less confusing because it is consistent with the assets shown on the conventional balance sheet and with net income computations.

When choosing between net and gross book value, companies should focus on the effect on managers' incentives. Managers evaluated using gross book value will tend to replace assets sooner than will managers in firms using net book value. Consider a division of **Nike** that has a 4-year-old machine with an original cost of $1,000 and net book value of $200. The division can replace the machine with a new one that also costs $1,000. The choice of net or gross book value does not affect net income. However, if Nike uses the net book value for measuring the investment base, replacement will increase the investment base from $200 to $1,000. In contrast, if Nike uses gross book value, the base is $1,000 irrespective of whether the asset is replaced. In summary, to maximize ROI, managers in firms using net book value have incentives to keep old assets with their low book value because the lower book value implies a lower measured investment. Managers in firms using gross book value have less incentive to keep old assets. Therefore, using gross book value will motivate managers to use more state-of-the-art production technology.

ASSET VALUES: BEGINNING, ENDING, OR AVERAGE?   If investment does not change throughout the year, it will not matter whether we measure assets at the beginning, the end, or average for the year. However, if investment changes throughout the year, we should measure invested capital as an average for the period. Why? Because income is a flow of resources over a period of time, and we should measure the effect of the flow on the average amount invested. The most accurate measures of average investment take into account the amount invested month-by-month, or even day-by-day. However, a simple average of the beginning and ending balances often provides nearly the same result without going to the trouble required to produce greater accuracy. Suppose division B had $800,000 of investment at the beginning of the year and the flow of income gradually increased it to $1,200,000 by the end of the year. The average of the beginning and ending investment amounts is ($800,000 + $1,200,000) ÷ 2 = $1,000,000.

SUMMARY   There are no universally correct answers with respect to such controversial issues as historical values versus current values, or gross versus net asset values, or beginning versus average versus ending values. Each organization must design its management control system to achieve the best possible decision making, taking into account the cost-benefit trade-off. This approach is not concerned with "truth" or "perfection" by itself. Instead, the design should ask questions such as the following: Will improvements in the system be worth the added cost? Will a different system achieve better goal congruence and managerial effort? Or, will our existing imperfect system provide about the same set of decisions at lower cost?

Incentives from ROI

Although evaluation based on ROI causes managers to consider both income and investment in their decisions, it still may not align the incentives for the manager with the goals of the firm. ROI-based performance evaluation may provide inappropriate incentives for managers to reject profitable investment opportunities or accept unprofitable investment opportunities. Consider a company with two divisions A and B, where currently division A has an

ROI of 5% and division B has an ROI of 15%. Suppose that the target return on investments is 10%—the corporate goal is to make investments where the return is 10% or more and reject investments where the return is less than 10%. If the company evaluates division managers based on ROI, their incentives will not be aligned with this corporate goal. For example, the division A manager has an incentive to adopt any investment that increases the division A return above its current value of 5%, including investments with returns between 5% and 10%, below the corporate target of 10%. Similarly, the division B manager has an incentive to reject any investment that decreases the division B return below its current value of 15%, including investments with returns between 10% and 15%, which are above the corporate target of 10%. The following sections explain how this issue is addressed by performance measures such as economic profit.

Economic Profit and Economic Value Added (EVA)

economic profit (residual income)

After-tax operating income less a capital charge.

net operating profit after-tax (NOPAT)

Income before interest expense but after tax.

capital charge

Company's cost of capital × average invested capital.

cost of capital

The cost of long-term liabilities and stockholders' equity weighted by their relative size.

Economic profit, also called **residual income**, is defined as net operating profit after-tax (NOPAT) less a capital charge. **Net operating profit after-tax (NOPAT)** is income before interest expense but after tax. The **capital charge** is the company's weighted-average cost of capital multiplied by the average invested capital, where the **cost of capital** is the after-tax cost of long-term liabilities and stockholders' equity weighted by their relative size. For example, a division with net operating profit after-tax of $250,000, average invested capital for the year of $1,000,000, and after-tax cost of capital of 10% has economic profit of $150,000:

Divisional net operating profit after-tax	$250,000
Minus charge for average invested capital (.10 × $1,000,000)	100,000
Equals economic profit (or residual income)	$150,000

Economic profit tells you the amount by which after-tax operating income exceeds the cost of the capital employed to generate that income. In the example, divisional income exceeds the cost of capital by $150,000.

Suppose a corporation has a goal to earn a return on investment greater than the cost of capital. Economic profit aligns incentives for individual managers with this corporate goal. Investments that earn a return in excess of the cost of capital will have positive economic profit while investments that earn a return below the cost of capital will have negative economic profit. Therefore, managers evaluated based on economic profit have incentives to make an investment if, and only if, its return exceeds the corporate cost of capital.

There are different ways to calculate measures of economic profit, depending on exactly how a company chooses to define the terms used. One popular variant developed and marketed by the consulting firm **Stern Stewart & Co.** is **economic value added (EVA)**. In formula form, Stern Stewart defines EVA as

economic value added (EVA)

Adjusted after-tax operating income minus the weighted-average cost of capital multiplied by the adjusted average invested capital.

$$\text{EVA} = \text{adjusted NOPAT} - (\text{weighted-average cost of capital} \times \text{adjusted average invested capital})$$

Stern Stewart's EVA measure incorporates adjustments to NOPAT and to invested capital. These adjustments are designed to convert after-tax operating income into a closer approximation of cash income and invested capital into a closer approximation of the cash invested in the economic resources the company uses to create value. Examples of these adjustments include the following:

- Use taxes paid rather than tax expense.
- Capitalize (rather than expense) research and development costs as an asset.
- Use FIFO for inventory valuation (thus companies using LIFO must add back the LIFO reserve to invested capital and add the increase or deduct the decrease in the LIFO reserve to after-tax operating income).
- If a company deducts interest expense in computing operating income, it must add back after-tax interest expense to find NOPAT.

Year	EP Operating Income	EVA Operating Income	EP Average Capital[†]	EVA Average Capital[†]	EP Capital Charge at 10%[‡]	EVA Capital Charge at 10%[§]	Economic Profit	Economic Value Added
Year 1	$ 8	$8 + 4 - 1 = \$11$*	$42	$42	$ 4.2	$ 4.2	$ 3.8	$ 6.8
Year 2	12	$12 - 1 = 11$	50	53	5.0	5.3	7.0	5.7
Year 3	12	$12 - 1 = 11$	62	64	6.2	6.4	5.8	4.6
Year 4	12	$12 - 1 = 11$	74	75	7.4	7.5	4.6	3.5
Total	$44	$44			$22.8	$23.4	$21.2	$20.6

[†]Income flows are assumed to occur at the end of each year so average capital for each year is equal to beginning capital. Beginning capital in year 1 is $42. In subsequent years, beginning capital increases by the corresponding income from the previous year. For example, year 2 EP beginning capital is $42 + 8 = 50 and year 2 EVA beginning capital is $42 + 11 = 53.
[‡]10% × EP average capital.
[§]10% × EVA average capital.
*Accounting operating income + R&D expense − R&D amortization = $8 + $4 − $1 = $11.

All amounts in this Exhibit are in millions of dollars.

Exhibit 9-4
Comparison of Economic Profit (EP) and Economic Value Added (EVA)

Exhibit 9-4 compares economic profit and EVA for an example where EVA incorporates an adjustment for research and development (R&D). Assume a division of Nike starts with invested capital of $42 (all amounts in this example are in millions of dollars) and ends each year with invested capital equal to beginning invested capital plus the income for the year. Further, to simplify the average capital calculations, assume that income flows do not increase invested capital during the year but instead are added to capital at the very end of the year. Under this assumption, average capital is simply the beginning capital. Finally, assume the division's operating income before accounting for R&D is $12 each year and that Nike's cost of capital is 10%. For simplicity, we ignore income taxes in our example, but remember that EVA uses after-tax numbers.

Suppose the division spent $4 during year 1 for R&D of a new shoe with a product life cycle of 4 years and there are no subsequent expenditures for R&D. Economic profit calculated according to U.S. financial reporting rules would show an expense equal to the entire $4 of R&D in the first year, and no subsequent expense for R&D, resulting in income after R&D for the 4 years of $8, $12, $12, and $12. Invested capital would grow by corresponding amounts from $42 at the beginning of year 1 to $50, $62, $74, and finally to $86 at the end of year 4. In contrast, EVA companies look upon R&D as a capital investment. For purposes of calculating EVA, Nike's division capitalizes R&D expenditures and expenses the $4 total cost as $1 of expense each year of the product's 4-year life cycle, resulting in income after R&D of $11, $11, $11, and $11. Invested capital would grow from $42 to $53, $64, $75, and $86 at the end of year 4. Thus, total operating income across the 4 years is $44 for either economic profit or EVA, and invested capital amounts at the beginning and at the end of the four-year example are the same under either economic profit or EVA. However, the timing of the recognition of income and the corresponding timing of the increases in capital during the four years of the example differ between EP and EVA, and therefore the capital charge differs between EP and EVA.

Economic profit over the 4 years is $21.2, or $44 less a capital charge of $22.8. EVA reflects the fact that capital is adjusted upward by $3 at the beginning of the second year ($4 investment in R&D less the $1 amortized in year 1) to reflect the capitalized investment in R&D and then declines by $1 per year as the company amortizes the remaining R&D. These adjustments in EVA imply a larger capital charge of $.3 in the second year, $.2 in the third year, and $.1 in the fourth year, so over the 4 years EVA deducts an additional $.6 capital charge for the capital invested in R&D and EVA = $44 − $23.4 = $20.6. After learning about present value in Chapter 12, you will also be able to show that although total EP and total EVA differ, the present value of the streams of EP and EVA discounted at the cost of capital are the same.

Stern Stewart has identified more than 160 different adjustments such as the adjustment illustrated for R&D but usually recommends only a few for a specific client. Many companies using economic profit for performance evaluation develop their own set of adjustments to income and capital, but all companies use the basic concept of net operating profit after-tax less a capital charge.

Economic profit and EVA have received much attention recently as scores of companies are adopting them as financial performance metrics. AT&T, Coca-Cola, CSX, FMC, and Quaker Oats claim that using EVA motivated managers to make decisions that increased shareholder value. Because EVA explicitly recognizes the cost of the capital deployed, it helps managers in these companies make better capital allocation decisions. Further, some investment companies, such as Manhattan-based broker-dealer Matrix USA, use economic profit to rate stocks for their investment clients.

Many companies are convinced that EVA has played a large role in their success. James M. Cornelius, chairman of Guidant Corporation—a medical device company, owned by Boston Scientific, that is focused on cardiovascular disease—paid tribute to EVA on Stern Stewart's Web site:

> *From day one at Guidant, we linked management bonuses to EVA performance targets. . . . If a target acquisition isn't EVA positive here, we don't do it. We pay EVA performance bonuses to Guidant technologists who develop new products within specified time frames, and we are seeing product innovation here that we've never seen before. All of our employees . . . are performing at levels we've never before experienced. I'm convinced these results are largely because of EVA. [Employees] keep looking for ways to improve our business because at the end of the day a significant share of their annual cash bonuses are tied to EVA improvement. . . . All that they have accomplished couldn't have been done without EVA.*

Siemens Corporation, Europe's largest electronics and electrical engineering firm and Stern Stewart's first EVA client in Europe, reported in its annual report that "Siemens focuses on EVA as the yardstick by which we measure the success of our efforts. The EVA performance standard encourages our people to be efficient, productive and proactive in thinking about our customers and their customers. These attributes translate into profitable growth and higher returns." Examples of actions taken by Siemens to improve EVA include the sale of Siecor, the fiber-optic cable business, to Corning, and the sale of its retail and banking business. As stated by Siemens, "Divesting selected businesses has generated funds for more strategic investments."

Making Managerial Decisions

One company that improved its EVA performance dramatically over the past two decades is IBM. In 1993, its EVA was a negative $13 billion. By 2000, the company improved its EVA to $2.2 billion. Like most companies, the economic downturn in the early 2000s hurt its EVA, dropping it into the negative range by 2002. By 2005, IBM again had a positive EVA at just under $1 billion, and it remained positive through 2010.

Compute the EVA for IBM for 2011 using the following data (in billions of dollars) without any of the specific adjustments recommended by Stern Stewart. As a manager, how would you explain the past history of EVA and the current EVA to investors?

	2011
Net operating profit after tax	$ 16.3
Invested capital	74
Cost of capital (assumed)	10%

Answer

Amounts are in billions as follows:

$$
\begin{aligned}
\text{EVA} &= \text{Net operating profit after tax} - \text{cost-of-capital} \\
&\quad \text{percentage} \times \text{capital invested} \\
&= \$16.3 - .10 \times \$74 \\
&= \$16.3 - \$7.4 = \$8.9 \text{ Billion}
\end{aligned}
$$

The improvement from 1993 to 2000 was dramatic as IBM moved from large negative EVA to positive EVA of $2.2 billion. The company continued to show strong improvements as EVA rose to $8.9 billion by 2011.

Incentives from Income, ROI, or Economic Profit

Objective 5

Compare the incentives created by income, ROI, and economic profit (or EVA) performance measures.

We have already discussed the main advantage of ROI relative to income measures—ROI provides incentives for segment managers to take into account the cost of resources used to generate income. But why do some companies prefer economic profit (or EVA) to ROI? After all, both take into account the cost of resources used to generate income. As explained

	Without Project		With Project	
	Division X	Division Y	Division X	Division Y
Net after-tax operating income	$ 200,000	$ 40,000	$ 275,000	$ 96,000
Invested capital	$1,000,000	$800,000	$1,500,000	$1,600,000
ROI (net operating income ÷ invested capital)	20%	5%	18.3%	6%
Capital charge (10% × invested capital)	$ 100,000	$ 80,000	$ 150,000	$ 160,000
Economic profit (net operating income – capital charge)	$ 100,000	$ (40,000)	$ 125,000	$ (64,000)

Exhibit 9-5
ROI and Economic Profit for Divisions X and Y

on p. 396, ROI can motivate segment managers to make investment decisions that are not in the best interests of the company as a whole. In contrast, when a company uses economic profit (or EVA) as a performance metric, managers have incentive to invest only in projects earning more than the cost of capital because only those projects increase the division's economic profit.

Consider two divisions of a company, division X with operating income of $200,000 and division Y with operating income of $40,000. Division X has average invested capital of $1 million and division Y has average invested capital of $800,000. Assume that the company's cost of capital is 10%, and, for simplicity, ignore taxes. Suppose each division is considering a new proposed project. Division X is considering Project A that will earn 15% annually on a $500,000 investment, or $75,000 a year. Division Y is considering Project B that will earn 7% annually on an $800,000 investment, or $56,000 a year. Exhibit 9-5 shows ROI and economic profit with and without the project for the two divisions.

Suppose performance evaluation is based on ROI. Would the manager of division X invest in Project A? No. Even though Project A earns a return of 15% (which is above the 10% cost of capital), it would decrease ROI for division X from 20% to 18.3%. Would the manager of division Y invest in Project B? Yes. Even though Project B earns a return of 7% (below the 10% cost of capital), it would increase ROI for division Y from 5% to 6%. In general, the ROI profitability metric provides an incentive for divisions to invest in new projects that earn a return in excess of their current return, rather than an incentive to invest in new projects with a return in excess of the cost of capital. Thus, performance evaluation based on ROI leads division X to reject a project with a 15% return and division Y to accept a project with a 7% return.

Now suppose performance evaluation is based on economic profit. For division X, investing in Project A would change economic profit from $100,000 to $125,000. This $25,000 increase in economic profit is the $75,000 annual return from the new project less the $50,000 annual cost of capital for the new project. In contrast to the decision under ROI, the manager of division X would accept Project A. For division Y, investing in Project B would change economic profit from $–40,000 to $–64,000. This $24,000 decrease is the $56,000 annual return from the new project less the $80,000 annual cost of capital for the new project. Thus, the manager of division Y would reject Project B. Evaluation based on economic profit motivates both managers to invest only in projects that earn a return in excess of the cost of capital, whereas evaluation based on ROI leads both managers to incorrect decisions— division A rejecting a desirable project and division B accepting an undesirable one. In general, use of economic profit or EVA will promote goal congruence and lead to better decisions than using ROI.

Despite the success of economic profit and EVA, many companies still use ROI. Why? Perhaps because it is simpler to compute, more readily understandable by managers, and easier to compare across divisions. Furthermore, in some cases, top management minimizes the dysfunctional incentives from ROI by emphasizing that managers should compare project ROI to the cost of capital, rather than to their existing ROI. Remember that companies try to choose a profitability measure to use in performance evaluation that aligns managers' incentives with organizational goals without being overly complex or too expensive to apply.

Summary Problem for Your Review

PROBLEM

Suppose a division of Google has assets of $2,000,000, invested capital of $1,800,000, and net operating income of $600,000. Ignore taxes.

1. What is the division's ROI?
2. If the weighted-average cost of capital is 14%, what is the EVA?
3. Suppose management uses ROI as a performance metric. What effects on management behavior do you expect?
4. Suppose management uses economic profit as a performance metric. What effects on management behavior do you expect?

SOLUTION

1. ROI = $600,000 ÷ $1,800,000 = 33%.
2. EVA = $600,000 − .14 ($1,800,000) = $600,000 − $252,000 = $348,000.
3. If the company uses ROI, the division manager has an incentive to reject new projects that do not earn an ROI of at least 33%, the division's current ROI. From the viewpoint of the organization as a whole, this is undesirable if the cost of capital is only 14%. If a division is enjoying a high ROI, it is less likely to expand if top management evaluates performance using ROI than if it evaluates performance using EVA.
4. If the company uses EVA, the manager is inclined to accept all projects whose expected rate of return exceeds the weighted-average cost of capital. The manager is more likely to expand the division because his or her goal is to maximize a dollar amount rather than a rate.

Transfer Pricing

Objective 6

Define *transfer prices* and identify their purpose.

When all the segments of a decentralized organization are independent of one another, segment managers can focus only on their own segments because what is best for their segment is generally best for the organization as a whole. In contrast, when segments interact, such as buying or selling in the same markets, there is a possibility that what helps one segment hurts another segment badly enough to have a negative net effect on the entire organization. For example, two Nike sales divisions may compete for the same customer by cutting prices, thereby reducing the company's overall margin on sales to the customer. The more customers (and suppliers) two segments have in common, the more a company should consider combining the two segments into one to minimize dysfunctional incentives for one segment to gain at the expense of the other.

Other potential interactions between segment and organizational interests occur when one segment sells products or services to another segment of the same organization for a price called the **transfer price**. For example, when one segment produces a component and sells it to another segment that then incorporates the component in a final product, a transfer price is required. Transfer prices also apply to services, such as when a product manager buys advertising services from the marketing support segment. The transfer price for the component or service is revenue to the producing segment and a cost to the acquiring segment. Thus, transfer prices allocate profit among segments—a change in the transfer price increases the computed profit for one segment and decreases the profit for the other segment—without affecting profit for the firm as a whole.

Transfer pricing policies are especially important in decentralized companies where top management believes that segment autonomy has important benefits. In such companies, segment managers decide how many products or services will be transferred from one segment to another. Delegating these decisions to segment managers creates benefits when the segment managers, being "closer to the action," have better information than top management about

transfer price

The price at which one segment of an organization sells products or services to another segment of the same organization.

the items being transferred. The challenge to such companies is to design a transfer pricing policy that motivates segment managers to transfer the quantity of products and services that both maximizes the segment's profitability metric and is also in the best interests of the company as a whole. There is seldom a perfect transfer pricing policy, so decentralization inevitably leads to some dysfunctional transfer decisions. But companies that adhere to a decentralization philosophy believe that the benefits of decentralization and the preservation of segment autonomy exceed the costs of occasional dysfunctional decisions.

When there is little information advantage at the segment level, companies generally centralize decisions and have top management dictate the quantity and price of products and services transferred between segments. This ensures that segment managers cannot make a decision to transfer an amount of a product or service that is not in the company's best interests.

Purposes of Transfer Pricing

What does a decentralized company want from its transfer pricing system? Ideally, it wants to ensure that managers who make decisions to improve their segment's performance also increase the performance of the company as a whole. Therefore, a company wants profitability metrics that reward the segment manager for decisions that increase the profitability of the entire company. For example, transfer prices should guide managers to make the best possible decisions regarding whether to buy or sell products and services inside or outside the total organization. Decisions by the buying and selling segment managers, acting without top-management intervention, should be the best decisions for their segment and for the entire organization. In other words, decisions that increase a segment's profitability metric should lead to increased profitability for the company as a whole.

Organizations use a variety of transfer prices. They use cost-based prices for some transfers, market-based prices for other transfers, and negotiated prices for others. Therefore, do not expect to find a single, universally applicable answer to the problem of transfer pricing. There is no perfect transfer-pricing system. Almost every manager in a decentralized organization has had experience with transfer-pricing systems that seem less than ideal. For example, a manager at Weyerhaeuser, a large wood-products firm, called transfer pricing his firm's most troublesome management control issue.

A General Rule for Transfer Pricing

Although no single rule always meets the goals of transfer pricing, a general rule can provide guidance:

$$\text{transfer price} = \text{outlay cost} + \text{opportunity cost}$$

As described earlier on page 346, outlay costs require a cash disbursement. They are essentially the additional amount the producing segment must pay to produce the product or service. Opportunity cost is the contribution to profit that the producing segment forgoes by transferring the item internally. For example, if capacity constraints prevent a segment from producing enough to meet both external demand and internal demand from the other segment, the opportunity cost is the contribution margin the producing segment could have received from selling in the external market rather than transferring internally.

Why does this rule provide incentives for segment decisions that also maximize profitability for the firm as a whole? Consider the following example of two hypothetical Nike divisions. The fabric division (the producing division) is considering transferring the fabric required for a golf shirt to the sportswear division (the buying division), as shown in Exhibit 9-6.

Objective 7

State the general rule for transfer pricing and use it to assess transfer prices based on total costs, variable costs, and market prices.

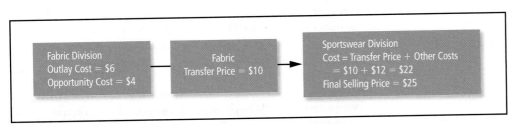

Exhibit 9-6
Transfer Pricing Example

Suppose the fabric division's $4 opportunity cost arises because it can get $10 by selling the fabric to a buyer outside the company. Thus, the foregone contribution by not selling to the outside buyer is $10 – $6 = $4. At any transfer price less than $10, the producing division is better off selling the fabrics to the outside buyer rather than transferring it. Thus, the minimum transfer price the fabric division would accept is $6 + $4 = $10.

Now consider how much the item is worth to the sportswear division. For the fabric to be profitable to the sportswear division, it must be able to sell the final product for more than the transfer price plus the other costs it must incur to finish and sell the product. Because it can sell the golf shirt for $25 and its other costs are $12, the maximum price the sportswear division would be willing to pay is $25 – $12 = $13. At any higher price, the sportswear division would choose not to produce the shirt at all. But there is a second constraint: The sportswear division will not pay more to the fabric division than it would have to pay an outside supplier. Thus, the largest transfer price acceptable to the sportswear division is the lesser of (1) $13 or (2) the cost charged by an outside supplier.

Now consider the transfer decision from the company's point of view. Transfer is desirable whenever (1) the total cost to the company for producing the fabric internally ($10, including opportunity cost, as determined by the fabric division) is less than its value to the company ($13 as determined by the sportswear division), and (2) the fabric division's costs (again including opportunity costs) are less than the price the sportswear division would have to pay to an outside supplier. The first criterion guarantees that the company does not decide to produce a product where the total cost to produce exceeds the final selling price to the end user. The second guarantees that it does not pay more to produce the fabric internally than it would have to pay to buy it in the marketplace. The only transfer price that will always meet these criteria is $10, the fabric division's outlay cost plus opportunity cost. Why? Any price between $10 and $13 meets the first criterion. However, only $10 meets the second because any transfer price above $10 opens the possibility that the sportswear division will buy the fabric externally when the company would be better off producing and transferring it from the fabric division.

Exhibit 9-7 summarizes the division's decision and the effect on Nike as a whole when an outside supplier offers the fabric at either greater than $10 or less than $10. At a $10 transfer price, regardless of what price outside suppliers offer, the division managers, acting independently, make the decision that is most profitable for the company as a whole. Any other transfer price creates a possibility of a manager making the decision that is best for his or her segment but not for the company as a whole. The fabric division would reject the transfer at less than $10 regardless of how much profit it creates for the sportswear division. The sportswear division would reject the transfer whenever the transfer price is greater than the price from alternative sources.

Note that any transfer price greater than the $10 price specified by the general rule runs the risk of the sportswear division purchasing outside the company even when the internal cost is lower. For example, with a transfer price of $12 and an outside purchase cost of $11, the sportswear division would pay $11 to the outside supplier when the company could have spent only $10 (including opportunity cost) to produce the fabric in the fabric division.

This general rule doesn't always provide a unique transfer price. For example, suppose there is no outside supplier for the fabric (but continue to assume there is an outside customer that will buy from the producing division for $10). Then the general rule tells us only that the transfer

Exhibit 9-7

Effects of a $10 Transfer Price on Decisions

Outside Supplier Price	Best Decision for Division	Best Decision for Company
Less than $10	Do not transfer—buying division rejects transfer because buying internally will reduce its profits	Do not transfer—buy from outside supplier because it is cheaper for the company as a whole
Greater than $10	If value to buying division is greater than $10: Transfer at $10—both divisions benefit	Transfer—cost of internal production is less than cost of buying externally
	If value to buying division is less than $10: Do not transfer—buying division rejects transfer	Do not transfer—value of the fabric to the company is less than its cost

price must be greater than $10 (the outlay cost plus opportunity cost for the producing division) and less than $13 (the final selling price minus the outlay costs for the sportswear division). Thus, the rule does not specify a specific price within this range. As another example, suppose that when selling the fabric to the outside buyer, there is a $.75 shipping and handling cost that is saved if the fabric is transferred internally. The general rule does not tell us how to allocate the $.75 savings between the two divisions.

Because transfer-pricing systems have multiple goals, there is no universally optimal transfer price. Nonetheless, the general rule provides a good benchmark by which to judge transfer-pricing systems. We analyze the following transfer-pricing systems, the most popular systems in practice, by examining how close the transfer price comes to the benchmark of outlay cost plus opportunity cost:

1. Market-based transfer prices
2. Cost-based transfer prices
   a. Variable cost
   b. Full cost (possibly plus profit)
3. Negotiated transfer prices

In addressing these transfer-pricing systems, we will assume that a company has multiple divisions that transfer items to one another, and that the company wants to preserve segment autonomy in a decentralized operation.

Market-Based Transfer Prices

When there is a ready market for an item or service transferred from one segment to another, transfer pricing policies are straightforward. The common maxim is "if a market price exists, use it." The more competitive the market, the better the maxim applies.

If there is a competitive market for the product or service being transferred internally, using the market price as a transfer price will generally lead to goal congruence. Why? Because the market price equals the variable cost plus opportunity cost.

$$\text{transfer price} = \text{variable cost} + \text{opportunity cost}$$
$$= \text{variable cost} + (\text{market price} - \text{variable cost})$$
$$= \text{market price} + \text{variable cost} - \text{variable cost}$$
$$= \text{market price}$$

If the selling division avoids some marketing and delivery costs when selling internally, many companies deduct these costs from the market price when computing the transfer price. That is, the transfer price is the net amount the selling division would receive selling the item on the market after deducting marketing and delivery costs.

To illustrate market-based transfer prices, reconsider the two hypothetical divisions of Nike. The fabric division makes fabrics it sells directly to external customers as well as to other Nike divisions, such as the sportswear division. The fabric division makes a particular fabric for an outlay cost of $6 and can sell it to external customers for $10. The sportswear division can buy that same fabric on the market for $10 and use it to make a golf shirt, spending an extra $12 in production costs. The golf shirt sells for $25. Should the sportswear division obtain the fabric from the fabric division of Nike or purchase it from an external supplier?

Assume for the moment that the fabric division can sell its entire production to external customers without incurring any marketing or shipping costs. The manager of the fabric division will not sell the fabric for less than $10. Why? Because he or she can sell it on the market for $10, so any price less than $10 will reduce the manager's division's profit. Furthermore, the sportswear division manager will refuse to pay a transfer price greater than $10 for the fabric for each golf shirt. Why? Because if the transfer price is greater than $10, he or she will purchase the fabric from the external supplier for the lower price of $10 in order to maximize his or her division's profit. The only transfer price that allows both managers to maximize their division's profit is $10, the market price. If the managers had autonomy to make decisions, at any transfer price other than $10 one of the managers would decline the internal transfer of the fabric.

Now suppose the fabric division incurs a $.75 per square yard marketing and shipping cost that it can avoid by transferring the fabric to the sportswear division instead of marketing it to outside customers. Most companies would then use a transfer price of $9.25, often called a "market-price-minus" transfer price. The fabric division would get the same net amount from the transfer ($9.25 with no marketing or shipping costs) as from an external sale ($10 less $.75 marketing and shipping costs), whereas the sportswear division saves $.75 per shirt. The fabric division will produce and transfer the fabric only if the transfer price is at least $9.25, and the sportswear division will buy the fabric internally only if it costs less than $10 and is worth at least $9.25 to the division. These criteria drive a decision to transfer only if it is in Nike's overall best interests.

While market-based transfer prices generally provide the correct incentives, market prices are not always available. Therefore, we next discuss some other systems commonly used in the absence of market-based prices.

Transfers at Cost

When market prices don't exist, most companies resort to cost-based transfer prices. In fact, about half the major companies in the world use a cost-based transfer-pricing system. However, there are many possible definitions of cost. Some companies use only variable cost, others use full cost, and still others use full cost plus a profit markup. Some use standard costs, and some use actual costs. Cost-based transfer prices are easy to understand and use, but they can easily lead to **dysfunctional decisions**—decisions in conflict with the company's goals. The key to successful cost-based transfer prices is to minimize such dysfunctional decisions. Let's examine some of these cost-based transfer-pricing systems.

dysfunctional decision
Any decision that is in conflict with organizational goals.

TRANSFERS AT VARIABLE COST Companies that transfer items at variable cost implicitly assume that the selling division has no opportunity cost. Why? Because the outlay cost is generally about equal to variable cost: transfer price = outlay (variable) cost + $0. Therefore, a variable-cost transfer-pricing system is most appropriate when the selling division forgoes no opportunities when it transfers the item internally, for example when there is plenty of excess capacity in the selling division.

Variable-cost transfer prices cause dysfunctional decisions when the selling segment has significant opportunity costs. In our fabric division–sportswear division example, there are two ways this could happen. First, if there are positive opportunity costs, the fabric division manager would turn down any transfer, preferring to pursue the alternative opportunities, perhaps selling the fabric on the open market or using facilities to make a different, more profitable, fabric. This would be dysfunctional if the sportswear division could make more profit from its golf shirt than the fabric division makes from pursuing its alternative opportunities. Second, realizing the lack of incentive for the fabric division to transfer the fabric, top management might insist that the fabric division produce and transfer the fabric. This would be against the company's interests if the fabric division passes up opportunities that yield more profit than the sportswear division's golf shirt. In addition, this policy violates segment autonomy.

TRANSFERS AT FULL COST OR FULL COST PLUS PROFIT Full-cost transfer prices include not only variable cost but also an allocation of fixed costs. In addition, some companies also add a markup for profit. This implicitly assumes the allocated fixed costs (and, if included, the profit markup) is a good approximation of the opportunity cost. In cases of constrained capacity, where the selling division cannot satisfy all internal and external demand for its products, the opportunity cost is positive. As explained in the previous section, when the opportunity cost is positive, variable-cost transfer prices are problematic. While there is no guarantee that adding an allocation of fixed cost is a good approximation of the opportunity cost, it may be a better approximation than assuming a zero opportunity cost. Some companies believe that using activity-based costing improves cost-based transfer prices, as described in the Business First box on page 353.

Dysfunctional decisions arise with full-cost transfer prices when the selling segment has opportunity costs that differ significantly from the allocation of fixed costs and profit. In our example, suppose the fabric division has excess capacity so that opportunity cost is zero. Nevertheless, it has large fixed costs so that the full cost of the transferred fabric includes $8 of fixed cost in addition to the $6 variable cost. At a transfer price of $14, and assuming an external supplier either doesn't exist or would also charge at least $14, the sportswear division would refuse the transfer unless it could sell the golf shirt for at least $14 + $12 = $26. Therefore, because the shirt sells for $25, the sportswear division would decide not to produce it.

But this decision costs Nike a contribution margin of $25 − ($6 + $12) = $7. The decision not to produce the shirt is dysfunctional—that is, it conflicts with Nike's goal of generating additional profit.

Cost-based transfer prices can create problems when a company uses actual cost rather than standard cost as a transfer price. Because the buying division will not know its actual cost in advance, it will not be able to accurately plan its costs. More importantly, a transfer price based on actual costs merely passes cost inefficiencies in the selling division along to the buying division. Therefore, the selling division lacks incentive to control its costs. Thus, we recommend using budgeted or standard costs instead of actual costs for cost-based transfer prices.

Finally, cost-based transfer prices can undercut segment autonomy and sometimes lead to conflicts between segment and organizational goals. Suppose managers believe it is best for the company to transfer an item internally rather than purchasing it externally but also believe that the transfer price is unfair to their segment. They may either do what they think top management wants but resent its negative effect on their segment, or they may do what is best for their segment, ignoring its negative impact on the organization as a whole. Neither alternative is desirable.

Supporters point out that cost-based transfer prices are easy to understand and inexpensive to implement. However, any cost-based transfer price can lead to dysfunctional decisions. Companies transferring goods or services in the absence of market prices must decide whether the effects of dysfunctional decisions are great enough to abandon cost-based transfer prices. One alternative is to give up decentralized decision making—essentially have top management dictate whether to transfer items internally or purchase them from external suppliers—but this also sacrifices the benefits of decentralization. Another alternative is negotiated transfer prices, which we discuss next.

Making Managerial Decisions

Consider the following data concerning a subassembly that Willamette Manufacturing Company produces in its fabricating division and uses in products assembled in its assembly division.

Fabricating Division	
Variable cost of subassembly	$35
Excess capacity (in units)	1,000
Assembly Division	
Market price for buying the subassembly from external sources	$50
Number of units needed	900

If you were the manager of the fabricating division, what is the lowest transfer price you would accept for the subassembly? If you were the manager of the assembly division, what is the most you would be willing to pay for the subassembly? Is there a transfer price that would motivate production and transfer of the subassembly? If so, what is the price?

Answer

The fabricating division has excess capacity, so its manager would be willing to accept any price above the variable cost of $35. The assembly division can buy the subassembly for $50 on the external market, so its manager would be willing to pay no more than $50 to buy it from the fabricating division. The transfer would take place at some price between $35 and $50.

Negotiated Transfer Prices

Companies heavily committed to segment autonomy often allow managers to negotiate transfer prices. The managers may consider both costs and market prices in their negotiations, though they are not required to do so. Supporters of negotiated transfer prices maintain that the managers involved have the best knowledge of what the company will gain or lose by producing and transferring the product or service, so open negotiation allows the managers to make optimal decisions. Critics of negotiated prices focus on the time and effort spent negotiating, an activity that adds nothing directly to the profits of the company.

Let's look at how our fabric division and sportswear division managers might approach a negotiation of a transfer price. The sportswear division manager might look at the selling price of the golf shirt, $25, less the additional cost the division incurs in making it, $12, and decide to purchase fabric at any transfer price less than $25 − $12 = $13. The sportswear division will add to its profit by making and selling the shirt if the transfer price is below $13. At a transfer price above $13, the sportswear division will choose to not make and sell the shirt, assuming there is no other supplier of fabric at a price below $13.

Similarly, the fabric division manager will look at what it costs to produce and transfer the fabric. If there is excess capacity and thus no opportunity cost, any transfer price above $6 will increase the fabric division's profit. Negotiation will result in a transfer if the maximum transfer price the sportswear division is willing to pay is greater than the minimum transfer price the fabric division is willing to accept. The fabric division manager is willing to accept any price above $6 and the sportswear division manager will pay up to $13. The exact transfer price will depend on the negotiating ability and power of the two division managers.

Now suppose there is no excess capacity in the fabric division and an outside customer is willing to pay $10 for the fabric. Transferring the fabric internally causes the division to give up a contribution of $4 as well as paying variable costs of $6, so the minimum transfer price acceptable to the fabric division is now $10. A transfer will take place at a price between $10 and $13.

If the opportunity cost had been more than $7, a transfer would not occur. Why? Because the fabric division's minimum price of $6 variable costs plus opportunity cost would now be greater than $13 and the sportswear division's maximum price would be just $13. This decision is exactly what Nike would prefer. When the fabric division's opportunity cost is less than $7, the golf shirt is more profitable than the fabric division's other business, and the transfer should occur. When the fabric division's opportunity cost is greater than $7, the additional contribution from the fabric division's other business will be greater than the sportswear division's contribution on the shirt, and the transfer should not occur. Therefore, the manager's decisions are congruent with the company's best interests.

What should top management of a decentralized organization do if it sees segment managers making dysfunctional decisions through their negotiations? As usual, the answer is, "It depends." Top management can step in and force the "correct" decision, but doing so undermines segment managers' autonomy and the overall notion of decentralization. It also assumes top management has the information necessary to determine the correct decision. Most important, frequent intervention results in recentralization. Indeed, if more centralization is desired, the organization might want to reorganize by combining segments.

Top managers who wish to encourage decentralization will often make sure that both producing and purchasing division managers understand all the facts and then allow the managers to negotiate a transfer price. Even when top managers suspect that the segments might make a dysfunctional decision, they may swallow hard and accept the segment manager's judgment as a cost of decentralization. (Repeated dysfunctional decision making may be a reason to change the organizational design or to change managers.)

Well-trained and informed segment managers who understand opportunity costs and the behavior of fixed and variable costs will often make better decisions than will top managers. The producing division manager knows best the various uses of its capacity, and the purchasing division manager knows best what profit can be made on the items to be transferred. In addition, negotiation allows segments to respond flexibly to changing market conditions when setting transfer prices. One transfer price may be appropriate in a time of idle capacity and another when demand increases and operations approach full capacity.

Multinational Transfer Pricing

Objective 8

Identify the factors affecting multinational transfer prices.

So far, we have focused on how transfer-pricing policies affect the motivation of managers. However, in multinational companies, other factors may dominate. For example, multinational companies use transfer prices to minimize worldwide income taxes, import duties, and tariffs. For example, Nike might prefer to make its profits in Singapore, where the marginal corporate tax rate is less than half the rate in the United States.

Suppose a division in a high-income-tax-rate country produces a component for another division in a low-income-tax-rate country. By setting a low transfer price, the company can recognize most of the profit from the production in the low-income-tax-rate country, thereby minimizing taxes. Likewise, items produced by divisions in a low-income-tax-rate country and transferred to a division in a high-income-tax-rate country should have a high transfer price to minimize taxes.

Sometimes import duties offset income tax effects. Most countries base import duties on the price paid for an item, whether bought from an outside company or transferred from another division. Therefore, low transfer prices generally lead to low import duties.

Business First

Activity-Based Costing and Transfer Pricing

Teva Pharmaceutical Industries Ltd. is a global health-care company specializing in pharmaceuticals. It is headquartered in Israel and had 2011 sales of $18.3 billion. Teva entered the lucrative generic drug market in the mid-1980s. Each of the marketing divisions purchases generic drugs from the manufacturing division. As part of its strategy, the company decentralized its pharmaceutical business into cost and profit centers. Prior to decentralization, each marketing division was a revenue center. With the new organizational structure, management had to decide how to measure marketing division costs because profits were now the key financial performance metric.

A key cost to the marketing divisions is the transfer price paid for drugs purchased from the manufacturing division. Management considered several alternative bases for the company's transfer prices. Market price was not a feasible basis for transfer pricing because there was no competitive market. Negotiated prices were rejected because management believed the resulting debates over the proper price would be lengthy and disruptive. Teva adopted variable cost (raw material and packaging costs) transfer pricing for a short time but eventually rejected it because it did not lead to congruent decisions—managers did not differentiate products using many scarce resources from those using few. Further, when a local source for the drug did exist, the market price was always above the variable-cost transfer price. Thus, managers in Teva's manufacturing division had little incentive to keep costs low.

Management also rejected traditional full cost that did not capture the actual cost structure of the manufacturing division. Specifically, the traditional full-cost system undercosted the low-volume products and overcosted the large-volume products. The system traced only raw materials directly to products. It divided the remaining manufacturing costs into two cost pools and allocated them based on labor hours and machine hours. One problem with the traditional system was its inability to capture and correctly allocate the non-value-added cost of setup activity. Management did not know the size of the errors in product cost, but the lack of confidence in the traditional cost system led to rejection of full cost as the transfer-pricing base.

Then Teva's management adopted an activity-based-costing (ABC) system to improve the accuracy of its product costs. The ABC system has five activity centers and related cost pools: receiving, manufacturing, packaging, quality assurance, and shipping. Because of the dramatic increase in costing accuracy, management was able to adopt full activity-based cost as the transfer price.

Teva's managers are pleased with their transfer-pricing system. The benefits include increased confidence that the costs being transferred are closely aligned with the actual short- and long-run costs being incurred, increased communication between divisions, and an increased awareness of the costs of low-volume products and the costs of capacity required to support these products. They believe their activity-based costs are the best approximation to outlay cost plus opportunity costs because the allocation of the fixed costs is a good measure of the value (opportunity cost) of the resources being consumed.

Sources: Adapted from Robert Kaplan, Dan Weiss, and Eyal Desheh, "Transfer Pricing with ABC," *Management Accounting*, May, 1997, pp. 20–28; and Teva Pharmaceutical Industries Ltd. *2011 Annual Report*.

Tax authorities also recognize the incentive to set transfer prices to minimize taxes and import duties. Therefore, most countries have restrictions on allowable transfer prices. U.S. multinationals must follow an Internal Revenue Code rule specifying that transfers be priced at "arm's-length" market values, or at the price one division would pay another if they were independent companies. Even with this rule, companies have some latitude in deciding an appropriate "arm's-length" price.

Consider a high-end running shoe produced by an Irish Nike division with a 12% income tax rate and transferred to a division in Germany with a 40% rate. In addition, suppose Germany imposes an import duty equal to 20% of the price of the item and that Nike cannot deduct this import duty for tax purposes. Suppose the full unit cost of a pair of the shoes (translated to U.S. dollars) is $100, and the variable cost is $60. If tax authorities allow either variable- or full-cost transfer prices, which should Nike choose? By transferring at $100 rather than at $60, the company gains $3.20 per unit:

Effect of Transferring at $100 Instead of at $60

Income of the Irish division is $40 higher; therefore, it pays 12% × $40 more income taxes	$(4.80)
Income of the German division is $40 lower; therefore, it pays 40% × $40 less income taxes	16.00
Import duty is paid by the German division on an additional $100 − $60 = $40; therefore, it pays 20% × $40 more duty	(8.00)
Net savings from transferring at $100 instead of $60	$ 3.20

Companies may also use transfer prices to avoid the financial restrictions imposed by some governments. For example, a country might restrict the amount of dividends paid to foreign owners. It may be easier for a company to get cash from a foreign division as payment for items transferred than as cash dividends.

In summary, transfer pricing becomes even more complex in a multinational company. Multinational companies try to achieve more objectives through transfer-pricing policies, and the objectives sometimes conflict with one another.

Summary Problem for Your Review

PROBLEM

Reconsider Nike's fabric division and sportswear division described earlier on page 332. In addition to the data there, suppose the fabric division has annual fixed manufacturing costs of $800,000 and expected annual production of enough fabric to make 100,000 golf shirts. The "fully-allocated cost" of the material for one golf shirt is as follows:

Variable costs	$ 6.00
Fixed costs, $800,000 ÷ 100,000 shirts	8.00
Fully allocated cost of the material for one golf shirt	$14.00

Assume that the fabric division has idle capacity. The sportswear division is considering whether to buy enough fabric for 10,000 golf shirts. It will sell each shirt for $25. The additional processing and selling costs in the sportswear division to produce and sell one shirt are $12. If Nike bases its transfer prices on fully-allocated cost, would the sportswear division manager buy? Explain. Would the company as a whole benefit if the sportswear division manager decided to buy? Explain.

SOLUTION

The sportswear division manager would not buy. The fully-allocated cost-based transfer price of $14 would make the acquisition of the fabric unattractive to the sportswear division:

Sportswear Division:		
Sales price of final product		$25
Deduct costs		
Transfer price paid to the fabric division (fully-allocated cost)	$14	
Additional processing and selling costs	12	
Total costs to the sportswear division		26
Contribution to profit of the sportswear division		$ (1)
Company as a whole:		
Sales price of final product		$25
Deduct variable costs and opportunity costs		
Fabric department	$ 6	
Sportswear department	12	
Total variable and opportunity costs		18
Contribution to company as a whole		$ 7

The company as a whole would benefit by $70,000 (10,000 shirts × $7) if the fabric division produces and transfers the fabric.

The major lesson here is that transfer prices based on fully-allocated costs may induce the wrong decisions when there is idle capacity in the supplier division. Working in his or her own best interests, the sportswear division manager has no incentive to buy from the fabric division.

Keys to Successful Management Control Systems

Like management in general, management control systems are more art than science. A company such as Nike will certainly include many subjective factors as well as more objective measures of profitability in its performance-evaluation system. Intelligent use of the available information is as important as generating the information itself. Next, we briefly explore three factors that help managers interpret and use management control information.

Objective 9

Explain how controllability and management by objectives (MBO) aid the implementation of management control systems.

Focus on Controllability

As Chapter 8 explained (see Exhibit 8-5, page 304), companies should distinguish between the performance of the division manager and the performance of the division as an investment by the corporation. Top management should evaluate segment managers on the basis of their controllable performance. However, management should base decisions such as increasing or decreasing investment in a division on the economic viability of the division, not on the performance of its managers.

This distinction helps to clarify some vexing difficulties. For example, top management may use an investment base to gauge the economic performance of a retail store, but judge the store's manager by focusing on income and ignoring any investment allocations. The aim is to evaluate the manager on controllable factors, but controllability depends on what decisions managers can make. In a highly decentralized company such as Johnson & Johnson or General Electric, for instance, managers can influence investments in assets and can exercise judgment regarding the appropriate amount of short-term credit and some long-term credit. Investment decisions that managers do not influence should not affect their performance evaluations.

Management by Objectives and Setting Expectations

Management by objectives (MBO) describes the joint formulation by managers and their superiors of a set of goals and plans for achieving the goals for a forthcoming period. For our purposes here, the terms *goals* and *objectives* are synonymous. The plans often take the form of a responsibility accounting budget (together with supplementary goals, such as levels of management training and safety that managers may not incorporate into the accounting budget). The company then evaluates a manager's performance in relation to these agreed-on budgeted objectives. It is important that managers' expectations be consistent with those of their superiors.

An MBO approach tends to reduce complaints about lack of controllability because managers first agree on a reasonable budget. That is, a particular manager and his or her superior negotiate a budget for a particular period and a particular set of expected outside and inside influences. For example, by evaluating results compared to expectations, a manager may more readily accept an assignment to a less successful segment. Why? Because a manager can reasonably expect to meet goals that recognize that the segment is economically struggling. Thus, an MBO system is preferable to a system that emphasizes absolute profitability for its own sake. Unless evaluation focuses on meeting reasonable expectations, able managers will be reluctant to accept responsibility for segments that are in economic trouble. Whether using MBO or not, skillful budgeting and intelligent performance evaluation will go a long way toward overcoming the common lament, "I'm being held responsible for items beyond my control."

MBO is also especially useful in nonprofit organizations where financial goals may be less important than nonfinancial goals. Managers can set objectives that fit well with overall organizational objectives. The accompanying Business First box on page 356 illustrates how an academic institution can use decentralization to further the university's financial and nonfinancial objectives.

management by objectives (MBO)
The joint formulation by managers and their superiors of a set of goals and plans for achieving the goals for a forthcoming period.

Budgets, Performance Targets, and Ethics

Organizations can minimize many of the troublesome motivational effects of performance evaluation systems by the astute use of budgets. We cannot overemphasize the desirability of tailoring budgets to a particular manager. For example, either an ROI or an economic profit system can promote goal congruence and managerial effort if top management gets everybody to focus on what is currently attainable in the forthcoming budget period.

Decentralization in Academia

Corporations are not the only types of organizations that decentralize. Many nonprofit organizations, such as universities, hospitals, and churches, also decentralize by delegating decision-making authority to segments of the organization. It is important for each segment to set objectives consistent with the overall organizational goals.

An example of such an organization is Harvard University. Using a philosophy of "every tub on its own bottom," Harvard is divided into 11 academic units: (1) Faculty of Arts and Sciences, which includes Harvard College, Graduate School of Arts and Sciences, and Division of Continuing Education; (2) Business School; (3) Design School; (4) Divinity School; (5) Graduate School of Education; (6) John F. Kennedy School of Government; (7) Law School; (8) Medical School; (9) Dental School; (10) School of Public Health; and (11) Radcliffe Institute for Advanced Study. At the head of each unit is a dean appointed by the president. The dean is directly responsible for his or her unit's finances and organization. In essence, each unit functions like a division of a decentralized corporation. Although the units have a great deal of independence, they must still set financial and nonfinancial objectives that are consistent with Harvard's goals, and their accomplishments will be measured against their objectives.

Because each unit at Harvard is responsible for its own revenues and expenses, many of the issues are similar to those of a for-profit corporation. The governing board that is responsible for the day-to-day operations at Harvard—called the Harvard Corporation and known formally as the President and Fellows of Harvard College—is a seven-member board headed by the president. To effectively manage the university, the board needs information from the units, but it intentionally does not directly make decisions for the units—that is left to the deans. Only when reports indicate that something is awry does the board intervene.

To the extent that the units are independent of one another, decentralization works well. But, just as in a for-profit organization, difficulties can arise when there are real or potential interactions among units. For example, how is tuition divided among units when students admitted to one unit take classes in another? This is a classic transfer-pricing problem. Or what about two units (for example the Law School and the Business School) competing for a particular faculty member. How is the good of the entire university reflected in such hiring decisions? Or how does the university encourage cross-functional programs and research involving more than one unit? Or how does the university choose whether to invest scarce funds into the Dental School or the Divinity School? These are all issues that arise from decentralization.

Like any organization, Harvard must balance overall organizational objectives versus the advantages of local decision making and superior motivation of divisional authority. While Harvard is an example of decentralization, other universities favor a more centralized approach.

Source: "Harvard at a Glance" (http://www.harvard.edu/Harvard-glance.html).

Using budgets as performance targets also has its dangers. On pages 374–376 of Chapter 6 we pointed out how misuse of budgets for performance evaluation can lead to lying and cheating. Companies that make meeting a budget too important when evaluating managers may motivate unethical behavior. Top management at companies such as WorldCom gave "making the numbers" such a high priority that when it became clear that a segment would not meet its goals, managers fabricated the accounting reports. At Enron, the consequences of poor performance evaluations were so great that managers played bookkeeping games and allegedly manipulated electricity prices to make their performance look better. The lesson is that "astute" use of budgets is good, but using budgets to put unreasonable pressure on managers can undermine the ethics of an organization.

As we said earlier in the chapter, "You get what you measure." It is important to use measures that are consistent with organizational goals. Yet, measurement is only part of the management control system. Managers should also think hard about how they use the measures to achieve the organization's objectives. Even good measures can lead to dysfunctional decisions when managers misuse them. A management control system is only as good as the managers who use it.

Highlights to Remember

1. **Define *decentralization* and identify its expected benefits and costs.** As companies grow, the ability of managers to effectively plan and control becomes more difficult because top managers are further removed from day-to-day operations. One approach to effective planning and control in large companies is to decentralize decision making. This means that top management gives mid- and lower-level managers the authority to make decisions that impact the subunit's performance. The more that decision-making authority is delegated, the greater the decentralization. Often, the subunit manager is most knowledgeable of the factors that management should consider in the decision-making process.

2. **Distinguish between responsibility centers and decentralization.** Top management must design the management control system so that it motivates managers to act in the best interests of the company. This is done through the choice of responsibility centers and the appropriate performance metrics and rewards. The degree of decentralization does not depend upon the type of responsibility center chosen. For example, a cost-center manager in one company may have more decision-making authority than does a profit-center manager in a highly centralized company.

3. **Explain how the linking of rewards to responsibility-center performance metrics affects incentives and risk.** It is generally a good idea to link managers' rewards to responsibility-center results to promote goal congruence. However, linking rewards to results creates risk for the manager. The greater the influence of uncontrollable factors on a manager's reward, the more risk the manager bears.

4. **Compute return on investment (ROI), economic profit, and economic value added (EVA).** It is typical to measure the results of investment centers using a set of performance metrics that include financial measures, such as return on investment (ROI), economic profit, or economic value added (EVA). ROI is any income measure divided by the dollar amount invested and is expressed as a percentage. Economic profit, or economic value added, is operating income less a capital charge based on the capital invested. It is an absolute dollar amount.

5. **Compare the incentives created by income, ROI, and economic profit (or EVA) performance measures.** Income performance measures create incentives to make decisions that increase income, without regard to the resources required. ROI creates incentives to adopt any and all projects with returns greater than existing ROI, rather than with returns greater than the cost of capital. EVA directly incorporates the cost of capital and provides incentives to adopt those projects with returns greater than the cost of capital.

6. **Define *transfer prices* and identify their purpose.** In large companies with many different segments, one segment often provides products or services to another segment. Deciding on the amount the selling division should charge the buying division for these transfers (the transfer price) is difficult. Companies use various types of transfer pricing policies. The overall purpose of transfer prices is to motivate managers to act in the best interests of the company, not just their segment.

7. **State the general rule for transfer pricing and use it to assess alternative transfer prices based on total costs, variable costs, or market prices.** As a general rule, transfer prices should approximate the outlay cost plus opportunity cost of the producing segment. Each type of transfer price has its own advantages and disadvantages. Each has a situation where it works best, and each can lead to dysfunctional decisions in some instances. When a competitive market exists for the product or service, transfer prices based on market prices usually lead to goal congruence and optimal decisions. When idle capacity exists in the segment providing the product or service, transfer prices based on variable cost usually lead to goal congruence. Cost-based transfer prices should usually be based on planned, rather than actual, costs. If a company uses actual costs, there is little incentive for the selling segment manager to minimize costs and the receiving segment manager does not know the cost in advance, which makes cost planning difficult.

8. **Identify the factors affecting multinational transfer prices.** Multinational organizations often use transfer prices as a means of minimizing worldwide income taxes, import duties, and tariffs.

9. **Explain how controllability and management by objectives (MBO) aid the implementation of management control systems.** Regardless of what measures a management control system uses, measures used to evaluate managers should focus on only the controllable aspects of performance. MBO can focus attention on performance compared to expectations, which is better than evaluations based on absolute profitability. Misuse of budgets and performance metrics can motivate managers to violate ethical standards.

Accounting Vocabulary

agency theory, p. 336
capital charge, p. 342
capital turnover, p. 339
centralization, p. 333
cost of capital, p. 342
decentralization, p. 333
dysfunctional
    decisions, p. 350
economic profit, p. 342

economic value added
    (EVA), p. 342
gross book value, p. 340
incentives, p. 336
management by objectives
    (MBO), p. 355
net book value, p. 340
net operating profit after-tax
    (NOPAT) , p. 342

performance metric, p. 336
residual income, p. 342
return on investment
    (ROI), p. 338
return on sales, p. 339
segment autonomy, p. 334
transfer price, p. 346

MyAccountingLab # Fundamental Assignment Material

9-A1 ROI and Economic Profit Calculations

Consider the following data (in thousands):

	Division		
	Hubert	**Duane**	**Louis**
Average invested capital	$2,000	$ 600	$1,800
Revenue	3,600	1,200	9,000
Income	180	84	216

1. For each division, compute the return on sales, the capital turnover, and the return on investment (ROI).
2. Which division is the best performer if evaluation is based on ROI? Explain.
3. Suppose each division is assessed a cost of capital of 10% on invested capital. Compute the economic profit for each division. Which division is the best performer based on economic profit? Explain.

9-A2 Transfer-Pricing Dispute

Zurich Équipement, SA, a Swiss transportation equipment manufacturer, is heavily decentralized. Each division head has full authority on all decisions regarding sales to internal or external customers. The Lucerne division has always acquired a certain equipment component from the Geneva division. The Geneva division recently acquired specialized equipment that is used primarily to make this component. The Geneva division has informed the Lucerne division that its fixed costs have increased by CHF 25 per unit because of the depreciation charges on the new equipment, so the unit price will be increased to CHF 325. However, the Lucerne division's management has now decided to purchase the component from outside suppliers at a price of CHF 300.

The Geneva division has supplied the following production cost data for this component:

Annual production of component (all for sale to Lucerne division)	3,000 units
Geneva's variable costs per unit	CHF 280
Geneva's fixed costs per unit	CHF 40

1. Suppose there are no alternative uses of the Geneva facilities and that fixed costs will continue if Geneva no longer produces the component for Lucerne. Will the company as a whole benefit if the Lucerne division buys from the outside suppliers for CHF 300 per unit? Show computations to support your answer.
2. Suppose there is an alternative use for the Geneva facilities. If the Geneva facilities are used to produce the component for the Lucerne division, the Geneva division will give up a contribution of CHF 85,000 from this alternative use. Should the Lucerne division purchase from outsiders at CHF 300 per unit?

3. Suppose that there are no alternative uses for Geneva's internal facilities and that the outsiders' selling price drops by CHF 50 to CHF 250. Should the Lucerne division purchase from outsiders?

4. As the president, how would you respond if the Geneva division manager requests that you require the Lucerne division to purchase the component from Geneva? Would your response differ depending on the specific situations described in numbers 1–3? Why?

9-A3 Transfer Pricing

Refer to problem 9-A2, number 1 only. Suppose the Geneva division could modify the component at an additional variable cost of CHF 25 per unit and sell the 3,000 units to other customers for CHF 330. Then, would the entire company benefit if the Lucerne division purchased the 3,000 components from outsiders at CHF 300 per unit?

9-A4 Rate of Return and Transfer Pricing

Consider the following data regarding budgeted operations for 20X7 of the Austin division of Texas Products:

Average total assets	
Receivables	$ 220,000
Inventories	290,000
Plant and equipment, net	450,000
Total	$ 960,000
Fixed overhead	$ 300,000
Variable costs	$.72 per unit
Desired rate of return on average total assets	20%
Expected volume	150,000 units

1. a. What average unit sales price does the Austin division need to obtain its desired rate of return on average total assets?
   b. What would be the expected capital turnover?
   c. What would be the return on sales?

2. a. If the selling price is as previously computed, what rate of return will the division earn on total assets if sales volume is 170,000 units?
   b. If sales volume is 130,000 units?

3. Assume that the Austin division plans to sell 45,000 units to the Galveston division of Texas Products and that it can sell only 105,000 units to outside customers at the price computed in requirement 1a. The Galveston division manager has balked at a tentative transfer price of $4. She has offered $2.25, claiming that she can manufacture the units herself for that price. The Austin division manager has examined his own data. He had decided that he could eliminate $60,000 of inventories, $90,000 of plant and equipment, and $22,500 of fixed overhead if he did not sell to the Galveston division and sold only 105,000 units to outside customers. Should the Austin division manager sell for $2.25? Show computations to support your answer.

9-B1 ROI or Economic Profit

Melbourne Co. is a large integrated Australian conglomerate with shipping, metals, and mining operations throughout Asia. Melbourne is just starting a new manufacturing division and the newly appointed general manager plans to submit a proposed capital budget for 20X8 for inclusion in the company-wide budget.

The division manager has for consideration the following projects, all of which require an outlay of capital. All projects have equal risk.

Project	Investment Required	Income
1	$4,800,000	$1,200,000
2	1,900,000	627,000
3	1,400,000	182,000
4	950,000	152,000
5	650,000	136,500
6	300,000	90,000

The division manager must decide which of the projects to take. The company has a cost of capital of 20%. An amount of $12 million is available to the division for investment purposes.

1. What will be the total investment, total return, return on capital invested, and economic profit of the rational division manager if
   a. the company has a rule that managers should accept all projects promising a return on investment of at least 15%?
   b. the company evaluates division managers on the return on capital invested (assume this is a new division so that invested capital will consist only of capital invested in new projects adopted by the manager)?
   c. the division manager is expected to maximize economic profit computed using the 20% cost of capital?
2. Which of the three approaches will induce the most effective investment policy for the company as a whole? Explain.

9-B2 Computing EVA

A company that uses EVA reported the following results for 20X4 and 20X5 (in millions):

	20X4	20X5
Pretax operating income	$6,105	$6,100
Cash taxes	1,686	1,620

Average adjusted invested capital was $16,125 million in 20X4 and $18,110 million in 20X5, and the cost of capital was 14% in both 20X4 and 20X5.

1. Compute the company's EVA for 20X4 and 20X5.
2. Compare the company's performance in creating value for its shareholders in 20X5 with that in 20X4.

9-B3 Transfer Pricing

Spartan Enterprises runs a chain of drive-in ice cream stands in Lansing during the summer season. Managers of all stands are told to act as if they owned the stand and are judged on their profit performance. Spartan Enterprises has rented an ice cream machine for the summer for $3,600 to supply its stands with ice cream. Spartan is not allowed to sell ice cream to other dealers because it cannot obtain a dairy license. The manager of the ice cream machine charges the stands $4 per gallon. Operating figures for the machine for the summer are as follows:

Sales to the stands (16,000 gallons at $4)		$64,000
Variable costs, at $2.00 per gallon	$32,000	
Fixed costs		
Rental of machine	3,600	
Other fixed costs	10,000	45,600
Operating margin		$18,400

The manager of the Okemos Drive-In, one of the Spartan drive-ins, is seeking permission to sign a contract to buy ice cream from an outside supplier at $3.35 a gallon. The Okemos Drive-In uses 4,000 gallons of ice cream during the summer. Elizabeth Chuk, controller of Spartan, refers this request to you. You determine that the other fixed costs of operating the machine will decrease by $900 if the Okemos Drive-In purchases from an outside supplier. Chuk wants an analysis of the request in terms of overall company objectives and an explanation of your conclusion. What is the appropriate transfer price?

9-B4 Rate of Return and Transfer Pricing

The Sendai division of Shusei Toy Company manufactures units of the game Shogi and sells them in the Japanese market for ¥7,350 each. The following data are from the Sendai division's 20X8 budget:

Variable cost	¥ 4,900 per unit
Fixed overhead	¥ 5,700,000
Total assets	¥16,000,000

Shusei has instructed the Sendai division to budget a rate of return on total assets (before taxes) of 24%.

1. Suppose the Sendai division expects to sell 3,350 games during 20X8.
   a. What rate of return will be earned on total assets?
   b. What would be the expected capital turnover?
   c. What would be the return on sales?
2. The Sendai division is considering adjustments in the budget to reach the desired 24% rate of return on total assets.
   a. How many units must be sold to obtain the desired return if no other part of the budget is changed?
   b. Suppose sales cannot be increased beyond 3,350 units. How much must total assets be reduced to obtain the desired return? Assume that for every ¥1,000 decrease in total assets, fixed costs decrease by ¥100.
3. Assume that only 2,950 units can be sold in the Japanese market. However, another 1,200 units can be sold to the European marketing division of Shusei. The Sendai manager has offered to sell the 1,200 units for ¥6,450 each. The European marketing division manager has countered with an offer to pay ¥6,150 per unit, claiming that she can subcontract production to an Italian producer at a cost equivalent to ¥6,150. The Sendai manager knows that if his production falls to 2,950 units, he could eliminate some assets, reducing total assets to ¥11 million and annual fixed overhead to ¥5.4 million. Should the Sendai manager sell for ¥6,150 per unit? Support your answer with the relevant computations. Ignore the effects of income taxes and import duties.

Additional Assignment Material

MyAccountingLab

QUESTIONS

9-1 "Decentralization has benefits and costs." Name three of each.

9-2 Sophisticated accounting and communications systems aid decentralization. Explain how they accomplish this.

9-3 Why is decentralization more popular in profit-seeking organizations than in nonprofit organizations?

9-4 "The essence of decentralization is the use of profit centers." Do you agree? Explain.

9-5 What kinds of organizations find decentralization to be preferable to centralization?

9-6 According to agency theory, employment contracts balance what three factors?

9-7 What is the major benefit of the ROI technique for measuring performance?

9-8 What two major items affect ROI?

9-9 How does economic profit differ from net income?

9-10 Define *economic value added (EVA)* and describe three ways a company can improve its EVA.

9-11 Division A's ROI is 20%, and B's is 10%. The company pays each division manager a bonus based on his or her division's ROI. Discuss whether each division manager would accept or reject a proposed project with a rate of return of 15%. Would either of them make a different decision if the company evaluated managers using economic profit with a capital charge of 11%? Explain.

9-12 Give three possible definitions of invested capital that we can use in measuring ROI or economic profit.

9-13 "Managers who use a historical-cost accounting system look backward at what something cost yesterday, instead of forward to what it will cost tomorrow." Do you agree? Why?

9-14 Ross Company uses net book value as a measure of invested capital when computing ROI. A division manager has suggested that the company change to using gross book value instead. What difference in motivation of division managers might result from such a change? Do you suppose most of the assets in the division of the manager proposing the change are relatively new or old? Why?

9-15 Why do companies need transfer-pricing systems?

9-16 Describe two problems that can arise when using actual full cost as a transfer price.

9-17 How does the presence or absence of idle capacity affect the optimal transfer-pricing policy?

9-18 "We use variable-cost transfer prices to ensure that we make no dysfunctional decisions." Discuss.

9-19 What is the major advantage of negotiated transfer prices? What is the major disadvantage?

9-20 Discuss two factors that affect multinational transfer prices but have little effect on purely domestic transfers.

9-21 Describe management by objectives (MBO).

9-22 How can performance measurement lead to unethical behavior by managers?

CRITICAL THINKING EXERCISES

9-23 Decentralization

Many companies implement organizational changes to centralize or decentralize operations only to follow with later changes in the opposite direction. Why might a company that at one time decentralizes decide later to centralize?

9-24 Comparing Financial Measures of Performance

"Both ROI and economic profit use profit and invested capital to measure performance. Therefore it really doesn't matter which we use." Do you agree? Explain.

9-25 Performance Metrics and Ethics

"Financial performance metrics cause managers to ignore ethics and focus just on meeting their profit targets. After all, look at what happened at Enron, Global Crossing, WorldCom, Tyco, HealthSouth, and several other companies." Evaluate this quote. Can financial performance metrics be compatible with ethical behavior?

9-26 Transfer Pricing and Organizational Behavior

The principle reason for transfer-pricing systems is to communicate data that will lead to goal-congruent decisions by managers of different business units. When managers take actions that conflict with organizational goals, dysfunctional behavior exists. Why does top management sometimes accept a division manager's judgments, even if the division manager appears to behave in a dysfunctional manner?

EXERCISES

9-27 Simple ROI Calculation

You are given the following data:

Sales	$227,500,000
Invested capital	$ 65,000,000
Net income	$ 9,100,000

Compute the following:

1. Turnover of capital
2. Return on sales
3. Return on investment (ROI)

9-28 Simple ROI Calculation

Fill in the blanks:

	Division		
	A	B	C
Return on sales	6%	4%	__%
Capital turnover	3	__	5
Rate of return on invested capital	__%	18%	20%

9-29 Simple ROI and Economic Profit Calculations

Consider the following data:

	Division		
	X	Y	Z
Invested capital	$1,050,000	$ _____	$1,200,000
Income	$ _____	$ 142,800	$ 210,000
Revenue	$2,310,000	$2,856,000	$ _____
Return on sales	3%	_____ %	_____ %
Capital turnover	_____	_____	3.5
Rate of return on invested capital	_____ %	10.5%	_____ %

1. Prepare a similar tabular presentation, filling in all blanks.
2. Suppose each division is assessed a capital charge based on a cost of capital of 10% of invested capital. Compute the economic profit for each division.
3. Which division is the best performer? Explain.

9-30 EVA

Lohmann Corporation is a major supplier to makers of outdoor power equipment. According to the company's annual report, "management subscribes to the premise that the value of our company is enhanced if the capital invested in its operations yields a cash return that is greater than that expected by the providers of capital."

The following data are from Lohmann's annual report that incorporate EVA adjustments to operating profit and average invested capital (amounts in thousands):

	20X1	20X2
Adjusted before tax operating profit	$ 78,000	$ 80,000
Cash taxes	20,500	22,600
Adjusted average invested capital	650,000	600,000
Cost of capital	9.4%	9.4%

1. Compute the EVA for Lohmann for 20X1 and 20X2.
2. Did Lohmann's overall performance improve from 20X1 to 20X2? Explain.

9-31 Comparison of Asset and Equity Bases

Hope Company has assets of $3 million and long-term, 12% debt of $1,240,000. Crosby Company has assets of $3 million and no long-term debt. The annual operating income (before interest) of both companies is $690,000. Ignore taxes.
1. Compute the rate of return on
   a. assets, and
   b. stockholders' equity.
2. Evaluate the relative merits of each base for appraising operating management.

9-32 Finding Unknowns

Consider the following data:

	Division		
	J	K	L
Income	$450,000	$ _____	$ _____
Revenue	$ _____	$ _____	$ _____
Invested capital	$ _____	$5,000,000	$20,000,000
Return on sales	5%	9%	_____ %
Capital turnover	6	_____	2
Rate of return on invested capital	_____ %	27%	16%
Cost of capital	7%	14%	_____ %
Economic profit	$ _____	$ _____	$ 200,000

1. Prepare a similar tabular presentation, filling in all blanks.
2. Which division is the best performer? Explain.

9-33 Gross Versus Net Asset Value

The Alexandria division of Atkinson Company just purchased an asset for $120,000. The asset has a 3-year life. Atkinson's top management evaluates Lisa LaVilla, manager of the Alexandria division, based on ROI for this asset. She can choose to measure the asset using either gross asset value or net asset value. Her operating income before depreciation each year is $100,000.

1. What is the Alexandria division's ROI for each of the 3 years using the gross asset value?
2. What is the Alexandria division's ROI for each of the 3 years using the net asset value?
3. If LaVilla expects Atkinson to transfer her to a different division in about a year, which asset valuation policy would she prefer?

9-34 Variable Cost as a Transfer Price

A chair's variable cost is $52 and its market value as a piece of unfinished furniture is $65 at a transfer point from the assembly division to the finishing division. The finishing division's variable cost of sanding and finishing the chair is $26, and the selling price of the chair after sanding and finishing is $83.

1. Prepare a tabulation of the contribution margin per unit for the finishing division's performance and overall company performance under the two alternatives of (a) selling to outsiders at the transfer point and (b) sanding and finishing the chair and then selling to outsiders.
2. As finishing division manager, which alternative would you choose? Explain.

9-35 Maximum and Minimum Transfer Price

Sherwin Company makes bicycles. Various divisions make components and transfer them to the Dayton division for assembly into final products. The Dayton division can also buy components from external suppliers. The Toledo division makes the wheels, and it also sells wheels to external customers. All divisions are profit centers, and managers are free to negotiate transfer prices. Prices and costs for the Toledo and Dayton divisions are as follows:

Toledo Division	
Sales price to external customers	$ 14
Internal transfer price	?
Costs	
Variable costs per wheel	$ 10
Total fixed costs	$320,000
Budgeted production	64,000 wheels*

*Includes production for transfer to Dayton

Dayton Division	
Sales price to external customers	$ 170
Costs	
Wheels, per bicycle	?
Other components, per bicycle	$ 85
Other variable costs, per bicycle	$ 45
Total fixed costs	$640,000
Budgeted production	16,000 bicycles

Fixed costs in both divisions will be unaffected by the transfer of wheels from Toledo to Dayton.

1. Compute the maximum transfer price per wheel the Dayton division would be willing to pay to buy wheels from the Toledo division.

2. Compute the minimum transfer price per wheel at which the Toledo division would be willing to produce and sell wheels to the Dayton division. Assume that Toledo has excess capacity.

9-36 Multinational Transfer Prices

Princeton International has production and marketing divisions throughout the world. It produces one particular product in Ireland, where the income tax rate is 24%, and transfers it to a marketing division in Japan, where the income tax rate is 45%. Assume that Japan places an import tax of 13% on the product and that import duties are not deductible for income tax purposes.

The variable cost of the product is £500 and the full cost is £800. Suppose the company can legally select a transfer price anywhere between the variable and full cost.

1. What transfer price should Princeton International use to minimize taxes? Explain why this is the tax-minimizing transfer price.
2. Compute the amount of taxes saved by using the transfer price in requirement 1 instead of the transfer price that would result in the highest taxes.

PROBLEMS

9-37 Agency Theory

The Tamura International Trading Company plans to hire a manager for its division in Mexico City. Tamura International's president and vice president of personnel are trying to decide on an appropriate incentive employment contract. The manager will operate far from the Tokyo corporate headquarters, so evaluation by personal observation will be limited. The president insists that a large incentive to produce profits is necessary; he favors a salary of ¥150,000 and a bonus of 10% of the profits above ¥1,200,000. If operations proceed as expected, profits will be ¥4,600,000, and the manager will receive ¥490,000. But both profits and compensation might be more or less than planned.

The vice president of personnel responds that ¥490,000 is more than most of Tamura International's division managers make. She is sure that the company can hire a competent manager for a guaranteed salary of ¥400,000. She argued, "Why pay ¥490,000 when we can probably hire the same person for ¥400,000?"

1. What factors would affect Tamura International's choice of employment contract? Include a discussion of the pros and cons of each proposed contract.
2. Why is the expected compensation more with the bonus plan than with the straight salary?

9-38 Margins and Turnover

Accountants often express ROI as the product of two components—capital turnover and return on sales. You are considering investing in one of three companies, all in the same industry, and are given the following information:

	Company		
	Adam	Basil	Collin
Sales	$8,500,000	$ 1,500,000	$29,000,000
Income	$ 765,000	$ 180,000	$ 180,000
Capital	$3,200,000	$12,000,000	$12,000,000

1. Why would you desire the breakdown of return on investment into return on sales and turnover on capital?
2. Compute the return on sales, turnover on capital, and ROI for the three companies, and comment on the relative performance of the companies as thoroughly as the data permit.
3. Notice that Basil and Collin have the same income and capital but vastly different levels of sales. Discuss the types of strategies that Basil and Collin might be employing.

9-39 ROI by Business Segment

ViaMedia does business in three different business segments: (1) entertainment, (2) publishing/information, and (3) consumer/commercial finance. Results for a recent year were as follows (in millions):

	Revenues	Operating Income	Total Assets
Entertainment	$1,050	$210	$1,000
Publishing/Information	$ 700	$140	$1,400
Consumer/Commercial Finance	$1,060	$265	$ 848

1. Compute the following for each business segment:
   a. Return on sales
   b. Capital turnover
   c. ROI
2. Comment on the differences in ROI among the business segments. Include reasons for the differences.

9-40 EVA Versus Economic Profit

The primary difference between the EVA and economic profit measures is the increased focus on cash flow by EVA. For example, economic profit generally uses the provision for income taxes from the income statement while EVA uses cash taxes paid. EVA companies typically make several adjustments (from 5 to 15 adjustments for the typical EVA company) to both operating income from the income statement and invested capital from the balance sheet. Common examples include adjustments for R&D, LIFO, and warranty costs.

The following data were taken from the 20X3 annual report of Burton Company (thousands of dollars):

Income from operations	$ 267,400
Provision for income taxes	57,455
Net EVA adjustments added to income from operations	5,398
Additional capital employed from EVA adjustments	234,159
Ending total shareholders' equity	845,632
Cash taxes	64,800
Ending total current liabilities	340,125
Ending total assets	1,834,456
Beginning total shareholders' equity	841,589
Beginning total current liabilities	471,859
Beginning total assets	1,889,321
Management's estimate of the cost-of-capital	11.3%

Prepare a schedule that calculates and compares EVA to economic profit for Burton Company.

9-41 EVA

The Jeske Company had the following financial results for two recent fiscal years (in millions):

	Year 2	Year 1
Revenues	$4,463	$4,510
Operating expenses	3,569	3,615
Cash income taxes	292	255
Average invested capital (total assets less current liabilities)	$2,854	$2,689

1. Suppose that Jeske's cost of capital is 11.5%. Compute the company's EVA for years 1 and 2. Assume definitions of after-tax operating income and invested capital as reported in Jeske's annual reports without adjustments advocated by Stern Stewart or others.
2. Discuss the change in EVA between years 1 and 2.

9-42 EVA and Cost of Capital

The Holt Company uses EVA to evaluate top management performance. In 20X8, Holt had net operating income of $8,210 million, income taxes of $1,395 million, and average noncurrent liabilities plus stockholders' equity of $27,555 million. The company's capital is about 55% long-term debt and 45% equity. Assume that the after-tax cost of debt is 10% and the cost of equity is 12%.

1. Compute Holt's EVA. Assume definitions of after-tax operating income and invested capital as reported in Holt's annual reports without adjustments advocated by Stern Stewart.
2. Explain what EVA tells you about the performance of the top management of Holt in 20X8.

9-43 Evaluation of Divisional Performance

As the CEO of Middling Hardware Company, you examined the following measures of the performance of three divisions (in thousands of dollars):

Division	Average Net Assets Based On		Operating Income Based On*	
	Historical Cost	**Replacement Cost**	**Historical Cost**	**Replacement Cost**
Tools	$15,000	$16,000	$2,600	$2,500
Appliances	44,000	55,000	6,750	6,150
Lighting	27,000	48,000	5,000	3,900

*The differences in operating income between historical and replacement cost are attributable to the differences in depreciation expenses.

1. Calculate for each division the rate of return on net assets and the economic profit based on historical cost and on replacement cost. For purposes of calculating economic profit, use 10% as the cost of capital.
2. Rank the performance of each division under each of the four different measures computed in number 1.
3. What do these measures indicate about the performance of the divisions? Of the division managers? Which measure do you prefer? Why?

9-44 Use of Gross or Net Book Value of Fixed Assets

Assume that a machine shop acquires $520,000 of fixed assets with a useful life of 4 years and no residual value. The shop uses straight-line depreciation. The company judges the shop manager based on income in relation to these fixed assets. Annual net income, after deducting depreciation, is $20,000.

Assume that sales, and all expenses except depreciation, are on a cash basis. Dividends equal net income. Thus, cash in the amount of the depreciation charge will accumulate each year. The plant manager's performance is judged in relation to fixed assets because all current assets, including cash, are considered under central-company control. Assume (unrealistically) that any cash accumulated remains idle. Ignore taxes.

1. Prepare a comparative tabulation of the plant's rate of return and the company's overall rate of return based on
   a. gross (i.e., original cost) assets.
   b. net book value of assets.
2. Evaluate the relative merits of gross assets and net book value of assets as investment bases.

9-45 Role of Economic Value and Replacement Value

(This problem requires understanding of the concept of present values.)

"To me, economic value is the only justifiable basis for measuring plant assets for purposes of evaluating performance. By economic value, I mean the present value of expected future services. Still, we do not even do this on acquisition of new assets—that is, we may compute a positive net present value, using discounted cash flow; but we record the asset at no more than its cost. In this way, the excess present value is not shown in the initial balance sheet. Moreover, the use of replacement costs in subsequent years is also unlikely to result in showing economic values. The replacement cost will probably be less than the economic value at any given instant of an asset's life.

"Market values are totally unappealing to me because they represent a second-best alternative value—that is, they ordinarily represent the maximum amount obtainable from an alternative that has been rejected. Obviously, if the market value exceeds the economic value of the assets in use, they should be sold. However, in most instances, the opposite is true; market values of individual assets are far below their economic value in use.

"The obtaining and recording of total present values of individual assets based on discounted-cash-flow techniques is an infeasible alternative. I, therefore, conclude that replacement cost (less accumulated depreciation) of similar assets producing similar services is the best practical approximation of the economic value of the assets in use. Of course, it is more appropriate for the evaluation of the division's performance than the division manager's performance."

Critically evaluate these comments. Please do not wander; concentrate on the issues described by the quotation.

9-46 Profit Centers and Transfer Pricing in an Automobile Dealership

A large automobile dealership in Chicago is installing a responsibility accounting system and three profit centers: parts and service, new vehicles, and used vehicles. Top management has told the three department managers to run their shops as if they were in business for themselves. However, there are interdepartmental dealings. For example,

    a. the parts and service department prepares new cars for final delivery and repairs used cars prior to resale.

    b. the used-car department's major source of inventory has been cars traded in as partial payment for new cars.

The owner of the dealership has asked you to draft a company policy statement on transfer pricing, together with specific rules to be applied to the examples cited. He has told you that clarity is of paramount importance because he will rely on your statement for settling transfer-pricing disputes.

9-47 Transfer Pricing

The shocks and struts division of Transnational Motors Company produces strut assemblies for automobiles. It has been the sole supplier of strut assemblies to the automotive division and charges $48 per unit, the current market price for very large wholesale lots. The shocks and struts division also sells to outside retail outlets, at $61 per unit. Normally, outside sales amount to 30% of a total sales volume of 1 million strut assemblies per year. Typical combined annual data for the division follow:

Sales	$51,900,000	
Variable costs, at $38.50 per strut assembly		$38,500,000
Fixed costs		4,200,000
Total costs	$42,700,000	
Gross margin	$ 9,200,000	

Flint Auto Parts Company, an entirely separate entity, has offered the automotive division comparable strut assemblies at a firm price of $42.70 per unit. The shocks and struts division of Transnational Motors claims that it cannot possibly match this price because it could not earn any margin at the price Flint is offering.

1. Assume that you are the manager of the automotive division of Transnational Motors. Comment on the shocks and struts division's claim. Assume that normal outside volume cannot be increased.

2. Now assume the shocks and struts division believes that it can increase outside sales by 700,000 strut assemblies per year by increasing fixed costs by $2.5 million and variable costs by $4.50 per unit while reducing the selling price to $58. Assume that maximum capacity is 1 million strut assemblies per year. Should the division reject intracompany business and concentrate solely on outside sales?

9-48 Transfer-Pricing Concession

You are the divisional controller of the U.S. division of Samtech Electronics. Your division is operating at capacity. The Australian division has asked the U.S. division to supply a sound system (chip and speaker), which it will use in a new model Game Box that it is introducing. The U.S. division currently sells identical sound systems to outside customers at $11.00 each.

The Australian division has offered to pay $7.00 for each sound system. The total cost of the Game Box is as follows:

Purchased parts from outside vendors	$28.10
Sound system from U.S. division	7.00
Other variable costs	17.50
Fixed overhead	10.00
Total	$62.60

The Australian division is operating at 50% of capacity, and this Game Box is an important new product introduction to increase its use of capacity. Based on a target-costing approach, the Australian division management has decided that paying more than $7.00 for the sound system would make production of the Game Box infeasible because the predicted selling price for the Game Box is only $62.00.

Samtech Electronics evaluates divisional managers on the basis of pretax ROI and dollar profits compared to the budget. Ignore taxes and tariffs.

1. As divisional controller of the U.S. division, would you recommend supplying the sound system to the Australian division for $7.00 each? Why or why not?
2. Would it be to the short-run economic advantage of Samtech Electronics for the U.S. division to supply the sound system to the Australian division? Explain your answer.
3. Discuss the organizational and behavioral difficulties, if any, inherent in this situation. As the U.S. division controller, what would you advise the Samtech Electronics president to do in this situation?

9-49 Transfer Prices and Idle Capacity

The Eugene division of Union Furniture purchases lumber, which it uses to fabricate tables, chairs, and other wood furniture. It purchases most of the lumber from Shasta Mill, also a division of Union Furniture. Both the Eugene division and Shasta Mill are profit centers.

The Eugene division proposes to produce a new Shaker-style chair that will sell for $95. The manager is exploring the possibility of purchasing the required lumber from Shasta Mill. Production of 800 chairs is planned, using capacity in the Eugene division that is currently idle.

The Eugene division can purchase the lumber needed for one chair from an outside supplier for $72. Union Furniture has a policy that internal transfers are priced at fully allocated cost.

Assume the following costs for the production of one chair and the lumber required for the chair:

Shasta Mill—Lumber Cost		Eugene Division—Chair Cost		
Variable cost	$48	Variable costs		
Allocated fixed cost	22	Lumber from Shasta Mill		$70
Fully allocated cost	$70	Eugene division variable costs		
		Manufacturing	$23	
		Selling	6	29
		Total variable cost		$99

1. Assume that the Shasta Mill has idle capacity and, therefore, would incur no additional fixed costs to produce the required lumber. Would the Eugene division manager buy the lumber for the chair from the Shasta Mill given the existing transfer-pricing policy? Why or why not? Would the company as a whole benefit if the manager decides to buy from the Shasta Mill? Explain.
2. Assume that there is no idle capacity at the Shasta Mill and the lumber required for one chair can be sold to outside customers for $72. Would the company as a whole benefit if the Eugene manager buys from Shasta? Explain.

9-50 Transfer-Pricing Principles

A law firm, Arno Legal Services, is decentralized with 25 offices around the state of California. The headquarters is based in San Francisco. Another operating division is located in San Jose, 50 miles away. A subsidiary printing operation, ArnoPrint, is located in the headquarters building. Top management has indicated the desirability of the San Jose office using ArnoPrint for printing reports. All charges are eventually billed to the client, but Arno Legal Services was concerned about keeping such charges competitive.

ArnoPrint charges San Jose the following:

Photographing page for offset printing (a setup cost)	$.200
Printing cost per page	.02

At this rate, ArnoPrint sales have a 50% contribution margin to fixed overhead.

Outside bids for 250 copies of a 180-page report needed immediately have been as follows:

Print 4U	$942.00
Jiffy Press	918.25
Kustom Print	923.50

These three printers are located within a 5-mile radius of Arno Legal Services' San Jose office and can have the reports ready in 2 days. A messenger would have to be sent to drop off the original and pick up the copies. The messenger usually goes to headquarters, but in the past, special trips have been required to deliver the original or pick up the copies. It takes 3–4 days to get the copies from ArnoPrint (because of the extra scheduling difficulties in delivery and pickup).

Quality control at ArnoPrint is poor. Reports received in the past have contained wrinkled pages, have occasionally been mis-collated, or have had pages deleted altogether. (In one instance, an intra-company memorandum including the San Jose Office's financial performance statistics was inserted in a report prepared for an outside client. Fortunately, the San Jose office detected the error before the report was distributed to the client.) The degree of quality control in the three outside print shops is unknown.

(Although the differences in costs may seem immaterial in this case, regard the numbers as significant for purposes of focusing on the key issues.)

1. If you were the decision maker at the San Jose office of Arno Legal Services, to which print shop would you give the business? Is this an optimal economic decision from the entire organization's viewpoint?
2. What would be the ideal transfer price in this case, if based only on economic considerations?
3. Time is an important factor in maintaining client goodwill. There is potential return business from this client. Given this perspective, what might be the optimal decision for the company?
4. Comment on the wisdom of top management in indicating that ArnoPrint should be used.

9-51 Negotiated Transfer Prices

The Lighting division of Ibex Office Furniture needs 1,200 units of a leaded-glass lamp shade from the fabricating division. The company has a policy of negotiated transfer prices. The fabricating division has enough excess capacity to produce 2,000 units of the lamp shade. Its variable cost of production is $23. The market price of the lamp shade to external customers is $39.

What is the natural bargaining range for a transfer price between the two divisions? Explain why no price below your range would be acceptable. Also explain why no price above your range would be acceptable.

9-52 Transfer Prices and Minority Shareholders

This chapter discussed transferring profits between divisions of a multinational company. Another situation where transfer prices have a similar effect is when a parent company transfers items to or from a subsidiary when there are minority shareholders in the subsidiary. Consider the **Michelin Group** and its Polish subsidiary, **Stomil Olsztyn**, of which Michelin owns 70%. Michelin buys tires from Stomil Olsztyn at a transfer price. Since Michelin owns a majority of Stomil Olsztyn, it controls the transfer-pricing policy. The holders of the other 30% of Stomil Olsztyn claim that Michelin sets the transfer prices too low, thereby reducing the profits of Stomil Olsztyn. They maintain that Stomil Olsztyn would be more profitable if it were allowed to sell its tires on the market rather than transfer them to Michelin. In reply, Michelin managers maintain that Stomil Olsztyn is more profitable than other members of the Michelin Group, and, therefore, the transfer prices must be fair.

Discuss the incentives for Michelin to transfer tires at a low price from Stomil Olsztyn to its Michelin parent. What transfer price do the minority shareholders in Stomil Olsztyn favor? Use an example of a tire that Stomil Olsztyn produces at a variable cost of €20 that is transferred to Michelin for €25. How should Michelin and Stomil Olsztyn establish a fair transfer price?

9-53 Multinational Transfer Prices

Minnesota Medical Instruments produces a variety of medical products at its plant in Minneapolis. The company has sales divisions worldwide. One of these sales divisions is located in Stockholm, Sweden. Assume that the U.S. income tax rate is 30%, the Swedish rate is 65%, and a 5% import duty is imposed on medical supplies brought into Sweden.

One product produced in Minneapolis and shipped to Sweden is a heart defibrillator. The variable cost of production is $200 per unit, and the fully allocated cost is $350 per unit.

1. Suppose the Swedish and U.S. governments allow either the variable or fully allocated cost to be used as a transfer price. Which price should Minnesota Medical Instruments choose to minimize the total of income taxes and import duties? Compute the amount the company saves if it uses your suggested transfer price instead of the alternative. Assume import duties are not deductible for tax purposes.
2. Suppose the Swedish parliament passed a law decreasing the income tax rate to 40% and increasing the duty on heart monitors to 15%. Repeat number 1, using these new facts.

9-54 Review of Major Points in This Chapter

The Canadian Instruments Company uses the decentralized form of organizational structure and considers each of its divisions as an investment center. The Toronto division is currently selling 15,000 air filters annually, although it has sufficient productive capacity to produce 21,000 units per year. Variable manufacturing costs amount to $21 per unit, while the total fixed costs amount to $90,000. These 15,000 air filters are sold to outside customers at $40 per unit.

The Montreal division, also a part of Canadian Instruments, has indicated that it would like to buy 1,500 air filters from the Toronto division, but at a price of $37 per unit. This is the price the Montreal division is currently paying an outside supplier.

1. Compute the effect on the operating income of the company as a whole if the Montreal division purchases the 1,500 air filters from the Toronto division.
2. What is the minimum price that the Toronto division should be willing to accept for these 1,500 air filters?
3. What is the maximum price that the Montreal division should be willing to pay for these 1,500 air filters?
4. Suppose instead that the Toronto division is currently producing and selling 21,000 air filters annually to outside customers. What is the effect on the overall Canadian Instruments Company operating income if the Toronto division is required by top management to sell 1,500 air filters to the Montreal division at (a) $21 per unit and (b) $37 per unit?
5. For this question only, assume that the Toronto division is currently earning an annual operating income of $36,000, and the division's average invested capital is $300,000. The division manager has an opportunity to invest in a proposal that will require an additional investment of $20,000 and will increase annual operating income by $2,000. (a) Should the division manager accept this proposal if the Canadian Instruments Company uses ROI in evaluating the performance of its divisional managers? (b) If the company uses economic profit? (Assume a cost of capital of 7%.)

CASES

9-55 Profit Centers and Central Services

Star Manufacturing, manufacturer of Starlite brand small appliances, has a process engineering department (PED). The department's major task has been to help the production departments improve their operating methods and processes.

For several years, Star Manufacturing has charged the cost of consulting services to the production departments based on a signed agreement between the managers involved. The agreement specifies the scope of the project, the predicted savings, and the number of consulting hours required. The charge to the production departments is based on the costs to the engineering department of the services rendered. For example, senior engineer hours cost more per hour than junior engineer hours. An overhead cost is included. The agreement is really a "fixed-price" contract. That is, the production manager knows the total cost of the project in advance. A recent survey revealed that production managers have a high level of confidence in the engineers.

The PED department manager oversees the work of about 40 engineers and 10 technicians. She reports to the engineering manager, who reports to the vice president of manufacturing. The PED manager has the freedom to increase or decrease the number of engineers under her supervision. The PED manager's performance evaluation is based on many factors including the annual incremental savings to the company in excess of the costs of operating the PED department.

The production departments are profit centers. Their goods are transferred to subsequent departments, such as a sales department or sales division, at prices that approximate market prices for similar products.

Top management is seriously considering a "no-charge" plan. That is, production departments would receive engineering services at absolutely no cost. Proponents of the new plan maintain that it would motivate the production managers to take better advantage of engineering talent. In all other respects, the new system would be unchanged from the present system.

1. Compare the present and proposed plans. What are their strong and weak points? In particular, will the PED manager tend to hire the "optimal" amount of engineering talent?
2. Which plan do you favor? Why?

9-56 Management by Objectives

Roger Ravenhill is the CEO of Haida Company. Ravenhill has a financial management background and is known throughout the organization as a "no-nonsense" executive. When Ravenhill became CEO, he emphasized cost reduction and savings and introduced a comprehensive cost control and budget system. The company goals and budget plans were established by Ravenhill and given to his subordinates for implementation. Some of the company's key executives were dismissed or demoted for failing to meet projected budget plans. Under the leadership of Roger Ravenhill, Haida has once again become financially stable and profitable after several years of poor performance.

Recently, Ravenhill has become concerned with the human side of the organization and has become interested in the management technique referred to as "management by objectives" (MBO). If there are enough positive benefits of MBO, he plans to implement the system throughout the company. However, he realizes that he does not fully understand MBO because he does not understand how it differs from the current system of establishing firm objectives and budget plans.

1. Briefly explain what MBO entails and identify its advantages and disadvantages.
2. Does Roger Ravenhill's management style incorporate the human-value premises and goals of MBO? Explain your answer.

NIKE 9-K PROBLEM

9-57 ROI and Economic Profit

Examine **Nike**'s segments as defined in Note 18 to its financial statements in the 10-K report. We will use the segment information from the first six segments listed to calculate approximations to ROI and economic profit. For purposes of this problem, define segment income as segment EBIT and define segment assets as the sum of the assets shown in note 18, namely receivables, inventory, and property plant and equipment. Therefore, pretax and pre-interest ROA is EBIT divided by segment assets and an approximation to economic profit is EBIT minus a charge for the cost of capital to finance segment assets.

Using these definitions, determine ROA and economic profit for each segment in 2010 and 2011 using EBIT from Note 18 in the 10-K and the information on segment assets in the following table. Assume that Nike's cost of capital is 10%. Use your results to evaluate the performance of each segment. Which segment management seems to be doing the best job? What subjective factors would you consider, in addition to ROA and economic profit, in assessing segment performance?

Ending Accounts Receivable, Inventories, and Property, Plant, and Equipment		
Segment	**2011**	**2010**
North America	$2,433	$1,941
Western Europe	1,272	1,031
Central and Eastern Europe	448	384
Greater China	471	379
Japan	595	568
Emerging Markets	953	683
Nike Total (includes corporate assets not in segments)	$7,968	$6,623

EXCEL APPLICATION EXERCISE

9-58 Return on Investment and Economic Profit

Goal: Create an Excel spreadsheet to calculate performance of divisional segments using the ROI and economic profit methods. Use the results to answer questions about your findings.

Scenario: The company has asked you to calculate ROI and economic profit for three divisions. The background data for your analysis appears in Fundamental Assignment Material 9-A1. Use an interest rate of 10% when calculating the capital charge.

When you have completed your spreadsheet, answer the following questions:

1. Which division has the best performance using the ROI method? Using the economic profit method?
2. Which division has the worst performance under both methods?
3. Which method would you suggest for evaluating the manager of each division?

Step-by-Step:

1. Open a new Excel spreadsheet.
2. In column A, create a bold-faced heading that contains the following:
   Row 1: Chapter 9 Decision Guideline
   Row 2: Divisions Hubert, Duane, and Louis
   Row 3: Measures of Profitability
   Row 4: Today's Date
3. Merge and center the four heading rows across columns A–I.
4. In row 7, create the following center-justified column headings:
   Column A: Division
   Column B: Invested Capital
   Column C: Revenue
   Column D: Income
   Column E: Capital Charge
   Column F: Economic Profit
   Column G: Return on Investment
   Column H: Return on Sales
   Column I: Capital Turnover
5. Change the format of Economic Profit and Return on Investment to bold-faced headings.
6. Change the format of the column headings in row 7 to permit the titles to be displayed on multiple lines within a single cell.

   Alignment tab: Wrap Text: Checked

   Note: Adjust column widths so the headings only use two lines.

   Adjust row height to insure that row is the same height as adjusted headings.

7. In column A, create the following center-justified row headings:
   Row 8: Hubert
   Skip a row.
   Row 10: Duane
   Skip a row.
   Row 12: Louis
8. Use the scenario data to fill in invested capital, revenue, and income amounts for each division.
9. Use the scenario data and appropriate formulas to calculate capital charge amounts for each division.
10. Use the appropriate formulas from this chapter to calculate economic profit, ROI, return on sales, and capital turnover amounts for each division.
11. Format amounts in columns B, C, D, E, and F for division A as follows:

Number tab:	Category:	Currency
	Decimal places:	0
	Symbol:	$
	Negative numbers:	Black with parentheses

12. Format amounts in columns B, C, D, E, and F for divisions B and C as follows:

	Number tab:	Category:	Currency
		Decimal places:	0
		Symbol:	None
		Negative numbers:	Black with parentheses

13. Format amounts in columns G and H to display as percentages without decimal places.

	Number tab:	Category:	Percentage
		Decimal places:	0

14. Format the capital turnover amounts to display two decimal places, followed by the word **times**.

	Number tab:	Category:	Custom

From the Type list, highlight the type shown next:

		Type:	0.00

Change the data in the Type field from 0.00 to the following:

		Type:	0.00 "times"

Click the OK button.

15. Save your work, and print a copy for your files.

Note: Print your spreadsheet using landscape in order to ensure that all columns appear on one page.

COLLABORATIVE LEARNING EXERCISE

9-59 ROI

Form groups of three to six students. Each student should select a company. Coordinate the selection of companies so that each group has companies from a wide variety of industries. For example, a good mix of industries for a group of five students would be a retail company, a basic manufacturing company, a computer software company, a bank, and an electric utility company.

1. Each student should find the latest annual report for his or her company. (If you cannot find the company's home page, try www.sec.gov, and search the Security and Exchange Commission's Edgar files for the company's 10-K report, which will contain its financial statements.) Compute the following:
   a. Return on sales
   b. Capital turnover
   c. ROI
2. As a group, compare these performance metrics for the chosen companies. Why do they differ across companies? What characteristic of the company and its industry might explain the differences in the measures?

INTERNET EXERCISE

9-60 Decentralization at Marriott International

Decentralization of an organization can occur for many reasons. It may be that the organization is involved in multiple activities that are not closely related to each other, such as construction and auto sales. In other cases, the decision may be due to the structure of the firm's ownership and how it chooses to manage its image. Let's look at a firm that falls under this category—**Marriott International**.

1. Go to Marriott International's Web site at www.marriott.com. Does the home page emphasize corporate information or promotional information?
2. How has Marriott decentralized its businesses? Click on "Explore Our Brands" near the bottom of the page to find a list of Marriott's divisions. Do you suppose the divisions are cost centers, profit centers, or investment centers?

3. Go to the most recent annual report by clicking on "About Marriott," "Investors," "Financial Information," and finally click on "Financial Reports & Proxy" to find the most recent annual report. Locate the information on business segments in the Notes to Financial Statements. How many segments does Marriott identify? What are these segments? What information does the firm report with respect to each of the different segments?

4. Marriott provides both income and assets for each of the segments. Calculate the return on average total assets for the past year for each of the segments.

5. What was the return on average total assets for the corporation as a whole for the past year? Given the different kinds of business segments the company has, do you think that operating return on average total assets would be a good measure for evaluating the individual segments? What factors might influence your answer?

6. Is Marriott likely to have any transfer prices? If Marriott has transfers, how do you suppose the company determines its transfer prices?

Interest Rates and Bond Valuation

LEARNING OBJECTIVES

When you have finished studying this chapter, you should be able to:

1. *Describe interest rate fundamentals, the term structure of interest rates, and risk premiums.*

2. Review the legal aspects of bond financing and bond cost.

3. Discuss the general features, yields, prices, ratings, popular types, and international issues of corporate bonds.

4. Understand the key inputs and basic model used in the bond valuation process.

5. Apply the basic valuation model to bonds, and describe the impact of required return and time to maturity on bond values.

6. Explain yield to maturity (YTM), its calculation, and the procedure used to value bonds that pay interest semiannually.

► WHY THIS CHAPTER MATTERS TO YOU

In your *professional* life

ACCOUNTING You need to understand interest rates and the various types of bonds to be able to account properly for amortization of bond premiums and discounts and for bond issues and retirements.

INFORMATION SYSTEMS You need to understand the data that is necessary to track bond valuations and bond amortization schedules.

MANAGEMENT You need to understand the behavior of interest rates and how they affect the types of funds the firm can raise and the timing and cost of bond issues and retirements.

MARKETING You need to understand how the interest rate level and the firm's ability to issue bonds may affect the availability of financing for marketing research projects and new-product development.

OPERATIONS You need to understand how the interest rate level may affect the firm's ability to raise funds to maintain and grow the firm's production capacity.

In your *personal* life
Interest rates have a direct impact on personal financial planning. Movements in interest rates occur frequently and affect the returns from and values of savings and investments. The rate of interest you are charged on credit cards and loans can have a profound effect on your personal finances. Understanding the basics of interest rates is important to your personal financial success.

THE FEDERAL DEBT
A Huge Appetite for Money

Who is the largest debtor in the world? The U.S. federal government, of course. As of October 6, 2010, the national debt was more than $13 trillion, more than $1 trillion of which accrued in 2009 alone. About half of the outstanding U.S. government debt is held by the U.S. Federal Reserve and other U.S. intragovernmental bodies, and another quarter is held by foreign investors. Interest on the national debt is one of the largest items in the federal budget, totaling $383 billion in 2009. With Congressional Budget Office estimates projecting that from 2010 to 2019 the cumulative deficits will exceed $7 trillion, the federal government has a huge need for outside financing, which dwarfs the capital needs of any corporation.

Sara Piaseczynski

To feed this huge demand, the U.S. Treasury Department can issue T-bills, debt securities that mature in less than 1 year, Treasury notes that mature in 1 to 10 years, Treasury bonds that mature in more than 10 years, and savings bonds. Treasury securities can be purchased at banks (EE- and I-series savings bonds), at public auctions, and through TreasuryDirect, a Web-based system that allows investors to establish accounts to conduct transactions in Treasury securities online. Despite the government's massive past and projected future deficits, U.S. Treasury securities are still regarded as the safest investments in the world. In this chapter, you'll learn about the pricing of these and other debt instruments.

LG 1   10.1 Interest Rates and Required Returns

Financial institutions and markets create the mechanism through which funds flow between savers (funds suppliers) and borrowers (funds demanders). All else being equal, savers would like to earn as much interest as possible, and borrowers would like to pay as little as possible. The interest rate prevailing in the market at any given time reflects the equilibrium between savers and borrowers.

Interest Rate Fundamentals

The *interest rate* or *required return* represents the cost of money. It is the compensation that a supplier of funds expects and a demander of funds must pay. Usually the term **interest rate** is applied to debt instruments such as bank loans or bonds, and the term **required return** is applied to equity investments, such as common stock, that give the investor an ownership stake in the issuer. In fact, the meaning of these two terms is quite similar because, in both cases, the supplier is compensated for providing funds to the demander.

A variety of factors can influence the equilibrium interest rate. One factor is **inflation**, a rising trend in the prices of most goods and services. Typically, savers demand higher returns (that is, higher interest rates) when inflation is high because they want their investments to more than keep pace with rising prices. A second factor influencing interest rates is risk. When people perceive that a particular investment is riskier, they will expect a higher return on that investment as compensation for bearing the risk. A third factor that can affect the interest rate is a **liquidity**

interest rate
Usually applied to debt instruments such as bank loans or bonds; the compensation paid by the borrower of funds to the lender; from the borrower's point of view, the cost of borrowing funds.

required return
Usually applied to equity instruments such as common stock; the cost of funds obtained by selling an ownership interest.

Matter of fact

Fear Turns T-Bill Rates Negative

Near the height of the financial crisis in December 2008, interest rates on Treasury bills briefly turned negative, meaning that investors paid more to the Treasury than the Treasury promised to pay back. Why would anyone put their money into an investment that they know will lose money? Remember that 2008 saw the demise of Lehman Brothers, and fears that other commercial banks and investments banks might fail were rampant. Evidently, some investors were willing to pay the U.S. Treasury to keep their money safe for a short time.

inflation

A rising trend in the prices of most goods and services.

liquidity preference

A general tendency for investors to prefer short-term (that is, more liquid) securities.

real rate of interest

The rate that creates equilibrium between the supply of savings and the demand for investment funds in a perfect world, without inflation, where suppliers and demanders of funds have no liquidity preferences and there is no risk.

nominal rate of interest

The actual rate of interest charged by the supplier of funds and paid by the demander.

preference among investors. The term *liquidity preference* refers to the general tendency of investors to prefer short-term securities (that is, securities that are more liquid). If, all other things being equal, investors would prefer to buy short-term rather than long-term securities, interest rates on short-term instruments such as Treasury bills will be lower than rates on longer-term securities. Investors will hold these securities, despite the relatively low return that they offer, because they meet investors' preferences for liquidity.

THE REAL RATE OF INTEREST   Imagine a *perfect world* in which there is no inflation, in which investors have no liquidity preferences, and in which there is no risk. In this world, there would be one cost of money—the **real rate of interest**. The real rate of interest creates equilibrium between the supply of savings and the demand for funds. It represents the most basic cost of money. Historically, the real rate of interest in the United States has averaged about 1 percent per year, but that figure does fluctuate over time. This supply–demand relationship is shown in Figure 10.1 by the supply function (labeled S_0) and the demand function (labeled D). An equilibrium between the supply of funds and the demand for funds ($S_0 = D$) occurs at a rate of interest r_0^*, the real rate of interest.

Clearly, the real rate of interest changes with changing economic conditions, tastes, and preferences. To combat a recession, the Board of Governors of the Federal Reserve System might initiate actions to increase the supply of credit in the economy, causing the supply function in Figure 10.1 to shift to, say, S_1. This could result in a lower real rate of interest, r_1^*, at equilibrium ($S_1 = D$). With a lower cost of money, firms might find that investments that were previously unattractive are now worth undertaking, and as firms hire more workers and spend more on plant and equipment, the economy begins to expand again.

NOMINAL OR ACTUAL RATE OF INTEREST (RETURN)   The **nominal rate of interest** is the actual rate of interest charged by the supplier of funds and paid by the demander. *Throughout this book, interest rates and required rates of return are nominal rates unless otherwise noted.* The nominal rate of interest differs from the real rate of interest, r^*, as a result of two factors, inflation and risk. When people save money and invest it, they are sacrificing consumption today (that is, they are spending less than they could) in return

**Figure 10.1
Supply–Demand
Relationship**

Supply of savings and demand for investment funds

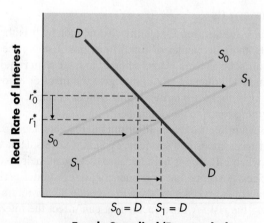

for higher future consumption. When investors expect inflation to occur, they believe that the price of consuming goods and services will be higher in the future than in the present. Therefore, they will be reluctant to sacrifice today's consumption unless the return they can earn on the money they save (or invest) will be high enough to allow them to purchase the goods and services they desire at a higher future price. That is, *investors will demand a higher nominal rate of return if they expect inflation*. This higher rate of return is called the expected inflation premium (*IP*).

Similarly, investors generally demand higher rates of return on risky investments as compared to safe ones. Otherwise, there is little incentive for investors to bear the additional risk. Therefore, *investors will demand a higher nominal rate of return on risky investments*. This additional rate of return is called the risk premium (*RP*). Therefore, the nominal rate of interest for security 1, r_1, is given in Equation 10.1:

$$r_1 = \underbrace{r^* + IP}_{\substack{\text{risk-free} \\ \text{rate, } R_F}} + \underbrace{RP_1}_{\substack{\text{risk} \\ \text{premium}}} \tag{10.1}$$

As the horizontal braces below the equation indicate, the nominal rate, r_1, can be viewed as having two basic components: a risk-free rate of return, R_F, and a risk premium, RP_1:

$$r_1 = R_F + RP_1 \tag{10.2}$$

For the moment, ignore the risk premium, RP_1, and focus exclusively on the risk-free rate. Equation 10.1 says that the risk-free rate can be represented as

$$R_F = r^* + IP \tag{10.3}$$

The risk-free rate (as shown in Equation 10.3) embodies the real rate of interest plus the expected inflation premium. The inflation premium is driven by investors' expectations about inflation—the more inflation they expect, the higher will be the inflation premium and the higher will be the nominal interest rate.

Three-month *U.S. Treasury bills* (*T-bills*) are short-term IOUs issued by the U.S. Treasury, and they are widely regarded as the safest investments in the world. They are as close as we can get in the real world to a risk-free investment. To estimate the real rate of interest, analysts typically try to determine what rate of inflation investors expect over the coming 3 months. Next, *they subtract the expected inflation rate from the nominal rate on the 3-month T-bill to arrive at the underlying real rate of interest*. For the risk-free asset in Equation 10.3, the real rate of interest, r^*, would equal $R_F - IP$. A simple personal finance example can demonstrate the practical distinction between nominal and real rates of interest.

Personal Finance Example 10.1

Marilyn Carbo has $10 that she can spend on candy costing $0.25 per piece. She could buy 40 pieces of candy ($10.00 ÷ $0.25) today. The nominal rate of interest on a 1-year deposit is currently 7%, and the expected rate of inflation over the coming year is 4%. Instead of buying the 40 pieces of candy today, Marilyn could invest the $10. After one year she would have $10.70 because she would have earned 7% interest—an additional $0.70 (0.07 × $10.00) —on her $10 deposit. During that year, inflation would have increased the cost of the candy by 4%—an additional $0.01 (0.04 × $0.25) —to $0.26 per piece. As a result, at the end of the 1-year period Marilyn would be able to buy about 41.2 pieces of candy ($10.70 ÷ $0.26), or roughly 3% more (41.2 ÷ 40.0 = 1.03) . The 3% increase in Marilyn's buying power represents her real rate of return. The nominal rate of return on her investment (7%), is partly eroded by inflation (4%), so her real return during the year is the difference between the nominal rate and the inflation rate (7% − 4% = 3%) .

I-Bonds Adjust for Inflation

One of the disadvantages of bonds is that they usually offer a fixed interest rate. Once a bond is issued, its interest rate typically cannot adjust as expected inflation changes. This presents a serious risk to bond investors because if inflation rises while the nominal rate on the bond remains fixed, the real rate of return falls.

The U.S. Treasury Department now offers the I-bond, which is an inflation-adjusted savings bond. A Series-I bond earns interest through the application of a composite rate. The composite rate consists of a fixed rate that remains the same for the life of the bond and an adjustable rate equal to the actual rate of inflation. The adjustable rate changes twice per year and is based on movements in the Consumer Price Index for All Urban Consumers (CPI-U). This index tracks the prices of thousands of goods and services, so an increase in this index indicates that inflation has occurred. As the rate of inflation moves up and down, I-bond interest rates adjust (with a short lag). Interest earnings are exempt from state and local income taxes, and are payable only when an investor redeems an I-bond.

I-bonds are issued at face value in denominations of $50, $75, $100, $200, $500, $1,000, $5,000, and $10,000.

The I-bond is not without its drawbacks. Any redemption within the first

5 years results in a 3-month interest penalty. Also, you should redeem an

I-bond only at the first of the month because none of the interest earned during a month is included in the redemption value until the first day of the following month. The adjustable-rate feature of I-bonds can work against investors (that is, it can lower their returns) if deflation occurs. Deflation refers to a general trend of falling prices, so when deflation occurs, the change in the CPI-U is negative, and the adjustable portion of an I-bond's interest also turns negative. For example, if the fixed-rate component on an

I-bond is 2 percent and prices fall 0.5 percent (stated equivalently, the inflation rate is –0.5 percent), then the nominal rate on an I-bond will be just 1.5 percent (2 percent minus 0.5 percent). Nevertheless, in the past 80 years, periods of deflation have been very rare, whereas inflation has been an almost ever-present feature of the economy, so investors are likely to enjoy the inflation protection that I-bonds offer in the future.

▶ What effect do you think the inflation-adjusted interest rate has on the price of an I-bond in comparison with similar bonds with no allowance for inflation?

deflation
A general trend of falling prices.

The premium for *expected inflation* in Equation 10.3 represents the average rate of *inflation* expected over the life of an investment. It is *not* the rate of inflation experienced over the immediate past, although investors' inflation expectations are undoubtedly influenced by the rate of inflation that has occurred in the recent past. Even so, the inflation premium reflects the expected rate of inflation. The expected inflation premium changes over time in response to many factors, such as changes in monetary and fiscal policies, currency movements, and international political events. For a discussion of a U.S. debt security whose interest rate is adjusted for inflation, see the *Focus on Practice* box.

Figure 10.2 illustrates the annual movement of the rate of inflation and the risk-free rate of return from 1961 through 2009. During this period the two rates tended to move in a similar fashion. Note that T-bill rates were slightly above the inflation rate most of the time, meaning

Figure 10.2
Impact of Inflation
Relationship between annual rate of inflation and 3-month U.S. Treasury bill average annual returns, 1961–2009

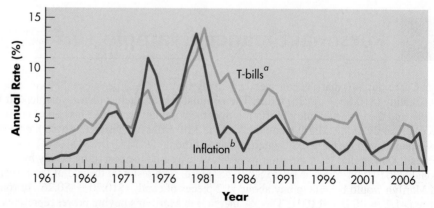

a Average annual rate of return on 3-month U.S. Treasury bills.
b Annual pecentage change in the consumer price index.

Sources: Data from selected *Federal Reserve Bulletins* and *U.S. Department of Labor Bureau of Labor Statistics.*

that T-bills generally offered a small positive real return. Between 1978 and the early 1980s, inflation and interest rates were quite high, peaking at over 13 percent in 1980–1981. Since then, rates have gradually declined. To combat a severe recession, the Federal Reserve pushed interest rates down to almost 0% in 2009, and for the first time in decades, the rate of inflation turned slightly negative (that is, there was slight deflation that year).

Term Structure of Interest Rates

The **term structure of interest rates** is the relationship between the maturity and rate of return for bonds with similar levels of risk. A graph of this relationship is called the **yield curve.** A quick glance at the yield curve tells analysts how rates vary between short-, medium-, and long-term bonds, but it may also provide information on where interest rates and the economy in general are headed in the future. Usually, when analysts examine the term structure of interest rates, they focus on Treasury securities because these are generally considered to be free of default risk.

YIELD CURVES A bond's **yield to maturity (YTM)** (discussed later in this chapter) represents the compound annual rate of return that an investor earns on the bond assuming that the bond makes all promised payments and the investor holds the bond to maturity. In a yield curve, the yield to maturity is plotted on the vertical axis and time to maturity is plotted on the horizontal axis. Figure 10.3 shows three yield curves for U.S. Treasury securities: one at May 22, 1981, a second at September 29, 1989, and a third at May 28, 2010.

Observe that both the position and the shape of the yield curves change over time. The yield curve of May 22, 1981, indicates that short-term interest rates at that time were above longer-term rates. For reasons that a glance at the figure makes obvious, this curve is described as *downward-sloping*. Interest rates in May 1981 were also quite high by historical standards, so the overall level of the yield curve is high. Historically, a downward-sloping yield curve, which is often called an **inverted yield curve,** occurs infrequently and is often a sign that the economy is weakening. Most recessions in the United States have been preceded by an inverted yield curve.

Usually, short-term interest rates are lower than long-term interest rates, as they were on May 28, 2010. That is, the **normal yield curve** is *upward-sloping*. Notice that the May 2010 yield curve lies entirely beneath the other two curves shown in Figure 10.3. In other words, interest rates in May 2010 were unusually low, largely because at that time the economy was just beginning to recover from a deep recession and inflation was very low. Sometimes, a **flat yield curve,** similar to that of September 29, 1989, exists. A flat yield curve simply means that rates do not vary much at different maturities.

The shape of the yield curve may affect the firm's financing decisions. A financial manager who faces a downward-sloping yield curve may be tempted to rely more heavily on cheaper, long-term financing. However, a risk in following this strategy is that interest rates may fall in the future, so long-term rates that seem cheap today may be relatively expensive tomorrow.

term structure of interest rates
The relationship between the maturity and rate of return for bonds with similar levels of risk.

yield curve
A graphic depiction of the term structure of interest rates.

yield to maturity (YTM)
Compound annual rate of return earned on a debt security purchased on a given day and held to maturity.

inverted yield curve
A *downward-sloping* yield curve indicates that short-term interest rates are generally higher than long-term interest rates.

normal yield curve
An *upward-sloping* yield curve indicates that long-term interest rates are generally higher than short-term interest rates.

flat yield curve
A yield curve that indicates that interest *rates* do not vary much at different maturities.

Figure 10.3
Treasury Yield Curves
Yield curves for U.S. Treasury securities: May 22, 1981; September 29, 1989; and May 28, 2010

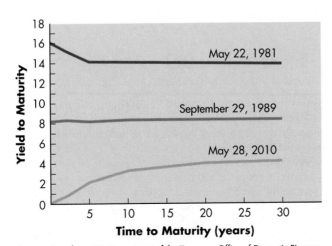

Sources: Data from U.S. Department of the Treasury, Office of Domestic Finance, Office of Debt Management.

expectations theory

The theory that the yield curve reflects investor expectations about future interest rates; an expectation of rising interest rates results in an upward-sloping yield curve, and an expectation of declining rates results in a downward-sloping yield curve.

Likewise, when the yield curve is upward-sloping, the manager may feel that it is wise to use cheaper, short-term financing. Relying on short-term financing has its own risks. Firms that borrow on a short-term basis may see their costs rise if interest rates go up. Even more serious is the risk that a firm may not be able to refinance a short-term loan when it comes due. A variety of factors influence the choice of loan maturity, but the shape of the yield curve is something that managers must consider when making decisions about borrowing short-term versus long-term.

THEORIES OF TERM STRUCTURE Three theories are frequently cited to explain the general shape of the yield curve: the expectations theory, the liquidity preference theory, and the market segmentation theory.

Expectations Theory One theory of the term structure of interest rates, the **expectations theory,** suggests that the yield curve reflects investor expectations about future interest rates. According to this theory, when investors expect short-term interest rates to rise in the future (perhaps because investors believe that inflation will rise in the future), today's long-term rates will be higher than current short-term rates, and the yield curve will be upward sloping. The opposite is true when investors expect declining short-term rates— today's short-term rates will be higher than current long-term rates, and the yield curve will be inverted.

To understand the expectations theory, consider this example. Suppose that the yield curve is flat. The rate on a 1-year Treasury note is 4 percent, and so is the rate on a 2-year Treasury note. Now, consider an investor who has money to place into a low-risk investment for 2 years. The investor has two options. First, he could purchase the 2-year Treasury note and receive a total of 8 percent (ignoring compounding) in 2 years. Second, he could invest in the 1-year Treasury earning 4 percent, and then when that security matures, he could reinvest in another 1-year Treasury note. If the investor wants to maximize his expected return, the decision between the first and second options above depends on whether he expects interest rates to rise, fall, or remain unchanged during the next year.

If the investor believes that interest rates will rise, that means next year's return on a 1-year Treasury note will be greater than 4 percent (that is, greater than the 1-year Treasury rate right now). Let's say the investor believes that the interest rate on a 1-year note next year will be 5 percent. If the investor expects rising rates, then his expected return is higher if he follows the second option, buying a 1-year Treasury note now (paying 4 percent) and reinvesting in a new security that pays 5 percent next year. Over 2 years, the investor would expect to earn about 9 percent (ignoring compounding) in interest, compared to just 8 percent earned by holding the 2-year bond.

If the current 1-year rate is 4 percent and investors generally expect that rate to go up to 5 percent next year, what would the 2-year Treasury note rate have to be right now to remain competitive? The answer is 4.5 percent. An investor who buys this security and holds it for 2 years would earn about 9 percent interest (again, ignoring compounding), the same as the expected return from investing in two consecutive 1-year bonds. In other words, *if investors expect interest rates to rise, the 2-year rate today must be higher than the 1-year rate today, and that in turn means that the yield curve must have an upward slope.*

Example 10.2

Suppose that a 5-year Treasury note currently offers a 3% annual return. Investors believe that interest rates are going to decline, and 5 years from now, they expect the rate on a 5-year Treasury note to be 2.5%. According to the expectations theory, what is the return that a 10-year Treasury note has to offer today? What does this imply about the slope of the yield curve?

Consider an investor who purchases a 5-year note today and plans to reinvest in another 5-year note in the future. Over the 10-year investment horizon, this investor expects to earn about 27.5%, ignoring compounding (that's 3% per year for the first 5 years and 2.5% per year for the next 5 years). To compete with that return, a 10-year bond today could offer 2.75% per year. That is, a bond that pays 2.75% for each of the next 10 years produces the same 27.5% total return that the series of two 5-year notes is expected to produce. Therefore, the 5-year rate today is 3% and the 10-year rate today is 2.75%, and the yield curve is downward sloping.

Liquidity Preference Theory   Most of the time, yield curves are upward sloping. According to the expectations theory, this means that investors expect interest rates to rise. An alternative explanation for the typical upward slope of the yield curve is the **liquidity preference theory.** This theory holds that, all else being equal, investors generally prefer to buy short-term securities, while issuers prefer to sell long-term securities. For investors, short-term securities are attractive because they are highly liquid and their prices are not particularly volatile.[1] Hence, investors will accept somewhat lower rates on short-term bonds because they are less risky than long-term bonds. Conversely, when firms or governments want to lock in their borrowing costs for a long period of time by selling long-term bonds, those bonds have to offer higher rates to entice investors away from the short-term securities that they prefer. Borrowers are willing to pay somewhat higher rates because long-term debt allows them to eliminate or reduce the risk of not being able to refinance short-term debts when they come due. Borrowing on a long-term basis also reduces uncertainty about future borrowing costs.

Market Segmentation Theory   The **market segmentation theory** suggests that the market for loans is totally segmented on the basis of maturity and that the supply of and demand for loans within each segment determine its prevailing interest rate. In other words, the equilibrium between suppliers and demanders of short-term funds, such as seasonal business loans, would determine prevailing short-term interest rates, and the equilibrium between suppliers and demanders of long-term funds, such as real estate loans, would determine prevailing long-term interest rates. The slope of the yield curve would be determined by the general relationship between the prevailing rates in each market segment. Simply stated, an upward-sloping yield curve indicates greater borrowing demand relative to the supply of funds in the long-term segment of the debt market relative to the short-term segment.

All three term structure theories have merit. From them we can conclude that at any time the slope of the yield curve is affected by (1) interest rate expectations, (2) liquidity preferences, and (3) the comparative equilibrium of supply and demand in the short- and long-term market segments. Upward-sloping yield curves result from expectations of rising interest rates, lender preferences for shorter-maturity loans, and greater supply of short-term loans than of long-term loans relative to demand. The opposite conditions would result in a downward-sloping yield curve. At any time, the interaction of these three forces determines the prevailing slope of the yield curve.

liquidity preference theory
Theory suggesting that long-term rates are generally higher than short-term rates (hence, the yield curve is upward sloping) because investors perceive short-term investments to be more liquid and less risky than long-term investments. Borrowers must offer higher rates on long-term bonds to entice investors away from their preferred short-term securities.

market segmentation theory
Theory suggesting that the market for loans is segmented on the basis of maturity and that the supply of and demand for loans within each segment determine its prevailing interest rate; the slope of the yield curve is determined by the general relationship between the prevailing rates in each market segment.

Risk Premiums: Issuer and Issue Characteristics

So far we have considered only risk-free U.S. Treasury securities. We now reintroduce the risk premium and assess it in view of risky non-Treasury issues. Recall Equation 10.1:

$$r_1 = \underbrace{r^* + IP}_{\substack{\text{risk-free} \\ \text{rate, } R_F}} + \underbrace{RP_1}_{\substack{\text{risk} \\ \text{premium}}}$$

In words, the nominal rate of interest for security 1 (r_1) is equal to the risk-free rate, consisting of the real rate of interest (r^*) plus the inflation expectation premium (IP), plus the risk premium (RP_1). The *risk premium* varies with specific issuer and issue characteristics.

Example 10.3

The nominal interest rates on a number of classes of long-term securities in May 2010 were as follows:

Security	Nominal interest rate
U.S. Treasury bonds (average)	3.30%
Corporate bonds (by risk ratings):	
High quality (Aaa–Aa)	3.95
Medium quality (A–Baa)	4.98
Speculative (Ba–C)	8.97

---

[1] Later in this chapter we demonstrate that debt instruments with longer maturities are more sensitive to changing market interest rates. For a given change in market rates, the price or value of longer-term debts will be more significantly changed (up or down) than the price or value of debts with shorter maturities.

Because the U.S. Treasury bond would represent the risk-free, long-term security, we can calculate the risk premium of the other securities by subtracting the risk-free rate, 3.30%, from each nominal rate (yield):

Security	Risk premium
Corporate bonds (by ratings):	
High quality (Aaa–Aa)	3.95% − 3.30% = 0.65%
Medium quality (A–Baa)	4.98 − 3.30 = 1.68
Speculative (Ba–C)	8.97 − 3.30 = 5.67

These risk premiums reflect differing issuer and issue risks. The lower-rated (speculative) corporate issues have a far higher risk premium than that of the higher-rated corporate issues (high quality and medium quality), and that risk premium is the compensation that investors demand for bearing the higher default risk of lower quality bonds.

The risk premium consists of a number of issuer- and issue-related components, including business risk, financial risk, interest rate risk, liquidity risk, and tax risk, as well as the purely debt-specific risks—default risk, maturity risk, and contractual provision risk, briefly defined in Table 10.1. In general, the highest risk premiums and therefore the highest returns result from securities issued by firms with a high risk of default and from long-term maturities that have unfavorable contractual provisions.

	Description
Default risk	The possibility that the issuer of debt will not pay the contractual interest or principal as scheduled. The greater the uncertainty as to the borrower's ability to meet these payments, the greater the risk premium. High bond ratings reflect low default risk, and low bond ratings reflect high default risk.
Maturity risk	The fact that the longer the maturity, the more the value of a security will change in response to a given change in interest rates. If interest rates on otherwise similar-risk securities suddenly rise as a result of a change in the money supply, the prices of long-term bonds will decline by more than the prices of short-term bonds, and vice versa.[a]
Contractual provision risk	Conditions that are often included in a debt agreement or a stock issue. Some of these reduce risk, whereas others may increase risk. For example, a provision allowing a bond issuer to retire its bonds prior to their maturity under favorable terms increases the bond's risk.

[a]A detailed discussion of the effects of interest rates on the price or value of bonds and other fixed-income securities is presented later in this chapter.

Table 10.1
Debt-Specific Issuer- and Issue-Related Risk Premium Components

→ **Review Questions**

10–1 What is the *real rate of interest?* Differentiate it from the *nominal rate of interest* for the risk-free asset, a 3-month U.S. Treasury bill.

10–2 What is the *term structure of interest rates,* and how is it related to the *yield curve?*

10–3 For a given class of similar-risk securities, what does each of the following yield curves reflect about interest rates: (**a**) downward-sloping; (**b**) upward-sloping; and (**c**) flat? What is the "normal" shape of the yield curve?

10–4 Briefly describe the following theories of the general shape of the yield curve: (**a**) expectations theory; (**b**) liquidity preference theory; and (**c**) market segmentation theory.

10–5 List and briefly describe the potential issuer- and issue-related risk components that are embodied in the risk premium. Which are the purely debt-specific risks?

LG 3 10.2 Corporate Bonds

A **corporate bond** is a long-term debt instrument indicating that a corporation has borrowed a certain amount of money and promises to repay it in the future under clearly defined terms. Most bonds are issued with maturities of 10 to 30 years and with a par value, or face value, of $1,000. The **coupon interest rate** on a bond represents the percentage of the bond's par value that will be paid annually, typically in two equal semiannual payments, as interest. The bondholders, who are the lenders, are promised the semiannual interest payments and, at maturity, repayment of the principal amount.

Legal Aspects of Corporate Bonds

Certain legal arrangements are required to protect purchasers of bonds. Bondholders are protected primarily through the indenture and the trustee.

BOND INDENTURE A **bond indenture** is a legal document that specifies both the rights of the bondholders and the duties of the issuing corporation. Included in the indenture are descriptions of the amount and timing of all interest and principal payments, various standard and restrictive provisions, and, frequently, sinking-fund requirements and security interest provisions. The borrower commonly must (1) *maintain satisfactory accounting records* in accordance with generally accepted accounting principles (GAAP); (2) periodically *supply audited financial statements;* (3) *pay taxes and other liabilities when due;* and (4) *maintain all facilities in good working order.*

Standard Provisions The **standard debt provisions** in the bond indenture specify certain record-keeping and general business practices that the bond issuer must follow.

Restrictive Provisions Bond indentures also normally include certain **restrictive covenants,** which place operating and financial constraints on the borrower. These provisions help protect the bondholder against increases in borrower risk. Without them, the borrower could increase the firm's risk but not have to pay increased interest to compensate for the increased risk.

The most common restrictive covenants do the following:

1. Require a *minimum level of liquidity,* to ensure against loan default.
2. *Prohibit the sale of accounts receivable* to generate cash. Selling receivables could cause a long-run cash shortage if proceeds were used to meet current obligations.
3. Impose *fixed-asset restrictions.* The borrower must maintain a specified level of fixed assets to guarantee its ability to repay the bonds.
4. *Constrain subsequent borrowing.* Additional long-term debt may be prohibited, or additional borrowing may be *subordinated* to the original loan. **Subordination** means that subsequent creditors agree to wait until all claims of the *senior debt* are satisfied.
5. *Limit the firm's annual cash dividend payments* to a specified percentage or amount.

Other restrictive covenants are sometimes included in bond indentures.

The violation of any standard or restrictive provision by the borrower gives the bondholders the right to demand immediate repayment of the debt. Generally, bondholders evaluate any violation to determine whether it jeopardizes the loan. They may then decide to demand immediate repayment, continue the loan, or alter the terms of the bond indenture.

Sinking-Fund Requirements Another common restrictive provision is a **sinking-fund requirement.** Its objective is to provide for the systematic retirement of bonds prior to their maturity. To carry out this requirement, the corporation makes semiannual or annual payments that are used to retire bonds by purchasing them in the marketplace.

Security Interest The bond indenture identifies any collateral pledged against the bond and specifies how it is to be maintained. The protection of bond collateral is crucial to guarantee the safety of a bond issue.

TRUSTEE A **trustee** is a third party to a *bond indenture.* The trustee can be an individual, a corporation, or (most often) a commercial bank trust department. The trustee is paid to act as a "watchdog" on behalf of the bondholders and can take specified actions on behalf of the bondholders if the terms of the indenture are violated.

---

corporate bond
A long-term debt instrument indicating that a corporation has borrowed a certain amount of money and promises to repay it in the future under clearly defined terms.

coupon interest rate
The percentage of a bond's par value that will be paid annually, typically in two equal semiannual payments, as interest.

bond indenture
A legal document that specifies both the rights of the bondholders and the duties of the issuing corporation.

standard debt provisions
Provisions in a *bond indenture* specifying certain record-keeping and general business practices that the bond issuer must follow; normally, they do not place a burden on a financially sound business.

restrictive covenants
Provisions in a *bond indenture* that place operating and financial constraints on the borrower.

subordination
In a bond indenture, the stipulation that subsequent creditors agree to wait until all claims of the senior debt are satisfied.

sinking-fund requirement
A restrictive provision often included in a bond indenture, providing for the systematic retirement of bonds prior to their maturity.

trustee
A paid individual, corporation, or commercial bank trust department that acts as the third party to a *bond indenture* and can take specified actions on behalf of the bondholders if the terms of the indenture are violated.

Cost of Bonds to the Issuer

The cost of bond financing is generally greater than the issuer would have to pay for short-term borrowing. The major factors that affect the cost, which is the rate of interest paid by the bond issuer, are the bond's maturity, the size of the offering, the issuer's risk, and the basic cost of money.

IMPACT OF BOND MATURITY Generally, as we noted earlier, long-term debt pays higher interest rates than short-term debt. In a practical sense, the longer the maturity of a bond, the less accuracy there is in predicting future interest rates, and therefore the greater the bondholders' risk of giving up an opportunity to lend money at a higher rate. In addition, the longer the term, the greater the chance that the issuer might default.

IMPACT OF OFFERING SIZE The size of the bond offering also affects the interest cost of borrowing but in an inverse manner: Bond flotation and administration costs per dollar borrowed are likely to decrease with increasing offering size. On the other hand, the risk to the bondholders may increase, because larger offerings result in greater risk of default.

IMPACT OF ISSUER'S RISK The greater the issuer's *default risk,* the higher the interest rate. Some of this risk can be reduced through inclusion of appropriate restrictive provisions in the bond indenture. Clearly, bondholders must be compensated with higher returns for taking greater risk. Frequently, bond buyers rely on bond ratings (discussed later) to determine the issuer's overall risk.

IMPACT OF THE COST OF MONEY The cost of money in the capital market is the basis for determining a bond's coupon interest rate. Generally, the rate on U.S. Treasury securities of equal maturity is used as the lowest-risk cost of money. To that basic rate is added a *risk premium* (as described earlier in this chapter) that reflects the factors mentioned above (maturity, offering size, and issuer's risk).

General Features of a Bond Issue

Three features sometimes included in a corporate bond issue are a conversion feature, a call feature, and stock purchase warrants. These features provide the issuer or the purchaser with certain opportunities for replacing or retiring the bond or supplementing it with some type of equity issue.

conversion feature
A feature of *convertible bonds* that allows bondholders to change each bond into a stated number of shares of common stock.

Convertible bonds offer a **conversion feature** that allows bondholders to change each bond into a stated number of shares of common stock. Bondholders convert their bonds into stock only when the market price of the stock is such that conversion will provide a profit for the bondholder. Inclusion of the conversion feature by the issuer lowers the interest cost and provides for automatic conversion of the bonds to stock if future stock prices appreciate noticeably.

call feature
A feature included in nearly all corporate bond issues that gives the issuer the opportunity to repurchase bonds at a stated *call price* prior to maturity.

The **call feature** is included in nearly all corporate bond issues. It gives the issuer the opportunity to repurchase bonds prior to maturity. The **call price** is the stated price at which bonds may be repurchased prior to maturity. Sometimes the call feature can be exercised only during a certain period. As a rule, the call price exceeds the par value of a bond by an amount equal to 1 year's interest. For example, a $1,000 bond with a 10 percent coupon interest rate would be callable for around $1,100 [$1,000 + (10% × $1,000)]. The amount by which the call price exceeds the bond's par value is commonly referred to as the **call premium.** This premium compensates bondholders for having the bond called away from them; to the issuer, it is the cost of calling the bonds.

call price
The stated price at which a bond may be repurchased, by use of a *call feature,* prior to maturity.

call premium
The amount by which a bond's *call price* exceeds its par value.

The call feature enables an issuer to call an outstanding bond when interest rates fall and issue a new bond at a lower interest rate. When interest rates rise, the call privilege will not be exercised, except possibly to meet *sinking-fund requirements.* Of course, to sell a callable bond in the first place, the issuer must pay a higher interest rate than on noncallable bonds of equal risk, to compensate bondholders for the risk of having the bonds called away from them.

stock purchase warrants
Instruments that give their holders the right to purchase a certain number of shares of the issuer's common stock at a specified price over a certain period of time.

Bonds occasionally have stock purchase warrants attached as "sweeteners" to make them more attractive to prospective buyers. **Stock purchase warrants** are instruments that give their holders the right to purchase a certain number of shares of the issuer's common stock at a specified price over a certain period of time. Their inclusion typically enables the issuer to pay a slightly lower coupon interest rate than would otherwise be required.

Bond Yields

The *yield,* or rate of return, on a bond is frequently used to assess a bond's performance over a given period of time, typically 1 year. Because there are a number of ways to measure a bond's yield, it is important to understand popular yield measures. The three most widely cited bond yields are (1) *current yield,* (2) *yield to maturity (YTM),* and (3) *yield to call (YTC).* Each of these yields provides a unique measure of the return on a bond.

The simplest yield measure is the **current yield,** the annual interest payment divided by the current price. For example, a $1,000 par value bond with an 8 percent coupon interest rate that currently sells for $970 would have a current yield of 8.25% [(0.08 × $1,000) ÷ $970]. This measure indicates the cash return for the year from the bond. However, because current yield ignores any change in bond value, it does not measure the total return. As we'll see later in this chapter, both the yield to maturity and the yield to call measure the total return.

Bond Prices

Because most corporate bonds are purchased and held by institutional investors, such as banks, insurance companies, and mutual funds, rather than individual investors, bond trading and price data are not readily available to individuals. Table 10.2 includes some assumed current data on the bonds of five companies, noted A through E. Looking at the data for Company C's bond, which is highlighted in the table, we see that the bond has a coupon interest rate of 7.200 percent and a maturity date of January 15, 2017. These data identify a specific bond issued by Company C. (The company could have more than a single bond issue outstanding.) The price represents the final price at which the bond traded on the current day.

Although most corporate bonds are issued with a *par,* or *face, value* of $1,000, *all bonds are quoted as a percentage of par.* A $1,000-par-value bond quoted at 94.007 is priced at $940.07 (94.007% × $1,000). Corporate bonds are quoted in dollars and cents. Thus, Company C's price of 103.143 for the day was $1,031.43—that is, 103.143% × $1,000.

The final column of Table 10.2 represents the bond's *yield to maturity (YTM),* which is the compound annual rate of return that would be earned on the bond if it were purchased and held to maturity. (YTM is discussed in detail later in this chapter.)

Bond Ratings

Independent agencies such as Moody's, Fitch, and Standard & Poor's assess the riskiness of publicly traded bond issues. These agencies derive their ratings by using financial ratio and cash flow analyses to assess the likely payment of bond interest and principal. Table 10.3 summarizes these ratings. For discussion of ethical issues related to the bond-rating agencies, see the *Focus on Ethics* box.

Normally an inverse relationship exists between the quality of a bond and the rate of return that it must provide bondholders: High-quality (high-rated) bonds provide lower returns than lower-quality (low-rated) bonds. This reflects the lender's risk–return trade-off. When considering bond financing, the financial manager must be concerned with the expected ratings of the bond issue, because these ratings affect salability and cost.

Company	Coupon	Maturity	Price	Yield (YTM)
Company A	6.125%	Nov. 15, 2011	105.336	4.788%
Company B	6.000	Oct. 31, 2036	94.007	6.454
Company C	7.200	Jan. 15, 2014	103.143	6.606
Company D	5.150	Jan. 15, 2017	95.140	5.814
Company E	5.850	Jan. 14, 2012	100.876	5.631

TABLE 10.2
Data on Selected Bonds

Can We Trust the Bond Raters?

Moody's Investors Service, Standard & Poor's, and Fitch Ratings play a crucial role in the financial markets. These credit-rating agencies evaluate and attach ratings to credit instruments (for example, bonds). Historically, bonds that received higher ratings were almost always repaid, while lower-rated, more speculative "junk" bonds experienced much higher default rates. The agencies' ratings have a direct impact on firms' cost of raising external capital and investors' appraisals of fixed-income investments.

Recently, the credit-rating agencies have been criticized for their role in the subprime crisis. The agencies attached ratings to complex securities that did not reflect the true risk of the underlying investments. For example, securities backed by mortgages issued to borrowers with bad credit and no documented income often received investment-grade ratings that implied almost zero probability of default. However, when home prices began to decline in 2006, securities backed by risky mort-

gages did default, including many that had been rated investment grade.

It is not entirely clear why the rating agencies assigned such high ratings to these securities. Did the agencies believe that complex financial engineering could create investment-grade securities out of risky mortgage loans? Did the agencies understand the securities they were rating? Were they unduly influenced by the security issuers, who also happened to pay for the ratings? Apparently, some within the rating agencies were suspicious. In a December, 2006 e-mail exchange between colleagues at Standard & Poor's, one individual proclaimed, "Let's hope we are all wealthy and retired by the time this house of cards falters."[a]

▶ What ethical issues may arise because the companies that issue bonds pay the rating agencies to rate their bonds?

[a]http://oversight.house.gov/images/stories/Hearings/Committee_on_Oversight/E-mail_from_Belinda_Ghetti_to_Nicole_ Billick_et_al._December_16_2006.pdf

Moody's	Interpretation	Standard & Poor's	Interpretation
Aaa	Prime quality	AAA	Investment grade
Aa	High grade	AA	
A	Upper medium grade	A	
Baa	Medium grade	BBB	
Ba	Lower medium grade or speculative	BB	Speculative
		B	
B	Speculative		
Caa	From very speculative	CCC	
Ca	to near or in default	CC	
C	Lowest grade	C	Income bond
		D	In default

[a]Some ratings may be modified to show relative standing within a major rating category; for example, Moody's uses numerical modifiers (1, 2, 3), whereas Standard & Poor's uses plus (+) and minus (−) signs.

Sources: Moody's Investors Service, Inc., and Standard & Poor's Corporation.

TABLE 10.3
Moody's and Standard & Poor's Bond Ratings[a]

debentures

subordinated debentures

income bonds

mortgage bonds

collateral trust bonds

equipment trust certificates
See Table 10.4.

zero- (or low-) coupon bonds

junk bonds

floating-rate bonds

extendible notes

putable bonds
See Table 10.5 on page 389.

Common Types of Bonds

Bonds can be classified in a variety of ways. Here we break them into traditional bonds (the basic types that have been around for years) and contemporary bonds (newer, more innovative types). The traditional types of bonds are summarized in terms of their key characteristics and priority of lender's claim in Table 10.4. Note that the first three types—**debentures, subordinated debentures,** and **income bonds**—are unsecured, whereas the last three—**mortgage bonds, collateral trust bonds,** and **equipment trust certificates**—are secured.

Table 10.5 (see page 389) describes the key characteristics of five contemporary types of bonds: **zero- (or low-) coupon bonds, junk bonds, floating-rate bonds, extendible notes,** and **putable bonds.** These bonds can be either unsecured or secured. Changing capital market conditions and investor preferences have spurred further innovations in bond financing in recent years and will probably continue to do so.

Bond type	Characteristics	Priority of lender's claim
Unsecured bonds		
Debentures	Unsecured bonds that only creditworthy firms can issue. Convertible bonds are normally debentures.	Claims are the same as those of any general creditor. May have other unsecured bonds subordinated to them.
Subordinated debentures	Claims are not satisfied until those of the creditors holding certain (senior) debts have been fully satisfied.	Claim is that of a general creditor but not as good as a senior debt claim.
Income bonds	Payment of interest is required only when earnings are available. Commonly issued in reorganization of a failing firm.	Claim is that of a general creditor. Are not in default when interest payments are missed, because they are contingent only on earnings being available.
Secured Bonds		
Mortgage bonds	Secured by real estate or buildings.	Claim is on proceeds from sale of mortgaged assets; if not fully satisfied, the lender becomes a general creditor. The first-mortgage claim must be fully satisfied before distribution of proceeds to second-mortgage holders, and so on. A number of mortgages can be issued against the same collateral.
Collateral trust bonds	Secured by stock and (or) bonds that are owned by the issuer. Collateral value is generally 25% to 35% greater than bond value.	Claim is on proceeds from stock and (or) bond collateral; if not fully satisfied, the lender becomes a general creditor.
Equipment trust certificates	Used to finance "rolling stock"—airplanes, trucks, boats, railroad cars. A trustee buys the asset with funds raised through the sale of trust certificates and then leases it to the firm; after making the final scheduled lease payment, the firm receives title to the asset. A type of leasing.	Claim is on proceeds from the sale of the asset; if proceeds do not satisfy outstanding debt, trust certificate lenders become general creditors.

TABLE 10.4
Characteristics and Priority of Lender's Claim of Traditional Types of Bonds

Bond type	Characteristics[a]
Zero- (or low-) coupon bonds	Issued with no (zero) or a very low coupon (stated interest) rate and sold at a large discount from par. A significant portion (or all) of the investor's return comes from gain in value (that is, par value minus purchase price). Generally callable at par value. Because the issuer can annually deduct the current year's interest accrual without having to pay the interest until the bond matures (or is called), its cash flow each year is increased by the amount of the tax shield provided by the interest deduction.
Junk bonds	Debt rated Ba or lower by Moody's or BB or lower by Standard & Poor's. Commonly used by rapidly growing firms to obtain growth capital, most often as a way to finance mergers and takeovers. High-risk bonds with high yields—often yielding 2% to 3% more than the best-quality corporate debt.
Floating-rate bonds	Stated interest rate is adjusted periodically within stated limits in response to changes in specified money market or capital market rates. Popular when future inflation and interest rates are uncertain. Tend to sell at close to par because of the automatic adjustment to changing market conditions. Some issues provide for annual redemption at par at the option of the bondholder.
Extendible notes	Short maturities, typically 1 to 5 years, that can be renewed for a similar period at the option of holders. Similar to a floating-rate bond. An issue might be a series of 3-year renewable notes over a period of 15 years; every 3 years, the notes could be extended for another 3 years, at a new rate competitive with market interest rates at the time of renewal.
Putable bonds	Bonds that can be redeemed at par (typically, $1,000) at the option of their holder either at specific dates after the date of issue and every 1 to 5 years thereafter or when and if the firm takes specified actions, such as being acquired, acquiring another company, or issuing a large amount of additional debt. In return for its conferring the right to "put the bond" at specified times or when the firm takes certain actions, the bond's yield is lower than that of a nonputable bond.

TABLE 10.5
Characteristics of Contemporary Types of Bonds

[a]The claims of lenders (that is, bondholders) against issuers of each of these types of bonds vary, depending on the bonds' other features. Each of these bonds can be unsecured or secured.

International Bond Issues

Companies and governments borrow internationally by issuing bonds in two principal financial markets: the Eurobond market and the foreign bond market. Both give borrowers the opportunity to obtain large amounts of long-term debt financing quickly, in the currency of their choice and with flexible repayment terms.

A **Eurobond** is issued by an international borrower and sold to investors in countries with currencies other than the currency in which the bond is denominated. An example is a dollar-denominated bond issued by a U.S. corporation and sold to Belgian investors. From the founding of the Eurobond market in the 1960s until the mid-1980s, "blue chip" U.S. corporations were the largest single class of Eurobond issuers. Some of these companies were able to borrow in this market at interest rates below those the U.S. government paid on Treasury bonds. As the market matured, issuers became able to choose the currency in which they borrowed, and European and Japanese borrowers rose to prominence. In more recent years, the Eurobond market has become much more balanced in terms of the mix of borrowers, total issue volume, and currency of denomination.

In contrast, a **foreign bond** is issued by a foreign corporation or government and is denominated in the investor's home currency and sold in the investor's home market. A Swiss-franc–denominated bond issued in Switzerland by a U.S. company is an example of a foreign bond. The three largest foreign-bond markets are Japan, Switzerland, and the United States.

Eurobond

A bond issued by an international borrower and sold to investors in countries with currencies other than the currency in which the bond is denominated.

foreign bond

A bond that is issued by a foreign corporation or government and is denominated in the investor's home currency and sold in the investor's home market.

→ **Review Questions**

10–6   What are typical maturities, denominations, and interest payments of a corporate bond? What mechanisms protect bondholders?

10–7   Differentiate between *standard debt provisions* and *restrictive covenants* included in a bond indenture. What are the consequences if a bond issuer violates any of these covenants?

10–8   How is the cost of bond financing typically related to the cost of short-term borrowing? In addition to a bond's maturity, what other major factors affect its cost to the issuer?

10–9   What is a *conversion feature?* A *call feature?* What are *stock purchase warrants?*

10–10   What is the *current yield* for a bond? How are bond prices quoted? How are bonds rated, and why?

10–11   Compare the basic characteristics of *Eurobonds* and *foreign bonds.*

LG 4 10.3 Valuation Fundamentals

valuation

The process that links risk and return to determine the worth of an asset.

Valuation is the process that links risk and return to determine the worth of an asset. It is a relatively simple process that can be applied to *expected* streams of benefits from bonds, stocks, income properties, oil wells, and so on. To determine an asset's worth at a given point in time, a financial manager uses the time-value-of-money techniques.

Key Inputs

There are three key inputs to the valuation process: (1) cash flows (returns), (2) timing, and (3) a measure of risk, which determines the required return. Each is described below.

CASH FLOWS (RETURNS)   The value of any asset depends on the cash flow(s) it is *expected* to provide over the ownership period. To have value, an asset does not have to provide an annual cash flow; it can provide an intermittent cash flow or even a single cash flow over the period.

Personal Finance Example 10.4

Celia Sargent wishes to estimate the value of three assets she is considering investing in: common stock in Michaels Enterprises, an interest in an oil well, and an original painting by a well-known artist. Her cash flow estimates for each are as follows:

Stock in Michaels Enterprises   *Expect* to receive cash dividends of $300 per year indefinitely.

Oil well   *Expect* to receive cash flow of $2,000 at the end of year 1, $4,000 at the end of year 2, and $10,000 at the end of year 4, when the well is to be sold.

Original painting   *Expect* to be able to sell the painting in 5 years for $85,000.

With these cash flow estimates, Celia has taken the first step toward placing a value on each of the assets.

TIMING In addition to making cash flow estimates, we must know the timing of the cash flows.[2] For example, Celia expects the cash flows of $2,000, $4,000, and $10,000 for the oil well to occur at the ends of years 1, 2, and 4, respectively. The combination of the cash flow and its timing fully defines the return expected from the asset.

RISK AND REQUIRED RETURN   The level of risk associated with a given cash flow can significantly affect its value. In general, the greater the risk of (or the less certain) a cash flow, the lower its value. Greater risk can be incorporated into a valuation analysis by using a higher required return or discount rate. The higher the risk, the greater the required return, and the lower the risk, the less the required return.

Personal Finance Example 10.5

Let's return to Celia Sargent's task of placing a value on the original painting and consider two scenarios.

Scenario 1—Certainty   A major art gallery has contracted to buy the painting for $85,000 at the end of 5 years. Because this is considered a certain situation, Celia views this asset as "money in the bank." She thus would use the prevailing risk-free rate of 3% as the required return when calculating the value of the painting.

Scenario 2—High risk   The values of original paintings by this artist have fluctuated widely over the past 10 years. Although Celia expects to be able to sell the painting for $85,000, she realizes that its sale price in 5 years could range between $30,000 and $140,000. Because of the high uncertainty surrounding the painting's value, Celia believes that a 15% required return is appropriate.

These two estimates of the appropriate required return illustrate how this rate captures risk. The often subjective nature of such estimates is also evident.

Basic Valuation Model

Simply stated, the value of any asset is *the present value of all future cash flows it is expected to provide over the relevant time period.* The time period can be any length, even infinity. The value of an asset is therefore determined by discounting the expected cash flows back to their present value, using the required return commensurate with the asset's risk as the appropriate discount rate. Using the present value techniques, we can express the value of any asset at time zero, V_0, as

$$V_0 = \frac{CF_1}{(1 + r)^1} + \frac{CF_2}{(1 + r)^2} + \cdots + \frac{CF_n}{(1 + r)^n} \qquad (10.4)$$

2. Although cash flows can occur at any time during a year, for computational convenience as well as custom, we will assume they occur at the *end of the year* unless otherwise noted.

where

$$V_0 = \text{value of the asset at time zero}$$
$$CF_t = \text{cash flow } expected \text{ at the end of year } t$$
$$r = \text{appropriate required return (discount rate)}$$
$$n = \text{relevant time period}$$

We can use Equation 10.4 to determine the value of any asset.

Personal Finance Example 10.6

Celia Sargent uses Equation 10.4 to calculate the value of each asset. She values Michaels Enterprises stock, which says that the present value of a perpetuity equals the annual payment divided by the required return. In the case of Michaels stock, the annual cash flow is $300, and Celia decides that a 12% discount rate is appropriate for this investment. Therefore, her estimate of the value of Michaels Enterprises stock is

$$\$300 \div 0.12 = \$2,500$$

Next, Celia values the oil well investment, which she believes is the most risky of the three investments. Using a 20% required return, Celia estimates the oil well's value to be

$$\frac{\$2,000}{(1 + 0.20)^1} + \frac{\$4,000}{(1 + 0.20)^2} + \frac{\$10,000}{(1 + 0.20)^4} = \$9,266.98$$

Finally, Celia estimates the value of the painting by discounting the expected $85,000 lump sum payment in 5 years at 15%:

$$\$85,000 \div (1 + 0.15)^5 = \$42,260.02$$

Note that, regardless of the pattern of the expected cash flow from an asset, the basic valuation equation can be used to determine its value.

→ Review Questions

10–12 Why is it important for financial managers to understand the valuation process?
10–13 What are the three key inputs to the valuation process?
10–14 Does the valuation process apply only to assets that provide an annual cash flow? Explain.
10–15 Define and specify the general equation for the value of any asset, V_0.

LG 5 LG 6 10.4 Bond Valuation

The basic valuation equation can be customized for use in valuing specific securities: bonds, common stock, and preferred stock. We describe bond valuation in this chapter, and valuation of common stock and preferred stock in Chapter 11.

Bond Fundamentals

As noted earlier in this chapter, *bonds* are long-term debt instruments used by business and government to raise large sums of money, typically from a diverse group of lenders. Most corporate bonds pay interest *semiannually* (every 6 months) at a stated *coupon interest rate,* have an initial *maturity* of 10 to 30 years, and have a *par value,* or *face value,* of $1,000 that must be repaid at maturity.

Example 10.7

Mills Company, a large defense contractor, on January 1, 2013, issued a 10% coupon interest rate, 10-year bond with a $1,000 par value that pays interest annually. Investors who buy this bond receive the contractual right to two cash flows: (1) $100 annual interest (10% coupon interest rate × $1,000 par value) distributed at the end of each year and (2) the $1,000 par value at the end of the tenth year.

We will use data for Mills's bond issue to look at basic bond valuation.

Basic Bond Valuation

The value of a bond is the present value of the payments its issuer is contractually obligated to make, from the current time until it matures. The basic model for the value, B_0, of a bond is given by Equation 10.5:

$$B_0 = I \times \left[\sum_{t=1}^{n} \frac{1}{(1 + r_d)^t} \right] + M \times \left[\frac{1}{(1 + r_d)^n} \right] \qquad (10.5)$$

where

$$B_0 = \text{value of the bond at time zero}$$
$$I = \textit{annual} \text{ interest paid in dollars}$$
$$n = \text{number of years to maturity}$$
$$M = \text{par value in dollars}$$
$$r_d = \text{required return on the bond}$$

We can calculate bond value by using Equation 10.5 and a financial calculator or by using a spreadsheet.

Personal Finance Example 10.8

Tim Sanchez wishes to determine the current value of the Mills Company bond. Assuming that interest on the Mills Company bond issue is paid annually and that the required return is equal to the bond's coupon interest rate, $I = \$100$, $r_d = 10\%$, $M = \$1,000$, and $n = 10$ years.

The computations involved in finding the bond value are depicted graphically on the following time line.

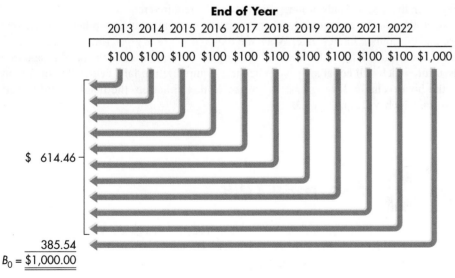

End of Year

2013 2014 2015 2016 2017 2018 2019 2020 2021 2022

$100 $100 $100 $100 $100 $100 $100 $100 $100 $100 $1,000

$ 614.46

385.54

$B_0 = \$1,000.00$

Time line for bond valuation (Mills Company's 10% coupon interest rate, 10-year maturity, $1,000 par, January 1, 2013, issue date, paying annual interest, and required return of 10%)

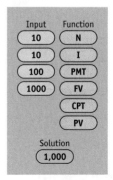

Input	Function
10	N
10	I
100	PMT
1000	FV
	CPT
	PV

Solution
1,000

Calculator Use   Using the Mills Company's inputs shown at the left, you should find the bond value to be exactly $1,000. Note that *the calculated bond value is equal to its par value; this will always be the case when the required return is equal to the coupon interest rate.*[3]

Spreadsheet Use   The value of the Mills Company bond also can be calculated as shown in the following Excel spreadsheet.

---

3. Note that because bonds pay interest in arrears, the prices at which they are quoted and traded reflect their value *plus* any accrued interest. For example, a $1,000 par value, 10% coupon bond paying interest semiannually and having a calculated value of $900 would pay interest of $50 at the end of each 6-month period. If it is now 3 months since the beginning of the interest period, three-sixths of the $50 interest, or $25 (that is, 3/6 × $50), would be accrued. The bond would therefore be quoted at $925—its $900 value plus the $25 in accrued interest. For convenience, *throughout this book, bond values will always be assumed to be calculated at the beginning of the interest period,* thereby avoiding the need to consider accrued interest.

	A	B
1	BOND VALUE, ANNUAL INTEREST, REQUIRED RETURN = COUPON INTEREST RATE	
2	Annual interest payment	$100
3	Coupon interest rate	10%
4	Number of years to maturity	10
5	Par value	$1,000
6	Bond value	$1,000.00

Entry in Cell B6 is
=PV(B3,B4,B2,B5,0)
Note that Excel will return a negative $1000
as the price that must be paid to acquire this bond.

Bond Value Behavior

In practice, the value of a bond in the marketplace is rarely equal to its par value. In the bond data (see Table 10.2 on page 387), you can see that the prices of bonds often differ from their par values of 100 (100 percent of par, or $1,000). Some bonds are valued below par (current price below 100), and others are valued above par (current price above 100). A variety of forces in the economy, as well as the passage of time, tend to affect value. Although these external forces are in no way controlled by bond issuers or investors, it is useful to understand the impact that required return and time to maturity have on bond value.

REQUIRED RETURNS AND BOND VALUES Whenever the required return on a bond differs from the bond's coupon interest rate, the bond's value will differ from its par value. The required return is likely to differ from the coupon interest rate because either (1) economic conditions have changed, causing a shift in the basic cost of long-term funds; or (2) the firm's risk has changed. Increases in the basic cost of long-term funds or in risk will raise the required return; decreases in the cost of funds or in risk will lower the required return.

discount
The amount by which a bond sells at a value that is less than its par value.

premium
The amount by which a bond sells at a value that is greater than its par value.

Regardless of the exact cause, what is important is the relationship between the required return and the coupon interest rate: When the required return is greater than the coupon interest rate, the bond value, B_0, will be less than its par value, M. In this case, the bond is said to sell at a **discount,** which will equal $M - B_0$. When the required return falls below the coupon interest rate, the bond value will be greater than par. In this situation, the bond is said to sell at a **premium,** which will equal $B_0 - M$.

Example 10.9

The preceding example showed that when the required return equaled the coupon interest rate, the bond's value equaled its $1,000 par value. If for the same bond the required return were to rise to 12% or fall to 8%, its value in each case could be found using Equation 10.5 or as follows.

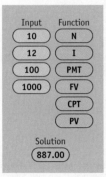

Input	Function
10	N
12	I
100	PMT
1000	FV
	CPT
	PV

Solution
887.00

Calculator Use Using the inputs shown at the left for the two different required returns, you will find the value of the bond to be below or above par. At a 12% required return, the bond would sell at a *discount* of $113.00 ($1,000 par value − $887.00 value). At the 8% required return, the bond would sell for a *premium* of $134.20 ($1,134.20 value − $1,000 par value). The results of these calculations for Mills Company's bond values are summarized in Table 10.6 and graphically depicted in Figure 10.4. The inverse relationship between bond value and required return is clearly shown in the figure.

Spreadsheet Use The values for the Mills Company bond at required returns of 12% and 8% also can be calculated as shown in the following Excel spreadsheet. Once this spreadsheet has been configured you can compare bond values for any two required returns by simply changing the input values.

	A	B	C
1	BOND VALUE, ANNUAL INTEREST, REQUIRED RETURN NOT EQUAL TO COUPON INTEREST RATE		
2	Annual interest payment	$100	$100
3	Coupon interest rate	10%	10%
4	Annual required return	12%	8%
5	Number of years to maturity	10	10
6	Par value	$1,000	$1,000
7	Bond value	$887.00	$1,134.20

Entry in Cell B7 is =PV(B4,B5,B2,B6,0)
Note that the bond trades at a discount (i.e., below par)
because the bond's coupon rate is below investors'
required return.

Entry in Cell C7 is =PV(C4,C5,C2,C6,0)
Note that the bond trades at a premium
because the bond's coupon rate is above investors'
required return.

Input — Function
10 — N
8 — I
100 — PMT
1000 — FV
— CPT
— PV

Solution
1,134.20

Required return, r_d	Bond value, B_0	Status
12%	$ 887.00	Discount
10	1,000.00	Par value
8	1,134.20	Premium

TABLE 10.6
Bond Values for Various Required Returns (Mills Company's 10% Coupon Interest Rate, 10-Year Maturity, $1,000 Par, January 1, 2013, Issue Date, Paying Annual Interest)

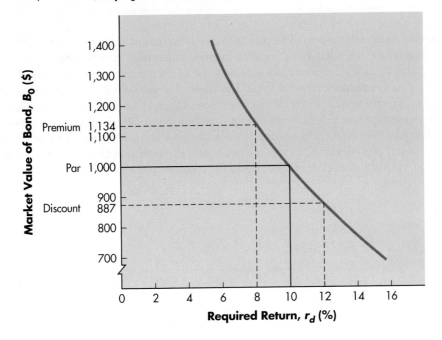

Figure 10.4
Bond Values and Required Returns

Bond values and required returns (Mills Company's 10% coupon interest rate, 10-year maturity, $1,000 par, January 1, 2013, issue date, paying annual interest)

TIME TO MATURITY AND BOND VALUES   Whenever the required return is different from the coupon interest rate, the amount of time to maturity affects bond value. An additional factor is whether required returns are constant or change over the life of the bond.

Constant Required Returns   When the required return is different from the coupon interest rate and is *constant until maturity,* the value of the bond will approach its par value as the passage of time moves the bond's value closer to maturity. (Of course, when the required return *equals* the coupon interest rate, the bond's value will remain at par until it matures.)

Example 10.10

Figure 10.5 depicts the behavior of the bond values calculated earlier and presented in Table 10.6 for Mills Company's 10% coupon interest rate bond paying annual interest and having 10 years to maturity. Each of the three required returns—12%, 10%, and 8%—is assumed to remain constant over the 10 years to the bond's maturity. The bond's value at both 12% and 8% approaches and ultimately equals the bond's $1,000 par value at its maturity, as the discount (at 12%) or premium (at 8%) declines with the passage of time.

Figure 10.5
Time to Maturity and Bond Values

Relationship among time to maturity, required returns, and bond values (Mills Company's 10% coupon interest rate, 10-year maturity, $1,000 par, January 1, 2013, issue date, paying annual interest)

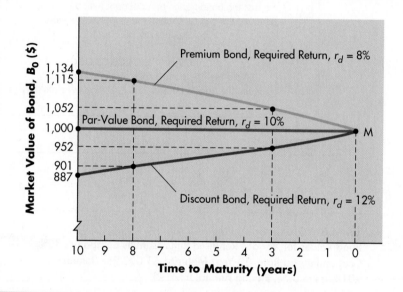

Changing Required Returns The chance that interest rates will change and thereby change the required return and bond value is called **interest rate risk**.[4] Bondholders are typically more concerned with rising interest rates because a rise in interest rates, and therefore in the required return, causes a decrease in bond value. The shorter the amount of time until a bond's maturity, the less responsive is its market value to a given change in the required return. In other words, *short maturities have less interest rate risk than long maturities when all other features (coupon interest rate, par value, and interest payment frequency) are the same.* This is because of the mathematics of time value; the present values of short-term cash flows change far less than the present values of longer-term cash flows in response to a given change in the discount rate (required return).

Example 10.11

The effect of changing required returns on bonds with differing maturities can be illustrated by using Mills Company's bond and Figure 10.5. If the required return rises from 10% to 12% when the bond has 8 years to maturity (see the dashed line at 8 years), the bond's value decreases from $1,000 to $901—a 9.9% decrease. If the same change in required return had occurred with only 3 years to maturity (see the dashed line at 3 years), the bond's value would have dropped to just $952—only a 4.8% decrease. Similar types of responses can be seen for the change in bond value associated with decreases in required returns. The shorter the time to maturity, the less the impact on bond value caused by a given change in the required return.

---

4. A more robust measure of a bond's response to interest rate changes is *duration*. Duration measures the sensitivity of a bond's prices to changing interest rates. It incorporates both the interest rate (coupon rate) and the time to maturity into a single statistic. Duration is simply a weighted average of the maturity of the present values of all the contractual cash flows yet to be paid by the bond. Duration is stated in years, so a bond with a 5-year duration will decrease in value by 5 percent if interest rates rise by 1 percent or will increase in value by 5 percent if interest rates fall by 1 percent.

Yield to Maturity (YTM)

When investors evaluate bonds, they commonly consider yield to maturity (YTM). This is the compound annual rate of return earned on a debt security purchased on a given day and held to maturity. (The measure assumes, of course, that the issuer makes all scheduled interest and principal payments as promised.)[5] The yield to maturity on a bond with a current price equal to its par value (that is,) will always equal the coupon interest rate. When the bond value differs from par, the yield to maturity will differ from the coupon interest rate.

Assuming that interest is paid annually, the yield to maturity on a bond can be found by solving Equation 10.5 for r_d. In other words, the current value, the annual interest, the par value, and the number of years to maturity are known, and the required return must be found. The required return is the bond's yield to maturity. The YTM can be found by using a financial calculator, by using an Excel spreadsheet, or by trial and error. The calculator provides accurate YTM values with minimum effort.

Example 10.12

Earl Washington wishes to find the YTM on Mills Company's bond. The bond currently sells for $1,080, has a 10% coupon interest rate and $1,000 par value, pays interest annually, and has 10 years to maturity.

Calculator Use   Most calculators require *either* the present value (B_0 in this case) or the future values (I and M in this case) to be input as negative numbers to calculate yield to maturity. That approach is employed here. Using the inputs shown at the left, you should find the YTM to be 8.766%.

Spreadsheet Use   The yield to maturity of Mills Company's bond also can be calculated as shown in the following Excel spreadsheet. First, enter all the bond's cash flows. Notice that you begin with the bond's price as an outflow (a negative number). In other words, an investor has to pay the price up front to receive the cash flows over the next 10 years. Next, use Excel's *internal rate of return* function. This function calculates the discount rate that makes the present value of a series of cash flows equal to zero. In this case, when the present value of all cash flows is zero, the present value of the inflows (interest and principal) equals the present value of the outflows (the bond's initial price). In other words, the internal rate of return function is giving us the bond's YTM, the discount rate that equates the bond's price to the present value of its cash flows.

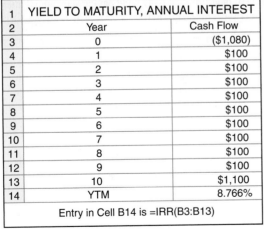

Input	Function
10	N
−1080	PV
100	PMT
1000	FV
	CPT
	I

Solution
8.766

	A	B
1	YIELD TO MATURITY, ANNUAL INTEREST	
2	Year	Cash Flow
3	0	($1,080)
4	1	$100
5	2	$100
6	3	$100
7	4	$100
8	5	$100
9	6	$100
10	7	$100
11	8	$100
12	9	$100
13	10	$1,100
14	YTM	8.766%
	Entry in Cell B14 is =IRR(B3:B13)	

---

5. Many bonds have a call feature, which means they may not reach maturity if the issuer, after a specified time period, calls them back. Because the call feature typically cannot be exercised until a specific future date, investors often calculate the yield to call (YTC). The yield to call represents the rate of return that investors earn if they buy a callable bond at a specific price and hold it until it is called back and they receive the call price, which would be set above the bond's par value. Here our focus is solely on the more general measure of yield to maturity.

Semiannual Interest and Bond Values

The procedure used to value bonds paying interest semiannually is similar for compounding interest more frequently than annually, except that here we need to find present value instead of future value. It involves

1. Converting annual interest, I, to semiannual interest by dividing I by 2.
2. Converting the number of years to maturity, n, to the number of 6-month periods to maturity by multiplying n by 2.
3. Converting the required stated (rather than effective)[6] annual return for similar-risk bonds that also pay semiannual interest from an annual rate, r_d, to a semiannual rate by dividing r_d by 2.

Substituting these three changes into Equation 10.5 yields

$$B_0 = \frac{I}{2} \times \left[\sum_{t=1}^{2n} \frac{1}{\left(1 + \dfrac{r_d}{2}\right)^t} \right] + M \times \left[\frac{1}{\left(1 + \dfrac{r_d}{2}\right)^{2n}} \right] \qquad (10.6)$$

Example 10.13

Input	Function
20	N
6	I
50	PMT
1000	FV
	CPT
	PV

Solution
885.30

Assuming that the Mills Company bond pays interest semiannually and that the required stated annual return, r_d, is 12% for similar-risk bonds that also pay semiannual interest, substituting these values into Equation 10.6 yields

$$B_0 = \frac{\$100}{2} \times \left[\sum_{t=1}^{20} \frac{1}{\left(1 + \dfrac{0.12}{2}\right)^t} \right] + \$1,000 \times \left[\frac{1}{\left(1 + \dfrac{0.12}{2}\right)^{20}} \right] = \$885.30$$

Calculator Use In using a calculator to find bond value when interest is paid semiannually, we must double the number of periods and divide both the required stated annual return and the annual interest by 2. For the Mills Company bond, we would use 20 periods (2 × 10 years), a required return of 6% (12% ÷ 2), and an interest payment of $50 ($100 ÷ 2). Using these inputs, you should find the bond value with semiannual interest to be $885.30, as shown at the left.

Spreadsheet Use The value of the Mills Company bond paying semiannual interest at a required return of 12% also can be calculated as shown in the following Excel spreadsheet.

	A	B
1	BOND VALUE, SEMIANNUAL INTEREST	
2	Semiannual interest payment	$50
3	Semiannual required return	6%
4	Number of periods to maturity	20
5	Par value	$1,000
6	Bond value	$885.30
	Entry in Cell B6 is =PV(B3,B4,B2,B5,0) Note that Excel will produce a negative value for the bond's price	

---

6. The effective annual rate of interest, EAR, for stated interest rate r, when interest is paid semiannually (m = 2), can be found by using Equation 5.17:

$$EAR = \left(1 + \frac{r}{2}\right)^2 - 1$$

For example, a bond with a 12% required stated annual return, r_d, that pays semiannual interest would have an effective annual rate of

$$1 = (1.06)^2 - 1 = 1.1236 - 1 = 0.1236 = 12.36\%$$

Because most bonds pay semiannual interest at semiannual rates equal to 50 percent of the stated annual rate, their effective annual rates are generally higher than their stated annual rates.

Comparing this result with the $887.00 value found earlier for annual compounding, we can see that the bond's value is lower when semiannual interest is paid. *This will always occur when the bond sells at a discount.* For bonds selling at a premium, the opposite will occur: The value with semiannual interest will be greater than with annual interest.

→ Review Questions

10–16 What basic procedure is used to value a bond that pays annual interest? Semiannual interest?

10–17 What relationship between the required return and the coupon interest rate will cause a bond to sell at a *discount?* At a *premium?* At its *par value?*

10–18 If the required return on a bond differs from its coupon interest rate, describe the behavior of the bond value over time as the bond moves toward maturity.

10–19 As a risk-averse investor, would you prefer bonds with short or long periods until maturity? Why?

10–20 What is a bond's *yield to maturity (YTM)?* Briefly describe the use of a financial calculator and the use of an Excel spreadsheet for finding YTM.

Summary

FOCUS ON VALUE

Interest rates and required returns embody the real cost of money, inflationary expectations, and issuer and issue risk. They reflect the level of return required by market participants as compensation for the risk perceived in a specific security or asset investment. Because these returns are affected by economic expectations, they vary as a function of time, typically rising for longer-term maturities. The yield curve reflects such market expectations at any point in time.

The value of an asset can be found by calculating the present value of its expected cash flows, using the required return as the discount rate. Bonds are the easiest financial assets to value; both the amounts and the timing of their cash flows are contractual and, therefore, known with certainty (at least for high-grade bonds). The financial manager needs to understand how to apply valuation techniques to bonds, stocks, and tangible assets (as we will demonstrate in the following chapters) to make decisions that are consistent with the firm's **share price maximization goal.**

REVIEW OF LEARNING GOALS

LG 1   **Describe interest rate fundamentals, the term structure of interest rates, and risk premiums.** The flow of funds between savers and borrowers is regulated by the interest rate or required return. In a perfect, inflation-free, certain world there would be one cost of money— the real rate of interest. The nominal or actual interest rate is the sum of the risk-free rate and a risk premium reflecting issuer and issue characteristics. The risk-free rate is the real rate of interest plus an inflation premium.

For any class of similar-risk bonds, the term structure of interest rates reflects the relationship between the interest rate or rate of return and the time to maturity. Yield curves can be downward sloping (inverted), upward sloping (normal), or flat. The expectations theory, liquidity preference theory, and market segmentation theory are cited to explain the shape of the yield curve. Risk premiums for non-Treasury debt issues result from business risk, financial risk, interest rate risk, liquidity risk, tax risk, default risk, maturity risk, and contractual provision risk.

LG 2   **Review the legal aspects of bond financing and bond cost.** Corporate bonds are long-term debt instruments indicating that a corporation has borrowed an amount that it promises to repay in the future under clearly defined terms. Most bonds are issued with maturities of 10 to 30 years and a par value of $1,000. The bond indenture, enforced by a trustee, states all conditions of the bond issue. It contains both standard debt provisions and restrictive covenants, which may include a sinking-fund requirement and/or a security interest. The cost of a bond to an issuer depends on its maturity, offering size, and issuer risk and on the basic cost of money.

LG 3 **Discuss the general features, yields, prices, ratings, popular types, and international issues of corporate bonds.** A bond issue may include a conversion feature, a call feature, or stock purchase warrants. The yield, or rate of return, on a bond can be measured by its current yield, yield to maturity (YTM), or yield to call (YTC). Bond prices are typically reported along with their coupon, maturity date, and yield to maturity (YTM). Bond ratings by independent agencies indicate the risk of a bond issue. Various types of traditional and contemporary bonds are available. Eurobonds and foreign bonds enable established creditworthy companies and governments to borrow large amounts internationally.

LG 4 **Understand the key inputs and basic model used in the valuation process.** Key inputs to the valuation process include cash flows (returns), timing, and risk and the required return. The value of any asset is equal to the present value of all future cash flows it is *expected* to provide over the relevant time period.

LG 5 **Apply the basic valuation model to bonds, and describe the impact of required return and time to maturity on bond values.** The value of a bond is the present value of its interest payments plus the present value of its par value. The discount rate used to determine bond value is the required return, which may differ from the bond's coupon interest rate. A bond can sell at a discount, at par, or at a premium, depending on whether the required return is greater than, equal to, or less than its coupon interest rate. The amount of time to maturity affects bond values. The value of a bond will approach its par value as the bond moves closer to maturity. The chance that interest rates will change and thereby change the required return and bond value is called interest rate risk. The shorter the amount of time until a bond's maturity, the less responsive is its market value to a given change in the required return.

LG 6 **Explain yield to maturity (YTM), its calculation, and the procedure used to value bonds that pay interest semiannually.** Yield to maturity is the rate of return investors earn if they buy a bond at a specific price and hold it until maturity. YTM can be calculated by using a financial calculator or by using an Excel spreadsheet. Bonds that pay interest semiannually are valued by using the same procedure used to value bonds paying annual interest, except that the interest payments are one-half of the annual interest payments, the number of periods is twice the number of years to maturity, and the required return is one-half of the stated annual required return on similar-risk bonds.

Opener-in-Review

In the chapter opener you learned that the United States government had more than $13 trillion in debt outstanding in the form of Treasury bills, notes, and bonds in 2010. From time to time, the Treasury changes the mix of securities that it issues to finance government debt, issuing more bills than bonds or vice versa.

a. With short-term interest rates near 0 percent in 2010, suppose the Treasury decided to replace maturing notes and bonds by issuing new Treasury bills, thus shortening the average maturity of U.S. debt outstanding. Discuss the pros and cons of this strategy.

b. The average maturity of outstanding U.S. Treasury debt is about 5 years. Suppose a newly issued 5-year Treasury note has a coupon rate of 2 percent and sells at par. What happens to the value of this bond if the inflation rate rises 1 percentage point, causing the yield-to-maturity on the 5-year note to jump to 3 percent shortly after it is issued?

c. Assume that the "average" Treasury security outstanding has the features described in part **b.** If total U.S. debt is $13 trillion and an increase in inflation causes yields on Treasury securities to increase by 1 percentage point, by how much would the market value of the outstanding debt fall? What does this suggest about the incentives of government policy makers to pursue policies that could lead to higher inflation?

Self-Test Problems   (Solutions in Appendix)

LG 5   **LG 6** **ST10–1 Bond valuation**   Lahey Industries has outstanding a $1,000 par-value bond with an 8% coupon interest rate. The bond has 12 years remaining to its maturity date.

a. If interest is paid annually, find the value of the bond when the required return is (1) 7%, (2) 8%, and (3) 10%.

b. Indicate for each case in part a whether the bond is selling at a discount, at a premium, or at its par value.

c. Using the 10% required return, find the bond's value when interest is paid semiannually.

LG 3   **LG 6** **ST10–2 Bond yields**   Elliot Enterprises' bonds currently sell for $1,150, have an 11% coupon interest rate and a $1,000 par value, pay interest annually, and have 18 years to maturity.

a. Calculate the bonds' current yield.

b. Calculate the bonds' yield to maturity (YTM).

c. Compare the YTM calculated in part b to the bonds' coupon interest rate and current yield (calculated in part a). Use a comparison of the bonds' current price and par value to explain these differences.

Warm-Up Exercises   All problems are available in *MyAccountingLab*

LG 1   **E10–1** The risk-free rate on T-bills recently was 1.23%. If the real rate of interest is estimated to be 0.80%, what was the expected level of inflation?

LG 1   **E10–2** The yields for Treasuries with differing maturities on a recent day were as shown in the table on this page.

a. Use the information to plot a yield curve for this date.

b. If the expectations hypothesis is true, approximately what rate of return do investors expect a 5-year Treasury note to pay 5 years from now?

Maturity	Yield
3 months	1.41%
6 months	1.71
2 years	2.68
3 years	3.01
5 years	3.70
10 years	4.51
30 years	5.25

c. If the expectations hypothesis is true, approximately (ignoring compounding) what rate of return do investors expect a 1-year Treasury security to pay starting 2 years from now?

d. Is it possible that even though the yield curve slopes up in this problem, investors do not expect rising interest rates? Explain.

LG 1   **E10–3** The yields for Treasuries with differing maturities, including an estimate of the real rate of interest, on a recent day were as shown in the following table:

Maturity	Yield	Real rate of interest
3 months	1.41%	0.80%
6 months	1.71	0.80
2 years	2.68	0.80
3 years	3.01	0.80
5 years	3.70	0.80
10 years	4.51	0.80
30 years	5.25	0.80

Use the information in the preceding table to calculate the inflation expectation for each maturity.

LG 1 **E10–4** Recently, the annual inflation rate measured by the Consumer Price Index (CPI) was forecast to be 3.3%. How could a T-bill have had a negative real rate of return over the same period? How could it have had a zero real rate of return? What minimum rate of return must the T-bill have earned to meet your requirement of a 2% real rate of return?

LG 1 **E10–5** Calculate the risk premium for each of the following rating classes of long-term securities, assuming that the yield to maturity (YTM) for comparable Treasuries is 4.51%.

Rating class	Nominal interest rate
AAA	5.12%
BBB	5.78
B	7.82

LG 4 **E10–6** You have two assets and must calculate their values today based on their different payment streams and appropriate required returns. Asset 1 has a required return of 15% and will produce a stream of $500 at the end of each year indefinitely. Asset 2 has a required return of 10% and will produce an end-of-year cash flow of $1,200 in the first year, $1,500 in the second year, and $850 in its third and final year.

LG 5 **E10–7** A bond with 5 years to maturity and a coupon rate of 6% has a par, or face, value of $20,000. Interest is paid annually. If you required a return of 8% on this bond, what is the value of this bond to you?

LG 5 **E10–8** Assume a 5-year Treasury bond has a coupon rate of 4.5%.
   a. Give examples of required rates of return that would make the bond sell at a discount, at a premium, and at par.
   b. If this bond's par value is $10,000, calculate the differing values for this bond given the required rates you chose in part a.

Problems   All problems are available in *MyAccountingLab*

LG 1 **P10–1** Interest rate fundamentals: The real rate of return   Carl Foster, a trainee at an investment banking firm, is trying to get an idea of what real rate of return investors are expecting in today's marketplace. He has looked up the rate paid on 3-month U.S. Treasury bills and found it to be 5.5%. He has decided to use the rate of change in the Consumer Price Index as a proxy for the inflationary expectations of investors. That annualized rate now stands at 3%. On the basis of the information that Carl has collected, what estimate can he make of the *real rate of return?*

LG 1 **P10–2 Real rate of interest** To estimate the real rate of interest, the economics division of Mountain Banks—a major bank holding company—has gathered the data summarized in the following table. Because there is a high likelihood that new tax legislation will be passed in the near future, current data as well as data reflecting the probable impact of passage of the legislation on the demand for funds are also

	Currently		With passage of tax legislation
Amount of funds supplied/demanded ($ billion)	Interest rate required by funds suppliers	Interest rate required by funds demanders	Interest rate required by funds demanders
$ 1	2%	7%	9%
5	3	6	8
10	4	4	7
20	6	3	6
50	7	2	4
100	9	1	3

included in the table. (Note: The proposed legislation will not affect the supply schedule of funds. Assume a perfect world in which inflation is expected to be zero, funds suppliers and demanders have no liquidity preference, and all outcomes are certain.)

a. Draw the supply curve and the demand curve for funds using the current data. (Note: Unlike the functions in Figure 10.1 on page 378, the functions here will not appear as straight lines.)

b. Using your graph, label and note the real rate of interest using the current data.

c. Add to the graph drawn in part a the new demand curve expected in the event that the proposed tax legislation is passed.

d. What is the new real rate of interest? Compare and analyze this finding in light of your analysis in part b.

Personal Finance Problem

LG 1 **P10–3 Real and nominal rates of interest** Zane Perelli currently has $100 that he can spend today on polo shirts costing $25 each. Alternatively, he could invest the $100 in a risk-free U.S. Treasury security that is expected to earn a 9% nominal rate of interest. The consensus forecast of leading economists is a 5% rate of inflation over the coming year.

a. How many polo shirts can Zane purchase today?

b. How much money will Zane have at the end of 1 year if he forgoes purchasing the polo shirts today?

c. How much would you expect the polo shirts to cost at the end of 1 year in light of the expected inflation?

d. Use your findings in parts b and c to determine how many polo shirts (fractions are OK) Zane can purchase at the end of 1 year. In percentage terms, how many more or fewer polo shirts can Zane buy at the end of 1 year?

e. What is Zane's real rate of return over the year? How is it related to the percentage change in Zane's buying power found in part d? Explain.

LG 1 **P10–4 Yield curve** A firm wishing to evaluate interest rate behavior has gathered yield data on five U.S. Treasury securities, each having a different maturity and all measured at the same point in time. The summarized data follow.

U.S. Treasury security	Time to maturity	Yield
A	1 year	12.6%
B	10 years	11.2
C	6 months	13.0
D	20 years	11.0
E	5 years	11.4

a. Draw the yield curve associated with these data.
b. Describe the resulting yield curve in part a, and explain the general expectations embodied in it.

LG 1 **P10–5 Nominal interest rates and yield curves** A recent study of inflationary expectations has revealed that the consensus among economic forecasters yields the following average annual rates of inflation expected over the periods noted. (Note: Assume that the risk that future interest rate movements will affect longer maturities more than shorter maturities is zero; that is, there is no maturity risk.)

Period	Average annual rate of inflation
3 months	5%
2 years	6
5 years	8
10 years	8.5
20 years	9

a. If the real rate of interest is currently 2.5%, find the nominal rate of interest on each of the following U.S. Treasury issues: 20-year bond, 3-month bill, 2-year note, and 5-year bond.
b. If the real rate of interest suddenly dropped to 2% without any change in inflationary expectations, what effect, if any, would this have on your answers in part a? Explain.
c. Using your findings in part a, draw a yield curve for U.S. Treasury securities. Describe the general shape and expectations reflected by the curve.
d. What would a follower of the liquidity preference theory say about how the preferences of lenders and borrowers tend to affect the shape of the yield curve drawn in part c? Illustrate that effect by placing on your graph a dotted line that approximates the yield curve without the effect of liquidity preference.
e. What would a follower of the market segmentation theory say about the supply and demand for long-term loans versus the supply and demand for short-term loans given the yield curve constructed for part c of this problem?

LG 1 **P10–6 Nominal and real rates and yield curves** A firm wishing to evaluate interest rate behavior has gathered data on the nominal rate of interest and on inflationary expectations for five U.S. Treasury securities, each having a different maturity and each measured at a different point in time during the year just ended. (Note: Assume that the risk that future interest rate movements will affect longer maturities more than shorter maturities is zero; that is, there is no maturity risk.) These data are summarized in the following table.

U.S. Treasury security	Point in time	Maturity	Nominal rate of interest	Inflationary expectation
A	Jan. 7	2 years	12.6%	9.5%
B	Mar. 12	10 years	11.2	8.2
C	May 30	6 months	13.0	10.0
D	Aug. 15	20 years	11.0	8.1
E	Dec. 30	5 years	11.4	8.3

a. Using the preceding data, find the real rate of interest at each point in time.
b. Describe the behavior of the real rate of interest over the year. What forces might be responsible for such behavior?
c. Draw the yield curve associated with these data, assuming that the nominal rates were measured at the same point in time.
d. Describe the resulting yield curve in part c, and explain the general expectations embodied in it.

LG 1 **P10–7 Term structure of interest rates**   The following yield data for a number of highest-quality corporate bonds existed at each of the three points in time noted.

	Yield		
Time to maturity (years)	5 years ago	2 years ago	Today
1	9.1%	14.6%	9.3%
3	9.2	12.8	9.8
5	9.3	12.2	10.9
10	9.5	10.9	12.6
15	9.4	10.7	12.7
20	9.3	10.5	12.9
30	9.4	10.5	13.5

a. On the same set of axes, draw the yield curve at each of the three given times.
b. Label each curve in part a with its general shape (downward-sloping, upward-sloping, flat).
c. Describe the general interest rate expectation existing at each of the three times.
d. Examine the data from 5 years ago. According to the expectations theory, what approximate return did investors expect a 5-year bond to pay as of today?

LG 1 **P10–8 Risk-free rate and risk premiums**   The real rate of interest is currently 3%; the inflation expectation and risk premiums for a number of securities follow.

Security	Inflation expectation Premium	Risk premium
A	6%	3%
B	9	2
C	8	2
D	5	4
E	11	1

a. Find the risk-free rate of interest, R$_F$, that is applicable to each security.
b. Although not noted, what factor must be the cause of the differing risk-free rates found in part a?
c. Find the nominal rate of interest for each security.

LG 1 **P10–9 Risk premiums**   Eleanor Burns is attempting to find the nominal rate of interest for each of two securities—A and B—issued by different firms at the same point in time. She has gathered the following data:

Characteristic	Security A	Security B
Time to maturity	3 years	15 years
Inflation expectation premium	9.0%	7.0%
Risk premium for:		
Liquidity risk	1.0%	1.0%
Default risk	1.0%	2.0%
Maturity risk	0.5%	1.5%
Other risk	0.5%	1.5%

a. If the real rate of interest is currently 2%, find the risk-free rate of interest applicable to each security.

b. Find the total risk premium attributable to each security's issuer and issue characteristics.

c. Calculate the nominal rate of interest for each security. Compare and discuss your findings.

LG 2 **P10–10** **Bond interest payments before and after taxes**   Charter Corp. has issued 2,500 debentures with a total principal value of $2,500,000. The bonds have a coupon interest rate of 7%.

a. What dollar amount of interest per bond can an investor expect to receive each year from Charter?

b. What is Charter's total interest expense per year associated with this bond issue?

c. Assuming that Charter is in a 35% corporate tax bracket, what is the company's net after-tax interest cost associated with this bond issue?

LG 4 **P10–11** **Bond prices and yields**   Assume that the Financial Management Corporation's $1,000-par-value bond had a 5.700% coupon, matures on May 15, 2020, has a current price quote of 97.708, and has a yield to maturity (YTM) of 6.034%. Given this information, answer the following questions:

a. What was the dollar price of the bond?

b. What is the bond's current yield?

c. Is the bond selling at par, at a discount, or at a premium? Why?

d. Compare the bond's current yield calculated in part b to its YTM and explain why they differ.

Personal Finance Problem

LG 4 **P10–12** Valuation fundamentals   Imagine that you are trying to evaluate the economics of purchasing an automobile. You expect the car to provide annual after-tax cash benefits of $1,200 at the end of each year and assume that you can sell the car for after-tax proceeds of $5,000 at the end of the planned 5-year ownership period. All funds for purchasing the car will be drawn from your savings, which are currently earning 6% after taxes.

a. Identify the cash flows, their timing, and the required return applicable to valuing the car.

b. What is the maximum price you would be willing to pay to acquire the car? Explain.

LG 4 **P10–13** Valuation of assets   Using the information provided in the following table, find the value of each asset.

Personal Finance Problem

LG 4 **P10–14** Asset valuation and risk   Laura Drake wishes to estimate the value of an asset expected to provide cash inflows of $3,000 per year at the end of years 1 through 4 and $15,000 at the end of year 5. Her research indicates that she must earn 10% on low-risk assets, 15% on average-risk assets, and 22% on high-risk assets.

a. Determine what is the most Laura should pay for the asset if it is classified as (1) low-risk, (2) average-risk, and (3) high-risk.

b. Suppose Laura is unable to assess the risk of the asset and wants to be certain she's making a good deal. On the basis of your findings in part a, what is the most she should pay? Why?

c. All else being the same, what effect does increasing risk have on the value of an asset? Explain in light of your findings in part a.

LG 5 **P10–15** **Basic bond valuation**   Complex Systems has an outstanding issue of $1,000-par-value bonds with a 12% coupon interest rate. The issue pays interest annually and has 16 years remaining to its maturity date.

Asset	Cash flow End of year	Amount	Appropriate required return
A	1	$ 5,000	18%
	2	5,000	
	3	5,000	
B	1 through ∞	$ 300	15%
C	1	$ 0	16%
	2	0	
	3	0	
	4	0	
	5	35,000	
D	1 through 5	$ 1,500	12%
	6	8,500	
E	1	$ 2,000	14%
	2	3,000	
	3	5,000	
	4	7,000	
	5	4,000	
	6	1,000	

a. If bonds of similar risk are currently earning a 10% rate of return, how much should the Complex Systems bond sell for today?

b. Describe the two possible reasons why the rate on similar-risk bonds is below the coupon interest rate on the Complex Systems bond.

c. If the required return were at 12% instead of 10%, what would the current value of Complex Systems' bond be? Contrast this finding with your findings in part a and discuss.

LG 5 **P10–16 Bond valuation—Annual interest** Calculate the value of each of the bonds shown in the following table, all of which pay interest *annually*.

Bond	Par value	Coupon interest rate	Years to maturity	Required return
A	$1,000	14%	20	12%
B	1,000	8	16	8
C	100	10	8	13
D	500	16	13	18
E	1,000	12	10	10

LG 5 **P10–17 Bond value and changing required returns** Midland Utilities has outstanding a bond issue that will mature to its $1,000 par value in 12 years. The bond has a coupon interest rate of 11% and pays interest annually.

a. Find the value of the bond if the required return is (1) 11%, (2) 15%, and (3) 8%.

b. Plot your findings in part a on a set of "required return (x axis)–market value of bond (y axis)" axes.

c. Use your findings in parts a and b to discuss the relationship between the coupon interest rate on a bond and the required return and the market value of the bond relative to its par value.

d. What two possible reasons could cause the required return to differ from the coupon interest rate?

LG 5 **P10–18** Bond value and time—Constant required returns   Pecos Manufacturing has just issued a 15-year, 12% coupon interest rate, $1,000-par bond that pays interest annually. The required return is currently 14%, and the company is certain it will remain at 14% until the bond matures in 15 years.

   a. Assuming that the required return does remain at 14% until maturity, find the value of the bond with (1) 15 years, (2) 12 years, (3) 9 years, (4) 6 years, (5) 3 years, and (6) 1 year to maturity.

   b. Plot your findings on a set of "time to maturity (x axis)–market value of bond (y axis)" axes constructed similarly to Figure 10.5 on page 396.

   c. All else remaining the same, when the required return differs from the coupon interest rate and is assumed to be constant to maturity, what happens to the bond value as time moves toward maturity? Explain in light of the graph in part b.

Personal Finance Problem

LG 5 **P10–19** **Bond value and time—Changing required returns**   Lynn Parsons is considering investing in either of two outstanding bonds. The bonds both have $1,000 par values and 11% coupon interest rates and pay annual interest. Bond A has exactly 5 years to maturity, and bond B has 15 years to maturity.

   a. Calculate the value of bond A if the required return is (1) 8%, (2) 11%, and (3) 14%.

   b. Calculate the value of bond B if the required return is (1) 8%, (2) 11%, and (3) 14%.

   c. From your findings in parts a and b, complete the following table, and discuss the relationship between time to maturity and changing required returns.

Required return	Value of bond A	Value of bond B
8%	?	?
11	?	?
14	?	?

   d. If Lynn wanted to minimize interest rate risk, which bond should she purchase? Why?

LG 6 **P10–20** **Yield to maturity**   The relationship between a bond's yield to maturity and coupon interest rate can be used to predict its pricing level. For each of the bonds listed, state whether the price of the bond will be at a premium to par, at par, or at a discount to par.

Bond	Coupon interest rate	Yield to maturity	Price
A	6%	10%	_____
B	8	8	_____
C	9	7	_____
D	7	9	_____
E	12	10	_____

LG 6 **P10–21** **Yield to maturity**   The Salem Company bond currently sells for $955, has a 12% coupon interest rate and a $1,000 par value, pays interest *annually*, and has 15 years to maturity.

   a. Calculate the yield to maturity (YTM) on this bond.

   b. Explain the relationship that exists between the coupon interest rate and yield to maturity and the par value and market value of a bond.

LG 6 **P10–22** **Yield to maturity**   Each of the bonds shown in the following table pays interest *annually*.

Bond	Par value	Coupon interest rate	Years to maturity	Current value
A	$1,000	9%	8	$ 820
B	1,000	12	16	1,000
C	500	12	12	560
D	1,000	15	10	1,120
E	1,000	5	3	900

   a. Calculate the yield to maturity (YTM) for each bond.

   b. What relationship exists between the coupon interest rate and yield to maturity and the par value and market value of a bond? Explain.

Personal Finance Problem

LG 2 **LG 5** **P10–23** Bond valuation and yield to maturity   Mark Goldsmith's broker has

LG 6

shown him two bonds. Each has a maturity of 5 years, a par value of $1,000, and a yield to maturity of 12%. Bond A has a coupon interest rate of 6% paid annually. Bond B has a coupon interest rate of 14% paid annually.

   a. Calculate the selling price for each of the bonds.

   b. Mark has $20,000 to invest. Judging on the basis of the price of the bonds, how many of either one could Mark purchase if he were to choose it over the other? (Mark cannot really purchase a fraction of a bond, but for purposes of this question, pretend that he can.)

   c. Calculate the yearly interest income of each bond on the basis of its coupon rate and the number of bonds that Mark could buy with his $20,000.

   d. Assume that Mark will reinvest the interest payments as they are paid (at the end of each year) and that his rate of return on the reinvestment is only 10%. For each bond, calculate the value of the principal payment plus the value of Mark's reinvestment account at the end of the 5 years.

   e. Why are the two values calculated in part d different? If Mark were worried that he would earn less than the 12% yield to maturity on the reinvested interest payments, which of these two bonds would be a better choice?

LG 6 **P10–24** Bond valuation—Semiannual interest   Find the value of a bond maturing in 6 years, with a $1,000 par value and a coupon interest rate of 10% (5% paid semi-annually) if the required return on similar-risk bonds is 14% annual interest (7% paid semiannually).

LG 6 **P10–25** Bond valuation—Semiannual interest Calculate the value of each of the bonds shown in the following table, all of which pay interest *semiannually*.

Bond	Par value	Coupon interest rate	Years to maturity	Required stated annual return
A	$1,000	10%	12	8%
B	1,000	12	20	12
C	500	12	5	14
D	1,000	14	10	10
E	100	6	4	14

LG 6 **P10–26** Bond valuation—Quarterly interest   Calculate the value of a $5,000-par-value bond paying quarterly interest at an annual coupon interest rate of 10% and having 10 years until maturity if the required return on similar-risk bonds is currently a 12% annual rate paid quarterly.

LG 1 **P10–27** ETHICS PROBLEM   Bond rating agencies have invested significant sums of money in an effort to determine which quantitative and nonquantitative factors best predict bond defaults. Furthermore, some of the raters invest time and money to meet privately with corporate personnel to get nonpublic information that is used in assigning the issue's bond rating. To recoup those costs, some bond rating agencies have tied their ratings to the purchase of additional services. Do you believe that this is an acceptable practice? Defend your position.

Spreadsheet Exercise

CSM Corporation has a bond issue outstanding at the end of 2012. The bond has 15 years remaining to maturity and carries a coupon interest rate of 6%. Interest on the bond is compounded on a semiannual basis. The par value of the CSM bond is $1,000 and it is currently selling for $874.42.

TO DO

Create a spreadsheet similar to the Excel spreadsheet examples located in the chapter for yield to maturity and semiannual interest to model the following:

a. Create a spreadsheet similar to the Excel spreadsheet examples located in the chapter to solve for the yield to maturity.

b. Create a spreadsheet similar to the Excel spreadsheet examples located in the chapter to solve for the price of the bond if the yield to maturity is 2% higher.

c. Create a spreadsheet similar to the Excel spreadsheet examples located in the chapter to solve for the price of the bond if the yield to maturity is 2% lower.

d. What can you summarize about the relationship between the price of the bond, the par value, the yield to maturity, and the coupon rate?

 Visit **www.myaccountinglab.com** for **Chapter Case: Evaluating Annie Hegg's Proposed Investment in Atilier Industries Bonds**, Group Exercises, and other numerous resources.

CHAPTER

11

Stock Valuation

LEARNING GOALS

1. Differentiate between debt and equity.

2. Discuss the features of both common and preferred stock.

3. Describe the process of issuing common stock, including venture capital, going public, and the investment banker.

4. Understand the concept of market efficiency and basic stock valuation using zero-growth, constant-growth, and variable-growth models.

5. Discuss the free cash flow valuation model and the book value, liquidation value, and price/earnings (P/E) multiple approaches.

6. Explain the relationships among financial decisions, return, risk, and the firm's value.

WHY THIS CHAPTER MATTERS TO YOU

In your *professional* life

ACCOUNTING You need to understand the difference between debt and equity in terms of tax treatment; the ownership claims of capital providers, including venture capitalists and stockholders; and the differences between book value per share and other market-based valuations.

INFORMATION SYSTEMS You need to understand the procedures used to issue common stock, the information needed to value stock, how to collect and process the necessary information from each functional area, and how to disseminate information to investors.

MANAGEMENT You need to understand the difference between debt and equity capital, the rights and claims of stockholders, the process of issuing common stock, and the effects each functional area has on the value of the firm's stock.

MARKETING You need to understand that the firm's ideas for products and services will greatly affect investors' beliefs regarding the likely success of the firm's projects; projects that are viewed as more likely to succeed are also viewed as more valuable and therefore lead to a higher stock value.

OPERATIONS You need to understand that the evaluations of venture capitalists and other would-be investors will in part depend on the efficiency of the firm's operations; more cost-efficient operations lead to better growth prospects and, therefore, higher stock valuations.

In your *personal* life
At some point, you are likely to hold stocks as an asset in your retirement program. You may want to estimate a stock's value. If the stock is selling below its estimated value, you may buy the stock; if its market price is above its value, you may sell it. Some individuals rely on financial advisors to make such buy or sell recommendations. Regardless of how you approach investment decisions, it will be helpful for you to understand how stocks are valued.

A123 SYSTEMS INC.

Going Green to Find Value

One of the most "hotly" debated topics of our day has been the issue of global warming and the benefits and costs of lower emissions. Many companies are investing in radical new technologies with the hope of capitalizing on the going green movement. On September 24, 2009, A123 Systems Inc. raised $378 million in its initial public offering (IPO) of common stock. A123, whose shares trade on the Nasdaq stock exchange, uses a patented nanotechnology developed at the Massachusetts Institute of Technology to produce more powerful and longer-lasting lithium ion batteries that go in products ranging from cordless hand tools to electric vehicles. Even though A123 reported a loss of $40.7 million on revenue of just $42.9 million in the first half of 2009, investors welcomed the IPO, boosting the share price 50 percent on the first day of trading.

Excitement about A123's prospects was fueled in part by major investments in the company from a few high-profile companies including General Electric, Qualcomm, and Motorola. Furthermore, the company secured almost $250 million in grants from the federal government as part of the American Recovery and Reinvestment Act of 2009, a bill passed by Congress designed to help the U.S. economy emerge from a deep recession. Some likely customers of A123 also received stimulus funds, including electric car makers Tesla Motors and Fisker Automotive. In the weeks following the IPO, A123's stock price was as high as $28 per share, but by the middle of 2010 it was trading below $10 a share. A123 is not a stock for the faint of heart. In the long run, A123's stock price will depend on its ability to generate positive cash flows and convince the market of its ability to do so into the future.

Reprinted with permission by A123 Systems

11.1 Differences between Debt and Equity

Although debt and equity capital are both sources of external financing used by firms, they are very different in several important respects. Most importantly, debt financing is obtained from creditors, and equity financing is obtained from investors who then become part owners of the firm. Creditors (lenders or debtholders) have a legal right to be repaid, whereas investors have only an expectation of being repaid. **Debt** includes all borrowing incurred by a firm, including bonds, and is repaid according to a fixed schedule of payments. **Equity** consists of funds provided by the firm's owners (investors or stockholders) and is repaid subject to the firm's performance. A firm can obtain equity either *internally*, by retaining earnings rather than paying them out as dividends to its stockholders, or *externally*, by selling common or preferred stock. The key differences between debt and equity capital are summarized in Table 11.1 and discussed in the following pages.

Voice in Management

Unlike creditors, holders of equity (stockholders) are owners of the firm. Stockholders generally have voting rights that permit them to select the firm's directors and vote on special issues. In contrast, debtholders do not receive voting privileges but instead rely on the firm's contractual obligations to them to be their voice.

debt
Includes all borrowing incurred by a firm, including bonds, and is repaid according to a fixed schedule of payments.

equity
Funds provided by the firm's owners (investors or stockholders) that are repaid subject to the firm's performance.

413

How Are Assets Divided in Bankruptcy?

According to the U.S. Securities and Exchange Commission, in bankruptcy assets are divided up as follows:

1. **Secured creditors:** Secured bank loans or secured bonds are paid first.
2. **Unsecured creditors:** Unsecured bank loans or unsecured bonds, suppliers, or customers have the next claim.
3. **Equityholders:** Equityholders or the owners of the company have the last claim on assets, and they may not receive anything if the secured and unsecured creditors' claims are not fully repaid.

Claims on Income and Assets

Equityholders' claims on income and assets are secondary to the claims of creditors. Their *claims on income* cannot be paid until the claims of all creditors, including both interest and scheduled principal payments, have been satisfied. After satisfying creditor's claims, the firm's board of directors decides whether to distribute dividends to the owners.

Equityholders' *claims on assets* also are secondary to the claims of creditors. If the firm fails, its assets are sold, and the proceeds are distributed in this order: secured creditors, unsecured creditors, and equityholders. Because equityholders are the last to receive any distribution of assets, they expect greater returns from their investment in the firm's stock than the returns creditors require on the firm's borrowings. The higher rate of return expected by equityholders leads to a higher cost of equity financing relative to the cost of debt financing for the firm.

In more depth

To read about *The Bankruptcy Process*, go to www.myaccountinglab.com
MyAccountingLab

Maturity

Unlike debt, equity is a *permanent form* of financing for the firm. It does not "mature," so repayment is not required. Because equity is liquidated only during bankruptcy proceedings, stockholders must recognize that, although a ready market may exist for their shares, the price that can be realized may fluctuate. This fluctuation of the market price of equity makes the overall returns to a firm's stockholders even more risky.

Tax Treatment

Interest payments to debtholders are treated as tax-deductible expenses by the issuing firm, whereas dividend payments to a firm's stockholders are not tax deductible. The tax deductibility

Characteristic	Type of capital	
	Debt	Equity
Voice in management[a]	No	Yes
Claims on income and assets	Senior to equity	Subordinate to debt
Maturity	Stated	None
Tax treatment	Interest deduction	No deduction

[a]Debtholders do not have voting rights, but instead they rely on the firm's contractual obligations to them to be their voice.

TABLE 11.1
Key Differences between Debt and Equity

of interest lowers the corporation's cost of debt financing, further causing it to be lower than the cost of equity financing.

→ Review Questions

11–1   What are the key differences between *debt* and *equity*?

LG 3 | 11.2 Common and Preferred Stock

A firm can obtain equity capital by selling either common or preferred stock. All corporations initially issue common stock to raise equity capital. Some of these firms later issue either additional common stock or preferred stock to raise more equity capital. Although both common and preferred stock are forms of equity capital, preferred stock has some similarities to debt that significantly differentiate it from common stock. Here we first consider the features of both common and preferred stock and then describe the process of issuing common stock, including the use of venture capital.

Common Stock

The true owners of a corporate business are the common stockholders. Common stockholders are sometimes referred to as *residual owners* because they receive what is left—the residual—after all other claims on the firm's income and assets have been satisfied. They are assured of only one thing: that they cannot lose any more than they have invested in the firm. As a result of this generally uncertain position, common stockholders expect to be compensated with adequate dividends and, ultimately, capital gains.

OWNERSHIP   The common stock of a firm can be **privately owned** by private investors or publicly owned by public investors. Private companies are often **closely owned** by an individual investor or a small group of private investors (such as a family). Public companies are **widely owned** by many unrelated individual or institutional investors. The shares of privately owned firms, which are typically small corporations, are generally not traded; if the shares are traded, the transactions are among private investors and often require the firm's consent. Large corporations, which are emphasized in the following discussions, are publicly owned, and their shares are generally actively traded in the broker or dealer markets.

PAR VALUE   The market value of common stock is completely unrelated to its par value. The **par value** of common stock is an arbitrary value established for legal purposes in the firm's corporate charter and is generally set quite low, often an amount of $1 or less. Recall that when a firm sells new shares of common stock, the par value of the shares sold is recorded in the capital section of the balance sheet as part of common stock. One benefit of this recording is that at any time the total number of shares of common stock outstanding can be found by dividing the book value of common stock by the par value.

Setting a low par value is advantageous in states where certain corporate taxes are based on the par value of stock. A low par value is also beneficial in states that have laws against selling stock at a discount to par. For example, a company whose common stock has a par value of $20 per share would be unable to issue stock if investors are unwilling to pay more than $16 per share.

PREEMPTIVE RIGHTS   The **preemptive right** allows common stockholders to maintain their proportionate ownership in the corporation when new shares are issued, thus protecting them from dilution of their ownership. A **dilution of ownership** is a reduction in each previous shareholder's fractional ownership resulting from the issuance of additional shares of common stock. Preemptive rights allow preexisting shareholders to maintain their preissuance voting control and protects them against the dilution of earnings. Preexisting shareholders experience a **dilution of earnings** when their claim on the firm's earnings is *diminished* as a result of new shares being issued.

In a *rights offering*, the firm grants **rights** to its shareholders. These financial instruments allow stockholders to purchase additional shares at a price below the market price, in direct pro-

---

privately owned (stock)
The common stock of a firm is owned by private investors; this stock is not publicly traded.

publicly owned (stock)
The common stock of a firm is owned by public investors; this stock is publicly traded.

closely owned (stock)
The common stock of a firm is owned by an individual or a small group of investors (such as a family); these are usually privately owned companies.

widely owned (stock)
The common stock of a firm is owned by many unrelated individual or institutional investors.

par-value common stock
An arbitrary value established for legal purposes in the firm's corporate charter and which can be used to find the total number of shares outstanding by dividing it into the book value of common stock.

preemptive right
Allows common stockholders to maintain their proportionate ownership in the corporation when new shares are issued, thus protecting them from dilution of their ownership.

dilution of ownership
A reduction in each previous shareholder's fractional ownership resulting from the issuance of additional shares of common stock.

dilution of earnings
A reduction in each previous shareholder's fractional claim on the firm's earnings resulting from the issuance of additional shares of common stock.

rights
Financial instruments that allow stockholders to purchase additional shares at a price below the market price, in direct proportion to their number of owned shares.

authorized shares

Shares of common stock that a firm's corporate charter allows it to issue.

outstanding shares

Issued shares of common stock held by investors, including both private and public investors.

treasury stock

Issued shares of common stock held by the firm; often these shares have been repurchased by the firm.

issued shares

Shares of common stock that have been put into circulation; the sum of *outstanding shares and treasury stock.*

portion to their number of owned shares. In these situations, rights are an important financing tool without which shareholders would run the risk of losing their proportionate control of the corporation. From the firm's viewpoint, the use of rights offerings to raise new equity capital may be less costly than a public offering of stock.

AUTHORIZED, OUTSTANDING, AND ISSUED SHARES   A firm's corporate charter indicates how many **authorized shares** it can issue. The firm cannot sell more shares than the charter authorizes without obtaining approval through a shareholder vote. To avoid later having to amend the charter, firms generally attempt to authorize more shares than they initially plan to issue.

Authorized shares become **outstanding shares** when they are issued or sold to investors. If the *firm* repurchases any of its outstanding shares, these shares are recorded as **treasury stock** and are no longer considered to be outstanding shares. **Issued shares** are the shares of common stock that have been put into circulation; they represent the sum of *outstanding shares* and *treasury stock.*

Example 11.1

Golden Enterprises, a producer of medical pumps, has the following stockholders' equity account on December 31:

Stockholders' Equity

Common stock—$0.80 par value:

Authorized 35,000,000 shares; issued 15,000,000 shares	$ 12,000,000
Paid-in capital in excess of par	63,000,000
Retained earnings	31,000,000
	$106,000,000
Less: Cost of treasury stock (1,000,000 shares)	4,000,000
Total stockholders' equity	$102,000,000

How many shares of additional common stock can Golden sell without gaining approval from its shareholders? The firm has 35 million authorized shares, 15 million issued shares, and 1 million shares of treasury stock. Thus 14 million shares are outstanding (15 million issued shares minus 1 million shares of treasury stock), and Golden can issue 21 million additional shares (35 million authorized shares minus 14 million outstanding shares) without seeking shareholder approval. This total includes the treasury shares currently held, which the firm can reissue to the public without obtaining shareholder approval.

VOTING RIGHTS   Generally, each share of common stock entitles its holder to one vote in the election of directors and on special issues. Votes are generally assignable and may be cast at the annual stockholders' meeting.

Because most small stockholders do not attend the annual meeting to vote, they may sign a **proxy statement** transferring their votes to another party. The solicitation of proxies from shareholders is closely controlled by the Securities and Exchange Commission to ensure that proxies are not being solicited on the basis of false or misleading information. Existing management generally receives the stockholders' proxies because it is able to solicit them at company expense.

proxy statement

A statement transferring the votes of a stockholder to another party.

Occasionally, when the firm is widely owned, outsiders may wage a **proxy battle** to unseat the existing management and gain control of the firm. To win a corporate election, votes from a majority of the shares voted are required. However, the odds of an outside group winning a proxy battle are generally slim.

In recent years, many firms have issued two or more classes of common stock with unequal voting rights. A firm can use different classes of stock as a defense against a *hostile takeover* in which an outside group, without management support, tries to gain voting control of the firm by buying its shares in the marketplace. **Supervoting shares**, which have multiple votes per share, allow "insiders" to maintain control against an outside group whose shares have only one vote each. At other times, a class of **nonvoting common stock** is issued when the firm wishes to raise capital through the sale of common stock but does not want to give up its voting control.

When different classes of common stock are issued on the basis of unequal voting rights, class A common typically—but not universally—has one vote per share, and class B common has supervoting rights. In most cases, the multiple share classes are equal with respect to all other aspects of ownership, although there are some exceptions to this general rule. In particular, there is usually no difference in the distribution of earnings (dividends) and assets. Treasury stock, which is held within the corporation, generally *does not* have voting rights, *does not* earn dividends, and *does not* have a claim on assets in liquidation.

DIVIDENDS   The payment of dividends to the firm's shareholders is at the discretion of the company's board of directors. Most corporations that pay dividends pay them quarterly. Dividends may be paid in cash, stock, or merchandise. Cash dividends are the most common, merchandise dividends the least.

Common stockholders are not promised a dividend, but they come to expect certain payments on the basis of the historical dividend pattern of the firm. Before firms pay dividends to common stockholders, they must pay any past due dividends owed to preferred stockholders. The firm's ability to pay dividends can be affected by restrictive debt covenants designed to ensure that the firm can repay its creditors.

Since passage of the *Jobs and Growth Tax Relief Reconciliation Act of 2003*, many firms now pay larger dividends to shareholders, who are subject to a maximum tax rate of 15 percent on dividends rather than the maximum tax rate of 39 percent in effect prior to passage of the act. Because of the importance of the dividend decision to the growth and valuation of the firm, dividends are discussed.

INTERNATIONAL STOCK ISSUES   Although the international market for common stock is not as large as the international market for bonds, cross-border issuance and trading of common stock have increased dramatically in the past 30 years.

Some corporations *issue stock in foreign markets*. For example, the stock of General Electric trades in Frankfurt, London, Paris, and Tokyo; the stocks of Time Warner and Microsoft trade in Frankfurt and London; and the stock of McDonalds trades in Frankfurt, London, and Paris. The Frankfurt, London, and Tokyo markets are the most popular. Issuing stock internationally broadens the ownership base and helps a company to integrate into the local business environment. Having locally traded stock can facilitate corporate acquisitions because shares can be used as an acceptable method of payment.

Foreign corporations have also discovered the benefits of trading their stock in the United States. The disclosure and reporting requirements mandated by the U.S. Securities and Exchange Commission have historically discouraged all but the largest foreign firms from directly listing their shares on the New York Stock Exchange or the American Stock Exchange.

As an alternative, most foreign companies choose to tap the U.S. market through **American depositary shares (ADSs)**. These are dollar-denominated receipts for the stocks of foreign companies that are held by a U.S. financial institution overseas. They serve as backing for **American depositary receipts (ADRs)**, which are securities that permit U.S. investors to hold shares of non-U.S. companies and trade them in U.S. markets. Because ADRs are issued, in dollars, to

proxy battle
The attempt by a nonmanagement group to gain control of the management of a firm by soliciting a sufficient number of proxy votes.

supervoting shares
Stock that carries with it multiple votes per share rather than the single vote per share typically given on regular shares of common stock.

nonvoting common stock
Common stock that carries no voting rights; issued when the firm wishes to raise capital through the sale of common stock but does not want to give up its voting control.

American depositary shares (ADSs)
Dollar-denominated receipts for the stocks of foreign companies that are held by a U.S. financial institution overseas.

American depositary receipts (ADRs)
Securities, backed by *American depositary shares (ADSs)*, that permit U.S. investors to hold shares of non-U.S. companies and trade them in U.S. markets.

U.S. investors, they are subject to U.S. securities laws. At the same time, they give investors the opportunity to diversify their portfolios internationally.

Preferred Stock

Preferred stock gives its holders certain privileges that make them senior to common stockholders. Preferred stockholders are promised a fixed periodic dividend, which is stated either as a percentage or as a dollar amount. How the dividend is specified depends on whether the preferred stock has a *par value*. **Par-value preferred stock** has a stated face value, and its annual dividend is specified as a percentage of this value. **No-par preferred stock** has no stated face value, but its annual dividend is stated in dollars. Preferred stock is most often issued by public utilities, by acquiring firms in merger transactions, and by firms that are experiencing losses and need additional financing.

BASIC RIGHTS OF PREFERRED STOCKHOLDERS   The basic rights of preferred stockholders are somewhat stronger than the rights of common stockholders. Preferred stock is often considered *quasi-debt* because, much like interest on debt, it specifies a fixed periodic payment (dividend). Preferred stock is unlike debt in that it has no maturity date. Because they have a fixed claim on the firm's income that takes precedence over the claim of common stockholders, preferred stockholders are exposed to less risk.

Preferred stockholders are also given *preference over common stockholders in the liquidation of assets* in a legally bankrupt firm, although they must "stand in line" behind creditors. The amount of the claim of preferred stockholders in liquidation is normally equal to the par or stated value of the preferred stock. Preferred stockholders are *not normally given a voting right*, although preferred stockholders are sometimes allowed to elect one member of the board of directors.

FEATURES OF PREFERRED STOCK   A preferred stock issue generally includes a number of features, which, along with the stock's par value, the amount of dividend payments, the dividend payment dates, and any restrictive covenants, are specified in an agreement similar to a *bond indenture*.

Restrictive Covenants   The restrictive covenants in a preferred stock issue focus on ensuring the firm's continued existence and regular payment of the dividend. These covenants include provisions about passing dividends, the sale of senior securities, mergers, sales of assets, minimum liquidity requirements, and repurchases of common stock. The violation of preferred stock covenants usually permits preferred stockholders either to obtain representation on the firm's board of directors or to force the retirement of their stock at or above its par or stated value.

Cumulation   Most preferred stock is **cumulative** with respect to any dividends passed. That is, all dividends in arrears, along with the current dividend, must be paid before dividends can be paid to common stockholders. If preferred stock is **noncumulative**, passed (unpaid) dividends do not accumulate. In this case, only the current dividend must be paid before dividends can be paid to common stockholders. Because the common stockholders can receive dividends only after the dividend claims of preferred stockholders have been satisfied, it is in the firm's best interest to pay preferred dividends when they are due.

Other Features   Preferred stock can be *callable or convertible*. Preferred stock with a **callable feature** allows the issuer to retire outstanding shares within a certain period of time at a specified price. The call price is normally set above the initial issuance price, but it may decrease as time passes. Making preferred stock callable provides the issuer with a way to bring the fixed-payment commitment of the preferred issue to an end if conditions make it desirable to do so.

Preferred stock with a **conversion feature** allows *holders* to change each share into a stated number of shares of common stock, usually anytime after a predetermined date. The conversion ratio can be fixed, or the number of shares of common stock that the preferred stock can be exchanged for changes through time according to a predetermined formula.

---

par-value preferred stock
Preferred stock with a stated face value that is used with the specified dividend percentage to determine the annual dollar dividend.

no-par preferred stock
Preferred stock with no stated face value but with a stated annual dollar dividend.

cumulative (preferred stock)
Preferred stock for which all passed (unpaid) dividends in arrears, along with the current dividend, must be paid before dividends can be paid to common stockholders.

noncumulative (preferred stock)
Preferred stock for which passed (unpaid) dividends do not accumulate.

callable feature (preferred stock)
A feature of *callable preferred stock* that allows the issuer to retire the shares within a certain period of time and at a specified price.

conversion feature (preferred stock)
A feature of *convertible preferred stock* that allows holders to change each share into a stated number of shares of common stock.

Issuing Common Stock

Because of the high risk associated with a business startup, a firm's initial financing typically comes from its founders in the form of a common stock investment. Until the founders have made an equity investment, it is highly unlikely that others will contribute either equity or debt capital. Early-stage investors in the firm's equity, as well as lenders who provide debt capital, want to be assured that they are taking no more risk than the founders. In addition, they want confirmation that the founders are confident enough in their vision for the firm that they are willing to risk their own money.

Typically, the initial nonfounder financing for business startups with attractive growth prospects comes from private equity investors. Then, as the firm establishes the viability of its product or service offering and begins to generate revenues, cash flow, and profits, it will often "go public" by issuing shares of common stock to a much broader group of investors.

Before we consider the initial *public* sale of equity, let's discuss some of the key aspects of early-stage equity financing in firms that have attractive growth prospects.

VENTURE CAPITAL The initial external equity financing privately raised by firms, typically early-stage firms with attractive growth prospects, is called **venture capital**. Those who provide venture capital are known as **venture capitalists (VCs)**. They typically are formal business entities that maintain strong oversight over the firms they invest in and that have clearly defined exit strategies. Less visible early-stage investors called **angel capitalists** (or **angels**) tend to be investors who do not actually operate as a business; they are often wealthy individual investors who are willing to invest in promising early-stage companies in exchange for a portion of the firm's equity. Although angels play a major role in early-stage equity financing, we will focus on VCs because of their more formal structure and greater public visibility.

Organization and Investment Stages   Venture capital investors tend to be organized in one of four basic ways, as described in Table 11.2. The *VC limited partnership* is by far the dominant structure. These funds have as their sole objective to earn high returns, rather than to obtain access to the companies in order to sell or buy other products or services.

VCs can invest in early-stage companies, later-stage companies, or buyouts and acquisitions. Generally, about 40 to 50 percent of VC investments are devoted to early-stage companies (for startup funding and expansion) and a similar percentage to later-stage companies (for marketing, production expansion, and preparation for public offering); the remaining 5 to 10 percent are devoted to the buyout or acquisition of other companies. Generally, VCs look for compound annual rates of return ranging from 20 to 50 percent or more, depending on both the development stage and the attributes of each company. Earlier-stage investments tend to demand higher returns than later-stage investments because of the higher risk associated with the earlier stages of a firm's growth.

venture capital
Privately raised external equity capital used to fund early-stage firms with attractive growth prospects.

venture capitalists (VCs)
Providers of venture capital; typically, formal businesses that maintain strong oversight over the firms they invest in and that have clearly defined exit strategies.

angel capitalists (angels)
Wealthy individual investors who do not operate as a business but invest in promising early-stage companies in exchange for a portion of the firm's equity.

Organization	Description
Small business investment companies (SBICs)	Corporations chartered by the federal government that can borrow at attractive rates from the U.S. Treasury and use the funds to make venture capital investments in private companies.
Financial VC funds	Subsidiaries of financial institutions, particularly banks, set up to help young firms grow and, it is hoped, become major customers of the institution.
Corporate VC funds	Firms, sometimes subsidiaries, established by nonfinancial firms, typically to gain access to new technologies that the corporation can access to further its own growth.
VC limited partnerships	Limited partnerships organized by professional VC firms, which serve as the general partner and organize, invest, and manage the partnership using the limited partners' funds; the professional VCs ultimately liquidate the partnership and distribute the proceeds to all partners.

TABLE 11.2
Organization of Venture Capital Investors

Deal Structure and Pricing   Regardless of the development stage, venture capital investments are made under a legal contract that clearly allocates responsibilities and ownership interests between existing owners (founders) and the VC fund or limited partnership. The terms of the agreement will depend on numerous factors related to the founders; the business structure, stage of development, and outlook; and other market and timing issues. The specific financial terms will, of course, depend on the value of the enterprise, the amount of funding, and the perceived risk. To control the VC's risk, various covenants are included in the agreement, and the actual funding may be pegged to the achievement of *measurable milestones*. The VC will negotiate numerous other provisions into the contract, both to ensure the firm's success and to control its risk exposure. The contract will have an explicit exit strategy for the VC that may be tied both to measurable milestones and to time.

The amount of equity to which the VC is entitled will, of course, depend on the value of the firm, the terms of the contract, the exit terms, and the minimum compound annual rate of return required by the VC on its investment. Although each VC investment is unique and no standard contract exists, the transaction will be structured to provide the VC with a high rate of return that is consistent with the typically high risk of such transactions. The exit strategy of most VC investments is to take the firm public through an initial public offering.

GOING PUBLIC   When a firm wishes to sell its stock in the primary market, it has three alternatives. It can make (1) a *public offering*, in which it offers its shares for sale to the general public; (2) a *rights offering*, in which new shares are sold to existing stockholders; or (3) a *private placement*, in which the firm sells new securities directly to an investor or group of investors. Here we focus on public offerings, particularly the **initial public offering (IPO)**, which is the first public sale of a firm's stock. IPOs are typically made by small, rapidly growing companies that either require additional capital to continue expanding or have met a milestone for going public that was established in a contract signed earlier in order to obtain VC funding.

To go public, the firm must first obtain the approval of its current shareholders, the investors who own its privately issued stock. Next, the company's auditors and lawyers must certify that all documents for the company are legitimate. The company then finds an investment bank will-

initial public offering (IPO)

The first public sale of a firm's stock.

**Figure 11.1
Cover of a Preliminary Prospectus for a Stock Issue**

Some of the key factors related to the 2010 common stock issue by Convio, Inc., are summarized on the cover of the preliminary prospectus. The disclaimer printed in red across the top of the page is what gives the preliminary prospectus its "red herring" name.

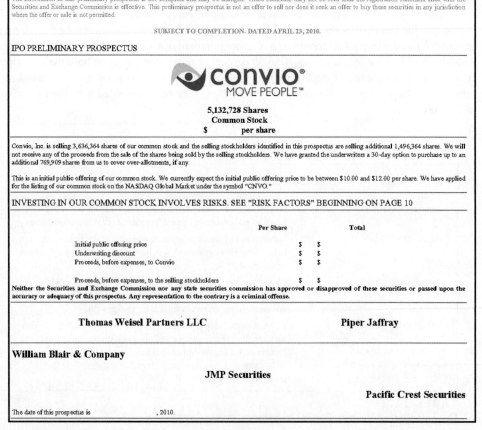

Source: SEC filing Form S-1/A, Convio, Inc., filed April 26, 2010, p. 4.

ing to *underwrite* the offering. This underwriter is responsible for promoting the stock and facilitating the sale of the company's IPO shares. The underwriter often brings in other investment banking firms as participants. We'll discuss the role of the investment banker in more detail in the next section.

The company files a registration statement with the SEC. One portion of the registration statement is called the **prospectus**. It describes the key aspects of the issue, the issuer, and its management and financial position. During the waiting period between the statement's filing and its approval, prospective investors can receive a preliminary prospectus. This preliminary version is called a **red herring**, because a notice printed in red on the front cover indicates the tentative nature of the offer. The cover of the preliminary prospectus describing the 2010 stock issue of Convio, Inc., is shown in Figure 11.1. Note the red herring printed across the top of the page.

After the SEC approves the registration statement, the investment community can begin analyzing the company's prospects. However, from the time it files until at least one month after the IPO is complete, the company must observe a *quiet period*, during which there are restrictions on what company officials may say about the company. The purpose of the quiet period is to make sure that all potential investors have access to the same information about the company—the information presented in the preliminary prospectus—and not to any unpublished data that might give them an unfair advantage.

The investment bankers and company executives promote the company's stock offering through a *road show*, a series of presentations to potential investors around the country and sometimes overseas. In addition to providing investors with information about the new issue, road show sessions help the investment bankers gauge the demand for the offering and set an expected pricing range. After the underwriter sets terms and prices the issue, the SEC must approve the offering.

THE INVESTMENT BANKER'S ROLE   Most public offerings are made with the assistance of an **investment banker**. The investment banker is a financial intermediary (such as Morgan Stanley or Goldman Sachs) that specializes in selling new security issues and advising firms with regard to major financial transactions. The main activity of the investment banker is **underwriting**. This process involves purchasing the security issue from the issuing corporation at an agreed-on price and bearing the risk of reselling it to the public at a profit. The investment banker also provides the issuer with advice about pricing and other important aspects of the issue.

In the case of very large security issues, the investment banker brings in other bankers as partners to form an **underwriting syndicate**. The syndicate shares the financial risk associated

prospectus
A portion of a security registration statement that describes the key aspects of the issue, the issuer, and its management and financial position.

red herring
A preliminary prospectus made available to prospective investors during the waiting period between the registration statement's filing with the SEC and its approval.

investment banker
Financial intermediary that specializes in selling new security issues and advising firms with regard to major financial transactions.

underwriting
The role of the *investment banker* in bearing the risk of reselling, at a profit, the securities purchased from an issuing corporation at an agreed-on price.

underwriting syndicate
A group of other bankers formed by an investment banker to share the financial risk associated with *underwriting* new securities.

Figure 11.2
The Selling Process for a Large Security Issue
The investment banker hired by the issuing corporation may form an underwriting syndicate. The underwriting syndicate buys the entire security issue from the issuing corporation at an agreed-on price. The underwriters then have the opportunity (and bear the risk) of reselling the issue to the public at a profit. Both the originating investment banker and the other syndicate members put together a selling group to sell the issue on a commission basis to investors.

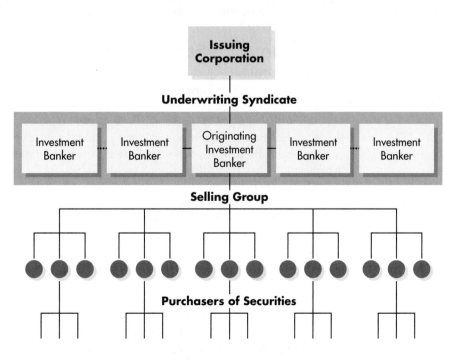

selling group

A large number of brokerage firms that join the originating investment banker(s); each accepts responsibility for selling a certain portion of a new security issue on a commission basis.

with buying the entire issue from the issuer and reselling the new securities to the public. The originating investment banker and the syndicate members put together a **selling group**, normally made up of themselves and a large number of brokerage firms. Each member of the selling group accepts the responsibility for selling a certain portion of the issue and is paid a commission on the securities it sells. The selling process for a large security issue is depicted in Figure 11.2.

Compensation for underwriting and selling services typically comes in the form of a discount on the sale price of the securities. For example, an investment banker may pay the issuing firm $24 per share for stock that will be sold for $26 per share. The investment banker may then sell the shares to members of the selling group for $25.25 per share. In this case, the original investment banker earns $1.25 per share ($25.25 sale price minus $24 purchase price). The members of the selling group earn 75 cents for each share they sell ($26 sale price minus $25.25 purchase price). Although some primary security offerings are directly placed by the issuer, the majority of new issues are sold through public offering via the mechanism just described.

→ **Review Questions**

11–2 What risks do common stockholders take that other suppliers of capital do not?

11–3 How does a *rights offering* protect a firm's stockholders against the *dilution of ownership?*

11–4 Explain the relationships among authorized shares, outstanding shares, treasury stock, and issued shares.

11–5 What are the advantages to both U.S.-based and foreign corporations of issuing stock outside their home markets? What are *American depositary receipts (ADRs)?* What are *American depositary shares (ADSs)?*

11–6 What claims do preferred stockholders have with respect to distribution of earnings (dividends) and assets?

11–7 Explain the *cumulative feature* of preferred stock. What is the purpose of a *call feature* in a preferred stock issue?

11–8 What is the difference between a *venture capitalist (VC)* and an *angel capitalist (angel)?*

11–9 What are the four ways that VCs are most commonly organized? How are their deals structured and priced?

11–10 What general procedures must a private firm follow to go public via an *initial public offering (IPO)?*

11–11 What role does an *investment banker* play in a public offering? Describe an underwriting syndicate.

LG 4 LG 5 # 11.3 Common Stock Valuation

Common stockholders expect to be rewarded through periodic cash dividends and an increasing share value. Some of these investors decide which stocks to buy and sell based on a plan to maintain a broadly diversified portfolio. Other investors have a more speculative motive for trading. They try to spot companies whose shares are *undervalued*—meaning that the true value of the shares is greater than the current market price. These investors buy shares that they believe to be undervalued and sell shares that they think are *overvalued* (that is, the market price is greater than the true value). Regardless of one's motive for trading, understanding how to value common stocks is an important part of the investment process. Stock valuation is also an important tool for financial managers— how can they work to maximize the stock price without understanding the factors that determine the value of the stock? In this section, we will describe specific stock valuation techniques. First, we will consider the relationship between market efficiency and stock valuation.

Market Efficiency

Economically rational buyers and sellers use their assessment of an asset's risk and return to determine its value. To a buyer, the asset's value represents the maximum purchase price, and to a seller it represents the minimum sale price. In competitive markets with many active participants, such as the New York Stock Exchange, the interactions of many buyers and sellers result in an equilibrium price—the *market value*—for each security. This price reflects the collective actions that buyers and sellers take on the basis of all available information. Buyers and sellers digest new information quickly as it becomes available and, through their purchase and sale activities, create a new market equilibrium price. Because the flow of new information is almost constant, stock prices fluctuate, continuously moving toward a new equilibrium that reflects the most recent information available. This general concept is known as *market efficiency*.

The Efficient-Market Hypothesis

Active broker and dealer markets, such as the New York Stock Exchange and the Nasdaq market, are *efficient*—they are made up of many rational investors who react quickly and objectively to new information. The **efficient-market hypothesis (EMH)**, which is the basic theory describing the behavior of such a "perfect" market, specifically states that

1. Securities are typically in equilibrium, which means that they are fairly priced and that their expected returns equal their required returns.
2. At any point in time, security prices fully reflect all information available about the firm and its securities, and these prices react swiftly to new information.
3. Because stocks are fully and fairly priced, investors need not waste their time trying to find mispriced (undervalued or overvalued) securities.

Not all market participants are believers in the efficient-market hypothesis. Some feel that it is worthwhile to search for undervalued or overvalued securities and to trade them to profit from market inefficiencies. Others argue that it is mere luck that would allow market participants to anticipate new information correctly and as a result earn *abnormal returns*—that is, actual returns greater than average market returns. They believe it is unlikely that market participants can *over the long run* earn abnormal returns. Contrary to this belief, some well-known investors such as Warren Buffett and Bill Gross *have* over the long run consistently earned abnormal returns on their portfolios. It is unclear whether their success is the result of their superior ability to anticipate new information or of some form of market inefficiency.

THE BEHAVIORAL FINANCE CHALLENGE Although considerable evidence supports the concept of market efficiency, a growing body of academic evidence has begun to cast doubt on the validity of this notion. The research documents various *anomalies*—outcomes that are inconsistent with efficient markets—in stock returns. A number of academics and practitioners have also recognized that emotions and other subjective factors play a role in investment decisions.

This focus on investor behavior has resulted in a significant body of research, collectively referred to as **behavioral finance**. Advocates of behavioral finance are commonly referred to as "behaviorists." Daniel Kahneman was awarded the 2002 Nobel Prize in economics for his work in behavioral finance, specifically for integrating insights from psychology and economics. Ongoing research into the psychological factors that can affect investor behavior and the resulting effects on stock prices will likely result in growing acceptance of behavioral finance. The *Focus on Practice* box further explains some of the findings of behavioral finance.

While challenges to the efficient market hypothesis, such as those presented by advocates of behavioral finance, are interesting and worthy of study, in this text we generally take the position that markets are efficient. This means that the terms *expected return* and *required return* will be used interchangeably because they should be equal in an efficient market. In other words, we will operate under the assumption that a stock's market price at any point in time is the best estimate of its value. We're now ready to look closely at the mechanics of common stock valuation.

Basic Common Stock Valuation Equation

Like the value of a bond, which we discussed in Chapter 10, *the value of a share of common stock is equal to the present value of all future cash flows (dividends) that it is expected to provide.* Although a stockholder can earn capital gains by selling stock at a price above that originally paid, what the buyer really pays for is the right to all future dividends. What about stocks that do not currently pay dividends? Such stocks have a value attributable to a future dividend stream or to the proceeds from the sale of the company. Therefore, *from a valuation viewpoint, future dividends are relevant.*

efficient-market hypothesis (EMH)
Theory describing the behavior of an assumed "perfect" market in which (1) securities are in equilibrium, (2) security prices fully reflect all available information and react swiftly to new information, and (3), because stocks are fully and fairly priced, investors need not waste time looking for mispriced securities.

In more depth

To read about *The Hierarchy of the Efficient-Market Hypothesis,* go to
www.myaccountinglab.com
MyAccountingLab

behavioral finance
A growing body of research that focuses on investor behavior and its impact on investment decisions and stock prices. Advocates are commonly referred to as "behaviorists."

focus on PRACTICE

Understanding Human Behavior Helps Us Understand Investor Behavior

Market anomalies are patterns inconsistent with the efficient market hypothesis. Behavioral finance has a number of theories to help explain how human emotions influence people in their investment decision-making processes.

Regret theory deals with the emotional reaction people experience after realizing they have made an error in judgment. When deciding whether to sell a stock, investors become emotionally affected by the price at which they purchased the stock. A sale at a loss would confirm that the investor miscalculated the value of the stock when it was purchased. The correct approach when considering whether to sell a stock is, "Would I buy this stock today if it were already liquidated?" If the answer is "no," it is time to sell. Regret theory also holds true for investors who passed up buying a stock that now is selling at a much higher price. Again, the correct approach is to value the stock today without regard to its prior value.

Herding is another market behavior affecting investor decisions. Some investors rationalize their decision to buy certain stocks with "everyone else is doing it." Investors may feel less embarrassment about losing money on a popular stock than about losing money on an unknown or unpopular stock.

People have a tendency to place particular events into *mental accounts*, and the difference between these compartments sometimes influences behavior more than the events themselves. Researchers have asked people the following question: "Would you purchase a $20 ticket at the local theater if you realize after you get there that you have lost a $20 bill?" Roughly 88 percent of people would do so. Under another scenario, people were asked whether they would buy a second $20 ticket if they arrived at the theater and realized that they had left at home a ticket purchased in advance for $20. Only 40 percent of respondents would buy another. In both scenarios the person is out $40, but mental accounting leads to a different outcome. In investing, compartmentalization is best illustrated by the hesitation to sell an investment that once had monstrous gains and now has a modest gain. During bull markets, people get accustomed to paper gains. When a market correction deflates investors' net worth, they are hesitant to sell, causing them to wait for the return of that gain.

Other investor behaviors are prospect theory and anchoring. According to *prospect theory*, people express a different degree of emotion toward gains than losses. Individuals are stressed more by prospective losses than they are buoyed by the prospect of equal gains. Anchoring is the tendency of investors to place more value on recent information. People tend to give too much credence to recent market opinions and events and mistakenly extrapolate recent trends that differ from historical, long-term averages and probabilities. Anchoring is a partial explanation for the longevity of some bull markets.

Most stock-valuation techniques require that all relevant information be available to properly determine a stock's value and potential for future gain. Behavioral finance may explain the connection between valuation and an investor's actions based on that valuation.

▶ *Theories of behavioral finance can apply to other areas of human behavior in addition to investing. Think of a situation in which you may have demonstrated one of these behaviors. Share your situation with a classmate.*

The basic valuation model for common stock is given in Equation 11.1:

$$P_0 = \frac{D_1}{(1 + r_s)^1} + \frac{D_2}{(1 + r_s)^2} + \cdots + \frac{D_\infty}{(1 + r_s)^\infty} \tag{11.1}$$

where

$$P_0 = \text{value today of common stock}$$
$$D_t = \text{per-share dividend } expected \text{ at the end of year } t$$
$$r_s = \text{required return on common stock}$$

The equation can be simplified somewhat by redefining each year's dividend, D_t, in terms of anticipated growth. We will consider three models here: zero growth, constant growth, and variable growth.

Zero-Growth Model

zero-growth model
An approach to dividend valuation that assumes a constant, nongrowing dividend stream.

The simplest approach to dividend valuation, the **zero-growth model**, assumes a constant, nongrowing dividend stream. In terms of the notation already introduced,

$$D_1 = D_2 = \cdots = D_\infty$$

When we let D_1 represent the amount of the annual dividend, Equation 11.1 under zero growth reduces to

$$P_0 = D_1 \times \sum_{t=1}^{\infty} \frac{1}{(1 + r_s)^t} = D_1 \times \frac{1}{r_s} = \frac{D_1}{r_s} \qquad (11.2)$$

The equation shows that with zero growth, the value of a share of stock would equal the present value of a perpetuity of D_1 dollars discounted at a rate r_s.

Personal Finance Example 11.2

Chuck Swimmer estimates that the dividend of Denham Company, an established textile producer, is expected to remain constant at $3 per share indefinitely. If his required return on its stock is 15%, the stock's value is $20 ($3 ÷ 0.15) per share.

Preferred Stock Valuation   Because preferred stock typically provides its holders with a fixed annual dividend over its assumed infinite life, Equation 11.2 can be used to find the value of preferred stock. The value of preferred stock can be estimated by substituting the stated dividend on the preferred stock for D_1 and the required return for rs in Equation 11.2. For example, a preferred stock paying a $5 stated annual dividend and having a required return of 13 percent would have a value of $38.46 ($5 ÷ 0.13) per share.

CONSTANT-GROWTH MODEL   The most widely cited dividend valuation approach, the **constant-growth model**, assumes that dividends will grow at a constant rate, but a rate that is less than the required return. (The assumption that the constant rate of growth, g, is less than the required return, r_s, is a necessary mathematical condition for deriving this model.[1]) By letting D_0 represent the most recent dividend, we can rewrite Equation 11.1 as follows:

$$P_0 = \frac{D_0 \times (1 + g)^1}{(1 + r_s)^1} + \frac{D_0 \times (1 + g)^2}{(1 + r_s)^2} + \cdots + \frac{D_0 \times (1 + g)^\infty}{(1 + r_s)^\infty} \qquad (11.3)$$

If we simplify Equation 11.3, it can be rewritten as:

$$P_0 = \frac{D_1}{r_s - g} \qquad (11.4)$$

The constant-growth model in Equation 11.4 is commonly called the **Gordon growth model**. An example will show how it works.

constant-growth model
A widely cited dividend valuation approach that assumes that dividends will grow at a constant rate, but a rate that is less than the required return.

In more depth

To read about *Deriving the Constant-Growth Model*, go to www.myaccountinglab.com
MyAccountingLab

Gordon growth model
A common name for the *constant-growth model* that is widely cited in dividend valuation.

Example 11.3

Lamar Company, a small cosmetics company, from 2007 through 2012 paid the following per-share dividends:

Year	Dividend per share
2012	$1.40
2011	1.29
2010	1.20
2009	1.12
2008	1.05
2007	1.00

---

1. Another assumption of the constant-growth model as presented is that earnings and dividends grow at the same rate. This assumption is true only in cases in which a firm pays out a fixed percentage of its earnings each year (has a fixed payout ratio). In the case of a declining industry, a negative growth rate ($g < 0\%$) might exist. In such a case, the constant-growth model, as well as the variable-growth model presented in the next section, remains fully applicable to the valuation process.

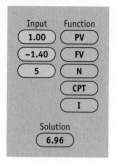

We assume that the historical annual growth rate of dividends is an accurate estimate of the future constant annual rate of dividend growth, g. To find the historical annual growth rate of dividends, we must solve the following for g:

$$D_{2012} = D_{2007} \times (1 + g)^5$$

$$\frac{D_{2007}}{D_{2012}} = \frac{1}{(1 + g)^5}$$

$$\frac{\$1.00}{\$1.40} = \frac{1}{(1 + g)^5}$$

Using a financial calculator or a spreadsheet, we find that the historical annual growth rate of Lamar Company dividends equals 7%.[2] The company estimates that its dividend in 2013, D_1, will equal $1.50 (about 7% more than the last dividend). The required return, r_s, is 15%. By substituting these values into Equation 11.4, we find the value of the stock to be

$$P_0 = \frac{\$1.50}{0.15 - 0.07} = \frac{\$1.50}{0.08} = \underline{\$18.75} \text{ per share}$$

Assuming that the values of D_1, r_s, and g are accurately estimated, Lamar Company's stock value is $18.75 per share.

---

variable-growth model

A dividend valuation approach that allows for a change in the dividend growth rate.

VARIABLE-GROWTH MODEL   The zero- and constant-growth common stock models do not allow for any shift in expected growth rates. Because future growth rates might shift up or down because of changing business conditions, it is useful to consider a **variable-growth model** that allows for a change in the dividend growth rate.[3] We will assume that a single shift in growth rates occurs at the end of year N, and we will use g_1 to represent the initial growth rate and g_2 for the growth rate after the shift. To determine the value of a share of stock in the case of variable growth, we use a four-step procedure:

Step 1   Find the value of the cash dividends at the end of *each year*, D_t, during the initial growth period, years 1 through N. This step may require adjusting the most recent dividend, D_0, using the initial growth rate, g_1, to calculate the dividend amount for each year. Therefore, for the first N years,

$$D_t = D_0 \times (1 + g_1)^t$$

Step 2   Find the present value of the dividends expected during the initial growth period. Using the notation presented earlier, we can give this value as

$$\sum_{t=1}^{N} \frac{D_0 \times (1 + g_1)^t}{(1 + r_s)^t} = \sum_{t=1}^{N} \frac{D_t}{(1 + r_s)^t}$$

Step 3   Find the value of the stock *at the end of the initial growth period*, $P_N = (D_{N+1})/(r_s - g_2)$, which is the present value of all dividends expected from year $N + 1$ to infinity, assuming a constant dividend growth rate, g_2. This value is found by applying the constant-growth model (Equation 11.4) to the dividends expected from year $N + 1$ to infinity.

The present value of P_N would represent the value today of all dividends that are expected to be received from year $N + 1$ to infinity. This value can be represented by

$$\frac{1}{(1 + r_s)^N} \times \frac{D_{N+1}}{r_s - g_2}$$

---

2. A financial calculator can be used. (*Note:* Most calculators require *either* the PV or FV value to be input as a negative number to calculate an unknown interest or growth rate. That approach is used here.) Using the inputs shown at the left, you should find the growth rate to be 6.96%, which we round to 7%.

   An electronic spreadsheet could also be used to make this computation. Given space considerations, we have forgone that computational aid here.

3. More than one change in the growth rate can be incorporated into the model, but to simplify the discussion we will consider only a single growth-rate change. The number of variable-growth valuation models is technically unlimited, but concern over all possible shifts in growth is unlikely to yield much more accuracy than a simpler model.

Step 4 Add the present value components found in Steps 2 and 3 to find the value of the stock, P_0, given in Equation 11.5:

$$P_0 = \sum_{t=1}^{N} \frac{D_0 \times (1 + g_1)^t}{(1 + r_s)^t} + \underbrace{\left[\frac{1}{(1 + r_s)^N} \times \frac{D_{N+1}}{r_s - g_2}\right]}_{} \qquad (11.5)$$

$\underbrace{\phantom{P_0 = \sum_{t=1}^{N} \frac{D_0 \times (1 + g_1)^t}{(1 + r_s)^t}}}_{\text{Present value of dividends during initial growth period}}$ $\underbrace{\phantom{\left[\frac{1}{(1 + r_s)^N} \times \frac{D_{N+1}}{r_s - g_2}\right]}}_{\text{Present value of price of stock at end of initial growth period}}$

The following example illustrates the application of these steps to a variable-growth situation with only one change in growth rate.

Personal Finance Example 11.4

Victoria Robb is considering purchasing the common stock of Warren Industries, a rapidly growing boat manufacturer. She finds that the firm's most recent (2012) annual dividend payment was $1.50 per share. Victoria estimates that these dividends will increase at a 10% annual rate, g_1, over the next 3 years (2013, 2014, and 2015) because of the introduction of a hot new boat. At the end of the 3 years (the end of 2015), she expects the firm's mature product line to result in a slowing of the dividend growth rate to 5% per year, g_2, for the foreseeable future. Victoria's required return, r_s, is 15%. To estimate the current (end-of-2012) value of Warren's common stock, $P_0 = P_{2012}$, she applies the four-step procedure to these data.

Step 1 The value of the cash dividends in each of the next 3 years is calculated in columns 1, 2, and 3 of Table 11.3. The 2013, 2014, and 2015 dividends are $1.65, $1.82, and $2.00, respectively.

t	End of year	$D_0 = D_{2012}$ (1)	$(1 + g_1)^t$ (2)	D_t [(1) × (2)] (3)	$(1 + r_s)^t$ (4)	Present value of dividends [(3) ÷ (4)] (5)
1	2013	$1.50	1.100	$1.65	1.150	$1.43
2	2014	1.50	1.210	1.82	1.323	1.37
3	2015	1.50	1.331	2.00	1.521	1.32

Sum of present value of dividends $= \displaystyle\sum_{t=1}^{3} \frac{D_0 \times (1 + g_1)^t}{(1 + r_s)^t} = \$4.12$

TABLE 11.3
Calculation of Present Value of Warren Industries Dividends (2013–2015)

Step 2 The present value of the three dividends expected during the 2013–2015 initial growth period is calculated in columns 3, 4, and 5 of Table 11.3. The sum of the present values of the three dividends is $4.12.

Step 3 The value of the stock at the end of the initial growth period ($N = 2015$) can be found by first calculating $D_{N+1} = D_{2016}$:

$$D_{2016} = D_{2015} \times (1 + 0.05) = \$2.00 \times (1.05) = \$2.10$$

By using $D_{2016} = \$2.10$, a 15% required return, and a 5% dividend growth rate, the value of the stock at the end of 2015 is calculated as follows:

$$P_{2015} = \frac{D_{2016}}{r_s - g_2} = \frac{\$2.10}{0.15 - 0.05} = \frac{\$2.10}{0.10} = \$21.00$$

Finally, in Step 3, the share value of $21 at the end of 2015 must be converted into a present (end-of-2012) value. Using the 15% required return, we get

$$\frac{P_{2015}}{(1 + r_s)^3} = \frac{\$21}{(1 + 0.15)^3} = \$13.81$$

Step 4   Adding the present value of the initial dividend stream (found in Step 2) to the present value of the stock at the end of the initial growth period (found in Step 3) as specified in Equation 11.5, the current (end-of-2012) value of Warren Industries stock is:

$$P_{2012} = \$4.12 + \$13.81 = \underline{\$17.93} \text{ per share}$$

Victoria's calculations indicate that the stock is currently worth $17.93 per share.

Free Cash Flow Valuation Model

As an alternative to the dividend valuation models presented earlier in this chapter, a firm's value can be estimated by using its projected *free cash flows (FCFs)*. This approach is appealing when one is valuing firms that have no dividend history or are startups or when one is valuing an operating unit or division of a larger public company. Although dividend valuation models are widely used and accepted, in these situations it is preferable to use a more general free cash flow valuation model.

free cash flow valuation model

A model that determines the value of an entire company as the present value of its expected *free cash flows* discounted at the firm's *weighted average cost of capital*, which is its expected average future cost of funds over the long run.

The **free cash flow valuation model** is based on the same basic premise as dividend valuation models: The value of a share of common stock is the present value of all future cash flows it is expected to provide over an infinite time horizon. However, in the free cash flow valuation model, instead of valuing the firm's expected dividends, we value the firm's expected *free cash flows*. They represent the amount of cash flow available to investors—the providers of debt (creditors) and equity (owners)—after all other obligations have been met.

The free cash flow valuation model estimates the value of the entire company by finding the present value of its expected free cash flows discounted at its *weighted average cost of capital*, which is its expected average future cost of funds, as specified in Equation 11.6:

$$V_C = \frac{FCF_1}{(1 + r_a)^1} + \frac{FCF_2}{(1 + r_a)^2} + \cdots + \frac{FCF_\infty}{(1 + r_a)^\infty} \qquad (11.6)$$

where

$$V_C = \text{value of the entire company}$$
$$FCF_t = \text{free cash flow } expected \text{ at the end of year } t$$
$$r_a = \text{the firm's weighted average cost of capital}$$

Note the similarity between Equations 11.6 and 11.1, the general stock valuation equation.

Because the value of the entire company, V_C, is the market value of the entire enterprise (that is, of all assets), to find common stock value, V_S, we must subtract the market value of all of the firm's debt, V_D, and the market value of preferred stock, V_P, from V_C:

$$V_S = V_C - V_D - V_P \qquad (11.7)$$

Because it is difficult to forecast a firm's free cash flow, specific annual cash flows are typically forecast for only about 5 years, beyond which a constant growth rate is assumed. Here we assume that the first 5 years of free cash flows are explicitly forecast and that a constant rate of free cash flow growth occurs beyond the end of year 5 to infinity. This model is methodologically similar to the variable-growth model presented earlier. Its application is best demonstrated with an example.

Example 11.5

Dewhurst, Inc., wishes to determine the value of its stock by using the free cash flow valuation model. To apply the model, the firm's CFO developed the data given in Table 11.4. Application of the model can be performed in four steps.

Step 1 Calculate the present value of the free cash flow occurring from the end of 2018 to infinity, measured at the beginning of 2018 (that is, at the end of 2017). Because a constant rate of growth in FCF is forecast beyond 2017, we can use the constant-growth dividend valuation model (Equation 11.4) to calculate the value of the free cash flows from the end of 2018 to infinity:

Free cash flow		Other data
Year (t)	(FCF_t)	
2013	$400,000	Growth rate of FCF, beyond 2017 to infinity, g_{FCF} = 3%
2014	450,000	Weighted average cost of capital, r_a = 9%
2015	520,000	Market value of all debt, V_D = $3,100,000
2016	560,000	Market value of preferred stock, V_P = $800,000
2017	600,000	Number of shares of common stock outstanding = 300,000

TABLE 11.4

Dewhurst, Inc.'s, Data for the Free Cash Flow Valuation Model

$$\text{Value of } FCF_{2018 \to \infty} = \frac{FCF_{2018}}{r_a - g_{FCF}}$$

$$= \frac{\$600,000 \times (1 + 0.03)}{0.09 - 0.03}$$

$$= \frac{\$618,000}{0.06} = \$10,300,000$$

Note that to calculate the FCF in 2018, we had to increase the 2017 FCF value of $600,000 by the 3% FCF growth rate, g_{FCF}.

Step 2 Add the present value of the FCF from 2018 to infinity, which is measured at the end of 2017, to the 2017 FCF value to get the total FCF in 2017.

$$\text{Total } FCF_{2017} = \$600,000 + \$10,300,000 = \$10,900,000$$

Step 3 Find the sum of the present values of the FCFs for 2013 through 2017 to determine the value of the entire company, V_C. This calculation is shown in Table 11.5.

Year (t)	FCF_t (1)	$(1 + r_a)^t$ (2)	Present value of FCF_t [(1) ÷ (2)] (3)
2013	$ 400,000	1.090	$ 366,972
2014	450,000	1.188	378,788
2015	520,000	1.295	401,544
2016	560,000	1.412	396,601
2017	10,900,000[a]	1.539	7,082,521
		Value of entire company, V_C =	$8,626,426[b]

[a]This amount is the sum of the FCF_{2017} of $600,000 from Table 11.4 and the $10,300,000 value of the $FCF_{2018 \to \infty}$ calculated in Step 1.

[b]This value of the entire company is based on the rounded values that appear in the table. The precise value found without rounding is $8,628,234.

TABLE 11.5

Calculation of the Value of the Entire Company for Dewhurst, Inc.

Step 4 Calculate the value of the common stock using Equation 11.7. Substituting into Equation 11.7 the value of the entire company, V_C, calculated in Step 3, and the market values of debt, V_D, and preferred stock, V_P, given in Table 11.4, yields the value of the common stock, V_S:

$$V_S = \$8,626,426 - \$3,100,000 - \$800,000 = \underline{\$4,726,426}$$

The value of Dewhurst's common stock is therefore estimated to be $4,726,426. By dividing this total by the 300,000 shares of common stock that the firm has outstanding, we get a common stock value of $15.76 per share ($4,726,426 ÷ 300,000).

It should now be clear that the free cash flow valuation model is consistent with the dividend valuation models presented earlier. The appeal of this approach is its focus on the free cash flow estimates rather than on forecasted dividends, which are far more difficult to estimate given that they are paid at the discretion of the firm's board. The more general nature of the free cash flow model is responsible for its growing popularity, particularly with CFOs and other financial managers.

Other Approaches to Common Stock Valuation

Many other approaches to common stock valuation exist. The more popular approaches include book value, liquidation value, and some type of price/earnings multiple.

book value per share
The amount per share of common stock that would be received if all of the firm's assets were *sold for their exact book (accounting) value* and the proceeds remaining after paying all liabilities (including preferred stock) were divided among the common stockholders.

BOOK VALUE   **Book value per share** is simply the amount per share of common stock that would be received if all of the firm's assets were *sold for their exact book (accounting) value* and the proceeds remaining after paying all liabilities (including preferred stock) were divided among the common stockholders. This method lacks sophistication and can be criticized on the basis of its reliance on historical balance sheet data. It ignores the firm's expected earnings potential and generally lacks any true relationship to the firm's value in the marketplace. Let us look at an example.

Example 11.6

At year-end 2012, Lamar Company's balance sheet shows total assets of $6 million, total liabilities (including preferred stock) of $4.5 million, and 100,000 shares of common stock outstanding. Its book value per share therefore would be

$$\frac{\$6,000,000 - \$4,500,000}{100,000 \text{ shares}} = \underline{\underline{\$15}} \text{ per share}$$

Because this value assumes that assets could be sold for their book value, it may not represent the minimum price at which shares are valued in the marketplace. As a matter of fact, although most stocks sell above book value, it is not unusual to find stocks selling below book value when investors believe either that assets are overvalued or that the firm's liabilities are understated.

LIQUIDATION VALUE   **Liquidation value per share** is the *actual amount* per share of common stock that would be received if all of the firm's assets were *sold for their market value*, liabilities (including preferred stock) were paid, and any remaining money were divided among the common stockholders. This measure is more realistic than book value—because it is based on the current market value of the firm's assets—but it still fails to consider the earning power of those assets. An example will illustrate.

Example 11.7

liquidation value per share
The *actual amount* per share of common stock that would be received if all of the firm's assets were *sold for their market value,* liabilities (including preferred stock) were paid, and any remaining money were divided among the common stockholders.

Lamar Company found on investigation that it could obtain only $5.25 million if it sold its assets today. The firm's liquidation value per share therefore would be

$$\frac{\$5,250,000 - \$4,500,000}{100,000 \text{ shares}} = \underline{\underline{\$7.50}} \text{ per share}$$

Ignoring liquidation expenses, this amount would be the firm's minimum value.

PRICE/EARNINGS (P/E) MULTIPLES   The *price/earnings (P/E) ratio*, introduced in Chapter 2, reflects the amount investors are willing to pay for each dollar of earnings. The average P/E ratio in a particular industry can be used as a guide to a firm's value—if it is assumed that investors value the earnings of that firm in the same way they do the "average" firm in the industry. The **price/earnings multiple approach** is a popular technique used to estimate the firm's share value; it is calculated by multiplying the firm's expected earnings per share (EPS) by the average price/earnings (P/E) ratio for the industry. The average P/E ratio for the industry can be obtained from a source such as *Standard & Poor's Industrial Ratios*.

The P/E ratio valuation technique is a simple method of determining a stock's value and can be quickly calculated after firms make earnings announcements, which accounts for its popularity. Naturally, this has increased the demand for more frequent announcements or "guidance" regarding future earnings. Some firms feel that pre-earnings guidance creates additional costs and can lead to ethical issues, as discussed in the *Focus on Ethics* box below.

The use of P/E multiples is especially helpful in valuing firms that are not publicly traded, but analysts use this approach for public companies too. In any case, the price/earnings multiple approach is considered superior to the use of book or liquidation values because it considers *expected* earnings. An example will demonstrate the use of price/earnings multiples.

price/earnings multiple approach
A popular technique used to estimate the firm's share value; calculated by multiplying the firm's expected earnings per share (EPS) by the average price/earnings (P/E) ratio for the industry.

Personal Finance Example 11.8

Ann Perrier plans to use the price/earnings multiple approach to estimate the value of Lamar Company's stock, which she currently holds in her retirement account. She estimates that Lamar Company will earn $2.60 per share next year (2013). This expectation is based on an analysis of the firm's historical earnings trend and of expected economic and industry conditions. She finds the price/earnings (P/E) ratio for firms in the same industry to average 7. Multiplying Lamar's

focus on ETHICS

Psst—Have You Heard Any Good Quarterly Earnings Forecasts Lately?

Corporate managers have long complained about the pressure to focus on the short term, and now business groups are coming to their defense. "The focus on the short term is a huge problem," says William Donaldson, former chairman of the Securities and Exchange Commission. "With all of the attention paid to quarterly performance, managers are taking their eyes off long-term strategic goals."

Donaldson, the U.S. Chamber of Commerce, and others believe that the best way to focus companies toward long-term goals is to do away with the practice of giving quarterly earnings guidance. In March 2007 the CFA Centre for Financial Market Integrity and the Business Roundtable Institute for Corporate Ethics proposed a template for quarterly earnings reports that would, in their view, obviate the need for earnings guidance.

Meanwhile, many companies are hesitant to give up issuing quarterly guidance. The practice of issuing earnings forecasts began in the early 1980s, a few years after the SEC's decision to allow companies to include forward-looking projections, provided they were accompanied by appropriate cautionary language. The result was what former SEC chairman Arthur Levitt once called a "game of winks and nods." Companies used earnings guidance to lower analysts' estimates; when the actual numbers came in higher, their stock prices jumped. The practice reached a

fever pitch during the late 1990s when companies that missed the consensus earnings estimate, even by just a penny, saw their stock prices tumble.

One of the first companies to stop issuing earnings guidance was Gillette, in 2001. Others that abandoned quarterly guidance were Coca-Cola, Intel, and McDonald's. It became a trend. By 2005, just 61 percent of companies were offering quarterly projections to the public; according to the National Investor Relations Institute, the number declined to 52 percent in 2006.

Not everyone agrees with eliminating quarterly guidance. A survey conducted by New York University's Stern School of Business finance professor Baruch Lev, along with University of Florida professors Joel Houston and Jennifer Tucker, showed that companies that ended quarterly guidance reaped almost no benefit from doing so. Their study found no evidence that guidance stoppers increased capital investments or research and development. So when should companies give up earnings guidance? According to Lev, they should do so only when they are not very good at predicting their earnings. "If you are not better than others at forecasting, then don't bother," he says.

▶ *What temptations might managers face if they have provided earnings guidance to investors and later find it difficult to meet the expectations that they helped create?*

Matter of fact

Problems with P/E Valuation

The P/E multiple approach is a fast and easy way to estimate a stock's value. However, P/E ratios vary widely over time. In 1980, the average stock had a P/E rato below 9, but by the year 2000, the ratio had risen above 40. Therefore, analyssts using the P/E approach in the 1980s would have come up with much lower estimates of value than analysts using the model 20 years later. In other words, when using this approach to estimate stock values, the estimate will depend more on whether stock market valuations generally are high or low rather than on whether stock market valuations generally are high or low rather than on whether the particular company is doing well or not.

expected earnings per share (EPS) of $2.60 by this ratio gives her a value for the firm's shares of $18.20, assuming that investors will continue to value the average firm at 7 times its earnings.

So how much is Lamar Company's stock really worth? That's a trick question because there's no one right answer. It is important to recognize that the answer depends on the assumptions made and the techniques used. Professional securities analysts typically use a variety of models and techniques to value stocks. For example, an analyst might use the constant-growth model, liquidation value, and a price/earnings (P/E) multiple to estimate the worth of a given stock. If the analyst feels comfortable with his or her estimates, the stock would be valued at no more than the largest estimate. Of course, should the firm's estimated liquidation value per share exceed its "going concern" value per share, estimated by using one of the valuation models (zero-, constant-, or variable-growth or free cash flow) or the P/E multiple approach, the firm would be viewed as being "worth more dead than alive." In such an event, the firm would lack sufficient earning power to justify its existence and should probably be liquidated.

→ **Review Questions**

11–12 Describe the events that occur in an *efficient market* in response to new information that causes the expected return to exceed the required return. What happens to the market value?

11–13 What does the *efficient-market hypothesis (EMH)* say about (**a**) securities prices, (**b**) their reaction to new information, and (**c**) investor opportunities to profit? What is the *behavioral finance* challenge to this hypothesis?

11–14 Describe, compare, and contrast the following common stock dividend valuation models: (**a**) zero-growth, (**b**) constant-growth, and (**c**) variable- growth.

11–15 Describe the *free cash flow valuation model* and explain how it differs from the dividend valuation models. What is the appeal of this model?

11–16 Explain each of the three other approaches to common stock valuation: (**a**) book value, (**b**) liquidation value, and (**c**) price/earnings (P/E) multiples. Which of these is considered the best?

 11.4 Decision Making and Common Stock Value

Valuation equations measure the stock value at a point in time based on expected return and risk. Any decisions of the financial manager that affect these variables can cause the value of the firm to change. Figure 11.3 depicts the relationship among financial decisions, return, risk, and stock value.

Changes in Expected Dividends

Assuming that economic conditions remain stable, any management action that would cause current and prospective stockholders to raise their dividend expectations should increase the firm's value. In Equation 11.4, we can see that P_0 will increase for any increase in D_1 or g. Any action of the financial manager that will increase the level of expected dividends without changing risk (the required return) should be undertaken, because it will positively affect owners' wealth.

Example 11.9

Using the constant-growth model in an earlier example (on pages 425 and 426), we found Lamar Company to have a share value of $18.75. On the following day, the firm announced a major technological breakthrough that would revolutionize its industry. Current and prospective stock-holders would not be expected to adjust their required return of 15%, but they would expect that future dividends will increase. Specifically, they expect that although the dividend next year, D_1, will remain at $1.50, the expected rate of growth thereafter will increase from 7% to 9%. If we substitute $D_1 = \$1.50$, $r_s = 0.15$, and $g = 0.09$ into Equation 11.4, the resulting share value is $25 [\$1.50 \div (0.15 - 0.09)]$. The increased value therefore resulted from the higher expected future dividends reflected in the increase in the growth rate.

Figure 11.3
Decision Making and Stock Value
Financial decisions, return, risk, and stock value

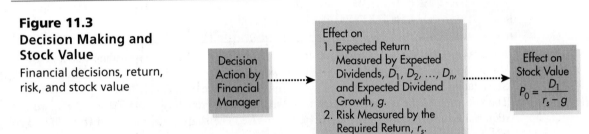

Changes in Risk

Any measure of required return consists of two components, a risk-free rate and a risk premium. We expressed this relationship as Equation 10.1 in the previous chapter, which we repeat here in terms of rs:

$$r_s = \underbrace{r^* + IP}_{\substack{\text{risk-free} \\ \text{rate, } R_F}} + \underbrace{RP_s}_{\substack{\text{risk} \\ \text{premium}}}$$

In the next chapter you will learn that the real challenge in finding the required return is determining the appropriate risk premium. We will discuss how investors and managers can estimate the risk premium for any particular asset. For now, recognize that r_s represents the minimum return that the firm's stock must provide to shareholders to compensate them for bearing the risk of holding the firm's equity.

Any action taken by the financial manager that increases the risk shareholders must bear will also increase the risk premium required by shareholders, and hence the required return. Additionally, the required return can be affected by changes in the risk free rate—even if the risk premium remains constant. For example, if the risk-free rate increases due to a shift in government policy, then the required return goes up too. In Equation 11.1, we can see that an increase in the required return, r_s, will reduce share value, P_0, and a decrease in the required return will increase share value. Thus, any action of the financial manager that increases risk contributes to a reduction in value, and any action that decreases risk contributes to an increase in value.

Example 11.10

Assume that Lamar Company's 15% required return resulted from a risk-free rate of 9% and a risk premium of 6%. With this return, the firm's share value was calculated in an earlier example (on page 425) to be $18.75.

Now imagine that the financial manager makes a decision that, without changing expected dividends, causes the firm's risk premium to increase to 7%. Assuming that *the risk-free rate remains at 9%, the new required return on Lamar stock will be 16% (9% + 7%),* substituting D_1 = \$1.50, r_s = 0.16, and g = 0.07 into the valuation equation (Equation 11.3), results in a new share value of \$16.67 [\$1.50 ÷ (0.16 − 0.07)]. As expected, raising the required return, without any corresponding increase in expected dividends, causes the firm's stock value to decline. Clearly, the financial manager's action was not in the owners' best interest.

Combined Effect

A financial decision rarely affects dividends and risk independently; most decisions affect both factors often in the same direction. As firms take on more risk, their shareholders expect to see higher dividends. The net effect on value depends on the relative size of the changes in these two variables.

Example 11.11

If we assume that the two changes illustrated for Lamar Company in the preceding examples occur simultaneously, the key variable values would be D_1 = \$1.50, r_s = 0.16, and g = 0.09. Substituting into the valuation model, we obtain a share price of \$21.43 [\$1.50 ÷ (0.16 − 0.09)]. The net result of the decision, which increased dividend growth (g, from 7% to 9%) as well as required return (rs, from 15% to 16%), is positive. The share price increased from \$18.75 to \$21.43. Even with the combined effects, the decision appears to be in the best interest of the firm's owners because it increases their wealth.

→ **Review Questions**

11–17 Explain the linkages among financial decisions, return, risk, and stock value.

11–18 Assuming that all other variables remain unchanged, what impact would *each* of the following have on stock price? (**a**) The firm's risk premium increases. (**b**) The firm's required return decreases. (**c**) The dividend expected next year decreases. (**d**) The rate of growth in dividends is expected to increase.

Summary

FOCUS ON VALUE

The price of each share of a firm's common stock is the value of each ownership interest. Although common stockholders typically have voting rights, which indirectly give them a say in management, their most significant right is their claim on the residual cash flows of the firm. This claim is subordinate to those of vendors, employees, customers, lenders, the government (for taxes), and preferred stockholders. The value of the common stockholders' claim is embodied in the future cash flows they are entitled to receive. The present value of those expected cash flows is the firm's share value.

To determine this present value, forecast cash flows are discounted at a rate that reflects their risk. Riskier cash flows are discounted at higher rates, resulting in lower present values than less risky expected cash flows, which are discounted at lower rates. The value of the firm's common stock is therefore driven by its expected cash flows (returns) and risk (certainty of the expected cash flows).

In pursuing the firm's goal of **maximizing the stock price**, the financial manager must carefully consider the balance of return and risk associated with each proposal and must undertake only those actions that create value for owners. By focusing on value creation and by managing and monitoring the firm's cash flows and risk, the financial manager should be able to achieve the firm's goal of share price maximization.

REVIEW OF LEARNING GOALS

LG 1 **Differentiate between debt and equity.** Holders of equity capital (common and preferred stock) are owners of the firm. Typically, only common stockholders have a voice in management. Equityholders' claims on income and assets are secondary to creditors' claims, there is no maturity date, and dividends paid to stockholders are not tax deductible.

LG 2 **Discuss the features of both common and preferred stock.** The common stock of a firm can be privately owned, closely owned, or publicly owned. It can be sold with or without a par value. Preemptive rights allow common stockholders to avoid dilution of ownership when new shares are issued. Not all shares authorized in the corporate charter are outstanding. If a firm has treasury stock, it will have issued more shares than are outstanding. Some firms have two or more classes of common stock that differ mainly in having unequal voting rights. Proxies transfer voting rights from one party to another. The decision to pay dividends to common stockholders is made by the firm's board of directors. Firms can issue stock in foreign markets. The stock of many foreign corporations is traded in U.S. markets in the form of American depositary receipts (ADRs), which are backed by American depositary shares (ADSs).

Preferred stockholders have preference over common stockholders with respect to the distribution of earnings and assets. They do not normally have voting privileges. Preferred stock issues may have certain restrictive covenants, cumulative dividends, a call feature, and a conversion feature.

LG 3 **Describe the process of issuing common stock, including venture capital, going public, and the investment banker.** The initial nonfounder financing for business startups with attractive growth prospects typically comes from private equity investors. These investors can be either angel capitalists or venture capitalists (VCs). VCs usually invest in both early-stage and later-stage companies that they hope to take public so as to cash out their investments.

The first public issue of a firm's stock is called an initial public offering (IPO). The company selects an investment banker to advise it and to sell the securities. The lead investment banker may form a selling syndicate with other investment bankers. The IPO process includes getting SEC approval, promoting the offering to investors, and pricing the issue.

LG 4 **Understand the concept of market efficiency and basic stock valuation using zero-growth, constant-growth, and variable-growth models.** Market efficiency assumes that the quick reactions of rational investors to new information cause the market value of common stock to adjust upward or downward quickly. The efficient-market hypothesis (EMH) suggests that securities are fairly priced, that they reflect fully all publicly available information, and that investors should therefore not waste time trying to find and capitalize on mispriced securities. Behavioral finance advocates challenge this hypothesis by arguing that emotion and other factors play a role in investment decisions.

The value of a share of stock is the present value of all future dividends it is expected to provide over an infinite time horizon. Three dividend growth models—zero-growth, constant-growth, and variable-growth—can be considered in common stock valuation. The most widely cited model is the constant-growth model.

LG 5 **Discuss the free cash flow valuation model and the book value, liquidation value, and price/earnings (P/E) multiple approaches.** The free cash flow valuation model values firms that have no dividend history, startups, or an operating unit or division of a larger public company. The model finds the value of the entire company by discounting the firm's expected free cash flow at its weighted average cost of capital. The common stock value is found by subtracting the market values of the firm's debt and preferred stock from the value of the entire company.

Book value per share is the amount per share of common stock that would be received if all of the firm's assets were *sold for their exact book (accounting) value* and the proceeds remaining after paying all liabilities (including preferred stock) were divided among the common stockholders. Liquidation value per share is the *actual amount* per share of common stock that would be received if all of the firm's assets were *sold for their market value*, liabilities (including preferred stock) were paid, and the remaining money were divided among the common stockholders. The price/earnings (P/E) multiple approach estimates stock value by multiplying the firm's expected earnings per share (EPS) by the average price/earnings (P/E) ratio for the industry.

LG 6 **Explain the relationships among financial decisions, return, risk, and the firm's value. In a** stable economy, any action of the financial manager that increases the level of expected dividends without changing risk should increase share value; any action that reduces the level of expected dividends without changing risk should reduce share value. Similarly, any action that increases risk (required return) will reduce share value; any action that reduces risk will increase share value. An assessment of the combined effect of return and risk on stock value must be part of the financial decision-making process.

Opener-in-Review

A123 shares were originally offered for sale at a price of $13.50. Three months later, the stock traded for about $18. What return did investors earn over this period? On November 10, 2009, A123 reported its 3rd quarter financial results. From November 9 to November 11, the firm's stock price fell from $17.85 to $16.88. Given that A123 has 102 million shares outstanding, what were the dollar and percentage losses that shareholders endured in the days surrounding the earnings release? Over the same three days (November 9–11), the Nasdaq stock index moved up 0.6%. How does this influence your thinking about A123's stock performance around this time?

Self-Test Problems   (Solutions in Appendix)

LG 4 **ST11–1 Common stock valuation**   Perry Motors' common stock just paid its annual dividend of $1.80 per share. The required return on the common stock is 12%. Estimate the value of the common stock under each of the following assumptions about the dividend:

   a. Dividends are expected to grow at an annual rate of 0% to infinity.
   b. Dividends are expected to grow at a constant annual rate of 5% to infinity.
   c. Dividends are expected to grow at an annual rate of 5% for each of the next 3 years, followed by a constant annual growth rate of 4% in years 4 to infinity.

LG 5 **ST11–2 Free cash flow valuation**   Erwin Footwear wishes to assess the value of its Active Shoe Division. This division has debt with a market value of $12,500,000 and no preferred stock. Its weighted average cost of capital is 10%. The Active Shoe Division's estimated free cash flow each year from 2013 through 2016 is given in the following table. Beyond 2016 to infinity, the firm expects its free cash flow to grow at 4% annually.

Year (t)	Free cash flow (FCF_t)
2013	$ 800,000
2014	1,200,000
2015	1,400,000
2016	1,500,000

   a. Use the free cash flow valuation model to estimate the value of Erwin's entire Active Shoe Division.
   b. Use your finding in part **a** along with the data provided above to find this division's common stock value.

c. If the Active Shoe Division as a public company will have 500,000 shares outstanding, use your finding in part **b** to calculate its value per share.

Warm-Up Exercises   All problems are available in *MyAccountingLab*

LG 1   **E11–1** A balance sheet balances assets with their sources of debt and equity financing. If a corporation has assets equal to $5.2 million and a debt ratio of 75.0%, how much debt does the corporation have on its books?

LG 2   **E11–2** Angina, Inc., has 5 million shares outstanding. The firm is considering issuing an additional 1 million shares. After selling these shares at their $20 per share offering price and netting 95% of the sale proceeds, the firm is obligated by an earlier agreement to sell an additional 250,000 shares at 90% of the offering price. In total, how much cash will the firm net from these stock sales?

LG 2   **E11–3** Figurate Industries has 750,000 shares of cumulative preferred stock outstanding. It has passed the last three quarterly dividends of $2.50 per share and now (at the end of the current quarter) wishes to distribute a total of $12 million to its shareholders. If Figurate has 3 million shares of common stock outstanding, how large a per-share common stock dividend will it be able to pay?

LG 3   **E11–4** Today the common stock of Gresham Technology closed at $24.60 per share, down $0.35 from yesterday. If the company has 4.6 million shares outstanding and annual earnings of $11.2 million, what is its P/E ratio today? What was its P/E ratio yesterday?

LG 4   **E11–5** Stacker Weight Loss currently pays an annual year-end dividend of $1.20 per share. It plans to increase this dividend by 5% next year and maintain it at the new level for the foreseeable future. If the required return on this firm's stock is 8%, what is the value of Stacker's stock?

LG 6   **E11–6** Brash Corporation initiated a new corporate strategy that fixes its annual dividend at $2.25 per share forever. If the risk-free rate is 4.5% and the risk premium on Brash's stock is 10.8%, what is the value of Brash's stock?

Problems   All problems are available in *MyAccountingLab*

LG 2   **P11–1 Authorized and available shares**   Aspin Corporation's charter authorizes issuance of 2,000,000 shares of common stock. Currently, 1,400,000 shares are outstanding, and 100,000 shares are being held as treasury stock. The firm wishes to raise $48,000,000 for a plant expansion. Discussions with its investment bankers indicate that the sale of new common stock will net the firm $60 per share.
   a. What is the maximum number of new shares of common stock that the firm can sell without receiving further authorization from shareholders?
   b. Judging on the basis of the data given and your finding in part a, will the firm be able to raise the needed funds without receiving further authorization?
   c. What must the firm do to obtain authorization to issue more than the number of shares found in part **a?**

LG 2   **P11–2** Preferred dividends   Slater Lamp Manufacturing has an outstanding issue of preferred stock with an $80 par value and an 11% annual dividend.
   a. What is the annual dollar dividend? If it is paid quarterly, how much will be paid each quarter?
   b. If the preferred stock is *noncumulative* and the board of directors has passed the preferred dividend for the last 3 quarters, how much must be paid to preferred stockholders in the current quarter before dividends are paid to common stockholders?

c. If the preferred stock is *cumulative* and the board of directors has passed the preferred dividend for the last 3 quarters, how much must be paid to preferred stockholders in the current quarter before dividends are paid to common stockholders?

LG 2 **P11–3** **Preferred dividends** In each case in the following table, how many dollars of preferred dividends per share must be paid to preferred stockholders in the current period before common stock dividends are paid?

Case	Type	Par value	Dividend per share per period	Periods of dividends passed
A	Cumulative	$ 80	$ 5	2
B	Noncumulative	110	8%	3
C	Noncumulative	100	$11	1
D	Cumulative	60	8.5%	4
E	Cumulative	90	9%	0

LG 2 **P11–4** **Convertible preferred stock** Valerian Corp. convertible preferred stock has a fixed conversion ratio of 5 common shares per 1 share of preferred stock. The preferred stock pays a dividend of $10.00 per share per year. The common stock currently sells for $20.00 per share and pays a dividend of $1.00 per share per year.

a. Judging on the basis of the conversion ratio and the price of the common shares, what is the current conversion value of each preferred share?

b. If the preferred shares are selling at $96.00 each, should an investor convert the preferred shares to common shares?

c. What factors might cause an investor not to convert from preferred to common stock?

Personal Finance Problem

LG 4 **P11–5** **Common stock valuation—Zero growth** Scotto Manufacturing is a mature firm in the machine tool component industry. The firm's most recent common stock dividend was $2.40 per share. Because of its maturity as well as its stable sales and earnings, the firm's management feels that dividends will remain at the current level for the foreseeable future.

a. If the required return is 12%, what will be the value of Scotto's common stock?

b. If the firm's risk as perceived by market participants suddenly increases, causing the required return to rise to 20%, what will be the common stock value?

c. Judging on the basis of your findings in parts a and b, what impact does risk have on value? Explain.

Personal Finance Problem

LG 4 **P11–6** **Common stock value—Zero growth** Kelsey Drums, Inc., is a well-established supplier of fine percussion instruments to orchestras all over the United States. The company's class A common stock has paid a dividend of $5.00 per share per year for the last 15 years. Management expects to continue to pay at that amount for the foreseeable future. Sally Talbot purchased 100 shares of Kelsey class A common 10 years ago at a time when the required rate of return for the stock was 16%. She wants to sell her shares today. The current required rate of return for the stock is 12%. How much capital gain or loss will Sally have on her shares?

LG 4 **P11–7** **Preferred stock valuation** Jones Design wishes to estimate the value of its outstanding preferred stock. The preferred issue has an $80 par value and pays an annual dividend of $6.40 per share. Similar-risk preferred stocks are currently earning a 9.3% annual rate of return.

a. What is the market value of the outstanding preferred stock?

b. If an investor purchases the preferred stock at the value calculated in part a, how much does she gain or lose per share if she sells the stock when the required return on similar-risk preferred stocks has risen to 10.5%? Explain.

LG 4 **P11–8** **Common stock value—Constant growth** Use the constant-growth model (Gordon growth model) to find the value of each firm shown in the following table.

Firm	Dividend expected next year	Dividend growth rate	Required return
A	$1.20	8%	13%
B	4.00	5	15
C	0.65	10	14
D	6.00	8	9
E	2.25	8	20

LG 4 **P11–9** **Common stock value—Constant growth** McCracken Roofing, Inc., common stock paid a dividend of $1.20 per share last year. The company expects earnings and dividends to grow at a rate of 5% per year for the foreseeable future.

a. What required rate of return for this stock would result in a price per share of $28?

b. If McCracken expects both earnings and dividends to grow at an annual rate of 10%, what required rate of return would result in a price per share of $28?

Personal Finance Problem

LG 4 **P11–10** **Common stock value—Constant growth** Elk County Telephone has paid the dividends shown in the following table over the past 6 years.

Year	Dividend per share
2012	$2.87
2011	2.76
2010	2.60
2009	2.46
2008	2.37
2007	2.25

The firm's dividend per share next year is expected to be $3.02.

a. If you can earn 13% on similar-risk investments, what is the most you would be willing to pay per share?

b. If you can earn only 10% on similar-risk investments, what is the most you would be willing to pay per share?

c. Compare and contrast your findings in parts a and b, and discuss the impact of changing risk on share value.

LG 4 **P11–11** **Common stock value—Variable growth** Newman Manufacturing is considering a cash purchase of the stock of Grips Tool. During the year just completed, Grips earned $4.25 per share and paid cash dividends of $2.55 per share $(D_0 = \$2.55)$. Grips' earnings and dividends are expected to grow at 25% per year for the next 3 years, after which they are expected to grow at 10% per year to infinity. What is the maximum price per share that Newman should pay for Grips if it has a required return of 15% on investments with risk characteristics similar to those of Grips?

Personal Finance Problem

LG 4 **P11–12** **Common stock value—Variable growth** Home Place Hotels, Inc., is entering into a 3-year remodeling and expansion project. The construction will have a limiting effect on earnings during that time, but when it is complete, it should allow the company to enjoy much improved growth in earnings and dividends. Last year, the company paid a dividend of $3.40. It expects zero growth in the next year. In years 2 and 3, 5% growth is expected, and in year 4, 15% growth. In year 5 and thereafter, growth should be a constant 10% per year. What is the maximum price per share that an investor who requires a return of 14% should pay for Home Place Hotels common stock?

LG 4 **P11–13 Common stock value—Variable growth** Lawrence Industries' most recent annual dividend was $1.80 per share ($D_0 = \$1.80$), and the firm's required return is 11%. Find the market value of Lawrence's shares when:

a. Dividends are expected to grow at 8% annually for 3 years, followed by a 5% constant annual growth rate in years 4 to infinity.

b. Dividends are expected to grow at 8% annually for 3 years, followed by a 0% constant annual growth rate in years 4 to infinity.

c. Dividends are expected to grow at 8% annually for 3 years, followed by a 10% constant annual growth rate in years 4 to infinity.

Personal Finance Problem

LG 4 **P11–14 Common stock value—All growth models** You are evaluating the potential purchase of a small business currently generating $42,500 of after-tax cash flow ($D_0 = \$42,500$). On the basis of a review of similar-risk investment opportunities, you must earn an 18% rate of return on the proposed purchase. Because you are relatively uncertain about future cash flows, you decide to estimate the firm's value using several possible assumptions about the growth rate of cash flows.

a. What is the firm's value if cash flows are expected to grow at an annual rate of 0% from now to infinity?

b. What is the firm's value if cash flows are expected to grow at a constant annual rate of 7% from now to infinity?

c. What is the firm's value if cash flows are expected to grow at an annual rate of 12% for the first 2 years, followed by a constant annual rate of 7% from year 3 to infinity?

LG 5 **P11–15 Free cash flow valuation** Nabor Industries is considering going public but is unsure of a fair offering price for the company. Before hiring an investment banker to assist in making the public offering, managers at Nabor have decided to make their own estimate of the firm's common stock value. The firm's CFO has gathered data for performing the valuation using the free cash flow valuation model.

The firm's weighted average cost of capital is 11%, and it has $1,500,000 of debt at market value and $400,000 of preferred stock at its assumed market value. The estimated free cash flows over the next 5 years, 2013 through 2017, are given below. Beyond 2017 to infinity, the firm expects its free cash flow to grow by 3% annually.

Year (t)	Free cash flow (FCF_t)
2013	$200,000
2014	250,000
2015	310,000
2016	350,000
2017	390,000

a. Estimate the value of Nabor Industries' entire company by using the *free cash flow valuation model*.

b. Use your finding in part *a*, along with the data provided above, to find Nabor Industries' common stock value.

c. If the firm plans to issue 200,000 shares of common stock, what is its estimated value per share?

Personal Finance Problem

LG 5 **P11–16** **Using the free cash flow valuation model to price an IPO** Assume that you have an opportunity to buy the stock of CoolTech, Inc., an IPO being offered for $12.50 per share. Although you are very much interested in owning the company, you are concerned about whether it is fairly priced. To determine the value of the shares, you have decided to apply the free cash flow valuation model to the firm's financial data that you've developed from a variety of data sources. The key values you have compiled are summarized in the following table.

Free cash flow		Other data
Year (t)	FCF_t	
2013	$ 700,000	Growth rate of FCF, beyond 2013 to infinity = 2%
2014	800,000	Weighted average cost of capital = 8%
2015	950,000	Market value of all debt = $2,700,000
2016	1,100,000	Market value of preferred stock = $1,000,000
		Number of shares of common stock outstanding = 1,100,000

a. Use the *free cash flow valuation model* to estimate CoolTech's common stock value per share.

b. Judging on the basis of your finding in part **a** and the stock's offering price, should you buy the stock?

c. On further analysis, you find that the growth rate in FCF beyond 2016 will be 3% rather than 2%. What effect would this finding have on your responses in parts **a** and **b**?

LG 5 **P11–17** **Book and liquidation value** The balance sheet for Gallinas Industries is as follows.

Gallinas Industries Balance Sheet December 31

Assets		Liabilities and Stockholders' Equity	
Cash	$ 40,000	Accounts payable	$100,000
Marketable securities	60,000	Notes payable	30,000
Accounts receivable	120,000	Accrued wages	30,000
Inventories	160,000	Total current liabilities	$160,000
Total current assets	$380,000	Long-term debt	$180,000
Land and buildings (net)	$150,000	Preferred stock	$ 80,000
Machinery and equipment	250,000	Common stock (10,000 shares)	260,000
Total fixed assets (net)	$400,000	Retained earnings	100,000
Total assets	$780,000	Total liabilities and stockholders' equity	$780,000

Additional information with respect to the firm is available:

(1) Preferred stock can be liquidated at book value.
(2) Accounts receivable and inventories can be liquidated at 90% of book value.
(3) The firm has 10,000 shares of common stock outstanding.
(4) All interest and dividends are currently paid up.
(5) Land and buildings can be liquidated at 130% of book value.
(6) Machinery and equipment can be liquidated at 70% of book value.
(7) Cash and marketable securities can be liquidated at book value.

Given this information, answer the following:

a. What is Gallinas Industries' *book value per share?*
b. What is its *liquidation value per share?*
c. Compare, contrast, and discuss the values found in parts **a** and **b**.

LG 5 **P11–18** **Valuation with price/earnings multiples** For each of the firms shown in the following table, use the data given to estimate its common stock value employing price/earnings (P/E) multiples.

Firm	Expected EPS	Price/earnings multiple
A	$3.00	6.2
B	4.50	10.0
C	1.80	12.6
D	2.40	8.9
E	5.10	15.0

LG 6 **P11–19 Management action and stock value** REH Corporation's most recent dividend was $3 per share, its expected annual rate of dividend growth is 5%, and the required return is now 15%. A variety of proposals are being considered by management to redirect the firm's activities. Determine the impact on share price for each of the following proposed actions, and indicate the best alternative.

a. Do nothing, which will leave the key financial variables unchanged.

b. Invest in a new machine that will increase the dividend growth rate to 6% and lower the required return to 14%.

c. Eliminate an unprofitable product line, which will increase the dividend growth rate to 7% and raise the required return to 17%.

d. Merge with another firm, which will reduce the growth rate to 4% and raise the required return to 16%.

e. Acquire a subsidiary operation from another manufacturer. The acquisition should increase the dividend growth rate to 8% and increase the required return to 17%.

LG 4 **LG 6** **P11–20 Integrative—Risk and Valuation** Given the following information for the stock of Foster Company, calculate the risk premium on its common stock.

Current price per share of common	$50.00
Expected dividend per share next year	$ 3.00
Constant annual dividend growth rate	9%
Risk-free rate of return	7%

LG 4 **LG 6** **P11–21 Integrative—Risk and valuation** Giant Enterprises' stock has a required return of 14.8%. The company, which plans to pay a dividend of $2.60 per share in the coming year, anticipates that its future dividends will increase at an annual rate consistent with that experienced over the 2006–2012 period, when the following dividends were paid:

Year	Dividend per share
2012	$2.45
2011	2.28
2010	2.10
2009	1.95
2008	1.82
2007	1.80
2006	1.73

a. If the risk-free rate is 10%, what is the risk premium on Giant's stock?

b. Using the constant-growth model, estimate the value of Giant's stock.

c. Explain what effect, if any, a decrease in the risk premium would have on the value of Giant's stock.

LG 4 **LG 6** **P11–22 Integrative—Risk and Valuation** Hamlin Steel Company wishes to determine the value of Craft Foundry, a firm that it is considering acquiring for cash. Hamlin wishes to determine the applicable discount rate to use as an input to the constant-growth valuation model. Craft's stock is not publicly traded. After studying the required returns of firms similar to Craft that are publicly traded, Hamlin believes that an appropriate risk premium on Craft stock is about 5%. The risk-free rate is currently 9%. Craft's dividend per share for each of the past 6 years is shown in the following table.

Year	Dividend per share
2012	$3.44
2011	3.28
2010	3.15
2009	2.90
2008	2.75
2007	2.45

a. Given that Craft is expected to pay a dividend of $3.68 next year, determine the maximum cash price that Hamlin should pay for each share of Craft.

b. Describe the effect on the resulting value of Craft of:

(1) A decrease in its dividend growth rate of 2% from that exhibited over the 2007–2012 period.

(2) A decrease in its risk premium to 4%.

LG 4 **P11–23** **ETHICS PROBLEM** Melissa is trying to value Generic Utility, Inc.'s, stock, which is clearly not growing at all. Generic declared and paid a $5 dividend last year. The required rate of return for utility stocks is 11%, but Melissa is unsure about the financial reporting integrity of Generic's finance team. She decides to add an extra 1% "credibility" risk premium to the required return as part of her valuation analysis.

a. What is the value of Generic's stock, assuming that the financials are trustworthy?

b. What is the value of Generic's stock, assuming that Melissa includes the extra 1% "credibility" risk premium?

c. What is the difference between the values found in parts a and b, and how might one interpret that difference?

Spreadsheet Exercise

You are interested in purchasing the common stock of Azure Corporation. The firm recently paid a dividend of $3 per share. It expects its earnings—and hence its dividends—to grow at a rate of 7% for the foreseeable future. Currently, similar-risk stocks have required returns of 10%.

TO DO

a. Given the data above, calculate the present value of this security. Use the constant-growth model (Equation 11.4) to find the stock value.

b. One year later, your broker offers to sell you additional shares of Azure at $73. The most recent dividend paid was $3.21, and the expected growth rate for earnings remains at 7%. If you determine that the appropriate risk premium is 6.74% and you observe that the risk-free rate, R_F, is currently 5.25%, what is the firm's current required return, r_{Azure}?

c. Applying Equation 11.4, determine the value of the stock using the new dividend and required return from part **b.**

d. Given your calculation in part **c,** would you buy the additional shares from your broker at $73 per share? Explain.

e. Given your calculation in part **c,** would you sell your old shares for $73? Explain.

 Visit **www.myaccountinglab.com** for **Chapter Case: Assessing the Impact of Suarez Manufacturing's Proposed Risky Investment on Its Stock Value,** Group Exercises, and numerous online resources.

Integrative Case

Encore International

In the world of trendsetting fashion, instinct and marketing savvy are prerequisites to success. Jordan Ellis had both. During 2012, his international casual-wear company, Encore, rocketed to $300 million in sales after 10 years in business. His fashion line covered the young woman from head to toe with hats, sweaters, dresses, blouses, skirts, pants, sweatshirts, socks, and shoes. In Manhattan, there was an Encore shop every five or six blocks, each featuring a different color. Some shops showed the entire line in mauve, and others featured it in canary yellow.

Encore had made it. The company's historical growth was so spectacular that no one could have predicted it. However, securities analysts speculated that Encore could not keep up the pace. They warned that competition is fierce in the fashion industry and that the firm might encounter little or no growth in the future. They estimated that stockholders also should expect no growth in future dividends.

Contrary to the conservative securities analysts, Jordan Ellis felt that the company could maintain a constant annual growth rate in dividends per share of 6% in the future, or possibly 8% for the next 2 years and 6% thereafter. Ellis based his estimates on an established long-term expansion plan into European and Latin American markets. Venturing into these markets was expected to cause the risk of the firm, as measured by the risk premium on its stock, to increase immediately from 8.8% to 10%. Currently, the risk-free rate is 6%.

In preparing the long-term financial plan, Encore's chief financial officer has assigned a junior financial analyst, Marc Scott, to evaluate the firm's current stock price. He has asked Marc to consider the conservative predictions of the securities analysts and the aggressive predictions of the company founder, Jordan Ellis.

Marc has compiled these 2012 financial data to aid his analysis:

Data item	2012 value
Earnings per share (EPS)	$6.25
Price per share of common stock	$40.00
Book value of common stock equity	$60,000,000
Total common shares outstanding	2,500,000
Common stock dividend per share	$4.00

TO DO

a. What is the firm's current book value per share?

b. What is the firm's current P/E ratio?

c. (1) What is the current required return for Encore stock?

   (2) What will be the new required return for Encore stock assuming that they expand into European and Latin American markets as planned?

d. If the securities analysts are correct and there is no growth in future dividends, what will be the value per share of the Encore stock? (Note: Use the new required return on the company's stock here.)

e. (1) If Jordan Ellis's predictions are correct, what will be the value per share of Encore stock if the firm maintains a constant annual 6% growth rate in future dividends? (Note: Continue to use the new required return here.)

   (2) If Jordan Ellis's predictions are correct, what will be the value per share of Encore stock if the firm maintains a constant annual 8% growth rate in dividends per share over the next 2 years and 6% thereafter?

f. Compare the current (2012) price of the stock and the stock values found in parts a, d, and e. Discuss why these values may differ. Which valuation method do you believe most clearly represents the true value of the Encore stock?

Capital Budgeting

LEARNING OBJECTIVES

When you have finished studying this chapter, you should be able to:

1. Describe capital-budgeting decisions and use the net-present-value (NPV) method to make such decisions.

2. Use sensitivity analysis to evaluate the effect of changes in predictions on investment decisions.

3. Calculate the NPV difference between two projects using both the total project and differential approaches.

4. Identify relevant cash flows for NPV analyses.

5. Compute the after-tax net present values of projects.

6. Explain the after-tax effect on cash received from the disposal of assets.

7. Use the payback model and the accounting rate-of-return model and compare them with the NPV model.

8. Reconcile the conflict between using an NPV model for making decisions and using accounting income for evaluating the related performance.

9. Compute the impact of inflation on a capital-budgeting project (Appendix 12).

▶ TOYOTA MOTOR CORPORATION

Toyota Motor Corporation was founded in 1937 by Japanese entrepreneur, Kiichiro Toyoda, to produce and sell Toyoda autos. Almost immediately the name was changed to Toyota because (according to Wikipedia) "it took eight brush strokes (a fortuitous number) to write in Japanese, was visually simpler (leaving off two ticks at the end), and sounded better with two 't's." In 1957 Toyota entered the U.S. market with a car called the Toyopet Crown. Unfortunately, U.S. consumers associated these cars with toys and pets, so Toyota quickly dropped the Toyopet name. Nevertheless, the company continued selling Toyotas in the United States. In 1963 Toyota built its first car outside of Japan (in Australia) and in 1982 began producing cars in the United States. In 2008, Toyota became the largest automobile company in the world, replacing **General Motors**. It has production or assembly plants in more than 25 countries.

Toyota was instrumental in developing lean manufacturing and just-in-time production. Its management philosophy focuses on four areas: 1) long-term thinking, 2) a process for problem-solving, 3) growth and development of employees, and 4) organizational learning. This has led to a variety of awards for quality, from the Deming Prize for Total Quality Management in 1965 to recent J.D. Power awards for automobile quality. This reputation for quality was instrumental in Toyota's worldwide growth.

Toyota invested heavily in U.S. manufacturing facilities, especially those for full-size pickup trucks and sports-utility vehicles. With the economic downturn beginning in 2008, Toyota found itself with excess manufacturing capacity. The company moved quickly to shut down two factories for several months each and to switch production in another from the Highlander SUV to the Prius. Every forward-looking company must make long-term investment decisions based on uncertain predictions. Despite using the best information available at the time the decision is made, some predictions subsequently turn out to be incorrect. Consequently, some investment decisions do not turn out well, as illustrated by some of Toyota's investments in production facilities. This chapter focuses on investment decisions, which are critical to the long-term success of most organizations. ■

© EPA European Pressphoto Agency B.V./Alamy

The Toyota Prius was the first mass-produced hybrid vehicle.

Capital Budgeting for Programs or Projects

Major corporations such as Toyota are not the only companies that face decisions about capital investment and expansion. Every company makes decisions about when and how to spend money on major projects. This chapter concentrates on investment decisions for programs or projects that affect financial results over a period longer than just the current year. Such decisions typically require commitment of relatively large amounts of resources—called capital outlays—in anticipation of future benefits that are often uncertain. The term **capital budgeting** describes the long-term planning for long-term investment decisions such as (1) investment in new equipment, (2) replacement of assets, (3) expansion of facilities, (4) investment in employee training programs, or (5) expenditures to improve process efficiency and reduce future costs. We discuss a number of specific investment examples in this chapter, but it is important to remember that capital-budgeting concepts apply to a wide variety of decisions.

Capital budgeting has three phases: (1) identifying potential investments, (2) choosing which investments to make (which includes gathering data to aid the decision), and (3) follow-up monitoring, or "post-audit," of the investments. The cost-management system often provides information to help managers assess the future cash flows needed as inputs to capital-budgeting models. In addition, accountants provide post-audit information to assess the success of projects. Let's take a look at how some capital-budgeting models work.

capital budgeting
The long-term planning for investment commitments with returns spread over time, typically over multiple years.

Discounted-Cash-Flow Models

The most widely used capital-budgeting models are **discounted-cash-flow (DCF) models**. These models focus on a project's cash inflows and outflows while taking into account the time value of money. The value of a dollar today is greater than the value of a dollar to be received in the future. Therefore, investors expect to be repaid more than the original amount invested, and the excess of the amount repaid over the original amount is interest. On the investor side of the transaction, this interest is income, while on the borrower's side of the transaction, this interest is expense. More than 85% of the large industrial firms in the United States evaluate investment decisions using the DCF model, which explicitly incorporates the time value of money.

discounted-cash-flow (DCF) models
Capital-budgeting models that focus on cash inflows and outflows while taking into account the time value of money.

Major Aspects of DCF

As the name suggests, DCF models focus on cash flows rather than on net income. These models convert future cash flows into the corresponding **present values**, the value today of a future cash flow. Companies invest cash today because they expect to receive a larger amount of cash in future periods. DCF models compare today's cash outflows with the predicted future cash inflows and outflows by converting all cash flows into present values based on the theory of compound interest. If your knowledge of compound interest and time value of money is a little rusty, before you continue with the rest of the discussion of DCF methods.

present value (PV)
The value today of a future cash flow.

Net Present Value (NPV)

net-present-value (NPV) method

A discounted-cash-flow approach to capital budgeting that computes the present value of all expected future cash flows using a required rate of return.

required rate of return (hurdle rate, discount rate)

The minimum acceptable rate of return, based on the firm's cost of capital.

We will focus on the most widely-used version of DCF, the **net-present-value (NPV) method**. The NPV method computes the present value of all cash flows using an interest rate called the **required rate of return**. This rate, also called the **hurdle rate** or **discount rate**, depends on the risk of a proposed project—the higher the risk, the higher the rate. It is often based on the cost of capital—what the firm pays to acquire more capital. This rate is applied to the cash flows for a project, which can be classified into one of three categories: 1) the net initial cash flow, the cash outflow for acquisition of assets less any offsetting cash inflows from disposal of existing assets; 2) periodic cash flows during the life of the project; and 3) net cash flow at termination of the project.

Using the required rate, managers sum the present values of all expected future cash flows associated with the project and subtract the initial investment. This total is the project's **net present value (NPV)**. A positive NPV means that the present value of the project's future cash flows exceeds the investment, so the project should be undertaken. Conversely, a negative NPV means the investment exceeds the present value (PV) of the future cash flows, so the project should not be undertaken.

Objective I

Describe capital-budgeting decisions and use the net-present-value (NPV) method to make such decisions.

net present value

The sum of the present values of all expected cash flows.

Applying the NPV Method

To illustrate how DCF models work, we will use the following example throughout the rest of this section: Managers at Toyota's Tupelo, Mississippi, plant are contemplating the purchase of new, more efficient auto painting equipment that they expect will increase efficiency and produce operating savings. The cash flows associated with this investment consist of 1) an initial investment outflow of $5,827 at time zero for the acquisition cost, followed by 2) annual cash savings (equivalent to a cash inflow) of $2,000 at the end of each year for the 4-year life of the equipment, and 3) no net cash flow at termination of the project. The required rate of return is 10% per year.

To apply the NPV method, you can use the following three steps, which we illustrate in Exhibit 12-1.

1. *Identify the amount and timing of relevant expected cash inflows and outflows:* The right-hand side of Exhibit 12-1 sketches these cash flows, with outflows shown in parentheses. Sketches like this one can help you visualize costs and cost relationships over time.

	Present Value of $1, Discounted at 10%	Total Present Value	Sketch of Cash Flows at End of Year				
			0	1	2	3	4
Approach 1: Discounting Each Year's Cash Flows Separately*							
Cash flows							
Annual savings	.9091	$1,818		$2,000			
	.8264	1,653			$2,000		
	.7513	1,503				$2,000	
	.6830	1,366					$2,000
Present value of future inflows		$6,340					
Initial outlay	1.0000	(5,827)	$(5,827)				
Net present value		$ 513					
Approach 2: Using Annuity Table†							
Annual savings	3.1699	$6,340		$2,000	$2,000	$2,000	$2,000
Initial outlay	1.0000	(5,827)	$(5,827)				
Net present value		$ 513					

*Present values from Table B-1.

†Present value of annuity from Table B-2. (Incidentally, calculators or computers may give slightly different answers than do the tables because of rounding differences.)

Exhibit 12-1

Net-Present-Value Method

Initial investment, $5,827. Useful life, 4 years. Annual cash inflow from operations, $2,000. Required rate of return, 10%. Cash outflows are in parentheses, while cash inflows are not. Total present values are rounded to the nearest dollar.

2. ***Find the present value of each expected cash inflow or outflow:*** Find the PV factor for each year's cash flow from the correct row and column of the table. Multiply each expected cash inflow or outflow by the appropriate PV factor. For example, the present value of the $2,000 cash savings that will occur 2 years hence is $2,000 × .8264 = $1,653. As another example, the initial acquisition cost outflow of $5,827 at time zero has a present value of $5,827.

3. ***Sum the individual present values:*** The sum is the project's NPV. Accept a project whose NPV is positive, and reject a project whose NPV is negative.

The present value of the initial cash investment is $5,827, the present value of the four annual cash inflows is $6,340, and there are no cash flows at termination. Thus, the net present value of all the cash flows is $6,340 − $5,827 = $513. Because the net present value is positive, Toyota's managers should accept the investment.

Choice of the Correct Table

Exhibit 12-1 also shows another way to calculate the NPV, shown as approach 2. The basic steps are the same as for approach 1. The only difference is that approach 2 uses Table B-2 in Appendix B to find the present value of the four annual amounts. Table B-2 is an annuity table that provides discount factors for computing the PV of a series of equal cash flows at equal intervals. Because the four annual cash flows in our example are all equal, you can use Table B-2 to make one PV computation instead of using Table B-1 to make four individual computations. Table B-2 merely sums up the pertinent PV factors of Table B-1. Therefore, the annuity factor for 4 years at 10% is[1]

$$.9091 + .8264 + .7513 + .6830 = 3.1698$$

Beware of using the wrong table. Use Table B-1 for discounting individual amounts and Table B-2 for a series of equal amounts spread evenly in time. Instead of using Tables B-1 and B-2, you can use the PV function on a handheld calculator or in a spreadsheet program. When you use a calculator or spreadsheet, you still need to be sure to choose the proper function to discount a single amount or to discount a series of equal amounts. While you are initially learning the NPV method, we encourage you to use the tables and explicitly draw out all the cash flows. This will help you better understand the process of PV computation. Once you are comfortable with the method, you can take advantage of the speed and convenience of calculators and spreadsheets.

Making Managerial Decisions

For major capital investments, managers usually prepare a detailed NPV analysis. For smaller items, sometimes they make a quick calculation or use intuition. Suppose you are in charge of a company's mail room. An employee has suggested the purchase of a $12,000 letter sorting machine. She says that it will save 1 hour per day for 250 working days a year for an employee making a total of $12 per hour. She indicates that the $12,000 expenditure will save $15,000 over the machine's 5-year life. Should you approve the purchase?

Answers

The employee's calculation of the $15,000 total savings is correct:

1 hour × 250 days × $12/hour × 5 years = $15,000

However, her calculation ignores the time value of money. The $12,000 must be paid immediately, and the $15,000 of savings is spread over the next 5 years at $3,000 per year. You know that the present value of the savings is less than the $15,000 total, but the exact amount depends on the required

rate of return. Therefore, you must know the required rate before you can answer the question.

Suppose the required rate is 10%. Using Table B-1, the NPV is negative, $(627.90):

.9091 × $3,000 + .8264 × $3,000 + .7513 × $3,000 +
.6830 × $3,000 + .6209 × $3,000 − $12,000 =
$2,727.30 + $2,479.20 + $2,253.90 + $2,049.00 +
$1,862.70 = $11,372.10 − 12,000 = $(627.90).

Using Table B-2, the NPV is 3.7908 × $3,000 − $12,000 = $11,372.40 − $12,000 = $(627.60), which differs from the Table B-1 result by $.30 due to rounding error. With a 10% required rate, the NPV is negative and the investment should not be accepted.

Now, suppose instead the required rate is 5%. The lower discount rate increases the present value of the annual cost savings and the NPV becomes positive. Using Table B-2, 4.3295 × $3,000 − $12,000 = $12,988.50 − $12,000 = $988.50. With this change in the required rate of return, the investment should be accepted.

---

[1]Rounding error causes a .0001 difference between the Table B-2 factor and the summation of Table B-1 factors..

Effect of Required Rate

We have just seen that a decrease in the required rate of return can change the NPV from negative to positive. In general, the higher the required rate of return, the lower the PV of each future cash inflow. Why? Because the higher the rate of return, the more it costs you to wait for the cash rather than having it available today. Thus, higher required rates lead to lower NPVs.

For example, at a rate of 16%, the NPV of the project in Exhibit 12-1 would be −$231. That is, $2,000 × 2.7982 = $5,596, which is $231 less than the investment of $5,827, instead of the +$513 computed with a 10% rate. When the required rate of return is 16% rather than 10%, the project should be rejected.

Assumptions of the NPV Model

We make two major assumptions when using the NPV model. First, we assume a world of certainty. That is, we act as if the predicted cash inflows and outflows are certain to occur at the times specified. Second, we assume perfect capital markets. That is, if we need to get extra cash or invest excess cash at any time, we can borrow or lend money at the same interest rate, which is our required rate of return. In a world that meets these assumptions, no model could possibly be better than the NPV model.

Unfortunately, the real world has neither certainty nor perfect capital markets. Nevertheless, the NPV model is usually preferred to other models because the assumptions of most other models are even less realistic. The NPV model is not perfect, but it generally meets our cost-benefit criterion. That is, the benefit of better decisions based on NPV is greater than the cost of applying it. More sophisticated models often do not improve decisions enough to be worth their cost.

Review of Decision Rules

Be sure that you understand why the NPV method works, not just how to apply it. The decision maker in our example cannot directly compare an immediate outflow of $5,827 with a series of four future inflows of $2,000 each because of the time value of money. The NPV model adds together the net monetary units (such as dollars, euros, or yen) after converting them to their present value at time zero. The required rate of return measures the cost of using money.

Internal Rate of Return (IRR) Model

internal rate of return (IRR) model

A capital-budgeting model that determines the interest rate, the IRR, at which the NPV equals zero.

Another popular DCF model is the **internal rate of return (IRR) model**. This model determines the interest rate at which the NPV equals zero. The rate that makes the NPV = 0 is called the IRR. For Toyota's painting equipment, we know that a rate of 10% yields a positive NPV (as shown in Exhibit 12-1) while a rate of 16% yields a negative NPV (as discussed in the Effect of Required Rate section). Therefore, we know that the IRR, the rate that yields a NPV=0, is somewhere between 10% and 16%. The following graph plots the relationship between NPV and required rate of return for our example:

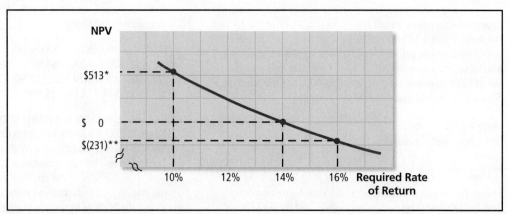

*($2,000 × 3.1699) − $5,827 = $513
**($2,000 × 2.7982) − $5,827 = $(231)

The IRR for our example can be found by trying values between 10% and 16%, converging on the return that yields a present value of zero. Most spreadsheets and many financial calculators include functions that solve for the IRR. As shown in the graph, the IRR for the painting equipment example is 14%. To confirm that this is the IRR, compute the NPV at a rate of 14%:

Outflow in today's dollars	$(5,827)
Inflows equivalent in today's dollars at 14%	5,827*
Net present value	$ 0

*$2,000 × 2.9137 from Table B-2 = $5,827.

The calculation confirms that at a required rate of return of 14%, the NPV is zero, and at this rate the decision maker is indifferent between having $5,827 now or having a stream of four annual inflows of $2,000 each.

Finance textbooks provide descriptions of the IRR method, and we will not go into details here. However, in most cases the IRR method gives equivalent decisions to the NPV method. In general, we find the following:

If IRR > required rate of return, then NPV > 0 and we should accept the project.

If IRR < required rate of return, then NPV < 0 and we should reject the project.

Because of the equivalence of NPV and IRR models for most investment proposals, we use only the NPV model for all the illustrations in this chapter.

Real Options

Whereas the IRR model is generally just an alternative formulation that yields decisions equivalent to the NPV model, the use of real options is an improvement on NPV. A **real options model** recognizes the value of contingent investments—that is, investments that a company can adjust as it learns more about their potential for success. For example, a project that a company can implement in stages, where investment in one stage occurs only if the previous stage was successful, has an advantage over an "all or nothing" project, one where the entire investment must take place up front.

The real options framework has some non-intuitive implications. For example, suppose that a project can either be implemented all at once or implemented in stages at greater cost. Despite the higher cost, staging the project might nonetheless be a preferred alternative if the company gains enough information in the early stages to make better decisions in the later stages. A real options model recognizes the value of such staging. Like the IRR model, we will leave the details of real options to the finance textbooks. However, real options models are an important innovation, and these models are becoming increasingly popular.

real options model
A capital-budgeting model that recognizes the value of contingent investments—that is, investments that a company can adjust as it learns more about its potential for success.

Sensitivity Analysis and Risk Assessment in DCF Models

The NPV model finds the present value of a set of predicted cash flows, but because the future is uncertain, actual cash inflows may differ from what was predicted. Managers often use sensitivity analysis to deal with this uncertainty. Sensitivity analysis determines what would occur if actual cash inflows and outflows differ from what was predicted. The analysis addresses what-if questions such as *What will happen to the NPV if my predictions of useful life or periodic cash flows or cash flows at termination change?*

Sensitivity analysis allows managers to find immediate answers about the effects of possible future events. It also helps managers evaluate prediction risk by showing how sensitive the decision is to changes in predictions. If only a small change in predicted cash flows would change the NPV for a project from positive NPV to negative, the project is subject to high prediction risk. The best way to understand sensitivity analysis is to see it in action, so let's apply sensitivity analysis to our example.

The Toyota managers know that the annual cash savings in Exhibit 12-1 could fall below the predicted level of $2,000. Suppose the managers want to know how far the annual cash savings could drop before the NPV becomes negative? The managers find the value of annual cash inflows that result in NPV = 0:

$$NPV = 0$$
$$(3.1699 \times cash flow) - \$5,827 = 0$$
$$cash flow = \$5,827 \div 3.1699$$
$$= \$1,838$$

Objective 2

Use sensitivity analysis to evaluate the effect of changes in predictions on investment decisions.

This sensitivity analysis shows that if the annual cash savings fall below $1,838, the NPV falls below zero, and the managers would reject the project. Therefore, annual cash savings can drop only $2,000 − $1,838 = $162, or 8.1% below the predicted amount, before the managers would change their decision.

Sensitivity analysis can become complicated very quickly, and manual calculations can be complex and tedious. Fortunately, there is a good deal of sensitivity analysis software available that does the calculations, thus, permitting managers and accountants to focus on interpreting the results of the analysis.

The NPV Comparison of Two Projects

Objective 3

Calculate the NPV difference between two projects using both the total project and differential approaches.

So far we have seen how to use the NPV method to evaluate a single project. In practice, managers rarely look at only one project or option at a time. Instead, managers compare several options to see which is the best or most profitable. We will now see how to use NPV to compare two or more alternatives.

Total Project Versus Differential Approach

Two common methods for comparing alternatives are (1) the total project approach and (2) the differential approach.

total project approach

A method for comparing alternatives that computes the total impact on cash flows for each alternative and then converts these total cash flows to their present values.

The **total project approach** computes the total impact on cash flows for each alternative and then converts these total cash flows to their present values. The alternative with the largest NPV of total cash flows is best. The total project approach is the most popular approach, and it can be used with any number of alternatives.

The **differential approach** computes the differences in cash flows between alternatives and then converts these differences to their present values. We cannot use this method to compare more than two alternatives.

differential approach

A method for comparing alternatives that computes the differences in cash flows between alternatives and then converts these differences in cash flows to their present values.

Let's compare the differential and total project approaches. Consider a motor that drives one of the assembly lines at Toyota's San Antonio plant. Assume that Toyota purchased the motor 3 years ago for $56,000. It has a remaining useful life of 5 years but will require a major overhaul at the end of two more years at a cost of $10,000. Its disposal value now is $20,000. Its predicted disposal value in 5 years is $8,000, assuming that the company does the scheduled $10,000 major overhaul. The predicted cash-operating costs of this motor are $40,000 annually. A sales representative has offered a substitute motor for $51,000. The new motor will reduce annual cash-operating costs by $10,000, will not require any overhauls, will have a useful life of 5 years, and will have a disposal value of $3,000. If the required rate of return is 14%, what should Toyota do to minimize long-run costs: keep the old machine or replace it with the new one? (Try to solve this problem yourself before examining the solution that follows.)

Regardless of the approach used, perhaps the hardest part of making capital-budgeting decisions is predicting the relevant cash flows accurately and completely. Seeing which events will cause money to flow either in or out can be complex, especially when there are many sources of cash flows. However, you cannot compare alternatives if you do not know their cash flows, so the first step for either the total project or differential approach is to estimate the relevant cash flows. Exhibit 12-2 sketches these cash flows for each approach.

Total Project Approach: For the total project approach we list the cash flows for each project, replace or keep, separately. We then determine the NPV of the cash flows for each individual project and choose the project with the largest positive NPV or smallest negative NPV. Exhibit 12-2 shows that the NPV of replacing the motor, −132,435, is better than the −$140,864 NPV of keeping the old motor. The advantage is $140,864 − $132,435 = $8,429. Most cash flows are negative because these are the costs of operating the motor. The alternative with the lowest cost—the smallest negative NPV—is the most desirable.

Differential Approach: For the differential approach, we first list the difference in cash flow for each year. In other words, assume implementation of one of the projects as a baseline and perform a differential analysis. Suppose we use keeping the old machine as the baseline. Then we subtract the cash flows for keeping from the cash flows for replacement. This isolates the advantages (cash inflows or cost savings) and disadvantages (cash outflows) of replacement compared to the baseline, keeping the machine. (Remember that cash inflows are positive numbers, while cash outflows are negative.) Next, calculate the NPV of the differential cash flows.

Exhibit 12-2
Total Project Versus Differential Approach to Net Present Value

	Present Value Discount Factor, at 14%	Total Present Value	Sketch of After-Tax Cash Flows at End of Year					
			0	1	2	3	4	5
I. Total Project Approach								
A. Replace								
Recurring cash operating costs, using an annuity table*	3.4331	$(102,993)		$(30,000)	$(30,000)	$(30,000)	$(30,000)	$(30,000)
Disposal value, end of year 5	.5194	1,558						$ 3,000
Initial required investment	1.0000	(31,000)	$(31,000)					
NPV of net cash flows		$(132,435)						
B. Keep								
Recurring cash operating costs, using an annuity table*	3.4331	$(137,324)		$(40,000)	$(40,000)	$(40,000)	$(40,000)	$(40,000)
Overhaul, end of year 2	.7695	(7,695)			$(10,000)			
Disposal value, end of year 5	.5194	4,155						$ 8,000
NPV of net cash flows		$(140,864)						
Difference in NPV between the alternatives		$ 8,429						
II. Differential Approach								
A–B. Analysis confined to differences								
Recurring cash operating savings, using an annuity table*	3.4331	$ 34,331		$ 10,000	$ 10,000	$ 10,000	$ 10,000	$ 10,000
Overhaul avoided, end of year 2	.7695	7,695			$ 10,000			
Difference in disposal values, end of year 5	.5194	(2,597)						$ (5,000)
Incremental initial investment	1.0000	(31,000)	$(31,000)					
Difference in NPV between alternatives		$ 8,429						

*Table B-2, Appendix B.

If the NPV is positive, choose the replacement alternative; if it is negative, choose the baseline alternative to keep the motor. Whereas the total project approach computed the difference in the NPVs of the two projects, the differential method computes the NPV of the difference in cash flows of the two projects. Both give the same total difference, an $8,429 advantage to replacement.

Exhibit 12-2 illustrates that both methods produce the same answer as long as you are considering only two alternatives. However, to compare more than two alternatives, you should use the total project approach.

Summary Problem for Your Review

PROBLEM

Review the example shown in Exhibit 12-2, page 453. Conduct three independent sensitivity analyses:

1. Compute the difference in the NPV of the alternatives if the required rate of return were 20% instead of 14%.
2. Compute the difference in the NPV of the alternatives if predicted cash operating costs of the new motor were $35,000 annually instead of $30,000, using the 14% discount rate.
3. By how much may the annual cash operating savings fall short of the $10,000 predicted amount before the difference in NPV between the alternatives reaches zero? Use the original discount rate of 14%.

SOLUTION

1. You can use either the total project approach or the differential approach. The differential approach shows the following:

	Present Value
Recurring cash operating savings, using an annuity table (Table B-2, p. A9): 2.9906 × $10,000 =	$ 29,906
Overhaul avoided: .6944 × $10,000 =	6,944
Difference in disposal values: .4019 × $5,000 =	(2,010)
Incremental initial investment	(31,000)
Difference in NPV between the alternatives	$ 3,840

With a 20% required rate of return, replacement is still the preferred alternative. However, the difference in NPV is reduced from the $8,429 shown in Exhibit 12-2 to $3,840.

2.

Difference in NPV value in Exhibit 12-2	$ 8,429
Present value of additional $5,000 annual operating costs 3.4331 × $5,000	(17,166)
Difference in NPV between the alternatives	$ (8,737)

With $5,000 less in annual savings, the new motor yields a negative difference in the NPV between the alternatives, and therefore is not desirable.

3. Let X = annual cash operating savings and find the value of X so that the difference in NPV between the two alternatives = 0. Then,

$$0 = 3.4331(X) + \$7,695 - \$2,597 - \$31,000$$
$$3.4331(X) = \$25,902$$
$$X = \$7,545$$

(Note that the $7,695, $2,597, and $31,000 are shown at the bottom of Exhibit 12-2.)

If the annual savings fall from $10,000 to $7,545, a decrease of $2,455 or almost 25%, the NPV will fall to zero.

An alternative way to obtain the same answer would be to divide the NPV of $8,429 (see bottom of Exhibit 12-2) by 3.4331, obtaining $2,455, the amount of the annual difference in savings that will eliminate the $8,429 of NPV.

Relevant Cash Flows

Predicting cash flows is often the hardest part of capital budgeting. We organize the discussion of predicting cash flows into three project phases: (1) cash flows at project initiation, (2) cash flows at project termination, and (3) periodic cash flows between project initiation and termination.

Objective 4

Identify relevant cash flows for NPV analyses.

Predicting Relevant Cash Flows

INITIAL CASH INFLOWS AND OUTFLOWS   These cash flows include both outflows for the purchase and installation of new equipment and other assets (such as additional investments in working capital) required by the project and cash inflows or outflows from disposal of any items that are replaced. For example, in Exhibit 12-2, we subtracted the $20,000 cash inflow from selling the old motor that was being replaced from the $51,000 cash outflow to purchase the new motor, resulting in the initial net cash outflow of $31,000. As another example, if instead of selling the old motor the company had to pay to dismantle it, the net cash outflow at project initiation would be $51,000 plus the cost of dismantling the old motor.

CASH INFLOWS AND OUTFLOWS AT TERMINATION   At project termination, assets may have cash disposal values that represent a cash inflow. In other cases, there may be costs at termination to dispose of an asset that represent a cash outflow.

OPERATING CASH FLOWS DURING THE LIFE OF THE PROJECT   The major purpose of most investments is to affect periodic cash inflows and outflows during the life of the project. Many of these effects are difficult to measure, and three points deserve special mention:

1. The only relevant cash flows are those that will differ among alternatives, and it is frequently difficult to identify exactly which costs will differ. Fixed overhead will often be the same under all the available alternatives. If so, you can safely ignore it.
2. We treat a reduction in a cash outflow (a cash savings) the same as a cash inflow—both signify increases in value. Similarly, we treat a reduction in a cash inflow the same as a cash outflow—both signify decreases in value.
3. Remember that you are predicting cash inflows and outflows, not revenues and expenses. When there are differences between accrual basis revenues and expenses versus the corresponding cash inflows and cash outflows, the DCF model requires you to use the cash flow. For example, we might record a $10,000 sale on credit as accrual revenue in one period but if the related cash inflow comes in a later period, the $10,000 cash inflow will be recognized in the DCF model in the later period. In this chapter, we generally assume that cash inflows are equivalent to accrual revenues and that cash outflows are equivalent to accrual expenses, except in two major areas—depreciation and gains or losses on disposal of assets.

There is no cash outflow corresponding to depreciation expense in NPV calculations. Why not? Because depreciation expense is not a cash flow. Depreciation is an accrual expense that allocates the cost of a long-lived asset across the periods during which the asset is used. It is easy to confuse depreciation and cash flows because they are related to a common set of facts. Suppose a company acquires a machine for $54,000 that will be used for 5 years and then sold for $4,000. For NPV purposes, the relevant cash flows are a $54,000 cash outflow at acquisition and a $4,000 cash inflow at disposal. For financial reporting purposes, depreciation expense is the $54,000 acquisition cost less the $4,000 disposal value, a total of $50,000 spread across the 5-year life of the asset. For NPV purposes, it is incorrect to account for the acquisition and disposal cash flows and then also deduct depreciation over the asset's life as cash outflows—this would be like counting the net of the acquisition cost and disposal value twice.

The accrual gain or loss on disposal of an asset being replaced is another potential source of confusion. The gain or loss calculated by comparing the disposal value of the asset with its depreciated book value is not the cash flow. Rather, the cash flow is the disposal value. For example, suppose the asset in the previous example was purchased to replace an asset with a book value of $5,000. If the actual cash disposal value of the asset being replaced is $6,000, there is a gain on disposal of $1,000. Is the relevant initial cash flow from disposal of the replaced asset the $1,000 gain, the $5,000 book value, or the $6,000 selling price? It is the $6,000 selling price, the cash inflow from selling the asset that is being replaced.

Business First

Does DCF Apply to Technology Investments?

Although DCF models are widely used, some have criticized them for leading to overly cautious investment decisions in information technology (IT). The critics maintain that the benefits of IT investments are difficult to quantify and such investments lead to unforeseen opportunities. By ignoring some of the potential benefits and opportunities, companies pass up desirable IT investments.

The economic shakeout in 2001 and 2002 identified the winners and losers—and there were plenty of both. Winners (identified by *BusinessWeek*) included Expedia, Amazon, eBay, Yahoo!, and Dell. Losers, at least in the short run, included Hewlett-Packard, Barnes & Noble, AOL Time Warner, drkoop.com, and many startups. What differentiated winners from losers? Partly it was how they evaluated capital investment decisions. Some were overly cautious in employing technology. But others forgot the basic economics of investment analysis. Instead of focusing on cash flows and DCF analysis, companies touted their revenue per dollar of investment or, even worse, Web site hits per dollar of investment. They forgot that only positive net cash flows generate value. Increasing revenues are worse than worthless if related expenses grow faster so that net cash flows are negative. No one becomes rich because of an increasing number of visits to their Web site if the visits do not translate into cash flows.

How did the winners approach capital-budgeting decisions? First, they identified ways that technology solutions could generate cash—either new inflows or savings of outflows. Their analysis showed whether technology investments would become profitable and how profitable they would be. Second, the companies did not try to protect existing business while simultaneously pursuing new technology. If new technology served customers better than existing technology, companies lagging in technology would lose them anyway. And finally, they used DCF analysis. They realized that dollars in the future are worth less than those today, so they needed large future profits to justify investments that would not pay off in the short term.

In the aftermath of the technology crash, many companies focused on how to correctly apply DCF to technology investments. Microsoft developed guides to its software that showed how to apply DCF to investments in technology and developed blogs to allow managers to share experiences applying DCF methods.

Companies also used new developments in finance and accounting to aid in the application of DCF analyses. For example, Scott Gamster of Grant Thornton's Performance Management Practice suggested using activity-based costing (ABC) to better estimate future cash flows. Analyses that focused primarily on how technology reduced direct costs ignored potentially large savings in indirect costs. Because an ABC system focuses on indirect costs, it can help identify other cost impacts of new technology systems. The attention to activities helps managers better assess the various impacts of new systems.

Many firms also began to apply real options theory to value technology investments. For example, the Yankee 24, a shared electronic banking network in New England that subsequently merged with NYCE Payments Network, applied real options theory to the decision on timing the deployment of point-of-sale debit services. The method explicitly recognized the future opportunities created by a current investment decision, and it used the complete range of possible outcomes to determine the investment's value.

Criticisms of using DCF for investment decisions were primarily criticisms of incorrect or incomplete applications of it. The criticisms have led to a better understanding of how to apply DCF to technology investments and to refinements in DCF analysis that are especially useful to investments in technology.

Sources: Adapted from S. Gamster, "Using Activity Based Management to Justify ERP Implementations," *Journal of Cost Management*, September/October 1999, pp. 24–33; M. Benaroch and R. J. Kauffman, "A Case for Using Real Options Pricing Analysis to Evaluate Information Technology Project Investments," *Information Systems Research*, March 1999, pp. 70–76; "The E-Business Surprise," *BusinessWeek*, May 12, 2003, pp. 60–68; Microsoft Dynamics, "Using ROI analysis to prioritize technology purchases," March 7, 2007, http://community.dynamics.com/blogs/articles/archive/2007/03/07/using-roi-analysis-to-prioritize-technology-purchases.aspx.

Cash Flows for Investments in Technology

Many capital-budgeting decisions compare a potential investment in improved technology versus the alternative of retaining the existing technology. For example, consider investment in a highly automated production system to replace a traditional system. Cash flows predicted for the automated system should be compared with those predicted for continuation of the existing system into the future. However, it is important to note that the current cash flows for the existing system may not be the expected future cash flows from the existing system. Why? Because the competitive environment is changing. If competitors invest in automated systems, continuing with an existing system that produces lower quality or less reliable output may cause a decline in sales and cash inflows.

Suppose a company currently has a $10,000 net cash inflow annually using a traditional system. Investing in an automated system will increase the net cash inflow to $12,000. Failure to switch to the automated system will result in lower quality output and cause net cash inflows to fall to $8,000. The relevant annual cash flow during the life of the investment is a net cash inflow of $12,000 − $8,000 = $4,000, not $12,000 − $10,000 = $2,000. Similar situations arise in many technology investments such as those described in the Business First box above.

Income Tax Effects

For companies that are subject to income taxes, another type of cash flow enters into capital-budgeting decisions: income taxes. (Tax-exempt organizations such as churches, schools, or governmental units do not pay income taxes and therefore do not have tax-related cash flows.) Income taxes paid by companies are cash outflows. Savings of income taxes that would have been paid are equivalent to cash inflows.

The basic role of tax-related cash flows in capital budgeting does not differ from that of any other cash outflow. However, income taxes modify the cash flows of projects for taxable entities by making the government a profit-sharing partner. For example, if the annual cash inflow from a project is $1 million, a 40% tax rate shrinks the net inflow to $600,000. Why? Because the company would have to pay 40% × $1 million = $400,000 of the inflow in taxes, leaving just $600,000 net inflow for the company. The cash flow before considering the effect of income taxes is called the pretax cash flow (in this example, $1 million), and the amount after the effect of taxes is the **after-tax cash flow** ($600,000). All of our previous examples in the chapter have ignored the effect of taxes so the cash flows discussed have been pretax cash flows.

Corporations in the United States pay both federal and state taxes on their income. Federal income tax rates rise as income rises. The current federal tax rate on ordinary corporate taxable income below $50,000 is 15%. Rates then increase until companies with taxable income over $335,000 pay between 34% and 38% on additional income. State tax rates vary widely from state to state. Therefore, the total tax rate a company has to pay, federal rates plus state rates, also varies widely.

In capital budgeting, the relevant tax rate is the **marginal income tax rate**, the tax rate paid on incremental cash flows from a project. Suppose a corporation pays income taxes of 15% on the first $50,000 of pretax income and 30% on pretax income over $50,000. What is the company's marginal income tax rate when it initially has $75,000 of pretax income? The marginal rate is 30%, because the company will pay 30% of any incremental income in taxes. In contrast, the company's average income tax rate is only 20% (that is, 15% × $50,000 + 30% × $25,000 = $15,000 of taxes on $75,000 of pretax income). The marginal tax rate generally depends on both the initial amount of income and the amount of incremental income. Suppose the initial pretax income had been $40,000 in our example. Then the marginal tax rate on incremental income up to $10,000 would be 15% but incremental income beyond $10,000 would increase the marginal rate to 30%. When we assess tax effects of capital-budgeting decisions in the examples that follow, we always assume a single marginal tax rate applies to all incremental cash flows for a project.

Effects of Depreciation Deductions

Organizations that pay income taxes generally keep two sets of books—one set that follows the rules for financial reporting and one set that follows the tax rules. This practice is not illegal or immoral—it is necessary. Tax reporting rules are designed to achieve certain social goals. These rules are in many instances different from the financial reporting rules designed to best measure an organization's financial results and position.

Managers have an obligation to stockholders to minimize taxes to the extent permitted by law. Minimization of taxes permitted by law is called tax avoidance. In contrast, reduction of taxes by illegally recording fictitious deductions or failing to report income is called tax evasion. Managers who avoid taxes get bonuses; those who evade taxes often land in jail. Because the line between tax evasion and tax avoidance is sometimes gray, it is important to act both legally and ethically when trying to minimize taxes.

One item that usually differs between tax reporting and financial reporting is depreciation. Recall that depreciation spreads the cost of an asset over its useful life. U.S. tax laws allow **accelerated depreciation**, which charges a larger proportion of an asset's cost to the earlier years and less to later years. In contrast, an asset's depreciation for financial reporting purposes is often the same each year, called straight-line depreciation. For example, a $10,000 asset depreciated over a 5-year useful life results in straight-line depreciation of $10,000 ÷ 5 = $2,000 each year. In contrast, accelerated depreciation provides more than $2,000 of depreciation per year in the early years and less than $2,000 in the later years. In addition, U.S. tax laws generally permit companies to spread the cost of an asset over a **recovery period**—the number of years over which a company can depreciate an asset for tax purposes—that is shorter than the assets' useful life that the company uses to calculate depreciation for financial reporting purposes.

<table>
<tr><td colspan="3" align="center">**Annual Income Statement Effects**</td></tr>
<tr><td>(S)</td><td>Sales</td><td>$130,000</td></tr>
<tr><td>(E)</td><td>Less: Expenses, excluding depreciation</td><td>$ 70,000</td></tr>
<tr><td>(D)</td><td>Depreciation (straight-line)</td><td>25,000</td></tr>
<tr><td></td><td>Total expenses</td><td>$ 95,000</td></tr>
<tr><td></td><td>Income before taxes</td><td>$ 35,000</td></tr>
<tr><td>(T)</td><td>Income taxes at 40%</td><td>14,000</td></tr>
<tr><td>(I)</td><td>Net income</td><td>$ 21,000</td></tr>
<tr><td></td><td colspan="2">Total after-tax effect on cash is</td></tr>
<tr><td></td><td colspan="2">either S − E − T = $130,000 − $70,000 − $14,000 = $46,000</td></tr>
<tr><td></td><td colspan="2">or I + D = $21,000 + $25,000 = $46,000</td></tr>
<tr><td colspan="3" align="center">**Annual Cash Flow Effects**</td></tr>
<tr><td></td><td>Cash effects of operations:</td><td></td></tr>
<tr><td>(S − E)</td><td>Pretax cash inflow from operations: $130,000 − $70,000</td><td>$ 60,000</td></tr>
<tr><td></td><td>Multiplied by (1 − tax rate)</td><td>× .60</td></tr>
<tr><td></td><td>After-tax cash inflow from operations</td><td>$ 36,000</td></tr>
<tr><td></td><td>Cash effects of depreciation tax deduction:</td><td></td></tr>
<tr><td>(D)</td><td>Depreciation tax deduction: $125,000 ÷ 5</td><td>$ 25,000</td></tr>
<tr><td></td><td>Multiplied by tax rate</td><td>× .40</td></tr>
<tr><td></td><td>Tax savings due to depreciation</td><td>10,000</td></tr>
<tr><td></td><td>Total after-tax effect on cash</td><td>$ 46,000</td></tr>
</table>

Exhibit 12-3
Toyota Machine
Basic Analysis of Income Statement, Income Taxes, and Cash Flows

Exhibit 12-3 shows the interrelationship of income before taxes, income taxes, and depreciation for a hypothetical asset owned by Toyota. Assume that Toyota's U.S. operation purchases for $125,000 cash a machine that produces replacement parts used in Lexus exhaust systems. The machine has a 5-year recovery period and also a 5-year useful life. Management expects the value of the machine at the end of its useful life to be zero. Toyota uses straight-line depreciation for both financial reporting and tax purposes, resulting in annual depreciation of $25,000. Using the machine produces annual sales revenue of $130,000 and expenses (excluding depreciation) of $70,000. For this example, and the remaining examples in this chapter, we assume that revenues equal cash inflows and that all expenses other than depreciation equal cash outflows. We also assume a marginal tax rate of 40% applies to all incremental cash flows and that the income tax flows occur at the same time as the related pretax cash flows. Here, we assume that both the net ($130,000 – $70,000) = $60,000 pretax cash inflow from the machine and the related tax payments occur at the end of each year during the 5-year life of the machine.

The bottom part of Exhibit 12-3 shows the three components of the after-tax cash flow: cash inflow from operations, income taxes on the inflows from operations, and income-tax savings from depreciation. Consider first the cash inflow from operations and the related tax effect. Each additional $1 of net cash inflow from operations also results in a cash outflow for income tax payments of $.40, leaving a net cash inflow of $.60. Thus, the after-tax effect of the $60,000 pretax net cash inflow from operations is an after-tax inflow of ($60,000 – (.4 × $60,000) = $60,000 × .6 = $36,000.

The cash flow effect of the depreciation tax deduction is a decrease in the cash outflow for income taxes, equivalent to a cash inflow. We compute the tax savings due to the depreciation tax deduction by multiplying the depreciation of $25,000 by the tax rate, or $25,000 × .40 = $10,000. The depreciation deduction reduces taxes, and thereby increases cash flows, by $10,000 annually.

Exhibit 12-4 analyzes the entire set of cash flows for Toyota's machine. The initial $125,000 investment buys two 5-year streams of cash: (1) net after-tax cash flows from operations of $36,000 annually plus (2) annual savings of $10,000 of income tax outflows due to the depreciation tax deduction over the recovery period. The after-tax NPV for the investment in this asset is $40,821, so Toyota management should accept it.

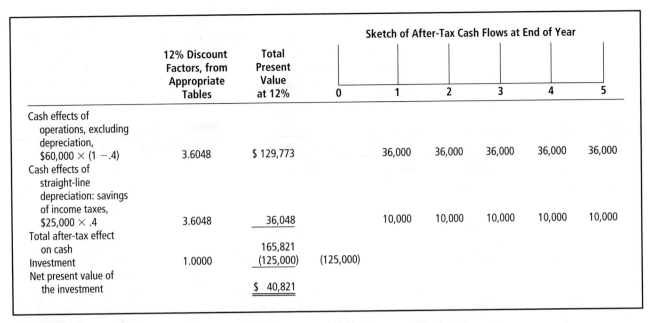

	12% Discount Factors, from Appropriate Tables	Total Present Value at 12%	Sketch of After-Tax Cash Flows at End of Year					
			0	1	2	3	4	5
Cash effects of operations, excluding depreciation, $60,000 × (1 − .4)	3.6048	$ 129,773		36,000	36,000	36,000	36,000	36,000
Cash effects of straight-line depreciation: savings of income taxes, $25,000 × .4	3.6048	36,048		10,000	10,000	10,000	10,000	10,000
Total after-tax effect on cash		165,821						
Investment	1.0000	(125,000)	(125,000)					
Net present value of the investment		$ 40,821						

Exhibit 12-4
Impact of Income Taxes on Capital-Budgeting Analysis
Assume: original cost of equipment, $125,000; 5-year recovery period with straight-line depreciation assumed for simplicity; 5-year useful life; zero terminal disposal value; pretax annual net cash inflow from operations, $60,000; income tax rate, 40%; required after-tax rate of return, 12%. All items are in dollars except discount factors. The after-tax cash flows are from Exhibit 12-3.

Summary Problem for Your Review

PROBLEM

Consider Toyota's purchase of the $125,000 machine analyzed in Exhibits 12-3 and 12-4. Suppose the machine had a useful life of 6 years, but the recovery period remains 5 years. What is the net present value of the investment?

SOLUTION

The present value of the tax savings will not change because only the recovery period, not the useful life, affects the depreciation deductions. The tax law specifies recovery periods for various types of depreciable assets. The economic useful life of the asset may be different than the recovery period permitted by tax law. Thus, a longer useful life for an asset increases the present value of the operating cash flows but does not change the PV of the tax savings.

There will be one extra year of operating savings in year 6. The present value of the additional operating savings in year 6 is $36,000 × .5066 = $18,238. Therefore, the net present value is $59,059:

Original NPV (from Exhibit 12-4)	$40,821
Added PV of savings in year 6	18,238
NPV	$59,059

Timing of Depreciation Tax Deductions and Cash Flow Effects

The value of the depreciation tax deduction depends not only on the amount of the reduction in cash payments for income taxes but also on the timing of the reduction. A $1 reduction now is worth more than a $1 reduction several years from now. To illustrate the importance of timing, reconsider the facts in Exhibit 12-4. Suppose that Toyota could deduct the entire initial investment immediately rather than spreading the cost over the 5-year life of the machine.

The immediate tax deduction of $125,000 would be the same as the total tax deduction of $5 \times$ $25,000 = $125,000 in Exhibit 12-4, and the total reduction in tax payments would be 40% $\times$ $125,000 = $50,000 in both cases. However, because the tax savings occur sooner, the present value of the immediate $125,000 deduction is $50,000 compared to only $36,048 when the deduction is spread over 5 years. As the following calculations show, when the entire $125,000 is deductible immediately the NPV will rise from $40,821 to $54,773:

	Present Values	
	As in Exhibit 12-4	Complete Write-Off Immediately
Cash effects of operations	$ 129,773	$ 129,773
Cash effects of depreciation	36,048	50,000
Total after-tax effect on cash	165,821	179,773
Investment	(125,000)	(125,000)
Net present value	$ 40,821	$ 54,773

In general, the earlier you can take a depreciation deductions, the greater the PV of the income tax savings. Therefore, a shorter recovery period and a depreciation method that takes more of the depreciation sooner during the recovery period will increase the PV of the tax deduction.

Modified Accelerated Cost Recovery System (MACRS)

modified accelerated cost recovery system (MACRS)

The method companies use to depreciate most assets under U.S. income tax laws.

Depreciation methods that take more depreciation sooner are called accelerated depreciation methods. The example discussed in Exhibits 12-3 and 12-4 assumed that Toyota used straight-line depreciation for tax purposes. However, under U.S. income tax laws, companies depreciate most assets using the **modified accelerated cost recovery system (MACRS)**. This system specifies a recovery period and an accelerated depreciation schedule for all types of assets. The MACRS system places each asset in one of the eight classes shown in Exhibit 12-5.

Exhibit 12-5

Examples of Assets in Modified Accelerated Cost Recovery System (MACRS) Classes

3-year	Special tools for several specific industries, tractor units for over-the-road
5-year	Automobiles, trucks, research equipment, computers, machinery and equipment in selected industries
7-year	Office furniture, railroad tracks, machinery and equipment in a majority of industries
10-year	Water transportation equipment, machinery and equipment in selected industries
15-year	Most land improvements, machinery and equipment in selected industries
20-year	Farm buildings, electricity generation and distribution equipment
27.5-year	Residential rental property
31.5-year	Nonresidential real property

Exhibit 12-6

Selected MACRS Depreciation Schedules

Tax Year	3-Year Property	5-Year Property	7-Year Property	10-Year Property
1	33.33%	20.00%	14.29%	10.00%
2	44.45	32.00	24.49	18.00
3	14.81	19.20	17.49	14.40
4	7.41	11.52	12.49	11.52
5		11.52	8.93	9.22
6		5.76	8.92	7.37
7			8.93	6.55
8			4.46	6.55
9				6.56
10				6.55
11				3.28

Exhibit 12-6 presents MACRS depreciation schedules for recovery periods of 3, 5, 7, and 10 years. Note that each schedule extends 1 year beyond the recovery period because MACRS assumes one half-year of depreciation in the first year and one half-year in the final year. For example, a 3-year MACRS depreciation schedule has one half-year of depreciation in years 1 and 4 and a full year of depreciation in years 2 and 3. We can apply MACRS depreciation to the example in Exhibit 12-4 as follows, assuming that the machine that Toyota purchased is a 5-year MACRS asset:

Year	Tax Rate (1)	PV Factor at 12% (2)	Depreciation (3)	PV of Tax Savings (1) × (2) × (3)
1	.40	0.8929	$125,000 × .2000 = $25,000	$ 8,929
2	.40	0.7972	125,000 × .3200 = 40,000	12,755
3	.40	0.7118	125,000 × .1920 = 24,000	6,833
4	.40	0.6355	125,000 × .1152 = 14,400	3,660
5	.40	0.5674	125,000 × .1152 = 14,400	3,268
6	.40	0.5066	125,000 × .0576 = 7,200	1,459
				$36,904

How much did Toyota gain by using MACRS instead of straight-line depreciation? The $36,904 present value of tax savings is $856 higher with MACRS than the $36,048 present value achieved with straight-line depreciation (see Exhibit 12-4 on page 459).

Present Value of MACRS Depreciation Tax Deduction

The present value of the tax savings from depreciation is often referred to as the **depreciation tax shield**. As explained earlier, the value of a depreciation deduction depends on timing. Because MACRS specifies the timing of deductions for each recovery period, we can easily compute the present value of the depreciation tax shield for any recovery period.

Exhibit 12-7 provides present values for the depreciation deductions from $1 of investment using MACRS schedules for 3-, 5-, 7-, and 10-year recovery periods for a variety of interest

depreciation tax shield
The tax savings due to depreciation deductions, generally the present value of the product of the tax rate and the depreciation deduction.

Discount Rate	3-year	5-year	7-year	10-year
3%	0.9439	0.9215	0.9002	0.8698
4%	0.9264	0.8975	0.8704	0.8324
5%	0.9095	0.8746	0.8422	0.7975
6%	0.8931	0.8526	0.8155	0.7649
7%	0.8772	0.8315	0.7902	0.7344
8%	0.8617	0.8113	0.7661	0.7059
9%	0.8468	0.7919	0.7432	0.6792
10%	0.8322	0.7733	0.7214	0.6541
12%	0.8044	0.7381	0.6810	0.6084
14%	0.7782	0.7055	0.6441	0.5678
15%	0.7657	0.6902	0.6270	0.5492
16%	0.7535	0.6753	0.6106	0.5317
18%	0.7300	0.6473	0.5798	0.4993
20%	0.7079	0.6211	0.5517	0.4702
22%	0.6868	0.5968	0.5257	0.4439
24%	0.6669	0.5740	0.5019	0.4201
25%	0.6573	0.5631	0.4906	0.4090
26%	0.6479	0.5526	0.4798	0.3985
28%	0.6299	0.5327	0.4594	0.3787
30%	0.6128	0.5139	0.4404	0.3606
40%	0.5381	0.4352	0.3632	0.2896

Exhibit 12-7
Present Value of MACRS Depreciation Deductions for $1 Investment

rates. To see how these present values are derived, consider a company with a 5-year asset and a 12% required rate of return. The PV of $1 of MACRS depreciation is as follows:

Year	Depreciation* (1)	PV Factor at 12% (2)	PV of Depreciation (1) × (2)
1	$0.2000	0.8929	$0.1786
2	0.3200	0.7972	0.2551
3	0.1920	0.7118	0.1367
4	0.1152	0.6355	0.0732
5	0.1152	0.5674	0.0654
6	0.0576	0.5066	0.0292
Total Depreciation	$1.0000		
Present Value of $1 depreciation, shown in Exhibit 12-7			$0.7381

*From the 5-Year Property column of Exhibit 12-6.

You can find the PV of the depreciation tax shield from an investment in three steps:

1. Find the factor for the present value of the depreciation tax deductions from Exhibit 12-7 for the appropriate recovery period and required rate of return.
2. Multiply the factor by the amount of the investment to find the PV of the total tax deductions.
3. Multiply the PV of the total tax deductions by the marginal tax rate to find the PV of the total tax savings.

Consider Toyota's investment of $125,000 in a machine with a 5-year MACRS recovery period. A 12% after-tax required rate of return and a 40% tax rate produce a tax savings with a present value of .7381 × $125,000 × .40 = $36,905. (This differs by $1 from the $36,904 calculated earlier due only to the cumulative effect of rounding in the earlier calculation.)

Making Managerial Decisions

Why do managers prefer accelerated depreciation for tax purposes? Consider an investment of $100,000 in an asset with a 10-year economic life and a 10-year MACRS recovery period. The asset has no salvage value at the end of 10 years. The tax rate is 40%, and the required rate of return is 10%. What is the PV of the depreciation tax savings using straight-line (SL) depreciation? What is the PV of the depreciation tax savings using MACRS depreciation? Which depreciation method would you prefer if you were managing the company?

Answers

Straight-line depreciation = $10,000 per year, so tax savings with SL is .40 × $10,000 = $4,000 per year. The present value of the SL tax savings is $4,000 × 6.1446 = $24,578.40.

The PV of MACRS depreciation tax savings using Exhibit 12-7 is .6541 × $100,000 × .40 = $26,164.00. Although the total tax savings is $40,000 regardless of the depreciation method, the tax savings occur earlier under the MACRS accelerated depreciation schedule, which creates a greater PV by $26,164.00 − $24,578.40 = $1,585.60. By choosing MACRS rather than straight-line depreciation, the manager saves $1,585.60 for the company.

Tax Effects of Gains or Losses on Disposal at Termination

Objective 6

Explain the after-tax effect on cash received from the disposal of assets.

The disposal of equipment for cash can also affect income taxes. Suppose Toyota sells its $125,000 machine at the end of year 3 after taking 3 years of straight-line depreciation. If Toyota sells it for its net book value, $125,000 − (3 × $25,000) = $50,000, there is no taxable gain and therefore no effect on tax payments. If Toyota receives more than $50,000, there is a gain and an additional tax payment. If the company receives less than $50,000, there is a loss and a tax savings. The following table shows the effects on cash flow for sales prices of $70,000 and $20,000:

(a)	Cash proceeds of sale	$70,000	$ 20,000
	Book value: [$125,000 − (3 × $25,000)]	50,000	50,000
	Gain (loss)	$20,000	$(30,000)
	Effect on income taxes at 40%:		
(b)	Tax savings, an inflow effect: .40 × loss		$ 12,000
(c)	Tax paid, an outflow: .40 × gain	$ (8,000)	
	Net cash inflow from sale:		
	(a) plus (b)		$ 32,000
	(a) minus (c)	$62,000	

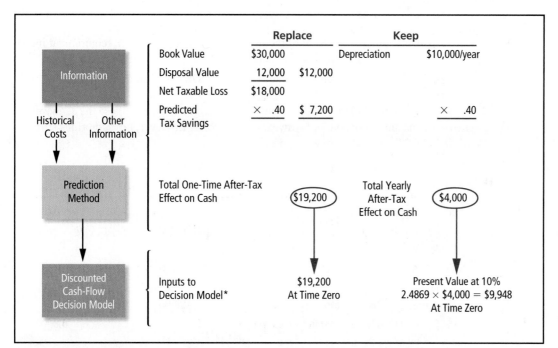

*There will be other related inputs to the replacement decision—for example, the cost of the new equipment, the tax effect of depreciation on the new equipment, and the differences in future annual cash flows from operations.

A second tax effect occurs when a company disposes of an asset before the end of its recovery period. In addition to taxable gains or losses, disposal eliminates future tax depreciation on the asset.

Suppose **General Electric** replaces some old copying equipment with a book value of $30,000, an expected terminal disposal value of zero, a current disposal value of $12,000, and 3 years remaining in its recovery period. For simplicity, assume that General Electric uses straight-line depreciation, amounting to $10,000 of depreciation per year. The tax rate is 40% and the required rate of return is 10%.

Exhibit 12-8 shows the cash flow effects due only to disposal of the old copying equipment. (That is, Exhibit 12-8 does not show the cost, annual cash flow effects, nor the depreciation tax savings related to the new copying equipment.) The cash inflow from disposal of the old copying equipment is $19,200, the disposal value plus the tax savings resulting from the tax loss on disposal. This immediate cash inflow is partially offset by the loss of future tax deductions of $10,000 per year for the next 3 years, which have a present value of 2.4869 × ($10,000 × 40%) = $9,948. The net cash inflow due to disposal of the old equipment is ($19,200 − $9,948) = $9,252.

Summary Problem for Your Review

PROBLEM

Consider the investment opportunity in Exhibit 12-4, page 459: original cost of machine, $125,000; 5-year useful life; zero terminal salvage value; pretax annual cash inflow from operations, $60,000; income tax rate, 40%; required after-tax rate of return, 12%. Assume the equipment is a 5-year MACRS asset for tax purposes. The NPV is as follows:

	Present Values (PV)
Cash effects of operations,*$60,000 × (1 − .40) × 3.6048	$129,773
Cash effects of depreciation on income tax savings using MACRS, $125,000 × .7381[†] × .40	36,905
Total after-tax effect on cash	$166,678
Investment	125,000
NPV	$ 41,678

*See Exhibit 12-4, page 459, for details.
[†]Factor .7381 is from Exhibit 12-7, page 461.

For each requirement, compute the NPV of the investment but consider each requirement independently. Assume the original depreciation schedule is not altered for either requirement.

1. Suppose Toyota ends up selling the equipment for $20,000 cash immediately after the end of year 5.
2. Ignore the assumption in number 1. Return to the original data. Suppose the economic life of the machine turns out to be 8 years, not 5 years. However, tax authorities still allow MACRS cost recovery over 5 years.

SOLUTION

1.

NPV as given		$41,678
Cash proceeds of sale	$20,000	
Book value	0	
Taxable gain	$20,000	
Income taxes at 40%	8,000	
Total after-tax effect on cash	$12,000	
PV of $12,000 to be received in 5 years at 12%, $12,000 × .5674		6,809
NPV of investment		$48,487

2.

NPV as given		$41,678
Add the PV of $36,000 per year for 8 years		
Discount factor of 4.9676* × $36,000 =	$178,834	
Deduct the PV of $36,000 per year for 5 years	129,773	
Increase in PV		49,061
NPV		$90,739

*Factor 4.9676 is from Table B-2.

The investment becomes more attractive with the increased economic life because there are operating savings for an additional three years and no reduction in the tax savings from depreciation.

Objective 7

Use the payback model and the accounting rate-of-return model and compare them with the NPV model.

Other Models for Analyzing Long-Range Decisions

Although most companies use DCF models to make major capital-budgeting decisions, some companies still use simpler models, either in place of or in addition to the NPV model. We will examine two such models, the payback and accounting rate-of-return models.

Payback Model

payback period (payback time)

The time it will take to recoup, in the form of cash inflows from operations, the initial dollars invested in a project.

Payback time or **payback period** is the time it will take to recoup, in the form of undiscounted cash inflows from operations, the initial dollars invested in a project. Assume that Toyota spends $12,000 for a forklift that has an estimated useful life of 4 years. Toyota expects the new forklift to reduce cash outflows by $4,000 each year. The payback period is 3 years, calculated as follows:

$$\text{payback time} = \frac{\text{initial incremental amount invested}}{\text{equal annual incremental cash inflow from operations}}$$

$$P = \frac{I}{O} = \frac{\$12,000}{\$4,000} = 3 \text{ years}$$

We can use this formula for payback time only when there are equal annual cash inflows from operations. When annual cash inflows are not equal, we must add up each year's net cash inflows until the point in time where the cumulative cash flows add up to the amount of the initial investment.

Assume the following cash flow pattern for the forklift:

End of Year	0	1	2	3	4
Investment	($12,000)				
Cash inflows		$4,000	$6,000	$5,000	$5,000

The calculation of the payback period is as follows:

Year	Initial Investment	Net Cash Inflows Each Year	Net Cash Inflows Cumulative
0	$12,000	—	—
1	—	$4,000	$ 4,000
2	—	6,000	10,000
2+	—	2,000	12,000

In this case, the payback time is slightly beyond the second year. Interpolation within the third year reveals that an additional 4/10 of a year is needed to recoup the final $2,000, making the payback period 2.4 years:

$$2 \text{ years} + \left(\frac{\$2,000}{\$5,000} \times 1 \text{ year} \right) = 2.4 \text{ years}$$

The major weakness of the payback model is that it merely measures how many years it takes to recover the original investment. The payback model ignores elements of timing and duration of cash flows that the DCF models recognize. For example, consider two investment projects with the same 3-year payback period and the same total cash flows for their 4-year lives. However, suppose most of the Project B cash flows occur in the first year of the 3-year payback period while most of the Project A cash flows occur in the third year. The payback periods for these two projects are identical, yet project B is superior because the cash flows arrive earlier. As another example, suppose Project C has the same cash flows over the first 4 years as Project A but the Project A cash flows stop after 4 years while the Project C cash flows continue for a total of 10 years. The payback period for these two projects is identical, yet project C is superior because the cash flows continue for a much longer period of time. The payback model measures only how quickly a company will recoup its investment dollars but ignores the time value of money and ignores cash flows beyond the payback period.

Despite its conceptual weaknesses, the payback model may be useful in certain circumstances. In some situations, managers use the payback model rather than DCF because of greater uncertainty about projections of cash flows further into the future. Suppose a company faces rapid technological changes so that cash flows beyond the first few years are extremely uncertain. In such a situation, managers may decide to base their decisions on the payback period because it emphasizes how quickly projects recoup their investment and ignores the highly uncertain cash flows farther into the future. In other situations, managers use the payback model because of cash constraints. We noted earlier that the DCF model assumes that additional funds can be borrowed at the required rate of return. Some firms, such as early-stage startups, may not be able to easily borrow additional funds, so managers may use the payback model because it focuses on how quickly the firm can recover its cash investments.

Accounting Rate-of-Return Model

The **accounting rate-of-return (ARR) model** expresses a project's return as the increase in expected average annual operating income divided by the initial required investment.

$$\text{accounting rate-of-return (ARR)} = \frac{\text{increase in expected average annual operating income}}{\text{initial required investment}}$$

accounting rate-of-return (ARR) model
A non-DCF capital-budgeting model expressed as the increase in expected average annual operating income divided by the initial required investment.

If operating income is the same as cash flow except for the effect of depreciation expense, then operating income = cash flow – depreciation, and the ARR becomes

$$ARR = \frac{\text{average annual incremental net cash inflow from operations} - \text{average incremental annual depreciation}}{\text{initial required investment}}$$

ARR computations dovetail most closely with conventional accounting models of calculating income and required investment, and they show the effect of an investment on an organization's financial statements.

To see how ARR works, assume the same facts as in Exhibit 12-1: Investment is $5,827, useful life is 4 years, estimated disposal value is zero, and expected annual cash inflow from operations is $2,000. Annual depreciation is $5,827 ÷ 4 = $1,456.75, rounded to $1,457. Substitute these values in the accounting rate-of-return equation:

$$ARR = \frac{(\$2,000 - \$1,457)}{\$5,827} = 9.3\%$$

Some companies use the "average" investment (often assumed to be the average book value over the useful life) instead of original investment in the denominator. The investment committed to the project would decline at a rate of $1,456.75 per year from $5,827 to zero; hence, the average investment would be the beginning balance plus the ending balance ($5,827 + 0) divided by 2, or $2,913.50. Therefore, the ARR using the average investment is

$$ARR = \frac{(\$2,000 - \$1,457)}{\$2,913.50} = 18.6\%$$

The accounting rate-of-return model has significant limitations. Like the payback model, the ARR model ignores important aspects of the timing and duration of cash flows. For example, consider two projects that require the same initial required investment and have the same average increase in operating income over the life of the projects, where most of the savings for Project B occur in the early years while most of the savings for Project A occur in later years. The ARRs for these two projects are identical, even though project B provides returns earlier. As another example, suppose Project C has the same ARR over a 10-year life as Project A has over a 4-year life. Although these two projects have identical ARRs, the return for project C continues for a much longer period of time.

Despite some obvious limitations, some firms still use the ARR and payback models in certain situations. The Business First box on page 467 describes the increasing use of DCF models as well as the continued use of alternative models, including the payback and accounting rate of return models.

Performance Evaluation

Potential Conflict

Objective 8

Reconcile the conflict between using an NPV model for making decisions and using accounting income for evaluating the related performance.

Many managers who are evaluated on the basis of accounting income or an ARR model are reluctant to accept DCF models as the best way to make capital-budgeting decisions. To illustrate, consider the potential conflict that might arise in the example of Exhibit 12-1. Recall that the NPV was $513 based on a 10% required rate of return, an investment of $5,827, cash savings of $2,000 for each of 4 years, and no terminal disposal value. Using ARR where accounting income is computed with straight-line depreciation, the evaluation of performance for years 1–4 would be as follows:

	Year 1	Year 2	Year 3	Year 4
Cash-operating savings	$2,000	$2,000	$2,000	$2,000
Straight-line depreciation, $5,827 ÷ 4	1,457	1,457	1,457	1,457*
Effect on operating income	543	543	543	543
Book value at beginning of year	5,827	4,370	2,913	1,456
ARR	9.3%	12.4%	18.6%	37.3%

*Total depreciation of 4 × $1,457 = $5,828 differs from $5,827 because of rounding error. Also, the ARR is based on the book value at the beginning of the year as a proxy for the investment.

Business First

Who Uses What Capital Budgeting Model?

Companies are increasingly using formal capital-budgeting models, and most use more than one model. Of the 1,000 largest U.S. companies, more than 95% use a DCF model for their large investment decisions, although about half of them use such methods only for investments over $500,000. The NPV model is the most popular DCF method, with many also using IRR. However, use of the payback model remains strong, with more than half of the companies using it for at least some decisions.

There is a clear relationship between size and capital-budgeting methods. The larger the company and the larger the investment, the more likely is the use of DCF methods. Smaller companies use the payback method more often. Companies that have high financial leverage and young, highly-educated CFOs are more likely to use DCF methods. Fast-growing companies use the payback method more than similar-sized, low-growth companies, due at least in part to constraints on the ability of fast-growing companies to raise additional capital.

DCF methods have also made inroads into nonprofit companies. For example, hospitals make huge capital investment decisions. A few years ago the payback model was the dominant capital budgeting model used, but recent studies show that DCF models are used as often as payback. Further, large, multihospital systems generally use DCF methods.

More companies in the United States use DCF methods than in other countries, but the usage is nearly as high in the United Kingdom, Australia, and the Netherlands. Even in China, nearly 90% of the large companies use DCF methods. However, in China the dominant DCF method is IRR and a larger percentage of companies continue to use the payback method for some investments. As companies become more sophisticated and more dependent on capital markets, they tend to progress from payback to IRR and then to NPV.

Companies are also using more sophisticated techniques to analyze capital investment decisions. The most popular is sensitivity analysis. However, the use of real options is growing quickly. In 2002 a quarter of large U.S. companies already used real options, as did a third of Australian firms in 2008. Within the next few years it is likely that half of the large companies in the developed world will use capital budgeting models based on real options for at least some of their major investments.

Sources: G. Truong, G. Partington, and M. Peat, "Cost-of-Capital Estimation and Capital-Budgeting Practices in Australia," *Australian Journal of Management*, June 2008, pp. 95–121; C. Kocher, "Hospital Capital Budgeting Practices and Their Relation to Key Hospital Characteristics: A Survey of U.S. Manager Practices," *Journal of Global Business Issues*, July 1, 2007, pp. 21–30 ; J. Graham and C. Harvey, "How Do CFOs Make Capital Budgeting and Capital Structure Decisions?" *Journal of Applied Corporate Finance*, Spring 2002, pp. 8–23; P. Ryan and G. Ryan, "Capital Budgeting Practices of the Fortune 1000: How Have Things Changed?" *Journal of Business and Management*, Winter 2002, pp. 355–364; and N. Hermes, P. Smid, and L. Yao, "Capital Budgeting Practices: A Comparative Study of The Netherlands and China," November 2005, available at SSRN: http://ssrn.com/abstract=881754.

Many managers would be reluctant to replace equipment, despite the positive NPV, if superiors evaluated their performance by accounting rate of return. They might be especially reluctant if they are likely to transfer to a new position (or retire) within the first year or two. Why? This accrual accounting system understates the return in early years, especially in year 1 when the return is below the required rate, and a manager who transfers will not be around to reap the benefits of the later overstatement of returns.

Managers are especially reluctant to replace assets if a heavy book loss on old equipment would appear in year 1's income statement—even though such a loss is irrelevant in a properly constructed decision model. Thus, performance evaluation based on typical accounting measures can lead to rejection of major, long-term projects where a large portion of the benefit does not appear in income immediately, such as investments in technologically advanced production systems. This pattern may help explain why many U.S. firms seem to be excessively short-term oriented.

Reconciliation of Conflict

The best way to reconcile the potential conflict between capital budgeting and performance evaluation is to use DCF for both capital-budgeting decisions and performance evaluation. Companies that use EVA for performance evaluation, as described in chapter 10, page 228 avoid some of the conflict. Although EVA has the weakness of relying on accrual accounting measures rather than cash flows, it is conceptually linked to the NPV method. Both EVA and NPV recognize that a firm creates value only when investment projects cover their cost of capital.

Another way to address this issue is to conduct a follow-up evaluation of capital-budgeting decisions, often called a **post-audit**. Most large companies (76% in a recent survey) post-audit at least some capital-budgeting decisions. The purposes of a post-audit include the following:

post-audit
A follow-up evaluation of capital-budgeting decisions.

1. Seeing that investment expenditures are proceeding on time and within budget
2. Comparing actual cash flows with those originally predicted, in order to motivate and reward careful and honest predictions

3. Providing information for improving future predictions of cash flows
4. Evaluating the continuation of the project

By focusing the post-audit on actual versus predicted cash flows, we can make the evaluation consistent with the decision process. However, post-auditing of all capital-budgeting decisions is costly. Most accounting systems are best at evaluating operating performances of products, departments, divisions, territories, and so on, year by year. In contrast, capital-budgeting decisions frequently deal with individual projects, not the collection of projects that are usually being managed at the same time by division or department managers. Therefore, most companies audit only selected capital-budgeting decisions.

The conflicts between the longstanding, pervasive accrual accounting model and various formal decision models create some of the most serious unsolved problems in the design of management control systems. Top management cannot expect goal congruence if it favors the use of one type of model for decisions and the use of another type for performance evaluation.

Highlights to Remember

1. **Describe capital-budgeting decisions and use the net-present-value (NPV) method to make such decisions.** Capital budgeting is long-term planning for investments where returns are spread over multiple years. The net-present-value (NPV) model aids this planning process by computing the present value (PV) of all expected future cash flows using a required rate of return. A company should accept projects with an NPV greater than zero.

2. **Use sensitivity analysis to evaluate the effect of changes in predictions on investment decisions.** Managers use sensitivity analysis to assess the effects of changes in predicted cash flows and other variables used in investment decisions.

3. **Calculate the NPV difference between two projects using both the total project and differential approaches.** The total project approach compares the NPVs of the total cash flows from each project, while the differential approach computes the NPV of the difference in cash flows between two projects. Both produce the same results when there are two alternatives. When there are more than two alternatives, you should use the total project approach.

4. **Identify relevant cash flows for NPV analyses.** Predicting cash flows is the hardest part of capital budgeting. Managers should consider three categories of cash flows: initial cash inflows and outflows at time zero, including additional required investments in working capital, future disposal values, and operating cash flows.

5. **Compute the after-tax net present values of projects.** Income taxes can have a significant effect on the desirability of an investment. Additional taxes are cash outflows, and tax savings are cash inflows. Accelerated depreciation speeds up a company's tax savings. In most cases, companies should take depreciation deductions as early as legally permitted.

6. **Explain the after-tax effect on cash received from the disposal of assets.** When companies sell assets for more than the tax book value, the gain generates additional taxes. When they sell assets for less than the tax book value, the loss generates tax savings.

7. **Use the payback model and the accounting rate-of-return model and compare them with the NPV model.** The payback model is simple to apply, but it does not measure profitability. The accounting rate-of-return model uses accounting measures of income and investment, but it ignores the time value of money. Both models have significant limitations relative to the NPV model.

8. **Reconcile the conflict between using an NPV model for making decisions and using accounting income for evaluating the related performance.** NPV is a summary measure of all the cash flows from a project. Accounting income is a one-period measure. A positive NPV project can have low (or even negative) accounting income in the first year. Managers may be reluctant to invest in such a project, despite its positive value to the company, especially if they expect to transfer to a new position before they can benefit from the positive returns that come later.

Appendix 11: Capital Budgeting and Inflation

Capital-budgeting decision makers should also consider the effects of inflation on their cash-flow predictions. **Inflation** is the decline in the general purchasing power of the monetary unit. For example, a dollar today will buy only a fraction of what it did in the late-1980s. At a 5% annual inflation rate, average prices rise more than 60% over 10 years and 165% over 20 years. The United States had double-digit inflation rates in the late 1970s, and some countries, such as Brazil and Argentina, have had triple-digit annual inflation rates (that is, average prices more than doubling each year). In the last decade, inflation rates in the United States have been low—generally around 3%—but it is possible that rates in the future might increase. If a company expects significant inflation over the life of a project, it should specifically and consistently recognize inflation in its capital-budgeting decisions.

Objective 9

Compute the impact of inflation on a capital-budgeting project.

inflation
The decline in the general purchasing power of the monetary unit.

Watch for Consistency

The key to appropriate consideration of inflation in capital budgeting is consistent treatment of the required rate of return and the predicted cash inflows and outflows. We can achieve such consistency by either 1) including an element for inflation in both the required rate and in the cash-flow predictions, or 2) excluding the effects of inflation in both the required rate and in the cash-flow predictions. We limit our discussion to the first approach, which is both simple and widely-used.

Many firms base their required rate of return on market interest rates, also called **nominal rates**, that include an inflation element. For example, consider three possible components of a 12% nominal rate:

nominal rate
Interest rate that includes an inflation element.

(a)	Risk-free element—the "pure" rate of interest	3%
(b)	Business-risk element—the "risk" premium that is demanded for taking larger risks	5
(a) + (b)	Often called the "real rate"	8%
(c)	Inflation element—the premium demanded because of expected deterioration of the general purchasing power of the monetary unit	4
(a) + (b) + (c)	Often called the "nominal rate"	12%

In this example, 4 percentage points out of the 12 percentage-point return compensate an investor for receiving future payments in inflated dollars, that is, in dollars with less purchasing power than those invested. Therefore, basing the required rate of return on quoted market rates automatically includes an inflation element in the rate. Companies that base their required rate of return on market rates should also adjust their cash-flow predictions for anticipated inflation. For example, suppose a company expects to sell 1,000 units of a product in each of the next 2 years. Assume this year's price is $50, and inflation causes next year's price to be $52.50. This year's predicted cash inflow is 1,000 × $50 = $50,000, and next year's inflation-adjusted cash inflow is 1,000 × $52.50 = $52,500. Inflation-adjusted cash flows are the inflows and outflows expected after adjusting prices to reflect anticipated inflation.

Consider another illustration: purchase cost of equipment, $200,000; useful life, 5 years; zero terminal salvage value; pretax operating cash savings per year, $83,333 (in 20X0 dollars); income tax rate, 40%. For simplicity, we assume ordinary straight-line depreciation of $200,000 ÷ 5 = $40,000 per year. The after-tax required rate, based on quoted market rates, is 25%. It includes an inflation factor of 10%.

Exhibit 12-9 displays correct and incorrect ways to analyze the effects of inflation. The key words are *internal consistency*. The correct analysis (1) uses a required rate that includes an element attributable to inflation and (2) explicitly adjusts the predicted operating cash flows for the effects of inflation. Note that the correct analysis favors the purchase of the equipment, but the incorrect analysis does not.

The incorrect analysis in Exhibit 12-9 is incorrect because it is internally inconsistent. The predicted cash inflows exclude adjustments for inflation. Instead, they are stated in 20X0 dollars. However, the discount rate includes an element attributable to inflation. An analytical mistake like this might lead to an unwise refusal to purchase.

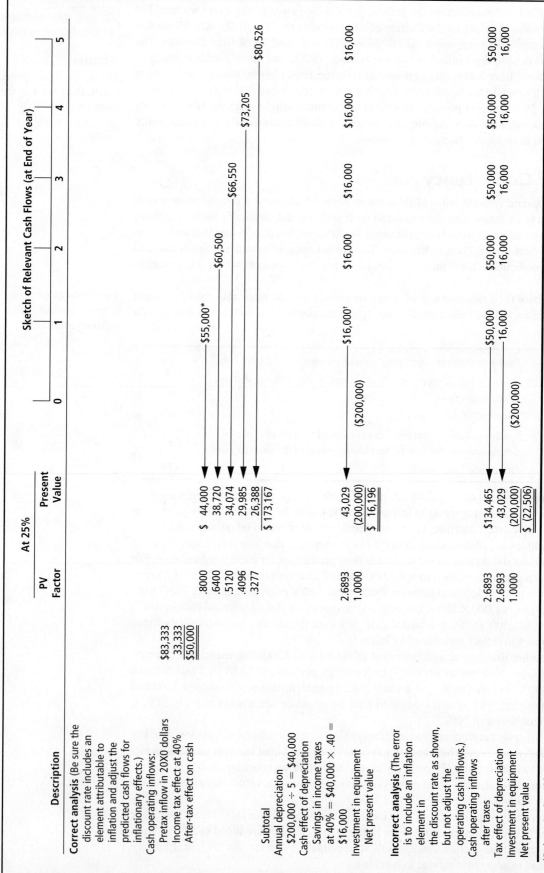

Sketch of Relevant Cash Flows (at End of Year)

Description	At 25% PV Factor	At 25% Present Value	0	1	2	3	4	5
Correct analysis (Be sure the discount rate includes an element attributable to inflation and adjust the predicted cash flows for inflationary effects.)								
Cash operating inflows:								
Pretax inflow in 20X0 dollars		$83,333						
Income tax effect at 40%		33,333						
After-tax effect on cash		$50,000						
	.8000	$ 44,000		$55,000*				
	.6400	38,720			$60,500			
	.5120	34,074				$66,550		
	.4096	29,985					$73,205	
	.3277	26,388						$80,526
Subtotal		$ 173,167						
Annual depreciation $200,000 ÷ 5 = $40,000								
Cash effect of depreciation								
Savings in income taxes at 40% = $40,000 × .40 = $16,000				$16,000†	$16,000	$16,000	$16,000	$16,000
	2.6893	43,029						
Investment in equipment	1.0000	(200,000)	($200,000)					
Net present value		$ 16,196						
Incorrect analysis (The error is to include an inflation element in the discount rate as shown, but not adjust the operating cash inflows.)								
Cash operating inflows after taxes				$50,000	$50,000	$50,000	$50,000	$50,000
	2.6893	$134,465						
Tax effect of depreciation	2.6893	43,029		16,000	16,000	16,000	16,000	16,000
Investment in equipment	1.0000	(200,000)	($200,000)					
Net present value		$ (22,506)						

*Each year is adjusted for anticipated inflation: $50,000 × 1.10 = $55,000 , $50,000 × 1.10² = $60,500, $50,000 × 1.10³ = $66,550, and so on.
†Inflation will not affect the annual savings in income taxes from depreciation. Why? Because the income tax deduction must be based on original cost of the asset in 20X0 dollars.

Exhibit 12-9
Inflation and Capital Budgeting

Role of Depreciation

While internally consistent analysis using nominal interest rates must adjust cash flows for inflation, you will notice that the correct analysis in Exhibit 12-9 shows that we did not adjust the tax effects of depreciation for inflation. Why? Because the depreciation deductions under U.S. income tax laws are based on the original dollars invested, not the inflation-adjusted amount of the investment.

Critics of U.S. income tax laws emphasize that such laws discourage capital investment by not allowing companies to adjust depreciation deductions for inflationary effects. For instance, the NPV in Exhibit 12-9 would be larger if depreciation for tax purposes were based on the inflation-adjusted value of the $200,000 investment. As shown in Exhibit 12-9, the unadjusted depreciation of $40,000 per year generates a $16,000 savings in 20X1 dollars, then $16,000 in 20X2 dollars, and so forth. If tax depreciation were based on the inflation-adjusted value of the investment which grows by 10% to $220,000 during the second year, the tax depreciation would grow to $220,000 ÷ 5 = $44,000 in the second year, generating a tax savings of $44,000 × 40% = $17,600. When the inflation-adjusted value of the investment grows by another 10% to $242,000 during the third year, the inflation-adjusted depreciation would grow to $242,000 ÷ 5 = $48,400, generating a tax savings of $48,400 × 40% = $19,360. On the other hand, defenders of existing U.S. tax laws point out that tax laws encourage capital investment in many other ways. The most prominent example is provision for accelerated depreciation over lives that are much shorter than the economic lives of the assets.

Summary Problems for Your Review

PROBLEM

Examine the correct analysis in Exhibit 12-9. Suppose the cash-operating inflows persisted for an extra year. Compute the PV of the inflow for the sixth year. Ignore depreciation.

SOLUTION

The cash operating inflow would be $50,000 × 1.10^6, or $80,526 × 1.10, or $88,579. Its PV would be $88,579 × .2621, the factor from Table B-1 of Appendix B (period 6 row, 25% column), or $23,217.

PROBLEM

Examine the MACRS depreciation schedule in Exhibit 12-7 on page 461. Assume an anticipated inflation rate of 7%. How would you change the PVs of depreciation to accommodate the inflation rate?

SOLUTION

The computations on page 461 would not change. Inflation does not affect the tax effects of depreciation. Income tax laws in the United States permit a deduction based on the original dollars invested, nothing more.

Accounting Vocabulary

Fundamental Assignment Material

Special note: In all assignment materials that include taxes, assume—unless directed otherwise—that (1) all income tax cash flows occur simultaneously with the pretax cash flows, and (2) the companies in question will have enough taxable income from other sources to use all income tax benefits from the situations described.

12-A1 Exercises in Compound Interest: Answers Supplied

Use the appropriate interest to complete the following exercises. The answers appear at the end of the assignment material for this chapter, page 479.

1. It is your sixtieth birthday. You plan to work 5 more years before retiring, at which point you and your spouse want to take $25,000 for a round-the-world tour. What lump sum do you have to invest now to accumulate the $25,000? Assume that your required rate of return is
   a. 5%, compounded annually.
   b. 10%, compounded annually.
   c. 20%, compounded annually.
2. You want to spend $2,000 on a vacation at the end of each of the next 5 years. What lump sum do you have to invest now to take the five vacations? Assume that your required rate of return is
   a. 5%, compounded annually.
   b. 10%, compounded annually.
   c. 20%, compounded annually.
3. At age 60, you find that your employer is moving to another location. You receive termination pay of $100,000. You have some savings and wonder whether to retire now.
   a. If you invest the $100,000 now at 5%, compounded annually, how much money can you withdraw from your account each year so that at the end of 5 years there will be a zero balance?
   b. Answer part a, assuming that you invest it at 10%.
4. Two NBA basketball players, LeBron and Kobe, signed 5-year, $60-million contracts. At 16%, compounded annually, which of the following contracts is more desirable in terms of present values? Show computations to support your answer.

Annual Cash Inflows (in thousands)		
Year	LeBron	Kobe
1	$20,000	$ 4,000
2	16,000	8,000
3	12,000	12,000
4	8,000	16,000
5	4,000	20,000
	$60,000	$60,000

12-A2 NPV for Investment Decisions

A manager of the engineering department of Manchester University is contemplating acquiring 120 computers. The computers will cost £240,000 cash, have zero terminal salvage value, and a useful life of 3 years. Annual cash savings from operations will be £110,000. The required rate of return is 14%. There are no taxes.

1. Compute the NPV.
2. Should the engineering department acquire the computers? Explain.

12-A3 Taxes, Straight-Line Depreciation, and Present Values

A manager of Cascade Mutual Funds is contemplating acquiring servers to operate its website. The servers will cost $660,000 cash and will have zero terminal salvage value. The recovery period and useful life are both 3 years. Annual pretax cash savings from operations will be $300,000. The income tax rate is 40%, and the required after-tax rate of return is 12%.

1. Compute the NPV, assuming straight-line depreciation of $220,000 yearly for tax purposes. Should Cascade acquire the computers? Explain.
2. Suppose the computers will be fully depreciated at the end of year 3 but can be sold for $90,000 cash. Compute the NPV. Should Cascade acquire the computers? Explain.
3. Ignore number 2. Suppose the required after-tax rate of return is 8% instead of 12%. Should Cascade acquire the computers? Show computations.

12-A4 **MACRS and Present Values**

Managers of Northwest Forge are considering whether to buy some equipment for the company's Fargo plant. The equipment will cost $2 million cash and will have a 10-year useful life and zero terminal salvage value. Annual pretax cash savings from operations will be $420,000. The income tax rate is 45%, and the required after-tax rate of return is 14%.

1. Compute the NPV, using a 7-year recovery period and MACRS depreciation for tax purposes. Should the company acquire the equipment?
2. Suppose the economic life of the equipment is 15 years, which means that there will be $420,000 additional annual cash savings from operations in each of the years from 11 to 15. Assume that a 7-year recovery period and MACRS depreciation is used. Should the company acquire the equipment? Show computations.

12-A5 **Gains or Losses on Disposal**

On January 1, 20X1, Melbourne Company sold an asset with a book value of $250,000 for cash.

Assume two selling prices: $305,000 and $230,000. For each selling price, prepare a tabulation of the gain or loss, the effect on income taxes, and the total after-tax effect on cash. The applicable income tax rate is 25%.

12-B1 **Exercises in Compound Interest**

Use the appropriate table to compute the following:

1. You have always dreamed of taking a safari in Africa. What lump sum do you have to invest today to have the $22,000 needed for the trip in 5 years? Assume that you can invest the money at
   a. 6%, compounded annually.
   b. 10%, compounded annually.
   c. 14%, compounded annually.
2. You are considering partial retirement. To do so you need to use part of your savings to supplement your income for the next 4 years. Suppose you need an extra $50,000 per year. What lump sum do you have to invest now to supplement your income for 4 years? Assume that your required rate of return is
   a. 6%, compounded annually.
   b. 10%, compounded annually.
   c. 14%, compounded annually.
3. You just won a lump sum of $6,000,000 in a state lottery. You have decided to invest the winnings and withdraw an equal amount each year for 20 years. How much can you withdraw each year and have a zero balance left at the end of 20 years if you invest at
   a. 4%, compounded annually?
   b. 8%, compounded annually?
4. An NHL hockey player is offered the choice of two 4-year salary contracts, contract X for $2.85 million and contract Y for $2.72 million:

	Contract X	Contract Y
End of year 1	$ 250,000	$ 550,000
End of year 2	750,000	820,000
End of year 3	850,000	650,000
End of year 4	1,000,000	700,000
Total	$2,850,000	$2,720,000

Which contract has the higher PV at 16% compounded annually? Show computations to support your answer.

12-B2 **NPV for Investment Decisions**

The head of the oncology department of FH Research Center is considering the purchase of some new equipment. The cost is $420,000, the economic life is 5 years, and there is no terminal disposal value. Annual cash inflows from operations would increase by $140,000, and the required rate of return is 14%. There are no taxes.

1. Compute the NPV.
2. Should the research center acquire the equipment? Explain.

12-B3 Taxes, Straight-Line Depreciation, and NPV

The president of Big Fish Games, an online gaming company, is considering the purchase of some equipment used for the development of new games. The cost is $400,000, the economic life and the recovery period are both 5 years, and there is no terminal disposal value. Annual pretax cash inflows from operations would increase by $130,000, giving a total 5-year pretax savings of $650,000. The income tax rate is 40%, and the required after-tax rate of return is 14%.

1. Compute the NPV, assuming straight-line depreciation of $80,000 yearly for tax purposes. Should Big Fish Games acquire the equipment?
2. Suppose the asset will be fully depreciated at the end of year 5 but is sold for $25,000 cash. Should Big Fish Games acquire the equipment? Show computations.
3. Ignore number 2. Suppose the required after-tax rate of return is 10% instead of 14%. Should Big Fish Games acquire the equipment? Show computations.

12-B4 MACRS and Present Values

The general manager of a New Mexico mining company has a chance to purchase a new drill at a total cost of $300,000. The recovery period is 5 years. Additional annual pretax cash inflow from operations is $75,000, the economic life of the drill is 5 years, there is no salvage value, the income tax rate is 45%, and the after-tax required rate of return is 10%.

1. Compute the NPV, assuming MACRS depreciation for tax purposes. Should the company acquire the drill?
2. Suppose the economic life of the drill is 6 years, which means that there will be a $75,000 cash inflow from operations in the sixth year. The recovery period is still 5 years. Should the company acquire the drill? Show computations.

12-B5 Income Taxes and Disposal of Assets

Assume that the combined federal and state income tax rate for Kafka Company is 30%.

1. The book value of an old machine is $40,000. Kafka sold the machine for $35,000 cash. What is the effect of this decision on after-tax cash flows?
2. The book value of an old machine is $40,000. Kafka sold the machine for $85,000 cash. What is the effect of this decision on after-tax cash flows?

MyAccountingLab Additional Assignment Material

QUESTIONS

12-1 Capital budgeting has three phases: (a) identification of potential investments, (b) selection of investments, and (c) post-audit of investments. What is the accountant's role in each phase?

12-2 Why is discounted cash flow a superior method for capital budgeting?

12-3 "The higher the required rate of return, the higher the price that a company will be willing to pay for cost-saving equipment." Do you agree? Explain.

12-4 "The DCF model assumes certainty and perfect capital markets. Thus, it is impractical to use it in most real-world situations." Do you agree? Explain.

12-5 "Double-counting of costs occurs if depreciation is separately considered in DCF analysis." Do you agree? Explain.

12-6 Does the IRR model make significantly different decisions than does the NPV model? Why or why not?

12-7 What does the real options model recognize that the NPV and IRR models do not?

12-8 "We can't use sensitivity analysis because our cash-flow predictions are too inaccurate." Comment.

12-9 Why should the differential approach to alternatives always lead to the same decision as the total project approach?

12-10 "The NPV model should not be used for investment decisions about advanced technology, such as computer-integrated manufacturing systems." Do you agree? Explain.

12-11 Distinguish between average and marginal tax rates.

12-12 "Congress should pass a law forbidding corporations to keep two sets of books." Do you agree? Explain.

12-13 Distinguish between tax avoidance and tax evasion.

12-14 "Companies that try to avoid taxes are unethical." Do you agree? Discuss.

12-15 Explain why accelerated depreciation methods are superior to straight-line methods for income tax purposes.

12-16 "An investment in equipment really buys two streams of cash." Do you agree? Explain.

12-17 Why should companies take tax deductions sooner rather than later?

12-18 "The MACRS half-year convention causes assets to be depreciated beyond the lives specified in the MACRS recovery schedules." Do you agree? Explain.

12-19 "When there are income taxes, depreciation is a cash outlay." Do you agree? Explain.

12-20 "If DCF approaches are superior to the payback and the accounting rate-of-return methods, why should we bother to learn the others? All it does is confuse things." Answer this contention.

12-21 What is the basic flaw in the pay-back model?

12-22 Explain how a conflict can arise between capital-budgeting decision models and performance evaluation methods.

12-23 Study Appendix 12. What are the three components of market (nominal) interest rates?

12-24 Study Appendix 12. Describe how internal consistency is achieved when considering inflation in a capital-budgeting model.

CRITICAL THINKING EXERCISES

12-25 Investment in R&D
"It is impossible to use DCF methods for evaluating investments in R&D. There are no cost savings to measure, and we don't even know what products might come out of our R&D activities." This is a quote from an R&D manager who was asked to justify investment in a major research project based on its expected NPV. Do you agree with her statement? Explain.

12-26 Business Valuation and NPV
When a company elects to invest in a project with a positive NPV, what will generally happen to the value of the company? What will happen to this value when the company invests in a negative NPV project?

12-27 Replacement of Production Facilities
A manufacturing company recently considered replacing one of its forming machines with a newer, faster, more accurate model. What cash flows would this decision be likely to affect? List both cash flows that would be easy to quantify and those for which measurement would be difficult.

12-28 Capital Budgeting, Taxes, and Ethics
The U.S. tax law is complex. Sometimes the line between tax avoidance and tax evasion is not clear. Discuss the legal and ethical implications of the following two capital investment decisions:

a. A company invested in an asset that it expects to grow rather than decline in value. Nevertheless, the tax law allows the company to deduct depreciation on the asset. Therefore, the company depreciated the asset for tax purposes using an accelerated MACRS schedule.

b. There are often tax advantages to investments "offshore." For example, in Bermuda there are no taxes on profits, dividends, or income, and there is no capital gains tax, no withholding tax, and no sales tax. A U.S. company decided to invest in a manufacturing plant in Bermuda and use transfer prices to move as much of the company's profits as possible to the Bermuda plant.

EXERCISES

12-29 Exercise in Compound Interest
Serena Madison wishes to purchase a $820,000 house. She has accumulated a $180,000 down payment, but she wishes to borrow $640,000 on a 15-year mortgage. For simplicity, assume annual mortgage payments occur at the end of each year and there are no loan fees.

1. What are Madison's annual payments if her interest rate is (a) 4%, (b) 8%, and (c) 12%, compounded annually?
2. Repeat number 1 for a 10-year mortgage.
3. Suppose Madison had to choose between a 15-year and a 10-year mortgage, either one at a 8% interest rate. Compute the total payments and total interest paid on (a) a 15-year mortgage and (b) a 10-year mortgage.

12-30 Exercise in Compound Interest
Suppose **Pfizer** wishes to borrow money from **Bank of America**. They agree on an annual rate of 4%.

1. Suppose Pfizer agrees to repay $750 million at the end of 10 years. How much will Bank of America lend Pfizer?
2. Suppose Pfizer agrees to repay a total of $750 million at a rate of $75 million at the end of each of the next 10 years. How much will Bank of America lend Pfizer?

CHAPTER 12

12-31 Exercise in Compound Interest

Suppose you are a loan officer for a bank. A start-up company has qualified for a loan. You are pondering various proposals for repayment:

1. Lump sum of $250,000 five years hence. How much will you lend if your required rate of return is (a) 8%, compounded annually, and (b) 12%, compounded annually?
2. Repeat number 1, but assume that the interest rates are compounded semiannually.
3. Suppose the loan is to be paid in full by equal payments of $50,000 at the end of each of the next 5 years. How much will you lend if your required rate of return is (a) 8%, compounded annually, and (b) 12%, compounded annually?

12-32 Basic Relationships in Interest Tables

1. Suppose you borrow $300,000 now at 10% interest, compounded annually. You will repay the borrowed amount plus interest in a lump sum at the end of 4 years. How much must you repay? Use Table B-1 (page A6) and the basic equation PV = future amount × conversion factor.
2. Assume the same facts as previously except that you will repay the loan in equal installments at the end of each of the 4 years. How much must you repay each year? Use Table B-2 (page A-9) and the basic equation: PV = future annual amounts × conversion factor.

12-33 PV and Sports Salaries

Because of a salary cap, **NBA** teams are not allowed to exceed a certain annual limit in total player salaries. Suppose the Minnesota Timberwolves had scheduled salaries exactly equal to their cap of $90 million for 2012. Kim Jenner, a star player, was scheduled to receive $15 million in 2012. To free up money to pay a prize rookie, Jenner agreed on July 1, 2012, to defer $8 million of his salary for 2 years, by which time the salary cap will have been increased. His contract called for salary payments of $15 million in 2012, $19 million in 2013, and $21 million in 2014, all on July 1 of the respective year. Now, he will receive $7 million in 2012, still $19 million in 2013, and $29 million in 2014. Jenner's required rate of return is 10%.

Did the deferral of salary cost Jenner anything? If so, how much? Compute the PV of the sacrifice as of July 1, 2012. Explain.

12-34 Simple NPV

Rajgopal Company expects to receive $600 at the end of each of the next 3 years and an additional $3,500 at the end of the third year. Therefore, the total payments will be $5,300. What is the NPV of the payments at an interest rate of 4%?

12-35 NPV Relationships

Fill in the blanks.

	Number of Years			
	7	**18**	**18**	**28**
Amount of annual cash inflow*	$8,000	$	$ 30,000	$16,000
Required initial investment	$	$70,000	$ 50,000	$29,000
Required rate of return	10%	18%	$	20%
NPV	$ 980	($10,009)	$231,157	$

*To be received at the end of each year.

12-36 New Equipment

The Montevideo Office Equipment Company has offered to sell some new packaging equipment to the Cortez Company. The list price is $65,000, but Montevideo has agreed to allow a trade-in allowance of $21,000 on some old equipment. The old equipment was carried at a book value of $21,300 and could be sold outright for $20,000 cash. Cash-operating savings are expected to be $22,000 annually for the next 8 years. The required rate of return is 14%. The old equipment has a remaining useful life of 8 years. Both the old and the new equipment will have zero disposal values 8 years from now.

Should Cortez buy the new equipment? Show your computations, using the NPV method. Ignore income taxes.

12-37 Present Values of Cash Inflows

City View Restaurant is about to open at a new location. Operating plans indicate the following expected cash flows:

		Outflows	Inflows
Initial investment now		$235,000	$ —
End of year:	1	$150,000	200,000
	2	$200,000	250,000
	3	$250,000	300,000
	4	$300,000	450,000
	5	$350,000	500,000

1. Compute the NPV for all these cash flows. This should be a single amount. Use a discount rate of 14%.
2. Suppose the required rate was 12%. Without further calculations, determine whether the NPV is positive or negative. Explain.

12-38 Effect of Required Rate

Blanchard Company has an opportunity to invest $15,000 in a new automated lathe that will reduce annual operating costs by $2,300 per year and will have an economic life of 12 years.

1. Suppose Blanchard Company has a required rate of return of 10%. Compute the NPV of the investment and recommend to Blanchard Company whether it should purchase the lathe.
2. Suppose Blanchard Company has a required rate of return of 12%. Compute the NPV of the investment and recommend to Blanchard Company whether it should purchase the lathe.
3. How does the required rate of return affect the NPV of a potential investment?

12-39 NPV and IRR

Czick Company is considering an investment in a machine that costs $36,048 and would result in cash savings of $10,000 per year for 5 years. The company's cost of capital is 10%.

1. Compute the project's NPV at 10%, 12%, and 14%.
2. Compute the project's IRR.
3. Suppose the company uses the NPV model. Would it accept the project? Why or why not?
4. Suppose the company uses the IRR model. Would it accept the project? Why or why not?

12-40 Sensitivity Analysis

Mack and Myer, LLP, a law firm, is considering the replacement of its old accounting system with new software that should save $10,000 per year in net cash operating costs. The old system has zero disposal value, but it could be used for the next 5 years. The estimated useful life of the new software is 5 years with zero salvage value, and it will cost $40,000. The required rate of return is 14%.

1. What is the payback period?
2. Compute the NPV.
3. Management is unsure about the useful life. What would be the NPV if the useful life were (a) 3 years instead of 5 or (b) 10 years instead of 5?
4. Suppose the life will be 5 years, but the savings will be $8,000 per year instead of $10,000. What would be the NPV?
5. Suppose the annual savings will be $9,000 for 4 years. What would be the NPV?

12-41 NPV and Sensitivity Analysis

Chippewa County Jail currently has its laundry done by a local cleaner at an annual cost of $46,000. It is considering a purchase of washers, dryers, and presses at a total installed cost of $52,000 so that inmates can do the laundry. The county expects savings of $15,000 per year, and it expects the machines to last 5 years. The required rate of return is 10%.

Answer each part separately.

1. Compute the NPV of the investment in laundry facilities.
2. a. Suppose the machines last only 4 years. Compute the NPV.
   b. Suppose the machines last 7 years. Compute the NPV.

3. a. Suppose the annual savings are only $12,000. Compute the NPV.

 b. Suppose the annual savings are $18,000. Compute the NPV.

4. a. Compute the most optimistic estimate of NPV, combining the best outcomes in numbers 2 and 3.

 b. Compute the most pessimistic estimate of NPV, combining the worst outcomes in numbers 2 and 3.

5. Accept the expected life estimate of 5 years. What is the minimum annual savings that would justify the investment in the laundry facilities?

12-42 Depreciation, Income Taxes, Cash Flows

Fill in the unknowns (in thousands of dollars):

(S)	Sales	750
(E)	Expenses excluding depreciation	275
(D)	Depreciation	200
	Total expenses	475
	Income before income taxes	?
(T)	Income taxes at 36%	?
(I)	Net income	?
	Cash effects of operations	
	Cash inflow from operations, before tax	?
	Cash inflow from operations, after tax	?
	Tax savings due to depreciation	?
	Total after-tax effect on cash	?

12-43 After-Tax Effect on Cash

The 20X9 income statement of United Cable Company included the following:

Sales		$1,700,000
Less: Expenses, excluding depreciation	$350,000	
Depreciation	425,000	
Total expenses		$ 775,000
Income before taxes		$ 925,000
Income taxes (37%)		342,250
Net income		$ 582,750

Compute the total after-tax effect on cash. Use the format of the second part of Exhibit 12-3, page 458, "Annual Cash Flow Effects."

12-44 MACRS Depreciation

In 20X8, Tebow Athletic Shoe Company acquired the following assets and immediately placed them into service.

1. Special tools (a 3-year-MACRS asset) that cost $55,000 on February 1.
2. A desktop computer that cost $3,500 on December 15.
3. Special calibration equipment that was used in running-shoe research and cost $16,000 on July 7.
4. A set of file cabinets that cost $9,500, purchased on March 1.

Compute the depreciation for tax purposes, under the prescribed MACRS method, in 20X8 and 20X9. Round amounts to the nearest whole dollar.

12-45 Present Value of MACRS Depreciation

Compute the PV of the MACRS tax savings for each of the following five assets: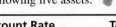

	Asset Cost	Recovery Period	Discount Rate	Tax Rate
(a)	$220,000	7-year	18%	33%
(b)	$640,000	7-year	12%	33%
(c)	$ 40,000	10-year	8%	29%
(d)	$950,000	10-year	5%	45%
(e)	$420,000	3-year	14%	25%

12-46 NPV, ARR, and Payback

Snuffy's Drive-In is considering a proposal to invest in a speaker system that would allow its employees to service drive-through customers. The cost of the system (including installation of special windows and driveway modifications) is $28,000. Brad Board, manager of Snuffy's, expects the drive-through operations to increase annual sales by $14,000, with a 25% contribution margin ratio. Assume that the system has an economic life of 10 years, at which time it will have no disposal value. The required rate of return is 10%. Ignore taxes.

1. Compute the payback period. Is this a good measure of profitability?
2. Compute the NPV. Should Brad Board accept the proposal? Why or why not?
3. Using the ARR model, compute the rate of return on the initial investment.

12-47 Weaknesses of the Payback Model

Stallone Company is considering two possible investments, each of which requires an initial investment of $36,000. Investment A will provide a cash flow of $4,000 at the end of each year for 20 years. Investment B will provide a cash flow of $4,500 at the end of each year for 8 years.

1. Determine the payback period for each investment. Which investment is most desirable using the payback method?
2. Compute the NPV of each investment using a required rate of return of 8%. Which investment is most desirable using the NPV method?
3. Explain why the payback method does not lead to an optimal decision for the Stallone Company.

12-48 Comparison of Capital-Budgeting Techniques

The City of Industry parks department is considering the purchase of a new, more efficient pool heater for its Campbell Swimming Pool at a cost of $28,000. It should save $7,000 in cash operating costs per year. Its estimated useful life is 10 years, and it will have zero disposal value. Ignore taxes.

1. What is the payback time?
2. Compute the NPV if the required rate of return is 10%. Should the department buy the heater? Why?
3. Using the ARR model, compute the rate of return on the initial investment.

12-49 Inflation and Capital Budgeting

Study Appendix 11. The head of the corporate tax division of a major public relations firm has proposed investing $290,000 in personal computers for the staff. The useful life and recovery period for the computers are both 5 years. The firm uses MACRS depreciation. There is no terminal salvage value. Labor savings of $140,000 per year (in year-zero dollars) are expected from the purchase. The income tax rate is 35%, and the after-tax required rate of return is 25%, which includes a 5% element attributable to inflation.

1. Compute the NPV of the computers. Use the nominal required rate of return and adjust the cash flows for inflation. (For example, year 1 cash flow = 1.05 × year 0 cash flow.)
2. Compute the NPV of the computers using the nominal required rate of return without adjusting the cash flows for inflation.
3. Compare your answers in numbers 1 and 2. Which is correct? Would using the incorrect analysis generally lead to overinvestment or underinvestment? Explain.

12-50 Sensitivity of Capital Budgeting to Inflation

Study Appendix 11. Enrique Mendoza, the president of a Mexican wholesale company, is considering whether to invest 420,000 pesos in new semiautomatic loading equipment that will last 5 years, have zero scrap value, and generate cash operating savings in labor usage of 150,000 pesos annually, using 20X0 prices and wage rates. It is December 31, 20X0.

   The required rate of return is 18% per year.

1. Compute the NPV of the project. Use 150,000 pesos as the savings for each of the 5 years. Assume a 40% tax rate and, for simplicity, assume ordinary straight-line depreciation of 420,000 pesos ÷ 5 = 84,000 pesos annually for tax purposes.
2. Mendoza is wondering if the model in number 1 provides a correct analysis of the effects of inflation. He maintains that the 18% rate embodies an element attributable to anticipated inflation. For purposes of this analysis, he assumes that the existing rate of inflation, 10% annually, will persist over the next 5 years. Repeat number 1, adjusting the cash operating savings upward by using the 10% inflation rate.
3. Which analysis, the one in number 1 or 2, is correct? Why?

PROBLEMS

12-51 Replacement of Office Equipment

Midwestern University is considering replacing some **Xerox** copiers with faster copiers purchased from **Brother**. The administration is very concerned about the rising costs of operations during the last decade.

To convert to Brother, two operators would have to be retrained. Required training and remodeling would cost $3,500. Midwestern's three Xerox machines were purchased for $8,000 each, 5 years ago. Their expected life was 15 years. Their resale value now is $1,750 each and will be zero in 10 more years. The total cost of the new Brother equipment will be $60,000; it will have zero disposal value in 10 years.

The three Xerox operators are paid $12 an hour each. They usually work a 40-hour week. Machine breakdowns occur monthly on each machine, resulting in repair costs of $75 per month and overtime of 6 hours, at time-and-one-half, per machine per month, to complete the normal monthly workload. Toner, supplies, and so on, cost $50 a month for each Xerox copier.

The Brother system will require only two regular operators, on a regular work week of 40 hours each, to do the same work. Rates are $14 an hour, and no overtime is expected. Toner, supplies, and so on, will cost a total of $4,500 annually. Maintenance and repairs are fully serviced by Brother for $600 annually. (Assume a 52-week year.)

1. Using DCF techniques, compute the PV of all relevant cash flows, under both alternatives, for the 10-year period discounted at 14%. As a nonprofit university, Midwestern does not pay income taxes.
2. Should Midwestern keep the Xerox copiers or replace them if the decision is based solely on the given data?
3. What other considerations might affect the decision?

12-52 Replacement Decision for Railway Equipment

Suppose the **Burlington Northern Railway** is considering replacement of a power jack tamper, used for maintenance of track, with a new automatic raising device that can be attached to a production tamper.

The present power jack tamper cost $35,000 seven years ago and had an estimated life of 15 years. Two years from now, the machine will require a major overhaul estimated to cost $6,500. It can be disposed of now via an outright cash sale for $5,500. There will be no value at the end of another 8 years.

The automatic raising attachment has a delivered selling price of $45,000 and an estimated life of 17 years. Because of anticipated future developments in combined maintenance machines, Burlington Northern management predicts that the company will dispose of the machine at the end of the eighth year to take advantage of newly developed machines. Estimated sales value at the end of 8 years is $6,500.

Tests have shown that the automatic raising machine will produce a more uniform surface on the track than does the power jack tamper now in use. The new equipment will eliminate one laborer whose annual compensation, including fringe benefits, is $36,000.

Track maintenance work is seasonal, and the equipment normally works from May 1 to October 31 each year. Machine operators and laborers are transferred to other work after October 31, at the same rate of pay.

The salesman claims that the annual normal maintenance of the new machine will run about $900 per year. Because the automatic raising machine is more complicated than the manually operated machine, it will probably require a thorough overhaul at the end of the third year, at an estimated cost of $5,500.

Records show the annual normal maintenance of the power jack tamper to be $1,500. Fuel consumption of the two machines is equal. Should Burlington Northern keep or replace the power jack tamper? The company requires a 14% rate of return. Compute PV. Ignore income taxes.

12-53 Discounted Cash Flow, Uneven Revenue Stream, Relevant Costs

Mildred Driver, the owner of a nine-hole golf course on the outskirts of a large city, is considering a proposal that the course be illuminated and operated at night. Ms. Driver purchased the course early last year for $480,000. Her receipts from operations during the 28-week season were $135,000. Total disbursements for the year, for all purposes, were $84,000.

The required investment in lighting this course is estimated at $90,000. The system will require 300 lamps of 1,000 watts each. Electricity costs $.08 per kilowatt-hour. The expected average hours of operation per night is 5. Because of occasional bad weather and the probable curtailment of night operation at the beginning and end of the season, it is estimated that there will be only 130 nights of operation per year. Labor for keeping the course open at night will cost $75 per night. Lightbulb cost is estimated at $1,500 per year; other maintenance and repairs, per year, will amount to 4% of the initial cost of the lighting system. Annual property taxes on this equipment will be about 1.7% of its initial cost. It is estimated that the average revenue, per night of operation, will be $420 for the first 2 years.

Considering the probability of competition from the illumination of other golf courses, Ms. Driver decides that she will not make the investment unless she can make at least 10% per annum on her investment. Because of anticipated competition, revenue is expected to drop to $300 per night for years 3–5. It is estimated that the lighting equipment will have a salvage value of $35,000 at the end of the 5-year period.

Using DCF techniques, determine whether Ms. Driver should install the lighting system.

12-54 Investment in Machine

The Soho Ale Company has an old brewing machine with a net disposal value of £12,000 now and £4,000 five years from now. A new brewing machine is offered for £57,000 cash or £45,000 with a trade-in. The new machine will result in an annual operating cash outflow of £40,000 as compared with the old machine's annual outflow of £50,000. The disposal value of the new machine 5 years hence will be £2,000.

The required rate of return is 20%. The company uses DCF techniques to guide these decisions.

Should Soho Ale acquire the new brewing machine? Show your calculations. Company procedures require the computing of the PV of each alternative. The most desirable alternative is the one with the least cost. Assume that the PV of £1 at 20% for 5 years is £.40; the PV of an annuity of £1 at 20% for 5 years is £3.

12-55 Replacement Decision

The **Metropolitan Transit Authority (MTA)** has included a cafeteria car on the passenger train it operates. Yearly operations of the cafeteria car have shown a consistent loss, which is expected to persist, as follows:

Revenue (in cash)		$200,000
Expenses for food, supplies, etc. (in cash)	$100,000	
Salaries	110,000	210,000
Net loss (ignore depreciation on the dining car itself)		$(10,000)

The Auto-Vend Company has offered to sell automatic vending machines to MTA for $22,000, less a $3,000 trade-in allowance on old equipment (which is carried at $3,000 book value, and which can be sold outright for $3,000 cash) now used in the cafeteria-car operation. The useful life of the vending equipment is estimated at 10 years, with zero scrap value. Experience elsewhere has led executives to predict that the equipment will serve 50% more food than the dining car, but prices will be 50% less, so the new revenue will probably be $150,000. The variety and mix of food sold are expected to be the same as for the cafeteria car. A catering company will completely service and supply food and beverages for the machines, paying 10% of revenue to MTA and bearing all costs of food, repairs, and so on. All dining-car employees will be discharged immediately. Their termination pay will total $35,000. However, an attendant who has some general knowledge of vending machines will be needed for one shift per day. The annual cost to MTA for the attendant will be $13,000.

For political and other reasons, the railroad will definitely not abandon its food service. The old equipment will have zero scrap value at the end of 10 years.

Using the preceding data, compute the following. Label computations. Ignore income taxes.

1. Use the NPV method to analyze the incremental investment. Assume a required rate of return of 10%. For this problem, assume that the PV of $1 at 10% to be received at the end of 10 years is $.400 and that the PV of an annuity of $1 at 10% for 10 years is $6.000.

2. What would be the minimum amount of annual revenue that MTA would have to receive from the catering company to justify making the investment? Show computations.

12-56 Minimization of Transportation Costs Without Income Taxes

Green Lighting Company produces industrial and residential lighting fixtures at its manufacturing facility located in Scottsdale, Arizona. The company currently ships products to an eastern warehouse via common carriers at a rate of $.27 per pound of fixtures. The warehouse is located in Atlanta, 1,900 miles from Scottsdale.

Alexis Azra, the treasurer of Green Lighting, is considering whether to purchase a truck for transporting products to the eastern warehouse. The following data on the truck are available:

Purchase price	$75,000
Useful life	4 years
Salvage value after 4 years	0
Capacity of truck	7,000 lb
Cash costs of operating truck	$.95 per mile

Azra feels that an investment in this truck is particularly attractive because of her successful negotiation with Jetson to back-haul Jetson's products from Atlanta to Scottsdale on every return trip from the warehouse. Jetson has agreed to pay Green Lighting $2,300 per load of Jetson's products hauled from Atlanta to Scottsdale up to and including 100 loads per year.

Green Lighting's marketing manager has estimated that the company will ship 385,000 pounds of fixtures to the eastern warehouse each year for the next 4 years. The truck will be fully loaded on each round trip.

Ignore income taxes.

1. Assume that Green Lighting requires a rate of return of 18%. Should it purchase the truck? Show computations to support your answer.
2. What is the minimum number of trips that Jetson must guarantee to make the deal acceptable to Green Lighting, based on the preceding numbers alone?
3. What qualitative factors might influence your decision? Be specific.

12-57 Straight-Line Depreciation, MACRS Depreciation, and Immediate Write-Off

Mr. Hiramatsu bought a new $50,000 freezer for his grocery store on January 2, 2013. The freezer has a 5-year economic life and recovery period, Mr. Hiramatsu's required rate of return is 12%, and his tax rate is 40%.

1. Suppose Mr. Hiramatsu uses straight-line depreciation for tax purposes. Compute the PV of the tax savings from depreciation. Assume that Mr. Hiramatsu takes a full year of depreciation at the end of 2013.
2. Suppose Mr. Hiramatsu uses MACRS depreciation for tax purposes. Compute the PV of the tax savings from depreciation.
3. Suppose Mr. Hiramatsu was allowed to immediately deduct the entire cost of the freezer for tax purposes. Compute the PV of the tax savings from depreciation.
4. Which of the three methods of deducting the cost of the freezer would Mr. Hiramatsu prefer if all three were allowable for tax purposes? Why?

12-58 MACRS, Residual Value

The Donald Company estimates that it can save $20,000 per year in annual operating cash costs for the next 3 years if it buys a special-purpose machine at a cost of $46,000. Residual value is expected to be $6,000, although no residual value is being provided for in using MACRS depreciation (3-year recovery period) for tax purposes. The company will sell the equipment at the end of the third year. The required rate of return is 16%. Assume the income tax rate is 30%.

Using the NPV method, show whether the investment is desirable.

12-59 Purchase of Equipment, MACRS

The Scranton Clinic, a for-profit medical facility, is planning to spend $35,000 for modernized MRI equipment. It will replace equipment that has zero book value and no salvage value, although the old equipment would have lasted another 10 years.

The new equipment will save $6,000 in cash operating costs for each of the next 10 years, at which time the clinic will sell it for $8,500. A major overhaul costing $9,000 will occur at the end of the seventh year; the old equipment would require no such overhaul. The entire cost of the overhaul is deductible for tax purposes in the seventh year. The equipment has a 3-year recovery period. The clinic uses MACRS depreciation for tax purposes.

The required rate of return is 8%. The applicable income tax rate is 44%.

Compute the after-tax NPV. Is the new equipment a desirable investment?

12-60 MACRS and Low-Income Housing

Aaron Hersch is a real estate developer who specializes in residential apartments. A complex of 20 run-down apartments has recently come on the market for $332,500. Hersch predicts that after remodeling, the 12 one-bedroom units will rent for $380 per month and the 8 two-bedroom apartments for

$440. He budgets 15% of the rental fees for repairs and maintenance. It should be 30 years before the apartments need remodeling again, if the work is done well. Remodeling costs are $15,000 per apartment. Both purchase price and remodeling costs qualify as 27.5-year MACRS property.

Assume that the MACRS schedule uses the straight-line method. It divides the total cost recovery amount by 27.5 and assigns a full year of depreciation to year 1 and a half year to year 28.

Hersch does not believe he will keep the apartment complex for its entire 30-year life. Most likely he will sell it just after the end of the tenth year. His predicted sales price is $980,000.

Hersch's required rate of return is 10%, and his tax rate is 38%.

Should Hersch buy the apartment complex? What is the after-tax NPV? Ignore tax complications, such as capital gains.

12-61 PV of After-Tax Cash Flows, Payback, and ARR

Suppose that Mitsubishi Chemical Corporation is planning to buy new equipment to expand its production of a popular solvent. Estimated data are as follows (monetary amounts are in thousands of Japanese yen):

Cash cost of new equipment now	¥400,000
Estimated life in years	10
Terminal salvage value	¥ 50,000
Incremental revenues per year	¥330,000
Incremental expenses per year other than depreciation	¥165,000

Assume a 60% flat rate for income taxes. The company receives all revenues and pays all expenses other than depreciation in cash. Use a 14% discount rate. Assume that the company uses ordinary straight-line depreciation based on a 10-year recovery period for tax purposes. Also assume that the company depreciates the original cost less the terminal salvage value.

Compute the following:

1. Depreciation expense per year
2. Anticipated net income per year
3. Annual net cash flow
4. Payback period
5. ARR on initial investment
6. NPV

12-62 Investment Justification Analysis and Graphs

Consider a new video game developed by Dynamic Gaming, Inc. (DGI). DGI's development team was formed at the end of 2009 and has been working on the development of the game for several years. After spending $175,000 on the development, the team has reached the point in 2013 where it must make a decision on whether to proceed with production of the game. Production of the game will require an initial investment in facilities of $199,500 at the end of 2013. The project has an expected life cycle of 7 years (end of 2013 through 2020). Predicted cash flows for the game are as follows (assuming that all cash flows occur at the end of the year):

End of Year	Cash Inflow	Cash Outflow
2013	$ 0	$199,500
2014	100,000	100,000
2015	220,000	180,000
2016	340,000	260,000
2017	460,000	320,000
2018	470,000	280,000
2019	410,000	200,000
2020	150,000	120,000

DGI's applicable tax rate is 40%, and DGI uses straight-line depreciation over the asset's expected life for tax purposes. The salvage value of the facilities will be zero in 7 years. DGI uses two criteria to evaluate potential investments: payback time and NPV. It wants a payback period of 3 years or less and an NPV greater than zero. DGI has a cost of capital of 18%.

1. Prepare a table that shows the after-tax annual net cash flows, cumulative net cash flow, and cumulative discounted net cash flow each year.
2. Would DGI invest in production of the game if it uses the payback period?
3. Would DGI invest in production of the game if it uses the NPV model?
4. Would you recommend that DGI invest in this project? Explain.

12-63 Fixed and Current Assets; Evaluation of Performance

Museum Clinic has been under pressure to keep costs down. The clinic administrator has been managing various revenue-producing centers to maximize contributions to the recovery of the operating costs of the clinic as a whole. The administrator has been considering whether to buy a special-purpose CAT scan machine for $251,000. Its unique characteristics would generate additional cash operating income of $50,000 per year for the clinic as a whole.

The clinic expects the machine to have a useful life of 8 years and a terminal salvage value of $35,000. The machine is delicate. It requires a constant inventory of various supplies and spare parts. When the clinic uses some of these items, it instantly replaces them so it maintains an investment of $7,000 at all times. However, the clinic fully recovers this investment at the end of the useful life of the machine.

1. Compute NPV if the required rate of return is 10%.
2. Compute the ARR on (a) the initial investment and (b) the "average" investment. Assume straight-line depreciation.
3. Why might the administrator be reluctant to base her decision on the DCF model?

12-64 Investment Before and After Taxes

Deer Valley Lodge, a ski area near Salt Lake City, has plans to eventually add five new chairlifts. Suppose that one of the lifts costs $2.2 million, and preparing the slope and installing the lift costs another $1.48 million. The lift will allow 300 additional skiers on the slopes, but there are only 40 days a year when the lodge needs the extra capacity. (Assume that Deer Valley will sell all 300 lift tickets on those 40 days.) Running the new lift will cost $500 a day for the entire 200 days the lodge is open. Assume that lift tickets at Deer Valley cost $65 a day and added cash expenses for each skier-day are $9. The new lift has an economic life of 20 years.

1. Assume that the before-tax required rate of return for Deer Valley is 14%. Compute the before-tax NPV of the new lift and advise the managers of Deer Valley about whether adding the lift will be a profitable investment.
2. Assume that the after-tax required rate of return for Deer Valley is 8%, the income tax rate is 40%, and the MACRS recovery period is 10 years. Compute the after-tax NPV of the new lift and advise the managers of Deer Valley about whether adding the lift will be a profitable investment.
3. What subjective factors would affect the investment decision?

12-65 After-Tax NPV

Berradi Corp. is considering the purchase of a new stamping machine to manufacture its product. The following information is available:

New Machine	
Purchase cost new	$85,000
Annual increase in cash revenues	60,000
Annual increase in cash operating costs	42,000
Salvage value—10 years from now	5,000

If Berradi purchases the new machine, it will use it for 10 years and then trade it in on another machine. The company computes depreciation on a straight-line basis, for both taxes and financial reporting purposes. Assume Berradi currently has an old stamping machine with a book value of $30,000 that it can currently dispose of for $8,000 if it buys the new machine. Assume Berradi's cost of capital is 14%, and its tax rate is 30%.

Should the new machine be purchased based on the NPV method?

12-66 Minimization of Transportation Costs After Taxes, Inflation

Study Appendix 11. (This problem is similar to Problem 12-56, but the numbers are different and it includes taxes and inflation elements.) The Green Lighting Company produces industrial and residential lighting fixtures at its manufacturing facility in Scottsdale. The company currently ships products to an eastern warehouse via common carriers at a rate of $.26 per pound of fixtures (expressed in year-zero dollars). The warehouse is located in Cleveland, 2,500 miles from Scottsdale. The rate will increase with inflation.

Alexis Azra, the treasurer of Green Lighting, is currently considering whether to purchase a truck for transporting products to the eastern warehouse. The following data on the truck are available:

Purchase price	$50,000
Useful life	5 years
Salvage value after 5 years	0
Capacity of truck	10,000 lb
Cash costs of operating truck	$.90 per mile

Azra feels that an investment in this truck is particularly attractive because of her successful negotiation with Jetson to back-haul Jetson's products from Cleveland to Scottsdale on every return trip from the warehouse. Jetson has agreed to pay Green Lighting $2,400 per load of Jetson's products hauled from Cleveland to Scottsdale for as many loads as Green Lighting can accommodate, up to and including 100 loads per year over the next 5 years.

Green Lighting's marketing manager has estimated that the company will ship 500,000 pounds of fixtures to the eastern warehouse each year for the next 5 years. The truck will be fully loaded on each round trip.

Make the following assumptions:

a. Green Lighting requires a 20% after-tax rate of return, which includes a 10% element attributable to inflation.

b. A 40% tax rate.

c. MACRS depreciation based on 5-year cost recovery period.

d. An inflation rate of 10%.

1. Should Green Lighting purchase the truck? Show computations to support your answer.
2. What qualitative factors might influence your decision? Be specific.

12-67 Inflation and Nonprofit Institution

Study Appendix 11. MLK Elementary School is considering the purchase of a photocopying machine for $7,000 on December 31, 20X0. The machine will have a useful life of 5 years and no residual value. The cash operating savings are expected to be $2,000 annually, measured in 20X0 dollars.

The required rate is 14%, which includes an element attributable to anticipated inflation of 6%. (Remember that the school district pays no income taxes.)

Use the 14% required rate for numbers 1 and 2:

1. Compute the NPV of the project without adjusting the cash operating savings for inflation.
2. Repeat number 1, adjusting the cash operating savings upward in accordance with the 6% inflation rate.
3. Compare your results in numbers 1 and 2. What generalization seems applicable about the analysis of inflation in capital budgeting?

CASES

12-68 Investment in CAD/CAM

Aswega AS is an Estonian manufacturer of electromagnetic flowmeters, heatmeters, and calibration equipment located in Tallinn. Suppose that it is considering the installation of a computer-aided design/computer-aided manufacturing (CAD/CAM) system. The current proposal calls for implementation of only the CAD portion of the system. The manager in charge of production design and planning has estimated that the CAD portion of CAD/CAM could do the work of five designers, who are each paid EEK 520,000 per year (52 weeks $\times$ 40 hours $\times$ EEK 250 per hour), where EEK is the symbol for the Estonian kroon.

Aswega can purchase the CAD/CAM system for EEK 2.8 million. (It cannot purchase the CAD portion separately.) The annual out-of-pocket costs of running the CAD portion of the system are EEK 1.8 million. The company expects to use the system for 8 years. The company's required rate of return is 12%. Ignore income taxes.

1. Compute the NPV of the investment in the CAD/CAM system. Should Aswega purchase the system? Explain.
2. Suppose the manager was not certain about her predictions of savings and economic life. Possibly the company will replace only four designers, but if everything works out well, it may replace as many as six. If better systems become available, the company may use the CAD/CAM system for

only 5 years, but it might last as long as 10 years. Prepare pessimistic, most likely, and optimistic predictions of NPV. Would this analysis make you more confident or less confident in your decision in number 1? Explain.

3. What subjective factors might influence your decision?

12-69 Investment in Technology

Nashville Tool Company is considering installation of a CIM system as part of its implementation of a JIT philosophy. Gretchen Torres, company president, is convinced that the new system is necessary, but she needs the numbers to convince the board of directors. This is a major move for the company, and approval at board level is required.

Maria, Gretchen's daughter, has been assigned the task of justifying the investment. She is a business school graduate and understands the use of NPV for capital-budgeting decisions. To identify relevant costs, she developed the following information.

Nashville Tool Company produces a variety of small automobile components and sells them to auto manufacturers. It has a 40% market share, with the following condensed results expected for 2011:

Sales		$12,000,000
Cost of goods sold		
Variable	$4,000,000	
Fixed	4,300,000	8,300,000
Selling and administrative expenses		
Variable	$2,000,000	
Fixed	400,000	2,400,000
Operating income		$ 1,300,000

Installation of the CIM system will cost $6 million, and the company expects the system to have a useful life of 6 years with no salvage value. Installation will occur at the beginning of 2012. In 2012, the training costs for personnel will exceed any cost savings by $400,000. In years 2013–2017, variable cost of goods sold will decrease by 35%, an annual savings of $1.4 million. There will be no savings in fixed cost of goods sold—it will increase by the amount of the straight-line depreciation on the new system. Selling and administrative expenses will not be affected. The required rate of return is 12%. Assume that all cash flows occur at the end of the year the revenue or expense is recognized, except the initial investment, which occurs at the beginning of 2012. Ignore income taxes.

1. Suppose that Maria assumes that production and sales would continue for the next 6 years as they are expected in 2011 in the absence of investment in the CIM. Compute the NPV of investing in the CIM.

2. Now suppose Maria predicts that it will be difficult to compete without installing the CIM. She has undertaken market research that estimates a drop in market share of three percentage points a year starting in 2012 in the absence of investment in the CIM (i.e., market share will be 37% in 2012, 34% in 2013, 31% in 2014, etc.). Her study also showed that the total market sales level will stay the same, and she does not expect market prices to change. Compute the NPV of investing in the CIM.

3. Prepare a memo from Maria to the board of directors of Nashville Tool Company. In the memo, explain why the analysis in number 2 is appropriate and why analyses such as that in number 1 cause companies to underinvest in high-technology projects. Include an explanation of qualitative factors that are not included in the NPV calculation.

12-70 Investment in Quality

The Sydney Manufacturing Company produces a single model of a high-quality DVD player that it sells to Australian manufacturers of sound systems. It sells each DVD player for $210, resulting in a contribution margin of $70 before considering any costs of inspection, correction of product defects, or refunds to customers.

On January 1, 2014, top management at Sydney is contemplating a change in its quality control system. Currently, the company spends $30,000 annually on quality control inspections for the 50,000 DVD players it produces and ships each year. In producing those DVD players, the company produces an average of 2,000 defective units. The inspection process identifies 1,500 of these, and the company spends an average of $85 on each to correct the defects. The company ships the other 500 defective players to customers. When a customer discovers a defective DVD player, Sydney Manufacturing refunds the $210 purchase price.

Many of Sydney's customers build the DVD players into home-entertainment units. As more of these customers change to JIT inventory systems and automated production processes, the receipt of defective goods poses greater and greater problems for them. Sometimes a defective DVD player causes them to delay their whole production line while they replace the DVD player. Companies competing with Sydney recognize this situation, and most have already begun extensive quality control programs. If Sydney does not improve quality, sales volume is expected to fall by 5,000 DVD players a year, beginning after 2014:

	Predicted Sales Volume in Units Without Quality Control Program	Predicted Sales Volume in Units with Quality Control Program
2014	50,000	50,000
2015	45,000	50,000
2016	40,000	50,000
2017	35,000	50,000

The proposed quality control program has two elements. First, Sydney would spend $950,000 immediately to train workers to recognize and correct defects at the time they occur. This is expected to cut the number of defective DVD players produced from 2,000 to 500 without incurring additional manufacturing costs. Second, an earlier inspection point would replace the current inspection. This would require purchase of an X-ray machine at a cost of $250,000 plus additional annual operating costs of $60,000 more than the current inspection costs. Early detection of defects would reduce the average amount spent to correct defects from $85 to $50, and only 50 defective DVD players would be shipped to customers. To compete, Sydney would refund one-and-one-half times the purchase price ($315) for defective DVD players delivered to customers.

Top management at Sydney has decided that a 4-year planning period is sufficient for analyzing this decision. The required rate of return is 20%. For simplicity, assume that under the current quality control system, if the volume of production decreases, the number of defective DVD players produced remains at 2,000. Also assume that all annual cash flows occur at the end of the relevant year. Should Sydney undertake the new quality control program? Explain using the NPV model. Ignore income taxes.

12-71 Make or Buy and Replacement of Equipment

International Hoists is one of the largest producers of hoists of all types. An especially complex part of a particular auto hoist needs special tools that are not useful for other products. The company purchased these tools on July 1, 20X0, for $2,000,000.

It is now July 1, 20X4. The manager of the auto hoists division, David Lee, is contemplating three alternatives. First, he could continue to produce the ship using the current tools; they will last another 5 years, at which time they would have zero terminal value. Second, he could sell the tools for $400,000 and purchase the parts from an outside supplier for $110 each. Third, he could replace the tools with new, more efficient tools costing $1,800,000.

Lee expects to produce 8,000 units of this particular hoist each of the next 5 years. Manufacturing costs for the hoist have been as follows, and no change in costs is expected:

Direct materials	$ 38
Direct labor	37
Variable overhead	17
Fixed overhead[*]	45
Total unit cost	$137

[*]Depreciation accounts for two-thirds of the fixed overhead. The balance is for other fixed overhead costs of the factory that require cash outlays, 60% of which would be saved if production of the parts were eliminated.

The outside supplier offered the $110 price on a 5-year contract as a once-only offer. It is unlikely it would make such a low price available later. International Hoists would also have to guarantee to purchase at least 7,000 parts for each of the next 5 years.

The new tools that are available would last for 5 years with a disposal value of $500,000 at the end of 5 years. The old tools are a 5-year MACRS property, the new tools are a 3-year MACRS property, and both use the current MACRS schedules. International Hoists uses straight-line depreciation for book purposes and MACRS for tax purposes. The sales representative selling the new tools stated, "The new tools will allow direct labor and variable overhead to be reduced by $21 per unit." Lee thinks this estimate is accurate. However, he also knows that a higher quality of materials would be necessary with the new tools. He predicts the following costs with the new tools:

Direct materials	$ 40
Direct labor	25
Variable overhead	8
Fixed overhead	60*
Total unit cost	$133

*The increase in fixed overhead is caused by depreciation on the new tools.

The company has a 40% marginal tax rate and requires a 12% after-tax rate of return.

1. Calculate the NPV of each of the three alternatives. Recognize the tax implications. Which alternative should Lee select?
2. What are some factors besides the NPV that should influence Lee's selection?

NIKE 10-K PROBLEM

12-72 Nike Capital Budgeting with NPV

Examine Nike's financial statements and notes 1 and 3 to those statements.

1. What method of depreciation does Nike use in reporting to shareholders? Do you think it uses the same method for tax purposes? If not, what method do you suppose they use for tax reporting? Why?
2. What is the original cost of the machinery and equipment currently used by Nike? If Nike generally invests about $400 million per year in machinery and equipment, what is the average useful life of its machinery and equipment?
3. Nike's Statement of Cash Flows shows that the company invested $432 million in property, plant, and equipment during fiscal 2011. Assume that these assets have a useful life of 5 years and that Nike requires a 14% pretax rate of return. Compute the minimum average annual pretax net cash inflow that would justify this investment.
4. Using the $432 million of investment and the net cash flow you computed in requirement 3 (and assuming zero residual value), determine the investment's a) payback period and b) accounting rate of return on average investment.

EXCEL APPLICATION EXERCISE

12-73 Net Present Value and Payback Period for a Purchase Decision

Goal: Create a spreadsheet to compute the NPV and payback period to assist with a purchase decision. Use the results to answer questions about your findings.

Scenario: Amazon.com is planning to purchase a new bar-coding machine for one of its warehouses. You have been asked to prepare a simple analysis to determine whether Amazon should purchase the machine. The bar-coding machine costs $60,000. It has a 5-year economic life and an estimated residual value of $10,000. The estimated annual net cash flow from the machine is $16,000. Amazon.com's required rate of return is 16%.

When you have completed your spreadsheet, answer the following questions:

1. What is the machine's NPV?
2. What is the machine's payback period?
3. Should Amazon.com purchase the machine? Why or why not?

Step-by-Step:
1. Open a new Excel spreadsheet.
2. In column A, create bold-faced headings that contain the following:
   Row 1: Chapter 12 Decision Guideline
   Row 2: Amazon.com
   Row 3: Analysis for Purchase of Bar-Coding Machine
   Row 4: Today's Date
3. Merge and center the four heading rows across columns A–H.

4. In row 7, create the following bold-faced headings:
   Column A: Cash Outflow
   Column B: Calculations
   Column D: Annualized Cash Flows

5. Center the heading in column A, row 7 and then shade the heading as follows:

   Patterns tab: Color: Lightest gray (above white)

   Note: Adjust column width as necessary.

6. Merge and center the heading in column B, row 7 across columns B–C.

7. Merge and center the heading in column D, row 7 across columns D–H and shade the heading as follows:

   Patterns tab: Color: Lightest gray (above white)

8. In row 8, create the following bold-faced, center-justified column headings:
   Column A: Investment
   Column B: Net Present Value
   Column C: Payback Period
   Column D: Year 1
   Column E: Year 2
   Column F: Year 3
   Column G: Year 4
   Column H: Year 5

   Note: Adjust the width of columns B and C as necessary.

9. Use the scenario data to fill in the investment and annualized cash flows for each of the 5 years.

   Note: The amount in the Investment column should be entered as a negative amount because it represents cash outflow. Be sure to include the machine's residual value in the appropriate column when entering the Annualized Cash Flows data.

10. Use the NPV function to calculate the NPV of the machine in column B, row 9.
    Click Insert on the tool bar and select Function. Then do the following:

    Function category: Financial

    Function name: NPV

    Complete the fill-in form that appears with the appropriate data from the scenario.

    Hint: Go to "Help" and search the topic "NPV." Review the help text that appears. Carefully read the examples given and their associated formulas. Use the formula that matches the scenario data for the problem.

11. Enter a formula to calculate the payback period in column C, row 9. Ensure a positive result by using the absolute value function in your payback formula. (The formula can be found in the chapter.)

12. Modify the format of the payback period result by clicking in the cell containing the results. At the end of the formula that appears in the formula bar, type the following: & "years".
    Right justify the result.

13. Format row 9, columns A–B and columns D–H as follows:

    Number tab: Category: Currency

    Decimal places: 2

    Symbol: $

    Negative numbers: Red with parentheses

14. Save your work, and print a copy for your files.

    Note: Print your spreadsheet using landscape to ensure that all columns appear on one page.

COLLABORATIVE LEARNING EXERCISE

12-74 Capital Budgeting, Sensitivity Analysis, and Ethics

Abrielle Rossi had recently been appointed controller of the soup division of a major food company. The division manager, Asim Sharma, was known as a hard-driving, intelligent, uncompromising manager. He had been very successful and was rumored to be on the fast track to corporate top management, maybe even in line for the company presidency. One of Abrielle's first assignments was to prepare the financial analysis for a new soup, Delhi Chicken. This product was especially important to Sharma because he was convinced that it would be a success and thereby a springboard for his ascent to top management.

Rossi discussed the product with the food lab that had designed it, with the market research department that had tested it, and with the finance people who would have to fund its introduction. After putting together all the information, she developed the following optimistic and pessimistic sales projections:

	Optimistic	Pessimistic
Year 1	$ 1,600,000	$ 800,000
Year 2	3,600,000	1,200,000
Year 3	5,000,000	1,000,000
Year 4	8,000,000	800,000
Year 5	10,000,000	400,000

The optimistic predictions assume a successful introduction of a popular product. The pessimistic predictions assume that the product is introduced but does not gain wide acceptance and is terminated after 5 years. Rossi thinks the most likely results are halfway between the optimistic and pessimistic predictions.

Rossi learned from finance that this type of product introduction requires a predicted pretax rate of return of 16% before top management will authorize funds for its introduction. She also determined that the contribution margin should be about 50% on the product but could be as low as 42% or as high as 58%. Initial investment would include $3.5 million for production facilities and $2.5 million for advertising and other product introduction expenses. The production facilities would have a value of $1.2 million after 5 years.

Based on her preliminary analysis, Rossi recommended to Sharma that the product not be launched. Sharma was not pleased with the recommendation. He claimed that Rossi was much too pessimistic and asked her to redo her numbers so that he could justify the product to top management.

Rossi carried out further analysis, but her predictions came out no different. She became even more convinced that her projections were accurate. Yet, she was certain that if she returned to Sharma with numbers that did not support introduction of the product, she would incur his wrath. And he could be right—that is, there is so much uncertainty in the forecasts that she could easily come up with believable numbers that would support going forward with the product. She would not believe them, but she believed she could convince top management that they were accurate.

The entire class could role-play this scenario or it could be done in teams of three to six persons. Here, it is acted out by a team.

Choose one member of the team to be Abrielle Rossi and one to be Asim Sharma.

1. With the help of the entire team except the person chosen to be Sharma, Rossi should prepare the capital-budgeting analysis used for her first meeting with Sharma.
2. Next, Rossi should meet again with Sharma. They should try to agree on the analysis to take forward to top management. As they discuss the issues and try to come to an agreement, the remaining team members should record all the ethical judgments each discussant makes.
3. After Rossi and Sharma have completed their role-playing assignment, the entire team should assess the ethical judgments made by each and recommend an appropriate position for Rossi to take in this situation.

INTERNET EXERCISE

12-75 Capital Budgeting at Carnival Corporation

Many companies strive to continue to grow and develop. Some companies grow through the expansion of existing operations and increased utilization of existing assets. Others grow through the acquisition of firms within their industry or by purchasing a firm that opens up new direction for them. No matter which method a company selects, capital budgeting is an important part of a systematic expansion plan. Consider the expansion activities of **Carnival Corporation**, the cruise ship company.

1. Go to Carnival Corporation's home page at www.carnivalcorp.com. What cruise lines does Carnival own or have an interest in? Now go to the page "Corporate Information." How many ships does Carnival currently operate? What type of plans does the firm list for future expansion? What does this information indicate about the intent of the firm?
2. As we can see, the firm has looked ahead to buying new ships. To get additional information, click on the link to "Investor Relations" and then "Financial Reports." Select the most recent annual report and open it. Go to the section on Highlights near the beginning of the report. Looking at passengers carried and passenger capacity, examine how capacity available and capacity used have changed over the past 5 years.
3. Now examine the CEO's letter. What does the letter tell the investor about new investment during the current year and investment plans for the future?
4. Let's look at the Statement of Cash Flows to see if we can determine where the firm got the cash to pay for the new ships. Based on your review of the cash flow statement, how much money did

the firm invest in new property and equipment? Did Carnival generate the cash to pay for this investment from operations or from financing activities?

Solutions to Exercises in Compound Interest, Problem 12-A1

The general approach to these exercises centers on one fundamental question: Which of the two basic tables am I dealing with? No calculations should be made until after this question is answered with assurance. If you made any errors, it is possible that you used the wrong table.

1. From Table B-1:
   a. $19,587.50
   b. $15,522.50
   c. $10,047.50

   The $25,000 is an amount of future worth. You want the PV of that amount:

   $$PV = \$25,000 \times \frac{1}{[(1+i)^n]}$$

   The conversion factor, $1/(1+i)^n$, is on line 5 of Table B-1. Substituting,

   $$PV = \$25,000(.7835) = \$19,587.50$$
   $$PV = \$25,000(.6209) = \$15,522.50$$
   $$PV = \$25,000(.4019) = \$10,047.50$$

   Note that the higher the interest rate, the lower the PV.

2. From Table B-2:
   a. $8,659.00
   b. $7,581.60
   c. $5,981.20

   The $2,000 withdrawal is a uniform annual amount, an annuity. You need to find the PV of an annuity for 5 years:

   $$PV_A = \text{annual withdrawal} \times F, \text{ where F is the conversion factor.}$$

   Substituting:

   $$PV_A = \$2,000(4.3295) = \$8,659.00$$
   $$PV_A = \$2,000(3.7908) = \$7,581.60$$
   $$PV_A = \$2,000(2.9906) = \$5,981.20$$

3. From Table B-2:
   a. $23,097.36
   b. $26,379.66

   You have $100,000, the PV of your contemplated annuity. You must find the annuity that will just exhaust the invested principal in 5 years:

   $$PV_A = \text{annual withdrawal} \times F$$
   $$\$100,000 = \text{annual withdrawal} \times 4.3295$$
   $$\text{annual withrawal} = \$100,000 \div 4.3295$$
   $$= \$23,097.36$$
   $$\$100,000 = \text{annual withdrawal} \times 3.7908$$
   $$\text{annual withdrawal} = \$100,000 \div 3.7908$$
   $$= \$26,379.66$$

4. Amounts are in thousands. From Table B-1: LeBron's contract is preferable; its PV exceeds that of Kobe's contract by $43,143 − $35,441 = $7,702. Note that the nearer dollars are more valuable than the distant dollars.

Year	Present Value at 16% from Table B-1	Present Value of LeBron's Contract	Present Value of Kobe's Contract
1	.8621	$17,242	$ 3,448
2	.7432	11,891	5,946
3	.6407	7,688	7,688
4	.5523	4,418	8,837
5	.4761	1,904	9,522
		$43,143	$35,441

Appendix A   Recommended Readings

The following readings will aid readers who want to pursue some topics in more depth than is possible in this book. There is a hazard in compiling a group of recommended readings. Inevitably, we will omit some worthwhile books or periodicals. Moreover, such a list cannot include books published subsequently to the compilation date. Although this list is not comprehensive, it includes many excellent readings.

Periodicals

Professional Journals

The following professional journals are typically available in university libraries and include articles on the application of management accounting:

- *Accounting Horizons.* Published by the American Accounting Association; stresses current practice-oriented articles in all areas of accounting
- *CMA Magazine.* Published by CMA Canada; includes much practice-oriented research in management accounting
- *Cost Management.* Published by Thompson Reuters; stresses cost management tools
- *Financial Executive.* Published by Financial Executives International; emphasizes general policy issues for accounting and finance executives
- *The Journal of Corporate Accounting & Finance.* Published by Wiley; directed to corporate accounting and finance executives and outside auditors and accountants working for the corporation
- *Harvard Business Review.* Published by Harvard Business School; directed to general managers but contains excellent articles on applications of management accounting
- *Journal of Accountancy.* Published by the American Institute of CPAs; emphasizes financial accounting and is directed at the practicing CPA
- *Management Accounting Quarterly.* An online journal published by the Institute of Management Accountants; practical articles with an academic focus
- *Strategic Finance.* Published by the Institute of Management Accountants; many articles on actual applications by individual organizations
- *BusinessWeek, Forbes, Fortune, the Economist, and the Wall Street Journal.* Popular publications that cover a variety of business and economics topics; often their articles relate to management accounting

Academic Journals

The academic journal that focuses most directly on current management and cost accounting research is the *Journal of Management Accounting Research*, published by the Management Accounting section of the American Accounting Association. *The Accounting Review*, the general research publication of the American Accounting Association; *Journal of Accounting Research*, published at the University of Chicago; and *Contemporary Accounting Research*, published by the Canadian Academic Association, cover all accounting topics at a more theoretical level. *Accounting, Organizations and Society*, a British journal, publishes research on behavioral aspects of management accounting. The *Journal of Accounting and Economics* covers economics-based accounting research. *Journal of Accounting, Ethics and Public Policy* and *Research on Professional Responsibility and Ethics in Accounting* are journals devoted to ethical issues.

Books in Management Accounting

Most of the topics in this text are covered in more detail in the many books on cost accounting, including *Cost Accounting: A Managerial Emphasis*, 14th edition, by C. T. Horngren, S. Datar, and M. Rajan (Prentice Hall, 2012). You can find more advanced coverage in *Advanced Management Accounting*, 3rd edition, by R. S. Kaplan and A. A. Atkinson (Prentice Hall, 1998). Current management accounting issues are discussed in *Issues in Management Accounting* by Trevor Hopper, Robert W. Scapens, and Deryl Northcott (Prentice Hall, 2007).

Financial Executives International, 1250 Headquarters Plaza, West Tower, 7th Floor, Morristown, NJ, 07960, and the IMA, 10 Paragon Drive, Suite 1, Montvale, NJ 07645-1760, have long lists of accounting research publications.

Handbooks, General Texts, and Case Books

The books in this list have wide application to management accounting issues. The handbooks are basic references. The textbooks are designed for classroom use but may be useful for self-study. The case books present applications from real companies.

- Adkins, T. C., *Case Studies in Performance Management: A Guide from the Experts*, Hoboken, NJ: John Wiley & Sons, 2006.
- Allen, B. R., E. R. Brownlee, M. E. Haskins, L. J. Lynch, and J. W. Rotch, *Cases in Management Accounting and Control Systems*, 4th ed. Upper Saddle River, NJ: Prentice Hall, 2004.
- Bahnub, B., *Activity-Based Management for Financial Institutions: Driving Bottom-Line Results*, New York: Wiley, 2010.
- Bierman, H., Jr., and S. Smidt, *The Capital Budgeting Decision: Economic Analysis of Investment Projects*, 9th ed. Routledge, 2006. This text expands the capital budgeting discussion from Chapter 11.
- Bierman, H., Jr., and S. Smidt, *Advanced Capital Budgeting: Refinements in the Economic Analysis of Investment Projects*, Routledge, 2007.
- Groot, T., and K. Lukka (eds.), *Cases in Management Accounting: Current Practices in European Companies*, Harlow: Prentice Hall/Pearson, 2000.
- Kaplan, R., and S. Anderson, *Time-Driven Activity-Based Costing: A Simpler and More Powerful Path to Higher Profits*, Boston: Harvard Business Review Press, 2007.
- Manning, G. A., *Financial Investigation and Forensic Accounting*, 3rd ed. Boca Raton, FL: CRC Press, 2010.
- Pryor, T., et al., *Activity Dictionary: A Comprehensive Reference Tool for ABM and ABC: 2000 Edition*, Arlington, TX: ICMS, Inc., 2000.
- Render, B., R. Stair, and M. Hanna, *Quantitative Analysis for Management*, 11th ed. Prentice Hall, 2011.
- Rogers, J., *Strategy, Value, and Risk: The Real Options Approach*, 2nd Ed., Basingstoke, UK: Palgrave Macmillan, 2009.
- Seitz, N., and M. Ellison, *Capital Budgeting and Long-Term Financing Decisions*, Cincinnati, OH: South-Western, 2004.
- Shank, J., and V. Govindarajan, *Strategic Cost Management: The New Tool for Competitive Advantage*, New York: Free Press, 2008.
- Smith, J., *Handbook of Management Accounting*, 4th ed. London: CIMA, 2007.
- Weil, R., and M. Maher, *Handbook of Cost Management*, New York: Wiley, 2005.
- Young, S. M., *Readings in Management Accounting*, 6th ed. Upper Saddle River, NJ: Prentice Hall, 2012.

Accounting Ethics

Integrity is essential for accountants. An increasing emphasis on ethics has led to a number of books devoted to the subject.

- Brooks, L. J., and P. Dunn, *Business and Professional Ethics for Directors, Executives, & Accountants*, 5th ed., Mason, OH: South-Western, 2009.
- Duska, R. F., and B. S. Duska, *Accounting Ethics*, 2nd ed., Malden, MA: Wiley-Blackwell, 2011.
- Mintz, S. M., and R. E. Morris, *Ethical Obligations and Decision Making in Accounting: Text and Cases*, 2nd ed., New York: McGraw-Hill/Irwin, 2010.
- Pakaluk, M, and M. L. Cheffers, *Accounting Ethics*, Manchaug, MA: Allen David Press, 2011.

The Strategic Nature of Management Accounting

Management accountants realize that cost and performance information is most useful to organizations when it helps define strategic alternatives and helps in the management of resources to achieve strategic objectives. The books in this list, though not necessarily accounting books, provide a valuable foundation to the interaction of strategy and accounting information.

- Ansari, S., and J. Bell, *Target Costing: The Next Frontier in Strategic Cost Management*, Mountain Valley Publishing, 2009.
- Carr, L., and A. Nanni Jr., *Delivering Results: Managing What Matters*, Springer, 2009.
- Cokins, G., *Performance Management: Integrating Strategy Execution, Methodologies, Risk, and Analytics*, New York: Wiley, 2009.
- Grant, J. L., *Foundations of Economic Value Added*, 2nd ed. New York: Wiley, 2002.
- Kaplan, R., and D. Norton, *The Execution Premium: Linking Strategy to Operations for Competitive Advantage*, Boston: Harvard Business School Press, 2008.
- Magretta, J., *Understanding Michael Porter: The Essential Guide to Competition and Strategy*, Boston: Harvard Business Review Press, 2011.
- Stern, J., J. Shiely, and I. Ross, *The EVA Challenge: Implementing Value-Added Change in an Organization*, New York: Wiley, 2003.

Modern Manufacturing

The following books provide background on the role of accounting in modern manufacturing environments.

- Atkinson, A. A., R. S. Kaplan, E. M. Matsumura, and S. M. Young, *Management Accounting*, 6th ed. Upper Saddle River, NJ: Prentice Hall, 2012.
- Byrne, A., *The Lean Turnaround: How Business Leaders Use Lean Principles to Create Value and Transform Their Company*, New York: McGraw-Hill, 2013.
- Carreira, B, and B. Trudell, *Lean Six Sigma That Works: A Powerful Action Plan for Dramatically Improving Quality, Increasing Speed, and Reducing Waste*, New York: AMACOM, 2006.
- Cooper, R., and R. Kaplan, *Design of Cost Management Systems*, 2nd ed. Upper Saddle River, NJ: Prentice Hall, 1999.
- Cox III, J., and J. Schleier, *Theory of Constraints Handbook*, New York: McGraw-Hill, 2010.
- Goldratt, E. M., *Theory of Constraints*, Croton-on-Hudson, NY: North River Press, Inc., 2000.
- Goldratt, E. M., and J. Cox, *The Goal*, 3rd ed. Croton-on-Hudson, NY: North River Press, 2004. This is a novel illustrating the new manufacturing environment.
- Jacobs, F. R., R. Chase, and N. Aquilano, *Operations and Supply Management*, 12th ed., Homewood, IL: McGraw-Hill/Irwin, 2008.
- Mann, D., *Creating a Lean Culture: Tools to Sustain Lean Conversions*, 2nd ed., London: Productivity Press, 2010.
- Morgan, J., and M. Brenig-Jones, *Lean Six Sigma for Dummies*, 2nd ed., New York: Wiley, 2012.
- Pyzdek, T., and P. Keller, *The Six Sigma Handbook*, 3rd ed. New York: McGraw-Hill, 2009.
- Rubrich, L., and M. Watson, *Implementing World Class Manufacturing*, 2nd ed., Fort Wayne, IN: WCM Associates, 2004.
- Wilson, L., *How to Implement Lean Manufacturing*, New York: McGraw-Hill, 2009.

Management Control Systems

The topics of Chapters 7–10 can be explored further in several books, including the following:

- Anthony, R. N., and V. Govindarajan, *Management Control Systems*, 12th ed. McGraw-Hill/Irwin, 2006.
- Arrow, K. J., *The Limits of Organization*, New York: Norton, 1974. [This is a readable classic by a Nobel laureate.]
- Blocher, E., D. Stout, and G. Cokins, *Cost Management: A Strategic Emphasis*, 5th ed., McGraw-Hill/Irwin, 2009.
- Eckerson, W., *Performance Dashboards: Measuring, Monitoring, and Managing Your Business*, New York: Wiley, 2010.
- Gupta, P., and A. W. Wiggenhorn, *Six Sigma Business Scorecard: Creating a Comprehensive Corporate Performance Measurement System*, 2nd ed. New York: McGraw-Hill, 2006.

- Kaplan, R. S., and D. P. Norton, *The Balanced Scorecard: Measures That Drive Performance*, Boston: Harvard Business School Press, 1996.
- Kaplan, R. S., and D. P. Norton, *Alignment: Using the Balanced Scorecard to Create Corporate Synergies*, Boston: Harvard Business School Press, 2006.
- Merchant K., and W. Van der Stede, *Management Control Systems: Performance Measurement, Evaluation and Incentives*, 3rd ed. Upper Saddle River, NJ: Prentice Hall, 2012.
- Niven, P. R., *Balanced Scorecard Step-by-Step: Maximizing Performance and Maintaining Results*, 2nd ed., Hoboken, NJ: John Wiley & Sons, 2006.
- Parmenter, D., *Key Performance Indicators (KPI): Developing, Implementing, and Using Winning KPIs*, New York: Wiley, 2010.
- Simons, R., *Performance Measurement and Control Systems for Implementing Strategy*, Upper Saddle River, NJ: Prentice Hall, 2000.
- Solomons, D., *Divisional Performance: Measurement and Control*, New York: Markus Wiener, 1983. [This is a reprint of a 1965 classic that is still relevant.]

Management Accounting in Nonprofit Organizations

Many books discuss management accounting in nonprofit organizations, especially in health care. Examples are as follows:

- Anthony, R. N., and D. W. Young, *Management Control in Nonprofit Organizations*, 7th ed. Homewood, IL: Irwin, 2003.
- Baker, J. J., and R. W. Baker, *Health Care Finance: Basic Tools for Nonfinancial Managers*, 3rd ed. Sudbury, MA: Jones and Bartlett, 2009.
- Brimson, J., and J. Antos, *Activity Based Management for Service Industries, Government Entities, and Non-Profit Organizations*, New York: John Wiley & Sons, 1998.
- Finkler, S. A., D. M. Ward, and J. J. Baker, *Essentials of Cost Accounting for Health Care Organizations*, 3rd ed. Sudbury, MA: Jones and Bartlett, 2007.
- Gapenski, L. C., *Healthcare Finance: An Introduction to Accounting and Financial Management*, 4th ed. Washington DC: Health Administration Press, 2008.
- Marr, B., *Managing and Delivering Performance: How Government, Public Sector and Not-for-Profit Organisations Can Measure and Manage What Really Matters*, Abingdon, UK: Taylor & Francis, 2009.
- Niven, P., *Balanced Scorecard: Step-by-Step for Government and Nonprofit Agencies*, 2nd ed., New York: John Wiley & Sons, 2008.
- Young, D., *Management Accounting in Health Care Organizations*, 2nd ed., Jossey-Bass, 2009.

Online Resources

The online resources related to management accounting are too extensive to create a comprehensive list. The best way to access them may be to use a good search engine. However, we list a few URLs that can help you get started.

- AICPA's Financial Management Center: Information for CPAs in business and industry, at http://fmcenter.aicpa.org/
- Balanced Scorecard Institute: Includes a variety of resources related to the balanced scorecard, at http://www.balancedscorecard.org
- CMA Canada: Many services, including strategic management accounting practices and management accounting standards, at http://www.cma-canada.org
- Consortium for Advanced Manufacturing International (CAM-I): Online library, at http://www.cam-i.org
- Financial Executives International: Information for corporate financial officers, at http://www.fei.org
- IMA: A variety of services, including an index of research publications, at http://www.imanet.org/
- Metrus Group: A variation of the balance scorecard, at http://www.metrus.com/products/balanced-scorecards.html
- Stern Stewart & Co.: Information about economic value added by the firm that developed the technique, at http://www.sternstewart.com/

Appendix B   Fundamentals of Compound Interest and the Use of Present-Value Tables

The Nature of Interest

Interest is the cost of using money. A lender who loans an initial amount to a borrower now and receives repayment from the borrower later expects to receive more than the amount loaned. The difference between the initial amount loaned and the amount repaid later is interest. Interest is the rental fee for money, similar to the rental fees charged for the use of equipment or land.

Suppose you invest $10,000 in a savings account in a financial institution. In this transaction, you are lending your money to the financial institution. Your initial $10,000 investment (or loan to the financial institution) is the *principal*. Interest is the amount you earn on the investment each period. In this appendix, we focus on compound interest, where we add each period's interest to the beginning-of-the-period principal to come up with the principal for the start of the next period. For example, suppose the financial institution promised to pay 10% interest per year on your $10,000 investment. The $10\% \times \$10,000 = \$1,000$ interest the first year would create a principal of $\$10,000 + \$1,000 = \$11,000$ at the start of the second year. If you let the amount accumulate for 3 years before withdrawing the full balance of the deposit, the deposit would accumulate to $13,310:

	Principal	Compound Interest	Balance, End of Year
Year 1	$10,000	$10,000 × 0.10 = $1,000	$11,000
Year 2	11,000	11,000 × 0.10 = 1,100	12,100
Year 3	12,100	12,100 × 0.10 = 1,210	13,310

Because compound interest accumulates on both the original principal and the previously accumulated interest that has been added to principal each period, the "force" of compound interest can be staggering. For example, the $10,000 deposit would accumulate at 10% interest compounded annually as follows:

	At End of		
3 Years	10 Years	20 Years	40 Years
$13,310	$25,937	$67,275	$452,593

Step-by-step calculations of compound interest quickly become burdensome. However, the calculations can be described compactly in the formulas outlined next. These formulas are built into many handheld calculators and computer software programs. Compound interest tables show the results for various combinations of parameters.

This appendix explains how to use the two compound interest tables most commonly used in capital budgeting. Both tables allow us to calculate *present value*, the value today of a future amount. In the previous example, the $10,000 amount is a present value. The calculations showed what the future value of this amount would be after 3 years, 10 years, and so on. Another way to interpret these same calculations is that $10,000 is the present value of $13,310 to be repaid 3 years in the future, or the present value of $25,937 to be repaid 10 years in the future, or the present value of $452,593 to be repaid 40 years in the future. The remainder of this chapter explains how to use the tables to find the present value of any set of future payments.

Table B-1: Present Value of $1

How do you express a future cash inflow or outflow in terms of its equivalent today? Table B-1 provides factors that give the present value at time 0 of a single, lump-sum cash flow that you will receive or pay at the end of n periods.

Suppose you invest $1.00 today at 6% interest. It will grow to $1.06 in 1 year; that is, $\$1 \times 1.06 = \$1.06$. At the end of the second year, its value is $(\$1 \times 1.06) \times 1.06 = \$1 \times (1.06)^2 = \$1.124$; and at the end of the third year it is $\$1 \times (1.06)^3 = 1.191$. In n years at i percent interest, $1.00 grows to $\$1 \times (1 + i)^n$.

To determine the present value, you invert this accumulation process. If you will receive $1.00 in 1 year, it is worth $\$1 \div 1.06 = \$0.9434$ today at an interest rate of 6%. Stated differently, if you invest $0.9434 today, in 1 year you will have $\$0.9434 \times 1.06 = \$1.00$. Thus, $0.9434 is the present value of $1.00 a year hence at 6%.

Suppose you will receive the $1 in 2 years instead of in 1 year. Its present value is then $\$1.00 \div (1.06)^2 = \$0.8900$. The general formula for the present value (PV) of $1 is the inverse of the previous formula for the future value of $1, i.e., $\$1 \div (1 + i)^n$. If you will receive or pay an amount S in n periods at an interest rate of $i\%$ per period, the formula for present value is:

$$PV = S\frac{1}{(1 + i)^n}$$

TABLE B-1 Present Value of $1

Period	3%	4%	5%	6%	7%	8%	10%	12%	14%	16%	18%	20%	22%	24%	25%	26%	28%	30%	40%
1	.9709	.9615	.9524	.9434	.9346	.9259	.9091	.8929	.8772	.8621	.8475	.8333	.8197	.8065	.8000	.7937	.7813	.7692	.7143
2	.9426	.9246	.9070	.8900	.8734	.8573	.8264	.7972	.7695	.7432	.7182	.6944	.6719	.6504	.6400	.6299	.6104	.5917	.5102
3	.9151	.8890	.8638	.8396	.8163	.7938	.7513	.7118	.6750	.6407	.6086	.5787	.5507	.5245	.5120	.4999	.4768	.4552	.3644
4	.8885	.8548	.8227	.7921	.7629	.7350	.6830	.6355	.5921	.5523	.5158	.4823	.4514	.4230	.4096	.3968	.3725	.3501	.2603
5	.8626	.8219	.7835	.7473	.7130	.6806	.6209	.5674	.5194	.4761	.4371	.4019	.3700	.3411	.3277	.3149	.2910	.2693	.1859
6	.8375	.7903	.7462	.7050	.6663	.6302	.5645	.5066	.4556	.4104	.3704	.3349	.3033	.2751	.2621	.2499	.2274	.2072	.1328
7	.8131	.7599	.7107	.6651	.6227	.5835	.5132	.4523	.3996	.3538	.3139	.2791	.2486	.2218	.2097	.1983	.1776	.1594	.0949
8	.7894	.7307	.6768	.6274	.5820	.5403	.4665	.4039	.3506	.3050	.2660	.2326	.2038	.1789	.1678	.1574	.1388	.1226	.0678
9	.7664	.7026	.6446	.5919	.5439	.5002	.4241	.3606	.3075	.2630	.2255	.1938	.1670	.1443	.1342	.1249	.1084	.0943	.0484
10	.7441	.6756	.6139	.5584	.5083	.4632	.3855	.3220	.2697	.2267	.1911	.1615	.1369	.1164	.1074	.0992	.0847	.0725	.0346
11	.7224	.6496	.5847	.5268	.4751	.4289	.3505	.2875	.2366	.1954	.1619	.1346	.1122	.0938	.0859	.0787	.0662	.0558	.0247
12	.7014	.6246	.5568	.4970	.4440	.3971	.3186	.2567	.2076	.1685	.1372	.1122	.0920	.0757	.0687	.0625	.0517	.0429	.0176
13	.6810	.6006	.5303	.4688	.4150	.3677	.2897	.2292	.1821	.1452	.1163	.0935	.0754	.0610	.0550	.0496	.0404	.0330	.0126
14	.6611	.5775	.5051	.4423	.3878	.3405	.2633	.2046	.1597	.1252	.0985	.0779	.0618	.0492	.0440	.0393	.0316	.0254	.0090
15	.6419	.5553	.4810	.4173	.3624	.3152	.2394	.1827	.1401	.1079	.0835	.0649	.0507	.0397	.0352	.0312	.0247	.0195	.0064
16	.6232	.5339	.4581	.3936	.3387	.2919	.2176	.1631	.1229	.0930	.0708	.0541	.0415	.0320	.0281	.0248	.0193	.0150	.0046
17	.6050	.5134	.4363	.3714	.3166	.2703	.1978	.1456	.1078	.0802	.0600	.0451	.0340	.0258	.0225	.0197	.0150	.0116	.0033
18	.5874	.4936	.4155	.3503	.2959	.2502	.1799	.1300	.0946	.0691	.0508	.0376	.0279	.0208	.0180	.0156	.0118	.0089	.0023
19	.5703	.4746	.3957	.3305	.2765	.2317	.1635	.1161	.0829	.0596	.0431	.0313	.0229	.0168	.0144	.0124	.0092	.0068	.0017
20	.5537	.4564	.3769	.3118	.2584	.2145	.1486	.1037	.0728	.0514	.0365	.0261	.0187	.0135	.0115	.0098	.0072	.0053	.0012
21	.5375	.4388	.3589	.2942	.2415	.1987	.1351	.0926	.0638	.0443	.0309	.0217	.0154	.0109	.0092	.0078	.0056	.0040	.0009
22	.5219	.4220	.3418	.2775	.2257	.1839	.1228	.0826	.0560	.0382	.0262	.0181	.0126	.0088	.0074	.0062	.0044	.0031	.0006
23	.5067	.4057	.3256	.2618	.2109	.1703	.1117	.0738	.0491	.0329	.0222	.0151	.0103	.0071	.0059	.0049	.0034	.0024	.0004
24	.4919	.3901	.3101	.2470	.1971	.1577	.1015	.0659	.0431	.0284	.0188	.0126	.0085	.0057	.0047	.0039	.0027	.0018	.0003
25	.4776	.3751	.2953	.2330	.1842	.1460	.0923	.0588	.0378	.0245	.0160	.0105	.0069	.0046	.0038	.0031	.0021	.0014	.0002
26	.4637	.3607	.2812	.2198	.1722	.1352	.0839	.0525	.0331	.0211	.0135	.0087	.0057	.0037	.0030	.0025	.0016	.0011	.0002
27	.4502	.3468	.2678	.2074	.1609	.1252	.0763	.0469	.0291	.0182	.0115	.0073	.0047	.0030	.0024	.0019	.0013	.0008	.0001
28	.4371	.3335	.2551	.1956	.1504	.1159	.0693	.0419	.0255	.0157	.0097	.0061	.0038	.0024	.0019	.0015	.0010	.0006	.0001
29	.4243	.3207	.2429	.1846	.1406	.1073	.0630	.0374	.0224	.0135	.0082	.0051	.0031	.0020	.0015	.0012	.0008	.0005	.0001
30	.4120	.3083	.2314	.1741	.1314	.0994	.0573	.0334	.0196	.0116	.0070	.0042	.0026	.0016	.0012	.0010	.0006	.0004	.0000
40	.3066	.2083	.1420	.0972	.0668	.0460	.0221	.0107	.0053	.0026	.0013	.0007	.0004	.0002	.0001	.0001	.0001	.0000	.0000

Table B-1 on page A6 provides factors computed using this formula for various combinations of n and i. Each factor shows the present value of a single, lump-sum cash flow of $1 at the end of n future periods at interest rate i.

Present values are also called *discounted values*, and the process of finding the present value is called *discounting*. You can think of this as discounting (decreasing) the value of a future cash inflow or outflow. Why is the value discounted? Because you will receive or pay the cash in the future, its value today is reduced or discounted from the future amount to be received.

Assume that a municipality issues a 3-year non-interest-bearing note payable that promises to pay you a lump sum of $1,000 exactly 3 years from the issue date. You desire a rate of return of 6%, compounded annually. How much would you be willing to pay now for the 3-year note? The situation is sketched as follows:

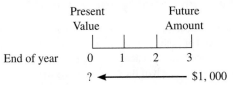

The factor in the period 3 row and 6% column of Table B-1 is 0.8396. The present value of the $1,000 payment is $1,000 × 0.8396 = $839.60. You would therefore be willing to pay $839.60 today for the $1,000 that you will receive in 3 years; $839.60 is the discounted value of the $1,000 future amount.

Compounding can occur more frequently than once per year. Suppose interest is compounded semiannually rather than annually. In our previous example, the 3 years become six semi-annual interest compounding periods. How much would you be willing to pay, assuming the rate of return you demand per semiannual period is half the annual rate, or 6% ÷ 2 = 3%? The factor in the period 6 row and 3% column of Table B-1 is 0.8375. You would be willing to pay $1,000 × 0.8375, or only $837.50.

Why is the present value lower when compounding occurs more frequently? Because money grows more quickly with more frequent compounding. Consider $1,000 invested at 6% interest compounded annually versus semi-annually:

	Annual Compounding	Semi-Annual Compounding
Year 0	$1,000.00	$1,000.00
½ year		$1,000.00 × 1.03 = $1,030.00
1 year	$1,000.00 × 1.06 = $1,060.00	$1,030.00 × 1.03 = $1,060.90
1 ½ years		$1,060.90 × 1.03 = $1,092.73
2 years	$1,060.00 × 1.06 = $1,123.60	$1,092.73 × 1.03 = $1,125.51
2 ½ years		$1,125.51 × 1.03 = $1,159.27
3 years	$1,123.60 × 1.06 = 1,190.16	$1,159.27 × 1.03 = $1,194.05

Notice that during the second half of year one, interest is paid on $1,000 with annual compounding, but interest is paid on $1,030 with semi-annual compounding. Compounding implies that interest is paid on interest, and with more frequent compounding, interest paid on interest starts sooner. Because money grows faster with semi-annual compounding, it doesn't require as many current dollars (present value) to grow to a given final value. This explains why a present value of $837.50 grows to $1,000 in 3 years at 6% compounded semi-annually, but if compounding occurs only annually, it requires a present value of $839.60 to grow to $1,000 in 3 years.

As a further check on your understanding, review the earlier example of your $10,000 investment. Suppose the financial institution promised to pay $13,310 at the end of 3 years. How much would you be willing to deposit at time zero if you required a 10% rate of return compounded annually? The period 3 row and 10% column factor is 0.7513 so the present value is this factor multiplied by the future amount of $13,310:

$$PV = 0.7513 \times \$13,310 = \$10,000$$

A diagram of this computation follows:

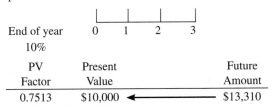

Pause for a moment. Use Table B-1 to obtain the present values of

1. $1,700 at 20% at the end of 20 years.
2. $8,300 at 10% at the end of 12 years.
3. $8,000 at 4% at the end of 4 years.

Answers:

1. $1,700 × 0.0261 = $44.37
2. $8,300 × 0.3186 = $2,644.38
3. $8,000 × 0.8548 = $6,838.40

Table B-2: Present Value of an Ordinary Annuity of $1

An annuity is a series of equal-sized cash flows spaced equally in time. An ordinary annuity has the equally spaced payments occurring at the end of each period. (We will not discuss the other type of annuity, an annuity due, which has payments at the beginning of each year.) Assume that you buy a note from a municipality that promises to pay $1,000 at the end of each of the next 3 years. How much should you be willing to pay if you desire a rate of return of 6%, compounded annually? This series of payments is a 3-year ordinary annuity. You denote the present value of an ordinary annuity as PV_A.

Before we introduce a computational method to deal with an annuity, note that you can always find the present value of the series of annuity payments by adding together the present values of the individual payments. That is, you can simply treat the annuity as a series of individual amounts, find the present values of each of the individual amounts using Table B-1, and then add the present values to find the present value of the entire series. For our example, you would be willing to pay $943.40 for the first payment, $890.00 for the second, and $839.60 for the third, so for the series of three payments, you are willing to pay a total of $2,673.00:

Payment	End of Year Table 1 Factor	0 Present Value	1	2	3
1	$\dfrac{1}{1.06} = .9434$	$ 943.40	$1,000		
2	$\dfrac{1}{(1.06)^2} = .8900$	890.00		1,000	
3	$\dfrac{1}{(1.06)^3} = .8396$	839.60			$1,000
Total		$2,673.00			

Although you can always treat an annuity as a series of individual amounts, this approach is computationally inconvenient for a long annuity. Instead, the factors in Table B-2 on page A9 provide a computational shortcut. Let's examine the conceptual basis for Table B-2 using our 3-year annuity. The three present value factors corresponding to the three annuity payments are the first three numbers from the 6% column of Table B-1. Because you multiply each of these factors by the $1,000 annuity payment, you can sum the factors and then multiply by $1,000 instead of multiplying each factor by $1,000 and then summing. For this example, the sum of the factors is .9434 + .8900 + .8396 = 2.6730, and this is the value that you find in Table B-2 for a three-period annuity with an interest rate of 6%. The present value of the annuity is simply the value from Table B-2, 2.6730, multiplied by $1,000: 2.6730 × $1,000 = $2,673.00. This shortcut is especially valuable if the cash payments or receipts extend over many periods. Consider an annual cash payment of $1,000 for 20 years at 6%. The present value, calculated from Table B-2, is $1,000 × 11.4699 = $11,469.90. To use Table B-1 for this calculation, you would have to perform 20 multiplications and then add the 20 products.

The factors in Table B-2 could be calculated by summing the factors in Table B-1, but they can instead be calculated using the following general formula:

$$PV_A = \frac{1}{i}\left[1 - \frac{1}{(1 + i)^n}\right]$$

Applied to our illustration,

$$PV_A = \frac{1}{.06}\left[1 - \frac{1}{(1.06)^3}\right] = \frac{1}{.06}(1 - .8396) = \frac{.1604}{.06} = 2.6730$$

There is also a potential accuracy advantage to using annuity Table B-2 rather than summing the factors from Table B-1 for individual amounts. If you round the individual numbers before summing them, you

TABLE B-2 Present Value of Ordinary Annuity of $1

Period	3%	4%	5%	6%	7%	8%	10%	12%	14%	16%	18%	20%	22%	24%	25%	26%	28%	30%	40%
1	.9709	.9615	.9524	.9434	.9346	.9259	.9091	.8929	.8772	.8621	.8475	.8333	.8197	.8065	.8000	.7937	.7813	.7692	.7143
2	1.9135	1.8861	1.8594	1.8334	1.8080	1.7833	1.7355	1.6901	1.6467	1.6052	1.5656	1.5278	1.4915	1.4568	1.4400	1.4235	1.3916	1.3609	1.2245
3	2.8286	2.7751	2.7232	2.6730	2.6243	2.5771	2.4869	2.4018	2.3216	2.2459	2.1743	2.1065	2.0422	1.9813	1.9520	1.9234	1.8684	1.8161	1.5889
4	3.7171	3.6299	3.5460	3.4651	3.3872	3.3121	3.1699	3.0373	2.9137	2.7982	2.6901	2.5887	2.4936	2.4043	2.3616	2.3202	2.2410	2.1662	1.8492
5	4.5797	4.4518	4.3295	4.2124	4.1002	3.9927	3.7908	3.6048	3.4331	3.2743	3.1272	2.9906	2.8636	2.7454	2.6893	2.6351	2.5320	2.4356	2.0352
6	5.4172	5.2421	5.0757	4.9173	4.7665	4.6229	4.3553	4.1114	3.8887	3.6847	3.4976	3.3255	3.1669	3.0205	2.9514	2.8850	2.7594	2.6427	2.1680
7	6.2303	6.0021	5.7864	5.5824	5.3893	5.2064	4.8684	4.5638	4.2883	4.0386	3.8115	3.6046	3.4155	3.2423	3.1611	3.0833	2.9370	2.8021	2.2628
8	7.0197	6.7327	6.4632	6.2098	5.9713	5.7466	5.3349	4.9676	4.6389	4.3436	4.0776	3.8372	3.6193	3.4212	3.3289	3.2407	3.0758	2.9247	2.3306
9	7.7861	7.4353	7.1078	6.8017	6.5152	6.2469	5.7590	5.3282	4.9464	4.6065	4.3030	4.0310	3.7863	3.5655	3.4631	3.3657	3.1842	3.0190	2.3790
10	8.5302	8.1109	7.7217	7.3601	7.0236	6.7101	6.1446	5.6502	5.2161	4.8332	4.4941	4.1925	3.9232	3.6819	3.5705	3.4648	3.2689	3.0915	2.4136
11	9.2526	8.7605	8.3064	7.8869	7.4987	7.1390	6.4951	5.9377	5.4527	5.0286	4.6560	4.3271	4.0354	3.7757	3.6564	3.5435	3.3351	3.1473	2.4383
12	9.9540	9.3851	8.8633	8.3838	7.9427	7.5361	6.8137	6.1944	5.6603	5.1971	4.7932	4.4392	4.1274	3.8514	3.7251	3.6059	3.3868	3.1903	2.4559
13	10.6350	9.9856	9.3936	8.8527	8.3577	7.9038	7.1034	6.4235	5.8424	5.3423	4.9095	4.5327	4.2028	3.9124	3.7801	3.6555	3.4272	3.2233	2.4685
14	11.2961	10.5631	9.8986	9.2950	8.7455	8.2442	7.3667	6.6282	6.0021	5.4675	5.0081	4.6106	4.2646	3.9616	3.8241	3.6949	3.4587	3.2487	2.4775
15	11.9379	11.1184	10.3797	9.7122	9.1079	8.5595	7.6061	6.8109	6.1422	5.5755	5.0916	4.6755	4.3152	4.0013	3.8593	3.7261	3.4834	3.2682	2.4839
16	12.5611	11.6523	10.8378	10.1059	9.4466	8.8514	7.8237	6.9740	6.2651	5.6685	5.1624	4.7296	4.3567	4.0333	3.8874	3.7509	3.5026	3.2832	2.4885
17	13.1661	12.1657	11.2741	10.4773	9.7632	9.1216	8.0216	7.1196	6.3729	5.7487	5.2223	4.7746	4.3908	4.0591	3.9099	3.7705	3.5177	3.2948	2.4918
18	13.7535	12.6593	11.6896	10.8276	10.0591	9.3719	8.2014	7.2497	6.4674	5.8178	5.2732	4.8122	4.4187	4.0799	3.9279	3.7861	3.5294	3.3037	2.4941
19	14.3238	13.1339	12.0853	11.1581	10.3356	9.6036	8.3649	7.3658	6.5504	5.8775	5.3162	4.8435	4.4415	4.0967	3.9424	3.7985	3.5386	3.3105	2.4958
20	14.8775	13.5903	12.4622	11.4699	10.5940	9.8181	8.5136	7.4694	6.6231	5.9288	5.3527	4.8696	4.4603	4.1103	3.9539	3.8083	3.5458	3.3158	2.4970
21	15.4150	14.0292	12.8212	11.7641	10.8355	10.0168	8.6487	7.5620	6.6870	5.9731	5.3837	4.8913	4.4756	4.1212	3.9631	3.8161	3.5514	3.3198	2.4979
22	15.9369	14.4511	13.1630	12.0416	11.0612	10.2007	8.7715	7.6446	6.7429	6.0113	5.4099	4.9094	4.4882	4.1300	3.9705	3.8223	3.5558	3.3230	2.4985
23	16.4436	14.8568	13.4886	12.3034	11.2722	10.3711	8.8832	7.7184	6.7921	6.0442	5.4321	4.9245	4.4985	4.1371	3.9764	3.8273	3.5592	3.3254	2.4989
24	16.9355	15.2470	13.7986	12.5504	11.4693	10.5288	8.9847	7.7843	6.8351	6.0726	5.4509	4.9371	4.5070	4.1428	3.9811	3.8312	3.5619	3.3272	2.4992
25	17.4131	15.6221	14.0939	12.7834	11.6536	10.6748	9.0770	7.8431	6.8729	6.0971	5.4669	4.9476	4.5139	4.1474	3.9849	3.8342	3.5640	3.3286	2.4994
26	17.8768	15.9828	14.3752	13.0032	11.8258	10.8100	9.1609	7.8957	6.9061	6.1182	5.4804	4.9563	4.5196	4.1511	3.9879	3.8367	3.5656	3.3297	2.4996
27	18.3270	16.3296	14.6430	13.2105	11.9867	10.9352	9.2372	7.9426	6.9352	6.1364	5.4919	4.9636	4.5243	4.1542	3.9903	3.8387	3.5669	3.3305	2.4997
28	18.7641	16.6631	14.8981	13.4062	12.1371	11.0511	9.3066	7.9844	6.9607	6.1520	5.5016	4.9697	4.5281	4.1566	3.9923	3.8402	3.5679	3.3312	2.4998
29	19.1885	16.9837	15.1411	13.5907	12.2777	11.1584	9.3696	8.0218	6.9830	6.1656	5.5098	4.9747	4.5312	4.1585	3.9938	3.8414	3.5687	3.3317	2.4999
30	19.6004	17.2920	15.3725	13.7648	12.4090	11.2578	9.4269	8.0552	7.0027	6.1772	5.5168	4.9789	4.5338	4.1601	3.9950	3.8424	3.5693	3.3321	2.4999
40	23.1148	19.7928	17.1591	15.0463	13.3317	11.9246	9.7791	8.2438	7.1050	6.2335	5.5482	4.9966	4.5439	4.1659	3.9995	3.8458	3.5712	3.3332	2.5000

run the risk of introducing more rounding error than you would by using Table B-2, where rounding occurs only after the numbers are summed. Therefore, computations are more accurate using the annuity factors in Table B-2.

Now, use Table B-2 to obtain the present values of the following ordinary annuities:

1. $1,600 at 20% for 20 years
2. $8,300 at 10% for 12 years
3. $8,000 at 4% for 4 years

Answers:

1. $1,600 × 4.8696 = $7,791.36
2. $8,300 × 6.8137 = $56,553.71
3. $8,000 × 3.6299 = $29,039.20

Note that the higher the interest rate, the lower the present value.

Appendix C   Excerpts from Form 10-K of NIKE, Inc.

UNITED STATES SECURITIES AND EXCHANGE COMMISSION
Washington, D.C. 20549

Form 10-K

(Mark One)

☑   **ANNUAL REPORT PURSUANT TO SECTION 13 OR 15(d) OF THE SECURITIES EXCHANGE ACT OF 1934**

For the fiscal year ended May 31, 2011

or

☐   **TRANSITION REPORT PURSUANT TO SECTION 13 OR 15(d) OF THE SECURITIES EXCHANGE ACT OF 1934**

For the transition period from   to   .

Commission File No. 1-10635

NIKE, Inc.

(Exact name of Registrant as specified in its charter)

Oregon	**93-0584541**
(State or other jurisdiction of incorporation)	*(IRS Employer Identification No.)*
One Bowerman Drive	**(503) 671-6453**
Beaverton, Oregon 97005-6453	*(Registrant's Telephone Number, Including Area Code)*
(Address of principal executive offices) (Zip Code)	

Securities registered pursuant to Section 12(b) of the Act:

Class B Common Stock	New York Stock Exchange
(Title of Each Class)	*(Name of Each Exchange on Which Registered)*

Securities registered pursuant to Section 12(g) of the Act:

None

DOCUMENTS INCORPORATED BY REFERENCE:

Parts of Registrant's Proxy Statement for the Annual Meeting of Shareholders to be held on September 19, 2011 are incorporated by reference into Part III of this Report.

Part I

Item 1. *Business*

GENERAL   NIKE, Inc. was incorporated in 1968 under the laws of the state of Oregon. As used in this report, the terms "we", "us", "NIKE" and the "Company" refer to NIKE, Inc. and its predecessors, subsidiaries and affiliates, unless the context indicates otherwise. Our Internet address is *www.nike.com.* On our NIKE Corporate web site, located at *www.nikebiz.com*, we post the following filings as soon as reasonably practicable after they are electronically filed with or furnished to the Securities and Exchange Commission: our annual report on Form 10-K, our quarterly reports on Form 10-Q, our current reports on Form 8-K and any amendments to those reports filed or furnished pursuant to Section 13(a) or 15(d) of the Securities and Exchange Act of 1934, as amended. All such filings on our NIKE Corporate web site are available free of charge. Also available on the NIKE Corporate web site are the charters of the committees of our board of directors, as well as our corporate governance guidelines and code of ethics; copies of any of these documents will be provided in print to any shareholder who submits a request in writing to NIKE Investor Relations, One Bowerman Drive, Beaverton, Oregon 97005-6453.

Our principal business activity is the design, development and worldwide marketing and selling of high quality footwear, apparel, equipment, and accessory products. NIKE is the largest seller of athletic footwear and athletic apparel in the world. We sell our products to retail accounts, through NIKE-owned retail stores and internet sales, which we refer to as our "Direct to Consumer" operations, and through a mix of independent distributors and licensees, in over 170 countries around the world. Virtually all of our products are manufactured by independent contractors. Virtually all footwear and apparel products are produced outside the United States, while equipment products are produced both in the United States and abroad.

PRODUCTS NIKE's athletic footwear products are designed primarily for specific athletic use, although a large percentage of the products are worn for casual or leisure purposes. We place considerable emphasis on high quality construction and innovation in products designed for men, women and children. Running, training, basketball, soccer, sport-inspired casual shoes, and kids' shoes are currently our top-selling footwear categories and we expect them to continue to lead in product sales in the near future. We also market footwear designed for baseball, cheerleading, football, golf, lacrosse, outdoor activities, skateboarding, tennis, volleyball, walking, wrestling, and other athletic and recreational uses.

We sell sports apparel and accessories covering most of the above categories, sports-inspired lifestyle apparel, as well as athletic bags and accessory items. NIKE apparel and accessories feature the same trademarks and are sold through the same marketing and distribution channels. We often market footwear, apparel and accessories in "collections" of similar design or for specific purposes. We also market apparel with licensed college and professional team and league logos.

We sell a line of performance equipment under the NIKE Brand name, including bags, socks, sport balls, eyewear, timepieces, electronic devices, bats, gloves, protective equipment, golf clubs, and other equipment designed for sports activities. We also sell small amounts of various plastic products to other manufacturers through our wholly-owned subsidiary, NIKE IHM, Inc.

In addition to the products we sell directly to customers through our Direct to Consumer operations, we have entered into license agreements that permit unaffiliated parties to manufacture and sell certain apparel, electronic devices and other equipment designed for sports activities.

Our wholly-owned subsidiary, Cole Haan ("Cole Haan"), headquartered in New York, New York, designs and distributes dress and casual footwear, apparel and accessories for men and women under the Cole Haan® trademark.

Our wholly-owned subsidiary, Converse Inc. ("Converse"), headquartered in North Andover, Massachusetts, designs, distributes and licenses athletic and casual footwear, apparel and accessories under the Converse®, Chuck Taylor®, All Star®, One Star®, Star Chevron and Jack Purcell® trademarks.

Our wholly-owned subsidiary, Hurley International LLC ("Hurley"), headquartered in Costa Mesa, California, designs and distributes a line of action sports and youth lifestyle apparel and accessories under the Hurley® trademark.

Our wholly-owned subsidiary, Umbro International Limited ("Umbro"), headquartered in Cheadle, United Kingdom, designs, distributes and licenses athletic and casual footwear, apparel and equipment, primarily for the sport of football (soccer), under the Umbro® trademark.

SALES AND MARKETING Financial information about geographic and segment operations appears in Note 18 of the accompanying Notes to the Consolidated Financial Statements.

We experience moderate fluctuations in aggregate sales volume during the year. Historically, revenues in the first and fourth fiscal quarters have slightly exceeded those in the second and third quarters. However, the mix of product sales may vary considerably as a result of changes in seasonal and geographic demand for particular types of footwear, apparel and equipment.

Because NIKE is a consumer products company, the relative popularity of various sports and fitness activities and changing design trends affect the demand for our products. We must therefore respond to trends and shifts in consumer preferences by adjusting the mix of existing product offerings, developing new products, styles and categories, and influencing sports and fitness preferences through aggressive marketing. Failure to respond in a timely and adequate manner could have a material adverse effect on our sales and profitability. This is a continuing risk.

We report our NIKE Brand operations based on our internal geographic organization. Each NIKE Brand geography operates predominantly in one industry: the design, development, marketing and selling of athletic footwear, apparel, and equipment. Effective June 1, 2009, we began operating under our new organizational structure for the NIKE Brand, which consists of the following six geographies: North America, Western Europe, Central & Eastern Europe, Greater China, Japan, and Emerging Markets. Previously, NIKE Brand operations were organized into the following four geographic regions: U.S., Europe, Middle East and Africa (collectively, "EMEA"), Asia Pacific, and Americas. Our NIKE Brand Direct to Consumer operations are managed within each geographic segment.

UNITED STATES MARKET   In fiscal 2011, sales in the United States including U.S. sales of our Other Businesses accounted for approximately 43% of total revenues, compared to 42% in fiscal 2010 and 2009. Our Other Businesses were primarily comprised of our affiliate brands; Cole Haan, Converse, Hurley and Umbro (which was acquired on March 3, 2008); and NIKE Golf. We estimate that we sell to more than 20,000 retail accounts in the United States. The NIKE Brand domestic retail account base includes a mix of footwear stores, sporting goods stores, athletic specialty stores, department stores, skate, tennis and golf shops, and other retail accounts. During fiscal 2011, our three largest customers accounted for approximately 23% of sales in the United States.

We make substantial use of our "futures" ordering program, which allows retailers to order five to six months in advance of delivery with the commitment that their orders will be delivered within a set time period at a fixed price. In fiscal 2011, 87% of our U.S. wholesale footwear shipments (excluding our Other Businesses) were made under the futures program, compared to 89% in fiscal 2010 and 2009. In fiscal 2011, 60% of our U.S. wholesale apparel shipments (excluding our Other Businesses) were made under the futures program, compared to 62% in fiscal 2010 and 60% in fiscal 2009.

We utilize 18 NIKE sales offices to solicit sales in the United States. We also utilize 4 independent sales representatives to sell specialty products for golf and 5 for skateboarding and snowboarding products. In addition, our Direct to Consumer operations sell NIKE Brand products through our internet website, *www.nikestore.com*, and the following retail outlets in the United States:

U.S. Retail Stores	Number
NIKE factory stores	150
NIKE stores	16
NIKETOWNs	9
NIKE employee-only stores	3
Cole Haan stores (including factory stores)	107
Converse stores (including factory stores)	58
Hurley stores (including factory and employee stores)	20
Total	363

NIKE's three significant distribution centers in the United States for NIKE Brand products, including NIKE Golf, are located in Memphis, Tennessee. NIKE also operates and leases one facility in Memphis, Tennessee for NIKE Brand product returns. NIKE Brand apparel and equipment products are also shipped from our Foothill Ranch, California distribution center. Cole Haan products are distributed primarily from Greenland, New Hampshire, and Converse and Hurley products are shipped primarily from Ontario, California.

INTERNATIONAL MARKETS In fiscal 2011, non-U.S. sales (including non-U.S. sales of our Other Businesses) accounted for 57% of total revenues, compared to 58% in fiscal 2010 and 2009. We sell our products to retail accounts, through our own Direct to Consumer operations, and through a mix of independent distributors and licensees around the world. We estimate that we sell to more than 20,000 retail accounts outside the United States, excluding sales by independent distributors and licensees. We operate 16 distribution centers outside of the United States. In many countries and regions, including Canada, Asia, some Latin American countries, and Europe, we have a futures ordering program for retailers similar to the United States futures program described above. During fiscal 2011, NIKE's three largest customers outside of the U.S. accounted for approximately 9% of total non-U.S. sales.

Our Direct to Consumer business operates the following retail outlets outside the United States:

Non-U.S. Retail Stores	Number
NIKE factory stores	243
NIKE stores	50
NIKETOWNs	3
NIKE employee-only stores	13
Cole Haan stores	83
Hurley stores	1
Total	393

International branch offices and subsidiaries of NIKE are located in Argentina, Australia, Austria, Belgium, Bermuda, Brazil, Canada, Chile, China, Croatia, Cyprus, the Czech Republic, Denmark, Finland, France, Germany, Greece, Hong Kong, Hungary, Indonesia, India, Ireland, Israel, Italy, Japan, Korea, Lebanon, Macau, Malaysia, Mexico, New Zealand, the Netherlands, Norway, the Philippines, Poland, Portugal, Russia, Singapore, Slovakia, Slovenia, South Africa, Spain, Sri Lanka, Sweden, Switzerland, Taiwan, Thailand, Turkey, the United Arab Emirates, the United Kingdom, Uruguay and Vietnam.

SIGNIFICANT CUSTOMER No customer accounted for 10% or more of our net sales during fiscal 2011.

ORDERS Worldwide futures and advance orders for NIKE Brand athletic footwear and apparel, scheduled for delivery from June through November 2011, were $10.3 billion compared to $8.8 billion for the same period last year. This futures and advance order amount is calculated based upon our forecast of the actual exchange rates under which our revenues will be translated during this period, which approximate current spot rates. Reported futures and advance orders are not necessarily indicative of our expectation of revenues for this period. This is because the mix of orders can shift between futures/advance and at-once orders and the fulfillment of certain of these futures/advance orders may fall outside of the scheduled time period noted above. In addition, foreign currency exchange rate fluctuations as well as differing levels of order cancellations and discounts can cause differences in the comparisons between futures and advance orders and actual revenues. Moreover, a significant portion of our revenue is not derived from futures and advance orders, including at-once and close-out sales of NIKE Brand footwear and apparel, sales of NIKE Brand equipment, sales from our Direct to Consumer operations, and sales from our Other Businesses.

PRODUCT RESEARCH AND DEVELOPMENT We believe our research and development efforts are a key factor in our past and future success. Technical innovation in the design of footwear, apparel, and athletic equipment receive continued emphasis as NIKE strives to produce products that help to reduce injury, enhance athletic performance and maximize comfort.

In addition to NIKE's own staff of specialists in the areas of biomechanics, chemistry, exercise physiology, engineering, industrial design, and related fields, we also utilize research committees and advisory boards made up of athletes, coaches, trainers, equipment managers, orthopedists, podiatrists, and other experts who consult with us and review designs, materials, concepts for product improvements and compliance with product safety regulations around the world. Employee athletes, athletes engaged under sports marketing contracts and other athletes wear-test and evaluate products during the design and development process.

MANUFACTURING   Virtually all of our footwear is produced by factories we contract with outside of the United States. In fiscal 2011, contract factories in Vietnam, China, Indonesia, and India manufactured approximately 39%, 33%, 24% and 2% of total NIKE Brand footwear, respectively. We also have manufacturing agreements with independent factories in Argentina, Brazil, India, and Mexico to manufacture footwear for sale primarily within those countries. The largest single footwear factory that we have contracted with accounted for approximately 6% of total fiscal 2011 NIKE Brand footwear production. Almost all of NIKE Brand apparel is manufactured outside of the United States by independent contract manufacturers located in 33 countries. Most of this apparel production occurred in China, Thailand, Vietnam, Malaysia, Sri Lanka, Indonesia, Turkey, Cambodia, El Salvador, and Mexico. The largest single apparel factory that we have contracted with accounted for approximately 7% of total fiscal 2011 apparel production.

The principal materials used in our footwear products are natural and synthetic rubber, plastic compounds, foam cushioning materials, nylon, leather, canvas, and polyurethane films used to make Air-Sole cushioning components. During fiscal 2011, NIKE IHM, Inc., a wholly-owned subsidiary of NIKE, as well as independent contractors in China and Taiwan, were our largest suppliers of the Air-Sole cushioning components used in footwear. The principal materials used in our apparel products are natural and synthetic fabrics and threads, plastic and metal hardware, and specialized performance fabrics designed to repel rain, retain heat, or efficiently transport body moisture. NIKE's independent contractors and suppliers buy raw materials in bulk for the manufacturing of our footwear, apparel and equipment products. Most raw materials are available and purchased by those independent contractors and suppliers in the countries where manufacturing takes place. We have thus far experienced little difficulty in satisfying our raw material requirements.

Since 1972, Sojitz Corporation of America ("Sojitz America"), a large Japanese trading company and the sole owner of our redeemable preferred stock, has performed significant import-export financing services for us. During fiscal 2011, Sojitz America provided financing and purchasing services for NIKE Brand products sold in Argentina, Uruguay, Canada, Brazil, India, Indonesia, the Philippines, Malaysia, South Africa, China, Korea, and Thailand, excluding products produced and sold in the same country. Approximately 19% of NIKE Brand sales occurred in those countries. Any failure of Sojitz America to provide these services or any failure of Sojitz America's banks could disrupt our ability to acquire products from our suppliers and to deliver products to our customers in those jurisdictions. Such a disruption could result in cancelled orders that would adversely affect sales and profitability. However, we believe that any such disruption would be short-term in duration due to the ready availability of alternative sources of financing at competitive rates. Our current agreements with Sojitz America expire on May 31, 2014.

INTERNATIONAL OPERATIONS AND TRADE   Our international operations and sources of supply are subject to the usual risks of doing business abroad, such as possible revaluation of currencies, export and import duties, anti-dumping measures, quotas, safeguard measures, trade restrictions, restrictions on the transfer of funds and, in certain parts of the world, political instability and terrorism. We have not, to date, been materially affected by any such risk, but cannot predict the likelihood of such developments occurring.

The global economic recession resulted in a significant slow-down in international trade and a sharp rise in protectionist actions around the world. These trends are affecting many global manufacturing and service sectors, and the footwear and apparel industries, as a whole, are not immune. Companies in our industry are facing trade protectionist challenges in many different regions, and in nearly all cases we are working together to address trade issues to reduce the impact to the industry, while observing applicable competition laws. Notwithstanding our efforts, such actions, if implemented, could result in increases in the cost of our products, which could adversely affect our sales or profitability and the imported footwear and apparel industry as a whole. Accordingly, we are actively monitoring the developments described below.

FOOTWEAR IMPORTS INTO THE EUROPEAN UNION   In 2005, at the request of the European domestic footwear industry, the European Commission ("EC") initiated investigations into leather footwear imported from China and Vietnam. Together with other companies in our industry, we took the position that Special Technology Athletic Footwear (STAF) (i) should not be within the scope of the investigation, and (ii) does not meet the legal requirements of injury and price in an anti-dumping investigation. Our arguments were successful and the EU agreed in October 2006 on definitive duties of 16.5% for China and 10% for Vietnam for non-STAF leather footwear, but excluded STAF from the final measures. Prior to the scheduled expiration in October 2008 of the measures imposed on the non-STAF footwear, the domestic industry requested and the EC agreed to review a petition to extend these restrictions on non-STAF leather footwear. In December 2009, following a review of the ongoing restrictions, EU member states voted to extend the measures for an additional 15 months, until March 31, 2011. In early 2011, the EC declined to further extend the measures and since April 1, 2011 these restrictions have been terminated. The EC noted that it will be monitoring leather footwear imports from Vietnam and China over the next 12 months and it is hoped that any increases will not result in renewed trade defense actions by the EC.

On February 3, 2010, the Chinese government announced it would seek to refer the EU decision (both on the original measures and subsequent review decision) to the World Trade Organization ("WTO") for its further review and decision. On May 18, 2010, the Dispute Settlement Body of the WTO agreed to establish a panel to rule on China's claims against the EU with respect to the above anti-dumping measures. The ruling from the WTO panel is expected in late July or August 2011, after which either party may accept or appeal the findings.

FOOTWEAR, APPAREL AND EQUIPMENT IMPORTS INTO BRAZIL AND ARGENTINA   At the request of certain domestic footwear industry participants, both Brazil and Argentina have initiated independent anti-dumping investigations against footwear made in China. Over the last two years, we have been working with a broad coalition of other companies in our industry to challenge these cases on the basis that the athletic footwear being imported from China (i) should not be within the scope of the investigation, and (ii) does not meet the legal requirements of injury and price in an anti-dumping investigation. In the case of Argentina, in 2010, the final determination made by the administering authorities was favorable to us. In the case of Brazil, the administering authorities agreed to impose an anti-dumping duty against nearly all footwear from China, which we believe will impact all brands in the footwear industry. Although we do not currently expect that this decision will materially affect us, we are working with the same broad coalition of footwear companies to challenge this decision in domestic Brazilian courts as well as international forums such as the WTO.

Many products, including footwear, apparel and equipment products, that we and others in our industry import into Argentina and Brazil are subject to the WTO non-automatic licensing requirements, which means that it may take up to 60 days for those products to clear customs and enter into those jurisdictions. From time to time, in addition to these WTO licensing requirements, these jurisdictions impose further importation restrictions or limitations. As a result, we have experienced delays in our ability to import our products or it has taken longer than the time allowed under the WTO for us to import our products. To date, our business has not been materially affected by these restrictions or delays. In the future, however, if we are unable to import our products into these jurisdictions due to these or other restrictions or if we experience increasing or more frequent delays beyond the WTO-permitted 60 days to import our products, our business could be materially affected.

FOOTWEAR, APPAREL AND EQUIPMENT IMPORTS INTO TURKEY   In 2006, Turkey introduced safeguard measures in the form of additional duties on all imported footwear into Turkey with the goal of protecting its local shoe manufacturing industry until August 2009. In June 2009, Turkish shoe-manufacturers submitted, and the Turkish Government agreed to review, a request for extension of the safeguard measures claiming that the rehabilitation process of the local Turkish industry was interrupted due to the continuing increase of footwear imports. Despite the importers opposition to the continuation of the safeguard measures, the Turkish authorities extended these safeguard measures until August 2012, but reduced the duty from $3 per pair of footwear to $1.60 per pair of footwear.

In 2011, two new safeguard measures and reviews were initiated by the Turkish Undersecretariat of Foreign Trade ("UFT") on apparel and equipment imports. In January 2011, the UFT began an investigation on apparel imports that could result in a 20-30% increase in import duties applied to imported apparel products, regardless of country of origin and with only a few exceptions for countries that currently have a Free Trade Agreement with Turkey. A decision is expected in late July 2011 and if approved, these higher import duties will be in place through July 2014. Together with other companies in our industry, we are advocating for exclusion of certain apparel products used for sporting activities that cannot be manufactured in Turkey and therefore should not be subject to a higher import duty. In February 2011, the UFT began a review of existing safeguard measure on travel goods, handbags and similar accessories and containers listed under applicable regulations. One Turkish bag manufacturers association has requested the continuation of the safeguard measures through April 2014, with the application of an additional import duty of 2.70 USD/kg (max. 4.25 USD/unit), regardless of country of origin. Together with other companies in our industry, we are advocating for the exclusion of non-leather bags from the scope of the continued safeguards.

TRADE RELATIONS WITH CHINA   China represents an important sourcing country and consumer marketing country for us. Many governments around the world are concerned about China's growing and fast-paced economy, compliance with WTO rules, currency valuation, and high trade surpluses. As a result, a wide range of legislative proposals have been introduced to address these concerns. While some of these concerns may be justified, we are working with broad coalitions of global businesses and trade associations representing a wide variety of sectors (e.g., services, manufacturing, and agriculture) to help ensure any legislation enacted and implemented (i) addresses legitimate and core concerns, (ii) is consistent with international trade rules, and (iii) reflects and considers China's domestic economy and the important role it has in the global economic community. We believe other companies in our industry as well as most other multinational companies are in a similar position regarding these trade measures.

In the event any of these trade protection measures are implemented, we believe that we have the ability to develop, over a period of time, adequate alternative sources of supply for the products obtained from our present suppliers. If events prevented us from acquiring products from our suppliers in a particular country, our operations could be temporarily disrupted and we could experience an adverse financial impact. However, we believe we could abate any such disruption, and that much of the adverse impact on supply would, therefore, be of a short-term nature. We believe our principal competitors are subject to similar risks.

COMPETITION   The athletic footwear, apparel, and equipment industry is keenly competitive in the United States and on a worldwide basis. We compete internationally with a significant number of athletic and leisure shoe companies, athletic and leisure apparel companies, sports equipment companies, and large companies having diversified lines of athletic and leisure shoes, apparel, and equipment, including Adidas, Puma, and others. The intense competition and the rapid changes in technology and consumer preferences in the markets for athletic and leisure footwear and apparel, and athletic equipment, constitute significant risk factors in our operations.

NIKE is the largest seller of athletic footwear and athletic apparel in the world. Performance and reliability of shoes, apparel, and equipment, new product development, price, product identity through marketing and promotion, and customer support and service are important aspects of competition in the athletic footwear, apparel, and equipment industry. To help market our products, we contract with prominent and influential athletes, coaches, teams, colleges and sports leagues to endorse our brands and use our products, and we actively sponsor sporting events and clinics. We believe that we are competitive in all of these areas.

TRADEMARKS AND PATENTS   We utilize trademarks on nearly all of our products and believe having distinctive marks that are readily identifiable is an important factor in creating a market for our goods, in identifying our brands and the Company, and in distinguishing our goods from the goods of others. We consider our NIKE® and Swoosh Design® trademarks to be among our most valuable assets and we have registered these trademarks in over 150 countries. In addition, we own many other trademarks that we utilize in marketing our products. We continue to vigorously protect our trademarks against infringement.

NIKE has an exclusive, worldwide license to make and sell footwear using patented "Air" technology. The process utilizes pressurized gas encapsulated in polyurethane. Some of the early NIKE AIR® patents have expired, which may enable competitors to use certain types of similar technology. Subsequent NIKE AIR® patents will not expire for several years. We also have hundreds of U.S. and foreign utility patents, and thousands of U.S. and foreign design patents covering components and features used in various athletic and leisure shoes, apparel, and equipment. These patents expire at various times, and patents issued for applications filed this year will last from now to 2025 for design patents, and from now to 2031 for utility patents. We believe our success depends primarily upon skills in design, research and development, production, and marketing rather than upon our patent position. However, we have followed a policy of filing applications for United States and foreign patents on inventions, designs, and improvements that we deem valuable.

EMPLOYEES   As of May 31, 2011, we had approximately 38,000 employees worldwide, which includes retail and part-time employees. Management considers its relationship with employees to be excellent. None of our employees is represented by a union, except for certain employees in the Emerging Markets geography, where local law requires those employees to be represented by a trade union, and in the United States, where certain employees of Cole Haan are represented by a union. Also, in some countries outside of the United States, local laws require representation for employees by works councils (such as in certain countries in the European Union, in which they are entitled to information and consultation on certain Company decisions) or other employee representation by an organization similar to a union, and in certain European countries, we are required by local law to enter into and/or comply with (industry wide or national) collective bargaining agreements. There has never been a material interruption of operations due to labor disagreements.

EXECUTIVE OFFICERS OF THE REGISTRANT   The executive officers of NIKE as of July 14, 2011 are as follows:

Philip H. Knight, Chairman of the Board—Mr. Knight, 73, a director since 1968, is a co-founder of NIKE and, except for the period from June 1983 through September 1984, served as its President from 1968 to 1990 and from June 2000 to December 2004. Prior to 1968, Mr. Knight was a certified public accountant with Price Waterhouse and Coopers & Lybrand and was an Assistant Professor of Business Administration at Portland State University.

Mark G. Parker, Chief Executive Officer and President—Mr. Parker, 55, was appointed CEO and President in January 2006. He has been employed by NIKE since 1979 with primary responsibilities in product research, design and development, marketing, and brand management. Mr. Parker was appointed divisional Vice President in charge of development in 1987, corporate Vice President in 1989, General Manager in 1993, Vice President of Global Footwear in 1998, and President of the NIKE Brand in 2001.

David J. Ayre, Vice President, Global Human Resources—Mr. Ayre, 51, joined NIKE as Vice President, Global Human Resources in 2007. Prior to joining NIKE, he held a number of senior human resource positions with PepsiCo, Inc. since 1990, most recently as head of Talent and Performance Rewards.

Donald W. Blair, Vice President and Chief Financial Officer—Mr. Blair, 53, joined NIKE in November 1999. Prior to joining NIKE, he held a number of financial management positions with PepsiCo, Inc., including Vice President, Finance of Pepsi-Cola Asia, Vice President, Planning of PepsiCo's Pizza Hut Division, and Senior Vice President, Finance of The Pepsi Bottling Group, Inc. Prior to joining PepsiCo, Mr. Blair was a certified public accountant with Deloitte, Haskins, and Sells.

Charles D. Denson, President of the NIKE Brand—Mr. Denson, 55, has been employed by NIKE since 1979. Mr. Denson held several management positions within the Company, including his appointments as Director of USA Apparel Sales in 1994, divisional Vice President, U.S. Sales in 1994, divisional Vice President European Sales in 1997, divisional Vice President and General Manager, NIKE Europe in 1998, Vice President and General Manager of NIKE USA in 2000, and President of the NIKE Brand in 2001.

Gary M. DeStefano, President, Global Operations—Mr. DeStefano, 54, has been employed by NIKE since 1982, with primary responsibilities in sales and regional administration. Mr. DeStefano was appointed Director of Domestic Sales in 1990, divisional Vice President in charge of domestic sales in 1992, Vice President of Global Sales in 1996, Vice President and General Manager of Asia Pacific in 1997, President of USA Operations in 2001, and President of Global Operations in 2006.

Trevor Edwards, Vice President, Global Brand and Category Management—Mr. Edwards, 48, joined NIKE in 1992. He was appointed Marketing Manager, Strategic Accounts, Foot Locker in 1993, Director of Marketing, the Americas in 1995, Director of Marketing, Europe in 1997,

Vice President, Marketing for Europe, Middle East and Africa in 1999, and Vice President, U.S. Brand Marketing in 2000. Mr. Edwards was appointed corporate Vice President, Global Brand Management in 2002 and Vice President, Global Brand and Category Management in 2006. Prior to NIKE, Mr. Edwards was with the Colgate-Palmolive Company.

Jeanne P. Jackson, President, Direct to Consumer—Ms. Jackson, 59, served as a member of the NIKE, Inc. Board of Directors from 2001 through 2009, when she resigned from our Board and was appointed President, Direct to Consumer. She is founder and CEO of MSP Capital, a private investment company. Ms. Jackson was CEO of Walmart.com from March 2000 to January 2002. She was with Gap, Inc., as President and CEO of Banana Republic from 1995 to 2000, also serving as CEO of Gap, Inc. Direct from 1998 to 2000. Since 1978, she has held various retail management positions with Victoria's Secret, The Walt Disney Company, Saks Fifth Avenue, and Federated Department Stores. Ms. Jackson is the past President of the United States Ski and Snowboard Foundation Board of Trustees, and is a director of McDonald's Corporation. She is a former director of Nordstrom, Inc., and Harrah's Entertainment, Inc.

Hilary K. Krane, Vice President and General Counsel—Ms. Krane, 47, joined NIKE as Vice President and General Counsel in April 2010. Prior to joining NIKE, Ms. Krane was General Counsel and Senior Vice President for Corporate Affairs at Levi Strauss & Co. where she was responsible for legal affairs and overseeing the global brand protection department from 2006 to 2010. From 1996 to 2006, she was a partner and assistant general counsel at PricewaterhouseCoopers LLP.

Bernard F. Pliska, Vice President, Corporate Controller—Mr. Pliska, 49, joined NIKE as Corporate Controller in 1995. He was appointed Vice President, Corporate Controller in 2003. Prior to NIKE, Mr. Pliska was with Price Waterhouse from 1984 to 1995. Mr. Pliska is a certified public accountant.

John F. Slusher, Vice President, Global Sports Marketing—Mr. Slusher, 42, has been employed by NIKE since 1998 with primary responsibilities in global sports marketing. Mr. Slusher was appointed Director of Sports Marketing for the Asia Pacific and Americas Regions in 2006, divisional Vice President, Asia Pacific & Americas Sports Marketing in September 2007 and Vice President, Global Sports Marketing in November 2007. Prior to joining NIKE, Mr. Slusher was an attorney at the law firm of O'Melveny & Myers from 1995 to 1998.

Eric D. Sprunk, Vice President, Merchandising and Product—Mr. Sprunk, 47, joined NIKE in 1993. He was appointed Finance Director and General Manager of the Americas in 1994, Finance Director, NIKE Europe in 1995, Regional General Manager, NIKE Europe Footwear in 1998, and Vice President & General Manager of the Americas in 2000. Mr. Sprunk was appointed corporate Vice President, Global Footwear in 2001 and Vice President, Merchandising and Product in 2009. Prior to joining NIKE, Mr. Sprunk was a certified public accountant with Price Waterhouse from 1987 to 1993.

Hans van Alebeek, Vice President, Global Operations and Technology—Mr. van Alebeek, 45, joined NIKE as Director of Operations of Europe in 1999, and was appointed Vice President, Operations & Administration in EMEA in 2001, Vice President, Global Operations in 2003, Vice President, Global Operations & Technology in 2004, and Corporate Vice President in November 2005. Prior to joining NIKE, Mr. van Alebeek worked for McKinsey & Company as a management consultant and at N.V. Indivers in business development.

Roger S. Wyett, President, Affiliates—Mr. Wyett, 54, joined NIKE in April 2005 as President and Chief Operating Officer of the Company's Hurley brand and was appointed Vice President, Global Apparel in 2006. In October 2007, Mr. Wyett returned to the Company's Hurley brand as President and Chief Executive Officer, and then in February 2011 was appointed President of Affiliates. Mr. Wyett first joined NIKE in 1994, holding a number of management positions in soccer and NIKE Team Sports. From 2000 to 2005, Mr. Wyett was employed by The Walt Disney Company where he was Senior Vice President for Global Apparel, Accessories and Footwear, and later promoted to Executive Vice President for Global Sales and Marketing for Consumer Products.

Item 2. *Properties*

The following is a summary of principal properties owned or leased by NIKE.

The NIKE World Campus, owned by NIKE and located in Beaverton, Oregon, USA, is a 176 acre facility of 18 buildings which functions as our world headquarters and is occupied by approximately 6,000 employees engaged in management, research, design, development, marketing, finance, and other administrative functions from nearly all of our divisions. We also lease various office facilities in the surrounding metropolitan area. We lease a similar, but smaller, administrative facility in Hilversum, the Netherlands, which serves as the headquarters for the Western Europe and Central & Eastern Europe geographies. There are three significant distribution and customer service facilities for NIKE Brand products, including NIKE Golf, in the United States. All three of them are located in Memphis, Tennessee, two of which are owned and one of which is leased. NIKE also operates and leases one facility in Memphis, Tennessee for NIKE Brand product returns. NIKE Brand apparel and equipment are also shipped from our Foothill Ranch, California distribution center, which we lease. Cole Haan also operates a distribution facility in Greenland, New Hampshire, which we lease. Smaller leased distribution facilities for other brands and non-NIKE Brand businesses are located in various parts of the United States. We also own or lease distribution and customer service facilities in many parts of the world, the most significant of which are the distribution facilities located in Tomisatomachi, Japan, Laakdal, Belgium, and Taicang, China, all of which we own.

We manufacture Air-Sole cushioning materials and components at NIKE IHM, Inc. manufacturing facilities located in Beaverton, Oregon and St. Charles, Missouri, which we own. We also manufacture and sell small amounts of various plastic products to other manufacturers through NIKE IHM, Inc.

Aside from the principal properties described above, we lease three production offices outside the United States, over 100 sales offices and showrooms worldwide, and approximately 65 administrative offices worldwide. We lease more than 700 retail stores worldwide, which consist primarily of factory outlet stores. See "United States Market" and "International Markets" starting on pages 2 and 3 of this Report, respectively. Our leases expire at various dates through the year 2035.

Item 7. *Management's Discussion and Analysis of Financial Condition and Results of Operations*

NIKE designs, develops, markets and sells high quality footwear, apparel, equipment and accessory products worldwide. We are the largest seller of athletic footwear and apparel in the world. We sell our products to retail accounts, through NIKE-owned retail stores and internet sales, which we refer to as our "Direct to Consumer" operations, and through a mix of independent distributors and licensees, worldwide. Our goal is to deliver value to our shareholders by building a profitable global portfolio of branded footwear, apparel, equipment and accessories businesses. Our strategy is to achieve long-term revenue growth by creating innovative, "must have" products, building deep personal consumer connections with our brands, and delivering compelling retail presentation and experiences.

In addition to achieving long-term revenue growth, we continue to strive to deliver shareholder value by driving operational excellence in several key areas:

- Making our supply chain a competitive advantage through operational discipline,
- Reducing product costs through a continued focus on lean manufacturing and product design that strives to eliminate waste,
- Improving selling and administrative expense productivity by focusing on investments that drive economic returns in the form of incremental revenue and gross margin, and leveraging existing infrastructure across our portfolio of brands to eliminate duplicative costs,
- Improving working capital efficiency, and
- Deploying capital effectively to create value for our shareholders.

Through execution of this strategy, our long-term financial goals continue to be:

- High single-digit revenue growth,
- Mid-teens earnings per share growth,
- Increased return on invested capital and accelerated cash flows, and
- Consistent results through effective management of our diversified portfolio of businesses.

Over the past ten years, we have achieved or exceeded all of these financial goals. During this time, NIKE, Inc's revenues and earnings per share have grown 8% and 15%, respectively, on an annual compounded basis. Our return on invested capital has increased from 14% to 22% and we expanded gross margins by more than 5 percentage points.

Our fiscal 2011 results demonstrated our continued focus toward meeting our financial goals, while positioning ourselves for sustainable, profitable long-term growth. Despite the uncertain macroeconomic environment in fiscal 2011, we delivered record high revenues and diluted earnings per share. Our revenues grew 10% to $20.9 billion, net income increased 12% to $2.1 billion, and we delivered diluted earnings per share of $4.39, a 14% increase from fiscal 2010.

Income before income taxes increased 13% for fiscal 2011 primarily as a result of the increase in revenues and leverage on selling and administrative expense, which more than offset a decrease in gross margin percentage. The increase in revenues is reflective of increased demand for NIKE Brand footwear and apparel products across most businesses, particularly in the North America, Emerging Markets and Greater China geographies. Demand for our NIKE Brand footwear and apparel was fueled by our innovative products as well as strong category focused retail presentations. The decrease in gross margin percentage was primarily driven by higher product input costs, increased transportation expenses and a lower mix of licensee revenue as certain markets within our Other Businesses transitioned to NIKE, Inc. owned markets. These factors more than offset the positive impact from the growth and expanding profitability of our NIKE Brand Direct to Consumer business and our ongoing product cost reduction initiatives.

Net income for fiscal 2011 was negatively impacted by a year-over-year increase of 80 basis points in our effective tax rate, driven primarily by an increase in the percentage of total pre-tax income earned from operations in the United States. The United States statutory tax rate is generally higher than the tax rate on operations outside the United States.

For the year, diluted earnings per share grew at a higher rate than net income due to a 2% decrease in the weighted average number of diluted common shares outstanding driven by our share repurchases during fiscal 2011. While we increased the use of working capital in fiscal 2011 to support the growth of our businesses, we returned larger amounts of cash to our shareholders through higher dividends and increased share repurchases compared to fiscal 2010.

While we continue to believe that the Company is well positioned from a business and financial perspective, our future performance is subject to the inherent uncertainty presented by volatile macroeconomic conditions that may have an impact on our operations around the world. Our future performance is subject to our continued ability to take appropriate actions to respond to these conditions.

RESULTS OF OPERATIONS

	Fiscal 2011	Fiscal 2010	FY11 vs. FY10 % Change	Fiscal 2009	FY10 vs. FY09 % Change
	(In millions, except per share data)				
Revenues	$20,862	$19,014	10%	$19,176	−1%
Cost of sales	11,354	10,214	11%	10,572	−3%
Gross margin	9,508	8,800	8%	8,604	2%
Gross margin %	45.6%	46.3%		44.9%	
Demand creation expense	2,448	2,356	4%	2,352	0%
Operating overhead expense	4,245	3,970	7%	3,798	5%
Total selling and administrative expense	6,693	6,326	6%	6,150	3%
% of Revenues	32.1%	33.3%		32.1%	
Restructuring charges	—	—	—	195	—
Goodwill impairment	—	—	—	199	—
Intangible and other asset impairment	—	—	—	202	—
Income before income taxes	2,844	2,517	13%	1,957	29%
Net income	2,133	1,907	12%	1,487	28%
Diluted earnings per share	4.39	3.86	14%	3.03	27%

CONSOLIDATED OPERATING RESULTS

Revenues

	Fiscal 2011	Fiscal 2010	FY11 vs. FY10 % Change	FY11 vs. FY10 % Change Excluding Currency Changes[1]	Fiscal 2009	FY10 vs. FY09 % Change	FY10 vs. FY09 % Change Excluding Currency Changes[1]
				(In millions)			
Revenues	$20,862	$19,014	10%	10%	$19,176	−1%	−2%

[1] Results have been restated using constant exchange rates for the comparative period to enhance the visibility of the underlying business trends excluding the impact of foreign currency exchange rate fluctuations.

Fiscal 2011 Compared to Fiscal 2010 On both a reported and currency neutral basis, revenues for NIKE, Inc. grew 10% for fiscal 2011, driven by increases in revenues for both the NIKE Brand and our Other Businesses. On a currency neutral basis, revenues for the NIKE Brand increased 10% for fiscal 2011, while revenues for our Other Businesses increased 8%. Excluding the effects of changes in currency exchange rates, every NIKE Brand geography except Japan delivered higher revenues for fiscal 2011, led by North America, which contributed approximately 5 percentage points to the NIKE Brand revenue increase. The Emerging Markets and Greater China contributed approximately 3 and 2 percentage points to the NIKE Brand revenue growth, respectively.

By product group, NIKE Brand footwear and apparel revenue increased 11% and 9%, respectively, while NIKE Brand equipment revenues declined 2% during fiscal 2011. Fueling the growth of our NIKE Brand footwear business was the increased demand in our performance products, including the NIKE Lunar and Free technologies which are used across multiple categories. The increase in NIKE Brand footwear revenue for fiscal 2011 was attributable to a high single-digit percentage increase in unit sales along with a low single-digit percentage increase in the average selling price per pair. The increase in unit sales was primarily driven by double-digit percentage growth in Running, Men's Training, Action Sports and Women's Training products, while the increase in average selling price per pair was primarily driven by price increases on selected products and fewer close-outs as a percentage of total sales. For NIKE Brand apparel, the increase in revenue for fiscal 2011 was primarily driven by a low double-digit percentage increase in unit sales attributable to strong category presentations and improved product lines, while the average selling price per unit was relatively flat. The increase in unit sales was driven by increased demand in all key categories.

While wholesale revenues remain the largest component of overall NIKE Brand revenues, we continue to see growth in revenue through our Direct to Consumer channels. Our NIKE Brand Direct to Consumer operations include NIKE owned in-line and factory stores, as well as online sales through NIKE owned websites. For fiscal 2011, Direct to Consumer channels represented approximately 16% of our total NIKE Brand revenues compared to 15% in fiscal 2010. On a currency neutral basis, Direct to Consumer revenues grew 16% for fiscal 2011 as we continue to expand our store network, increase comparable store sales and build our e-commerce business. Comparable store sales grew 11% for fiscal 2011. Comparable store sales include revenues from NIKE owned in-line and factory stores for which all three of the following requirements have been met: the store has been open at least one year, square footage has not changed by more than 15% within the past year, and the store has not been permanently repositioned within the past year.

Revenues for our Other Businesses consist of results from our affiliate brands; Cole Haan, Converse, Hurley and Umbro; and NIKE Golf. Excluding the impact of currency changes, revenues for these businesses increased by 8% in fiscal 2011, reflecting double-digit percentage revenue growth at Converse, Cole Haan and Hurley, and a low single-digit growth at Umbro, which more than offset a mid single-digit revenue decline at NIKE Golf.

Fiscal 2010 Compared to Fiscal 2009 Excluding the effects of changes in currency exchange rates, revenues for NIKE, Inc. declined 2%, driven primarily by a 2% decline in revenues for the NIKE Brand. All of our geographies delivered lower revenues with the exception of Emerging Markets, reflecting a challenging economic environment across most markets, most notably in our Western Europe and Central & Eastern Europe geographies. By product group, revenues for our worldwide NIKE Brand footwear business were down 1% compared to the prior year.

Worldwide NIKE Brand apparel and equipment revenues declined 5% and 7%, respectively. Our Direct to Consumer operations represented approximately 15% of our total NIKE Brand revenues in fiscal 2010 as compared to 13% in fiscal 2009.

Excluding the impact of currency changes, revenues for our Other Businesses increased by 4% for fiscal 2010, driven by increased revenues at Converse, Umbro and Hurley, which more than offset revenue declines at NIKE Golf and Cole Haan.

Futures Orders Futures and advance orders for NIKE Brand footwear and apparel scheduled for delivery from June through November 2011 were 15% higher than the orders reported for the comparable prior year period. This futures and advance order amount is calculated based upon our forecast of the actual exchange rates under which our revenues will be translated during this period, which approximate current spot rates. Excluding the impact of currency changes, futures orders increased 12%, primarily driven by a high single-digit percentage increase in unit sales volume and a low single-digit percentage increase in average price per unit for both footwear and apparel products.

By geography, futures orders growth was as follows:

	Reported Futures Orders Growth	Futures Orders Excluding Currency Changes[1]
North America	+14%	+14%
Western Europe	+11%	+1%
Central & Eastern Europe	+13%	+10%
Greater China	+24%	+17%
Japan	−13%	−6%
Emerging Markets	+25%	+23%
Total NIKE Brand Futures Orders	+15%	+12%

[1] Growth rates have been restated using constant exchange rates for the comparative period to enhance the visibility of the underlying business trends excluding the impact of foreign currency exchange rate fluctuations.

The reported futures and advance orders growth is not necessarily indicative of our expectation of revenue growth during this period. This is due to year-over-year changes in shipment timing and because the mix of orders can shift between advance/futures and at-once orders and the fulfillment of certain orders may fall outside of the schedule noted above. In addition, exchange rate fluctuations as well as differing levels of order cancellations and discounts can cause differences in the comparisons between advance/futures orders and actual revenues. Moreover, a significant portion of our revenue is not derived from futures and advance orders, including at-once and close-out sales of NIKE Brand footwear and apparel, sales of NIKE Brand equipment, sales from our Direct to Consumer operations, and sales from our Other Businesses.

Gross Margin

	Fiscal 2011	Fiscal 2010	FY11 vs. FY10 % Change	Fiscal 2009	FY10 vs. FY09 % Change
			(In millions)		
Gross Margin	$9,508	$8,800	8%	$8,604	2%
Gross Margin %	45.6%	46.3%	(70) bps	44.9%	140 bps

Fiscal 2011 Compared to Fiscal 2010 For fiscal 2011, our consolidated gross margin percentage was 70 basis points lower than the prior year. The primary factors contributing to this decrease were as follows:

- Higher input costs across most businesses,
- Increased transportation costs, including additional air freight incurred to meet strong demand for NIKE Brand products across most businesses, most notably in North America, Western Europe, and Central & Eastern Europe geographies, and
- A lower mix of licensee revenue as distribution for certain markets within our Other Businesses transitioned from licensees to operating units of NIKE, Inc.

Together, these factors decreased consolidated gross margins by approximately 130 basis points for fiscal 2011, with the most significant erosion in the second half of the fiscal year. These decreases were partially offset by the positive impact from the growth and expanding profitability of our NIKE Brand Direct to Consumer business, a higher mix of full-price sales and favorable impacts from our ongoing product cost efficiency initiatives.

As we head into fiscal 2012, we anticipate that our gross margins will continue to face pressure from macroeconomic factors, most notably rising product input costs as well as higher transportation costs, which may more than offset the favorable impact from our planned price increases and ongoing production cost efficiency initiatives.

Fiscal 2010 Compared to Fiscal 2009 For fiscal 2010, our consolidated gross margin percentage was 140 basis points higher than the prior year. The primary factors contributing to this improvement were as follows:

- Improved in-line product margins across most geographies, driven by reduced raw material and freight costs as well as favorable changes in product mix,
- Improved inventory positions, most notably in North America and Western Europe, which drove a shift in mix from discounted close-out to higher margin in-line sales, and
- Growth of NIKE-owned retail as a percentage of total revenue, across most NIKE Brand geographies, driven by an increase in both new store openings and comparable store sales.

Together, these factors increased consolidated gross margins by approximately 160 basis points for fiscal 2010. These increases were partially offset by the impact of unfavorable currency exchange rates, primarily affecting our Emerging Markets and Central & Eastern Europe geographies.

Selling and Administrative Expense

	Fiscal 2011	Fiscal 2010	FY11 vs. FY10 % Change	Fiscal 2009	FY10 vs. FY09 % Change
			(In millions)		
Demand creation expense[1]	$2,448	$2,356	4%	$2,352	0%
Operating overhead expense	4,245	3,970	7%	3,798	5%
Selling and administrative expense	$6,693	$6,326	6%	$6,150	3%
% of Revenues	32.1%	33.3%	(120) bps	32.1%	120 bps

[1] Demand creation consists of advertising and promotion expenses, including costs of endorsement contracts.

Fiscal 2011 Compared to Fiscal 2010 In fiscal 2011, the effect of changes in foreign currency exchange rates did not have a significant impact on selling and administrative expense.

Demand creation expense increased 4% compared to the prior year, primarily driven by a higher level of brand event spending around the World Cup and World Basketball Festival in the first half of fiscal 2011, as well as increased spending around key product initiatives and investments in retail product presentation with wholesale customers.

Operating overhead expense increased 7% compared to the prior year. This increase was primarily attributable to increased investments in our Direct to Consumer operations as well as growth in our wholesale operations, where we incurred higher personnel costs and travel expenses as compared to the prior year.

Fiscal 2010 Compared to Fiscal 2009 In fiscal 2010, changes in currency exchange rates had a minimal impact on demand creation expense. Demand creation expense remained flat compared to the prior year, as increases in sports marketing and digital marketing expenses were offset by reductions in advertising.

Excluding changes in exchange rates, operating overhead expense increased 4% compared to the prior year due primarily to increases in performance-based compensation and investments in our Direct to Consumer operations. These increases were partially offset by reductions in compensation spending in fiscal 2010 as a result of restructuring activities that took place in the fourth quarter of fiscal 2009.

Restructuring Charges

During fiscal 2009, we restructured the organization to streamline our management structure, enhance consumer focus, drive innovation more quickly to market and establish a more scalable cost structure. As a result of these actions, we reduced our global workforce by approximately 5% and incurred pre-tax restructuring charges of $195 million in fiscal 2009, primarily consisting of cash severance costs. These charges are included in "Corporate" for segment reporting purposes.

Goodwill, Intangibles and Other Assets Impairment

In fiscal 2009, we recognized non-cash impairment charges of $199 million and $202 million relating to Umbro's goodwill, intangibles and other assets, respectively. Although Umbro's financial performance for fiscal 2009 was slightly better than we had originally expected, projected future cash flows had fallen below the levels we expected at the time of acquisition. This erosion was a result of both the unprecedented decline in global consumer markets, particularly in the United Kingdom, and our decision to adjust the level of investment in the business.

For additional information about our impairment charges, see Note 4–Acquisition, Identifiable Intangible Assets, Goodwill and Umbro Impairment in the accompanying Notes to the Consolidated Financial Statements.

Other (Income), net

	Fiscal 2011	Fiscal 2010	FY11 vs. FY10 % Change	Fiscal 2009	FY10 vs. FY09 % Change
			(In millions)		
Other (income), net	$(33)	$(49)	−33%	$(89)	−45%

Fiscal 2011 Compared to Fiscal 2010 Other (income), net is comprised of foreign currency conversion gains and losses from the re-measurement of monetary assets and liabilities in non-functional currencies and the impact of certain foreign currency derivative instruments, as well as unusual or non-recurring transactions that are outside the normal course of business. For fiscal 2011, other (income), net was primarily comprised of net foreign currency gains.

For fiscal 2011, we estimate that the combination of translation of foreign currency-denominated profits from our international businesses and the year-over-year change in foreign currency related net gains included in other (income), net had an unfavorable impact of approximately $33 million on our income before income taxes.

Fiscal 2010 Compared to Fiscal 2009 For fiscal 2010 and 2009, other (income), net was primarily comprised of net foreign currency gains and the recognition of previously deferred licensing income related to our fiscal 2008 sale of NIKE Bauer Hockey.

For fiscal 2010, we estimate that the combination of translation of foreign currency-denominated profits from our international businesses and the year-over-year change in foreign currency related net gains included in other (income), net increased our income before income taxes by approximately $34 million.

Income Taxes

	Fiscal 2011	Fiscal 2010	FY11 vs. FY10 % Change	Fiscal 2009	FY10 vs. FY09 % Change
Effective tax rate	25.0%	24.2%	80 bps	24.0%	20 bps

Fiscal 2011 Compared to Fiscal 2010 Our effective tax rate for fiscal 2011 was 80 basis points higher than the effective rate for fiscal 2010 due primarily to the change in geographic mix of earnings. A larger percentage of our earnings in fiscal 2011 were attributable to operations in the U.S., where the statutory tax rate is generally higher than the tax rate on operations outside of the U.S. This impact was partially offset by changes to uncertain tax positions.

Fiscal 2010 Compared to Fiscal 2009 Our effective tax rate for fiscal 2010 was 20 basis points higher than the effective rate for fiscal 2009. Our effective tax rate for fiscal 2009 includes a tax benefit related to charges recorded for the impairment of Umbro's goodwill, intangible and other assets. Excluding this tax benefit, our effective rate for fiscal 2009 would have been 26.5%, 230 basis points higher than our effective tax rate for fiscal 2010. The decrease in our effective tax rate for fiscal 2010 was primarily attributable to our international operations, as tax rates for these operations are generally lower than the U.S. statutory rate.

OPERATING SEGMENTS The Company's reportable operating segments are based on our internal geographic organization. Each NIKE Brand geography operates predominantly in one industry: the design, development, marketing and selling of athletic footwear, apparel, and equipment. Our reportable operating segments for the NIKE Brand are: North America, Western Europe, Central & Eastern Europe, Greater China, Japan, and Emerging Markets. Our NIKE Brand Direct to Consumer operations are managed within each geographic segment.

As part of our centrally managed foreign exchange risk management program, standard foreign currency rates are assigned to each NIKE Brand entity in our geographic operating segments and are used to record any non-functional currency revenues or product purchases into the entity's functional currency. Geographic operating segment revenues and cost of sales reflect use of these standard rates. For all NIKE Brand operating segments, differences between assigned standard foreign currency rates and actual market rates are included in Corporate together with foreign currency hedge gains and losses generated from our centrally managed foreign exchange risk management program. Prior to fiscal 2010, all foreign currency results, including hedge results and other conversion gains and losses generated by the Western Europe and Central & Eastern Europe geographies were recorded in their respective geographic results.

Certain prior year amounts have been reclassified to conform to fiscal 2011 presentation, as South Africa became part of the Emerging Markets operating segment beginning June 1, 2010. Previously, South Africa was part of the Central & Eastern Europe operating segment.

The breakdown of revenues follows:

	Fiscal 2011	Fiscal 2010[1]	FY11 vs. FY10 % Change	FY11 vs. FY10 % Change Excluding Currency Changes[2]	Fiscal 2009[1]	FY10 vs. FY09 % Change	FY10 vs. FY09 % Change Excluding Currency Changes[2]
				(In millions)			
North America	$ 7,578	$ 6,696	13%	13%	$ 6,778	−1%	−1%
Western Europe	3,810	3,892	−2%	4%	4,139	−6%	−6%
Central & Eastern Europe	1,031	993	4%	7%	1,247	−20%	−19%
Greater China	2,060	1,742	18%	16%	1,743	0%	0%
Japan	766	882	−13%	−21%	926	−5%	−12%
Emerging Markets	2,736	2,199	24%	19%	1,828	20%	17%
Global Brand Divisions	123	105	17%	21%	96	9%	12%
Total NIKE Brand Revenues	18,104	16,509	10%	10%	16,757	−1%	−2%
Other Businesses	2,747	2,530	9%	8%	2,419	5%	4%
Corporate[3]	11	(25)	—	—	—	—	—
Total NIKE, Inc. Revenues	$20,862	$19,014	10%	10%	$19,176	−1%	−2%

[1] Certain prior year amounts have been reclassified to conform to fiscal year 2011 presentation. These changes had no impact on previously reported results of operations or shareholders' equity.

[2] Results have been restated using constant exchange rates for the comparative period to enhance the visibility of the underlying business trends excluding the impact of foreign currency exchange rate fluctuations.

[3] Corporate revenues primarily consist of foreign currency hedge gains and losses generated by entities within the NIKE Brand geographic operating segments but managed through our central foreign exchange risk management program, and foreign currency gains and losses resulting from the difference between actual foreign currency rates and standard rates assigned to these entities, which are used to record any non-functional currency revenues into the entity's functional currency.

The primary financial measure used by the Company to evaluate performance of individual operating segments is earnings before interest and taxes (commonly referred to as "EBIT") which represents net income before interest expense (income), net and income taxes in the consolidated statements of income. As discussed in Note 18—Operating Segments and Related Information in the accompanying Notes to the Consolidated Financial Statements, certain corporate costs are not included in EBIT of our operating segments.

The breakdown of earnings before interest and taxes is as follows:

	Fiscal 2011	Fiscal 2010[1]	FY11 vs. FY10 % Change	Fiscal 2009[1]	FY10 vs. FY09 % Change
			(In millions)		
North America	$1,750	$1,538	14%	$1,429	8%
Western Europe	721	856	−16%	939	−9%
Central & Eastern Europe	233	253	−8%	394	−36%
Greater China	777	637	22%	575	11%
Japan	114	180	−37%	205	−12%
Emerging Markets	688	521	32%	364	43%
Global Brand Divisions	(998)	(867)	−15%	(811)	−7%
Total NIKE Brand	3,285	3,118	5%	3,095	1%
Other Businesses	334	299	12%	(193)	—
Corporate	(771)	(894)	14%	(955)	6%
Total Consolidated Earnings Before Interest and Taxes	$2,848	$2,523	13%	$1,947	30%
Interest expense (income), net	4	6	−33%	(10)	—
Total Consolidated Income Before Income Taxes	$2,844	$2,517	13%	$1,957	29%

[1] Certain prior year amounts have been reclassified to conform to fiscal year 2011 presentation. These changes had no impact on previously reported results of operations or shareholders' equity.

North America

	Fiscal 2011	Fiscal 2010	FY11 vs. FY10 % Change	FY11 vs. FY10 % Change Excluding Currency Changes	Fiscal 2009	FY10 vs. FY09 % Change	FY10 vs. FY09 % Change Excluding Currency Changes
				(In millions)			
Revenues							
Footwear	$5,109	$4,610	11%	11%	$4,694	−2%	−2%
Apparel	2,105	1,740	21%	21%	1,740	0%	0%
Equipment	364	346	5%	5%	344	1%	0%
Total Revenues	$7,578	$6,696	13%	13%	$6,778	−1%	−1%
Earnings Before Interest and Taxes	$1,750	$1,538	14%		$1,429	8%	

Fiscal 2011 Compared to Fiscal 2010 Revenues for North America increased 13%, driven by double-digit percentage growth in both wholesale and Direct to Consumer revenues. Contributing to the wholesale revenue growth was strong product category presentations at our wholesale customers, improved product lines and earlier shipments of summer season products. North America's Direct to Consumer revenues grew 19%, which contributed approximately 4 percentage points to North America's revenue increase. The growth in the Direct to Consumer business was fueled by 14% growth in comparable store sales.

For fiscal 2011, the increase in North America footwear revenue was primarily driven by double-digit percentage growth in Running, Men's and Women's Training and Football (Soccer) categories and a single-digit percentage growth in Basketball, partially offset by a low single-digit percentage decline in sales of our NIKE Brand Sportswear products.

The year-over-year increase in North America apparel revenues was primarily driven by double-digit percentage growth in most key categories, most notably Men's Training, Running, Basketball and Women's Training.

For fiscal 2011, the increase in North America's EBIT was primarily the result of revenue growth and leverage on selling and administrative expense, which more than offset a lower gross margin percentage. The decline in gross margin percentage was due primarily to increased air freight and product input costs, which more than offset the favorable impact from the growth of our Direct to Consumer business and fewer close-out sales.

Fiscal 2010 Compared to Fiscal 2009 Excluding the changes in currency exchange rates, revenues for North America declined 1%, driven primarily by a decrease in revenue from our wholesale business. This decrease was partially offset by an increase in our NIKE-owned retail business, driven primarily by an increase in comparable store sales.

During fiscal 2010, the decrease in North America footwear revenue was primarily attributable to a low single-digit percentage decrease in unit sales, while average selling price per pair remained flat. The decline in unit sales was primarily driven by lower sales for our Kids' and Running categories in the first half of fiscal 2010.

North America apparel revenue during fiscal 2010 was flat when compared to fiscal 2009, which was reflective of a high single-digit percentage increase in average selling price per unit, offset by a low double-digit percentage decrease in unit sales. Both the increase in average selling price per unit and the decrease in unit sales were primarily a result of fewer close-out sales compared to the prior year.

For fiscal 2010, the increase in North America's EBIT was primarily the result of improved gross margins combined with a slight decrease in selling and administrative expense, driven by a reduction in demand creation expense compared to prior year. The improvement in gross margin was mainly attributable to a shift in mix from close-out to in-line sales, growth of our Direct to Consumer business as a percentage of total sales, improved in-line product margins and lower warehousing costs.

Western Europe

	Fiscal 2011	Fiscal 2010	FY11 vs. FY10 % Change	FY11 vs. FY10 % Change Excluding Currency Changes	Fiscal 2009	FY10 vs. FY09 % Change	FY10 vs. FY09 % Change Excluding Currency Changes
				(In millions)			
Revenues							
Footwear	$2,327	$2,320	0%	7%	$2,385	−3%	−3%
Apparel	1,266	1,325	−4%	2%	1,463	−9%	−9%
Equipment	217	247	−12%	−6%	291	−15%	−15%
Total Revenues	$3,810	$3,892	−2%	4%	$4,139	−6%	−6%
Earnings Before Interest and Taxes	$ 721	$ 856	−16%		$ 939	−9%	

Fiscal 2011 Compared to Fiscal 2010 On a currency neutral basis, revenues for Western Europe increased 4% for fiscal 2011, attributable to growth in most territories. Revenues for the U.K. & Ireland, the largest market in Western Europe, grew 5% for fiscal 2011. Western Europe's Direct to Consumer revenues grew 10%, which contributed approximately 1 percentage point to Western Europe's revenue increase. The growth in the Direct to Consumer business was fueled by 6% growth in comparable store sales.

Excluding changes in currency exchange rates, footwear revenue in Western Europe increased 7%, driven by double-digit percentage growth in our Running, Football (Soccer) and Action Sports categories, which more than offset a slight revenue decline in our NIKE Brand Sportswear category.

On a currency neutral basis, apparel revenue in Western Europe increased 2%, primarily driven by double-digit percentage growth in our Football (Soccer) and Running categories, which more than offset a mid single-digit revenue decline in our NIKE Brand Sportswear category.

For fiscal 2011, the decrease in Western Europe's EBIT was driven by unfavorable foreign currency translation and a lower gross margin percentage, all of which more than offset the increase in revenues and improved leverage on selling and administrative expense. The decline in the gross margin percentage was significantly impacted by the unfavorable year-over-year standard currency rates. Also contributing to the decrease in the gross margin percentage was higher product input and air freight costs, higher royalty expenses related to sales of endorsed team products and higher full price discounts. These factors more than offset the favorable impact of fewer close-out sales.

Fiscal 2010 Compared to Fiscal 2009 On a currency neutral basis, most markets in Western Europe experienced lower revenues during fiscal 2010, reflecting a difficult retail environment throughout the geography. Our largest market, the U.K. & Ireland, declined 4%.

Excluding changes in currency exchange rates, the decrease in footwear revenue during fiscal 2010 was primarily the result of low single-digit decreases in both average selling price and unit sales. The decrease in average selling price was attributable to higher customer discounts provided to manage inventory levels, while the reduction in unit sales was due to lower sales for most NIKE Brand product categories.

The year-over-year decrease in apparel revenue was primarily driven by a high single-digit decline in unit sales combined with a mid single-digit decrease in average selling price. The decrease in unit sales was due to lower sales for most NIKE Brand product categories, while the decrease in average selling price was a result of higher discounts provided to retailers to manage their inventory levels.

For fiscal 2010, EBIT for Western Europe declined at a faster rate than revenues, as the increase in selling and administrative expense as a percentage of revenues more than offset the improvements in gross margin percentage. The increase in selling administrative expense was primarily driven by a higher level of both demand creation spending around the 2010 World Cup and operating overhead expense as a result of investments in our Direct to Consumer operations and higher performance-based compensation. The gross margin improvement in fiscal 2010 was primarily attributable to higher in-line product margins, a smaller proportion of close-out sales and reduced inventory obsolescence expense as a result of our leaner inventory positions.

Central & Eastern Europe

	Fiscal 2011	Fiscal 2010	FY11 vs. FY10 % Change	FY11 vs. FY10 % Change Excluding Currency Changes	Fiscal 2009	FY10 vs. FY09 % Change	FY10 vs. FY09 % Change Excluding Currency Changes
				(In millions)			
Revenues							
Footwear	$ 600	$558	8%	11%	$ 673	−17%	−16%
Apparel	356	354	1%	4%	468	−24%	−24%
Equipment	75	81	−7%	−5%	106	−24%	−21%
Total Revenues	$1,031	$993	4%	7%	$1,247	−20%	−19%
Earnings Before Interest and Taxes	$ 233	$253	−8%		$ 394	−36%	

Fiscal 2011 Compared to Fiscal 2010 Led by Russia and Turkey, most territories within Central & Eastern Europe reported revenue growth during fiscal 2011 as economic conditions in the geography continued to show signs of recovery.

The growth in Central & Eastern Europe's footwear revenues was mainly driven by double-digit percentage growth in our Football (Soccer), Running and Action Sports categories, while the growth in apparel revenues was primarily driven by double-digit percentage growth in our Running category.

For fiscal 2011, the decrease in Central & Eastern Europe's EBIT was primarily driven by unfavorable foreign currency translation and a lower gross margin percentage, which more than offset the increase in revenues and improved leverage on selling and administrative expense. The decline in the gross margin percentage was primarily due to unfavorable year-over-year standard currency rates, higher air freight costs and an increase in product input costs.

Fiscal 2010 Compared to Fiscal 2009 Economic conditions in Central & Eastern Europe remained difficult as most markets within the geography experienced lower revenues in fiscal 2010 as compared to fiscal 2009.

The decrease in footwear revenue was due to a decline in average selling price, while unit sales remained flat compared to fiscal 2009. The decline in average selling price was primarily the result of higher discounts provided to retailers to manage their inventory levels.

The year-over-year decrease in apparel revenue was primarily driven by a double-digit decrease in average selling price and a mid single-digit decline in unit sales. The decline in average selling price was primarily the result of higher discounts provided to retailers to manage their inventory levels, while the decline in unit sales was due to lower sales in most key product categories.

The year-over-year decrease in Central & Eastern Europe's EBIT during fiscal 2010 was the result of lower revenues, a decline in gross margin percentage and higher selling and administrative expense. The decline in gross margin percentage was primarily attributable to less favorable year-over-year standard currency rates, as well as higher discounts provided to customers. The increase in selling and administrative expense was primarily due to an increase in the reserve for bad debts along with increased investments in our Direct to Consumer operations.

Greater China

	Fiscal 2011	Fiscal 2010	FY11 vs. FY10 % Change	FY11 vs. FY10 % Change Excluding Currency Changes	Fiscal 2009	FY10 vs. FY09 % Change	FY10 vs. FY09 % Change Excluding Currency Changes
				(In millions)			
Revenues							
Footwear	$1,164	$ 953	22%	19%	$ 940	1%	1%
Apparel	789	684	15%	13%	700	−2%	−3%
Equipment	107	105	2%	0%	103	2%	0%
Total Revenues	$2,060	$1,742	18%	16%	$1,743	0%	0%
Earnings Before Interest and Taxes	$ 777	$ 637	22%		$ 575	11%	

Fiscal 2011 Compared to Fiscal 2010 Excluding changes in currency exchange rates, Greater China revenues increased 16% for fiscal 2011, driven by expansion in the number of partner-owned stores selling NIKE products, as well as improvement in comparable store sales for partner-owned stores.

For fiscal 2011, the increase in Greater China's footwear revenue was primarily driven by double-digit percentage growth in our Running and NIKE Brand Sportswear categories, while the growth in apparel revenue was mainly driven by double-digit percentage increases in our NIKE Brand Sportswear, Basketball and Men's Training categories.

For fiscal 2011, EBIT for Greater China grew at a faster rate than revenue as a result of a higher gross margin percentage, improved leverage on selling and administrative expense and favorable foreign currency translation. The improvement in the gross margin percentage was primarily attributable to higher product prices, favorable product mix and lower inventory obsolescence expense, which more than offset higher product input costs and warehousing costs from our new China distribution center.

Fiscal 2010 Compared to Fiscal 2009 For fiscal 2010, revenues for Greater China were flat, primarily attributable to comparisons against strong revenue growth in the first half of fiscal 2009 driven by the Beijing Olympics. Greater China began to gain momentum in the second half of fiscal 2010, as revenues increased 11% as compared to the second half of fiscal 2009.

The increase in footwear revenue was primarily driven by a mid single-digit increase in average selling price, partially offset by a mid single-digit decrease in unit sales. The increase in average selling price was primarily due to strategic price increases, while the decrease in unit sales was primarily driven by lower discounts on in-line products compared to the prior year.

The decrease in apparel revenue for fiscal 2010 was primarily due to a mid single-digit decrease in unit sales across most major categories, which more than offset a low single-digit increase in average selling price primarily driven by strategic price increases.

EBIT for Greater China increased at a faster rate than revenue as a result of higher gross margins and reductions in demand creation spending attributable to comparisons against higher prior year spending around the Beijing Olympics.

Japan

	Fiscal 2011	Fiscal 2010	FY11 vs. FY10 % Change	FY11 vs. FY10 % Change Excluding Currency Changes	Fiscal 2009	FY10 vs. FY09 % Change	FY10 vs. FY09 % Change Excluding Currency Changes
				(In millions)			
Revenues							
Footwear	$396	$433	−9%	−16%	$430	1%	−7%
Apparel	302	357	−15%	−23%	397	−10%	−17%
Equipment	68	92	−26%	−32%	99	−7%	−13%
Total Revenues	$766	$882	−13%	−21%	$926	−5%	−12%
Earnings Before Interest and Taxes	$114	$180	−37%		$205	−12%	

Fiscal 2011 Compared to Fiscal 2010 Macroeconomic conditions in Japan remain difficult. On March 11, 2011, Japan experienced a major earthquake and resulting tsunami. While the Company's organization and assets in Japan were not materially damaged, business results for the month of March 2011 were significantly eroded by the natural disaster. As we enter fiscal 2012, we anticipate macroeconomic conditions in Japan to remain difficult as consumer confidence continues to recover.

Excluding changes in currency exchange rates, both footwear and apparel revenues in Japan declined, driven by decreases across most key categories. Partially offsetting the decreases was a double-digit percentage growth in revenues from Running apparel.

The decrease in Japan's EBIT for fiscal 2011 was primarily due to lower revenues and higher selling and administrative expense as a percentage of revenue, partially offset by an improvement in the gross margin percentage. The improvement in the gross margin percentage was primarily driven by favorable year-over-year standard currency rates and positive impacts from fewer discounts on close-out sales, which more than offset higher product input costs and inventory obsolescence expense.

Fiscal 2010 Compared to Fiscal 2009 Excluding changes in currency exchange rates, both footwear and apparel revenues in Japan declined during fiscal 2010 due to decreases in unit sales across most major categories. The decline in revenues was reflective of a difficult and highly promotional marketplace in Japan.

For fiscal 2010, the decrease in Japan's EBIT was primarily due to lower revenues and higher selling and administrative expense, driven by increased investments in our Direct to Consumer operations, which more than offset improved gross margins.

Emerging Markets

	Fiscal 2011	Fiscal 2010	FY11 vs. FY10 % Change	FY11 vs. FY10 % Change Excluding Currency Changes	Fiscal 2009	FY10 vs. FY09 % Change	FY10 vs. FY09 % Change Excluding Currency Changes
				(In millions)			
Revenues							
Footwear	$1,897	$1,458	30%	24%	$1,185	23%	20%
Apparel	657	577	14%	9%	477	21%	17%
Equipment	182	164	11%	6%	166	−1%	−3%
Total Revenues	$2,736	$2,199	24%	19%	$1,828	20%	17%
Earnings Before Interest and Taxes	$ 688	$ 521	32%		$ 364	43%	

Fiscal 2011 Compared to Fiscal 2010 Excluding the changes in currency exchange rates, revenues for Emerging Markets increased 19% for fiscal 2011. Most territories in the geography reported double-digit revenue growth for the fiscal year, led by Brazil, Argentina, Mexico, and Korea.

For fiscal 2011, both footwear and apparel revenue growth in the Emerging Markets was primarily driven by strong demand in nearly all key categories, most notably NIKE Brand Sportswear and Running.

For fiscal 2011, EBIT for Emerging Markets grew at a faster rate than revenue as a result of higher gross margin percentage, improved leverage on selling and administrative expense and favorable foreign currency translation. The increase in the gross margin percentage was primarily due to a higher mix of in-line product sales, lower warehousing costs and favorable year-over-year standard currency rates, which more than offset the increase in product input costs and higher full-price discounts.

Fiscal 2010 Compared to Fiscal 2009 Excluding changes in currency exchange rates, fiscal 2010 revenue growth for the Emerging Markets geography was driven by growth in all product categories and all territories, most notably Brazil, Mexico and Korea.

Footwear revenue growth was primarily driven by a double-digit growth in unit sales and a mid single-digit increase in average selling price per pair during fiscal 2010, reflective of strong demand for most NIKE Brand product categories in all markets within the geography.

For fiscal 2010, the increase in Emerging Markets' EBIT was primarily the result of revenue growth combined with lower selling and administrative expense, which more than offset a decrease in gross margin percentage. The decrease in selling and administrative expense was primarily due to lower operating overhead expense resulting from fiscal 2009 restructuring activities. The decline in gross margin was primarily due to less favorable year-over-year standard currency rates compared to the prior year, which more than offset improved in-line product margins.

Global Brand Divisions

	Fiscal 2011	Fiscal 2010	FY11 vs. FY10 % Change	FY11 vs. FY10 % Change Excluding Currency Changes	Fiscal 2009	FY10 vs. FY09 % Change	FY10 vs. FY09 % Change Excluding Currency Changes
				(In millions)			
Revenues	$123	$105	17%	21%	$ 96	9%	12%
(Loss) Before Interest and Taxes	(998)	(867)	−15%		(811)	−7%	

Global Brand Divisions primarily represent demand creation and operating overhead expenses that are centrally managed for the NIKE Brand. Revenues for the Global Brand Divisions are attributable to NIKE Brand licensing businesses that are not part of a geographic operating segment.

Fiscal 2011 Compared to Fiscal 2010 For fiscal 2011, the increase in Global Brand Division expense was primarily due to an increase in both operating overhead and centrally managed demand creation expense. The increase in operating overhead expense was mainly driven by increased investments in our Direct to Consumer infrastructure along with higher wages and travel expense. The increase in demand creation expense was primarily driven by a higher level of brand event spending around the World Cup and World Basketball Festival in the first half of fiscal 2011, as well as increased investments in sports marketing.

Fiscal 2010 Compared to Fiscal 2009 For fiscal 2010, the increase in Global Brand Division expense was largely due to increases in centrally managed demand creation expense and performance-based compensation, which more than offset an increase in licensing revenues. The increase in demand creation expense was primarily driven by the centralization of certain marketing production costs.

Other Businesses

	Fiscal 2011	Fiscal 2010	FY11 vs. FY10 % Change	FY11 vs. FY10 % Change Excluding Currency Changes	Fiscal 2009	FY10 vs. FY09 % Change	FY10 vs. FY09 % Change Excluding Currency Changes
				(In millions)			
Revenues							
Converse	$1,130	$ 983	15%	15%	$ 915	7%	7%
NIKE Golf	623	638	−2%	−4%	648	−2%	−4%
Cole Haan	518	463	12%	12%	472	−2%	−2%
Hurley	252	221	14%	14%	203	9%	9%
Umbro	224	225	0%	2%	174	29%	30%
Other	—	—	—	—	7	—	—
Total Revenues	$2,747	$2,530	9%	8%	$2,419	5%	4%
Earnings Before Interest and Taxes	$ 334	$ 299	12%		$(193)	—	

Fiscal 2011 Compared to Fiscal 2010 Our Other Businesses are comprised of our affiliate brands; Cole Haan, Converse, Hurley and Umbro; and NIKE Golf. The revenue growth at Converse was primarily driven by increased licensing revenue in China, as well as increased sales in the U.K. as we transitioned that market to a Converse owned distribution model. Revenues for Cole Haan increased 12%, driven by double-digit percentage growth in our wholesale operations as well as high single-digit percentage growth in our Direct to Consumer operations. Revenues declined at NIKE Golf, where we experienced significant erosion in our Japan business following the earthquake and tsunami in March 2011.

For fiscal 2011, EBIT for our Other Businesses grew at a faster rate than revenues, primarily as a result of more favorable foreign currency exchange impacts. The gross margin percentage remained relatively flat for fiscal 2011, as the favorable impact from improved product mix was offset by a lower mix of licensee revenues. Selling and administrative expense as a percentage of revenues remained relatively flat for fiscal 2011.

Fiscal 2010 Compared to Fiscal 2009 For fiscal 2010, the increase in Other Businesses' revenue was primarily driven by revenue growth at Converse, Umbro and Hurley, which more than offset the declines at NIKE Golf and Cole Haan due to reductions in consumer discretionary spending in their respective markets.

In fiscal 2009, EBIT for our Other Businesses included a $401 million pre-tax non-cash charge relating to the impairment of goodwill, intangible and other assets of Umbro. Excluding this impairment charge, EBIT for our Other Businesses would have increased 43%, as a result of higher revenues, improved gross margins across most businesses, and lower demand creation spending.

For additional information about our impairment charges, see Note 4—Identifiable Intangible Assets, Goodwill and Umbro Impairment in the Notes to the Consolidated Financial Statements.

Corporate

	Fiscal 2011	Fiscal 2010	FY11 vs. FY10 % Change	Fiscal 2009	FY10 vs. FY09 % Change
			(In millions)		
Revenues	$ 11	$(25)	—	$ —	—
(Loss) Before Interest and Taxes	(771)	(894)	14%	(955)	6%

Corporate consists largely of unallocated general and administrative expenses, which includes expenses associated with centrally managed departments, depreciation and amortization related to our corporate headquarters, unallocated insurance, benefit and compensation programs, including stock-based compensation, certain foreign currency gains and losses, including certain hedge gains and losses, corporate eliminations and other items.

Corporate revenues primarily consist of (1) foreign currency hedge gains and losses related to revenues generated by entities within the NIKE Brand geographic operating segments but managed through our central foreign exchange risk management program and (2) foreign currency gains and losses resulting from the difference between actual foreign currency rates and standard rates assigned to these entities, which are used to record any non-functional currency revenues into the entity's functional currency.

In addition to the foreign currency gains and losses recognized in Corporate revenues, foreign currency results include all other foreign currency hedge results generated through our centrally managed foreign exchange risk management program, other conversion gains and losses arising from re-measurement of monetary assets and liabilities in non-functional currencies, and gains and losses resulting from the difference between actual foreign currency rates and standard rates assigned to each entity in NIKE Brand geographic operating segments, which are used to record any non-functional currency product purchases into the entity's functional currency. Prior to fiscal 2010, all foreign currency results, including hedge results and other conversion gains and losses, generated by the Western Europe and Central & Eastern Europe geographies were recorded in their respective geographic results.

Fiscal 2011 Compared to Fiscal 2010 For fiscal 2011, the decrease in Corporate expense was primarily driven by year-over-year net foreign currency gains generated by our centrally managed foreign exchange risk management program. Also contributing to the decrease in Corporate expense for fiscal 2011 was a $54 million year-over-year reduction in stock options expense primarily due to a change in accelerated vesting provisions that took effect in the first quarter of fiscal 2011 and a lower estimated fair value for stock options granted in the current year. These benefits more than offset an increase in corporate operating overhead expenses, primarily driven by higher wage-related expense.

Fiscal 2010 Compared to Fiscal 2009 In fiscal 2009, results for Corporate included a pre-tax restructuring charge of $195 million. Excluding this restructuring charge, loss before interest and taxes for Corporate would have increased by 18% for fiscal 2010, primarily driven by an increase in performance-based compensation.

LIQUIDITY AND CAPITAL RESOURCES

Cash Flow Activity Cash provided by operations was $1.8 billion for fiscal 2011 compared to $3.2 billion for fiscal 2010. Our primary source of operating cash flow for fiscal 2011 was net income of $2.1 billion. Our working capital was a net cash outflow of $708 million for fiscal 2011 as compared to a positive net cash inflow of $694 million for fiscal 2010. Our investments in working capital increased primarily due to an increase in inventory and higher accounts receivable. Inventory at the end of fiscal 2011 increased 33% compared to fiscal 2010, primarily driven by a 15% increase in futures orders, growth in replenishment programs for high-turnover styles, early purchases of key seasonal items with longer production lead times as well as the growth of Direct to Consumer operations. Changes in currency exchange rates and higher product costs also contributed to the increase in dollar inventory. The increase in accounts receivable was mainly attributable to the increase in revenues during fiscal 2011.

Cash used by investing activities was $1.0 billion during fiscal 2011, compared to $1.3 billion for fiscal 2010. The year-over-year decrease was primarily due to lower net purchases of short-term investments. Net purchases of short-term investments were $537 million (net of sales and maturities) in fiscal 2011 compared to $937 million during fiscal 2010.

Cash used by financing activities was $2.0 billion for fiscal 2011 compared to $1.1 billion used in fiscal 2010. The increase in cash used by financing activities was primarily due to an increase in share repurchases and dividends paid, partially offset by an increase in notes payable.

In fiscal 2011, we purchased 23.8 million shares of NIKE's class B common stock for $1.9 billion. These repurchases were made under the four-year, $5 billion program approved by our Board of Directors which commenced in December 2009 and as of the end of fiscal 2011, we have repurchased 30.4 million shares for $2.3 billion under this program. We continue to expect funding of share repurchases will come from operating cash flow, excess cash, and/or debt. The timing and the amount of shares purchased will be dictated by our capital needs and stock market conditions.

Off-Balance Sheet Arrangements

In connection with various contracts and agreements, we provide routine indemnifications relating to the enforceability of intellectual property rights, coverage for legal issues that arise and other items where we are acting as the guarantor. Currently, we have several such agreements in place. However, based on our historical experience and the estimated probability of future loss, we have determined that the fair value of such indemnifications is not material to our financial position or results of operations.

Contractual Obligations

Our significant long-term contractual obligations as of May 31, 2011, and significant endorsement contracts entered into through the date of this report are as follows:

Description of Commitment	Cash Payments Due During the Year Ending May 31,						
	2012	**2013**	**2014**	**2015**	**2016**	**Thereafter**	**Total**
	(In millions)						
Operating Leases	$ 374	$ 310	$ 253	$198	$174	$ 535	$ 1,844
Long-term Debt	200	48	58	8	109	37	460
Endorsement Contracts[1]	800	806	742	615	463	1,018	4,444
Product Purchase Obligations[2]	3,175	—	—	—	—	—	3,175
Other[3]	277	137	22	4	1	—	441
Total	$4,826	$1,301	$1,075	$825	$747	$1,590	$10,364

[1] The amounts listed for endorsement contracts represent approximate amounts of base compensation and minimum guaranteed royalty fees we are obligated to pay athlete and sport team endorsers of our products. Actual payments under some contracts may be higher than the amounts listed as these contracts provide for bonuses to be paid to the endorsers based upon athletic achievements and/or royalties on product sales in future periods. Actual payments under some contracts may also be lower as these contracts include provisions for reduced payments if athletic performance declines in future periods.

In addition to the cash payments, we are obligated to furnish our endorsers with NIKE product for their use. It is not possible to determine how much we will spend on this product on an annual basis as the contracts generally do not stipulate a specific amount of cash to be spent on the product. The amount of product provided to the endorsers will depend on many factors including general playing conditions, the number of sporting events in which they participate, and our own decisions regarding product and marketing initiatives. In addition, the costs to design, develop, source, and purchase the products furnished to the endorsers are incurred over a period of time and are not necessarily tracked separately from similar costs incurred for products sold to customers.

[2] We generally order product at least 4 to 5 months in advance of sale based primarily on advanced futures orders received from customers. The amounts listed for product purchase obligations represent agreements (including open purchase orders) to purchase products in the ordinary course of business, that are enforceable and legally binding and that specify all significant terms. In some cases, prices are subject to change throughout the production process. The reported amounts exclude product purchase liabilities included in accounts payable on the consolidated balance sheet as of May 31, 2011.

[3] Other amounts primarily include service and marketing commitments made in the ordinary course of business. The amounts represent the minimum payments required by legally binding contracts and agreements that specify all significant terms, including open purchase orders for non-product purchases. The reported amounts exclude those liabilities included in accounts payable or accrued liabilities on the consolidated balance sheet as of May 31, 2011.

The total liability for uncertain tax positions was $212 million, excluding related interest and penalties, at May 31, 2011. We are not able to reasonably estimate when or if cash payments of the long-term liability for uncertain tax positions will occur.

We also have the following outstanding short-term debt obligations as of May 31, 2011. Please refer to the accompanying Notes to the Consolidated Financial Statements (Note 7—Short-Term Borrowings and Credit Lines) for further description and interest rates related to the short-term debt obligations listed below.

	Outstanding as of May 31, 2011
	(In millions)
Notes payable, due at mutually agreed-upon dates within one year of issuance or on demand	$187
Payable to Sojitz America for the purchase of inventories, generally due 60 days after shipment of goods from a foreign port	$111

As of May 31, 2011, letters of credit of $99 million were outstanding, generally for the purchase of inventory.

Capital Resources

In December 2008, we filed a shelf registration statement with the Securities and Exchange Commission under which $760 million in debt securities may be issued. As of May 31, 2011, no debt securities had been issued under this shelf registration.

As of and for the year ended May 31, 2011, we had no amounts outstanding under our multi-year, $1 billion revolving credit facility in place with a group of banks. The facility matures in December 2012. Based on our current long-term senior unsecured debt ratings of A+ and A1 from Standard and Poor's Corporation and Moody's Investor Services, respectively, the interest rate charged on any outstanding borrowings would be the prevailing London Interbank Offer Rate ("LIBOR") plus 0.15%. The facility fee is 0.05% of the total commitment.

If our long-term debt rating were to decline, the facility fee and interest rate under our committed credit facility would increase. Conversely, if our long-term debt rating were to improve, the facility fee and interest rate would decrease. Changes in our long-term debt rating would not trigger acceleration of maturity of any then outstanding borrowings or any future borrowings under the committed credit facility. Under this committed credit facility, we have agreed to various covenants. These covenants include limits on our disposal of fixed assets and the amount of debt secured by liens we may incur as well as a minimum capitalization ratio. In the event we were to have any borrowings outstanding under this facility, failed to meet any covenant, and were unable to obtain a waiver from a majority of the banks, any borrowings would become immediately due and payable. As of May 31, 2011, we were in full compliance with each of these covenants and believe it is unlikely we will fail to meet any of these covenants in the foreseeable future.

Liquidity is also provided by our $1 billion commercial paper program. As of and for the year ended May 31, 2011, no amounts were outstanding under this program. We currently have short-term debt ratings of A1 and P1 from Standard and Poor's Corporation and Moody's Investor Services, respectively.

As of May 31, 2011, we had cash, cash equivalents and short term investments totaling $4.5 billion, including amounts held in the U.S. and foreign jurisdictions. Cash equivalents and short term investments consist primarily of deposits held at major banks, money market funds, Tier-1 commercial paper, corporate notes, U.S. Treasury obligations, U.S. government agency obligations and government sponsored enterprise obligations, and other investment grade fixed income securities. Our fixed income investments are exposed to both credit and interest rate risk. All of our investments are investment grade to minimize our credit risk. While individual securities have varying durations, the average duration of our entire cash equivalents and short term investment portfolio is less than 120 days as of May 31, 2011.

Despite recent uncertainties in the financial markets, to date we have not experienced difficulty accessing the credit markets or incurred higher interest costs. Future volatility in the capital markets, however, may increase costs associated with issuing commercial paper or other debt instruments or affect our ability to access those markets. We utilize a variety of tax planning and financing strategies in an effort to manage our worldwide cash and deploy funds to locations where it is needed. We believe that existing cash, cash equivalents, short-term investments and cash generated by operations, together with access to external sources of funds as described above, will be sufficient to meet our domestic and foreign capital needs in the foreseeable future.

Item 8. *Financial Statements and Supplemental Data*

Management of NIKE, Inc. is responsible for the information and representations contained in this report. The financial statements have been prepared in conformity with the generally accepted accounting principles we considered appropriate in the circumstances and include some amounts based on our best estimates and judgments. Other financial information in this report is consistent with these financial statements.

Our accounting systems include controls designed to reasonably assure assets are safeguarded from unauthorized use or disposition and provide for the preparation of financial statements in conformity with generally accepted accounting principles. These systems are supplemented by the selection and training of qualified financial personnel and an organizational structure providing for appropriate segregation of duties.

An Internal Audit department reviews the results of its work with the Audit Committee of the Board of Directors, presently consisting of three outside directors. The Audit Committee is responsible for the appointment of the independent registered public accounting firm and reviews with the independent registered public accounting firm, management and the internal audit staff, the scope and the results of the annual examination, the effectiveness of the accounting control system and other matters relating to the financial affairs of NIKE as they deem appropriate. The independent registered public accounting firm and the internal auditors have full access to the Committee, with and without the presence of management, to discuss any appropriate matters.

Management's Annual Report on Internal Control Over Financial Reporting

Management is responsible for establishing and maintaining adequate internal control over financial reporting, as such term is defined in Rule 13a-15(f) and Rule 15d-15(f) of the Securities Exchange Act of 1934, as amended. Internal control over financial reporting is a process designed to provide reasonable assurance regarding the reliability of financial reporting and the preparation of the financial statements for external purposes in accordance with generally accepted accounting principles in the United States of America. Internal control over financial reporting includes those policies and procedures that: (i) pertain to the maintenance of records that, in reasonable detail, accurately and fairly reflect the transactions and dispositions of assets of the company; (ii) provide reasonable assurance that transactions are recorded as necessary to permit preparation of financial statements in accordance with generally accepted accounting principles, and that receipts and expenditures of the company are being made only in accordance with authorizations of our management and directors; and (iii) provide reasonable assurance regarding prevention or timely detection of unauthorized acquisition, use or disposition of assets of the company that could have a material effect on the financial statements.

While "reasonable assurance" is a high level of assurance, it does not mean absolute assurance. Because of its inherent limitations, internal control over financial reporting may not prevent or detect every misstatement and instance of fraud. Controls are susceptible to manipulation, especially in instances of fraud caused by the collusion of two or more people, including our senior management. Also, projections of any evaluation of effectiveness to future periods are subject to the risk that controls may become inadequate because of changes in conditions, or that the degree of compliance with the policies or procedures may deteriorate.

Under the supervision and with the participation of our Chief Executive Officer and Chief Financial Officer, our management conducted an evaluation of the effectiveness of our internal control over financial reporting based upon the framework in *Internal Control—Integrated Framework* issued by the Committee of Sponsoring Organizations of the Treadway Commission (COSO). Based on the results of our evaluation, our management concluded that our internal control over financial reporting was effective as of May 31, 2011.

PricewaterhouseCoopers LLP, an independent registered public accounting firm, has audited (1) the consolidated financial statements and (2) the effectiveness of our internal control over financial reporting as of May 31, 2011, as stated in their report herein.

Mark G. Parker
Chief Executive Officer and President

Donald W. Blair
Chief Financial Officer

Report of Independent Registered Public Accounting Firm

To the Board of Directors and Shareholders of NIKE, Inc.:

In our opinion, the consolidated financial statements listed in the index appearing under Item 15(a)(1) present fairly, in all material respects, the financial position of NIKE, Inc. and its subsidiaries at May 31, 2011 and 2010, and the results of their operations and their cash flows for each of the three years in the period ended May 31, 2011 in conformity with accounting principles generally accepted in the United States of America. In addition, in our opinion, the financial statement schedule listed in the appendix appearing under Item 15(a)(2) presents fairly, in all material respects, the information set forth therein when read in conjunction with the related consolidated financial statements. Also in our opinion, the Company maintained, in all material respects, effective internal control over financial reporting as of May 31, 2011, based on criteria established in *Internal Control—Integrated Framework* issued by the Committee of Sponsoring Organizations of the Treadway Commission (COSO). The Company's management is responsible for these financial statements and financial statement schedule, for maintaining effective internal control over financial reporting and for its assessment of the effectiveness of internal control over financial reporting, included in Management's Annual Report on Internal Control Over Financial Reporting appearing under Item 8. Our responsibility is to express opinions on these financial statements, on the financial statement schedule, and on the Company's internal control over financial reporting based on our integrated audits. We conducted our audits in accordance with the standards of the Public Company Accounting Oversight Board (United States). Those standards require that we plan and perform the audits to obtain reasonable assurance about whether the financial statements are free of material misstatement and whether effective internal control over financial reporting was maintained in all material respects. Our audits of the financial statements included examining, on a test basis, evidence supporting the amounts and disclosures in the financial statements, assessing the accounting principles used and significant estimates made by management, and evaluating the overall financial statement presentation. Our audit of internal control over financial reporting included obtaining an understanding of internal control over financial reporting, assessing the risk that a material weakness exists, and testing and evaluating the design and operating effectiveness of internal control based on the assessed risk. Our audits also included performing such other procedures as we considered necessary in the circumstances. We believe that our audits provide a reasonable basis for our opinions.

A company's internal control over financial reporting is a process designed to provide reasonable assurance regarding the reliability of financial reporting and the preparation of financial statements for external purposes in accordance with generally accepted accounting principles. A company's internal control over financial reporting includes those policies and procedures that (i) pertain to the maintenance of records that, in reasonable detail, accurately and fairly reflect the transactions and dispositions of the assets of the company; (ii) provide reasonable assurance that transactions are recorded as necessary to permit preparation of financial statements in accordance with generally accepted accounting principles, and that receipts and expenditures of the company are being made only in accordance with authorizations of management and directors of the company; and (iii) provide reasonable assurance regarding prevention or timely detection of unauthorized acquisition, use, or disposition of the company's assets that could have a material effect on the financial statements.

Because of its inherent limitations, internal control over financial reporting may not prevent or detect misstatements. Also, projections of any evaluation of effectiveness to future periods are subject to the risk that controls may become inadequate because of changes in conditions, or that the degree of compliance with the policies or procedures may deteriorate.

/s/ PRICEWATERHOUSECOOPERS LLP

Portland, Oregon
July 22, 2011

NIKE, INC.
CONSOLIDATED STATEMENTS OF INCOME

	Year Ended May 31,		
	2011	**2010**	**2009**
	(In millions, except per share data)		
Revenues	$20,862	$19,014	$19,176
Cost of sales	11,354	10,214	10,572
Gross margin	9,508	8,800	8,604
Demand creation expense	2,448	2,356	2,352

	Year Ended May 31,		
	2011	2010	2009
	(In millions, except per share data)		
Operating overhead expense	4,245	3,970	3,798
Total selling and administrative expense	6,693	6,326	6,150
Restructuring charges (Note 16)	—	—	195
Goodwill impairment (Note 4)	—	—	199
Intangible and other asset impairment (Note 4)	—	—	202
Interest expense (income), net (Notes 6, 7 and 8)	4	6	(10)
Other (income), net (Note 17)	(33)	(49)	(89)
Income before income taxes	2,844	2,517	1,957
Income taxes (Note 9)	711	610	470
Net income	$ 2,133	$ 1,907	$ 1,487
Basic earnings per common share (Notes 1 and 12)	$ 4.48	$ 3.93	$ 3.07
Diluted earnings per common share (Notes 1 and 12)	$ 4.39	$ 3.86	$ 3.03
Dividends declared per common share	$ 1.20	$ 1.06	$ 0.98

The accompanying notes to consolidated financial statements are an integral part of this statement.

NIKE, INC.

CONSOLIDATED BALANCE SHEETS

	May 31,	
	2011	2010
	(In millions)	
ASSETS		
Current assets:		
Cash and equivalents	$ 1,955	$ 3,079
Short-term investments (Note 6)	2,583	2,067
Accounts receivable, net (Note 1)	3,138	2,650
Inventories (Notes 1 and 2)	2,715	2,041
Deferred income taxes (Note 9)	312	249
Prepaid expenses and other current assets	594	873
Total current assets	11,297	10,959
Property, plant and equipment, net (Note 3)	2,115	1,932
Identifiable intangible assets, net (Note 4)	487	467
Goodwill (Note 4)	205	188
Deferred income taxes and other assets (Notes 9 and 17)	894	873
Total assets	$14,998	$14,419

LIABILITIES AND SHAREHOLDERS' EQUITY

Current liabilities:		
Current portion of long-term debt (Note 8)	$ 200	$ 7
Notes payable (Note 7)	187	139
Accounts payable (Note 7)	1,469	1,255
Accrued liabilities (Notes 5 and 17)	1,985	1,904
Income taxes payable (Note 9)	117	59
Total current liabilities	3,958	3,364
Long-term debt (Note 8)	276	446
Deferred income taxes and other liabilities (Notes 9 and 17)	921	855
Commitments and contingencies (Note 15)	—	—
Redeemable Preferred Stock (Note 10)	—	—

	May 31,	
	2011	**2010**
	(In millions)	
Shareholders' equity:		
Common stock at stated value (Note 11):		
Class A convertible—90 and 90 shares outstanding	—	—
Class B—378 and 394 shares outstanding	3	3
Capital in excess of stated value	3,944	3,441
Accumulated other comprehensive income (Note 14)	95	215
Retained earnings	5,801	6,095
Total shareholders' equity	9,843	9,754
Total liabilities and shareholders' equity	$14,998	$14,419

The accompanying notes to consolidated financial statements are an integral part of this statement.

NIKE, INC.
CONSOLIDATED STATEMENTS OF CASH FLOWS

	Year Ended May 31,		
	2011	**2010**	**2009**
	(In millions)		
Cash provided by operations:			
Net income	$2,133	$1,907	$1,487
Income charges (credits) not affecting cash:			
Depreciation	335	324	335
Deferred income taxes	(76)	8	(294)
Stock-based compensation (Note 11)	105	159	171
Impairment of goodwill, intangibles and other assets (Note 4)	—	—	401
Amortization and other	23	72	48
Changes in certain working capital components and other assets and liabilities excluding the impact of acquisition and divestitures:			
(Increase) decrease in accounts receivable	(273)	182	(238)
(Increase) decrease in inventories	(551)	285	32
(Increase) decrease in prepaid expenses and other current assets	(35)	(70)	14
Increase (decrease) in accounts payable, accrued liabilities and income taxes payable	151	297	(220)
Cash provided by operations	1,812	3,164	1,736
Cash used by investing activities:			
Purchases of short-term investments	(7,616)	(3,724)	(2,909)
Maturities of short-term investments	4,313	2,334	1,280
Sales of short-term investments	2,766	453	1,110
Additions to property, plant and equipment	(432)	(335)	(456)
Disposals of property, plant and equipment	1	10	33
Increase in other assets, net of other liabilities	(30)	(11)	(47)
Settlement of net investment hedges	(23)	5	191
Cash used by investing activities	(1,021)	(1,268)	(798)
Cash used by financing activities:			
Reductions in long-term debt, including current portion	(8)	(32)	(7)
Increase (decrease) in notes payable	41	(205)	177
Proceeds from exercise of stock options and other stock issuances	345	364	187

	Year Ended May 31,		
	2011	2010	2009
	(In millions)		
Excess tax benefits from share-based payment arrangements	64	58	25
Repurchase of common stock	(1,859)	(741)	(649)
Dividends—common and preferred	(555)	(505)	(467)
Cash used by financing activities	(1,972)	(1,061)	(734)
Effect of exchange rate changes	57	(47)	(47)
Net (decrease) increase in cash and equivalents	(1,124)	788	157
Cash and equivalents, beginning of year	3,079	2,291	2,134
Cash and equivalents, end of year	$1,955	$3,079	$2,291
Supplemental disclosure of cash flow information:			
Cash paid during the year for:			
Interest, net of capitalized interest	$ 32	$ 48	$ 47
Income taxes	736	537	765
Dividends declared and not paid	145	131	121

The accompanying notes to consolidated financial statements are an integral part of this statement.

NIKE, INC.
CONSOLIDATED STATEMENTS OF SHAREHOLDERS' EQUITY

	Common Stock				Capital in Excess of Stated Value	Accumulated Other Comprehensive Income	Retained Earnings	Total
	Class A		Class B					
	Shares	Amount	Shares	Amount				
	(In millions, except per share data)							
Balance at May 31, 2008	**97**	**$ —**	**394**	**$ 3**	**$ 2,498**	**$ 251**	**$ 5,073**	**$ 7,825**
Stock options exercised			4		167			167
Conversion to Class B Common Stock	(2)		2					—
Repurchase of Class B Common Stock			(11)		(6)		(633)	(639)
Dividends on Common stock ($0.98 per share)							(475)	(475)
Issuance of shares to employees			1		45			45
Stock-based compensation (Note 11):					171			171
Forfeiture of shares from employees			—		(4)		(1)	(5)
Comprehensive income:								
Net income							1,487	1,487

NIKE, INC.
CONSOLIDATED STATEMENTS OF SHAREHOLDERS' EQUITY

| | Common Stock | | | | Capital in Excess of Stated Value | Accumulated Other Comprehensive Income | Retained Earnings | Total |
| | Class A | | Class B | | | | | |
	Shares	Amount	Shares	Amount				
					(In millions, except per share data)			
Other comprehensive income:								
Foreign currency translation and other (net of tax benefit of $178)						(335)		(335)
Net gain on cash flow hedges (net of tax expense of $168)							454	454
Net gain on net investment hedges (net of tax expense of $55)						106		106
Reclassification to net income of previously deferred net gains related to hedge derivatives (net of tax expense of $40)						(108)	—	(108)
Total comprehensive income	—	—	—	—	—	117	1,487	1,604
Balance at May 31, 2009	**95**	**$ —**	**390**	**$ 3**	**$ 2,871**	**$ 368**	**$ 5,451**	**$ 8,693**
Stock options exercised			9		380			380
Conversion to Class B Common Stock	(5)		5					—
Repurchase of Class B Common Stock			(11)		(7)		(747)	(754)
Dividends on Common stock ($1.06 per share)							(515)	(515)
Issuance of shares to employees			1		40			40
Stock-based compensation (Note 11):					159			159
Forfeiture of shares from employees			—		(2)		(1)	(3)
Comprehensive income:								
Net income							1,907	1,907
Other comprehensive income (Notes 14 and 17):								
Foreign currency translation and other (net of tax benefit of $72)						(159)		(159)
Net gain on cash flow hedges (net of tax expense of $28)						87		87

NIKE, INC.
CONSOLIDATED STATEMENTS OF SHAREHOLDERS' EQUITY

	Common Stock				Capital in Excess of Stated Value	Accumulated Other Comprehensive Income	Retained Earnings	Total
	Class A		Class B					
	Shares	Amount	Shares	Amount				
	(In millions, except per share data)							
Net gain on net investment hedges (net of tax expense of $21)						45		45
Reclassification to net income of previously deferred net gains related to hedge derivatives (net of tax expense of $42)						(122)		(122)
Reclassification of ineffective hedge gains to net income (net of tax expense of $1)						(4)		(4)
Total comprehensive income						(153)	1,907	1,754
Balance at May 31, 2010	**90**	**$ —**	**394**	**$ 3**	**$ 3,441**	**$ 215**	**$ 6,095**	**$ 9,754**
Stock options exercised			7		368			368
Repurchase of Class B Common Stock			(24)		(14)		(1,857)	(1,871)
Dividends on Common stock ($1.20 per share)							(569)	(569)
Issuance of shares to employees			1		49			49
Stock-based compensation (Note 11):					105			105
Forfeiture of shares from employees			—		(5)		(1)	(6)
Comprehensive income:								
Net income							2,133	2,133
Other comprehensive income (Notes 14 and 17):								
Foreign currency translation and other (net of tax expense of $121)						263		263
Net loss on cash flow hedges (net of tax benefit of $66)						(242)		(242)
Net loss on net investment hedges (net of tax benefit of $28)						(57)		(57)

NIKE, INC.
CONSOLIDATED STATEMENTS OF SHAREHOLDERS' EQUITY

	Common Stock				Capital in Excess of Stated Value	Accumulated Other Comprehensive Income	Retained Earnings	Total
	Class A		Class B					
	Shares	Amount	Shares	Amount				
	(In millions, except per share data)							
Reclassification to net income of previously deferred net gains related to hedge derivatives (net of tax expense of $24)						(84)		(84)
Total comprehensive income						(120)	2,133	2,013
Balance at May 31, 2011	90	$ —	378	$ 3	$ 3,944	$ 95	$ 5,801	$ 9,843

The accompanying notes to consolidated financial statements are an integral part of this statement.

NIKE, INC.
NOTES TO CONSOLIDATED FINANCIAL STATEMENTS

Note 1—Summary of Significant Accounting Policies

Description of Business

NIKE, Inc. is a worldwide leader in the design, marketing and distribution of athletic and sports-inspired footwear, apparel, equipment and accessories. Wholly-owned NIKE subsidiaries include Cole Haan, which designs, markets and distributes dress and casual shoes, handbags, accessories and coats; Converse Inc., which designs, markets and distributes athletic and casual footwear, apparel and accessories; Hurley International LLC, which designs, markets and distributes action sports and youth lifestyle footwear, apparel and accessories; and Umbro International Limited, which designs, distributes and licenses athletic and casual footwear, apparel and equipment, primarily for the sport of soccer.

Basis of Consolidation

The consolidated financial statements include the accounts of NIKE, Inc. and its subsidiaries (the "Company"). All significant intercompany transactions and balances have been eliminated.

Recognition of Revenues

Wholesale revenues are recognized when title passes and the risks and rewards of ownership have passed to the customer, based on the terms of sale. This occurs upon shipment or upon receipt by the customer depending on the country of the sale and the agreement with the customer. Retail store revenues are recorded at the time of sale. Provisions for sales discounts, returns and miscellaneous claims from customers are made at the time of sale. As of May 31, 2011 and 2010, the Company's reserve balances for sales discounts, returns and miscellaneous claims were $423 million and $371 million, respectively.

Shipping and Handling Costs

Shipping and handling costs are expensed as incurred and included in cost of sales.

Demand Creation Expense

Demand creation expense consists of advertising and promotion costs, including costs of endorsement contracts, television, digital and print advertising, brand events, and retail brand presentation. Advertising production costs are expensed the first time an advertisement is run.

Advertising placement costs are expensed in the month the advertising appears, while costs related to brand events are expensed when the event occurs. Costs related to retail brand presentation are expensed when the presentation is completed and delivered. A significant amount of the Company's promotional expenses result from payments under endorsement contracts. Accounting for endorsement payments is based upon specific contract provisions. Generally, endorsement payments are expensed on a straight-line basis over the term of the contract after giving recognition to periodic performance compliance provisions of the contracts. Prepayments made under contracts are included in prepaid expenses or other assets depending on the period to which the prepayment applies.

Through cooperative advertising programs, the Company reimburses retail customers for certain costs of advertising the Company's products. The Company records these costs in selling and administrative expense at the point in time when it is obligated to its customers for the costs, which is when the related revenues are recognized. This obligation may arise prior to the related advertisement being run.

Total advertising and promotion expenses were $2,448 million, $2,356 million, and $2,352 million for the years ended May 31, 2011, 2010 and 2009, respectively. Prepaid advertising and promotion expenses recorded in prepaid expenses and other assets totaled $291 million and $261 million at May 31, 2011 and 2010, respectively.

Cash and Equivalents

Cash and equivalents represent cash and short-term, highly liquid investments with maturities of three months or less at date of purchase. The carrying amounts reflected in the consolidated balance sheet for cash and equivalents approximate fair value.

Short-Term Investments

Short-term investments consist of highly liquid investments, including commercial paper, U.S. treasury, U.S. agency, and corporate debt securities, with maturities over three months from the date of purchase. Debt securities that the Company has the ability and positive intent to hold to maturity are carried at amortized cost. At May 31, 2011 and 2010, the Company did not hold any short-term investments that were classified as trading or held-to-maturity.

At May 31, 2011 and 2010, short-term investments consisted of available-for-sale securities. Available-for-sale securities are recorded at fair value with unrealized gains and losses reported, net of tax, in other comprehensive income, unless unrealized losses are determined to be other than temporary. The Company considers all available-for-sale securities, including those with maturity dates beyond 12 months, as available to support current operational liquidity needs and therefore classifies all securities with maturity dates beyond three months at the date of purchase as current assets within short-term investments on the consolidated balance sheet.

See Note 6—Fair Value Measurements for more information on the Company's short term investments.

Allowance for Uncollectible Accounts Receivable

Accounts receivable consists primarily of amounts receivable from customers. We make ongoing estimates relating to the collectability of our accounts receivable and maintain an allowance for estimated losses resulting from the inability of our customers to make required payments. In determining the amount of the allowance, we consider our historical level of credit losses and make judgments about the creditworthiness of significant customers based on ongoing credit evaluations. Accounts receivable with anticipated collection dates greater than 12 months from the balance sheet date and related allowances are considered non-current and recorded in other assets. The allowance for uncollectible accounts receivable was $124 million and $117 million at May 31, 2011 and 2010, respectively, of which $50 million and $43 million was classified as long-term and recorded in other assets.

Inventory Valuation

Inventories are stated at lower of cost or market and valued on a first-in, first-out ("FIFO") or moving average cost basis.

Property, Plant and Equipment and Depreciation

Property, plant and equipment are recorded at cost. Depreciation for financial reporting purposes is determined on a straight-line basis for buildings and leasehold improvements over 2 to 40 years and for machinery and equipment over 2 to 15 years. Computer software (including, in some cases, the cost of internal labor) is depreciated on a straight-line basis over 3 to 10 years.

Impairment of Long-Lived Assets

The Company reviews the carrying value of long-lived assets or asset groups to be used in operations whenever events or changes in circumstances indicate that the carrying amount of the assets might not be recoverable. Factors that would necessitate an impairment assessment include a significant adverse change in the extent or manner in which an asset is used, a significant adverse change in legal factors or the business climate that could affect the value of the asset, or a significant decline in the observable market value of an asset, among others. If such facts indicate a potential impairment, the Company would assess the recoverability of an asset group by determining if the carrying value of the asset group exceeds the sum of the projected undiscounted cash flows expected to result from the use and eventual disposition of the assets over the remaining economic life of the primary asset in the asset group. If the recoverability test indicates that the carrying value of the asset group is not recoverable, the Company will estimate the fair value of the asset group using appropriate valuation methodologies which would typically include an estimate of discounted cash flows. Any impairment would be measured as the difference between the asset groups carrying amount and its estimated fair value.

Identifiable Intangible Assets and Goodwill

The Company performs annual impairment tests on goodwill and intangible assets with indefinite lives in the fourth quarter of each fiscal year, or when events occur or circumstances change that would, more likely than not, reduce the fair value of a reporting unit or an intangible asset with an indefinite life below its carrying value. Events or changes in circumstances that may trigger interim impairment reviews include significant changes in business climate, operating results, planned investments in the reporting unit, or an expectation that the carrying amount may not be recoverable, among other factors. The impairment test requires the Company to estimate the fair value of its reporting units. If the carrying value of a reporting unit exceeds its fair value, the goodwill of that reporting unit is potentially impaired and the Company proceeds to step two of the impairment analysis. In step two of the analysis, the Company measures and records an impairment loss equal to the excess of the carrying value of the reporting unit's goodwill over its implied fair value should such a circumstance arise.

The Company generally bases its measurement of fair value of a reporting unit on a blended analysis of the present value of future discounted cash flows and the market valuation approach. The discounted cash flows model indicates the fair value of the reporting unit based on the present value of the cash flows that the Company expects the reporting unit to generate in the future. The Company's significant estimates in the discounted cash flows model include: its weighted average cost of capital; long-term rate of growth and profitability of the reporting unit's business; and working capital effects. The market valuation approach indicates the fair value of the business based on a comparison of the reporting unit to comparable publicly traded companies in similar lines of business. Significant estimates in the market valuation approach model include identifying similar companies with comparable business factors such as size, growth, profitability, risk and return on investment, and assessing comparable revenue and operating income multiples in estimating the fair value of the reporting unit.

The Company believes the weighted use of discounted cash flows and the market valuation approach is the best method for determining the fair value of its reporting units because these are the most common valuation methodologies used within its industry; and the blended use of both models compensates for the inherent risks associated with either model if used on a stand-alone basis.

Indefinite-lived intangible assets primarily consist of acquired trade names and trademarks. In measuring the fair value for these intangible assets, the Company utilizes the relief-from-royalty method. This method assumes that trade names and trademarks have value to the extent that their owner is relieved of the obligation to pay royalties for the benefits received from them. This method requires the Company to estimate the future revenue for the related brands, the appropriate royalty rate and the weighted average cost of capital.

Foreign Currency Translation and Foreign Currency Transactions

Adjustments resulting from translating foreign functional currency financial statements into U.S. dollars are included in the foreign currency translation adjustment, a component of accumulated other comprehensive income in shareholders' equity.

The Company's global subsidiaries have various assets and liabilities, primarily receivables and payables, that are denominated in currencies other than their functional currency. These balance sheet items are subject to remeasurement, the impact of which is recorded in other (income), net, within our consolidated statement of income.

Accounting for Derivatives and Hedging Activities

The Company uses derivative financial instruments to limit exposure to changes in foreign currency exchange rates and interest rates. All derivatives are recorded at fair value on the balance sheet and changes in the fair value of derivative financial instruments are either recognized in other comprehensive income (a component of shareholders' equity), debt or net income depending on the nature of the underlying exposure, whether the derivative is formally designated as a hedge, and, if designated, the extent to which the hedge is effective. The Company classifies the cash flows at settlement from derivatives in the same category as the cash flows from the related hedged items. For undesignated hedges and designated cash flow hedges, this is within the cash provided by operations component of the consolidated statements of cash flows. For designated net investment hedges, this is generally within the cash used by investing activities component of the cash flow statement. As our fair value hedges are receive-fixed, pay-variable interest rate swaps, the cash flows associated with these derivative instruments are periodic interest payments while the swaps are outstanding, which are reflected in net income within the cash provided by operations component of the cash flow statement.

See Note 17—Risk Management and Derivatives for more information on the Company's risk management program and derivatives.

Stock-Based Compensation

The Company estimates the fair value of options and stock appreciation rights granted under the NIKE, Inc. 1990 Stock Incentive Plan (the "1990 Plan") and employees' purchase rights under the Employee Stock Purchase Plans ("ESPPs") using the Black-Scholes option pricing model. The Company recognizes this fair value, net of estimated forfeitures, as selling and administrative expense in the consolidated statements of income over the vesting period using the straight-line method.

See Note 11—Common Stock and Stock-Based Compensation for more information on the Company's stock programs.

Income Taxes

The Company accounts for income taxes using the asset and liability method. This approach requires the recognition of deferred tax assets and liabilities for the expected future tax consequences of temporary differences between the carrying amounts and the tax basis of assets and liabilities. United States income taxes are provided cur.rently on financial statement earnings of non-U.S. subsidiaries that are expected to be repatriated. The Company determines annually the amount of undistributed non-U.S. earnings to invest indefinitely in its non-U.S. operations. The Company recognizes interest and penalties related to income tax matters in income tax expense.

See Note 9—Income Taxes for further discussion.

Earnings Per Share

Basic earnings per common share is calculated by dividing net income by the weighted average number of common shares outstanding during the year. Diluted earnings per common share is calculated by adjusting weighted average outstanding shares, assuming conversion of all potentially dilutive stock options and awards.

See Note 12—Earnings Per Share for further discussion.

Management Estimates

The preparation of financial statements in conformity with generally accepted accounting principles requires management to make estimates, including estimates relating to assumptions that affect the reported amounts of assets and liabilities and disclosure of contingent assets and liabilities at the date of financial statements and the reported amounts of revenues and expenses during the reporting period. Actual results could differ from these estimates.

Note 2—Inventories

Inventory balances of $2,715 million and $2,041 million at May 31, 2011 and 2010, respectively, were substantially all finished goods.

Note 3—Property, Plant and Equipment

Property, plant and equipment included the following:

	As of May 31,	
	2011	2010
	(In millions)	
Land	$ 237	$ 223
Buildings	1,124	952
Machinery and equipment	2,487	2,217
Leasehold improvements	931	821
Construction in process	127	177
	4,906	4,390
Less accumulated depreciation	2,791	2,458
	$2,115	$1,932

Capitalized interest was not material for the years ended May 31, 2011, 2010, and 2009.

Note 4—Identifiable Intangible Assets, Goodwill and Umbro Impairment

Identified Intangible Assets and Goodwill

The following table summarizes the Company's identifiable intangible asset balances as of May 31, 2011 and 2010:

	May 31, 2011			May 31, 2010		
	Gross Carrying Amount	Accumulated Amortization	Net Carrying Amount	Gross Carrying Amount	Accumulated Amortization	Net Carrying Amount
	(In millions)					
Amortized intangible assets:						
Patents	$ 80	$(24)	$ 56	$ 69	$(21)	$ 48
Trademarks	44	(25)	19	40	(18)	22
Other	47	(22)	25	32	(18)	14
Total	$171	$(71)	$100	$141	$(57)	$ 84
Unamortized intangible assets—Trademarks			387			383
Identifiable intangible assets, net			$487			$467

The effect of foreign exchange fluctuations for the year ended May 31, 2011 increased unamortized intangible assets by approximately $4 million.

Amortization expense, which is included in selling and administrative expense, was $16 million, $14 million, and $12 million for the years ended May 31, 2011, 2010, and 2009, respectively. The estimated amortization expense for intangible assets subject to amortization for each of the years ending May 31, 2012 through May 31, 2016 are as follows: 2012: $16 million; 2013: $14 million; 2014: $12 million; 2015: $8 million; 2016: $7 million.

All goodwill balances are included in the Company's "Other" category for segment reporting purposes. The following table summarizes the Company's goodwill balance as of May 31, 2011 and 2010:

	Goodwill	Accumulated Impairment	Goodwill, net
		(In millions)	
May 31, 2009	$393	$(199)	$194
Other[1]	(6)	—	(6)
May 31, 2010	387	(199)	188
Umbro France[2]	10	—	10
Other[1]	7	—	7
May 31, 2011	$404	$(199)	$205

[1] Other consists of foreign currency translation adjustments on Umbro goodwill.

[2] In March 2011, Umbro acquired the remaining 51% of the exclusive licensee and distributor of the Umbro brand in France for approximately $15 million.

Umbro Impairment in Fiscal 2009

The Company performs annual impairment tests on goodwill and intangible assets with indefinite lives in the fourth quarter of each fiscal year, or when events occur or circumstances change that would, more likely than not, reduce the fair value of a reporting unit or intangible assets with an indefinite life below its carrying value. As a result of a significant decline in global consumer demand and continued weakness in the macroeconomic environment, as well as decisions by Company management to adjust planned investment in the Umbro brand, the Company concluded sufficient indicators of impairment existed to require the performance of an interim assessment of Umbro's goodwill and indefinite lived intangible assets as of February 1, 2009. Accordingly, the Company performed the first step of the goodwill impairment assessment for Umbro by comparing the estimated fair value of Umbro to its carrying amount, and determined there was a potential impairment of goodwill as the carrying amount exceeded the estimated fair value. Therefore, the Company performed the second step of the assessment which compared the implied fair value of Umbro's goodwill to the book value of goodwill. The implied fair value of goodwill is determined by allocating the estimated fair value of Umbro to all of its assets and liabilities, including both recognized and unrecognized intangibles, in the same manner as goodwill was determined in the original business combination.

The Company measured the fair value of Umbro by using an equal weighting of the fair value implied by a discounted cash flow analysis and by comparisons with the market values of similar publicly traded companies. The Company believes the blended use of both models compensates for the inherent risk associated with either model if used on a stand-alone basis, and this combination is indicative of the factors a market participant would consider when performing a similar valuation. The fair value of Umbro's indefinite-lived trademark was estimated using the relief from royalty method, which assumes that the trademark has value to the extent that Umbro is relieved of the obligation to pay royalties for the benefits received from the trademark. The assessments of the Company resulted in the recognition of impairment charges of $199 million and $181 million related to Umbro's goodwill and trademark, respectively, for the year ended May 31, 2009. A tax benefit of $55 million was recognized as a result of the trademark impairment charge. In addition to the above impairment analysis, the Company determined an equity investment held by Umbro was impaired, and recognized a charge of $21 million related to the impairment of this investment. These charges are included in the Company's "Other" category for segment reporting purposes.

The discounted cash flow analysis calculated the fair value of Umbro using management's business plans and projections as the basis for expected cash flows for the next 12 years and a 3% residual growth rate thereafter. The Company used a weighted average discount rate of 14% in its analysis, which was derived primarily from published sources as well as our adjustment for increased market risk given current market conditions. Other significant estimates used in the discounted cash flow analysis include the rates of projected growth and profitability of Umbro's business and working capital effects. The market valuation approach indicates the fair value of Umbro based on a comparison of Umbro to publicly traded companies in similar lines of business. Significant estimates in the market valuation approach include identifying similar companies with comparable business factors such as size, growth, profitability, mix of revenue generated from licensed and direct distribution, and risk of return on investment.

Holding all other assumptions constant at the test date, a 100 basis point increase in the discount rate would reduce the adjusted carrying value of Umbro's net assets by an additional 12%.

Note 5—Accrued Liabilities

Accrued liabilities included the following:

	May 31,	
	2011	2010
	(In millions)	
Compensation and benefits, excluding taxes	$ 628	$ 599
Endorser compensation	284	267
Taxes other than income taxes	214	158
Fair value of derivatives	186	164
Dividends payable	145	131
Advertising and marketing	139	125
Import and logistics costs	98	80
Other[1]	291	380
	$1,985	$1,904

[1] Other consists of various accrued expenses and no individual item accounted for more than 5% of the balance at May 31, 2011 and 2010.

Note 7—Short-Term Borrowings and Credit Lines

Notes payable to banks and interest-bearing accounts payable to Sojitz Corporation of America ("Sojitz America") as of May 31, 2011 and 2010, are summarized below:

	May 31,			
	2011		2010	
	Borrowings	Interest Rate	Borrowings	Interest Rate
	(In millions)			
Notes payable:				
U.S. operations	35	—[1]	18	—[1]
Non-U.S. operations	152	7.05%[1]	121	6.35%[1]
	$187		$139	
Sojitz America	$111	0.99%	$ 88	1.07%

[1] Weighted average interest rate includes non-interest bearing overdrafts.

The carrying amounts reflected in the consolidated balance sheet for notes payable approximate fair value.

The Company purchases through Sojitz America certain athletic footwear, apparel and equipment it acquires from non-U.S. suppliers. These purchases are for the Company's operations outside of the United States, Europe and Japan. Accounts payable to Sojitz America are generally due up to 60 days after shipment of goods from the foreign port. The interest rate on such accounts payable is the 60-day London Interbank Offered Rate ("LIBOR") as of the beginning of the month of the invoice date, plus 0.75%.

As of May 31, 2011 and 2010, the Company had no amounts outstanding under its commercial paper program.

In December 2006, the Company entered into a $1 billion revolving credit facility with a group of banks. The facility matures in December 2012. Based on the Company's current long-term senior unsecured debt ratings of A+ and A1 from Standard and Poor's Corporation and Moody's Investor Services, respectively, the interest rate charged on any outstanding borrowings would be the prevailing LIBOR plus 0.15%. The facility fee is 0.05% of the total commitment. Under this agreement, the Company must maintain, among other things, certain minimum specified financial ratios with which the Company was in compliance at May 31, 2011. No amounts were outstanding under this facility as of May 31, 2011 and 2010.

Note 8—Long-Term Debt

Long-term debt, net of unamortized premiums and discounts and swap fair value adjustments, is comprised of the following:

	May 31,	
	2011	2010
	(In millions)	
5.66% Corporate bond, payable July 23, 2012	$ 26	$ 27
5.40% Corporate bond, payable August 7, 2012	16	16
4.70% Corporate bond, payable October 1, 2013	50	50
5.15% Corporate bond, payable October 15, 2015	114	112
4.30% Japanese Yen note, payable June 26, 2011	130	116
1.52% Japanese Yen note, payable February 14, 2012	62	55
2.60% Japanese Yen note, maturing August 20, 2001 through November 20, 2020	54	53
2.00% Japanese Yen note, maturing August 20, 2001 through November 20, 2020	24	24
Total	476	453
Less current maturities	200	7
	$276	$446

The scheduled maturity of long-term debt in each of the years ending May 31, 2012 through 2016 are $200 million, $48 million, $58 million, $8 million and $109 million, at face value, respectively.

The Company's long-term debt is recorded at adjusted cost, net of amortized premiums and discounts and interest rate swap fair value adjustments. The fair value of long-term debt is estimated based upon quoted prices for similar instruments. The fair value of the Company's long-term debt, including the current portion, was approximately $482 million at May 31, 2011 and $453 million at May 31, 2010.

In fiscal years 2003 and 2004, the Company issued a total of $240 million in medium-term notes of which $190 million, at face value, were outstanding at May 31, 2011. The outstanding notes have coupon rates that range from 4.70% to 5.66% and maturity dates ranging from July 2012 to October 2015. For each of these notes, except the $50 million note maturing in October 2013, the Company has entered into interest rate swap agreements whereby the Company receives fixed interest payments at the same rate as the notes and pays variable interest payments based on the six-month LIBOR plus a spread. Each swap has the same notional amount and maturity date as the corresponding note. At May 31, 2011, the interest rates payable on these swap agreements ranged from approximately 0.3% to 1.0%.

In June 1996, one of the Company's wholly owned Japanese subsidiaries, NIKE Logistics YK, borrowed ¥10.5 billion (approximately $130 million as of May 31, 2011) in a private placement with a maturity of June 26, 2011. Interest is paid semi-annually. The agreement provides for early retirement of the borrowing.

In July 1999, NIKE Logistics YK assumed a total of ¥13.0 billion in loans as part of its agreement to purchase a distribution center in Japan, which serves as collateral for the loans. These loans mature in equal quarterly installments during the period August 20, 2001 through November 20, 2020. Interest is also paid quarterly. As of May 31, 2011, ¥6.3 billion (approximately

$78 million) in loans remain outstanding. In February 2007, NIKE Logistics YK entered into a ¥5.0 billion (approximately $62 million as of May 31, 2011) term loan that replaced certain intercompany borrowings and matures on February 14, 2012. The interest rate on the loan is approximately 1.5% and interest is paid semi-annually.

Note 9—Income Taxes

Income before income taxes is as follows:

	Year Ended May 31,		
	2011	**2010**	**2009**
	(In millions)		
Income before income taxes:			
United States	$1,084	$ 699	$ 846
Foreign	1,760	1,818	1,111
	$2,844	$2,517	$1,957

The provision for income taxes is as follows:

	Year Ended May 31,		
	2011	**2010**	**2009**
	(In millions)		
Current:			
United States			
Federal	$289	$200	$410
State	57	50	46
Foreign	441	349	308
	787	599	764
Deferred:			
United States			
Federal	(61)	18	(251)
State	—	(1)	(8)
Foreign	(15)	(6)	(35)
	(76)	11	(294)
	$711	$610	$470

A reconciliation from the U.S. statutory federal income tax rate to the effective income tax rate follows:

	Year Ended May 31,		
	2011	**2010**	**2009**
Federal income tax rate	35.0%	35.0%	35.0%
State taxes, net of federal benefit	1.3%	1.3%	1.2%
Foreign earnings	−10.2%	−13.6%	−14.9%
Other, net	−1.1%	1.5%	2.7%
Effective income tax rate	25.0%	24.2%	24.0%

The effective tax rate for the year ended May 31, 2011 of 25.0% increased from the fiscal 2010 effective tax rate of 24.2% due primarily to the change in geographic mix of earnings. A larger percentage of our earnings before income taxes in the current year are attributable to operations in the United States where the statutory tax rate is generally higher than the tax rate on operations outside of the U.S. This impact was partially offset by changes to uncertain tax positions. Our effective tax rate for the year ended May 31, 2010 of 24.2% increased from the fiscal 2009 effective rate of 24.0%. The effective tax rate for fiscal 2009 includes a tax benefit related to charges recorded for the impairment of Umbro's goodwill, intangible and other assets.

Deferred tax assets and (liabilities) are comprised of the following:

	May 31,	
	2011	**2010**
	(In millions)	
Deferred tax assets:		
Allowance for doubtful accounts	$ 19	$ 17
Inventories	63	47
Sales return reserves	72	52
Deferred compensation	152	144
Stock-based compensation	148	145
Reserves and accrued liabilities	66	86
Foreign loss carry-forwards	60	26
Foreign tax credit carry-forwards	236	148
Hedges	21	1
Undistributed earnings of foreign subsidiaries	—	128
Other	86	37
Total deferred tax assets	923	831
Valuation allowance	(51)	(36)
Total deferred tax assets after valuation allowance	872	795
Deferred tax liabilities:		
Undistributed earnings of foreign subsidiaries	(40)	—
Property, plant and equipment	(151)	(99)
Intangibles	(97)	(99)
Hedges	(1)	(72)
Other	(20)	(8)
Total deferred tax liability	(309)	(278)
Net deferred tax asset	$ 563	$ 517

The following is a reconciliation of the changes in the gross balance of unrecognized tax benefits:

	May 31,		
	2011	**2010**	**2009**
	(In millions)		
Unrecognized tax benefits, as of the beginning of the period	$282	$274	$251
Gross increases related to prior period tax positions	13	87	53
Gross decreases related to prior period tax positions	(98)	(122)	(62)
Gross increases related to current period tax positions	59	52	72
Gross decreases related to current period tax positions	(6)	—	—
Settlements	(43)	(3)	(29)
Lapse of statute of limitations	(8)	(9)	(4)
Changes due to currency translation	13	3	(7)
Unrecognized tax benefits, as of the end of the period	$212	$282	$274

As of May 31, 2011, the total gross unrecognized tax benefits, excluding related interest and penalties, were $212 million, $93 million of which would affect the Company's effective tax rate if recognized in future periods. Total gross unrecognized tax benefits, excluding interest and penalties, as of May 31, 2010 and 2009 was $282 million and $274 million, respectively.

The Company recognizes interest and penalties related to income tax matters in income tax expense. The liability for payment of interest and penalties increased $10 million, $6 million, and $2 million during the years ended May 31, 2011, 2010, and 2009, respectively. As of May 31, 2011 and 2010, accrued interest and penalties related to uncertain tax positions was $91 million and $81 million, respectively (excluding federal benefit).

The Company is subject to taxation primarily in the U.S., China and the Netherlands as well as various state and other foreign jurisdictions. The Company has concluded substantially all U.S. federal income tax matters through fiscal year 2009. The Company is currently under audit by the Internal Revenue Service for the 2010 tax year. The Company's major foreign jurisdictions, China and the Netherlands, have concluded substantially all income tax matters through calendar 2000 and fiscal 2005, respectively. The Company estimates that it is reasonably possible that the total gross unrecognized tax benefits could decrease by up to $69 million within the next 12 months as a result of resolutions of global tax examinations and the expiration of applicable statutes of limitations.

The Company has indefinitely reinvested approximately $4.4 billion of the cumulative undistributed earnings of certain foreign subsidiaries. Such earnings would be subject to U.S. taxation if repatriated to the U.S. Determination of the amount of unrecognized deferred tax liability associated with the indefinitely reinvested cumulative undistributed earnings is not practicable.

A portion of the Company's foreign operations are benefitting from a tax holiday that will phase out in 2019. The decrease in income tax expense for the year ended May 31, 2011 as a result of this arrangement was approximately $36 million ($0.07 per diluted share) and $30 million ($0.06 per diluted share) for the year ended May 31, 2010.

Deferred tax assets at May 31, 2011 and 2010 were reduced by a valuation allowance relating to tax benefits of certain subsidiaries with operating losses where it is more likely than not that the deferred tax assets will not be realized. The net change in the valuation allowance was an increase of $15 million and $10 million for the years ended May 31, 2011 and 2010, respectively and a decrease of $15 million for the year ended May 31, 2009.

The Company does not anticipate that any foreign tax credit carry-forwards will expire. The Company has available domestic and foreign loss carry-forwards of $183 million at May 31, 2011. Such losses will expire as follows:

	Year Ending May 31,						
	2013	**2014**	**2015**	**2016**	**2017-2028**	**Indefinite**	**Total**
	(In millions)						
Net Operating Losses	$7	$10	$4	$10	$91	$61	$183

During the years ended May 31, 2011, 2010, and 2009, income tax benefits attributable to employee stock-based compensation transactions of $68 million, $57 million, and $25 million, respectively, were allocated to shareholders' equity.

Note 10—Redeemable Preferred Stock

Sojitz America is the sole owner of the Company's authorized Redeemable Preferred Stock, $1 par value, which is redeemable at the option of Sojitz America or the Company at par value aggregating $0.3 million. A cumulative dividend of $0.10 per share is payable annually on May 31 and no dividends may be declared or paid on the common stock of the Company unless dividends on the Redeemable Preferred Stock have been declared and paid in full. There have been no changes in the Redeemable Preferred Stock in the three years ended May 31, 2011, 2010, and 2009. As the holder of the Redeemable Preferred Stock, Sojitz America does not have general voting rights but does have the right to vote as a separate class on the sale of all or substantially all of the assets of the Company and its subsidiaries, on merger, consolidation, liquidation or dissolution of the Company or on the sale or assignment of the NIKE trademark for athletic footwear sold in the United States.

Note 11—Common Stock and Stock-Based Compensation

The authorized number of shares of Class A Common Stock, no par value, and Class B Common Stock, no par value, are 175 million and 750 million, respectively. Each share of Class A Common Stock is convertible into one share of Class B Common Stock. Voting rights of Class B Common Stock are limited in certain circumstances with respect to the election of directors.

In 1990, the Board of Directors adopted, and the shareholders approved, the NIKE, Inc. 1990 Stock Incentive Plan (the "1990 Plan"). The 1990 Plan provides for the issuance of up to 163 million previously unissued shares of Class B Common Stock in connection with stock options and other awards granted under the plan. The 1990 Plan authorizes the grant of non-statutory stock options, incentive stock options, stock appreciation rights, restricted stock, restricted stock units, and performance-based awards. The exercise price for stock options and stock appreciation rights may not be less than the fair market value of the underlying shares on the date of grant. A committee of the Board of Directors administers the 1990 Plan. The committee has the authority to determine the employees to whom awards will be made, the amount of the awards, and the other terms and conditions of the awards. Substantially all stock option grants outstanding under the 1990 Plan were granted in the first quarter of each fiscal year, vest ratably over four years, and expire 10 years from the date of grant.

The following table summarizes the Company's total stock-based compensation expense recognized in selling and administrative expense:

	Year Ended May 31,		
	2011	**2010**	**2009**
	(in millions)		
Stock options[1]	$ 77	$135	$129
ESPPs	14	14	14
Restricted stock	14	10	8
Subtotal	105	159	151
Stock options and restricted stock expense—restructuring [2]	—	—	20
Total stock-based compensation expense	$105	$159	$171

[1] Expense for stock options includes the expense associated with stock appreciation rights. Accelerated stock option expense is recorded for employees eligible for accelerated stock option vesting upon retirement. In the first quarter of fiscal 2011, the Company changed the accelerated vesting provisions of its stock option plan. Under the new provisions, accelerated stock option expense for year ended May 31, 2011 was $12 million. The accelerated stock option expense for the years ended May 31, 2010 and 2009 was $74 million and $59 million, respectively.

[2] In connection with the restructuring activities that took place during fiscal 2009, the Company recognized stock-based compensation expense relating to the modification of stock option agreements, allowing for an extended post-termination exercise period, and accelerated vesting of restricted stock as part of severance packages. See Note 16—Restructuring Charges for further details.

As of May 31, 2011, the Company had $111 million of unrecognized compensation costs from stock options, net of estimated forfeitures, to be recognized as selling and administrative expense over a weighted average period of 2.2 years.

The weighted average fair value per share of the options granted during the years ended May 31, 2011, 2010, and 2009, as computed using the Black-Scholes pricing model, was $17.68, $23.43, and $17.13, respectively. The weighted average assumptions used to estimate these fair values are as follows:

	Year Ended May 31,		
	2011	**2010**	**2009**
Dividend yield	1.6%	1.9%	1.5%
Expected volatility	31.5%	57.6%	32.5%
Weighted average expected life (in years)	5.0	5.0	5.0
Risk-free interest rate	1.7%	2.5%	3.4%

The Company estimates the expected volatility based on the implied volatility in market traded options on the Company's common stock with a term greater than one year, along with other factors. The weighted average expected life of options is based on an analysis of historical and expected future exercise patterns. The interest rate is based on the U.S. Treasury (constant maturity) risk-free rate in effect at the date of grant for periods corresponding with the expected term of the options.

The following summarizes the stock option transactions under the plan discussed above:

	Shares[1]	Weighted Average Option Price
	(In millions)	
Options outstanding May 31, 2008	36.6	$40.14
Exercised	(4.0)	35.70
Forfeited	(1.3)	51.19
Granted	7.5	58.17
Options outstanding May 31, 2009	38.8	$43.69
Exercised	(8.6)	37.64
Forfeited	(0.6)	51.92
Granted	6.4	52.79
Options outstanding May 31, 2010	36.0	$46.60
Exercised	(7.0)	42.70
Forfeited	(0.5)	58.08
Granted	6.3	69.20
Options outstanding May 31, 2011	34.8	$51.29
Options exercisable at May 31,		
2009	21.4	$36.91
2010	20.4	41.16
2011	20.1	$44.05

[1] Includes stock appreciation rights transactions.

The weighted average contractual life remaining for options outstanding and options exercisable at May 31, 2011 was 6.0 years and 4.5 years, respectively. The aggregate intrinsic value for options outstanding and exercisable at May 31, 2011 was $1,154 million and $811 million, respectively. The aggregate intrinsic value was the amount by which the market value of the underlying stock exceeded the exercise price of the options. The total intrinsic value of the options exercised during the years ended May 31, 2011, 2010, and 2009 was $267 million, $239 million, and $108 million, respectively.

In addition to the 1990 Plan, the Company gives employees the right to purchase shares at a discount to the market price under employee stock purchase plans ("ESPPs"). Employees are eligible to participate through payroll deductions up to 10% of their compensation. At the end of each six-month offering period, shares are purchased by the participants at 85% of the lower of the fair market value at the beginning or the end of the offering period. Employees purchased 0.8 million shares during the years ended May 31, 2011 and 2010, and 1.0 million shares during the year ended May 31, 2009.

From time to time, the Company grants restricted stock and unrestricted stock to key employees under the 1990 Plan. The number of shares granted to employees during the years ended May 31, 2011, 2010, and 2009 were 0.2 million, 0.5 million, and 0.1 million with weighted average values per share of $70.23, $53.16, and $56.97, respectively. Recipients of restricted shares are entitled to cash dividends and to vote their respective shares throughout the period of restriction. The value of all of the granted shares was established by the market price on the date of grant. During the years ended May 31, 2011, 2010, and 2009, the fair value of restricted shares vested was $15 million, $8 million, and $10 million, respectively, determined as of the date of vesting.

Note 12—Earnings Per Share

The following is a reconciliation from basic earnings per share to diluted earnings per share. Options to purchase an additional 0.2 million, 0.2 million, and 13.2 million shares of common stock were outstanding at May 31, 2011, 2010, and 2009, respectively, but were not included in the computation of diluted earnings per share because the options were anti-dilutive.

| | **Year Ended May 31,** | | |
	2011	**2010**	**2009**
	(In millions, except per share data)		
Determination of shares:			
Weighted average common shares outstanding	475.5	485.5	484.9
Assumed conversion of dilutive stock options and awards	10.2	8.4	5.8
Diluted weighted average common shares outstanding	485.7	493.9	490.7
Basic earnings per common share	$ 4.48	$ 3.93	$ 3.07
Diluted earnings per common share	$ 4.39	$ 3.86	$ 3.03

Note 13—Benefit Plans

The Company has a profit sharing plan available to most U.S.-based employees. The terms of the plan call for annual contributions by the Company as determined by the Board of Directors. A subsidiary of the Company also has a profit sharing plan available to its U.S.-based employees. The terms of the plan call for annual contributions as determined by the subsidiary's executive management. Contributions of $39 million, $35 million, and $28 million were made to the plans and are included in selling and administrative expense for the years ended May 31, 2011, 2010, and 2009, respectively. The Company has various 401(k) employee savings plans available to U.S.-based employees. The Company matches a portion of employee contributions. Company contributions to the savings plans were $39 million, $34 million, and $38 million for the years ended May 31, 2011, 2010, and 2009, respectively, and are included in selling and administrative expense.

The Company also has a Long-Term Incentive Plan ("LTIP") that was adopted by the Board of Directors and approved by shareholders in September 1997 and later amended in fiscal 2007. The Company recognized $31 million, $24 million, and $18 million of selling and administrative expense related to cash awards under the LTIP during the years ended May 31, 2011, 2010, and 2009, respectively.

The Company has pension plans in various countries worldwide. The pension plans are only available to local employees and are generally government mandated. The liability related to the unfunded pension liabilities of the plans was $93 million and $113 million at May 31, 2011 and 2010, respectively, which was primarily classified as long-term in other liabilities.

Note 14—Accumulated Other Comprehensive Income

The components of accumulated other comprehensive income, net of tax, are as follows:

| | **May 31,** | |
	2011	**2010**
	(In millions)	
Cumulative translation adjustment and other	$168	$(95)
Net deferred gain on net investment hedge derivatives	50	107
Net deferred (loss) gain on cash flow hedge derivatives	(123)	203
	$ 95	$215

Note 15—Commitments and Contingencies

The Company leases space for certain of its offices, warehouses and retail stores under leases expiring from 1 to 24 years after May 31, 2011. Rent expense was $446 million, $416 million, and $397 million for the years ended May 31, 2011, 2010 and 2009, respectively. Amounts of minimum future annual rental commitments under non-cancelable operating leases in each of the five years ending May 31, 2012 through 2016 are $374 million, $310 million, $253 million, $198 million, $174 million, respectively, and $535 million in later years.

As of May 31, 2011 and 2010, the Company had letters of credit outstanding totaling $99 million and $101 million, respectively. These letters of credit were generally issued for the purchase of inventory.

In connection with various contracts and agreements, the Company provides routine indemnifications relating to the enforceability of intellectual property rights, coverage for legal issues that arise and other items where the Company is acting as the guarantor. Currently, the Company has several such agreements in place. However, based on the Company's historical experience and the estimated probability of future loss, the Company has determined that the fair value of such indemnifications is not material to the Company's financial position or results of operations.

In the ordinary course of its business, the Company is involved in various legal proceedings involving contractual and employment relationships, product liability claims, trademark rights, and a variety of other matters. The Company does not believe there are any pending legal proceedings that will have a material impact on the Company's financial position or results of operations.

Note 16—Restructuring Charges

During fiscal 2009, the Company took necessary steps to streamline its management structure, enhance consumer focus, drive innovation more quickly to market and establish a more scalable, long-term cost structure. As a result, the Company reduced its global workforce by approximately 5% and incurred pre-tax restructuring charges of $195 million, primarily consisting of severance costs related to the workforce reduction. As nearly all of the restructuring activities were completed in fiscal 2009, the Company did not recognize additional costs relating to these actions. The restructuring charge is reflected in the corporate expense line in the segment presentation of earnings before interest and taxes in Note 18—Operating Segments and Related Information. The restructuring accrual included in accrued liabilities in the consolidated balance sheet was $3 million and $8 million as of May 31, 2011 and 2010, respectively.

Note 18—Operating Segments and Related Information

Operating Segments. The Company's operating segments are evidence of the structure of the Company's internal organization. The major segments are defined by geographic regions for operations participating in NIKE Brand sales activity excluding NIKE Golf. Each NIKE Brand geographic segment operates predominantly in one industry: the design, development, marketing and selling of athletic footwear, apparel, and equipment. In fiscal 2009, the Company initiated a reorganization of the NIKE Brand into a new model consisting of six geographies. Effective June 1, 2009, the Company's new reportable operating segments for the NIKE Brand are: North America, Western Europe, Central and Eastern Europe, Greater China, Japan, and Emerging Markets. Previously, NIKE Brand operations were organized into the following four geographic regions: U.S., Europe, Middle East and Africa (collectively, "EMEA"), Asia Pacific, and Americas. The Company's NIKE Brand Direct to Consumer operations are managed within each geographic segment.

The Company's "Other" category is broken into two components for presentation purposes to align with the way management views the Company. The "Global Brand Divisions" category primarily represents NIKE Brand licensing businesses that are not part of a geographic operating segment, selling, general and administrative expenses that are centrally managed for the NIKE Brand and costs associated with product development and supply chain operations. The "Other Businesses" category primarily consists of the activities of our affiliate brands; Cole Haan, Converse Inc., Hurley International LLC and Umbro International Limited; and NIKE Golf. Activities represented in the "Other" category are immaterial for individual disclosure.

Revenues as shown below represent sales to external customers for each segment. Intercompany revenues have been eliminated and are immaterial for separate disclosure.

Corporate consists of unallocated general and administrative expenses, which includes expenses associated with centrally managed departments, depreciation and amortization related to the Company's headquarters, unallocated insurance and benefit programs, including stock-based compensation, certain foreign currency gains and losses, including hedge gains and losses, certain corporate eliminations and other items.

Effective June 1, 2009, the primary financial measure used by the Company to evaluate performance of individual operating segments is Earnings Before Interest and Taxes (commonly referred to as "EBIT") which represents net income before interest expense (income), net and income taxes in the consolidated statements of income. Reconciling items for EBIT represent corporate expense items that are not allocated to the operating segments for management reporting. Previously, the Company evaluated performance of individual operating segments based on pre-tax income or income before income taxes.

As part of the Company's centrally managed foreign exchange risk management program, standard foreign currency rates are assigned to each NIKE Brand entity in our geographic operating segments and are used to record any non-functional currency revenues or product purchases into the entity's functional currency. Geographic operating segment revenues and cost of sales reflect use of these standard rates. For all NIKE Brand operating segments, differences between assigned standard foreign currency rates and actual market rates are included in Corporate together with foreign currency hedge gains and losses generated from the centrally managed foreign exchange risk management program and other conversion gains and losses. Prior to June 1, 2010, foreign currency results, including hedge results and other conversion gains and losses generated by the Western Europe and Central & Eastern Europe geographies were recorded in their respective geographic results.

Additions to long-lived assets as presented in the following table represent capital expenditures.

Accounts receivable, inventories and property, plant and equipment for operating segments are regularly reviewed by management and are therefore provided below.

Certain prior year amounts have been reclassified to conform to fiscal 2011 presentation, as South Africa became part of the Emerging Markets operating segment beginning June 1, 2010. Previously, South Africa was part of the Central & Eastern Europe operating segment.

	Year Ended May 31,		
	2011	**2010**	**2009**
	(In millions)		
Revenue			
North America	$ 7,578	$ 6,696	$ 6,778
Western Europe	3,810	3,892	4,139
Central & Eastern Europe	1,031	993	1,247
Greater China	2,060	1,742	1,743
Japan	766	882	926
Emerging Markets	2,736	2,199	1,828
Global Brand Divisions	123	105	96
Total NIKE Brand	18,104	16,509	16,757
Other Businesses	2,747	2,530	2,419
Corporate	11	(25)	—
Total NIKE Consolidated Revenues	$20,862	$19,014	$19,176
Earnings Before Interest and Taxes			
North America	$ 1,750	$ 1,538	$ 1,429
Western Europe	721	856	939
Central & Eastern Europe	233	253	394
Greater China	777	637	575
Japan	114	180	205
Emerging Markets	688	521	364
Global Brand Divisions	(998)	(867)	(811)
Total NIKE Brand	3,285	3,118	3,095
Other Businesses[1]	334	299	(193)
Corporate[2]	(771)	(894)	(955)

	Year Ended May 31,		
	2011	**2010**	**2009**
	(In millions)		
Total NIKE Consolidated Earnings Before Interest and Taxes	2,848	2,523	1,947
Interest expense (income), net	4	6	(10)
Total NIKE Consolidated Earnings Before Taxes	$ 2,844	$ 2,517	$ 1,957
Additions to Long-lived Assets			
North America	$ 79	$ 45	$ 99
Western Europe	75	59	70
Central & Eastern Europe	5	4	7
Greater China	43	80	59
Japan	9	12	10
Emerging Markets	21	11	12
Global Brand Divisions	44	30	37
Total NIKE Brand	276	241	294
Other Businesses	38	52	90
Corporate	118	42	72
Total Additions to Long-lived Assets	$ 432	$ 335	$ 456
Depreciation			
North America	$ 70	$ 65	$ 64
Western Europe	52	57	51
Central & Eastern Europe	4	4	4
Greater China	19	11	7
Japan	22	26	30
Emerging Markets	14	12	10
Global Brand Divisions	39	33	43
Total NIKE Brand	220	208	209
Other Businesses	44	46	38
Corporate	71	70	88
Total Depreciation	$ 335	$ 324	$ 335

[1] During the year ended May 31, 2009, the Other category included a pre-tax charge of $401 million for the impairment of goodwill, intangible and other assets of Umbro, which was recorded in the third quarter of fiscal 2009. See Note 4—Identifiable Intangible Assets, Goodwill and Umbro Impairment for more information.

[2] During the year ended May 31, 2009, Corporate expense included pre-tax charges of $195 million for the Company's restructuring activities, which were completed in the fourth quarter of fiscal 2009. See Note 16—Restructuring Charges for more information.

	Year Ended May 31,	
	2011	**2010**
	(In millions)	
Accounts Receivable, net		
North America	$1,069	$ 848
Western Europe	500	402
Central & Eastern Europe	290	271
Greater China	140	129
Japan	153	167
Emerging Markets	466	350
Global Brand Divisions	23	22
Total NIKE Brand	2,641	2,189
Other Businesses	471	442
Corporate	26	19
Total Accounts Receivable, net	$3,138	$2,650
Inventories		
North America	$1,034	$ 768
Western Europe	434	347
Central & Eastern Europe	145	102
Greater China	152	104
Japan	82	68
Emerging Markets	429	285
Global Brand Divisions	25	20
Total NIKE Brand	2,301	1,694
Other Businesses	414	347
Corporate	—	—
Total Inventories	$2,715	$2,041
Property, Plant and Equipment, net		
North America	$ 330	$325
Western Europe	338	282
Central & Eastern Europe	13	11
Greater China	179	146
Japan	360	333
Emerging Markets	58	48
Global Brand Divisions	116	99
Total NIKE Brand	1,394	1,244
Other Businesses	164	167
Corporate	557	521
Total Property, Plant and Equipment, net	$2,115	$1,932

Revenues by Major Product Lines.

Revenues to external customers for NIKE Brand products are attributable to sales of footwear, apparel and equipment. Other revenues to external customers primarily include external sales by Cole Haan, Converse, Hurley, NIKE Golf, and Umbro.

	Year Ended May 31,		
	2011	**2010**	**2009**
	(In millions)		
Footwear	$11,493	$10,332	$10,307
Apparel	5,475	5,037	5,245
Equipment	1,013	1,035	1,110
Other	2,881	2,610	2,514
	$20,862	$19,014	$19,176

Revenues and Long-Lived Assets by Geographic Area.

Geographical area information is similar to what was shown previously under operating segments with the exception of the Other activity, which has been allocated to the geographical areas based on the location where the sales originated. Revenues derived in the United States were $8,956 million, $7,914 million, and $8,020 million for the years ended May 31, 2011, 2010, and 2009, respectively. The Company's largest concentrations of long-lived assets primarily consist of the Company's world headquarters and distribution facilities in the United States and distribution facilities in Japan, Belgium and China. Long-lived assets attributable to operations in the United States, which are comprised of net property, plant & equipment, were $1,115 million, $1,070 million, and $1,143 million at May 31, 2011, 2010, and 2009, respectively. Long-lived assets attributable to operations in Japan were $363 million, $336 million, and $322 million at May 31, 2011, 2010 and 2009, respectively. Long-lived assets attributable to operations in Belgium were $182 million, $164 million, and $191 million at May 31, 2011, 2010, and 2009, respectively. Long-lived assets attributable to operations in China were $175 million, $144 million, and $76 million at May 31, 2011, 2010, and 2009, respectively.

Major Customers.

No customer accounted for 10% or more of the Company's net sales during the years ended May 31, 2011, 2010, and 2009.

Glossary

absorption approach (absorption costing) A costing approach that considers all indirect manufacturing costs (both variable and fixed) to be product (inventoriable) costs that become an expense in the form of manufacturing cost of goods sold only as sales occur (p. 184).

accelerated depreciation A pattern of depreciation that charges a larger proportion of an asset's cost to the earlier years and less to later years (p. 445).

account analysis Classifying each account as a variable cost or as a fixed cost with respect to a selected cost driver (p. 95).

account Each item in a financial statement (p. 620).

accounting rate-of-return (ARR) model A non-DCF capital-budgeting model expressed as the increase in expected average annual operating income divided by the initial required investment (p. 453).

accounting system A formal mechanism for gathering, organizing, and communicating information about an organization's activities (p. 5).

accounts payable Amounts owed to vendors for purchases on open accounts (p. 619).

accounts receivable Amounts due from customers for sales charged to an account instead of being paid for in cash (p. 619).

accrual basis A process of accounting that recognizes the impact of transactions on the financial statements in the time periods when revenues and expenses occur instead of when the company pays or receives cash (p. 624).

accrue To accumulate a receivable or payable during a given period, even though no explicit transaction occurs (p. 629).

accrued expenses Expenses reported on the income statement before a company pays for them with cash (p. 629).

accrued revenues Revenues that a company has earned but has not yet received in cash (p. 631).

accumulated depreciation The sum of all depreciation charged to past periods (p. 240).

activity analysis The process of identifying appropriate cost drivers and their effects on the costs of making a product or providing a service (p. 92).

activity-based budget (ABB) A budget that focuses on the budgeted cost of activities required to produce and sell products and services (p. 289).

activity-based costing (ABC) system A system that first accumulates indirect resource costs for each of the activities of the area being costed and then assigns the costs of each activity to the products, services, or other cost objects that require that activity (p. 135).

activity-based flexible budget A budget based on budgeted costs for each activity using the related cost driver (p. 313).

activity-based management (ABM) Using the output of an activity-based cost accounting system to aid strategic decision making and to improve operational control of an organization (p. 142).

activity-level variances The differences between the static budget amounts and the amounts in the flexible budget (p. 315).

adjustments (adjusting entries) Entries that record implicit transactions such as unpaid wages, prepaid rent, interest owed, and the like (p. 625).

after-tax cash flow The cash flow after the effect of income taxes, generally the pretax cash flow multiplied by $(1 - \text{marginal tax rate})$ (p. 445).

agency theory A theory that deals with relationships where one party (the principal) delegates decision-making authority to another party (the agent) (p. 394).

annual report A report prepared by management for the company's shareholders (p. 687).

assets Economic resources that a company owns and expects to provide future benefits (p. 620).

attention directing Reporting and interpreting information that helps managers to focus on operating problems, imperfections, inefficiencies, and opportunities (p. 5).

audit An "examination" or in-depth inspection of financial statements and companies' records made in accordance with auditing standards (p. 635).

available-for-sale securities Investments that the investor company does not intend to sell in the near future (p. 717).

avoidable costs Costs that will not continue if an ongoing operation is changed or deleted (p. 235).

backflush costing An accounting system that applies costs to products only when the production is complete (p. 598).

balanced scorecard (BSC) A performance measurement and reporting system that strikes a balance between financial and nonfinancial measures, links performance to rewards, and gives explicit recognition to the link between performance measurement and organizational goals and objectives (p. 370).

balance sheet (statement of financial position) A snapshot of the financial status of an organization at a point in time (p. 620).

behavioral implications The accounting system's effect on the behavior, specifically the decisions, of managers (p. 9).

benchmark comparisons Comparison of a company's financial ratios with general rules of thumb (p. 731).

benchmarking The continuous process of comparing products, services, and activities against the best industry standards (p. 142).

book value (net book value) The original cost of equipment less accumulated depreciation (p. 240).

break-even point The level of sales at which revenue equals total cost and net income is zero (p. 46).

budget A quantitative expression of a plan of action and an aid to coordinating and implementing the plan (p. 7).

budgetary slack (budget padding) Overstatement of budgeted cost or understatement of budgeted revenue to create a budget goal that is easier to achieve (p. 274).

budgeted factory-overhead rate The budgeted total overhead for each cost pool divided by the budgeted cost-allocation base level (p. 534).

business-to-business (B2B) Electronic commerce from one business to another business (p. 16).

business-to-consumer (B2C) Electronic commerce from business to consumer (p. 16).

business process reengineering The fundamental rethinking and radical redesign of business processes to improve performance in areas such as cost, quality, service, and speed (p. 16).

by-product A product that, like a joint product, is not individually identifiable until manufacturing reaches a split-off point, but has relatively insignificant total sales value (p. 509).

capacity costs The fixed costs of being able to achieve a desired level of production or to provide a desired level of service while maintaining product or service attributes, such as quality (p. 88).

capital budget A budget that details the planned expenditures for facilities, equipment, new products, and other long-term investments (p. 277).

capital budgeting The long-term planning for investment commitments with returns spread over time, typically over multiple years (p. 435).

capital charge Company's cost of capital × average invested capital (p. 400).

capital turnover Revenue divided by invested capital (p. 397).

capitalize To record an amount as an asset rather than as an expense (p. 665).

cash basis A process of accounting where revenue and expense recognition occur when the company receives and pays out cash (p. 624).

cash budget A statement of planned cash receipts and disbursements (p. 283).

cash dividends (dividends) Distributions of cash to stockholders that reduce retained earnings (p. 632).

cash equivalents Short-term investments that a company can easily convert into cash with little delay (p. 663).

cash flows from financing activities The section in the statement of cash flows that lists the cash-flow effects of obtaining cash from creditors and owners, repaying creditors or buying back stock from owners, and paying cash dividends (p. 675).

cash flows from investing activities The section in the statement of cash flows that lists the cash-flow effects of (1) lending and collecting on loans and (2) acquiring and selling long-term assets (p. 675).

cash flows from operating activities The section in the statement of cash flows that lists the cash-flow effects of transactions that affect the income statement (p. 675).

centralization Concentration of decision-making authority only at the highest levels of an organization (p. 391).

certified management accountant (CMA) The management accountant's counterpart to the CPA (p. 4).

certified public accountant (CPA) In the United States, independent accountants who assure the reliability of companies' published financial statements (p. 4).

chartered accountant (CA) In many countries, the equivalent to the CPA in the United States—independent accountants who assure the reliability of companies' financial statements (p. 4).

chief financial officer (CFO) The top executive who deals with all finance and accounting issues in an organization. The CFO generally oversees the accounting function (p. 14).

code of conduct A document specifying the ethical standards of an organization (p. 8).

coefficient of determination (R^2) A measurement of how much of the fluctuation of a cost is explained by changes in the cost driver (p. 101).

committed fixed costs Costs arising from the possession of facilities, equipment, and a basic organization (p. 89).

common costs Those costs of facilities and services that are shared by users (p. 235).

common stock Stock that has no predetermined rate of dividends and is the last to obtain a share in the assets when the corporation liquidates. It usually confers voting power to elect the board of directors of the corporation (p. 668).

common-size statements Financial statements expressed in component percentages (p. 730).

comparability A characteristic of information produced when all companies use similar concepts and measurements and use them consistently (p. 642).

component percentages Analysis and presentation of financial statements in percentage form to aid comparability, frequently used when companies differ in size (p. 730).

compound entry A transaction that affects more than two accounts (p. 622).

computer-aided design (CAD) The use of computer technology for the design of real or virtual objects (p. 16).

computer-aided manufacturing (CAM) The use of computer-based software tools in manufacturing or prototyping (p. 16).

computer-integrated manufacturing (CIM) systems Systems that use computer-aided design, computer-aided manufacturing, robots, and computer-controlled machines (p. 16).

confirmatory value A quality of information that allows it to confirm or change existing expectations (p. 642).

conservatism convention Selecting the method of measurement that yields the gloomiest immediate results (p. 642).

consistency Using the same accounting policies and procedures from period to period (p. 642).

consolidated financial statements Financial statements that combine the books of two or more separate legal entities into one set of financial statements (p. 716).

continuity convention (going concern convention) The assumption that an organization will continue to exist and operate (p. 641).

continuous budget (rolling budget) A common form of master budget that adds a month in the future as the month just ended is dropped (p. 277).

contribution approach A method of internal (management accounting) reporting that emphasizes the distinction between variable and fixed costs for the purpose of better decision making (p. 185).

contribution margin A term used for either total contribution margin, unit contribution margin, or contribution margin percentage (p. 49).

contribution-margin percentage Total contribution margin divided by sales or 100% minus the variable cost percentage (p. 48).

contribution-margin ratio Contribution margin percentage expressed as a ratio (p. 48).

control Implementing plans and using feedback to evaluate the attainment of objectives (p. 6).

controllable cost Any cost that a manager's decisions and actions can influence (p. 360).

controller (comptroller) The accounting officer of an organization who deals mainly with operating matters, such as aiding management decision making (p. 14).

corporation A business organized as a separate legal entity and owned by its stockholders (p. 619).

cost A sacrifice or giving up of resources for a particular purpose (p. 124).

cost accounting That part of the cost management system that measures costs for the purposes of management decision making and financial reporting (p. 124).

cost accounting systems The techniques used to determine the cost of a product, service, customer, or other cost object (p. 124).

cost accumulation Collecting costs by some natural classification, such as activities performed, labor, or materials (p. 125).

cost allocation Assigning indirect costs to cost objects in proportion to the cost object's use of a particular cost-allocation base (p. 126).

cost-allocation base A measure of input or output that determines the amount of cost to be allocated to a particular cost object. An ideal cost-allocation base measures how much of the particular cost is caused by the cost object (p. 126).

cost application The allocation of total departmental costs to the revenue-producing products or services (p. 490).

cost assignment Attaching costs to one or more cost objects, such as activities, departments, customers, or products (p. 125).

cost behavior How the activities of an organization affect its costs (p. 37).

cost-benefit balance Weighing estimated costs against probable benefits, the primary consideration in choosing among accounting systems and methods (p. 9).

cost-benefit criterion An approach that implicitly underlies the decisions about the design of accounting systems. As companies change their accounting systems, the potential benefits should exceed the costs of gathering and interpreting the information (p. 643).

cost of capital The cost of long-term liabilities and stockholders' equity weighted by their relative size (p. 400).

cost center A responsibility center in which managers are responsible for costs only (p. 360).

cost driver A measure of activities that requires the use of resources and thereby cause costs (p. 37).

cost function An algebraic equation used by managers to describe the relationship between a cost and its cost driver(s) (p. 91).

cost of goods sold The cost of the merchandise that a company acquires or produces and sells (p. 58).

cost management system (CMS) A collection of tools and techniques that identify how management's decisions affect costs (p. 123).

cost measurement Estimating or predicting costs as a function of appropriate cost drivers (p. 91).

cost object (cost objective) Anything for which decision makers desire a separate measurement of costs. Examples include departments, products, activities, and territories (p. 124).

cost pool A group of individual costs that a company allocates to cost objects using a singlecost-allocation base (p. 128).

cost of quality report A report that displays the financial impact of quality (p. 366).

cost recovery A concept in which companies carry forward as assets such items as inventories, prepayments, and equipment because they expect to recover the costs of these assets in the form of cash inflows (or reduced cash outflows) in future periods (p. 638).

cost structure The combination of variable- and fixed-cost resources used to carry out the organization's activities (p. 55).

cost-volume-profit (CVP) analysis The study of the effects of output volume on revenue (sales), expenses (costs), and net income (net profit) (p. 45).

credit An entry on the right side of an account (p. 644).

cross-sectional comparisons Comparisons of a company's financial ratios with ratios of similar companies, with industry averages, or "best-practices" ratios for the same period (p. 731).

current assets Cash and all other assets that a company reasonably expects to convert to cash or sell or consume within one year or during the normal operating cycle, if longer than a year (p. 661).

current liabilities An organization's debts that fall due within the coming year or within the normal operating cycle if longer than a year (p. 666).

currently attainable standards Levels of performance that managers can achieve by realistic levels of effort (p. 318).

cycle time (throughput time) The time taken to complete a product or service (p. 367).

debentures Formal certificates of indebtedness that are accompanied by a promise to pay interest at a specified annual rate (p. 666).

debit An entry on the left side of an account (p. 644).

decentralization The delegation of decision-making authority to lower levels of the organization. The lower in the organization that authority is delegated, the greater the decentralization (p. 391).

decision context The circumstances surrounding the decision for which the cost will be used (p. 42).

decision making Choosing among alternative courses of action designed to achieve some objective (p. 5).

decision model Any method for making a choice, sometimes requiring elaborate quantitative procedures (p. 182).

degree of operating leverage The ratio of contribution margin to profit, defined at a specific volume of sales (p. 56).

denominator level The expected cost-allocation base activity selected to determine the fixed-overhead rate (p. 543).

depreciation The periodic cost of equipment that a company spreads over the future periods in which the company will use the equipment (p. 240).

depreciation tax shield The tax savings due to depreciation deductions, generally the present value of the product of the tax rate and the depreciation deduction (p. 449).

differential analysis A decision process that compares the differential revenues and costs of alternatives (p. 227).

differential approach A method for comparing alternatives that computes the differences in cash flows between alternatives and then converts these differences in cash flows to their present values (p. 440).

differential cost The difference in total cost between two alternatives (p. 227).

differential revenue The difference in total revenue between two alternatives (p. 227).

direct costs Costs that accountants can identify specifically and exclusively with a given cost object in an economically feasible way (p. 126).

direct-labor costs The wages of all labor that a company can trace specifically and exclusively to the manufactured goods (p. 131).

direct-material costs The acquisition costs of raw materials that a company traces to the manufactured goods (p. 131).

direct method A method for allocating service department costs that ignores other service departments when allocating any given service department's costs to the operating departments (p. 487).

direct method for operating cash flows A method for computing cash flows from operating activities that subtracts operating cash disbursements from cash collections to arrive at cash flows from operations (p. 680).

discounted-cash-flow (DCF) models Capital-budgeting models that focus on cash inflows and outflows while taking into account the time value of money (p. 435).

discretionary fixed costs Costs determined by management as part of the periodic planning process in order to meet the organization's goals. They have no obvious relationship with levels of capacity or output activity (p. 89).

discriminatory pricing Charging different prices to different customers for the same product or service (p. 194).

double-entry system A method of record keeping in which each transaction affects at least two accounts (p. 644).

dysfunctional decision Any decision that is in conflict with organizational goals (p. 408).

earnings per share (EPS) Net income divided by the average number of common shares outstanding during the year (p. 671).

economic profit (residual income) After-tax operating incomeless a capital charge (p. 400).

economic value added (EVA) Adjusted after-tax operating income minus the weighted-average cost of capital multiplied by the adjusted average invested capital (p. 400).

effectiveness The degree to which an organization meets an objective (p. 99).

efficiency The degree to which an organization minimizes the resources used to achieve an objective (p. 319).

efficient capital market A market in which market prices fully reflect all information available to the public (p. 735).

electronic commerce (e-commerce) Conducting business online (p. 16).

engineering analysis The systematic review of materials, supplies, labor, support services, and facilities needed for products and services; measuring cost behavior according to what costs should be, not by what costs have been (p. 93).

enterprise resource planning (ERP) systems Integrated information systems that support all functional areas of a company (p. 16).

equity method A method of accounting for an investment by adjusting the acquisition cost of the investment for the investor's share of earnings or losses of the investee after the date of investment and for dividends received (p. 718).

equivalent units The number of completed (whole) units that could have been produced from the resources required for the partially completed units (p. 591).

ethics The field that deals with human conduct in relation to what is morally good and bad, right and wrong. It is the application of values to decision making. These values include honesty, fairness, responsibility, respect, and compassion (p. 18).

expected cost The cost most likely to be attained (p. 318).

expenses Decreases in ownership claims arising from delivering goods or services or using up assets (p. 622).

explicit transactions Transactions that record day-to-day routine events—such as credit sales, credit purchases, cash received on account, and cash disbursed on account—that are supported by source documents (p. 625).

eXtensible Business Reporting Language (XBRL) An XML-based accounting language that helps communicate financial information electronically (p. 16).

faithful representation A quality of information that ensures that it captures the economic substance of the transactions, events, or circumstances it describes. It requires information to be complete, neutral, and free from material errors (p. 642).

favorable cost variance A variance that occurs when actual costs are less than budgeted costs (p. 312).

favorable profit variance A variance that occurs when actual profit exceeds budgeted profit (p. 311).

favorable revenue variance A variance that occurs when actual revenue exceeds budgeted revenue (p. 312).

financial accounting The branch of accounting that develops information for external decision makers, such as stockholders, suppliers, banks, and government regulatory agencies (p. 3).

Financial Accounting Standards Board (FASB) The body that sets GAAP in the United States (p. 636).

financial budget The part of a master budget that focuses on the effects that the operating budget and other plans (such as capital budgets and repayments of debt) have on cash balances (p. 277).

financial planning model A mathematical model of the master budget that can incorporate any set of assumptions about sales, costs, or product mix (p. 290).

financial statements Summarized reports of accounting transactions (p. 619).

finished-goods inventory Goods fully completed but not yet sold (p. 132).

first-in, first-out (FIFO) An inventory method that assumes that a company sells or uses up first the stock acquired earliest (p. 693).

fiscal year The year established for accounting purposes for the preparation of annual reports (p. 663).

fixed assets (tangible assets) Physical items that a person can see and touch, such as property, plant, and equipment (p. 663).

fixed cost A cost that is not affected by changes in the cost-driver level (p. 39).

fixed-overhead rate The amount of fixed manufacturing overhead applied to each unit of production. It is determined by dividing the budgeted fixed overhead by the expected cost-allocation base activity for the budget period (p. 543).

fixed-overhead spending variance The difference between actual fixed overhead and budgeted fixed overhead (p. 329).

flexible budget (variable budget) A budget that adjusts to different levels of activity (p. 312).

flexible-budget variance The difference between actual results and the flexible budget for the actual level of output achieved (p. 315).

Foreign Corrupt Practices Act A U.S. law forbidding bribery and other corrupt practices. The law also requires all publicly held companies to maintain their accounting records in reasonable detail and accuracy and have an appropriate system of internal controls (p. 8).

free cash flow Cash flows from operations less capital expenditures (p. 685).

full cost The total of all manufacturing costs plus the total of all selling and administrative costs (p. 195).

functional budgeting Budgeting process that focuses on preparing budgets for various functions, such as production, selling, and administrative support (p. 289).

general ledger A collection of the group of accounts that supports the items shown in the major financial statements (p. 644).

generally accepted accounting principles (GAAP) A set of standards to which public companies' published financial statements must adhere (p. 8).

goal congruence A condition where employees, responding to the incentives created by the control system, make decisions that help meet the overall goals of the organization (p. 355).

goodwill The excess of the cost of an acquired company over the sum of the fair market values of its identifiable individual assets less its liabilities (p. 665).

Grenzplankostenrechnung (GPK) A German cost accounting system that goes a step further than ABC systems (p. 143).

gross book value The original cost of an asset before deducting accumulated depreciation (p. 398).

gross margin (gross profit) The excess of sales over the total cost of goods sold (p. 58).

high-low method A simple method for measuring a linear-cost function from past cost data, focusing on the highest-activity and lowest-activity points and fitting a line through these two points (p. 98).

hybrid costing systems An accounting system that is a blend of ideas from both job costing and process costing (p. 577).

IMA Statement of Ethical Professional Practice A code of conduct developed by the Institute of Management Accountants; this code includes competence, confidentiality, integrity, and credibility (p. 18).

imperfect competition A market in which the price a firm charges for a unit influences the quantity of units it sells (p. 192).

implicit transactions Transactions that record events that day-to-day recording procedures temporarily ignore, such as expiration of prepaid rent or accrual of interest due to the passage of time (p. 625).

incentives Rewards, both implicit and explicit, for managerial effort and actions (p. 393).

income (net income, profits, earnings) The excess of revenues over expenses (p. 622).

income statement A statement that summarizes a company's revenues and expenses. It measures the performance of an organization by matching its accomplishments (revenue from customers) and its efforts (cost of goods sold and other expenses) (p. 622).

incremental analysis An analysis of the incremental (additional) costs and benefits of a proposed alternative compared with the current situation (p. 227).

incremental benefits The additional revenues or reduced costs generated by the proposed alternative in comparison with the current situation (p. 227).

incremental costs The additional costs or reduced benefits generated by the proposed alternative in comparison with the current situation (p. 227).

incremental effect The change in total results (such as revenue, expenses, or income) under a new condition in comparison with some given or known condition (p. 51).

independent opinion The accountant's assurance that management's financial statements are in conformity with GAAP (p. 635).

indirect costs Costs that accountants cannot identify specifically and exclusively with a given cost object in an economically feasible way (p. 126).

indirect method for operating cash flows A method for computing cash flows from operating activities that adjusts the previously calculated accrual net income from the income statement to reflect only cash receipts and cash disbursements (p. 680).

indirect production costs (indirect manufacturing costs, factory burden, factory overhead, manufacturing overhead) All costs associated with the production process that a company cannot trace to the goods or services produced in an economically feasible way; usually all production costs except direct materials and direct labor (p. 131).

inflation The decline in the general purchasing power of the monetary unit (p. 457).

Institute of Management Accountants (IMA) The largest U.S. professional organization of accountants focused on internal accounting (p. 3).

intangible assets Long-lived assets that are not physical in nature. Examples are goodwill, franchises, patents, trademarks, and copyrights (p. 665).

internal auditors Accountants who review and evaluate accounting systems, including their internal controls (p. 8).

internal controls Policies to protect and make the most efficient use of an organization's assets (p. 8).

internal rate of return (IRR) model A capital-budgeting model that determines the interest rate, the IRR, at which the NPV equals zero (p. 438).

International Accounting Standards Board (IASB) The group that establishes international GAAP (p. 636).

inventory turnover The number of times the average inventory is sold per year (p. 237).

investment center A responsibility center where managers are responsible for investment as well as profits (p. 361).

job-cost record (job-cost sheet, job order) A document that shows all costs for a particular product, service, or batch of products (p. 577).

job-order costing (job costing) The method of allocating costs to heterogeneous products that are readily identified by individual units or batches, each of which requires differential (sometimes custom) amounts of materials, labor, and overhead (p. 577).

joint costs The costs of manufacturing joint products prior to the split-off point (p. 238).

joint products Two or more manufactured products that (1) have relatively significant sales values and (2) are not separately identifiable as individual products until their split-off point (p. 238).

just-in-time (JIT) philosophy A philosophy to eliminate waste by reducing the time products spend in the production process and eliminating the time products spend on activities that do not add value (p. 16).

kaizen costing The Japanese term for continuous improvement during manufacturing (p. 202).

key performance indicators Measures that drive the organization to achieve its goals (p. 371).

key success factors Characteristics or attributes that managers must achieve in order to drive the organization toward its goals (p. 354).

labor time tickets (time cards) The record of the time a particular direct laborer spends on each job (p. 577).

last-in, first-out (LIFO) An inventory method that assumes that a company sells or uses up the stock acquired most recently first (p. 693).

lean manufacturing Applying continuous process improvements to eliminate waste from the entire enterprise (p. 17).

least-squares regression (regression analysis) Measuring a cost function objectively by using statistics to fit a cost function to all the data (p. 100).

ledger accounts A method of keeping track of how transactions affect each particular asset, liability, revenue, and expense (p. 643).

liabilities The entity's economic obligations to nonowners (p. 620).

LIFO layers (LIFO increments) Separately identifiable additions to a LIFO inventory (p. 694).

limited liability A provision that a company's creditors cannot seek payment from stockholders as individuals if the corporation itself cannot pay its debts (p. 668).

limiting factor (scarce resource) The item that restricts or constrains the production or sale of a product or service (p. 236).

linear-cost behavior Activity that can be graphed with a straight line because costs are assumed to be either fixed or variable (p. 87).

line managers Managers who are directly involved with making and selling the organization's products or services (p. 13).

liquidation Converting assets to cash and using the cash to pay off outside claims (p. 667).

long-lived assets Assets that will provide services for more than a year (p. 626).

long-range plan Forecasted financial statements for 5- to 10-year periods (p. 277).

lower-of-cost-or-market (LCM) An inventory method in which accountants compare the current market price of inventory with its cost (derived by specific identification, FIFO, LIFO, or weighted average) and select the lower of the two as the inventory value (p. 695).

management accounting The branch of accounting that produces information for managers within an organization. It is the process of identifying, measuring, accumulating, analyzing, preparing, interpreting, and communicating information that helps managers fulfill organizational objectives (p. 3).

management audit A review to determine whether managers are implementing the policies and procedures specified by top management (p. 8).

management by exception Concentrating more on areas that deviate from the plan and less on areas that conform with plans and are presumed to be running smoothly (p. 7).

management by objectives (MBO) The joint formulation by managers and their superiors of a set of goals and plans for achieving the goals for a forthcoming period (p. 413).

management control system An integrated set of techniques for gathering and using information to make planning and control decisions, for motivating employee behavior, and for evaluating performance (p. 353).

management's discussion and analysis (MD&A) A section of annual reports and 10-K filings that concentrates on explaining the major changes in the income statement, changes in liquidity and capital resources, and the impact of inflation from one year to the next (p. 730).

managerial effort Exertion toward a goal or objective, including all conscious actions (such as supervising, planning, and thinking) that result in more efficiency and effectiveness (p. 355).

marginal cost The additional cost resulting from producing and selling one additional unit (p. 192).

marginal income tax rate The tax rate paid on incremental taxable income (p. 445).

marginal revenue The additional revenue resulting from the sale of an additional unit (p. 192).

margin of safety Planned unit sales less the break-even unit sales; a measure of how far sales can fall below the planned level before losses occur (p. 55).

market-value method The method of accounting for investments in equity securities that shows the investment on the balance sheet at market value (p. 717).

markup The amount by which price exceeds cost (p. 195).

master budget An extensive analysis of the first year of the long-range plan. It summarizes the planned activities of all subunits of an organization (p. 277).

matching The linking of revenues (as measured by the selling prices of goods and services delivered) with the expenses incurred to generate them (as measured by the cost of goods and services used) (p. 638).

materiality The accounting convention that justifies the omission of insignificant information when its omission or misstatement would not mislead a user of the financial statements (p. 642).

materials requisitions Records of materials used in particular jobs (p. 577).

measurement of cost behavior Understanding and quantifying how activities of an organization affect its levels of costs (p. 86).

mixed cost A cost that contains elements of both fixed- and variable-cost behavior (p. 44).

modified accelerated cost recovery system (MACRS) The method companies use to depreciate most assets under U.S. income tax laws (p. 448).

motivation The drive that creates effort and action toward a goal (p. 356).

net book value The original cost of an asset less any accumulated depreciation (p. 398).

net operating profit after-tax (NOPAT) Income before interest expense but after tax (p. 400).

net present value The sum of the present values of all expected cash flows (p. 436).

net-present-value (NPV) method A discounted-cash-flow approach to capital budgeting that computes the present value of all expected future cash flows using the required rate of return (p. 436).

net worth A synonym for owners' equity (p. 634).

nominal rate Interest rate that includes an inflation element (p. 457).

noncontrolling interests An account that summarizes the outside stockholders' interest, as opposed to the parent's interest, in a subsidiary corporation (p. 721).

noncurrent liabilities (long-term liabilities) An organization's debts that fall due beyond one year (p. 666).

non-value-added costs Costs that a company can eliminate without affecting a product's value to the customer (p. 142).

normal costing system The cost system in which the cost of the manufactured product is composed of actual direct material, actual direct labor, and normal applied overhead (p. 536).

operating budget (profit plan) A major part of a master budget that focuses on the income statement and its supporting schedules (p. 277).

operating cycle The time span during which a company spends cash to acquire goods and services that it uses to produce the organization's output, which it in turn sells to customers, who in turn pay for their purchases with cash (p. 661).

operating leverage The sensitivity of a firm's profit to changes in volume of sales (p. 55).

opportunity cost For a resource that a company already owns or that it has already committed to purchase, the maximum available benefit forgone (or passed up) by using such a resource for a particular purpose (p. 228).

other comprehensive income A few special types of gains and losses that do not appear on the income statement and thus do not become part of retained earnings (p. 668).

outlay cost A cost that requires a future cash disbursement (p. 227).

outsourcing Purchasing products or services from an outside supplier (p. 229).

overapplied overhead The difference between actual and applied overhead when the amount applied exceeds the amount incurred (p. 537).

owners' equity The excess of the assets over the liabilities (p. 620).

paid-in capital The ownership claim arising from funds paid in by the owners (p. 620).

parent company A company that has effective control over another company. Usually this means owning more than 50% of the company's stock (p. 719).

participative budgeting Budgets formulated with the active participation of all affected employees (p. 274).

partnership An organization that joins two or more individuals together as co-owners (p. 634).

par value (stated value) The value often printed on the face of stock certificates (p. 668).

payback period (payback time) The time it will take to recoup, in the form of cash inflows from operations, the initial dollars invested in a project (p. 452).

perfect competition A market in which a firm can sell as much of a product as it can produce, all at a single market price (p. 191).

perfection standards (ideal standards) Expressions of the most efficient performance possible under the best conceivable conditions, using existing specifications and equipment (p. 318).

performance metric A specific measure of management accomplishment (p. 393).

performance reports Feedback provided by comparing results with plans and by highlighting variances (p. 7).

period costs Costs that become expenses during the current period without becoming part of inventory (p. 131).

planning Setting objectives for an organization and determining how to attain them (p. 6).

post-audit A follow-up evaluation of capital-budgeting decisions (p. 455).

predatory pricing Establishing prices so low that they drive competitors out of the market. The predatory pricer then has no significant competition and can raise prices dramatically (p. 194).

predictive value A quality of information that allows it to help users form their expectations about the future (p. 642).

preferred stock Stock that typically has some priority over other shares in the payment of dividends or the distribution of assets upon liquidation (p. 668).

present value (PV) The value today of a future cash flow (p. 435).

price elasticity The effect of price changes on sales volume (p. 193).

price variance The difference between actual input prices and standard input prices multiplied by the actual quantity of inputs used (p. 323).

problem solving Analysis of possible courses of action and identification of the best course to follow (p. 5).

process costing The method of allocating costs to homogeneous products by averaging costs over large numbers of nearly identical products (p. 577).

process map A schematic diagram capturing interrelationships between cost objects, activities, and resources (p. 135).

producing departments Departments where employees work on the organization's products or services (p. 481).

product costs (inventoriable costs) Costs identified with goods produced or purchased for resale (p. 131).

product life cycle The various stages through which a product passes, from conception and development to introduction into the market to maturation and, finally, withdrawal from the market (p. 9).

production-volume variance A variance that appears whenever actual production deviates from the expected volume of production used in computing the fixed overhead rate. It is calculated as (actual volume − expected volume) × fixed-overhead rate (p. 543).

productivity A measure of outputs divided by inputs (p. 368).

profit center A responsibility center in which managers are responsible for revenues as well as costs—that is, profitability (p. 360).

proration To assign underapplied overhead or overapplied overhead to cost of goods sold, work-in-process inventory, and finished-goods inventory in proportion to the ending balances of each account (p. 537).

quality control The effort to ensure that products and services perform to customer requirements (p. 365).

quality-control chart The statistical plot of measures of various product quality dimensions or attributes (p. 366).

quantity variance The difference between the actual quantity of inputs used and the standard quantity allowed for the good output achieved multiplied by the standard price of the input (p. 323).

rate variance An alternative name for the price variance applied to labor (p. 326).

raw material The basic material from which a product is made (p. 131).

raw-material inventory Raw material on hand and awaiting use in the production process (p. 132).

real options model A capital-budgeting model that recognizes the value of contingent investments—that is, investments that a company can adjust as it learns more about its potential for success (p. 439).

recognition The principle that specifies when a company should record revenue in the accounting records (p. 638).

recognize To formally record in the accounting records during the current period (p. 622).

recovery period The number of years over which a company can depreciate an asset for tax purposes (p. 445).

relevance The capability of information to make a difference to the decision maker (p. 642).

relevant information The predicted future costs and revenues that will differ among alternative courses of action (p. 181).

relevant range The limits of the cost-driver level within which a specific relationship between costs and the cost driver is valid (p. 42).

required rate of return (hurdle rate, discount rate) The minimum acceptable rate of return, based on the firm's cost of capital (p. 436).

residual value The predicted sales value of a long-lived asset at the end of its useful life (p. 626).

responsibility accounting Identifying what parts of the organization have primary responsibility for each action, developing performance measures and targets, and designing reports of these measures by responsibility center (p. 360).

responsibility center A set of activities and resources assigned to a manager, a group of managers, or other employees (p. 360).

retained earnings (retained income) The ownership claim arising from the reinvestment of previous profits (p. 620).

return on investment (ROI) A measure of income divided by the investment required to obtain that income (p. 396).

return on sales Income divided by revenue (p. 397).

revenue Increases in ownership claims arising from the delivery of goods or services (p. 622).

sales-activity variances The activity-level variances when sales is used as the cost driver (p. 315).

sales budget The sales forecast that is the result of decisions to create conditions that will generate a desired level of sales (p. 276).

sales forecast A prediction of sales under a given set of conditions (p. 276).

sales mix The relative proportions or combinations of quantities of products that constitute total sales (p. 47).

sales revenue (sales) Revenue from customers (p. 622).

Sarbanes-Oxley Act A 2002 law that requires top-management oversight of a company's accounting policies and procedures (p. 8).

scorekeeping The accumulation, classification, and reporting of data that help users understand and evaluate performance (p. 5).

Securities and Exchange Commission (SEC) A government agency that regulates the financial markets in the United States, including financial reporting (p. 635).

segment autonomy The delegation of decision-making power to managers of segments in an organization (p. 392).

segments Responsibility centers for which a company develops separate measures of revenues and costs (p. 361).

sensitivity analysis The systematic varying of decision input assumptions to examine the effect on a decision (p. 293).

separable costs Any cost beyond the split-off point (p. 238).

service departments Units that exist only to support other departments or customers (p. 481).

service organizations Organizations that do not make or sell tangible goods but instead provide other forms of value (p. 15).

short-term investments Temporary investments in marketable securities (p. 663).

Six Sigma A data-driven continuous process improvement effort designed to eliminate defects and improve quality (p. 17).

sole proprietorship A business entity with a single owner (p. 634).

source documents Clear evidence of transactions, such as sales slips and purchase invoices (p. 625).

specific identification An inventory method that recognizes the actual cost paid for the specific physical item sold (p. 692).

split-off point The juncture of manufacturing where the joint products become individually identifiable (p. 238).

staff managers Managers who are advisory to the line managers. They have no authority over line managers, but they support the line managers by providing information and advice (p. 13).

standard cost A cost that should be achieved (p. 318).

statement of cash flows A statement that reports the cash receipts and cash payments of an organization during a particular period (p. 674).

statement of stockholders' equity A statement that shows the changes in each stockholders' equity account during the period (p. 634).

static budget A budget that is prepared for only one expected level of activity (p. 312).

static-budget variance The difference between actual results and the static budget for the original planned level of output (p. 314).

step cost A cost that changes abruptly at different intervals of activity because the resources and their costs come in indivisible chunks (p. 43).

step-down method A method for allocating service department costs that recognizes that some service departments support the activities in other service departments as well as those in operating departments (p. 488).

stockholders' equity The owners' equity of a corporation (p. 620).

straight-line method A method that depreciates an asset by the same amount each year (p. 627).

strategic plan A plan that sets the overall goals and objectives of the organization (p. 277).

subordinated A creditor claim that is junior to the other creditors in exercising claims against assets (p. 667).

subsidiary A company controlled by a parent company that generally owns more than 50% of its stock (p. 719).

sunk cost A historical or past cost, that is, a cost that the company has already incurred and, therefore, is irrelevant to the decision-making process (p. 240).

T-accounts Simplified versions of ledger accounts that take the form of the capital letter *T* (p. 643).

target costing Taking a product's market price as given and determining the maximum cost the company can spend to make the product and still achieve the desired profitability (p. 201).

timeliness The quality that information must reach decision makers while it can still influence their decisions (p. 642).

time-series comparisons Comparison of a company's financial ratios with its own historical ratios (p. 731).

total quality management (TQM) An approach to quality that focuses on prevention of defects and on customer satisfaction (p. 366).

total contribution margin Total number of units sold times the unit contribution margin (p. 48).

total project approach A method for comparing alternatives that computes the total impact on cash flows for each alternative and then converts these total cash flows to their present values (p. 440).

tracing Physically identifying the amount of a direct cost that relates exclusively to a particular cost object (p. 126).

trading securities Investments "held for current resale," that is, investments that the investor company intends to sell in the near future (p. 717).

traditional costing systems Accounting systems that do not accumulate or report costs of individual activities or processes. They often use a single cost pool for all indirect production costs with a labor-based cost-allocation base (p. 135).

transaction Any event that affects the financial position of an organization and requires recording (p. 619).

transfer price The price at which one segment of an organization sells products or services to another segment of the same organization (p. 404).

transferred-in costs In process costing, costs incurred in a previous department for items that have been received by a subsequent department (p. 596).

treasurer The executive who is concerned mainly with the company's financial matters, such as raising and managing cash (p. 14).

treasury stock A corporation's own stock that it has issued and subsequently repurchased but has not permanently retired (p. 668).

two-stage ABC system A costing system with two stages of allocation to get from the original indirect resource cost to the final product or service cost. The first stage allocates indirect resource costs to activity-cost pools. The second stage allocates activity costs to products or services (p. 138).

unallocated costs Costs that an accounting system records but does not allocate to any cost object (p. 129).

unavoidable costs Costs that will continue even if a company discontinues an operation (p. 235).

uncontrollable cost Any cost that the management of a responsibility center cannot affect within a given time span (p. 360).

underapplied overhead The difference between actual and applied overhead when the amount applied is less than the amount incurred (p. 537).

understandable A criterion that requires accountants to present information clearly and concisely (p. 642).

unearned revenue (deferred revenue) Collections from customers that companies receive and record before they earn the revenue (p. 629).

unexpired cost Any asset that managers expect to become an expense in future periods, for example, inventory and prepaid rent (p. 626).

unfavorable cost variance A variance that occurs when actual costs exceed budgeted costs (p. 312).

unfavorable profit variance A variance that occurs when actual profit falls below budgeted profit (p. 312).

unfavorable revenue variance A variance that occurs when actual revenue falls below budgeted revenue (p. 312).

unit contribution margin (marginal income per unit) The sales price per unit minus the variable cost per unit (p. 48).

usage variance (efficiency variance) Alternative names for the quantity variance (p. 326).

useful life The number of years the company expects to use an asset (p. 626).

value-added cost The necessary cost of an activity that cannot be eliminated without affecting a product's value to the customer (p. 142).

value chain The set of business functions or activities that add value to the products or services of an organization (p. 10).

value engineering A cost-reduction technique, used primarily during design, that uses information about all value-chain functions to satisfy customer needs while reducing costs (p. 202).

variable cost A cost that changes in direct proportion to changes in the cost-driver level (p. 39).

variable-cost percentage Total variable costs divided by total sales (p. 48).

variable-cost ratio Variable cost percentage expressed as a ratio (p. 48).

variable-overhead efficiency variance The difference between actual cost-driver activity and the standard amount allowed for the actual output achieved multiplied by the standard variable-overhead rate per cost-driver unit (p. 328).

variable-overhead spending variance The difference between the actual variable overhead cost and the amount predicted for the actual level of cost-driver activity (p. 328).

variances Deviations from plans (p. 7).

verifiability A characteristic of information that can be checked to ensure it is correct (p. 642).

visual-fit method A method in which the cost analyst visually fits a straight line through a plot of all the available data (p. 100).

volume variance A common name for the production-volume variance (p. 546).

weighted-average cost An inventory method that assigns the same unit cost to each unit available for sale (p. 694).

weighted-average (WA) process-costing method A process-costing method that determines total cost by adding together the cost of (1) all work done in the current period and (2) the work done in the preceding period on the current period's beginning inventory of work in process, and divides the total by the equivalent units of work done to date (p. 595).

working capital Current assets less current liabilities (p. 666).

work-in-process inventory Goods undergoing the production process but not yet fully completed (p. 132).

zero-base budget A budget that requires justification of expenditures for every activity, including continuing activities (p. 272).